Readings in Philosophy of Psychology

The Language and Thought Series

Series Editors
Jerrold J. Katz
D. Terence Langendoen
George A. Miller

Readings in Philosophy of Psychology, Volume 1
NED BLOCK,
Editor

Readings in Philosophy of Psychology, Volume 2
NED BLOCK,
Editor

Surface Structure: The Interface of Autonomous Components
ROBERT FIENGO

Semantics: Theories of Meaning in Generative Grammar
JANET DEAN FODOR

The Language of Thought
JERRY A. FODOR

Propositional Structure and Illocutionary Force
JERROLD J. KATZ

An Integrated Theory of Linguistic Ability
THOMAS BEVER, JERROLD J. KATZ, AND D. TERENCE LANGENDOEN,
Editors (Distributed by Harper & Row, Publishers)

Readings in
Philosophy of Psychology

Volume 2

Edited by Ned Block

HARVARD UNIVERSITY PRESS
Cambridge, Massachusetts
1981

Library of Congress Cataloging in Publication Data

Main entry under title:

Readings in philosophy of psychology.

  (Language and thought series)
  Includes index.
  1. Psychology—Philosophy—Addresses, essays,
lectures. I. Block, Ned Joel, 1942-
BF38.R35   150'.1   79-25593
ISBN 0-674-74875-1 (v. 1.)
ISBN 0-674-74877-8 (v. 2.)

Preface

IT IS INCREASINGLY CLEAR that progress in philosophy of mind is greatly facilitated by knowledge of many areas of psychology and also that progress in psychology is facilitated by knowledge of philosophy. What makes this interrelationship most obvious to practitioners in these fields is that in order to keep up with the current literature on the problems on which they work, they find that they must be able to read the technical literature of one another's fields. The simple fact is that lines of research in many areas of philosophy and psychology have tended to converge on the same clusters of issues.

This convergence reflects a deeper mesh of the fields. A host of crucial issues do not "belong" to either philosophy or psychology, but rather fall equally well in both disciplines because they reflect the traditional concerns or require the traditional methods of both fields. The problems will yield only to philosophically sophisticated psychologists or to psychologically sophisticated philosophers.

The interest and viability of approaching these problems from the joint perspective of philosophy and psychology are widely acknowledged, as is indicated by the number of people engaged in joint research, by the existence of journals wholly or partly devoted to it, by the existence of at least one learned society and a number of less formal discussion groups, and by conferences too numerous to mention. Although there have been a number of books of proceedings of philosophy of psychology conferences, until now there has been no general anthology intended as a text in philosophy of psychology. It is this gap that the present book, which appears in two volumes, is intended to fill.

This is the second volume of *Readings in Philosophy of Psychology*. It covers mental representation, imagery, the subject matter of grammar, and innate ideas—topics that are closely related to current psychological research. The first volume covers mainly the chief "isms" of contemporary theory of the nature of the mind: behaviorism, reductionism, physicalism, and functionalism—topics that are more distant from the day-to-day empirical concerns of psychology. Since the anthology has been divided into two volumes, I want to stress that neither volume on its own gives a picture of the field.

It should be said, moreover, that this anthology is *not* intended as a survey. No single book could be comprehensive and at the same time present its topics in any depth. The topics covered here were chosen because they are especially interesting, because they have been a focus of current activity, because they allowed the selection of high-caliber articles, and because they fit together in a coherent way.

Details of the original publication of the articles appear at the foot of the first page. All the introductions appear here for the first time. Throughout the an-

thology, nonstandard symbols have been used instead of common symbols such as the arrow, double arrow, backward "E," upside-down "A," square, and diamond. Explanations of the notation are repeated in each chapter where they appear.

I would like to thank Edward Stabler for making the index for this volume. The preparation of this volume was indirectly supported by National Endowment for the Humanitities grant ED00009-79-554.

Contents

Introduction
What Is Philosophy of Psychology?
Ned Block

PHILOSOPHY OF PSYCHOLOGY is the study of conceptual issues in psychology. For the most part, these issues fall equally well in psychology as in philosophy. But this is not to say these issues are always on the *borderline* between philosophy and psychology, peripheral to both fields.

How can it be that a set of issues falls in the mainstream of two such different disciplines? Part of the answer is that progress in science involves the solution of various sorts of conceptual puzzles, often requiring substantial conceptual articulation and sometimes the ferreting out of serious conceptual confusions. For example, Aristotelian physics conflated instantaneous velocity with average velocity, creating paradoxes and contradictions—as Galileo showed (see Kuhn, 1964). Newton's mechanics required resolving the ordinary notion of weight into force and mass, and Cannizzaro's breakthrough in chemistry involved distinguishing among atomic weight, mo-

An earlier version of this introduction appeared as "Philosophy of Psychology" in Peter D. Asquith and Henry E. Kyburg, Jr., eds., *Current Research in Philosophy of Science* (East Lansing: Philosophy of Science Association, 1979), pp. 450-462. Reprinted by permission.

lecular weight, and equivalent weight. Normally, the scientists themselves solve conceptual problems in science. Although the skills involved are of the sort in which philosophers are trained (and in which scientists are typically not trained), only those at the frontiers of scientific knowledge are in a position to see the issues with the requisite degree of clarity.

What is different about conceptual issues in psychology is mainly that the frontiers of knowledge in the field are so close to the heartland of folk psychology that the conceptual issues about the mind that philosophers have long discussed are very nearly the same as the issues that impede theoretical progress in psychology. Indeed, the majority of topics of concern to contemporary philosophers of psychology would have been intelligible and, in many cases, even familiar to philosophers who lived long before the rise of modern psychology. Consider for example such topics of current controversy as the nature of mental representation in general and mental images in particular; whether there are innate ideas; whether perception is inferential; what it is to have a concept; the subject matter of grammar; and what the difference is between rule-governed and rule-described action (all discussed in this anthology). It is worth noting by contrast that a philosopher who lived before the rise of modern physics (albeit long before the rise of modern psychology) would be utterly baffled by most of the issues of concern to contemporary philosophers of physics. (Imagine Aristotle being asked whether the psi function of quantum mechanics is a probability wave.) The difference is that advances in physics have involved strikingly new concepts, and thus new conceptual issues, while advances in psychology have not.

This being said, it should also be conceded that the old issues typically appear in new and often more tractable forms. Indeed, some of the old issues are hardly recognizable in their new forms. For example, the issue of whether the subject matter of grammar is rules in the mind has been considerably altered by the advances in transformational-generative grammar and Chomsky's distinction between competence and performance. Moreover, since psychology does contain *some* new theoretical apparatus, new conceptual questions arise in connection with that apparatus: for example, the philosophical issues concerning Freudian theory (Wollheim, 1974). Also, new experimental techniques sometimes reveal previously unrecognized human capacities whose nature involves recognizably philosophical difficulties. For example, the experimental techniques of psychophysics reveal that people can make a series of judgments of relative brightness of lights that are stable and coherent and that allow experimenters to conclude that brightness is a certain function of a physical parameter (intensity). But this result raises the question of what brightness is, and what it means for one light to be twice as bright as another (see Savage, 1970). The claims of psychometricians to measure intelligence, personality, and so on, have attracted the attention of philosophers of psychology (Block and Dworkin, 1974; Block, 1976).

What makes this issue of interest to philosophers (aside from its moral and political implications) is, first, that arguments for the claims made on behalf of the tests have gone unformulated and unexamined, and it is a typically philosophical task to formulate arguments and examine them, and, second, that psychometric practice and ideology presuppose dubious philosophical doctrines.

The sort of problem described in the last paragraph is the exception rather than the rule, however. As I said, the problems of philosophy of psychology are, by and large, traditional problems in new guises. In some cases, hindsight reveals that an old philosophical problem was largely empirical: for example, the question of whether the differences between different emotions are differences of feeling or attitude. Current work by psychologists (Schachter and Singer, 1962), though flawed, suggests that while all emotions involve states of physiological arousal, the differences between them are indeed cognitive differences. Similarly, the old issue of inference in the formation of perceptual beliefs seems (to me at least) to have been resolved in the affirmative (Neisser, 1967; but see Anscombe, 1974; Neisser, 1976). Even in this case, some of the old disputes are played out once again among psychologists of different stripes. Thus we have J. J. Gibson and his followers adducing empirical considerations supplemented by traditional philosophical arguments against inferential views.

To illustrate how old issues take on new forms, I shall briefly sketch some of the issues having to do with what is currently philosophy of psychology's hottest topic: mental representation. Issues of current interest include the following: how mental representations refer; how representations that express concepts combine to form representations that have truth value; whether mental representation requires a system of mental representations; whether the meaning of a mental representation is a matter of its role in inference, decision making, and other mental processes (and, if not, what the meaning of a mental representation does consist in); whether natural languages (such as English) are the major systems of mental representation, or whether we have to translate from English into our internal systems; whether the processes that manipulate mental representations take account of their meaning or of their shape only; what the identity conditions on mental representations are; what the difference is between discursive representations and imagistic or pictorial representations; whether images exist and, if so, whether they can refer, and, if so, whether they can refer in virtue of resemblance to their causes (as William of Ockham apparently thought). (These issues are discussed in part one, "Mental Representation," and part two, "Imagery.")

Difficulties about imagery provide a good example of issues that have been changed not one iota by new theory; rather, they have been altered (in the direction of intractability, I fear) by striking new evidence. Roger Shepard and his students (see Shepard and Metzler, 1971) have put together an impressive array of evidence that people perform certain tasks by generating mental images (a process that can be timed) and rotating them at constant angular velocity. For example, when subjects are presented with two figures that clearly differ in their orientation and then are asked whether the figures have identical shapes, the time it takes subjects to answer is proportional to the angular displacement of the figures — independently of whether the rotation is in the plane of the page or at right angles to it.

In another experiment (described in chapter 8), subjects were asked to form an image of a map of an (imaginary) island containing seven small pictured objects (a house, a well, a tree, and so forth). Sub-

jects were asked to "zoom in" on (as it might be) their image of the tree, and then answer, *by consulting their image*, the question "Does the island contain a house?" It was found that the time it took to answer was highly correlated with the distance between the tree and the house. Distances between objects varied considerably, and all of the pairs of objects (21) were used. These and many other results make it seem for all the world as if subjects are secretly manipulating drawings or models. Compelling as these experiments are, they do not cast much light on the traditional philosophical issues about images. We still want to know: What are images? Are the images of perception the same sort of thing as the images we "conjure up"? Are images like pictures in the head? If so, in what respects? How can an image be the end product in perception, for then there would have to be a perceiver of the image, and who would perceive *his* images? But what other role could an image have in perception? How can it be that an image of a tiger has no definite number of stripes? Is an image a neural entity? If so, what about the traditional Leibniz's Law problems — for instance, that images can be pink and green striped while the brain is mainly gray?

Another familiar issue having to do with mental representation is the question of what the difference is between behavior being rule-described and behavior being rule-governed. This distinction is at least as old as Aristotle and is also a major issue with respect to Kant's Categorical Imperative: "Act only according to a maxim which can at the same time be willed a universal law." Is a maxim of your action one that merely describes it, or one that governs it as well?

One major issue is whether behavior can be rule-governed, even in cases where one is not conscious of acting in accordance with a rule. Many philosophers of psychology are convinced that in an important class of rule-governed behaviors, we have no conscious knowledge of the rule. Here is an example of the sort of case that provides evidence for that view. Speakers of most dialects of English pronounce the 'g' differently in 'finger' and 'singer'. The first 'g' might be described as "hard," the second as "soft."[1] There is a regularity here: roughly, the 'g' in 'nger' words formed from verbs is soft; otherwise, it is hard. What is the explanation of the fact that the rule "use soft 'g' in 'nger' words formed from verbs — otherwise use hard 'g' " describes our pronunciation behavior? One possible explanation is that we have in effect memorized the pronunciation of each 'nger' word. Another explanation is that the rule mentioned above (or some other rule — a possibility I will ignore) governs the behavior as well as describing it. Here is one item of evidence that rules out the former hypothesis and thus makes the latter more plausible. Let us coin the word 'ming': to ming is to look to the east. Someone who habitually looks to the east is a minger — with a *soft* 'g'. Since the rule applies to new cases, we have some reason to think the behavior is rule-governed.

It has been suggested (Fodor, 1975) that what the distinction between rule-governed and rule-described behavior comes to is that behavior is governed by a rule just in case a mental representation of the rule causally influences the behavior so as to make it described by the rule. This proposal raises a traditional bogeyman, described below.

Carroll (1895) pointed out that principles of logic cannot be applied without the use of reasoning that itself embodies logical principles. This fact creates difficulties for a view that says that all reasoning is rule-governed — that is, causally controlled by mentally represented rules. For example, suppose one reasons as follows:

The Argument: All men are mortal; Socrates is a man; therefore Socrates is mortal.

If all reasoning is causally controlled by mentally represented rules, it is plausible that the rule involved in this case is something like this:

The Rule: If an argument is of the form 'for any x, if x is F, then x is G; a is F; therefore a is G', then the argument is valid.

But how could The Rule play a causal role in one's reaching The Argument's conclusion that Socrates is mortal? It is hard to see how The Rule could be involved here if not in something like the following reasoning. The Rule says every argument of a certain specified form is valid; The Argument is of that form; so The Argument is valid. But this bit of reasoning *itself involves the application of The Rule*. (This can be made explicit by putting the reasoning so that it is clear that it fits the specified form, with F = being of the specified form, and G = validity: for any x, if x is of a certain form then x is valid; a is of that form; therefore, a is valid.) Thus it seems that in order to apply our mental representation of The Rule to The Argument, we require *another* application of a mental representation of The Rule. And so on. It is hard to see how a mental representation of The Rule can be applied at all. This traditional puzzle can be seen as a serious problem for the foundations of psychology.[2]

I described this puzzle partly to illustrate the traditional aspect of issues of contemporary philosophy of psychology, but partly also to indicate a way in which new approaches often differ from the old. The way the new approach differs here has perhaps as much to do with new technology as with new theory (though this distinction is of less note with regard to psychology than to some other fields). The new technology is that of the digital computer; the new theoretical concept is that of the Turing machine. The example of the digital computer shows us the rough outlines of a solution to this problem (and also suggests a way out of the problem of the infinite regress of image perceivers mentioned above. A digital computer is a device one knows to be rule-governed, for the rules are inserted by us as part of the program. In the digital computer, some operations are accomplished "automatically," by hard-wired circuitry, and not via the application of any represented rules. Minsky (1967) describes two primitive operations 'add 1' and 'subtract 1 or if register $= 0$, jump to the nth (where n is indicated) instruction'; he then shows that these two operations will suffice for the power of a universal Turing machine. In a commercial digital computer, the operations referred to in the rules that one programs into the computer are ultimately defined in terms of such primitive operations, the terms for which constitute a "machine language" that the machine is *built* to use, in the sense that when a primitive instruction appears in the appropriate register, the hard-wired circuitry accomplishes the operation. There is no regress because the machine's primitive operations are not rule-governed. The claimed solution, then, is that there are mental operations analogous to the primitive operations of the computer, and also mental operations analogous to the programmed operations, the latter being composed of the former in the mind as in the computer.

The fallacy in the argument in the paragraph before last can be blamed on the assumption that all reasoning is rule-governed (causally controlled by mentally represented rules). Some reasoning is "automatic" in the manner of the primitive operations of digital computers. Alternatively, one could hold on to the claim that all reasoning is rule-governed and blame the unsoundness of the argument on the premise (implicit in the sentence "It is hard to see how The Rule could be involved here . . .") that a rule can govern

reasoning only via an application that itself involves reasoning. Sometimes a rule causally controls reasoning "automatically," in the way the machine language command "ADD 1" causes the representation in a register to change, by the operation of hard-wired circuitry, and not by any process involving reasoning.

I have left out many issues that are closely related to those described above, involving perception, memory, attention, intentionality, innate ideas, conceptual development (such as issues arising from the work of Jean Piaget and Lawrence Kohlberg) and the foundations of artificial intelligence. But had these been described in more detail, the picture of philosophy of psychology sketched here would be even more skewed toward cognitive psychology. Psychology is a very fragmented field — cognitive psychology, mathematical psychology, and social psychology, for example, have little in common; those who work in or know about one rarely have much expertise in the other. I have given little indication of the interest and activity in topics on the borderline of psychology with physiology, such as split brains (Nagel, 1971; Puccetti, 1973); mathematical psychology; traits (Alston, 1976); non-cognitive states of mind; and the foundations of social psychology (Harre and Secord, 1973). The emotions, especially, have been the topic of a veritable flurry of books and articles (Solomon, 1976; Thalberg, 1977; Rorty, forthcoming) on such topics as the intentionality of the emotions; whether emotions are voluntary; whether the expression of an emotion is part of the emotional state; the relation of emotions to character traits; and problems in the cross-cultural identification of the emotions.

The discussion above is also misleading in that it scants what might be called traditional philosophy of mind, including such topics as mind-body identity, other minds, privacy, consciousness, and the like. Some philosophers might consider this omission fortunate, appealing to the idea that philosophy of mind has as little to do with philosophy of psychology as metaphysics has to do with philosophy of physics. On the contrary, however, I see good reason to count philosophy of mind as part of philosophy of psychology (rather than conversely, as is commonly supposed). For one thing, as I have argued above, most of the problems in philosophy of psychology simply *are* versions of traditional problems. Second, even rather rarefied problems in philosophy of mind such as the status of "qualia" often have rather more direct relations to central conceptual issues in psychology than one might think at first glance. For example, functionalism (the view that mental states are functional states, states defined by their causal role) is currently the dominant view of the nature of mind. While some philosophers regard functionalism as providing a foundation for mental sentence theories of belief (Harman, 1973; Fodor, 1979); others think functionalism counts against mental sentence theories of belief (Stalnaker, 1976). The latter group regards the claim that belief is a functional state as a *rival* of the claim that belief is a relation to a sentence in the language of thought (see Field, chapter 5, for a critique of such arguments). At least there is wide agreement among philosophers of radically different points of view that functionalism is *relevant* to the foundations of psychology. The problems of qualia are in turn relevant to functionalism because there is reason to think that two states can be functionally identical, even though one lacks and the other has qualitative character (Block and Fodor, volume 1, chapter 20; Block, volume 1, chapter 22); hence qualia are the basis for an argument that functionalism is false. Of course, there is a great deal of disagreement about this matter (Shoemaker, volume 1, chapter 21; Block, 1980). Dennett has gone so far as

to argue that qualia can be explained by psychological models of the sort currently in vogue in cognitive psychology (Dennett, 1978).

Traditional philosophy of mind is often taken to include issues that more properly belong in metaphysics (personal identity) or epistemology (some issues about sense data), but the other issues in philosophy of mind, the ones that are genuinely about the mind, seem best classified as part of philosophy of psychology, even though some of them are related to empirical issues in a very abstract way.

The variety of problems in the philosophy of psychology is sufficiently great that no single anthology on the subject could possibly be comprehensive. The best one can do is pick a few topics and cover them in moderate depth. Inevitably, many major issues must be entirely omitted. Thus, for example, this anthology has no part devoted to problems of perception or to whether children's conceptual systems differ from those of adults. I have tried to pick disparate topics that at the same time fit together coherently.

All of the parts have something to do with empirical psychology, although much of the material in volume 1 could as easily fit into a book on traditional philosophy of mind. The issues raised in the "Functionalism" section of volume 1 lead naturally into those in "Mental Representation" (this volume, part one), since one of the plausible answers to the question of what makes mental representations represent is their functional role. Although they are not all in the same part, the articles by Nagel (volume 1, chapter 11), Shoemaker (volume 1, chapter 21), and Block (volume 1, chapter 22) are a natural group, since they are all concerned with problems of consciousness. "Mental Representation" and "Imagery" (parts one and two) go naturally together, images and mental language be-

ing the leading candidate mental representations. The issues discussed in "Mental
Representation" have natural applications
in "The Subject Matter of Grammar" and
"Innate Ideas" (parts three and four). The
former is about the issue of whether grammars are theories of mental representations, and the latter is about the issue of
whether (or to what degree) our mental
representations of grammar are innate.

Notes

1. Actually, the 'g' in the "soft" cases is
deleted, and the 'n' is velar.
2. I am indebted to a discussion with
Hartry Field and David Hills.

References

Alston, W. 1976. "Traits, Consistency, and
Conceptual Alternatives for Personality
Theory." *Journal for the Theory of Social
Behavior* 5, no. 1: 17-48.

Anscombe, G. E. M. 1974. "Comment on Pro-
fessor R. L. Gregory's Paper." In S. C.
Brown, ed., *Philosophy of Psychology*.
New York: Barnes and Noble.

Block, N. 1976. "Fictionalism, Functionalism,
and Factor Analysis." In R. S. Cohen, C. A.
Hooker, and A. C. Michalos, eds., *PSA
1974. Boston Studies in Philosophy of Science*, vol. 32. Dordrecht: Reidel.

———— 1978. "Troubles With Functionalism."
In C. W. Savage, ed., *Minnesota Studies in
the Philosophy of Science*. Vol. 9. Minneapolis: University of Minnesota Press. Reprinted as volume 1, chapter 22.

———— 1980. "Are Absent Qualia Impossible?" *Philosophical Review* 89.

Block, N., and G. Dworkin. 1974. "IQ, Heri-
tability and Inequality." *Philosophy and
Public Affairs* 3, no. 4: 331-409; 4, no. 1:
40-99.

Block, N., and J. A. Fodor. 1972. "What Psychological States Are Not." *Philosophical
Review* 81: 159-181. Reprinted as volume 1,
chapter 20.

Brown, S. C., ed. 1974. *Philosophy of Psychology*. New York: Barnes and Noble.

Carroll, L. 1895: "What the Tortoise Said to
Achilles." *Mind* 4: 278-280.

Cummins, R. 1975. "Functional Analysis."
Journal of Philosophy 72: 741-764. Reprinted in part as volume 1, chapter 12.

Dennett, D. 1969. *Content and Consciousness*.
London: Routledge & Kegan Paul. A section
of this book is reprinted as chapter 6, this
volume.

———— 1977. "Critical Notice: *The Language
of Thought* by Jerry Fodor." *Mind* 86: 265-
280. Reprinted as "A Cure for the Common
Code?" chapter 4, this volume.

———— 1978. "A Cognitive Theory of Consciousness." In C. W. Savage, ed., *Minnesota Studies in the Philosophy of Science*.
Vol. 9. Minneapolis: University of Minnesota Press.

———— In press. "Why a Computer Can't Feel
Pain." *Synthese*.

Field, H. 1978. "Mental Representation." *Erkenntnis* 13: 19-61. Reprinted as chapter 5,
this volume.

Fodor, J. A. 1975. *The Language of Thought*.
New York: Crowell.

———— 1978a. "Computation and Reduction."
In C. W. Savage, ed., *Minnesota Studies in
the Philosophy of Science*. Vol. 9. Minneapolis: University of Minnesota Press.

———— 1978b. "Propositional Attitudes." *Monist* 61, no. 4: 501-523. Reprinted as chapter
3, this volume.

———— 1980. "Methodological Solipsism." *Behavioral and Brain Sciences*.

Harman, G., 1973. *Thought*. Princeton:
Princeton University Press.

———— 1975. "Language, Thought and Communication." In K. Gunderson, ed., *Language, Mind, and Knowledge. Minnesota
Studies in the Philosophy of Science*. Vol. 7.
Minneapolis: University of Minnesota Press.

Harre, R., and P. Secord. 1973. *The Explanation of Social Behavior*. Oxford: Blackwell.

Kosslyn, S., and J. Pomerantz. 1977. "Imagery, Propositions, and the Form of Internal
Representations." *Cognitive Psychology* 9:
52-76. Reprinted as chapter 8, this volume.

Kuhn, T. S. 1964. "A Function for Thought
Experiments." In *Mélanges Alexandre
Koyré*, 41, *L'aventure de l'esprit*. Paris:
Herman.

Minsky, M. 1967. *Computation*. Englewood
Cliffs, N.J.: Prentice-Hall.

Nagel, T. 1971. "Brain Bisection and the Unity
of Consciousness." *Synthese* 22: 396-413.

Neisser, U. 1967. *Cognitive Psychology*, New
York: Appleton-Century-Crofts.

————— 1976. *Cognition and Reality.* San Francisco: Freeman.

Puccetti, R. 1973. "Brain Bisection and Personal Identity." *British Journal for the Philosophy of Science* 24: 339-355.

Rorty, A. Forthcoming. *A Natural History of the Emotions.*

Savage, C. W. 1970. *The Measurement of Sensation.* Berkeley and Los Angeles: University of California Press.

Savage, C. W., ed. 1978. *Perception and Cognition: Issues in the Foundations of Psychology. Minnesota Studies in the Philosophy of Science.* Vol 9. Minneapolis: University of Minnesota Press.

Schachter, S., and Singer, J. E. 1962. "Cognitive, Social and Physiological Determinants of Emotional States." *Psychological Review* 69: 379-399.

Shepard, R., and J. Metzler. 1971. "Mental Rotation of Three-Dimensional Objects." *Science* 171: 701-703.

Shoemaker, S. 1975. "Functionalism and Qualia." *Philosophical Studies* 22: 291-313. Reprinted as volume 1, chapter 21.

Sober, E. 1976. "Mental Representations." *Synthese* 33: 101-148.

Solomon, R. 1976. *The Passions.* New York: Doubleday, Anchor.

Stalnaker, R. 1976. "Propositions." In A. McKay and D. Merrill, eds., *Issues in the Philosophy of Language.* New Haven: Yale University Press.

Thalberg, I. 1977. *Perception, Emotion and Action.* Oxford: Blackwell.

Wollheim, R., ed. 1974. *Freud.* New York: Doubleday, Anchor.

Part One
Mental Representation

Introduction: Mental Representations and Languages of Thought

David Hills

I

Utterances and inscriptions in human languages are capable of serving as a medium of communication and intercourse among us in part because they are capable of *representing* things as being one way rather than another. I can tell you that the cat is on the mat, ask you whether the cat is on the mat, order you to put the cat on the mat, and so on by uttering English sentences only because English sentences are capable of representing the cat as being on the mat. This much ought to be uncontroversial. But if we try to ask ourselves what this "representing" involves we will quickly face most of the controversial questions in philosophy of language and some of the controversial questions in metaphysics: questions about the status of "states of affairs" like the cat's

being on the mat, questions about the connection between the way language represents and the way pictures represent their subjects, questions about the "correspondence theory of truth," and so on.

One much simpler situation in which we sometimes speak of an object's representing things as being one way rather than another is the case of natural indicators or "natural signs." Some of the special complexities of linguistic representation will come out if we compare the two situations. Suppose I can read off the approximate speed of the wind by judging the angle at which the smoke rises from a factory smokestack. Then we can say that the angle *represents* the speed of the wind to me by virtue of this ability of mine. If we like, we can think of various possible angles as going together to form a rudimentary *system* of representation, different angles going in a systematic manner with different ways the wind can be blowing.

Yet the states of affairs a plume of smoke can represent to us in this way are severely limited in variety and novelty, whereas by varying elements of a sentence like 'The cat is on the mat' we can represent to ourselves a wide variety of further states of affairs, including ones that

I am indebted to Ned Block, Edwin McCann, Martha Nussbaum, and Naomi Scheman for various sorts of advice on earlier drafts. [*Editor's note:* Both Jerry A. Fodor's "Propositional Attitudes" and Harry Field's "Mental Representation" were written after David Hills had prepared this introduction. "Propositional Attitudes" covers much the same ground as the sections of Fodor's *Language of Thought* (pp. 28-34, 55-78, and 197-199) that were to be reprinted here and are discussed in this introduction.]

neither we nor our listeners have encountered before ('The samovar is on the mat'; 'The cat is on the samovar'). In fact there seem to be no bounds—at least no well-defined bounds—to the complexity and variety of things we can make English sentences represent, by simply recombining elements that English speakers already understand. (This is what linguists are alluding to when they speak of the *productivity* of language.)

Smoke represents speed because of simple and reliable relationships between speeds and angles, relations I can use to infer speeds. But 'the cat is on the mat' does not represent the cat's being on the mat to me by virtue of anything as simple and easy to specify as my being able to infer the cat is on the mat whenever I hear it. Its utterer may be lying, expressing a supposition, or doing any of a dozen other things that keep what is said from being a reliable indicator of the cat's position, while still representing the cat as being on the mat. Furthermore, our sentence can represent what it does in a larger sentence that does not itself purport to locate our cat at all. 'If the cat is on the mat that floor must have been pretty cold last night'. A sentence can represent a *mere possibility* in ways a plume of smoke cannot. (We can even make suppositions about imaginary cats!) Finally, speaking of linguistic representations as *true* or *false* and speaking of their elements as *referring* to particular objects ('the cat', perhaps, referring on this occasion to Joe's old tom Oscar) will play a large role in describing how they function. Truth and reference have no such clear application—in fact, no such clear *sense*—in connection with natural signs.

II

All this has been about language; what about the mind?

In the selections in this part, philosophers are concerned with the ways *the mind* represents things as being one way

rather than another. I can *judge that* the cat is on the mat, *wonder whether* the cat is on the mat, *be afraid that* the cat might get on the mat, and so on, they suggest, in part because I am capable of in some sense *mentally representing* the cat as being on the mat. What does this sort of representation involve?

For each of these philosophers, an important guide to how the mind represents is the way *language* represents. But they pursue this guide in various directions and to various distances. Daniel C. Dennett is probably the most cautious. Peter Geach wants to regard some of our psychological concepts as derived by analogy from concepts relating to speech and our practice of reporting what he calls "the content of mental acts" as derived by analogy from the practice of reporting overt discourse, though he regards the analogy as sharply limited in certain ways. Jerry A. Fodor goes so far as to regard his task as that of producing a speculative description of the inner language in which thought takes place, the syntax and semantics of an internal code. Such a "language" must be very different from natural languages like English in many ways, but Fodor argues in his discussion of concept learning that it must share the features of linguistic representation noted above: it is systematic and productive; mere possibilities can be represented in it; it contains referring elements; representations can be importantly true and false. In fact, in *The Language of Thought* (1975 pp. 65-97), Fodor argues that the internal code must possess from the beginning the full expressive power of any possible natural language! Gilbert Harman goes just as far in a slightly different direction. He suggests that there is an important sense in which an adult user of English uses *English* as a medium in which to think. More specifically, he wants to suggest that the *principal* use of a natural language is for thought rather than speech, and that to learn a natural language is to "incorporate" it into one's language of thought.

These positions certainly *look* different. Still, it is hard to say what the differences really amount to at this stage, since the shape of any of these pictures depends so much on what sort of philosophy of *natural* language accompanies it. In their current form, the issues are extremely hard and extremely new.

In another form, the issues are quite old, being the same ones that were traditionally discussed under the head of *intentionality*. Intentionality was the characteristic "object-directedness" or "aboutness" that philosophers like Franz Brentano (1838-1917) took to be an important mark of the mental. But if the focus of the traditional discussions was on how the mental could be "about" things, the focus has shifted to how the mental could "say" one thing rather than another. Instead of concentrating on Jones's fear of *lions* or his imagining *a stately pleasure dome*, our philosophers take as primary his fear *that a lion will eat him* or his imagining *that a stately pleasure dome has been built in his back yard*. This shift of primary examples makes the analogy between fears, imaginings, and so on, and assertings, questionings, and so on—between thought and language—much more accessible and much more tempting.

If we take a wider and longer view, however, we will see that such an analogy is not so new after all. Geach draws on views of thought as inner speech that he finds in William of Ockham and Saint Thomas, and Brentano drew heavily on medieval writers. Conceptions of thinking as a kind of talking to oneself have a long and varied history in psychology, for instance in the work of J. B. Watson. In Aristotle himself we get hints like this: "Now spoken sounds are symbols of affections in the soul, and written marks symbols of spoken sounds. But what these are in the first place signs of—affections of the soul—are the same for all; and what these affections are likenesses of—actual things—are also the same."[1]

III

It would be a mistake to think these are issues about the proper understanding of *ordinary* mental talk that empirical psychologists and philosophers reflecting on psychological theory can safely leave to one side. However illuminating it may be for some limited purposes to compare human beings to Turing machines or finite automata, it does not seem possible to formulate substantive hypotheses about human mental life in terms of a small number of unstructured *total* states succeeding each other according to simple rules. There are too many possible states and no reason to think anyone is ever in the same state twice. This remains equally true whatever our views (dualist, identity-theoretic, functionalist, or whatnot) about the nature of the individual states.

This is particularly apparent if, like the authors in this section, we do think psychology must concern itself with ordinary or "commonsense" mental concepts like believing, wanting, fearing, perceiving, concluding, and so on, or theoretical refinements of these. For a person at a time is characterized by a *number* of beliefs, wants, and so on—a *vast* number, in fact. Moreover, at least one way of specifying a particular belief or want is to offer a *sentence* (I believe *that p*; I want it to become true *that p*). Systematically vary *p* and you systematically vary the content of the belief you report: here a cat, there a samovar. So if we want to make beliefs and so forth into possible states in a psychological model in even the crudest way, we must conceive of psychological states in the plural and we must conceive of at least some of them as structured like sentences. That is, vast numbers of these states must be able to coexist and some possible states must be subject to systematic variations that at least roughly parallel the systematic variations among possible sentences. For picturesqueness, we may want to think of these possible states *as sentences*, as long as we avoid thinking they must consist of "words laid end to end" in some literal way. Pursuing this picture, we can try to think of the changes our beliefs, wants, and so on undergo over time as interpretable as derivations, where derivations are systematic *manipulations* of sentences or collections of sentences. Get some rules for these derivations to follow and you have a crude psychological theory, if all goes well.

Of the philosophers who appear below, Harman is the one who is most ready to appeal to considerations like these. With a special eye to the ordinary notions of believing and desiring or wanting, he argues boldly:

We know that people have beliefs and desires, that beliefs and desires influence action, that interaction with the environment can give rise to new beliefs, and that needs and drives can give rise to desires. Adequate psychological theories must reflect this knowledge and add to it. So adequate psychological models must have states that correspond to beliefs, desires, and thoughts such that these states function in the model as psychological states function in the person modeled, and such that they are representational in the way that psychological states are representational. Where there is such representation, there is a system of representation; and that system may be identified with the inner language in which a person thinks. (chapter 2)

(Fodor makes more detailed and more carefully hedged arguments to a similar conclusion.)[2]

There are a number of points where someone might want to resist this argument. One might deny, for instance, that the commonplaces Harman recites at the beginning really are things we know or that they really make sense, dismissing the notions of belief, desire, and so on, as

so much prescientific mythology. B. F. Skinner occasionally sounds like this.

One might also regard these commonplaces as in order as they stand but misleading in *form*. Following this line, we would say it is perfectly in order to say that people "have" beliefs and desires, that beliefs and desires "influence" action, and so on, if we understand these remarks as they are understood in ordinary language. But when we do so we will see that "have," "influence," and so on have to be understood in such a way as to avoid the impression that we are describing two different sorts of thing—people and their actions, on the one hand, and "ghostly" entities like beliefs and desires, on the other—actually standing in relations of causation and possession. The commonplaces are misleading to the extent that they call up the image of inner or hidden happenings *actually* brought about by inner and environmental causes and *actually* issuing in inner and behavioral effects. Ordinary mental talk is not about *actual inner goings-on* at all but rather about *hypothetical behavior*, though we may need a more liberal conception of behavior than Skinner's to make this out.

This sort of position is associated with Gilbert Ryle and *The Concept of Mind.*[3] On such a view, Jones's believing such and such simply consists in its being the case that *if* Jones were placed in various hypothetical situations *then* he would overtly act in such and such ways. So the truth conditions of commonsense psychological ascriptions are exhausted by matters of *overt* fact of very familiar kinds. They do not involve anything that either purports to be or could turn out to be an "internal state" of the kind that would interest someone trying to produce a scientific account of why behavior happens. "Commonsense psychology" properly understood does not *explain* behavior, even in a sketchy way; it *summarizes* behavior. To think such talk could be a guide to the inner causes of behavior is to misunderstand what it is about in the first place. Thus defenders of ambitious proposals about mental representation consider Ryle an important opponent.

Yet a third way of dissenting from Harman's argument is represented by Dennett. Suppose we grant that commonsense talk about beliefs, desires, and so on is properly interpreted as telling a story about how behavior is actually caused by inner happenings of some kind. Suppose we grant that systematic psychological theories are supposed to "reflect and add to" the knowledge we *now* express in talking about beliefs, desires, and so on. Then the task of psychological theories would be to explain systematically and comprehensively what is now explained or at least described more fragmentarily using these commonsense notions. Suppose we even grant that for theoretical or practical reasons these theories must involve describing *systems of representations* for ways things can be and describing the deployment of these systems in organisms, after the fashion of "information-processing" schools of cognitive psychology. (We might have reasons for this claim that are fairly independent of Harman's. After all, even *neurophysiological* results are sometimes best summarized in a "representational" way: "This neuron-firing represents the visual field as containing an edge moving in such and such a direction.")

Dennett wants to argue that with all this granted we do not have to say (with Harman) that a psychological model needs to have particular states in it that "correspond to" beliefs and desires in any straightforward way. Nor do we need to say (with Fodor) that belief that *p*, desire that *p*, and so on, consist in one's being in appropriate "computational relations" to a formula that means *p*. For it is one thing to say that belief and desire specify part of what we want psychology to account for

and quite another to say that psychology itself is required to talk about (or provide materials for defining) beliefs and desires. It might be that none of the representations a good psychological theory uses corresponds in any simple way to ordinary ascriptions. A chess-playing program can be correctly criticized for "wanting to get its queen out early" without there being any representation *in* the program that can appropriately be described as *saying* "Get your queen out early." Why couldn't *our* beliefs, wants, and so on, be related to *our* "program" in a similarly indirect way?

In dealing with the first two objections, Harman and Fodor have the help and blessings of much twentieth-century philosophy of mind. The third objection is more novel and considerably harder to evaluate. Some questions to bear in mind in doing so are these: Just what should a psychologist's attitude to "commonsense psychology" be? If human information processing can be described at many different levels of detail, how will the representations we talk about at different levels be related? (Are we *sure* "Get your queen out early" does *not* appear in Dennett's program?) How much is the chess program's "want" like *our* wants? It is certainly a good deal more limited in the ways it manifests itself; does this difference undermine the comparison?

IV

Among the chapters in this part of the volume, the selection from Geach's *Mental Acts* (chapter 1) is the earliest by nearly twenty years. It illustrates the fact that many current issues in philosophy of psychology have been explored quite sensitively by philosophers of mind who were not directly concerned with empirical psychology at all. (Another figure who was discussing similar issues with similar philosophical resources in the same period was Wilfrid Sellars; see 1963a, 1963b, 1968.) Geach conceives of his task as that of describing what he calls, after Wittgenstein, the "logic" of ordinary psychological concepts. In other words, he wants to describe what controls our application of these concepts as things now stand.

It is also important to notice that the mental descriptions that principally concern Geach are not the same ones that principally concern Harman and Fodor. We can draw a rough distinction between mental descriptions that are used to assign standing attitudes to us (what we believe, want, and so on) and those that describe temporally localized episodes in our mental life that occur against the background of these attitudes, occasionally altering the background in one way or another. This latter, episodic class would include descriptions of what we are now seeing, hearing, recalling, imagining, mentally rehearsing, and so on. (Sometimes the same verb can be used in both ways. Compare *hoping* in a general way — for years on end, perhaps — that California will not sink into the Pacific with Geach's hero's *hoping* "with a sudden pang of hope" for a letter from his sweetheart.) Harman and Fodor worry primarily about attitudes, Geach about episodes — what he calls "mental acts." Among these he is particularly concerned with acts of *judgment*, as when we judge, for example, that the carburetor needs adjusting from the way our engine sounds.

Given these divergences, the number of claims, concerns, and even arguments he shares with someone like Fodor is remarkable. The two argue against behaviorist and Rylean views of mental notions in very similar terms. Geach's discussion of Dr. Johnson's penance in Uttoxeter square could but for its bookishness have come from Fodor's discussion of the explanation of action. They also share the conviction that various themes from empiricism have seriously obscured our thinking about mental representation: the view that we have

some sort of quasi-sensory (and perhaps infallible) access to our own mental operations, the view that all our knowledge consists in inferences from ultimate premises that talk only of objects of "direct acquaintance" describable in some sort of sense-datum language, the view that the concepts employed in mental representations can and must themselves be "derived from experience" by selectively noticing repeated features and performing an act of abstraction.

There are of course important differences. For instance, Geach relates concepts, judgment, and the mental representations that concern *him* far more closely to the possession of a natural language than Fodor does. Thus Fodor speaks of "organisms" where Geach always speaks of just "men," that is, people who can speak. The difference reflects Geach's conviction that the sensible application of the same psychological notions to ourselves and speechless organisms would depend on our having similar or broadly analogous capacities and practices in many different areas, and that for most psychological notions the necessary similarities and analogies simply are not there.

To what extent are mental acts really episodes, comparable to overt physical episodes like a flash of lightning or a spilling of ink? On this question Geach argues against Ryle that descriptions of mental acts cannot be disguised hypotheticals about overt behavior, but at the same time he wants to deny that the analogy between mental acts and physical occurrences is perfect. It makes no sense, for instance, to ask how long an act of judging takes to run to completion.

To what extent are acts of judgment a matter of asserting a sentence "inwardly"? And to what extent is the assembling of concepts in a judgment like the assembling of words in a sentence? In other parts of *Mental Acts* Geach offers a rather detailed account of the relation between the indirect discourse (*oratio obliqua*) we use to report acts of judgment and the direct quotation (*oratio recta*) we use in reporting people's actual spoken words. This much should be said here: for Geach a *concept* is an ability to use particular words or constructions in speaking and thinking. An act of judgment consists of appropriately related exercises of various concepts; what counts as "appropriately related" depends on the form of the judgment. (Geach calls the dated exercises of concepts in acts of judgment "Ideas.") He sketches a further account of how "intellectually identical" judgments, ones involving the same concepts exercised in the same way, could manage to be about different particular objects—first one cat, then another. But he does not think of concepts in a judgment as related to one another in a spatial or temporal sequence; nor does he think there is any unique decomposition of a judgment into constituent concepts. A single judgment can be assigned as many different "structures" as there are different correct ways of reporting it in indirect discourse.

V

Let us return to the problem of modeling a scientific psychology on commonsense ascriptions of beliefs, wants, fears, and so on, as I sketched it in III. Fodor and Harman agree that there is more to be said about the nature and structure of mental representations than a view like Geach's would indicate. They suggest that empirical work in psychology and linguistics can help us decide what more to say, and that in the process we uncover further similarities between mental representations and linguistic representations. For instance, in his discussion of concept learning Fodor cites evidence that the same supposition about an experimental situation can be expressed in *different* but *logically equivalent* forms that cannot be used by the subject with equal speed and facility, one intuitively "conjunctive" and the other intuitively "disjunctive."

Presumably this is a case in which Geach would have a single possible "act of supposition," which we on the outside can carve into concept-exercises in different, equally good ways. But Fodor's evidence suggests that on any particular occasion one carving *is* better, more accurately reflects what actually went on, than the other.

How languagelike do mental representations get? Here Harman is more specific; according to him, thought may be regarded as consisting in large part of operations on what he calls "sentences under analysis," disambiguated deep structures. It is important, however, to note that Fodor and Harman claim only that some mental representations are highly languagelike, not that all are. In *Thought*, Harman remarks that "not all human thought is in words. Our conception of ourselves in the world is more like a map than a story, and in perception our view of the world is more like a picture" (1973, p. vii). (See also Fodor, chapter 7.)

To make responsible use of this evidence we need a working conception of how philosopher-talk about mental representations is to link up with psychologist-talk about the storage, processing, and flow of what is usually and obscurely called "information." Here it is Fodor who is more explicit, and his basic idea is that of a derivation as I used it above in III. By trying to construct a psychological theory that employs states modeled on sentences and trying to find general principles about how combinations of these states succeed one another, we are in effect trying to define a formal system and a notion of derivation or computation for that system. Possible transitions of states (or at least the psychologically explicable ones) will correspond to legal derivations in the formal system. Proposals about "how information is processed" are proposals about how derivations generate new mental formulae from old. (Of course, *derivation* will not be *deduction* in general, since what we conclude is not in general implied by the things from which we conclude it. There may be interesting regularities concerning derivation and truth but derivation is not in general truth-preserving.) In *The Language of Thought*, Fodor develops the idea this way:

> When we think of an organism as a computer, we attempt to assign formulae in the vocabulary of a psychological theory to physical states of the organism (e.g., to states of its nervous system). Ideally, the assignment should be carried through in such fashion that some (at least) of the sequences of states that are causally implicated in the production of behavior can be interpreted as computations which have appropriate descriptions of the behavior as their 'last line.' The idea is that, in the case of organisms as in the case of real computers, if we get the right way of assigning formulae to the states it will be feasible to interpret the sequence of events that *causes* the output as a computational derivation of the output. (pp. 73-74)

He speaks here of derivations rather than simply of formal transformations because the states to which we assign formulae (or which we regard *as* formulae) are importantly sentencelike and because the "last lines" of these derivations are interpretable as our *concluding* that this or that is the case, that this or that bodily movement should be executed, and so forth.

Of course, most psychological theorizing proceeds without benefit of physiological descriptions of these states. This troubles many philosophers and many psychologists. The psychologist can often claim acquaintance with states *only* as tokens of certain formulae or, if you like, *psychofunctionally*: as whatever states they may be that bear the appropriate causal relations to each other and to things outside the organism. Fodor is eager to show that we can develop and

test plausible theories about formulae and derivations nonetheless, and that psycholinguists are doing just that (see 1975, chap. 3).

On the picture I have been following, which I shall call the *derivation picture*, states *are* formulae. Or if one wants one's formulae to be strings of ink marks, different states correspond to different formulae. In particular, believing something and wanting that same thing will involve the occurrence of different formulae in one's mental life. But Fodor *also* uses (sometimes in adjacent passages) a *relational picture* that is quite different (p. 75). According to the relational picture, believing something and wanting that same thing will involve an organism's being in different relations to (possibly different tokens of) the *same* formula. States are no longer identifiable with formulae, and psychologically explicable changes of state are no longer identifiable with derivations.

It is a weakness of Fodor's account that he switches back and forth between these pictures without notice, but so far as I can see he *can* use both, if he takes different items as "formulae of the internal code" on the two different pictures. If on the relational picture we take believing such and such to be a matter of the organism's standing in one of several possible relations—the "belief-relation"—to a formula P that means such and such, then on the derivation picture we will need to trade a multiplicity of relations for a multiplicity of formulae. We will need a number of different formulae with the same "propositional content" but tagged to indicate whether they are "beliefs that such and such," "desires that such and such," or something else.[4] In naming these formulae on paper we might write 'P_B,' 'P_D,' and so on. Our derivation rules will, of course, have to "pay attention to subscripts."

We might diagram the two conceptions of a total psychological state thus, with B = belief; D = desire; and F = fear:

Relational picture   Derivation picture

Organism O

B-relation   D-relation   F-relation

O's
formulae $= \{ \quad P, \quad\quad Q, \quad\quad R, \ldots \}$

O's
formulae $= \{ \quad P_B, Q_D, R_F, \ldots \quad \}$

The relational picture has the virtue of making our mental formulae more fully analogous to declarative sentences. It also permits us to think (as we are bound to anyway) of the mind as a quasi-spatial mechanism whose "parts" take in representations from each other, perform operations on them, and pass on the results. To be *really* crude about it we could think of the different kinds of arrow in the figure as leading to different boxes of token formulae, with "processors" connecting one box with another like siphons. A processor sucks up tokens from one or more boxes, performs manipulations that result in new tokens, and distributes them to one or more other boxes. One box might be "what I believe." Of course, we do not *need* to be this crude about it, and that is important. Dennett's worries about whether there would be room in our brains for all our beliefs if Fodor were right can be allayed if we recognize that being in a "computational relation" to a formula need not involve having a token of that formula present in the "computer" at all. It could involve no more than (for example) a readiness to compute such a token under special circumstances.

Another worry expressed by Dennett—the worry about infinite regress in explanation—is one psychologists need to take more seriously. It may be easy enough to tell a plausible tale about "boxes" and "tokens in boxes" as long as

we do not task ourselves with saying how the "processors" work. Moreover, not all explicit stories about what the processors are like and what they do are equally explanatory. We would feel as if we had made some progress if we could get by with processors that behaved like adding machines, but not if they had to behave like a grown woman at the breakfast table reading a newspaper, talking to her husband, and all the time contriving not to spill cigarette ashes on the tablecloth. In the latter case, we would feel that the boxes and tokens had not made things a bit less mysterious.

This point would be of limited and questionable significance if it were merely a point about what would explain what, or what would make what less mysterious. (Whatever the correct account of scientific explanation may be, a phenomenon can perfectly well serve as evidence for a theory without thereby being explained by the theory. Besides, it is unfortunately the case that scientific explanations of phenomena often make them look much more complicated and indeed much more mysterious than they seemed pretheoretically. Look at twentieth-century physics!) It is a point about *testing* as well. After all, *any* logically possible and reasonably systematic notation could be handled by *some* sort of processor and to almost any effect. We simply do not know how to test a hypothesis about how the mind represents things without at least some views about the mental operations in which these representations figure. To switch pictures: views about the syntax and semantics of the internal code and views about the mind's derivation rules must come together. This is important to bear in mind, since it is much easier to think up systems of representations than it is to think up workable accounts of human inference and action that would use them.

The apparition of the little man in the head perusing our brainwriting should not scare us away from the whole conception of mental representations or languages of thought. Not yet, at least. The moral is that however analogous mental and linguistic representations may turn out to be in *structure*, their *employments* by human organisms are as different as they can be, and the employment of neither is at all well understood. If we forget this we can easily fool ourselves into thinking we understand a lot more than we do.

Notes

1. *De Interpretatione* 16ᵃ3. From *Aristotle's Categories and De Interpretatione*, trans. with notes and glossary by J. L. Ackrill (London: Oxford University Press, 1963), p. 43. Of course, our philosophers will not find it so obvious that the "affections of the soul" are in any simple sense the same for all, or that their relation to things they represent is anything as straightforward as "likeness."

2. In Fodor, 1975, he summarizes his approach this way (p. 27):

1. The only psychological models of cognitive processes that seem even remotely plausible represent such processes as computational.
2. Computation presupposes a medium of computation: a representational system.
3. Remotely plausible theories are better than no theories at all.
4. We are thus provisionally committed to attributing a representational system to organisms. 'Provisionally committed' means: committed insofar as we at-

tribute cognitive processes to organisms and insofar as we take seriously such theories of these processes as are currently available.
5. It is a reasonable research *goal* to try to characterize the representational system to which we thus find ourselves provisionally committed.
6. It is a reasonable research *strategy* to try to infer this characterization from the details of such psychological theories as seem likely to prove true.
7. This strategy may actually work: it is possible to exhibit specimen inferences along the lines of item 6 which, if not precisely apodictic, have at least an air of prima facie plausibility.

3. Dennett argues that Ryle is sometimes misconstrued on these matters in "A Cure for the Common Code?" (chapter 4).

4. Psychology may need more or different "propositional attitudes" than commonsense does, but it is convenient to forget this here.

References

Dennett, D. C. 1969. *Content and Consciousness.* London: Routledge and Kegan Paul.

Fodor, J. A. 1975. *The Language of Thought.* New York: Crowell.

Gunderson, K., ed. 1975. *Language, Mind, and Knowledge. Minnesota Studies in the Philosophy of Science*, vol. 7. Minneapolis: University of Minnesota Press.

Harman, G. 1973. *Thought.* Princeton: Princeton University Press.

Putnam, H. 1973. "Reference and Understanding." In *Meaning and the Moral Sciences.* London: Routledge and Kegan Paul.

Sellars, W. 1963a. "Being and Being Known." In *Science, Perception, and Reality.* London: Routledge and Kegan Paul.

—— 1963b. "Empiricism and the Philosophy of Mind," sections 46-62. In *Science, Perception, and Reality.* London: Routledge and Kegan Paul.

—— 1968. *Science and Metaphysics*, chap. 3. London: Routledge and Kegan Paul.

Vendler, Z. 1972. *Res Cogitans.* Ithaca: Cornell University Press.

Ziff, P. 1972. *Understanding Understanding.* Ithaca: Cornell University Press.

1

Selections from *Mental Acts*

Peter Geach

1. Act, Content, and Object

The title I have chosen for this work is a mere label for a set of problems; the controversial views that have historically been expressed by using the terms "act", "content", and "object" ought not at the outset to be borne in mind. My own use of the term "mental act" may be explained, sufficiently for present purposes, as follows. In historical or fictional narrative there occur reports, not only of what human beings overtly said and did, but also of what they thought, how they felt, what they saw and heard, and so on; I shall call the latter kind of reports "reports of mental acts". The psychological character or, as I shall say, the *content* of mental acts is expressed by the use of various psychological verbs, such as "see", "hear", "hope", "think". Many of these psychological verbs require a grammatical object — a noun, noun-phrase, or noun-clause — to complete their sense. The hero sees *the postman coming*, hears *his knock*, hopes (has a sudden pang of hope) for *a letter from his sweetheart*, thinks *that his letter to her may have been open-*

From *Mental Acts* (London: Routledge and Kegan Paul, 1957), sections 1-5, 17, 23-25. Reprinted by permission of Routledge and Kegan Paul and Humanities Press. Notes have been renumbered for this edition.

ed by her guardian, and so on. The use of such expressions is thus essential in stating the content of many mental acts; we may call them "object-expressions".

I shall avoid such uses of the term "object" as "A letter from his sweetheart is an object of the hero's hope" or "The possibility of his letters' being intercepted by her guardian is an object of his thought". Familiar and understandable as such uses are, they raise logical difficulties that I prefer to avoid. (One of these difficulties is that the so-called object may not exist; in my examples, there may be no letter from the hero's sweetheart such as he hopes for, and no such possibility as he thinks, of her guardian's intercepting his letters; so the use of "object" that I shall avoid might easily lead us on to such odd statements as "some objects of mental acts do not exist".) I shall accordingly state my problems not in the form "What sort of objects do these mental acts have?" but rather in the form "Such-and-such object-expressions are used in describing these mental acts; what is the logical role of these expressions?"

2. Wittgenstein's Alleged Rejection of Mental Acts

The existence of mental acts, as I have explained the term, ought not to be a

matter of controversy. According to the
Gospel story, something happened to St
Peter when the cock crew; he heard it
crow, and he remembered Christ's proph-
ecy of his three denials; his hearing and
his remembering were mental acts. There
is indeed a danger that when we speak of
mental acts or mental events or what happened in a person's mind, we may be led
to an illegitimate assimilation of psychological to physical reports. There are
logical similarities between the two kinds
of reports, but there are no less important
logical differences; these differences, on
which Wittgenstein continually insisted,
were already noticed by Aquinas, who
remarked that when people speak of the
mind as a 'subject of change' the meaning
(ratio) of "subject" and "change" is quite
other than it is in discourse about physical
processes (Ia q. 75 art. 5 ad 2 um). But
since such logical differences are just what
we are looking out for in our enquiry,
there is little risk of our forgetting that
they may exist.

Wittgenstein has been understood as
denying the existence of mental acts; and
certain remarks of his about 'private objects' (Wittgenstein, Part I, Section 293;
Part II, p. 207) are very easily taken this
way. I am sure, however, that I have not
so far maintained anything Wittgenstein
would have attacked. Of course Wittgenstein did not want to deny the obvious
truth that people have a 'private' mental
life, in the sense that they have for example thoughts they do not utter and pains
they do not show; nor did he try to
analyse away this truth in a neo-
behaviouristic fashion. In one of his lectures he mentioned Lytton Strachey's imaginative description of Queen Victoria's
dying thoughts. He expressly repudiated
the view that such a description is meaningless because 'unverifiable'; it has meaning, he said, but only through its connexion with a wider, public, 'language-game'
of describing people's thoughts; he used
the simile that a chess-move worked out

in a sketch of a few squares on a scrap of
paper has significance through its connexion with the whole practice of playing
chess. It is useful to observe Frege's
distinction of sense (Sinn) and reference
(Bedeutung) in stating Wittgenstein's position; what Wittgenstein wanted to deny
was not the private reference of psychological expressions—e.g. that "pain"
stands for a kind of experience that may
be quite 'private'—but the possibility of
giving them a private sense—e.g. of giving sense to the word "pain" by just attending to one's own pain-experiences, a performance that would be private and un-
checkable. The view that psychological
words are given a sense in this way is part
of a theory (abstractionism, as I shall call
it) which Wittgenstein rejected in toto and
not only as regards psychological terms.
Another view he rejected (one closely
bound up, I believe, with an abstractionist view of psychological terms) is the
view that such relations as that between a
pain and its symptoms or a thought and
the words expressing it have nothing to do
with our concept of pain or thought and
are just established inductively. We shall
discuss both these topics later on.

3. Ryle's Rejection of Mental Acts

Although I shall try to show that
reports of mental acts are logically different from reports of physical events, I
hold that reports of both kinds are categorical. This view is sharply opposed to
Ryle's view that psychological statements
are not reports of private events (mental
acts) but are hypothetical or semi-
hypothetical statements about overt behaviour. (Ryle, pp. 33, 46.) I shall not
criticize Ryle's attempted analyses in detail; the entire programme seems to me
misconceived. In the first place, he makes
no serious attempt to carry out his programme consistently; he leaves some reports of mental acts standing, without offering any analysis of them into hypothetical or semi-hypothetical statements

about behaviour. The mental acts in question are indeed referred to throughout in a highly depreciatory style, as "itches", "tingles", "tweaks", "agitations", etc.; but this rhetorical trick proves nothing. If reports of these mental acts cannot be reduced to hypothetical or semi-hypothetical statements about overt behaviour, then the view that the distinction between categoricals and hypotheticals is *the* logical distinction between physical and psychological statements must be *completely* wrong. A logical principle allows of no exceptions — not even if the exceptions are events that only James Joyce would put into a novel.

Secondly, when Ryle explains a statement of an *actual* difference between two men's mental states as really asserting only that there are circumstances in which one *would* act differently from the other, and apparently holds that this could be *all* the difference there is between the two, he is running counter to a very deep-rooted way of thinking. When two agents differ in their behaviour, we look for some actual, not merely hypothetical, difference between them to account for this; as the scholastics said, *omne agens agit in quantum est in actu.* Ryle explicitly and repeatedly compares psychological accounts of behaviour to saying that a glass broke because it was brittle (had the dispositional property of brittleness); in so doing, however, he is setting them on a level with the statement that opium puts people to sleep because it has a dormitive power — which I believe was not his intention. (Ryle, pp. 50, 86-7, 88-9, *et al.*)

The principle expressed in the scholastic tag just cited is of importance in scientific investigation. A physicist would be merely impatient if somebody said to him: "Why look for, or postulate, any *actual* difference between a magnetized and an unmagnetized bit of iron? Why not just say that if certain things are done to a bit of iron certain hypotheticals become true of it?" He would be still more impatient at

being told that his enquiries were vitiated by the logical mistake of treating "*x* is magnetized" as categorical, whereas it is really hypothetical or semi-hypothetical. Of course there may be people prepared to say that, although men of science regularly look for differences already existing between the agents in order to explain differences of behaviour, there is no reason to expect that such differences always do exist; the principle on which men of science proceed might be as unsound as any gambling system, and their success up to now mere luck. I shall not argue the point.

We may well be reluctant, then, to expound in Ryle's fashion even psychological accounts of *actual* differences in behaviour. Our reluctance should be still greater when we are invited to regard a statement that two men, whose overt behaviour was not actually different, were in different states of mind (e.g. that one checked a column of figures with his mind on the job, the other with his mind on his domestic troubles) as being really a statement that the behaviour of one man *would have been* different from that of the other in hypothetical circumstances that never arose. It ought to be, but plainly is not, generally known to philosophers that the logic of counterfactual conditionals is a very ill-explored territory; no adequate formal logic for them has yet been devised, and there is an extensive literature on the thorny problems that crop up. It is really a scandal that people should count it a philosophical advance to adopt a programme of analysing ostensible categoricals into unfulfilled conditionals, like the programmes of phenomenalists with regard to 'physical-object' statements and of neo-behaviourists with regard to psychological statements.

With specious lucidity, Ryle describes the counterfactual conditionals he uses as having the 'sentence-job' not of stating facts but of licencing inferences. The terms "inference-licence" and "inference-ticket" seem to be explanatory because we associate them with very familiar institutions. In order to see that nothing has been explained at all, we need only ask the question what inferences from fact to fact a counterfactual conditional does give us licence to perform. I need hardly comment on Ryle's view that "the rubber has begun to lose its elasticity" has to do not with a change in the rubber but with the (incipient?) expiry of an inference-ticket. (See Ryle, pp. 120-5.)

4. Acts of Judgment

The sort of mental acts that I shall chiefly investigate are acts of judgment. This is not an arbitrary choice. Concepts, as we shall see, are capacities exercised in acts of judgment—psychological concepts, in psychological judgments about oneself and others; and one of the chief obstacles we shall encounter is a tangle of mistakes and confusions about judgments and concepts generally, by reason of which people go widely astray in their account of psychological judgments and concepts in particular. I hope my work on the nature of judgment will do something to clear away the tangle.

Many readers may wish to object *in limine* that even if there are mental acts, there certainly are not acts of judgment. However difficult the logic of dispositional words may be, it is surely clear both that "believe" is such a word, and that the acts which make it true to say that So-and-so believes such-and-such are not only, perhaps not at all, acts of judgment. A gardener's belief that it will rain is a disposition exercised in suitable acts of preparation rather than in intermittent mental acts of judgment. (Ryle, pp. 175-6.)

But is there in fact any behaviour characteristic of a given belief? Can action be described as "acting as if you held such-and-such a belief" unless we take for granted, or are somehow specially informed about, the needs and wants of the

agent? In Ryle's example this information is smuggled in by his speaking of a *gardener's* rain-expecting behaviour (and tacitly assuming that the gardener is not e.g. a discontented or corrupt servant who wants the garden to be ruined). When Dr Johnson did penance in Uttoxeter market-place, he may have begun by standing around bareheaded until the threatened shower should fall; this would not be recognizable as rain-expecting behaviour without a knowledge of Johnson's wish to do penance. There is indeed one sort of behaviour that does characterize a belief—namely, putting it into words; lying is necessarily the exception, not the rule. But putting your belief into words is one of those 'intellectualistic' activities that Ryle seeks to depreciate. In this instance, his doing so is very understandable; for on the face of it if somebody puts his belief into words, not parrotwise but with consideration, then there occurs a mental act, of the sort that I call an act of judgment. Anybody performs an act of judgment at least as often as he makes up his mind how to answer a question; and acts of judgment in this sense are plainly episodic—have a position in a time-series. (We shall see, indeed, that we cannot—cannot in principle, not for lack of information or technique—assign positions in time to acts of judgment in the same way as we do to physical events, nor even in the same way as we do to sensations. But this is irrelevant to our present discussion.)

In very many languages, a report of an act of judgment is expressed by using the *oratio obliqua* construction—i.e. the same construction as is used with 'verbs of saying' to report the gist or upshot of somebody's remark rather than the actual words he used. Thus, in English and Latin and many other languages (including, as a pupil once told me, some African languages), there need be no difference except in the main verb between a statement that James *said* it was time for everybody to go home and a statement that James *judged* it was time for everybody to go home. And for every judgment whose content can thus be given by means of a piece of *oratio obliqua*, there is some form of words, in the language considered, that would be suitable to *express* the act of judgment—namely, some form of words whose gist is given in the piece of *oratio obliqua*. (We must of course distinguish between expressing a judgment and expressing a *report* of a judgment. "James judged that the crevasse was too wide for him to jump" expresses a *report* of James's judgment; a form of words suitable to express this act of judgment would be "the crevasse is too wide for me to jump".)

Now given a statement made by James in a language L, the grammatical rules of L generally allow us to construct a piece of *oratio obliqua* that preserves the gist of the statement. (Schoolboys often do this as an exercise in Latin grammar.) Having done this, we need only tack on the expression in L for "James judged (that . . .)", and we have a report in L of the judgment expressed in James's original statement. Moreover, if we have sufficient mastery of L to understand both the expression for "James judged (that . . .)" and the piece of *oratio obliqua*, we shall understand the report so constructed, no matter what the actual sense of the remark done into *oratio obliqua* may be.

Nonsense cannot be turned into *oratio obliqua*; for *oratio obliqua*, which serves to report the upshot of what is said, cannot be used to report nonsense. So an attempt to report that somebody judges nonsense is itself nonsense. A British pupil of Heidegger might say "Nothing noths" in a tone of conviction; assuming that this is nonsense, "he judged that Nothing nothed" would also be nonsense. (We ought rather to say: "he judged that 'Nothing noths' was the expression of a truth".)

These remarks about the expression of judgments and the reports of judgments may appear very obvious; but in fact, as we shall see, they impose severe logical restrictions upon analyses of judgment.

5. The Nature of Concepts

Concepts, the old-fashioned logic-books tell us, are presupposed to, and exercised in, acts of judgment. Of course this is psychology, not logic; but I think that it is correct psychology.

It has been argued, however, that, so far from concepts' being presupposed to judgments, the common feature of judgments in which one and the same concept is supposed to be exercised is something that appears on its own account only in subsequent reflection on the judgments. I do not, it is said, first acquire a concept of *man* and then put it to work in forming judgments about *man* (judgments whose natural expression in English would contain a use of the word "man"); on the contrary, I first of all form certain judgments and then, reflecting upon them, bring them under the head "judgments about *man*"; this feature that I now attend to on its own account did not exist as an independent factor in the original judgments.

My reply is as follows. Any reportable act of judgment is apt for verbal expression, in a form of words whose gist is contained in the *oratio obliqua* of the report. (I am not asserting, nor do I think, that an act of judgment is always put into words, even 'in the head'). Let us concentrate, for the moment, on judgments that are verbally expressed. The sentence expressing a judgment will consist of a number of words; and the significant utterance of the sentence therefore brings into exercise various relatively simple skills—the abilities to use the various expressions that occur in the sentence. It is important to notice that as applied to whole sentences the philosophical slogan "the meaning of an expression is its use" is seriously mistaken; at any rate if "use" is here taken to mean "established usage". For in general there is no established usage for a sentence as a whole; e.g. the sentences in this book do not get their meaning from any established usage, nor have I learned to use them in circles where they were commonly used. It is words and phrases that have an established usage; a language is mastered not by learning whole sentences out of a guidebook but by learning to make up sentences in it and to understand sentences not previously heard. That is how we learn foreign languages, and how children come to understand and speak their native language.[1] The ability to express a judgment in words thus presupposes a number of capacities, previously acquired, for intelligently using the several words and phrases that make up the sentence. I shall apply the old term "concepts" to these special capacities — an application which I think lies fairly close to the historic use of the term. It will be a *sufficient* condition for James's having the concept of *so-and-so* that he should have mastered the intelligent use (including the use in made-up sentences) of a word for *so-and-so* in some language. Thus: if somebody knows how to use the English word "red", he has a concept of red; if he knows how to use the first-person pronoun, he has a concept of *self*; if he knows how to use the negative construction in some language, he has a concept of negation.

An analogy from playing chess may help to show how concepts and acts of judgment are related. Making an appropriate move from a certain position may be, and at the opening of the game very likely will be, a learned response; but in the middle game it will certainly not be so, for the position may well occur only once in a life-time of play. On the other hand, the ability to make an appropriate move from a given position always presupposes a number of simpler, previously acquired, skills — the capacities to carry out the moves and captures that are lawful for the pawns and the various pieces. As these skills are related to the

chess-move, so concepts are related to the act of judgment.

I have stated only a sufficient, not a necessary, condition for somebody's having a given concept. If a man struck with aphasia can still play bridge or chess, I certainly wish to say he still has the concepts involved in the game, although he can no longer exercise them verbally. But it would be hard to devise non-verbal criteria for the patient's having retained a concept of *the day after tomorrow*. The central and typical applications of the term "having a concept" are those in which a man is master of a bit of linguistic usage; we can then reasonably extend the term to cases sufficiently like these, e.g. where the man can play 'intellectual' games like bridge and chess. I shall not try to draw any sharp line between what is 'sufficiently like' the central and typical cases and what is not; I do not think we shall go far wrong if we concentrate henceforward on concepts exercised linguistically.

A concept, as I am using the term, is subjective—it is a mental capacity belonging to a particular person. (My use of "concept" is thus to be contrasted e.g. with Russell's use of it in *The Principles of Mathematics* and again with the use of it to translate Frege's *"Begriff"*; Russell's 'concepts' and Frege's *Begriffe* were supposed to be objective entities, not belonging to a particular mind.) The subjective nature of concepts does not however imply that it is improper to speak of two people as "having the same concept"; conformably to my explanation of the term "concept", this will mean that they have the same mental capacity, i.e. can do essentially the same things. Thus, if each of two men has mastered the intelligent use of the negative construction in his own language, we may say that they have the same mental capacity, the same concept; they both have the concept of negation. There are of course all degrees of transition between cases where we should say unhesitatingly "they have different words, but they use them in the same way; they have the same concept", and where we should rather say "it's not just a verbal difference; they have different concepts".

I thus accept the psychology of the old logic-books, to the extent of recognizing the possession of concepts as presupposed to acts of judgment, and regarding a judgment as the exercise of a number of concepts. A feature of the traditional theory that I find unacceptable is the doctrine that there are acts of 'simple apprehension', in which concepts are somehow exercised *singly* without being applied to anything. I think these acts are mythical; in chess one can practise the moves of a solitary man on the board, but I think there is no analogous exercise of a single unapplied concept.

Having criticized Ryle for his reckless use of the term "disposition", I may myself be criticized for introducing concepts, which are supposed to be capacities. But to say that a man has a certain concept is to say that he *can* perform, because he sometimes *does* perform, mental exercises of a specifiable sort. This way of using the modal word "can" is a minimal use, confined to a region where the logic of the word is as clear as possible. *Ab esse ad posse valet consequentia* — what is can be, what a man does he can do; that is clear if anything in modal logic is clear, and no more than this is involved in my talking of concepts. Ryle's attempt to expound ostensible statements about actual mental states in terms of complicated sets of subjunctive conditionals is a far more dubious undertaking.

The exercise of a given concept in an act of judgment is not in general a definite, uniform sort of mental act; it does not even make sense to ask just how many concepts are exercised in a given judgment. Our chess analogy may here again be of service, in showing why this question is unreasonable. Playing chess in-

volves a number of abilities, which are not only distinguishable but can actually exist separately; for one way of teaching chess would be to play first just with the kings and the pawns and then add the other pieces successively in later games. It would, however, be absurd to ask just how many of these abilities there were, or just how many were exercised in a particular move; although one might perfectly well say that somebody knew the knight's move, and that this knowledge was or was not exercised in a particular move. Our language about the concepts exercised in a given act of judgment makes sense or does not make sense in much the same way.

In discussing (as for the most part I shall) concepts that are involved in the intelligent use of words, I shall often have to use the phrases "to know the use of the word ———", "to know the way to use the word ———", and the like. These phrases are irritatingly ambiguous, but practically indispensable. One ambiguity of them is notorious: ambiguity as between being able to use a word intelligently and being able to give an account of its use — between *knowing how* and *knowing that*; I shall consistently keep to the *knowing how* sense unless the contrary is expressly stated. Another, trickier, ambiguity may be brought out by this question: if a Frenchman who knows no English knows the use of the French adjective "rouge", does he know the use of the English adjective "red"? In one sense of "knowing the use of the word" he must know the use of the word "red", because it is *the same as* the (relevant) use of the word "rouge", which *ex hypothesi* he knows. In another sense, he does not 'know the use of' any English word, because he knows no English. The former sense of the phrase "know the use of the word "red" " might be brought out by saying: "know how to use *some* word in the way that the word "red" is in fact used in English"; but to avoid clumsily long clauses I shall express this sense just by saying: "know the use of the word "red" ", and shall avoid using such expressions in the sense in which they are truly predicable only of English-speaking persons. (I am afraid some recent philosophers have often been ensnared by this latter ambiguity of "knowing the use of a word"; and so they give us tedious and inaccurate supplements to *Modern English Usage*, instead of philosophical discussion of a 'way of using a word' which could be found in many languages.)

Many psychologists, wishing to use the term "concept" far more widely than I do, would strongly object to my concentrating on concepts expressed in language: they would say that an animal has acquired a concept if it has learned a discriminative response to some feature of its environment. If a rat or a dog is trained to react in a certain way whenever it has a triangle shown to it (rather than some other shape), then they would say it has acquired a concept of *triangle*. (Earthworms, we are told, regularly pull bits of paper into their burrows by the sharpest angles; I do not know whether any psychologist would be prepared on this account to say earthworms have an innate concept of angular magnitude.) What is at issue here is not just the way the term "concept" is to be used, but the desirability of comparing these achievements of rats and dogs with the performances of human beings who possess a concept of *triangle*; the psychologists I am criticizing want to play down the differences between human and animal performances, and I want to stress them. The life of brutes lacks so much that is integral to human life that it can only be misleading to say that they have concepts like us — as misleading as it would be to say that men have tails and women lay eggs (as I have actually heard someone of strong 'evolutionist' opinions say in discussion) or to call the noises made by brutes "language". Experience in training dogs to 'recognize' triangles can

be no guide in (let us say) teaching geometry. It is scholasticism in the worst sense of the word to argue that if men are descended from brutes they *cannot* have anything that the brutes did not already possess (*nihil dat quod non habet!*); the argument is just as bad whether it is used to disprove evolution (as it actually once used to be—James, vol. 2, pp. 670-1), or to prove that brutes, from whom man is descended, *must* have concepts at least in a 'rudimentary' form.

*   *   *

17. Analogy Theories of Psychological Concepts

I now turn to a theory of judgment *prima facie* very different from the one sketched in Section 14. As I remarked in Section 4, there are many languages in which, as in English, the only difference between the statements "James said that *p*" and "James judged that *p*" is that they have different main verbs. The theory I am now going to discuss takes this as its clue to the nature of judgment; the concept *judging* is viewed as an analogical extension of the concept *saying*. I must begin, then, with some general remarks about the 'analogy' theory of psychological concepts. This theory is *not* to be supported by appealing to the etymology of words for mental acts. Such etymologies are often very obscure (e.g. that of "credere", "to believe", in Latin) and often have no apparent relevance when they are clear (what has *standing under* to do with *understanding*?). Again we must distinguish between what may be called *casual* and *systematic* analogies. In casual analogies, a particular epithet may be suggestive or even 'inevitable' in its metaphorical use, but this gives us no indication for the transferred use of another epithet of the same family; an understanding of "yellow — that's the only word for him!" does not give us a clue as to what would be meant if another colourword were substituted for "yellow". The sort of analogy that is important is that in which a whole system of description is transferred to an analogical use; the *oratio obliqua* construction, for example, whose primary use is to report actual speech, is transferred to describing the content of judgments.

What is the meaning of calling a description of a mental act "analogical" or "metaphorical", except by contrast with a literal description? and if the literal description is available, how can the analogy be of any importance for the concept of the mental act? This objection to the expression "analogy" or "metaphor" is easily got over. What makes the description to be analogical is not that there is a literal description of the mental act, to replace the metaphor, but that there is another application of the description, and of the whole system of description to which it belongs; an application that may be called literal, in contrast to the transferred application to mental acts. We may agree that if a metaphorical description of a mental act is replaceable by a non-metaphorical description of that very act, then the metaphor can have little importance for the concept of that sort of act.

Someone may, however, argue thus: "Even if in our actual language there is no way of replacing a metaphor used to describe a mental act (except perhaps by another metaphor), this can only be an accident of language. For, in order to see that the metaphorical system of description is appropriate to the facts it is used to describe, we must already be able to discern those characteristics of mental acts which make the description appropriate. Now the characteristics (for example) of a judgment that is described by a transferred use of the *oratio obliqua* construction will be characteristics not to be found in the pieces of language that this construction is primarily used to report; so a concept of the mental characteristics must be an entirely new concept, which it

is merely misleading to call an 'analogical' extension of the concept exercised in the primary use of *oratio obliqua*. And if we can discern, and form a concept of, these mental characteristics on their own account, then we could if we chose invent a special word, which would be used *only* to express our exercise of the new psychological concept. So the analogy of mental judgments to actually uttered statements cannot be an indispensable part of our concept *judgment*; and in general psychological concepts cannot be irreducibly analogous in character."

If forming a concept consisted in extracting a repetitive feature from our experience and becoming able to recognize its recurrences, then indeed psychological concepts extracted from 'inner sense' would be in no way dependent on the analogies afforded by other concepts extracted from sense-experience; only when we already possessed the psychological concepts could we go on to observe the appropriateness of such analogies. I have argued, however, that no concept whatsoever is to be identified with a recognitional capacity. In all cases it is a matter of fitting my concept to my experience – of exercising the appropriate concept – not of picking out the feature I am interested in from among others simultaneously given in experience. Now exercise of a particular set of concepts in a particular way (e.g. the exercise involved in describing something by means of a particular set of words in the *oratio obliqua* construction) may be appropriate both as applied to A and as applied to B, although A is not 'like' B; and we may perfectly well know its appropriateness in both cases (in the 'knowing-how' sense; that is to say, we may know when to exercise our concepts thus, whether or not we can formulate to ourselves a rule as to when we ought to do so).

On our theory of concepts, there is no reason that can be offered in advance why psychological concepts, or some of

them, should not be irreducibly analogous. It might very well be that we
always get the know-how of a particular
set of concepts first of all in application to
sensible things (e.g. human utterances),
and then in psychological applications.
Any alleged example of this would have
to be investigated on its own account before we could decide about its gen-
uineness. On the other hand, our theory
destroys the old grounds for saying that
psychological concepts *must* be irreducibly analogous. Somebody who held
abstractionist views, and at the same time
held that sense-experience offered all the
material we have for performing abstraction upon — a combination of views
expressed in the old maxim *"Nihil in in-
tellectu nisi prius in sensu"* — would be
obliged to maintain that we first extract
concepts from sense-experience and then
give them an extended psychological use;
his position would, in my opinion, both
involve very unplausible accounts of
certain psychological concepts, and be extremely hard to maintain on an abstractionist footing. Our rejection of abstractionism means that we are not antece-
dently committed either way as to the
analogousness of a given psychological
concept.

It is a mere matter of terminology
whether we say that the psychological
concept is a new concept derived by
'analogy' from a previous concept, or that
we exercise an old concept in new,
psychological applications 'analogous' to
our former exercise of it. A concept is a
capacity for certain exercises of the mind;
and as regards capacities generally, if a
man formerly capable of certain performances in one domain comes to perform
similarly in another domain, it is quite arbitrary whether we say that his former
capacity now extends to a new domain of
exercise or that he has acquired a new
capacity closely related to his old one. I
shall say indifferently "analogical concepts" and "analogous exercises of concepts".

*   *   *

23. Dangers of the 'Inner Language' Analogy

The important thing about analogical
extensions of a concept is that we should
know (in practice at any rate) how far to
carry the analogy. Some people have certainly carried the analogy of thought to
language too far. Thus, for William of
Ockham, besides the spoken, conventional, languages, all men have a common, natural, language; for convenience,
I shall call it "Mental". The grammar of
Mental turns out to be remarkably like
Latin grammar. There are nouns and
verbs in Mental; nouns have cases and
numbers, and verbs have voice, mood,
tense, number, and person. On the other
hand, there is nothing in Mental corresponding to the different Latin declensions and conjugations; nor are there any
deponent verbs in Mental. Ockham's
criterion for transferring Latin grammatical terms to Mental was very simple-
minded. Nouns of different declensions,
or verbs of different conjugations, may be
synonyms, and then presumably correspond to the same Mental noun or verb;
so there is no reason to ascribe differences
of declension or conjugation to Mental
words. But a change of case or number or
voice may quite alter the sense of a Latin
sentence; so Mental words must have
case, number, and voice.

Without being able to say just how
far the analogy of inner language can be
carried, I think men of good sense would
see immediately that Ockham carries it
much too far. He merely transfers features
of Latin grammar to Mental, and then
regards this as explaining why such
features occur in Latin — they are needed
there if what we say inwardly in Mental is
to be outwardly got across to others in
Latin. But clearly nothing is explained at
all. Presumably Ockham's reasons for
thinking that the supposed grammar of
Mental had explanatory force were that
Mental is a natural and universal

language, and that Mental words, unlike Latin words, are immaterial entities. But if all men had a natural and universal *spoken* language, that would not mean that its grammar was any more self-explanatory than Latin grammar. And what carries significance in a language is its structure, not its medium — the structure that can be transferred from spoken to written language and to Morse code; but Ockham takes for granted the grammatical structure of Latin, and supposes that Mental, unlike Latin, is intrinsically intelligible, simply because its medium is not material but spiritual. In point of fact, any problems that arise as to the significance of a grammatical device will arise equally for the alleged Mental uses of this device; and Ockham's saying that the words of Mental are immaterial would merely raise such footling problems as how something immaterial can be in the genitive case, without throwing any light on the use of the genitive. To do Ockham justice, he wastes little time on such futilities; most of his, often acute, enquiries into the logical syntax of Latin are undisturbed by the reflection that Latin is really an imperfect reproduction of the Mental original, which on his view is the proper study of a logician.

A little consideration will show us various points at which the analogy of inner language must break down. The grammatical properties ascribed by Ockham to Mental words may all be easily dismissed, except mood and tense. "The farmer has one donkey, which is white" and "the farmer's one donkey is white" plainly both express the same judgment, although the cases of "farmer" and "donkey" are different in the two sentences; and so for most of the grammatical attributes. Tense, however, does enter into the content of our thoughts; "the farmer has often been drunk" cannot be replaced by any sentence to the same effect in which the tense is future instead of past. And I am inclined to think that there are also modal differences between

thoughts — though the moods of a natural language like Latin are a very inadequate indication of this, being cluttered with a lot of logically insignificant idiomatic uses.

What is more important is the difference between speech and thought as regards temporal duration. Spoken words last so long in physical time, and one word comes out after another; the time they take is, as Aquinas would say, the sort of time that is the measure of local motion — one could sensibly say that the utterance of the words was simultaneous with the movement of a body, e.g. the hand of a clock, from one place to another. The same would go for the duration of mental images of words, or any other mental images; one could sensibly say "I rehearsed the words in my head as I watched the beetle crawl from one side of the table to the other".

With a thought it is quite different. Even if we accepted the view sketched in Section 14 that a judgment is a complex of Ideas, we could hardly suppose that in a thought the Ideas occur successively, as the words do in a sentence; it seems reasonable to say that unless the whole complex content is grasped all together — unless the Ideas, if Ideas there are, are all simultaneously present — the thought or judgment just does not exist at all. All the same, when we read of the French politician who maintained that in French the word-order perfectly represented the order in thought (Wittgenstein, Part I, Section 336), our first reaction may be e.g. to think of the French negative "ne . . . pas", and protest that even a Frenchman could not negate the 'verb' part of his judgment in two bits, half an act of negation preceding the 'verb' part and half an act following it; that is to say, we are inclined to think that the Ideas do have *a* temporal order, only not quite the same order as that of the French words expressing them. Only on further reflection do we come to the view that there can be no question of their occurring in *any* temporal order. On my analysis of judgment in terms of Ideas that which corresponded to the 'main verb' in the verbal expression of judgment would be, not an Idea, but the relation binding the Ideas together; and it would be plainly absurd to enquire which position of the main verb best corresponded to the temporal position of this relation as compared with the Ideas it relates. Of course that analysis was only tentative and provisional; at the same time, it was suggested to me by the rather stringent requirements of logic, which became apparent in criticizing Russell's theory; it seems most unlikely that analysis of a judgment as a temporal succession of Ideas could meet these requirements, whatever temporal order we assume.

If a judgment is a non-successive unity, it seems to follow that we cannot assign to judgment more than a loose connexion with physical time. First, could a judgment be regarded as occupying a mere moment of physical time? If so, then either in any finite stretch of time there would be an illimitable number of judgments (or other thoughts), or there would be flashes of thought at discrete instants separated by gaps of thoughtlessness; the first alternative at least is plainly false, but the second might seem possible. Let us consider, however, the time-relation between an act of judgment and the words that express it. Once the words have been spoken, we suppose, the man goes on to think of other matters; so the act cannot be put later than the utterance of the end of the last word. If the man was not in a position to rehearse his words mentally before he said them, the act of judgment might be said not to come before the beginning of the utterance. Let us further suppose that the man's attention is not distracted while he speaks. Are we now to say that the judgment occurs in just one instant of the utterance, the rest of the time being taken up with uttering parrotwise? or, that it is repeated in a

series of flashes, so as to keep the utterance on the right track?

Or are we rather to say that the judging is going on continuously during the utterance? That is worse nonsense than ever: one can say "at 12.10 I had a sudden stab of pain, and the pain went on for two minutes", but not: "at 12.10 I had a sudden thought, and the thought lasted just long enough for me to utter it — it went on all the while that I was uttering it, and then it stopped". All that we can say is that the judgment is loosely bound up with physical time, in that (e.g.) it did not occur before the beginning or after the end of the words in which it is uttered; if we try to assign it to a definite moment or moments, or to a definite stretch of time, we find ourselves in a bog of nonsense.

What I have just said about the 'loose' relation of judgments to physical time is a logical point about applying time-specifications in our discourse about judgments; it does not imply e.g. that judgments are really performed in a super-physical realm. Excluding certain questions about the time of judgments as unreasonable can have no such momentous consequences; and for judgments to be tied loosely to physical time is still for them to be tied.

24. The Notion of 'Inner Sense'

In investigating some other psychological concepts, I shall approach them from the side of psychological judgments in which they are exercised. Psychological judgments have very often been held to be based primarily on the deliverances of an 'inner sense' whereby we are cognizant every one of his own psychical states; just as judgments about physical realities are based on the evidence of our senses. The supposed 'inner sense' is compared sometimes to looking ('introspection'), sometimes to feeling.

With the ordinary senses there is associated the power of forming mental images; I see in my mind's eye past scenes that are no longer before me, or things that I might see now in another position, or even quite imaginary scenes. No mental images, however, are commonly assigned to 'inner sense' in the same way. People have ridiculed the idea of McTaggart that I may have mental images of my own past mental states which I have introspectively perceived, of other people's mental states which I happen to be unable to inspect (a removable limitation, McTaggart believed), and of purely imaginary mental states that nobody has actually been in. (McTaggart, pp. 106–8.) Of course McTaggart's idea is quite wrong, but why is it absurd? If "looking into the mind" has a genuine logical similarity to "looking into the box", then it ought to make sense to talk about introspective mental images as we do about visual images; lack of introspective imagery would be an idiosyncrasy like being unable to visualize, and might be expected to disable a man for some tasks. If McTaggart's idea is absurd, then it ought to make us suspect the comparison of introspection to real looking.

Hume seems to have supposed that there were mental images of past mental states — less vivid copies of them, related to them as a perfume I 'smell' in memory is to something I really smell. But what Hume says is shot all through with his confusion between two senses of "idea" — the mental image of something, and the exercise of a concept of it in judgment. This exercise is in no way dependent on the presence of a pale replica of the thing judged about; if it were, then, as St Augustine remarked, we should habitually feel a certain reluctance to use the words "grief", "fear", "pain", lest they should arouse in our minds faint reproductions of the unwelcome experiences so called (*Confessions*, book X, chap. xiv).[2]

People suppose that I can give meaning to such words as "seeing", "hearing", "thinking", "hoping", etc., only by observing in my own case sample occurrences of

what these words refer to; failing the relevant experiences, or failing attention to them when I have had them, I must either lack a concept altogether or possess it in a very imperfect form, comparable to a colour-blind man's concept of colours. Let us fasten upon this comparison. The defect colour-blindness can be tested for, not only by looking for oddities in a man's colour-concepts, which show in his use of colour-words, but also by a non-linguistic investigation of what colours he is practically able to discriminate, without using words. We can even investigate what colour-discriminations brutes are capable of, although of course they cannot tell us and have no colour-concepts at all. Now could there be, let us say, anger-fear emotion-blindness, as there can be red-green colour-blindness? Could a man's introspective 'sense' be unable to discriminate between his being angry and his being afraid, so that his use of the words "anger" and "fear" depended precariously on other people's use of them, in the way that a colour-blind man's use of colour-words does? In regard to colours, we can distinguish between a colour-blind man with a sensory defect and a mentally defective man who is unable to form colour-concepts and learn the use of colour-words; could we make a similar distinction about emotions? Could we say of somebody: "He's very intelligent, but he keeps on using words for emotions wrongly; the psychiatrist says he has a congenital defect of the 'inner sense' that discriminates emotions from each other"?

I chose to set emotion-words and colour-words side by side, because there really is a considerable logical similarity. Both colours and emotions can occur in different intensities, and can wax and wane in intensity; there can be an emotion that is a blend of anger and fear, as there is a colour that is a blend of red and blue; you can ask of a feeling of fear, as you can of a coloured light, whether it came on suddenly or gradually, and how long it lasted, etc. If in spite of this we find a radical dissimilarity between colour-language and emotion-language, in that we could not apply a term "emotion-blindness" comparably to "colour-blindness", then the conclusion we ought to draw is surely that the idea of an introspective 'sense' is an illusion.

Somebody might try saying that the reason why we have no use for the term "emotion-blindness" is that our 'inner sense' is not liable to such defects as our eyesight is; our inner sense represents our emotions just as they occur, even if we are unable to describe them correctly. Now a sense that was *in fact* not affected by any illusions, any failure to discriminate, etc., is indeed conceivable; but plainly what our present objection is really after is a sense that merely does not but *cannot* mislead us. But this "cannot" would be a logical "cannot"; and the inclination to use "cannot" here points to a logical difference between our knowledge of the outer world by our senses and our knowledge of the mind by 'inner sense'. Of *bona fide* sense-faculties, it is impossible to say that they *cannot* be defective or inaccurate.

If anyone should think that in criticizing the idea of 'inner sense' I am flogging a dead horse, or knocking down a stuffed dummy of my own creation, I may reply by instancing Freud's use of the idea. "What role is there now left, in our representation of things, to the phenomena of consciousness, once so all-powerful and overshadowing all else? None other than *that of a sense-organ for the perception of psychic qualities.*" (Freud, p. 544; his italics.) "The unconscious is the true psychic reality; *in its inner nature it is just as much unknown to us as the reality of the external world, and it is just as imperfectly communicated to us by the data of consciousness as is the external world by the reports of our sense-organs.*" (Freud, p. 542; his italics.) Freud, as may be seen, transfers a naive 'representative' theory of perception from its

usual application (to the bodily senses, that is), and holds it to be no less valid of 'inner sense'. Presumably on his view 'inner sense' would *not* be inerrant; but I find in him no clear account of what an error of 'inner sense' would be like.

25. Could Sensuous Experiences Occur apart from an Organism?

'Inner sense' is supposed to show us, and to be the only thing that shows us, what it is like to see, hear, be afraid, etc. With this there goes a view that the connexion between such 'sensuous' experiences and a bodily organism is only a well-established empirical generalization. Such experiences are indeed dependent upon material things in the sense of being occupied with them; but they are not identifiable with any describable physiological processes in a living organism, and their connexion with such processes is only something empirically determined. There is no necessary, conceptual, connexion between the experience we call "seeing" and the processes that physiologists tell us happen in eye and brain; the statement "James can still see, although his optic centres are destroyed" is very unlikely on inductive grounds but perfectly intelligible — after all, people used the word "see" long before they had any idea of things happening in the optic centres of the brain. It therefore appears to be clearly conceivable that seeing and other 'sensuous' experiences might go on continuously even after the death of the organism with which they are now associated, and that the inductive reasons for doubting whether this ever happens might be outweighed by the evidence of Psychical Reseach.

I think it is an important conceptual enquiry to consider whether *really* disembodied seeing, hearing, pain, hunger, emotion, etc., are so clearly intelligible as is supposed in this common philosophical point of view. (I stress "really disembodied". Some people believe that there is a subtle body endowed with its own sense-organs, which persists after the dissolution of the body commonly so called. This view, so far as I can see, is philosophically speaking both unobjectionable and uninteresting. It is clear off-hand that the 'mind-body problem' is just the same whether the body is gross or subtle.)

"The verb 'to see' has its meaning for me because I *do* see—I have that experience!" Nonsense. As well suppose that I can come to know what a minus quantity is by setting out to lose weight. What shows a man to have the concept *seeing* is not merely that he sees, but that he can take an intelligent part in our everyday use of the word "seeing". Our concept of sight has its life only in connexion with a whole set of other concepts, some of them relating to the physical characteristics of visible objects, others relating to the behaviour of people who see things. (I express exercise of this concept in such utterances as "I can't see, it's too far off—now it's coming into view!" "He couldn't see me, he didn't look round", "I caught his eye", etc., etc.) It would be merely silly to be frightened off admitting this by the bogy of behaviourism; you can very well admit it without also thinking that "seeing" stands for a kind of behaviour.

Our investigation is put on the wrong track by an abstractionist prejudice. For an abstractionist, the possession of the concept *seeing* must be taken to be a capacity for finding and recognizing some recurrent feature—or at least to be that primarily; and I can find instances of seeing only in my own mind, by 'inner sense'; in other people I find nothing but characteristic pieces of behaviour, from which however it could justifiably be inferred (how?) that they also see.—In fact, of course, I learn to use the word "see" of others and of myself simultaneously; and if we reject the doctrine of abstractionism, we need not distinguish between exercises of the concept *seeing* as primary ones,

when I catch myself in the act of seeing something, and secondary ones, when I (with great rashness, surely, on this view) form the judgment that others likewise see. To have the concept *seeing* is not even primarily a matter of being able to spot instances of a characteristic repeatedly given in my ('inner-sense') experiences; *no* concept is primarily a recognitional capacity. And the exercise of one concept is intertwined with the exercise of others; as with a spider's web, some connexions may be broken with impunity, but if you break enough the whole web collapses—the concept becomes unusable. Just such a collapse happens, I believe, when we try to think of seeing, hearing, pain, emotion, etc., going on independently of a body.

When I apply this sort of concept to a human being, I do so in connexion with a whole lot of other concepts that I apply to human beings and their natural environment. It is easy enough to extend the concepts of 'sensuous' experience to creatures fairly like human beings, such as cats, dogs, and horses; when we try to extend them to creatures extremely unlike human beings in their style of life, we feel, if we are wise, great uncertainty—not just uncertainty as to the facts, or as to the possibility of finding them out, but uncertainty as to the *meaning* of saying: "I now know how to tell when an earthworm is angry". One is of course tempted to say: "That's easy; an earthworm is angry if it is feeling the way I feel when I am angry!" But this is just like saying: "Of course I know what it is for the time on the Sun to be five o'clock; it is five o'clock on the Sun when it is the same time as when it is five o'clock here!" (Wittgenstein, Part I, Section 350)—which clearly gets us no for'arder. There is just the same difficulty in extending the concept *the same time* as in extending the concept *five o'clock*. So in the psychological case: I know how to apply the concept *anger* to myself and to James, and I know how to apply the concept *feeling the same way* as between myself and James, or James and Smith; I get into the same difficulties if I try applying the concept *feeling the same way* as between myself and an earthworm as I do over applying the concept *anger* to it.[3]

Even an earthworm, though, affords some handholds for the application of 'sensuous' psychological concepts; we connect its writhings when injured with our own pain-reactions. But when it comes to an automaton, or again if we are invited to apply the concepts to a supposed disembodied existence, then we may be sure that we are right in refusing to play; too many threads are broken, and the conceptual web has collapsed. An automaton, by all sorts of criteria, is not even alive; we know this, though we may be uncertain whether to call a virus (say) alive or not. (Doctors may not agree whether a patient is yet dead; but we know that Queen Anne is dead.) Between what is certainly inanimate and ourselves there is far too little similarity for us to be able to pick out anything in its behaviour corresponding to the context in which we judge that human beings are in pain, or hungry, or afraid; we know that any particular movement which might even remotely suggest similarity is performed because the designer of the automaton intended such an imitation, and we ought to be no more inclined to ascribe feelings to the automaton than, after childhood, we think that a doll is in pain because it has been so constructed as to cry when it is smacked. — As for disembodied sensations and feelings, even more connexions are broken in this case; there is no handhold for applying 'sensuous' concepts to disembodied existence at all — we just do not know what we are doing if we try.

A good illustration, I think, of a concept's losing its applicability through connexions being broken is the following. Certain hysterics claimed to have magnetic sensations; it was discovered, however, that their claim to be having them at

a given time did not go with the presence of a magnet in their neighbourhood but with their belief, true or false, that a magnet was there. It would now have been possible to say: "We must take the patients' word for it that they have these peculiar sensations, which are quite different from ordinary people's sense-modalities; it is merely the term "magnetic sensations" that has turned out to be inappropriate; they had formed a wrong hypothesis about the physical cause of their sensations". But nobody even considered saying this; it was decided that the patients had just been indulging in the sort of pointless talk that hysterics often indulge in. This decision just to drop the idea of magnetic sensations and to ignore the patients' 'reports' of them was taken after a much smaller breakdown of the ordinary connexions than we are asked to tolerate when it is attempted to apply sensation-concepts to automata or to disembodied existence.

Denying sense to the attempt to think of feelings, sensations, emotions, etc., apart from a living organism may seem to be practically the same as denying disembodied mind altogether. Such a denial does not follow, nor has it historically always been held to follow. Aquinas, for example, believed that there were wholly disembodied intelligences, but that they were not liable to any such experiences as seeing and hearing and feeling afraid and having a pain: the evil spirits in hell are tormented not by aches but by the frustration of their wicked will. (Ia q. 54 art. 6, q. 59 art. 4, q. 64 art. 3.) Sensuous experiences are possible only in connexion with a living organism (Ia q. 77 art. 8). Only since Descartes has the main problem become: "How is *cogitatio* related to bodily processes?" (*"cogitatio"* covering, for him, everything 'in the mind', from a toothache to a metaphysical meditation); the old problem was rather: "How can a being that thinks and judges and decides *also* have sensuous experiences?" It was 'intellectual' acts like judgment, not just *anything* that would now be called 'consciousness', which seemed to Aquinas to be wholly incommensurable with events in the physical world; for him, the 'unbridgeable gulf' was at a different place. The usefulness of historical knowledge in philosophy, here as elsewhere, is that the prejudices of our own period may lose their grip on us if we imaginatively enter into another period, when people's prejudices were different.

Notes

1. Psychologists appear not to take this fact sufficiently into account. Thus, Humphrey takes as his example of the use of language, not a sentence devised for a new situation, but an ejaculation "Rain!" when it is raining; not surprisingly he concludes that the problem of meaning is just a case of the problem of learned responses. (Humphrey, pp. 227-34.)

2. Augustine here uses the term *"notiones"* for the mental acts involved in an understanding of such words as "fear", and denies that *notiones* are *imagines*. I wonder if this is the origin of Berkeley's puzzling talk about 'notions' as opposed to 'ideas'.

3. On a point of interpretation, I think it is a mistake to read Wittgenstein as having intended to show that I cannot apply a concept like *anger* both to myself and to others, and that it is meaningless to speak of others' feeling the same way as I do (unless indeed I just mean that they behave as I do). The difficulty of transferring the concept *anger* from myself to others is a spurious one, arising from the abstractionism that Wittgenstein consistently rejected; and the solution that the term "anger" is an equivocal term, applied in my own case to a recurrent experience and in other cases to a recurrent pattern of behaviour, is plausible, I think, only on abstractionist presuppositions; I do not believe, as some people I have had discussion with apparently do, that Wittgenstein really held this view and only shrank from a brash statement of it.

References

Aquinas, St. T., *Summa Theologica*.

Freud, S., *Basic Writings*, The Modern Library, New York, 1938.

Humphrey, G., *Thinking*, Methuen, 1951.

James, W., *The Principles of Psychology*, Macmillan, 1901.

McTaggart, J. E., *The Nature of Existence*, Vol. 2, Cambridge, 1927.

Ryle, G., *The Concept of Mind*, Hutchinson, 1949.

Wittgenstein, L., *Philosophical Investigations*, Blackwell, 1953.

Language Learning

Gilbert Harman

Let us suppose that there is an "inner language" of thought that may or may not be distinct from the "outer language" one speaks. I wish to contrast two views of what it is to learn a natural language. A code breaking conception might be provisionally formulated thus:

(CB)   One's inner language, which one thinks in, is distinct from one's outer language, which one speaks. Communication involves coding or translation between inner and outer languages. Learning language is a matter of learning an outer language and involves acquiring the ability to to do such coding or translation.

An incorporation view might be stated as follows:

(IV)   Knowledge of a language is the ability to use that language; and the primary use of language is in thought. Knowing a language is being able to think in it. Learning an outer language involves the incorporation of that language into one's inner language.

From *Nous* 4, no. 1 (February 1970): 33-43. Reprinted by permission of Wayne State University Press and the author. This work was supported in part by a grant from the National Science Foundation.

If space permitted, I would try to associate CB with such people as Jerrold Katz, the Port-Royal Grammarians, and Aristotle. I would try to connect IV with Wilfrid Sellars, Quine, Wittgenstein, Whorf, and Humboldt. On this occasion I must restrict myself to the attempt to say what the issue between CB and IV amounts to in the last analysis.

I shall begin with the notion of a psychological model. Such a model conceives a person as a nondeterministic automaton, whose input is the result of interaction with the environment and whose output consists in actions and reactions, including speech. Any plausible model makes use of a system of representation for framing beliefs, desires, etc. In a simple model, there might be two places in which representations are stored. Representations of things believed would be stored in one place; representations of things desired in the other. Interaction with the environment would produce new representations that would be stored as beliefs. Needs for food, love, etc. would produce representations to be stored as desires. Inferences could produce changes in both the set of beliefs and the set of desires.

Let us use the term "thoughts" to

stand for states and occurrences such as thoughts, beliefs, desires, etc. Then we might interpret CP and IV as the following proposals about psychological models:

(CBPM) A psychological model of a speaker of a language should use a system of representation for thoughts that is distinct from the language spoken by the person modeled. In a model of communication, the model of the speaker converts an element of this inner system of representation into a sentence of the language; and the model of the hearer converts this sentence back into the proper element of the inner system of representation. A model of a language learner must come to acquire the ability to thus convert elements of the inner system to sentences of the outer language; and vice versa.

(IVPM) A psychological model of a speaker of a language should use a system of representation for thoughts that includes the language spoken by the person modeled. A model of communication need not involve the sort of conversion mentioned in CBPM. A model of a language learner does not acquire the ability to do such conversion; instead it comes to incorporate the outer language into its inner system of representation.

There is no question that relevant models must thus make use of a system of representation. We know that people have beliefs and desires, that beliefs and desires influence action, that interaction with the environment can give rise to new beliefs, and that needs and drives can give rise to desires. Adequate psychological theories must reflect this knowledge and add to it. So adequate psychological models must have states that correspond to beliefs, desires, and thoughts such that these states function in the model as psychological states function in the person modeled, and such that they are representational in the way that psychologi-

cal states are representational. Where there is such representation, there is a system of representation; and that system may be identified with the inner language in which a person thinks.

This reduces the claim that there is an inner language, which one thinks in, to the trivial assertion that psychological states have a representational character. But it leaves obscure CBPM and IVPM, which respectively deny and assert that one's inner language contains one's outer language. What could it mean to assert or deny that psychological states involve, or even are, instances (i.e. tokens) of sentences of one's language? How can it be serious whether or not to include sentences of a person's language among the representations used in the way suggested above as part of a psychological model of that person?

In reply, one can agree that it is not clear what it is for a person's psychological states to be or include tokens of his language. But that is at least partially because it is unclear what it is for *anything* to be a token of a sentence. Compare uttered and written tokens, tokens in different dialects, different handwriting, and different styles of type, tokens uttered aloud and said to oneself.

What do all the various instances of a sentence have in common? It is not easy to say; but the following conditions seem necessary. First, any two tokens of the same sentence must have similar (potential) representational properties. Second, the tokens must each be analyzable as an ordered sequence of the same words in the same order.

A generalization of the second condition allows us to distinguish tokens of the same old sentences appearing in a new form (e.g. the new written tokens as opposed to the old spoken tokens) from tokens of sentences in another language which are only translations of sentences in the original language. In a language that can be both spoken and written, for every possible spoken word, there is a corresponding written word. Every spoken sentence is a temporal sequence of spoken words; and the corresponding written sentence is a spatial sequence of corresponding written words in the same order, where corresponding written and spoken sentences have the same potential representational properties. This sort of general correspondence does not hold between distinct languages. One cannot, for example, correlate English and Russian words so that whenever a sequence of English words forms a sentence, the corresponding sequence of Russian words forms a sentence that translates the English sentence.

This suggests that we formulate the two conceptions of language learning as follows (recall that we are using "thoughts" to include beliefs, desires, etc.):

(IVT) The relationship between one's thoughts and the sentences of one's language is relevantly more like the relationship between spoken and written English than it is like the relationship between English and Russian. Thoughts may be analyzed as sequences of elements; and some of the elements may be corre-lated with words in one's language so that corresponding sequences of elements and sequences of words have similar representational characteristics. To learn a language is to acquire thoughts that are (at least in part) tokens of sentences of that language.

(CBT) The relationship between one's thoughts and the sentences of one's language is relevantly more like the relationship between English and Russian than it is like the relation-ship between spoken and written English. The sort of analysis envisioned in IVT is not possible. To learn a language is not to acquire thoughts that are tokens of sentences of the language but is in part to acquire the ability to encode one's thoughts in such tokens.

Notice, by the way, that so formulated IVT does not commit one to the view that thoughts that are "in words" have such words occurring in temporal sequence. One can think in words without those words passing through one's head in the proper temporal order. An uttered sentence is a temporal sequence; but a written sentence is a spatial sequence; and a thought sentence need not be a spatio-temporal sequence at all.

However, a moment's reflection suffices to show that, when formulated in this way, IVT is false and CBT is true, because of ambiguity in natural language. Thoughts are not ambiguous in the way that sentences in English are. So there can be no analysis like that suggested in IVT which correlates sentences and thoughts that have *similar representational characteristics.* IVT is trivially false; and CBT, the relevant denial of IVT, is trivially true.

The ambiguity of a sentence may derive either from the ambiguity of certain words in the sentence, from the ambiguity of the grammatical structure of the sentence, or from some combination of factors. Let us make the controversial assumption that the relevant grammatical structure is what transformational linguists refer to as "deep structure," which reveals relations such as underlying first argument of a predicate, etc. (and also, I would maintain, scope of quantifiers and negation, etc.). Let us also assume that the deep structure of a sentence represents in some form or other the words (or morphemes) relevant to the meaning of the sentence. Finally, let us assume that different senses of words are distinguished by subscripts on those words in deep structure but that deep structure contains no other purely semantic information. Then, by a sentence under analysis, I shall mean a sentence viewed (or "heard") as having a particular deep structure in the sense just described.

We may now state the incorporation

view and the code breaking conception of language learning in such a way that there is a real nontrivial issue between them.

(IVA)   To acquire a language is to acquire thoughts that are, at least in part, instances of sentences of that lan-guage under analysis. Spontaneous speech is thinking out loud: one utters a sentence under analysis. Two such sentences sound the same if they contain the same words in the same order, even if their deep structures are different. For someone to understand what is said is for him to hear it as a sentence under analysis.

(CBA)   To learn a language is not to acquire thoughts that are instances of sentences of the language under analysis, but is in part to acquire the ability to encode one's thoughts in such instances.

Although I have defended IVA elsewhere, I now find that it is false. A recent article reports that

Our data show that children make discriminations that are not reflected in their speech. Children whose speech is telegraphic readily obey well-formed commands, and less readily obey telegraphic commands. Thus a description of the child's spontaneous utterances does not do justice to his linguistic organization. In some fairly clear sense, comprehension seems to precede the production of well-formed sentences. . . . What is truly surprising is that those utterances which a description of natural speech would specify as TYPICAL for the child are just those utterances which are LESS EFFECTIVE to him as commands. (Shipley, Smith, and Gleitman, "A Study in the Acquisition of Language," *Language*, 45 (1969): 322-342, quoting from pp. 336-7.)

If some of the child's thoughts are to be analyzed as sentences of his language under analysis, these sentences are either (1) the telegraphic ones of the sort he spontaneously produces or (2) the well formed ones of the sort he understands. On alternative (1), the child does not understand what is said by hearing it under analysis. And it would seem absurd to suggest that the child hears a well formed sentence as a telegraphic sentence under analysis, since the child has greater difficulty understanding telegraphic sentences than well formed ones. On the other hand, on alternative (2) the sentences the child spontaneously produces are not, even under analysis, sentences the child thinks in; and speech is not simply a matter of thinking out loud. Neither alternative (1) nor alternative (2) seems consistent with IVA.

The experimental results cited definitely favor CBA. Understanding is a matter of decoding what is said; spontaneous speech is a matter of encoding one's thoughts. Neither of these processes is trivial; and in learning a language, the former process is easier than the latter.

However, even if all this is granted to the code breaking conception, a defender of the incorporation view will want to claim that the relevant thoughts are language dependent. If thoughts are not sentences under analysis, i.e. sentences with deep structures, perhaps they are simply the deep structures without the sentences (but with the relevant words). Some defenders of the code breaking conception will want to argue that thoughts are not thus dependent on one's language. Therefore, I am led to a second way of stating the incorporation view and the code breaking conception such that there is a real and nontrivial issue between them.

(IVDS)   To understand what is said is to hear what is said as a sentence under analysis. That is because certain of one's thoughts are instances of deep structures of such sentences. Thoughts may be analyzed as structures of elements; and the elements can be correlated with subscripted words, the structures with deep structures, so that corresponding structures of elements and sentences under analysis have the same representational characteristics. To acquire a language is to acquire thoughts that are, at least in part, instances of deep structures of sentences of that language.

(CBDS)   In order to understand what is said, one must do more than hear the sentence uttered as having the proper deep structure; one must also interpret that deep structure by decoding it or translating it into the language of thought. The sort of analysis envisioned in IVDS is not possible. To learn a language is not to acquire thoughts that are instances of deep structures of sentences of that language.

Now, consider the following objection, which a defender of CBDS might make to IVDS: "If IVDS were true, thoughts expressed in one language could not be expressed in another, since thoughts are taken to be deep structures of sentences. But an English sentence under analysis can be translated into French sentence under analysis; and a criterion of good translation is that the translation should express the same thought as the sentence translated. The possibility of good translation shows that the same thoughts can be expressed in different languages. Therefore, IVDS must be false."

One might think it enough to respond to this objection by citing Quine's thesis of the indeterminacy of radical translation. Quine points out that adequate translation is a matter of pairing sentences from one language with sentences from another in such a way that the general correlation satisfies certain conditions. He claims that, when one considers all reasonable constraints on translation, one discovers that various nonequivalent general schemes of translation will satisfy these conditions. Thus he claims that the translation of one language into another resembles the "transla-tion" of number theory into set theory, in that there are many different equally good nonequivalent ways in which such translation may be carried out.

If Quine were right, it would make no sense to say that two sentences of different languages express the same thought, except relative to one or another general scheme of translation between the two languages. For, although one scheme might count sentence A the translation of sentence B, an alternative, but equally good, scheme would count sentence C as B's translation, where A and C need not express the "same thought." Given indeterminacy of radical translation, the possibility of good translation does not establish that the same thoughts can be said to be expressed by different sentences in different languages apart from specification of a general scheme of translation. And to say that relative to a specified scheme of translation the same thoughts are expressed by sentence A and sentence B would not be to say something incompatible with IVDS. If Quine were right, IVDS would seem definitely preferable to CBDS.

In *Word and Object* Quine argues that the meaning of a sentence in a single speaker's idiolect is a matter of what sentences he would be disposed to accept or reject as the result of being placed in various perceptual situations. Let me abbreviate this by saying that for the Quine meaning is a matter of a speaker's dispositions to accept sentences, where this is meant also to include rejection of sentences. If meaning were only a matter of a speaker's dispositions to accept sentences, then there would almost certainly be indeterminacy of radical translation. For it would seem obvious that there will be many different, equally simple ways to correlate sentences of two different languages which preserve a speaker's dispositions to accept sentences equally well.

The assumption that meaning is

essentially a matter of a speaker's dispositions to accept sentences does seem to capture the essence of the approach to the theory of meaning exemplified in the writings of Carnap, Ayer, Lewis, Firth, Hempel, Sellars, et al. This approach seems definitely committed to the indeterminacy of radical translation. But is it obvious that the basic assumption of this approach is correct?

The only argument for the assumption that I have been able to find appears in my contribution to the *Synthese* issue on Quine (in Vol. 19). I say,

> Meaning is not very much a matter of what words a person actually uses. What words he could have used are more relevant. Different people have different ways of speaking, different favorite phrases, etc. This obvious fact does not mean that the sentences of such different people are to be translated differently. To require similarity in actual usage (rather than possible usage) as a criterion of translatability would almost certainly rule out all translation, since any two people use their words differently. I do not mean something different by sentences of set theory from what you mean just because you and I use these sentences differently, e.g. just because I count with the von Neumann numbers while you count with Zermelo's, since I *could* always do it your way (18-19).

But this argument is obviously invalid. Preservation of similarity in actual usage can be a criterion of translation without ruling out all translation on the grounds that people use words differently. Preservation of similarity in belief is a criterion of translation even though no two people believe the same things. It tells us that, other things equal, we should prefer one general scheme of translation over a second if the first has us ascribe to speakers of another language beliefs that are more similar to our own beliefs than are the beliefs we would have to ascribe to them on the second scheme. A criterion of translation that appeals to similarity in

actual usage can be given an analogous formulation: other things equal, we should prefer one general scheme of translation over a second if translations of things actually said by speakers of another language are more like things we would say on the first scheme than on the second. The latter principle would rule out schemes of translation not ruled out by the appeal to a speaker's dispositions to accept sentences. For example, it might rule out a general scheme of translation according to which speakers of another language regularly refer to rabbit-stages rather than rabbits, people-stages rather than people, etc., in favor of a scheme according to which they regularly refer to rabbits, people, etc., although both these schemes might be equally good in terms of preservation of dispositions to accept sentences. Furthermore, I can think of no reason why preservation of similarity of actual usage, so understood, shouldn't be permitted to be just as much a criterion of good translation as preservation of similarity in belief. And, if it is allowed as a criterion, Quine's thesis of indeterminacy of radical translation no longer seems obviously true. Therefore, one cannot defend IVDS by appealing to this sort of indeterminacy.

Nevertheless, Quine's overall approach to meaning and translation is a good one; and it tends to support IVDS rather than CBDS even without the indeterminacy thesis. One general scheme of translation is better than another to the extent that it is simpler, preserves dispositions to accept sentences, and preserves similarity of actual usage. Each of these things is a matter of degree; and they can compete with each other. One could achieve perfect correspondence between another person's dispositions to accept sentences and one's own if one were willing to give up on simplicity. And sometimes one gives up the simplest scheme, e.g. the homophonic scheme with respect to a compatriot, in order to preserve more dispositions to accept sentences or to gain more similarity of actual usage. The fit is never perfect; but, let us assume, there is sometimes a best fit — a best general scheme of translation from one language to another.

Since the fit is only a matter of degree, the translation relation is not an "equivalence relation" in the mathematical sense. For it is not transitive. If x is the translation of y and y the translation of z, x need not be the translation of z. For there may be three languages L, M, and N, such that the best scheme of translation from L to N is not equivalent to the scheme one gets by first translating by the best scheme from L to M and then by the best scheme from M to N. This poses a problem for CBDS, which takes the possibility of good translation to show that the same thoughts can be expressed in different languages. If the thought expressed by x is the same identical thing as that expressed by y, which is the same as that expressed by z, the thought expressed by x is the same as that expressed by z, by the transitivity of identity. On CBDS, the translation relation ought to be an equivalence relation. So, even if Quine's thesis of the indeterminacy of radical translation is not accepted, his theory of translation gives us reason to be skeptical of CBDS, since CBDS implies that thoughts are linguistically neutral states that may be expressed in various languages in a way that is not relative to translation.

IVDS says that certain of one's psychological states may be treated as deep structures of sentences of one's language. This is done by constructing a psychological model in which certain beliefs are represented by the storage in a given place of instances of the appropriate deep structures. Similarly for desires, etc. The acquisition of language is treated in the first instance as the acquisition of a system of representation for the storage of beliefs, desires, etc. I think that IVDS gives the beginnings of the correct account of language learning. It might have been supposed that the possibility of good translation tells against IVDS in favor of a view like CBDS. However, I have argued that this is not so and that, as of now, a view like IVDS looks more promising than one like CBDS.

We cannot say simply whether the code breaking conception is or is not better than the incorporation view. On the one hand, language learning appears to involve the acquisition of coding and decoding abilities, as is revealed by the child's being better at decoding than he is at coding. CBA is true and IVA is false. On the other hand, the thoughts that a language encodes may themselves be highly dependent on that language, even to the point of being or involving deep structures of sentences of that language. Language learning may involve the incorporation of a system of language specific deep structure into one's language of thought. In that case IVDS will be true, and CBDS will be false.

3

Propositional Attitudes

Jerry A. Fodor

Some philosophers (John Dewey, for example, and maybe John Austin) hold that philosophy is what you do to a problem until it's clear enough to solve it by doing science. Others (Gilbert Ryle, for example, and maybe Ludwig Wittgenstein) hold that if a philosophical problem succumbs to empirical methods, that shows it wasn't *really* philosophical to begin with. Either way, the facts seem clear enough: questions first mooted by philosophers are sometimes coopted by people who do experiments. This seems to be happening now to the question 'what are propositional attitudes?' and cognitive psychology is the science of note.

One way to elucidate this situation is to examine theories that cognitive psychologists endorse, with an eye to explicating the account of propositional attitudes that the theories presuppose. That was my strategy in Fodor (1975). In this chapter, however, I'll take another tack. I want to outline a number of a priori conditions which, on my view, a theory of propositional attitudes (PAs) ought to meet. I'll argue that, considered together,

From *Monist* 61, no. 4 (October 1978): 501-523. Reprinted by permission of the publisher and the author.

these conditions pretty clearly demand a treatment of PAs as relations between organisms and internal representations; precisely the view that the psychologists have independently arrived at. I'll thus be arguing that we have good reasons to endorse the psychologists' theory even aside from the empirical exigencies that drove them to it. I take it that this convergence between what's plausible a priori and what's demanded *ex post facto* is itself a reason for believing that the theory is probably true.

Three preliminary remarks: First, I'm not taking "a priori" all that seriously. Some of the points I'll be making are, I suppose, strictly conceptual, but others are merely self-evident. What I've got is a set of glHring facts about propositional attitudes. I don't doubt that we might rationally adopt an account of the attitudes which contravenes some, or maybe even all of them. But the independent evidence for such an account would have to be extremely persuasive or I, for one, would get the jitters. Second, practically everything I'll say about the attitudes has been said previously in the philosophical literature. All I've done is bring the stuff together. I do think, however, that the various constraints that I'll discuss illuminate each other; it is only when one attempts to satisfy them all at once that one sees how univocal their demands are. Finally, though I intend what I say to apply, *mutatis mutandis*, to PAs at large, I shall run the discussion pretty much exclusively on beliefs and wants. These seem to be the root cases for a systematic cognitive psychology; thus learning and perception are presumably to be treated as varieties of the fixation of belief, and the theory of action is presumably continuous with the theory of utility.[1]

Here, then, are my conditions, with comments.

I. Propositional attitudes should be analyzed as relations. In particular, the verb in a sentence like 'John believes it's raining' expresses a relation between John and something else, and a token of that sentence is true iff John stands in the belief-relation to that thing.[2] Equivalently, for these purposes, 'it's raining' is a term in 'John believes it's raining'.[3] I have three arguments for imposing condition I, all of them inconclusive.

Ia. It's intuitively plausible: 'believes' looks like a two-place relation, and it would be nice if our theory of belief permitted us to save the appearances.

No doubt, appearances sometimes deceive. The ' 's' in 'Mary's sake' looks like expressing a relation (of possession) between Mary and a sake; but it doesn't, or so we're told. In fact, 'Mary's sake' doesn't look *very* relational, since *x's sake* would surely qualify as an idiom even if we had no ontological scruples to placate. There's something syntactically wrong with: #Mary's sake is *Fer* than Bill's#, 'Mary has a (little) sake', etc. [*Editor's note:* In this anthology, "#" is used instead of the corner quote.] For that matter, there's something syntactically wrong with 'a sake' *tout court*. Yet, we'd expect all such expressions to be well-formed if 'Mary's sake' contained a true possessive. 'Mary's sake' doesn't bear comparison with 'Mary's lamb'.

Still, there are some cases of *non-idiomatic* expressions which appear to be relational, but which, upon reflection, maybe aren't. 'Mary's voice' goes through the transformations even if 'Mary's sake' does not (Dennett, 1969). Yet there aren't, perhaps, such *things* as voices; and, if there aren't, 'Mary's voice' can't refer in virtue of a relation between Mary and one of them.[4] I think it is fair to view the "surface" grammar as ontologically misleading in *these* cases, but only because we know how to translate into more parsimonious forms. 'Mary has a good voice (bad voice; little voice; better voice than Bill's)' goes over, pretty much without residue, into 'Mary sings well (badly, weakly, less well than Bill)'. If, however, we were *unable* to provide (or, anyhow, to envision providing) the relevant translations, what right would we have to view such expressions as ontologically promiscuous? 'Bill believes it's raining' is not an idiom, and there is, so far as anybody knows, no way of translating sentences nominally about believing into sentences of reduced ontological load. (Behaviorists used to think such translations might be forthcoming, but they were wrong.) We must, then, either take the apparent ontological commitments seriously or admit to playing fast and loose.

Ib. Existential Generalization (*EG*) applies to the syntactic objects of verbs of propositional attitude; from 'John believes it's raining' we can infer 'John believes something' and 'there is something that John believes' (viz., that it's raining). *EG* may not be *criterial* for ontological commitment, but it is surely a straw in the wind.[5]

Ic. The only known alternative to the view that verbs of propositional attitude express relations is that they are (semantically) "fused" with their objects and that view would seem to be hopeless.[6]

The fusion story is the proposal that sentences like 'John believes it's raining' ought really to be spelled 'John believes-it's-raining'; that the logical form of such sentences acknowledges a referring expression ('John') and a one-place predicate with no internal structure ('believes-it's-raining'). 'John believes it's raining' is thus an atomic sentence, similar *au fond* to 'John is purple'.

Talk about counter-intuitive! Moreover:

1. There are infinitely many (semantically distinct) sentences of the form *a believes complement*. If all such sentences are atomic, how is English learned? (Davidson, 1965).

2. Different propositional attitudes are often "focused" on the same content; for example, one can both fear and believe that it will rain on Tuesday. But, on the fusion view, 'John fears that it will rain on Tuesday' has nothing in common with 'John believes that it will rain on Tuesday' save only the reference to John. In particular, it's an *accident* that the form of words 'it will rain on Tuesday' occurs in both.

3. Similarly, different beliefs can be related in such ways as the following: John thinks Sam is nice; Mary thinks Sam is nasty. Under ordinary English representation these beliefs overlap at the 'Sam' position, so the notation sustains the intuition that John and Mary disagree about Sam. But, if the fusion view is correct, 'John thinks Sam is nice' and 'Mary thinks Sam is nasty' have no more in common at the level of canonical notation than, say, 'John eats' and 'Mary swims'. Talk about imperspicuous! In respect of saving the intuitions, the recommended reconstruction does *worse* than the undisciplined orthography that we started with.[7] (For that matter, there's nothing in #believes-that-S# to suggest that it's about believing. Here too #believes that S# does much better.)

4. It could hardly be an accident that the declarative sentences of English constitute the (syntactic) objects of verbs like 'believe'. Whereas, on the fusion view it's *precisely* an accident; the complement of 'believes' in 'John believes it's raining' bears no more relation to the sentence 'It's raining' than, say, the word 'dog' bears to the first syllable of 'dogmatic'.

5. On the fusion view, it's a sheer accident that if 'John believes it's raining' is true, then what John believes is true iff 'it's raining' is true. But this, surely, is one accident too many. Surely the identity between the truth conditions on John's belief when he belies *Fa*, and those on the corresponding sentence #a is F# must be what connects the theory of sentence interpretation with the theory of PAs (and what explains our using 'it's raining', and not some other form of words, to specify *which* belief John has when he believes it's raining).

It's the mark of a bad theory that it makes the data look fortuitous. I conclude that the fusion story is not to be taken very seriously; that neither the philosophy of language nor the philosophy of mind is advanced just by proliferating hyphens. But the fusion story is (*de facto*) the only alternative to the view that 'believe' expresses a relation. Hence, at first blush, we had better assume that 'believe' expresses a relation. Hence, at first blush, we had better assume that 'believe' *does* express a relation and try to find an account of propositional attitudes which comports with that assumption.

II. A theory of PAs should explain the parallelism between verbs of PA and verbs of saying ("Vendler's condition").

Rather generally, the things we can be said to *believe* (want, hope, regret, etc.) are the very things that we can be said to *say* (assert, state, etc.). So, John can either believe or assert that it's about to blow; he can either hope that or inquire whether somebody has reefed the main; he can either doubt or demand that the crew should douse the Genny. Moreover, as Zeno Vendler (1972) has shown, there are interesting consequences of classifying verbs of PA (on the one hand) and verbs of saying (on the other) by reference to the syntax of their object complements. It turns out that the taxonomies thus engendered are isomorphic down to surprisingly fine levels of grain. Now, of course, this *could* be just an accident, as could the semantic and syntactic parallelisms between the complements of verbs of PA and free-standing declaratives (see above). Certainly, it's a substantial inference from the syntactic similarities that Vendler observes to the conclusion he draws: that the object of assertion is identical with the object of belief. Suffice it for now to make the less ambitious point: we should prefer a theory which explains the facts to one which merely shrugs its shoulders; viz., a theory which satisfies Vendler's condition to a theory which does not.

III. A theory of propositional attitudes should account for their opacity ("Frege's condition").

Thus far, I have stressed logico-syntactic analogies between the complements of belief clauses and the corresponding free-standing declaratives. However, it has been customary in the philosophical literature since Gottlob Frege to stress one of their striking *dis*analogies: the former are, in general, opaque to inferential operations to which the latter are, in general, transparent. Since this aspect of the behavior of sentences that ascribe propositional attitudes has so dominated the philosophical discussion, I shall make the point quite briefly here. Sentences containing verbs of PA are not, normally, truth functions of their complements. Moreover, contexts subordinated to verbs of PA are normally themselves non-truth functional, and *EG* and substitution of identicals may apply at syntactic positions in a free-standing declarative while failing at syntactically comparable positions in belief sentences. A theory of PAs should explain why all this is so.

It should be acknowledged that, however gross the inadequacies of the fu-

sion view, it does at least provide an account of propositional attitudes which meets Frege's condition. If *S* doesn't so much as occur in #John believes *S*# it's hardly surprising that the one should fail to be a truth function of the other; similarly, if 'Mary' doesn't occur in 'Bill believes that John bit Mary', it's hardly surprising that the sentence doesn't behave the way it would if 'Mary' occurred referentially. The methodological moral is perhaps that Frege's condition underconstrains a theory of PAs; ideally, an acceptable account of opacity should follow from a theory that is independently plausible.

IV. The objects of propositional attitudes have logical form ("Aristotle's condition").

Mental states (including, especially, token havings of propositional attitudes) interact causally. Such interactions constitute the mental processes which eventuate (*inter alia*) in the behaviors of organisms. Now, it is crucial to the whole program of explaining behavior by reference to mental states that the propositional attitudes belonging to these chains are typically *non*arbitrarily related in respect of their content (taking the "content" of a propositional attitude, informally, to be whatever it is that the complement of the corresponding PA-ascribing sentence expresses).

This is not an a priori claim, though perhaps it is a transcendental one. For, though one can imagine the occurrence of causal chains of mental states which are not otherwise related (as, e.g., a thought that two is a prime number, causing a desire for tea, causing an intention to recite the alphabet backwards, causing an expectation of rain) and though such sequences doubtless actually occur (in dreams, say, and in madness) still if *all* our mental life were like this, it's hard to see what point ascriptions of contents to mental states would have. Even phenomenology presupposes some correspondence between the content of our beliefs and the content of our beliefs about our beliefs; else there would be no coherent introspections for phenomenologists to report.

The paradigm situation — the grist for the cognitivist's mill — is the one where propositional attitudes interact causally and do so *in virtue of* their content. And the paradigm of this paradigm is the practical syllogism. Since it is part of my point that the details matter not at all, I shall take liberties with Aristotle's text.

John believes that it will rain if he washes his car. John wants it to rain. So John acts in a manner intended to be a car-washing.

I take it that this might be a true, if informal, etiology of John's "car-washing behavior"; the car-washing is an effect of the intention to car-wash, and the intention to car-wash is an effect of the causal interaction between John's beliefs and his utilities. Moreover, the etiological account might be counterfactual-supporting in at least the following sense: John wouldn't have car-washed had the content of his beliefs, utilities, and intentions been other than they were. Or, if he did, he would have done so unintentionally, or for different reasons, or with other ends in view. To say that John's mental states interact causally *in virtue of* their content is, in part, to say that such counterfactuals hold.

If there are true, contingent counterfactuals which relate mental state *tokens* in virtue of their contents, that is presumably because there are true, contingent generalizations which relate mental state *types* in virtue of their contents. So, still following Aristotle at a distance, we can schematize etiologies like the one above to get the underlying generalization: if *x* believes that *A* is an action *x* can perform; and if *x* believes that a performance of *A* is sufficient to bring it about that *Q*; and if *x* wants it to be the case that *Q*; then *x* acts in a fashion intended to be a performance of *A*.

I am not, for present purposes, interested in whether this is a plausible decision theory; still less in whether it is the decision theory that Aristotle thought plausible. What interests me here is rather: (a) that any decision theory we can now contemplate will surely look rather like this one in that (b) it will entail generalizations about the causal relations among content-related beliefs, utilities, and intentions; and (c) such generalizations will be specified by reference to the form of the propositional attitudes which instantiate them. (This remains true even if, as some philosophers suppose, an adequate decision theory is irremediably in need of *ceteris paribus* clauses to flesh out its generalizations. See, for example, Grice, 1975.) So, in particular, we can't state the theory-relevant generalization that is instantiated by the relations among John's mental states unless we allow reference to beliefs *of the form if X then Y*, desires of the form *that Y*; intentions of the form *that X should come about*; and so forth. Viewed one way (material mode) the recurrent schematic letters require identities of content among propositional attitudes. Viewed the other way (linguistically) they require formal identities among the complements of the PA-ascribing sentence which instantiate the generalizations of the theory that explains John's behavior. Either way, the form of the generalization determines how the theory relates to the events that it subsumes. There is nothing remarkable about this, of course, except that form is here being ascribed *inside* the scope of verbs of PA.

To summarize: our commonsense psychological generalizations relate mental states in virtue of their content, and canonical representation does what it can to reconstruct such content relations as relations of form. "Aristotle's condition" requires that our theory of propositional attitudes should rationalize this process by construing verbs of PA in a way that permits reference to the form of their objects. To do this is to legitimize the presuppositions of commonsense psychology and, for that matter, of real (viz., cognitive) psychology as well. (See Fodor, 1975.)

In fact, we can state (and satisfy) Aristotle's condition in a still stronger version. Let anything be a *belief sentence* if it is of the form *a believes (that) S*. Define the *correspondent* of such a sentence as the formula which consists of the sentence *S* standing alone.[8] I remarked above that there is the following relation between the truth conditions on the belief that a belief sentence ascribes and the truth conditions on the correspondent of the belief sentence: the belief is true iff the correspondent is. This is, presumably, at least part of what is involved in viewing the correspondent of a belief sentence as *expressing* the ascribed belief.

It should not, therefore, be surprising to find that our intuitions about the form of the belief ascribed by a given belief sentence are determined by the logical form of its correspondent. So, intuitively, John's belief that Mary and Bill are leaving is a conjunctive belief (cf. the logical form of 'Mary and Bill are leaving'); John's belief that Alfred is a white swan is a singular belief (cf. the logical form of 'Alfred is a white swan'); and so on. It is, of course, essential that we understand 'belief' *opaquely* in such examples; otherwise, the belief that *P* will have the logical form of any sentence equivalent to *P*. But this is as it should be: it is in virtue of its *opaque* content that John's belief that *P* plays its systematic role in John's mental life: e.g., in the determination of his actions and in the causation of his other mental states. Hence it is the opaque construal that operates in such patterns of explanation as the practical syllogism and its spiritual heirs.

I am now in position to state Aristotle's condition in its strongest (and final) form. A theory of propositional attitudes should legitimize the ascription of form to objects of propositional attitudes. In particular, it should explain why the form of a belief is identical to the logical form of the correspondent of a sentence which (opaquely) ascribes that belief.[9]

I digress. One may feel inclined to argue that the satisfaction of Aristotle's condition is incompatible with the satisfaction of Frege's condition; that the opacity of belief sentences shows the futility of assigning logical form to their objects. The argument might go as follows. Sentences have logical form in virtue of their behavior under logical transformations; the logical form of a sentence is that aspect of its structure in virtue of which it provides a domain for such transformations. But Frege shows us that the objects of verbs of propositional attitude are inferentially inert. Hence, it's a sort of charade to speak of the logical form of the objects of PAs; what's the force of saying that a sentence has the form $P \mathbin{\&} Q$ if one must also say that simplification of conjunction does not apply?

Perhaps some such argument supplies the motive force of fusion theories. It is, in any event, misled. In particular, it muddles the distinction between what's entailed by what's believed, and what's entailed by believing what's believed. Less cryptically: if John believes $P \mathbin{\&} Q$, then what John believes entails P and what John believes entails Q. This is surely incontestable; $P \mathbin{\&} Q$ is what John believes, and $P \mathbin{\&} Q$ entails P, Q. Full stop. It would thus be highly ill advised to put Frege's condition as "$P \mathbin{\&} Q$ is semantically inert when embedded to the context 'John believes . . .' "; for this makes it sound as though $P \mathbin{\&} Q$ entails P only from time to time. (A parallel bad argument: $P \mathbin{\&} Q$ sometimes doesn't entail P: viz., when it's in the scope of the operator 'not'.) What falls under Frege's condition, then, is not the sentence that expresses what John believes (viz., $P \mathbin{\&} Q$) but the sentence that expresses John's believing what he believes (viz., the sentence #John believes that $P \mathbin{\&} Q$#). Note that the inertness of this latter sentence isn't an exception to simplification of conjunction since simplification of conjunction isn't defined for sentences of the form *a believes that P & Q*; only for sentences of the form *P & Q*.

"Still," one might say, "if the form of words #*P & Q*# is logically inert when embedded to the form of words 'John believes . . .', what's the *point* of talking about the logical form of the complement of belief sentences?" This isn't an argument, of course, but it's a fair question. Answers: (a) because we may want to satisfy Aristotle's condition (e.g., in order to be in a position to state the practical syllogism); (b) because we may want to compare beliefs in respect of their form (John's belief that all *F*s are *G*s is a generalization of Mary's belief that *a* is *F* and *G*; Sam's belief that *P* is incompatible with Bill's belief that not-*P*; etc.); (c) because we may wish to speak of the consequences of a belief, even while cheerfully admitting that the consequences of a belief may not themselves be objects of belief (viz., believed in). Indeed, we need the notion of the consequences of a belief if only in order to say that belief isn't closed under the consequence relation.

I cease to digress.

V. A theory of propositional attitudes should mesh with empirical accounts of mental processes.

We want a theory of PAs to say what (tokens) propositional attitudes *are*; or, at least, what the facts are in virtue of which PA ascriptions are true. It seems to me self-evident that no such theory could be acceptable unless it lent itself to explanations of the data — gross and commonsensical or subtle and experimental — about mental states and processes. This is not, of course, to require that a theory of PAs legitimize our current empirical psychology; only that it comport with some psychology or other that is independently warranted. I hear this as analogous to: the theory that water is H_2O couldn't be acceptable unless, taken together with appropriate empirical

premises, it leads to explanations of the macro- and micro-properties of water. Hence, I hear it as undeniable.

I think, in fact, that the requirement that a theory of propositional attitudes should be empirically plausible can be made to do quite a lot of work; much more work than philosophers have usually realized. I'll return to this presently, when we have some theories in hand.

Those, then, are the conditions that I want a theory of propositional attitudes to meet. I shall argue that, taken together, they strongly suggest that propositional attitudes are relations between organisms and formulae in an internal language; between organisms and internal sentences, as it were. It's convenient, however, to give the arguments in two steps; first, to show that conditions I-V comport nicely with the view that the objects of PAs are sentences, and then to show that these sentences are plausibly internal.

I begin by anticipating a charge of false advertising. The arguments to be reviewed are explicitly nondemonstrative. All I claim for the internal language theory is that it works (a) surprisingly well, and (b) better than any of the available alternatives. The clincher comes at the end: even if we didn't need the internal sentence story for purposes of I-V, we'd need it to do our psychology. Another nondemonstrative argument, no doubt, but one I find terrifically persuasive.

Carnap's Theory

Rudolf Carnap suggested, in *Meaning and Necessity* (1947), that PAs might be construed as relations between people and sentences they are disposed to utter; e.g., between people and sentences of English. What Carnap had primarily in mind was coping with the opacity problem, but it's striking and instructive that his proposal does pretty well with *all* the conditions I've enumerated. Consider:

I. If propositional attitudes are relations to sentences, then they are relations *tout court.* Moreover, assume that the relation ascribed by a sentence of the form *a believes . . .* holds between the individual denoted by '*a*' and the correspondent of the complement clause. It is then immediately clear why the belief ascribed to *a* is true iff the correspondent is; the correspondent is the *object* of the belief (i.e., the correspondent is what's believed-true) if Carnap's story is right.

II. Vendler's condition is presumably satisfiable, though how the details go will depend on how we construe the objects of verbs of saying. A natural move for a neo-Carnapian to make would be to take John said that *P* to be true in virtue of some relation between John and a token of the type *P*. Since, on this account, saying *P* and believing *P* involve relations to tokens of the very same sentence, it's hardly surprising that formulae which express the object of the *says-that* relation turn out to be logico-syntactically similar to formulae which express the object of the *believes-that* relation.

III. Frege's condition is satisfied; the opacity of belief is construed as a special case of the opacity of quotation. To put it slightly differently: 'John said "Bill bit Mary"' expresses a relation between John and a (quoted) sentence, so we're unsurprised by the fact that John may bear *that* relation to *that* sentence, while not bearing it to some arbitrarily similar but distinct sentence; e.g., to the sentence 'somebody bit Mary' or to the sentence 'Bill bit somebody', etc. But ditto, *mutatis mutandis*, if 'John believes Bill bit Mary' *also* expresses a relation between John and a quoted sentence.

IV. Aristotle's condition is satisfied in the strong form. The logical form of the object of a belief sentence is inherited from the logical form of the correspondent of the belief sentence. Of course it is, since on the Carnap view, the correspondent of the belief sentence *is* the object of the belief that it ascribes.

V. Whether you think that Carnap's theory can claim empirical plausibility depends on what you take the empirical facts about propositional attitudes to be and how ingenious you are in exploiting the theory to provide explanations of the facts. Here's one example of how such an explanation might go.

It's plausible to claim that there is a fairly general parallelism between the complexity of beliefs and the complexity of the sentences that express them. So, for example, I take it that 'the Second Punic War was fought under conditions which none of the combatants could have desired or foreseen' is a more complex sentence than, e.g., 'it's raining'; and, correspondingly, I take it that the thought that the Second Punic War was found under conditions which neither of the combatants could have desired or foreseen is a more complicated thought than the thought that it's raining. Carnap's theory explains this parallelism,[10] since, according to the theory what makes a belief ascription true is a relation between an organism and the correspondent of the belief-ascribing sentence. To hold the belief that the Second Punic War . . . , etc., is thus to be related to a more complex sentence than the one you are related to when you hold the belief that it's raining.

Some people need to count noses before they will admit to having one. In which case, see the discussion of "codability" in Brown and Lenneberg (1954) and Brown (1976). What the experiments showed is that the relative complexity of the descriptions which subjects supply for color chips predicts the relative difficulty that the subjects have in identifying the chips in a recognition-recall task. Brown and Lenneberg explain the finding along strictly (though inadvertently) Carnapian lines: complex descriptions correspond to complex memories because it's the description which the subject (opaquely) remembers when he (transparently) remembers the color of the chip.

We can now begin to see *one* of the ways in which condition V is supposed to work. A theory of propositional attitudes specifies a construal of the objects of the attitudes. It tells for such a theory if it can be shown to mesh with an independently plausible story about the "cost accounting" for mental processes. A cost-accounting function is just a (partial) ordering of mental states by their relative complexity. Such an ordering is, in turn, responsive to a variety of types of empirical data, both intuitive and experimental. Roughly, one has a "mesh" between an empirically warranted cost accounting and a theory of the objects of PAs when one can predict the relative complexity of a mental state (or process) from the relative complexity of whatever the theory assigns as its object (or domain). (So, if Carnap is right, then the relative complexity of beliefs should be predictable from the relative linguistic complexity of the correspondents of belief-ascribing sentences, all other things being equal.

There's a good deal more to be said about all this than I have space for here. Again, roughly: to require that the complexity of the putative objects of PAs predict the cost accounting for the attitudes is to impose empirical constraints on the *notation* of (canonical) belief-ascribing sentences. So, for example, we would clearly get different predictions about the relative complexity of beliefs if we took the object of a PA to be the correspondent of the belief-ascribing sentence than if we took it to be, e.g., the correspondent transformed into disjunctive form. The fact that there are empirical consequences of the notation we use to specify the objects of PAs is, of course, part and parcel of the fact that we are construing the attitude ascriptions *opaquely*; it is precisely under opaque construal that we distinguish (e.g.) the mental state of believing that $P \& Q$ from

the mental state of believing that neither not-P nor not-Q.

In short, Carnap's theory fares rather well with conditions I–V; there's more to be said in its favor than one might gather from the muted enthusiasm which philosophers have generally accorded it. Nevertheless, I think the philosophical consensus is warranted; Carnap's theory won't do. Here are some of the reasons.

1. Carnap has a theory about the objects of the propositional attitudes (viz., they're sentences) and a theory about the character of the relation to those objects in virtue of which one has a belief, desire, etc. Now, the latter theory is blatantly behaviorist; on Carnap's view, to believe that so and so is to be disposed (under presumably specifiable conditions) to utter tokens of the correspondent of the belief-ascribing sentence. But, patently, beliefs aren't behavioral dispositions; *a fortiori*, they aren't dispositions to utter. Hence, something's wrong with at least part of Carnap's account of the attitudes.

I put this objection first because it's the easiest to meet. So far as I can see, nothing prevents Carnap from keeping his account of the *objects* of belief while scuttling the behaviorist analysis of the belief relation. This would leave him wanting an answer to such questions as: what relation to the sentence 'it's raining' is such that you believe that it's raining iff you are in that relation? In particular, he'd want some answer other than the behaviorist: "It's the relation of being disposed to utter tokens of that sentence when . . ."

The natural solution would be for Carnap to turn functionalist; to hold that to believe it's raining is to have a token of 'it's raining' play a certain role in the causation of your behavior and of your (other) mental states, said role eventually to be specified in the course of the detailed working out of empirical psychology . . . , etc., etc. This is, perhaps, not much of a story, but it's fashionable, I know of nothing better, and it does have the virtue of explaining why propositional attitudes are opaque. Roughly, you wouldn't expect to be able to infer from 'tokens of the sentence S_1 have the causal role R' to 'tokens of the sentence S_2 have the causal role R' on the basis of any logical relation between S_1 and S_2 (except, of course, identity). More generally, so far as I can see, a functionalist account of the way quoted sentences figure in the having of PAs will serve as well as a disposition-to-utter account in coping with all of conditions I-V. From now on, I'll take this emendation for granted.

2.   The natural way to read the Carnap theory is to take type identity of the correspondents of belief-ascribing sentences as necessary and sufficient for type identity of the ascribed beliefs; and it's at least arguable that this cuts the PAs too thin. So, for example, one might plausibly hold that 'John believes Mary bit Bill' and 'John believes Bill was bitten by Mary' ascribe the same belief.[11] In effect, this is the sinister side of the strategy of inheriting the opacity of belief from the opacity of quotation. The strategy fails whenever the identity conditions on beliefs are *different* from the identity conditions on sentences.

A way to cope would be to allow that the objects of beliefs are, in effect, *translation sets* of sentences; something like this seems to be the impetus for Carnap's doctrine of intentional isomorphism. In any event, the problems in this area are well known. It may well be, for example, that the right way to characterize a translation relation for sentences is by referring to the communicative intentions of speaker/hearers of whatever language the sentences belong to. (S_1 translates S_2 iff the two sentences are both standardly used with the same communicative intentions.) But, of course, we can't both identify translations by reference to intentions and individuate propositional attitudes (in-

cluding, N.B., intentions) by reference to translations. This problem holds quite independent of epistemological worries about the facticity of ascriptions of propositional attitudes, the determinacy or otherwise of translations, etc.; which suggests that it may be serious.

3.   You can believe that it's raining even if you don't speak English. This is a variant of the thickness of slice problem just mentioned; it again suggests that the appropriate objects of belief are translation sets and raises the specters that haunt that treatment.

4.   You can, surely, believe that it's raining even if you don't speak any language at all. To say this is to say that at least *some* human cognitive psychology generalizes to infrahuman organisms; if it didn't, we would find the behavior of animals *utterly* bewildering, which, in fact, we don't.

Of course, relations are cheap; there must be *some* relation which a dog bears to 'it's raining' iff the dog believes that it's raining; albeit, perhaps, some not very interesting relation. So, why not choose *it* as the relation in virtue of which the belief ascription holds of the dog? The problem is condition V. It would simply be a miracle if there were a relation between dogs and tokens of 'it's raining' such that any of the empirical facts about the propositional attitudinizing of dogs proved explicable in terms of that relation. (We can't, for example, choose any functional/causal relation because the behavior of dogs is surely not in any way caused by tokens of English sentences.) To put it generally if crudely, satisfying condition V depends on assuming that whatever the theory takes to be the object of a PA plays an appropriate role in the mental processes of the organism to which the attitude is ascribed. But English sentences play no role in the mental life of dogs. (Excepting, perhaps, such sentences as 'Down, Rover!' which, in any event, don't play the kind of role envisaged.)

5. I argued that the truth conditions on beliefs are inherited from the truth conditions on the correspondents of belief-ascribing sentences, but this won't work if, for example, there are inexpressible beliefs. This problem is especially serious for behaviorist (or functionalist) accounts of the belief relation; to believe that *P* can't be a question of being disposed to utter (or of having one's behavior caused by) tokens of the sentence *P* if, as a matter of fact, there is no such sentence. Yet it is the appeal to quoted sentences which does the work in such theories: which allows them to satisfy I–V.

6. I remarked that there's a rough correspondence between the complexity of thoughts and the complexity of the sentences which express them, and that the (neo-)Carnapian theory provides for this; more generally, that the view that the objects of PAs are natural-language sentences might mesh reasonably well with an empirically defensible cost accounting for mental states and processes. Unfortunately this argument cuts both ways if we assume—as seems plausible—that the correspondence is no better than partial. Whenever it fails, there's prima facie evidence *against* the theory that sentences are the objects of propositional attitudes.

In fact, we can do rather better than appealing to intuitions here. For example: I noted above that the "codability" (viz., mean simplicity of descriptions in English) of colors predicts their recallability in a population of English-speakers, and that this comports with the view that what one remembers when one remembers a color is (at least sometimes) its description: i.e., with the view that descriptions are the objects of (at least some) propositional attitudes. It thus comes as a shock to find that codability *in English* also predicts recall for a Dani subject population. We

can't explain this by assuming a correlation between codability-in-English and codability-in-Dani (i.e., by assuming that the colors that English-speakers find easy to describe are the ones that Dani-speakers also find easy to describe) since, as it turns out, Dani has no vocabulary *at all* for chromatic variation; all such variation is *infinitely* uncodable in Dani. This comes close to being the paradox dreaded above: how could *English* sentences be the objects of the propositional attitudes of (monolingual) Dani? And, if they are not, how could a property defined over English sentences mesh with a theory of cost accounting for the mental processes of the Dani? It looks as though either: (a) some propositional attitudes are *not* relations to sentences, or (b) if they are—if English sentences are somehow the objects of Dani PAs—then sentences which constitute the objects of PAs need play no functional/causal role in the having of the attitudes. (For discussion of the cross-cultural results on codability, see Brown, 1976. For details of the original studies, see Heider, 1972, and Berlin and Kay, 1969.)

7. If (token) sentences of a natural language are the objects of propositional attitudes, how are (first) languages learned? On any theory of language learning we can now imagine, that process must involve the collection of data, the formulation of hypotheses, the checking of the hypotheses against the data, and the decision about which of the hypotheses the data best confirm. That is, it must involve such mental states and processes as beliefs, expectation, and perceptual integration. It's important to realize that *no* account of language learning which does not thus involve propositional attitudes and mental processes has ever been proposed by anyone, barring only behaviorists. And behaviorist accounts of language learning are, surely, not tenable. So, on pain of circularity,

there must be *some* propositional attitudes which are not functional/causal relations to natural-language sentences. I see no way out of this which isn't a worse option than rejecting the Carnap theory.

So, the situation looks discouraging. On the one hand, we have a number of plausible arguments in favor of accepting the Carnap story (viz., I-V) and, on the other, we have a number of equally plausible arguments in favor of not (viz., 1-7). Never mind; for, at second blush, it seems we needn't accept the whole Carnap theory to satisfy I-V and we needn't reject the whole Carnap theory to avoid 1-7. Roughly, all that I-V require is the part of the story that says that the objects of PAs are *sentences* (hence have logical forms, truth conditions, etc.). Whereas what causes the trouble with 1-7 is only that part of the story which says that they are *natural-language* sentences (hence raising problems about nonverbal organisms, first language learning, etc.). The recommended solution is thus to take the objects of PAs to be sentences of a *non*natural language; in effect, formulae in an Internal Representational System.

The first point is to establish that this proposal does what it is supposed to: copes with I-V without running afoul of 1-7. In fact, I propose to do less than that since, so far as I can see, the details would be extremely complicated. Suffice it here to indicate the general strategy.

Conditions I and III are relatively easy to meet. Condition I demands that propositional attitudes be relations, and so they are if they are relations to internal representations. Condition III demands a construal of opacity. Carnap met this demand by reducing the opacity of belief to the opacity of quotation, and so do we: the only difference is that, whereas for Carnap, 'John believes it's raining' relates John to a sentence of English, for us it relates John to an internal formula.

Conditions II and IV stress logico-syntactic parallelism between the complements and the correspondents of belief-ascribing sentences; such relations are epitomized by the identity between the truth conditions on 'it's raining' and those on what is believed when it's believed that it's raining. (Neo-)Carnap explained these symmetries by taking the correspondents of belief ascriptions to be the objects of beliefs. The present alternative is spiritually similar but one step less direct: we assume that the correspondent of a belief-ascriber inherits its logico-semantic properties from the same internal formula which functions as the object of the belief ascribed.

There are three pieces in play: there are (a) *belief-ascribers* (like 'John believes it's raining'); (b) *complements* of belief-ascribers (like the phrase 'it's raining' in 'John believes it's raining'); and (c) *correspondents* of belief-ascribers (like the sentence 'it's raining' standing free). The idea is to get all three to converge (though, of course, by different routes) on the same internal formula (call it 'F(it's raining)')[12] thereby providing the groundwork for explaining the analogies that II and IV express. To get this to work out right would be to supply detailed instructions for connecting the theory of PAs with the theory of sentence interpretation, and I have misplaced mine. But the general idea is apparent. Belief-ascribers are true in virtue of functional/causal (call them 'belief-making') relations between organisms and tokens of internal formulae. Thus, in particular, 'John believes it's raining' is true in virtue of a belief-making relation between John and a token of F(it's raining). It is, of course, the complement of a belief-ascriber that determines *which* internal formula is involved in its truth conditions; in effect 'it's raining' in 'John believes it's raining' functions as an index which picks out F(it's raining) (and not, for example, F(elephants have wings)) as the internal formula that John is related to iff 'John believes it's raining' is true.

So, viewed along one vector, the complement of a belief-ascriber connects it to an internal formula. But, simultaneously, the complement of a belief-ascriber connects it to its correspondent: if the correspondent of 'John believes it's raining' is 'it's raining', that is because the form of words 'it's raining' constitutes its complement. And now we can close the circle, since, of course, F(it's raining) is *also* semantically connected with the correspondent of 'John believes it's raining', viz., by the principle that 'it's raining' is the sentence that English-speakers use when they are in the belief-making relation to a token of F(it's raining) and wish to use a sentence of English to say what it is that they believe.

There are various ways of thinking about the relation between internal formulae and the correspondents of belief-ascribers. One is to think of the conventions of a natural language as functioning to establish a pairing of its verbal forms with the internal formulae that mediate the propositional attitudes of its users; in particular, as pairing the internal objects of beliefs with the form of words that speaker/hearers use to express their beliefs. This is a natural way to view the situation if you think of a natural language as a system of conventional vehicles for the expression of thought (a view to which I know of no serious objections). So, in the present case, the conventions of English pair: 'it's raining' with F(it's raining) (viz., with the object of the belief that it's raining); 'elephants have wings' with F(elephants have wings) (viz., with the object of the belief that elephants have wings); and, generally, the object of each belief with the correspondent of some belief-ascribing sentence.[13]

Another option is to assume that F(it's raining) is distinguished by the fact that its tokens play a causal/functional role (not only as the object of the belief that it's raining, but also) in the production of linguistically regular utterances of 'it's raining'. Indeed, this option would plausibly be exercised in tandem with the one mentioned just above since it would be reasonable to construe "linguistically regular" utterances as the ones that are produced in light of the speaker's knowledge of the linguistic conventions. The basic idea, in any event, would be to implicate F(it's raining) as the object of the communicative intentions that utterances of 'it's raining' standardly function to express; hence, as among the mental causes of such utterances. I take it that, given this relation, it ought to be possible to work out detailed tactics for the satisfaction of conditions II and IV, but this is the bit I propose to leave to the ingenuity of the reader. What I want to emphasize here is the way the linguistic structure of the complement of a belief-ascriber connects it with free declaratives (in one direction) and with internal formulae (in the other). Contrary to the fusion story, it's no accident that 'it's raining' occurs in 'John believes it's raining'. Rather, the availability of natural languages for saying *both* what one believes *and* that one believes it turns on the exploitation of this elegant symmetry.

What about condition V? I shall consider this in conjunction with 2-7, since what's noteworthy about the latter is that they all register *empirical* complaints against the Carnap account. For example, 3, 4, and 6 would be without force if only everybody (viz., every subject of true propositional attitude ascriptions) talked English; 2 and 5 depend upon the empirical likelihood that English sentences fail to correspond one to one to objects of propositional attitudes; 7 would be met if only English were innate. Indeed, I suppose an ultra-hard-line-neo-Carnapian might consider saving the bacon by claiming that — appearances to the contrary notwithstanding—English *is* innate, universal, just rich enough, etc. My point is that this is the right *kind* of move to make; all we have against it is its palpable untruth.

Whereas, it's part of the charm of the internal language story that, since practically nothing is known about the details of cognitive processes, we can make the corresponding assumptions about the internal representational system risking no more than gross implausibility at the very worst.

So, let's assume—what we don't, at any event, *know* to be false—that the internal language is innate, that it's formulae correspond one to one with the contents of propositional attitudes (e.g., that 'John bit Mary' and 'Mary was bitten by John' correspond to the same "internal sentence"), and that it is *as* universal as human psychology; viz., that to the extent that an organism shares our mental processes, it also shares our system of internal representations. On these assumptions, everything works. It's no longer paradoxical, for example, that codability *in English* predicts the relative complexity of the mental processes of the Dani; for, by assumption, it's not *really* the complexity of English sentences that predicts *our* cost accounting; we wouldn't expect *that* correspondence to be better than partial (see objection 6). What really predicts our cost accounting is the relative complexity of the internal representations that we use English sentences to express. And, again by assumption, the underlying system of internal representations is common to the Dani and to us. If you don't like this assumption, try and find some other hypothesis that accounts for the facts about the Dani.

Notice that to say that we have our empirical assumptions isn't to say that we can have them for free. They carry a body of empirical commitments which, if untenable, will defeat the internal representation view. Imagine, for example, that cost accounting for English-speakers proves utterly unrelated to cost accounting for (e.g.) speakers of Latvian. (Imagine, in effect, that the Whorf-Sapir hypothesis turns out to be more or less true.) It's then hard to see how the system of internal representations could be universal. But if it's not universal, it's presumably not innate. And if it's not innate, it's not available to mediate the learning of first languages. And if it's not available to mediate the learning of first languages, we lose our means of coping with objection 7. There are plenty of ways in which we could find out that the theory's wrong if, in fact, it is.

Where we've gotten to is this: the general characteristics of propositional attitudes appear to demand sentencelike entities to be their objects. And broadly empirical conditions appear to preclude identifying these entities with sentences of *natural* languages; hence internal representations and private languages. How bad is it to have gotten here? I now want to argue that the present conclusion is independently required because it is presupposed by the best—indeed the only—psychology that we've got. Not just, as one philosopher has rather irresponsibly remarked, that "some psychologists like to talk that way," but that the best accounts of mental processes we have are quite unintelligible unless something like the internal representation story is true.

The long way of making this point is via a detailed discussion of such theories, but I've done that elsewhere and enough is enough. Suffice it here to consider a single example which is, however, prototypical. I claim again that the details don't matter; that one could make the same points by considering phenomena drawn from any area of cognitive psychology which is sufficiently well worked out to warrant talk of a theory *in situ*.

So, consider a fragment of contemporary (psycho)linguistics; consider the explanation of the ambiguity of a sentence like 'they are flying planes' (hereinafter, frequently *S*). The conventional story goes as follows: the sentence is ambiguous because there are two ways of grouping the word sequence into phrases, two ways of "bracketing" it. One bracketing, corresponding to the reading of the sentence which answers 'what are those things?', goes: (they) (are) (flying planes). Viz., the sentence is copular, the main verb is 'are' and 'flying' is an adjectival modifier of 'planes'. Whereas, on the other bracketing, corresponding to the reading on which the sentence answers 'what are those guys doing?', the bracketing goes: (they) (are flying) (planes); viz., the sentence is transitive, the main verb is 'flying' and 'are' belongs to the auxiliary. I assume without argument that something like this is, or at least contributes to, the explanation of the ambiguity of *S*. The evidence for such treatments is overwhelming and there is, literally, no alternative theory in the field.

But what could it mean to speak of *S* as "having" two bracketings? I continue to tread the well-worn path: *S* has two bracketings in that there exists a function (call it *G-proper*) from (as it might be) the word 'sentence' onto precisely those bracketed word strings which constitute the sentences of English. And both '(they) (are) (flying planes)' and '(they) (are flying) (planes)' are in the range of that function. (Moreover, no other bracketing of that word sequence is in the range of *G-proper* . . . , etc.)

Now, the trouble with this explanation, as it stands, is that it is either enthymematic or silly. For, one wants to ask, how *could* the mere, as it were Platonic, existence of *G-proper* account for the facts about the ambiguity of English sentences? Or, to put it another way, sure there is, Platonically, a function under which *S* gets two bracketings.

But there is also, Platonically, a function *G'* under which it gets sixteen; and a function *G''* under which it gets seven; and a function *G'''* under which it gets none. Since *G'*, *G''*, and *G'''* are all, qua functions, just as good as *G-proper*, how could the mere *existence* of the latter explain the linguistic properties of *S*? (You may feel inclined to say: "Ah, but *G-proper* is the (or perhaps is *the*) grammar of English, and that distinguishes it from *G'*, *G''*, and the rest." But this explanation takes one nowhere, since it invites the question: why does the grammar of English play a special role in the explanation of English sentences? Or, to put the same question minutely differently: call *G'* the schmammar of English. We now want to know how come it's the bracketing assigned by English grammar and not the bracketing assigned by English schmammar, which predicts the ambiguity of 'they are flying planes'.

So far as I can see, there's only one way such questions can conceivably be answered; viz., by holding that *G-proper* (not only exists but) is the very system of (internal (what else?)) formulae that English speaker/hearers use to represent the sentences of their language. But, then, if we accept this, we are willy-nilly involved in talking of at least *some* mental processes (processes of understanding and producing sentences) as involving at least some relations to at least some internal representations. And, if we have to have internal representations anyhow, why not take them to be the objects of propositional attitudes, thereby placating I–V? I say "if we accept this"; but really we have no choice. For the account is well evidenced, not demonstrably incoherent, and, again, it's the only one in the field. A working science is *ipso facto* in philosophical good repute.

So, by a series of nondemonstrative arguments: there are internal representations and propositional attitudes are relations that we bear to them. It remains to discuss two closely related objections.

Objection 1: Why not take the object of propositional attitudes to be *propositions*?

This suggestion has, no doubt, a ring of etymological plausibility; in fact, for all I know, it may be right. The mistake is in supposing it somehow conflicts with the present proposal.

I am taking seriously the idea that the system of internal representations constitutes a (computational) language. Qua language, it presumably has a syntax and a semantics; specifying the language involves saying what the properties are in virtue of which its formulae are well formed, and what relation(s) obtain between the formulae and things in the (nonlinguistic) world. I have no idea what an adequate semantics for a system of internal representations would look like; suffice it that, if propositions come in at all, they come in here. In particular, nothing stops us from specifying a semantics for the IRS by saying (*inter alia*) that some of its formulae express propositions. If we do say this, then we can make sense of the notion that propositional attitudes are relations to propositions; viz., they are *mediated* relations to propositions, with internal representations doing the mediating.

This is, quite generally, the way that representational theories of the mind work. So, in classical versions, thinking of John (construed opaquely) is a relation to an "idea"; viz., to an internal representation of John. But this is quite compatible with its also being (transparently) construable as a relation *to John*. In particular, when Smith is thinking of John, he (normally) stands in relation to John and does so *in virtue* of his standing in relation to an idea of John. Similarly, *mutatis mutandis*, if thinking that it will rain is standing in relation to a proposition, then, on the present account, you stand in that relation in virtue of your

(functional/causal) relation to an internal formula which expresses the proposition. No doubt, the "expressing" bit is obscure; but that's a problem about propositions, not a problem about internal representations.

"Ah, but if you are going to allow propositions as the *mediate* objects of propositional attitudes, why bother with internal representations as their immediate objects? Why not just say: 'Propositional attitudes are relations to propositions. Punkt!' " There's a small reason and a big reason. The small reason is that propositions don't have the right properties for our purposes. In particular, one anticipates problems of cost accounting. Condition V, it will be remembered, permits us to choose among theories of PAs in virtue of the form of the entities they assign as objects of the attitudes. Now, the problem with propositions is that they are the sorts of things which, presumably, don't *have* forms. Propositions are sheer contents; they neutralize the lexico-syntactic differences between various ways of saying the same thing. That's what they're *for*. I say that this is a small problem but it looms prodigious if you hanker after a theory of the object of PAs which claims empirical repute. After all, it's not just cost accounting which is supposed to be determined by formal aspects of the objects of PAs; it's *all* the mental processes and properties that cognitive psychology explains. That's what it *means* to speak of a *computational* psychology. Computational principles are ones that apply in virtue of the form of entities in their domain.

But my main reason for not saying "Propositional attitudes are relations to propositions. Punkt!" is that I don't understand it. I don't see how an organism can stand in an (interesting epistemic) relation to a proposition except by standing in a (causal/functional) relation to some token of a formula which expresses the proposition. I am aware that there is a philosophical tradition to the contrary. Plato says (I think) that there is a special intellectual faculty (*theoria*) wherewith one peers at abstract objects. Frege says that one *apprehends* (what I'm calling) propositions, but I can find no doctrine about what apprehension comes to beyond the remark (in "The Thought") that it's not sense perception because its objects are abstract and it's not introspection because its objects aren't mental. (He also says that grasping a thought isn't much like grasping a hammer. To be sure.) As for me, I want a mechanism for the relation between organisms and propositions, and the only one I can think of is mediation by internal representations.[14]

Objection 2: Surely its *conceivable* that propositional attitudes are *not* relations to internal representations.

I think it is; the theory that propositional attitudes are relations to internal representations is a piece of empirical psychology, not an analysis. For, there might have been angels, or behaviorism might have been true, and then the internal representation story would have been false. The moral is, I think, that we ought to give up asking for analyses; psychology is all the philosophy of mind that we are likely to get.

But, moreover, it may be *empirically* possible that there should be creatures which have the same propositional attitudes we do (e.g., the same beliefs) but *not* the same system of internal representations; creatures which, as it were, share our epistemic states but not our psychology. Suppose, for example, it turns out that Martians, or porpoises, believe what we do but have a very different sort of cost accounting. We might then want to say that there are translation relations among systems of internal representation (viz., that formally distinct representations can express the same proposition). Whether we can make sense of saying this remains to be seen; we can barely think about the question prior to the elabora-

tion of theories about how such systems are semantically interpreted and as things now stand, we haven't got semantic theories for natural languages, to say nothing of languages of thought. Perhaps it goes without saying that it's no objection to a doctrine that it *may* run us into incoherencies. Or, rather, if it is an objection, there's an adequate reply: "Yes, but also it may not."

I'll end on the note just sounded. Contemporary cognitive psychology is, in effect, a revival of the representational theory of the mind. The favored treatment of PAs arises in this context. So, in particular, the mind is conceived of as an organ whose function is the manipulation of representations, and these, in turn, provide the domain of mental processes and the (immediate) objects of mental states. That's what it is to see the mind as something like a computer. (Or rather, to put the horse back in front of the cart, that's what it is to see a computer as something like the mind. We give sense to the analogy by treating selected states of the machine as formulae and by specifying which semantic interpretations the formulae are to bear. It is in the context of such specifications that we speak of machine processes as computations and of machine states as intensional.)

If the representational theory of the mind is true, then we know what propositional attitudes are. But the net total of philosophical problems is surely not decreased thereby. We must now face what has always been *the* problem for representational theories to solve: what relates internal representations to the world? What is it for a system of internal representations to be semantically interpreted? I take it that this problem is now the main content of the philosophy of mind.

Notes

1. I shall have nothing at all to say about knowing, discovering, recognizing, or any

other of the "factive" attitudes. The justification for this restriction is worth discussing, but not here.

2. I am not distinguishing between the relation story and the one that takes 'John believes' to be an operator on 'it's raining'; it's the 'it's raining' bit, not the 'John believes' bit, that I'm primarily concerned about.

3. I assume that this is approximately correct: given a sentence of the syntactic form NP_1 $(V (NP_2))_{VP}$, V expresses a relation iff NP_1 and NP_2 refer. So, for present purposes, the question whether 'believes' expresses a relation in 'John believes it's raining' comes down to the question whether there are such things as objects of beliefs. I shan't, therefore, bother to distinguish among these various ways of putting the question in the discussion which follows.

4. Of course, it might refer by virtue of a relation between Mary and something other than a voice. 'John is taller than the average man' isn't true in virtue of a relation between John and the average man ('the average man' doesn't refer). But the sentence is relational for all that. It's for this sort of reason that such principles as the one announced in note 3 hold only to a first approximation.

5. N.B.: verbs of propositional attitude are transparent, in this sense, only when their objects are *complements*; one can't infer 'there is something Ponce de Leon sought' from 'Ponce de Leon sought the Fountain of Youth'. It may, however, be worth translating 'seek' to 'try to find' to save the generalization. This would give us: 'Ponce de Leon tried to find the Fountain of Youth', which does, I suppose, entail that there is something that Ponce de Leon tried (viz., tried to do; viz., to find the Fountain of Youth).

Also, to say that *EG* applies *to* the complement of verbs of PA is, of course, not to say that it applies *in* the complement of verbs of PA. 'John wants to marry Marie of Rumania' implies that there is something that John wants (viz., wants to do; viz., to marry Marie of Rumania); it notoriously does *not* imply that there is someone whom John wants to marry (see III below).

6. Fusion has been contemplated as a remedy for untransparency in several philosophical contexts; see Nagel, 1965; Goodman,

1968; Dennett, 1969. Note: 'contemplated', not 'embraced'.

7. 3. is not a point about *EG*. On the fusion view, there's no representation of the fact that 'the belief that Sam is nice' is about Sam even when 'belief' and 'about' are both construed *opaquely*.

8. Defining 'correspondent' gets complicated where verbs of PA take *transformed* sentences as their objects, but the technicalities needn't concern us here. Suffice it that we want the correspondent of 'John wants to leave' to be 'John leaves'; the correspondent of 'John objects to Mary and Bill being elected' to be 'Mary and Bill are elected', etc.

9. I am assuming that two sentences with correspondents of *different* logico-syntactic form cannot assign the same (opaque) belief, and someone might wish to challenge this; consider 'John believes that Mary bit Bill' and 'John believes that Bill was bitten by Mary'. This sort of objection is serious and will be accommodated later on.

10. In speaking of Carnap's theory, I don't wish to imply that Carnap would endorse the uses to which I'm putting it; quite the contrary, I should imagine.

11. See note 9 above.

12. Where *F* might be thought of as a function from (e.g., English) sentences onto internal formulae.

13. Assuming, as we may but now needn't do, that all beliefs are expressible in English. It is, of course, a consequence of the present view that all the beliefs we can entertain are expressible in the internal code.

14. The notion that the apprehension of propositions is mediated by linguistic objects is not entirely foreign even to the Platonist tradition. Church says: "The preference of (say) seeing over *understanding* as a method of observation seems to me capricious. For just as an opaque body may be seen, so a concept may be understood or grasped . . . In both cases the observation is not direct but through intermediaries . . . linguistic expressions in the case of the concept" (1951); see also the discussion in Dummett (1973, pp. 156-157).

References

Berlin, B., and P. Kay. 1969. *Basic Color*

3. Propositional Attitudes   63

Terms. Berkeley and Los Angeles: University of California Press.

Brown, R. 1976. "Reference — In Memorial Tribute to Eric Lenneberg." *Cognition* 4: 125-153.

Brown, R., and E. Lenneberg. 1954. "A Study in Language and Cognition." *Journal of Abnormal and Social Psychology* 49: 454-462.

Carnap, R. 1947. *Meaning and Necessity.* Chicago: University of Chicago Press, Phoenix Books.

Church, A. 1951. "The Need for Abstract Entities in Semantic Analysis." In *Contributions to the Analysis and Synthesis of Knowledge.* Proceedings of the American Academy of Arts and Sciences, no. 80, pp. 100-112.

Davidson, D. 1965. "Theories of Meaning and Learnable Languages." In Y. Bar-Hillel, ed., *Logic, Methodology and Philosophy of Science.* Proceedings of the 1964 International Congress, pp. 383-394. Amsterdam: North Holland.

Dennett, D. 1969. *Content and Consciousness.* London: Routledge and Kegan Paul.

Dummett, M. 1973. *Frege.* London: Duckworth.

Fodor, J. A. 1975. *The Language of Thought.* New York: Crowell.

Goodman, N. 1968. *Languages of Art.* Indianapolis: Bobbs-Merrill.

Grice, H. P. 1975. "Method in Philosophical Psychology." *Proceedings and Addresses of the American Philosophical Association,* vol. 48, pp. 23-53.

Heider, E. 1972. "Universals in Color Naming and Memory." *Journal of Experimental Psychology* 93: 10-20.

Nagel, T. 1965. "Physicalism." *Philosophical Review* 74: 339-356.

Vendler, Z. 1972. *Res Cogitans.* Ithaca: Cornell University Press.

A Cure for the Common Code?

Daniel C. Dennett

We and other creatures exhibit intelligent behavior, and since the regular production of such behavior requires thought, and since thought requires representation, and since nothing can represent except within a system, we must be endowed with and utilize a system of internal representation having its own "grammar" and "vocabulary", which we might call the language of thought.

This argument has seldom been brought into the open and examined, but behind the scenes it has motivated and flavored large bodies of philosophical doctrine, and strongly influenced research strategies and theories in psychology, linguistics, computer science and neurophysiology. It is worth asking why such an influential move has been so comfortably ignored until recently. It is not plausibly one of those drifts of thought that seem too obvious to need spelling out; perhaps it has been avoided because once one attempts to put the argument in proper and explicit shape, incoherencies,

From *Mind* 86 (April 1977): 265-280. Originally entitled "Critical Notice: *The Language of Thought* by Jerry Fodor." Reprinted by permission of Basil Blackwell, Publisher, and the author. Notes have been numbered for this edition.

paradoxes, infinite regresses and other alarming implications seem to arise at every turning. Now Jerry Fodor, in *The Language of Thought*, Crowell, 1975, has done us the fine service of propounding and defending a vigorous, unblinking, and ingenious version of the argument. Many of his conclusions seem outrageous, and the threats of incoherency are now close to the surface, but Fodor argues with great persuasiveness that these are in fact parts of the foundation of deservedly esteemed schools of thought in philosophy, cognitive psychology and linguistics. If he has produced an unintended *reductio ad absurdum* (a possibility he cheerfully admits), some of our favorite edifices will topple with him. He may be wrong, of course, but the challenge is well presented, and since recently thinkers in all the jeopardized fields have been converging on just the perplexities Fodor discusses, the challenge will not be ignored. The main issue treated in Fodor's book is fast becoming a major topic of interdisciplinary interest, and philosophers of mind who have squeezed the last drops of enlightenment out of the debate over the identity theory or the individuation of actions should be pleased to find here some important and fascinating problems to engage their talents. What is needed is nothing less than a completely general theory of representation, with which we can explain how words, thoughts, thinkers, pictures, computers, animals, sentences, mechanisms, states, functions, nerve impulses, and formal models (*inter alia*) can be said to represent one thing or another. It will not do to divide and conquer here—by saying that these various things do not represent in the same sense. Of course that is true, but what is important is that there is something that binds them all together, and we need a theory that can unify the variety. Producing such a theory is surely a philosophical endeavor, but philosophers must recognize that some of the most useful and suggestive work currently being done on the problems is being done by psychologists, linguists, and workers in artificial intelligence.

For what it is worth, Fodor probably holds uniquely strong professional credentials for the task of consolidating the insights from these fields, for he holds a joint appointment in psychology and philosophy (at M.I.T., a major centre for work in linguistics and artificial intelligence) and has made important contributions to experimental psycholinguistics and linguistics in addition to his work in philosophy. Fodor is not beset by the philosophical naiveté of many of his colleagues in psychology and he has as powerful a grasp of current thinking in linguistics and psychology as anyone in philosophy. Indeed, the overall savvy of his book is one of its most striking characteristics, mainly for good but also for ill. There cannot be many readers well equipped or disposed to appreciate all his knowing nudges; the uninitiated will perhaps be the unpersuaded (and unamused) as well. I fear that Fodor's unfailing high spirits and jocosity may hurt his cause by irritating as many readers as they amuse. I find the book genuinely wit-

ty, however, and can only urge those who resent being tickled while engaged in such serious business to make an extra effort to distinguish the medium from the message.

Fodor's message has three parts. First he describes and promotes a brand of theorizing he calls cognitive psychology, but clearly he means to cast his net wider, and in places narrower, than that term would suggest. The distinguishing mark of this theorizing is the unapologetic utilization of intentional characterizations of processes and "intellectualist" analyses of perception and other "cognitive processes" in terms of information-flow, hypothesis-testing, inference and decision-making. Within its boundaries fall much current psychology, linguistics, artificial intelligence, and some strains of thought in current philosophy. Let us call it neocognitivism, for it is not markedly continuous with earlier schools of cognitive psychology, nor is it all clearly psychology. It has developed largely in recognition of the impotence of (psychological and logical) behaviorism, and its inspiration is drawn largely from linguistics, computer science and (come to think of it) the last three hundred years of epistemology. Fodor attempts to establish the credentials of neocognitivism by showing how it avoids the doldrums of Rylean logical behaviorism, steers between the Scylla of dualism and the Charybdis of reductionism to emerge as the only straw floating—as Jerome Lettvin once put it. In this first part Fodor has a strong and persuasive case on almost all counts.

Fodor's second task is to show that this best hope for a confirmed, powerful psychological theory inescapably requires the postulation of internal representational systems. These systems, though designed for computation rather than communication, have structures—and other features—so like those of natural languages that we may—and should—

speak of the language of thought: the medium in which the computational transactions are performed that ultimately govern our behavior and the behavior of other intelligent creatures as well. This is the philosophic heart of Fodor's book, and will receive detailed attention below.

Third, Fodor completes his book with two lengthy chapters purporting to show how evidence from linguistics and psychology establishes answers to an impressive variety of questions about 'the structure of the internal code'. Having proved the existence of Planet X, he proceeds to detail its climate and geography for us, using data that had been available but hitherto mute. These chapters are undeniably compelling, for every now and then one gets glimmers of the sort of fruitful falling-into-place so seldom encountered in psychology or philosophy of mind. Whereas, for instance, behaviorism has always worn the guise of a properly endorsed method (a "methodology") in dogged search of results, here we seem to see an abundance of results and tempting hypotheses to test for which we must somehow concoct methodological permission.

For example, linguists have devised a variety of competing formal systems for more or less algorithmically generating or analysing sentences, and a question the psycholinguist asks is which if any proposed formalism has "psychological reality", or in other words describes or mirrors real psychological processes occurring in the production or comprehension of sentences. This empirical question is to be settled independently of the elegance or power of the formal systems. (One way of dividing 67 by 12 is to subtract 12 from 67, then subtract 12 from 55, and so forth, while counting the subtractions; another is long division; which if either has "psychological reality" for an individual human calculator is surely an empirical question, and *asking the calculator* is not the only, or always the best, way of

answering the question.) Subtle studies of reaction times, relative difficulty of comprehension, patterns of errors, and so forth often provide satisfyingly clearcut verdicts on these questions, but often only if we make just the sorts of assumptions about representational machinery Fodor is attempting to vindicate. Whether these investigations will continue to ramify nicely is far from assured, however, and there is an abundance of danger signals for skeptics to make of what they can.

The conclusion Fodor wishes to draw from his examination is bracingly unqualified: " . . . having a propositional attitude is being in some *computational* relation to an internal representation". "Attitudes to propositions are . . . 'reduced' to attitudes to formulae, though the formulae are couched in a proprietary inner code" (p. 198). The inner code is innate, and one's innate vocabulary of predicates must be sufficient to represent, by logical construction, any predicate of any natural language one can learn. Once one learns such a predicate one may augment one's inner code with a synonym, as it were, of the natural language predicate and henceforward use this non-native inner word as an abbreviation for the cumbersome truth-functional molecule of native mentalese (p. 152). We are not born with an inner code word for "airplane" but if we couldn't form at the outset a predicate of inner mentalese at least coextensive with "airplane" we could never learn what "airplane" meant, could never add an "airplane"-synonym to our basic stock. So there is a sense in which one cannot "acquire new concepts" by learning a language, even one's mother tongue.

All this (and there is more) is hard to swallow, but what are the alternatives? Thinkers as diverse as B. F. Skinner, Norman Malcolm and Hubert Dreyfus have insisted that the very concept of neural systems of representation is a monstrous error. Let us call that the extreme right wing view. On the extreme left, then, would be researchers such as McConnell and Ungar, who take brain-writing so literally that they suppose one might physically extract token sentences of the inner code from one creature and teach another by injection or ingestion. (Ungar reports he has trained cats to fear the dark and then isolated a substance in them, "scotophobin", which injected into untrained cats causes them to fear the dark!) Middle-of-the-road positions have yet to be formulated in satisfactory detail, but it is safe to say that Fodor has laid claim to a position far to the left of center and is insisting that no less extreme position can provide the foundations for the promising theories of neo-cognitivism.

Let us return to the beginning and examine Fodor's case in some detail. Fodor takes his first task to be protecting neo-cognitivism from two philosophic threats: Ryle's attack on intellectualist theorizing, and the physicalist demand that all theoretical terms be reducible somehow to the terms of physics. Fodor sees these as in different ways suggesting the charge that neo-cognitivism is dualistic (a verdict Fodor would view as at least discouraging and probably fatal). The charge is familiar: the characteristic predicates of cognitive psychology are intentional or "mentalistic" idioms, and since mentalism is dualism, cognitive psychology is dualistic. Certainly in the past this has been an influential train of thought; Brentano did after all reintroduce the concept of intentionality precisely as the distinguishing mark of the non-physical, and (though probably not influenced by Brentano) Skinner has for years seen the spectre of dualism in every variety of "mentalistic" theorizing. The claim has not however figured influentially in recent philosophic work in the area. On the contrary, the coexistence of physicalistic doctrine with intentional or mentalistic vocabulary, while perhaps not having

received the justification it ought to have, is a typically undefended and unattacked feature of current discussions.

It is a bit curious then that a rebuttal of the dualism charge should find pride of place in Fodor. Perhaps he is addressing the many psychologists who haven't heard and are still swayed by Skinner's suspicions. More curious still is Fodor's choice of Ryle as the initial target of his rebuttal. In *Psychological Explanation* (1968) Fodor went to great lengths to refute his version of Ryle's "logical behaviorism" and in 1975 he has still not been able to remove his hands from this tar-baby. Now it is clearer why Ryle should exercise him so, for he has clarified his interpretation with a cute example: "Why are Wheaties (as the ads say) the breakfast of champions?" "Because," says the dietician, "they contain vitamins, etc." "Because," says the Rylean, "they are eaten for breakfast by a non-negligible number of champions." The former is a "causal" explanation, the latter a "conceptual" explanation and, according to Fodor, Ryle's view is that the latter explanation is in competition with the former. When a question should have a conceptual answer, it cannot have a causal answer as well. Questions like "What makes the clown's clowning clever?" have conceptual answers and, according to Fodor's Ryle, therefore cannot have causal answers—"Alas for the psychology of clever clowning."

Fodor's demolition of this notion should be, and is, obvious, and as an interpretation of Ryle it is almost right: the Wheaties example does most effectively illuminate a central Rylean distinction, and there are many passages in *The Concept of Mind* that could be cited to support the claim that Ryle deserves to be so interpreted. But Ryle does not, as Fodor thinks, offer *The Concept of Mind* as a psychological theory or as a substitute for psychology or as a proof that psychology can't be done. Fodor seems to be pointing out that questions like "What makes the clowning clever?" are ambiguous, but he does not see, or accept, the implication that in such cases there are two questions one can be asking. If there are two questions, it can be true that one cannot answer a question requiring a conceptual answer with a causal answer, which is Ryle's point, without it being true that psychology and philosophy of mind are in competition. Fodor has construed Ryle's attack on intellectualist theorizing (involving the postulation of inner cognitive processes) as an attack on intellectualist solutions to problems in psychology, while Ryle intended it primarily as an attack on intellectualist solutions to the conceptual problems of philosophy. In fairness to Fodor's interpretation, Ryle does strongly suggest that cognitivistic or "para-mechanical" hypotheses and the like are bankrupt as psychology as well (see especially the last chapter of *The Concept of Mind*) and against that excessive strain in Ryle's thought Fodor's arguments — and indeed the whole book — are a welcome antidote. But in the process of magnifying and rebutting the worst in Ryle, Fodor misconstrues Ryle in another fashion that leads him to overlook a more penetrating Rylean objection to his enterprise. "Ryle assumes", Fodor tells us, " . . . that a mentalist must be a dualist; in particular, that mentalism and materialism are mutually exclusive." Hence the "tendency to see the options of dualism and behaviorism as exhaustive in the philosophy of mind" (p. 4). Were we to replace "Ryle" with "Skinner" and "philosophy of mind" with "psychology" in this passage there would be no quarrel, but in the sense of the term in which behaviorism is the chief rival empirical theory to Fodor's mentalism, Ryle is no behaviorist but a sort of mentalist himself. Ryle does not attempt, as Skinner does, to explicate mentalistic predicates "(just) in terms of stimulus and response variables" (p. 8). On the contrary, his

explications are typically replete with intentional idioms. Ryle's familiar account of vanity, for instance (whatever its problems) is not that vanity is a disposition to perform certain locomotions, utter certain sounds, respond to certain stimuli, but that it is a disposition to try to make oneself prominent, to ignore criticism, talk about oneself, avoid recalling past failures, "indulge in roseate daydreams about his own successes" (*The Concept of Mind*, p. 86). What kind of behaviorism is that? Not any kind to be found in psychology. Ryle's disagreements with Fodor are fundamental, but they are not to be discovered by allying Ryle with Skinner.

Perhaps Ryle's view can again be illuminated by a fanciful example. Suppose someone were benighted enough to think the monthly bank statement he received was a historical description of actual transfers of currency among thousands of labelled boxes in bank vaults. He is informed of an overdraft and puts forward a theory of anti-dollars, vacuums and vortices to explain it. The Rylean explains that *nothing like that* is what makes it the case that the account is overdrawn and gives a "conceptual" account of the situation. The "logical behaviorist" account of overdrafts is the one we are usually interested in. Of course there is a mechanical story about what happens at the bank that can be told as well, and perhaps knowing it will help us understand the conceptual account, but the two are distinct.

Fodor does not seem to see this point in application to psychology, for he wishes to maintain with regard to the clever clown "that it is the fact that the behavior was caused by such [inner cognitive] events that makes it the kind of behavior it is; that intelligent behavior *is* intelligent because it has the kind of etiology it has" (p. 3 — but see also n. 2 of p. 29, where Fodor qualifies this). This claim burkes Ryle's distinction and leads

Fodor, I hope to show later, to a mistaken account of what makes it the case that something represents something.

Setting aside this difficulty, Fodor has shown, *contra* Ryle, that there is some real work that the mentalistic terms of cognitive psychology might do, but could they do this work while being faithful to the spirit of materialism? Fodor argues that the reasonable belief in the generality of physics, and the reasonable desire that the various sciences be somehow unified, have engendered unreasonably strong demands that the theoretical predicates of the "special" sciences, and psychology in particular, be "reducible" to the predicates of physics. Fodor's critique of reductionism and concomitant defence of functionalism is consonant with other recent accounts, especially Putnam's, but makes important additions of detail to this emerging orthodoxy. The unreasonableness of reductionism is nicely illustrated by a discussion of its application to Gresham's Law; a very clear account is given of type and token physicalism and natural kinds, and there is an especially useful development of the claim that it is a mistake to try to make the laws of the unreduced sciences exceptionless. We should look for the laws of physics to be exceptionless, but these laws should not, as the reductionist requires, guarantee that the laws of the reduced sciences have no exceptions, but rather provide an explanation of the exceptions encountered. To reconstrue the laws of the special sciences so that their predicates were locked with the predicates of physics would be to abandon the very utility of the predicates that gave birth to the special sciences in the first place.

Fodor offers a specific positive account of the logical relations that may hold between the terms of a special science (say psychology) and a reducing science (either physiology or physics) which goes far toward establishing the proper independence of the former. I think it could go farther. Fodor shows how a special science can be neutral with regard to variation in physical realization, and can tolerate variety in the physical tokenings of its types even within the individual, but I think he unnecessarily rules out the possibility that there could be a law of a special science, even an exceptionless law, where there were no *laws* of the reducing sciences relating all the tokenings (because the regularities in token sequences could only be described by conditionals with highly disjunctive antecedents and consequents). It seems essential that he allow for and explain this possibility, for it is fundamental to the capacity of well designed systems to "absorb" random or merely fortuitous noise, malfunction, interference. The account Fodor gives does not permit the brain to tolerate typographical errors in the inner code, so far as I can see.

Fodor supposes his arguments obtain methodological permission to use mentalistic predicates in theory construction. Why should we want them? Because it is "self-evident that organisms often believe the behavior they produce to be of a certain kind and that it is often part of the explanation of the way that an organism behaves to advert to the beliefs it has about the kind of behavior it produces" (p. 28). In other words, Fodor does not believe another reasoned obituary of behaviorism would be worth space in his book. Very well, but what, exactly, is "self-evident"? Fodor believes that the everyday, lay explanations of behavior (of both people and beasts) in terms of beliefs and desires are of a piece with the sophisticated information-flow explanations of the neo-cognitivists, so that the self-evident acceptability of "the dog bit me because he thought I was someone else" ensures the inevitable theoretical soundness of something like "the dog's executive routine initiated the attack subroutine because in the course of perceptual analysis it generated and misconfirmed a false hypothesis about the identity of an object in its environment". Fodor recognizes that it is a fairly large step from everyday, personal-level intentional explanations to theory-bound subpersonal level intentional explanations but impatiently dismisses the worry that anything important to his enterprise might hinge on how he took the step: "There is, obviously, a horribly difficult problem about what determines what a person (as distinct from his body, or parts of his body) did. Many philosophers care terrifically about drawing this distinction . . . but . . . there is no particular reason to suppose that it is relevant to the purpose of cognitive psychology" (p. 52). We shall see.

Fodor's next task is to show how neo-cognitivist theory is unavoidably committed to a language of thought. He begins by offering three different but related demonstrations, and similar problems attend each. First, Fodor presents a schema for neo-cognitivist theories of "considered action". Any such theory will suppose the

> agent finds himself in a certain situation (S) . . . believes that a certain set of behavioral options . . . are available to him . . ., computes a set of hypotheticals roughly of the form if B_1 is performed in S, then, with a certain probability, C_1 . . . A preference ordering is assigned to the consequences . . . The organism's choice of behavior is determined as a function of the preferences and the probabilities assigned (p. 28-29).

In other words, a normative decision theory is to be adapted as a natural history of cognitive processes in the organism, and for such a history to be true, agents must "have means for representing their behavior to themselves". "For, according to the model, deciding is a computational process; the act the agent performs is the consequence of computations defined over representations of possible actions. No representations, no computations. No computations, no model" (p. 31). Moreover, "an infinity of distinct representations must belong to the system" for "there is no upper bound to the complexity of the representation that may be required to specify the behavioral options available to the agent" (p. 31).

Note that this argument assumes there is a clear line between computational processes and other processes, and another between considered action and mere reactivity. Fodor does not intend his argument to apply only to the psychology of human beings, but how plausible is it that a mole or a chicken or a fish is capable of representing behavioral options of unbounded complexity? The famous four F's (fighting, fleeing, feeding and sexual intercourse) would seem to be a plausible initial tally of options, and even if we allow, say, a dozen variations on each theme, we hardly need a productive representation system to provide internal vehicles for them all, and the process that led to the appropriate "choice" in such a case would not often appear to be computational, unless all processes are. Presumably a diving bell does not compute its equilibrium depth in the water, though it arrives at it by a process of diminishing "corrections". Does a fish compute its proper depth of operations? Is there an important qualitative difference between the processes in the fish and the diving bell?

Fodor's way of dealing with these problems is best understood by contrast with the paths not taken. Fodor could have claimed that only the behavior of human beings (and other smart creatures of his choosing) is governed by truly computational processes, or he could have gone to the other extreme and granted the diving bell its computational processes. Or he could have defended an intermediate position along these lines: all creatures of noticeable intelligence make decisions (I who "care terrifically" would insist that at best something decisionlike occurs within them) and as we ascend the phylogenetic scale the decision-processes are more and more aptly characterized as computational; all creatures of noticeable intelligence have at least rudimentary representational systems, but only in higher creatures are these systems language-like in being productive or generative. Instead, he adopts the line that there is a radical discontinuity between computational and non-computational processes: "What distinguishes what organisms do . . . is that a *representation of the rules they follow constitutes one of the causal determinants of their behavior*" (p. 74, n. 15). If Fodor is to distinguish this claim from the other options he must mean that these rules are *explicitly* represented (not implicitly represented in virtue of functional organization, that is), and this is the radical heart of Fodor's position. I will discuss some problems with it later.

Fodor's second demonstration concerns what he calls concept learning: roughly, coming to distinguish and attach importance to some particular class of things or stimuli in one's environment (e.g., learning about green apples, or learning not to press the bar until the buzzer sounds, or learning to put the red circles in one pile and everything else in another). Fodor claims that "there is only one kind of theory that has ever been proposed for concept learning — indeed, there would seem to be only one kind of theory that is conceivable — and this theory [that concept learning proceeds by hypothesis formation and confirmation] is incoherent unless there is a language of thought" (p. 36). Why? Because the hypotheses formed must be "couched" in representations. A striking point Fodor makes about this is that experiments can distinguish between *logically equivalent* but "notationally" different formulations of hypotheses in concept learning. The idea is that taking the spades out of a deck of cards is easier, oddly enough, than leaving all the cards

that are not spades in the deck. When presented with the latter task if one does not think "in other words . . ." one's performance will suffer. Does this consideration, and similar ones, not establish beyond a shadow of a doubt the "psychological reality" of the representations? As in the first case, it all depends on how far Fodor is prepared to descend with his talk of representations. What is somewhat plausible in the case of human beings is not at all plausible in the case of lower animals, and it seems that even insects can achieve *some* concept learning. Either some very primitive concept learning does not require hypothesis formation and confirmation, or if it all does, some hypotheses are formed but not "couched", or just about any feature on the inside of a creature can be considered a representation. Certainly the psychological reality of something functioning in some ways rather like a representation is established by the results Fodor cites, but Fodor has prepared a buttered slide for us and anyone who does not want to get on it might well dig in the heels at this point and ask for more details.

Fodor's third demonstration concerns perception. Here his point is that, as empiricists have insisted (for all the wrong reasons) "the sensory data which confirm a given perceptual hypothesis are typically internally represented in a vocabulary that is impoverished compared to the vocabulary in which the hypotheses themselves are couched" (p. 44). For instance, the empiricists would say that my hypothesis is that there is an apple out there, and my data are that I seem to see this red round patch. Fodor likes the idea of perception proceeding by a series of computational processes taking descriptions in one vocabulary and using them to confirm hypothesized descriptions in another vocabulary, and the main thing he sees wrong with empiricist versions of this is their penchant for couching the given in the "theory-free language of qualia" rather than the "theory-laden language of values of physical parameters" (p. 48). What is given is the excitation of a sensory mechanism sensitive to a physical property. "Hence, there is no reason to believe that the organism cannot be mistaken about what sensory descriptions apply in any given case" (p. 48). But here Fodor seems to me to have lost track of the important distinction between the content of a signal to the system it informs, and the content we on the outside can assign it when we describe the signal and the system of which it is a part. For instance, one badly misconceives the problem of perception if one views the retinal receptors as "telling" the first level of hypotheses testers "red wavelength light at location L again", for that level does not utilize or understand (in *any* impoverish sense) information of that sort. What it gets in the way of data are at best reports with uninterpreted dummy predicates ("it is intensely F at location L again") and out of these it must confirm its own dummy hypotheses.[1] In fact is either way of talking appropriate? The *vocabulary* of the signals is not something that is to be settled by an examination of tokens, at least at this level, and when we turn to indirect evidence of "psychological reality" any evidence we turn up will perforce be neutral between interpreted and uninterpreted predicates.

What content is to be assigned to events in the nervous system subserving perception? That, I take it, is a rather important question for cognitive psychology to answer. It cannot be answered, I submit, until one gets quite careful about who (or what, if anything) has access to the candidate representation — for whom or for what the thing in question is a representation. As Michael Arbib has suggested, what the frog's eye tells the frog's brain is not what the frog's eye tells the frog.

Fodor rather nonchalantly dismisses such distinctions. Why are they impor-

tant? Suppose we make the following extension of his main argument. The only psychology that could possibly succeed is neo-cognitivist, which requires the postulation of an internal system of representations. However, nothing is intrinsically a representation of anything; something is a representation only *for* or *to* someone; any representation or system of representations requires at least one *user* of the system who is external to the system. Call such a user an *exempt agent.* Hence, in addition to a system of internal representations, neo-cognitivism requires the postulation of an inner exempt agent or agents — in short, undischarged homunculi. Any psychology with undischarged homunculi is doomed to circularity or infinite regress, hence psychology is impossible (see my *Brainstorms,* Chapters 5 and 7, where these claims are expanded and examined at length).

The problem is an old one. Hume wisely shunned the notion of an inner self that would intelligently manipulate the ideas and impressions, but this left him with the necessity of getting the ideas to "think for themselves". His associationistic couplings of ideas and impressions, his pseudo-chemical bonding of each idea to it predecessor and successor, is a notorious non-solution to the problem. Fodor's analogous problem is to get the internal representations to "understand themselves", and one is initially inclined to view Hume's failure as the harbinger of doom for all remotely analogous enterprises. But perhaps the *prima facie* absurd notion of self-understanding representations is an idea whose time has come, for what are the "data structures" of computer science if not just that: representations that understand themselves? In a computer, a command to dig goes straight to the shovel, as it were, eliminating the comprehending and obeying middleman. Not *straight* to the shovel, of course, for a lot of sophisticated switching is required to get the right command going to the right tools, and for some purposes it is illuminating to treat parts of this switching machinery as analogous to the displaced shovellers, subcontractors and contractors. The beauty of it all, and its importance for psychology, is precisely that it promises to solve Hume's problem by giving us a model of vehicles of representation that function without exempt agents for whom they are ploys. Alternatively, one could insist that the very lack of exempt agents in computers to be the users of the putative representations shows that computers do not contain representations — real representations — at all, but unless one views this as a rather modest bit of lexicographical purism, one is in danger of discarding one of the most promising conceptual advances ever to fall into philosophers' hands.

Fodor almost parenthetically makes these points (in a footnote on p. 74, where he roundly rebuts an ill-considered version of the homunculus argument of mine). He is justly unafraid of homunculi, for they are at most just picturesquely described parts of the switching machinery that ensures the functional roles of the inner messages, but fails to recognize that they still play the theoretical role of fixing the "topic" and "vocabulary" of the messages they communicate. If viewing messages of the inner code as self-understanding representations in this fashion can save Fodor's enterprise from incoherence — and in principle I think it can — it does so by adding constraints to the notion of an internal representation system that emphasize rather than eliminate the distinction between personal level attributions of beliefs and desires and sub-personal level attributions of content to intrasystemic transactions. If there is any future for internal systems of representation it will not be for languages of thought that "represent our beliefs to us", except in the most strained sense. Fodor notices the strain (p. 52) but decides to tolerate it. The result, for all its

vividness, is at least misleading in a way that has an analogy in the history of science. The problem of genetic inheritance used to look all but insoluble. Did the sperm cell contain a tiny man, and if so did the tiny man have sperm cells containing tiny men and so forth *ad infinitum*? Or did the sperm cell contain a picture or description of a human being, and if so, what looked at the picture or read the description? The truth turns out to be scarcely less marvellous than the "absurd" speculations, what with self-reading, self-duplicating codes and their supporting machinery, but anyone who had insisted all along that somehow the mother finds out from the sperm what sort of baby the father wants would not have been pointing in just the right direction. (This sidelong glance at DNA serves the additional purpose of reminding the skeptics who view the contraptions of artificial intelligence as hopelessly inefficient and 'inorganic' that nature has proved not to be stingy when it comes to micro-engineering solutions to hard problems.)

Earlier I claimed that Fodor's view of computational processes commits him to a radical view of representation. The problems with this hard line on the psychological reality of explicit representations are apparent — indeed, are deliberately made apparent, to Fodor's credit — in his discussion of language learning. His argument is that the process of learning the meaning of a word, even the initial words of one's native tongue, is and must be a process of hypothesis formation and confirmation, and in particular,

among the generalizations about a language that the learner must hypothesize and confirm are some which determine the extensions of the predicates of that language. A generalization that effects such a determination is, by stipulation, a *truth rule* (p. 59).

For instance, the truth rule for "is a chair" a "#y is a chair# is true iff[2] Gx" where "G" is a predicate of one's internal code. [*Editor's note:* In this anthology, "#" is used instead of the corner quote.] Fodor seems to think that the only hypotheses which could *determine* the extension of a natural language predicate would have to be confirmed hypotheses explicitly about that predicate and having the explicit form of a truth rule. But to play Fodor's own game for a moment, couldn't a child learn *something that determined* the extension of "is a chair" by *disconfirming* the following hypotheses (and others):

#x is a chair# is true iff the referent of x is red

#x is a chair# is true iff the referent of x is in the living room

#x is a chair# is true iff the referent x has a cushion

and, perhaps, confirming — even *misconfirming* — others, e.g., "#x is a chair# is true if the referent of x is this object here or that object there", and "#x is a chair# is true only if the referent of x would support Daddy's weight", without ever *explicitly* representing a confirmed truth rule for "is a chair"? I suspect that Fodor's reply would be that to learn something determining the extension of "is a chair" the child must explicitly conjoin all the confirmed hypotheses and the negations of the disconfirmed hypotheses and that somehow this amounts to the confirmation of the explicit truth rule for "is a chair", but aside from the implausiblity of this as a story of real computational processes (but remember DNA) one wants to know what could conceivably count against the presumably empirical claim that whatever could determine the extension of a predicate has the explicit form of a truth rule, if this example did not.

Perhaps Fodor has gratuitously overstated his own best case, for it seems as if he is committed to the impossible view that only explicit representation is representation, and (roughly) nothing can be believed, thought about or learned without being explicitly represented.

> That is, one might think of cognitive theories as filling in explanation schema[ta] of, roughly, the form: *having the attitude R to proposition P is contingently identical to being in computational relation C to the formula (or sequence of formulae) F.* A cognitive theory, insofar as it was both true and general, would presumably explain the productivity of propositional attitudes by entailing infinitely many substitution instances of this schema: one for each of the propositional attitudes that the organism can entertain (p. 77).

Perhaps we "entertain" propositional attitudes either seriatim or at least in manageably small numbers at any one time, but the propositional attitudes we *have* far outstrip those we (in some sense) actively entertain. For instance, it should come as no news to any of you that zebras in the wild do not wear overcoats, but I hazard the guess that it *hadn't occurred* to any of you before just now. We all have believed it for some time but were not born believing it, so we must have come to believe it between birth and, say, age fifteen, but it is not at all plausible that this is a hypothesis any of us has explicitly formed or confirmed in our childhood, even unconsciously. It is not even plausible that having formed and confirmed other hypotheses entailing this fact about zebras, we (in our spare time?) explicitly *computed* this implication.

Fodor does seem to be committed to some such view as this, however. He backs into this corner by underestimating the viability of what he takes to be the only alternative, which he characterizes as a dispositional behavioral analysis of propositional attitudes. "A number of philosophers who ought to know better do, apparently, accept such views" Fodor says, never doubting that he has seen clearly to the very heart of such silliness. His version of dispositional analysis is so simplistic, however, that he thinks the notion is adequately buried by a quip: "Pay me enough and I will stand on my head iff you say chair. But I know what 'is a chair' means all the same" (p. 63). It is of course true that the arduous piecemeal composition of dispositional definitions of propositional attitudes would be a bootless methodology for psychology (Ryle knew better than to attempt to say, precisely, just what his "multi-track" dispositions were), but if, as Fodor supposes, the representation-talk of cognitive psychology ultimately gets vindicated by such ploys as computer modelling of cognitive systems and processes, he must be committed in spite of himself to a version of Rylism. For a computer program is just a very complicated specification of a multi-track disposition (a disposition to be disposed under conditions A, B, C to be disposed under conditions X, Y, Z to be disposed . . . to give output O . . . etc.). Notationally distinct but equivalent programs are equivalent precisely in that they determine the same multi-track disposition.

Suppose research reveals all the psychologically real computational processes in Mary, and artifical intelligencers program a robot, Ruth, whose internal processes "model" Mary's as perfectly as you like. Suppose that Mary believes that *p.* So then does Ruth. But suppose the artificial intelligencers then give another robot, Sally, a program equivalent to Ruth's, but notationally and computationally different. Sally may not be a good psychological model of Mary, but Sally, like Ruth and Mary, believes that *p.*[3] That is, the ascription of all Mary's beliefs and desires (etc.) to Sally will be just as predictive as their ascription to Ruth so far as prediction of action goes. Sally's response delays, errors, and the like may not match Mary's, but this it not what belief ascription is supposed to predict or explain (cf. Fodor, p. 123). If one agrees with Fodor that it is the job of cognitive psychology to map the

psychologically real processes in people, then since the ascription of belief and desire is only indirectly tied to such processes, one might well say that beliefs and desires are not the proper objects of study of cognitive psychology. Put otherwise, cognitivist theories are or should be theories of the subpersonal level, where beliefs and desires disappear, to be replaced with representations of other sorts on other topics.

But unless I am misreading Fodor, he will have none of this. His position simply is that since believing that snow is white could not be having a disposition to behave, it must be having a token of the mentalese translation of "snow is white" installed in some wonderful way in one's head. Perhaps I am misreading him by interpreting "being in a computational relation to a formula of the inner code" as implying the existence of a real token of that formula in some functionally characterized relation to the rest of the machinery, but the weaker alternative, *viz.,* that one is in a computational relation to a formula if one *can or would produce or use* a token of that formula in some way under some circumstance, invokes dispositionalism of just the sort Fodor has presumably forsworn.

None of this is to say that neural representations, even tokens of brain-writing, are impossible. It is not even to deny that the existence of such representations is a necessary condition for cognition. It may well turn out to be. But Fodor, by making explicit coding *criterial* for representation or contentfulness, has committed the very sin he imputes to Ryle: he has confused a conceptual answer with a causal answer. Like neo-cognitivists generally, Fodor wants to be able to assign content to events or other features of systems, to treat them as information-bearers or messages. What makes it the case ultimately that something in this sense represents something within a system is that it has a function within the system, in principle globally specifiable.⁴ To say that it has the function of bearing a certain message or transmitting certain information is to talk in circles, but often in useful circles for the time being. Content is a function of function, then, but not every structure can realize every function, can reliably guarantee the normal relationships required. So function is a function of structure. There are, then, strong indirect structural constraints on things that can be endowed with content. If our brains were as homogeneous as jelly we could not think. Fodor, however, makes a direct leap from content to structure and seems moreover to make structure in the end criterial for content.

On his view a prescriptive theory (e.g., natural deduction or decision theory) can be predictive of behavior only if it is descriptive of inner processes. When we predict and explain the behavior of a system at the intentional level *our* calculations have a certain syntactic structure: to oversimplify, they are formal proofs or derivations, e.g., of descriptions of best actions to take given certain beliefs and preferences. We predict that the physical states or events to which we assign the premises as formulae will *cause* those states or events whose formulae are the later lines of our calculations (see, e.g., p. 73). Fodor seems to suppose that the only structures that could guarantee and explain the predictive power of our intentionalistic calculations (and permit us to assign formulae to states or events in a principled way) *must* mirror the syntax of those calculations. This is either trivially true (because the "syntactic" structure of events or states is defined simply by their function) or an empirical claim that is very interesting, not entirely implausible, and as yet not demonstrated or even argued for, so far as I can tell. For instance, suppose hamsters are interpretable as good Bayesians when it comes to the decisions they make. Must we in principle

be able to find some saliencies in the hamsters' controls that are interpretable as tokens of formulae in some Bayesian calculus? If that is Fodor's conclusion, I don't see that he has given it the support it needs, and I confess to disbelieving it utterly.

In a recent conversation with the designer of a chess-playing program I heard the following criticism of a rival program: "It thinks it should get its queen out early." This ascribes a propositional attitude to the program in a very useful and predictive way, for as the designer went on to say, one can usually count on chasing that queen around the board. But for all the many levels of explicit representation to be found in that program, nowhere is anything roughly synonymous with "I should get my queen out early" explicitly tokened. The level of analysis to which the designer's remark belongs describes features of the program that are, in an entirely innocent way, emergent properties of the computational processes that have "engineering reality". I see no reason to believe that the relation between belief-talk and psychological-process talk will be any more direct.

Are all these doubts about Fodor's radical view swept away by the material in the second half of this book, where evidence is adduced about the structure, vocabulary and utilization of the inner code? The challenge of these chapters to the skeptic is to find a way of recasting what cannot be denied in them in terms less radical than Fodor's. I do not see that this cannot be done, but saying it is not doing it, and doing it would require a monograph. Fodor's account of the inner code in action is packed with detail and bold speculation, and is supported by a variety of elegant experiments and ingenious arguments. Fodor puts together a more or less Gricean theory of communication and a more or less Chomskyan view of the relation between surface features of utterances and deeper levels, but comes out forcefully against semantic primitives (at least in their familiar role in the production and comprehension of sentences). He defends images as inner representational vehicles in addition to his code formulae, and claims to show that the inner code can represent its own representations and has a vocabulary about as rich as that of English — to mention a few highlights. There are a few dubious links in the argumentation (e.g., Fodor's cat and mouse example on p. 142 seems obviously mis-analysed, but it may not matter), but time and again Fodor succeeds, in my estimation, in parrying the "obvious" philosophical objections. One exception is in his account of communication. Unless I am reading him too literally, he seems committed to the view that for A to communicate verbally with B, A and B must not only share a natural language but have the same version of mentalese as well. Once again this is a claim that might be trivial or might be almost certainly false, and we can't tell until Fodor is more explicit.

Faulting Fodor for not being sufficiently explicit in this instance is a bit ungenerous, for Fodor has offered a detailed theory in an area hitherto bereft of detailed theories, and has been more explicit than anybody else about many of the murky issues. The book is exceptionally clear, with excellent summaries of arguments and conclusions at just the right places. The view Fodor has put forward is a remarkably full view; seldom have stands on so many different issues been so staunchly taken in this area, and even where I think he is wrong, it is usually the crispness of his expression that suggests for the first time just exactly what is wrong. Fodor challenges us to find a better theory, and I fully expect that challenge to be met, but when better theories emerge they will owe a good deal to Fodor's reconnaissance.

Notes

1. Cf. J. J. C. Smart, *Philosophy and Scientific Realism* (London: Routledge & Kegan Paul, 1963), on "topic-neutral reports". The epistemic status of reports with uninterpreted predicates and reports with qualia-predicates would seem to be the same.

2. The term "iff" is logicians' shorthand for "if and only if".

3. Perfect equivalence of programs is a very strong condition. I would hold it is a sufficient but not necessary condition for sharing intentional characterizations.

4. Ignoring for the moment the normative element in all intentional attributions.

Mental Representation

Hartry H. Field

Any interesting version of materialism requires not only that there be no irreducibly mental *objects,* but also that
there be no irreducibly mental *properties:*
the idea that although people and certain
higher animals do not contain any immaterial substance, nonetheless they have
certain mental properties that are completely unexplainable in physical terms, is
an idea that very few people who regard
themselves as materialists would find
satisfying.[1] The unsatisfactoriness of
postulating irreducibly mental properties
is the source of the two main problems in
the philosophy of mind. The first and
more widely discussed problem is the
problem raised by *experiential* properties,
for instance the property of feeling pain: a
materialist needs to provide a believable
account of such properties according to
which those properties are not irreducibly
mental. The second problem, raised by
Brentano,[2] is the problem of *intentionality.* Many mental properties—believing,
desiring, and so forth — appear to be *rela-*

From *Erkenntnis* 13, no. 1 (1978): 9-61.
Copyright © 1978 by D. Reidel Publishing Company. Reprinted by permission of D. Reidel
Publishing Company and the author. The postscript
was added by the author for this edition. Notes have
been renumbered for this edition.

tional properties: more precisely, they appear to relate people to non-linguistic
entities called *propositions.* So any
materialist who takes believing and desiring at face value — any materialist who admits that belief and desire *are* relations
between people and propositions — any
such materialist must show that the relations in question are not irreducibly mental. Brentano felt that this could not be
done; and since he saw no alternative to
viewing belief and desire as relations to
propositions, he concluded that materialism must be false.

The first half of this paper is an
examination of Brentano's problem—that
is, of the problem (which Brentano believed to be unsolvable) of giving a
materialistically adequate account of
believing, desiring, and so forth. Unlike
Brentano, I take it as unquestionable
(given what we know about the world)
that materialism is true; I also take it as
unquestioned for the purposes of this
paper that people do believe and desire.
These two assumptions together amount
to the assumption that Brentano's problem *can* be solved; what I shall be interested in is the question of *how* it can be
solved, that is, of *what the assumption
that it can be solved shows about the*

nature of belief and desire. I will be particularly concerned to show that one cannot solve Brentano's problem merely by adopting the kind of functionalist theory of belief and desire that Robert Stalnaker and David Lewis have advocated.[3] In the second half of the paper I shall elaborate on the position suggested in the first half, and discuss some implications of my conclusions about intentionality for the theory of meaning.

I should say at the outset that my presupposition that people do in fact believe and desire is intended to be a presupposition that an instrumentalistic view of belief-talk and desire-talk is inappropriate. I am presupposing in other words that belief and desire ascriptions can be literally true, rather than being merely useful devices that we adopt for various purposes but for which talk of truth and falsity is inappropriate. It is clear that belief in materialism even together with the view that belief-talk and desire-talk are highly useful instruments is not sufficient to entail that Brentano's problem is solvable;[4] so the adoption of an instrumentalistic view of belief-talk and desire-talk is a possible way to save materialism and yet avoid having to solve Brentano's problem. To my mind, however, instrumentalism is unappealing: it seems to me that if a psychological theory that postulates beliefs and desires works well, and there is no available theory that works better, then barring strong specific reasons to the contrary, we should regard that theory as literally true. That it should be so regarded is a working hypothesis under which I am operating in this paper.

I. The Basic Argument

One way to reply to Brentano's argument would be to develop a theory of belief, desire, etc. according to which the objects of belief and desire were not propositions, but something more 'accessible', say sentences. If we construed belief and desire as relations between people and sentences, then—at least if we also demanded that the sentences a believer or desirer were related to were sentences in a language he was familiar with—it would presumably be possible to give an account of these relations in a materialistically impeccable way. I will have more to say about this method of dealing with Brentano's problem later on. For now I want to ignore it.

Suppose then that we accept the idea that belief and desire are relations between people and propositions; and suppose, for definiteness, that we follow Lewis and Stalnaker in taking propositions to be sets of possible worlds. The question arises, how can one give a materialistically acceptable account of a relation between a person and a proposition so construed?

The question is neither silly nor impossible to answer. One might think it were silly: "If you accept the ontology of propositions, plus a minimal amount of set theory, then a relation between people and propositions is merely a set of ordered pairs whose first members are people and whose second members are propositions. Or better—since the same person can be in the belief relation at one time but not at another—the belief relation is merely a function that assigns to each time a set of ordered pairs of people and propositions. A function assigning sets of ordered pairs is not a mental entity at all, let alone an irreducibly mental one, so what's the problem?" Needless to say, this misses the point. If this way of dismissing Brentano's question were legitimate, we could equally well dismiss any other *prima facie* difficulty for materialism without doing any substantive work, so that materialism would be a totally vacuous doctrine. For instance, if someone asked how to give a materialist account of pain, one could say, "What's the problem? Pain is simply a set of people, viz. those people that we say 'feel pain' or 'are in pain'. Or better—since the same person can feel pain at one time but not at others — pain is a function that assigns to each time the set of people who are in pain at that time. Such a function is a purely set-theoretic entity; it is not mental, let alone irreducibly mental, hence it carries no problem for materialism." I take it to be obvious that this set-theoretic approach to the theory of pain is totally unsatisfying. And I can't think of any reason why the set-theoretic approach to the theory of belief and desire should be thought to be any better.

Part of the explanation of why the set-theoretic account of pain is unsatisfying is that it treats pain as a set rather than a property. What is needed is an account of that property of people that 'pain' stands for which is materialistically acceptable — we need to show that property is not irreducibly mental. What the set-theoretic account does is to ignore the question of the *property* altogether, and to focus instead on the *set of things that have that property*. (Or — since the same thing can have the property at one time but not another — it focusses on the function-in-extension mapping each time into the set of things that have the property at the time.) Obviously there is no substantive question of this set (or this function) being irreducibly mental; but that just shows that the interesting question concerns not the set but the property. This diagnosis extends to the case of belief: the interesting question about belief is a question about the relation that 'belief' stands for, where by 'relation' I mean not 'set of ordered pairs' but '2-place property'. What a materialist needs to show is that that property is not irreducibly mental.

But is there any hope of giving a materialistically acceptable account of the belief relation? In particular, is there any hope of doing this when we take belief to be a relation between people and propositions, and construe propositions in terms of possible worlds? It might be thought

that the answer is 'obviously no', and that this fact shows the untenability of treating belief as a relation between a person and a set of possible worlds. I believe however that such a dismissal of the possible-worlds view of belief would be too quick: for I believe that it *is* possible to give a materialistically adequate account of the belief relation, even if that relation is construed as a relation to sets of possible worlds. I will now sketch a possible such account. We will see later that the main elements of this account can be preserved even if we abandon the assumption that belief is a relation between people and sets of possible worlds.

The account involves the assumption that the belief relation is a composite of two other relations: first, a relation between a person and a *sentence* that the person understands; second, a relation between the sentence and a set of possible worlds. This will be refined shortly, but unrefined, the claim is this:

(1)   X believes that *p* if and only if there is a sentence *S* such that X believes* *S* and *S* means that *p*.

Here *believes** is a relation between a person and a sentence in his own language: I believe* the English sentence 'Snow is white' but not the sentence 'Snow is green', and no one ignorant of English believes* either of these sentences.[5] The effect of adopting (1) is to divide the problem of giving a materialistically adequate account of the belief relation into two subproblems:

subproblem (a): the problem of explaining what it is for a person to believe* a sentence (of his or her own language).

subproblem (b): the problem of explaining what it is for a sentence to mean that *p*.

(The problem of giving a materialistically adequate account of the desire relation would be split into two subproblems in the analogous way, by introducing a notion of desiring*.)

The rough idea of how to give an account of (a) should be clear enough: I believe* a sentence of my language if and only if I am disposed to employ that sentence in a certain way in reasoning, deliberating, and so on. This is very vague of course, but providing that the vagueness can be eliminated and providing that a physical basis can be found for the dispositions invoked, then believing* will not be a relation that poses any problems for the materialist. Later on in this section I will state a more precise version of a dispositional account of believing*, one which will make it pretty clear what a physical basis for the disposition invoked would have to be like. But I hope that even the vague remarks above are enough to predispose the reader to think that believing* is not a relation that should be a particular worry to a materialist (even a materialist impressed by Brentano's problem). On the other hand, anyone impressed with Brentano's problem *is* likely to be impressed with subproblem (b), for unlike (a), (b) invokes a *semantic* relation (of *meaning that*).

Before looking into the question of whether it is reasonable to expect that a materialistically acceptable account of (b) could be given, let me note two auxiliary advantages of adhering to (1), and then go on to consider a necessary refinement in what I have said. The first auxiliary advantage of approaching the problem of explaining what it is to believe that *p* via (1) is that with this approach we need not assume from the outset the controversial assumption that the objects of belief are propositions. That is, if we later come up with a way to explain what it is to mean that *p* which does not make *meaning that* a relation between sentences and propositions, then if we also adopted (1) we would have an account of *believing that* according to which it was not a relation between people and propositions either. In fact, one can adhere to (1) without assuming that the occurrences of '*p*' in it

are occurrences of a quantifiable variable; they can be taken to be just instances of a schematic letter, so that talk of the objects of belief (as such talk has heretofore been construed) makes no literal sense. Such a possibility will be discussed in Section III; for now however I will continue to adopt Lewis' and Stalnaker's assumption that '*p*' is a quantifiable variable and stands for entities that are to be explained in terms of possible worlds.

A second auxiliary advantage of (1), for possible world theorists, is that it would give them a plausible way to make distinctions of belief which are intuitively there but which cannot be made on the possible worlds account as it stands. Consider any set theorist (who believes the axiom of choice) who has never heard of the Banach-Tarski theorem; if someone now formulates the theorem for him (without telling him that it is a theorem), he will almost surely not believe it to be true. (In fact, he is almost sure to believe it false;[6] to believe it true in the circumstances described would be a more likely sign of irrationality than to believe it false.) There is a big difference, then, between believing set theory and believing set theory plus the Banach-Tarski theorem; yet set theory and set-theory-plus-Banach-Tarski are logically equivalent, hence must be represented by the same set of possible worlds. Now, David Lewis has pointed out that a possible-worlds theorist need not say that the conjunction of the axioms of set theory[7] *means the same as* the conjunction of those axioms plus the Banach-Tarski theorem: he can recognize finer grades of *meaning* than sets of possible worlds.[8] A set of possible worlds can be called a *coarse-grained proposition;* a *fine-grained proposition* is a certain complicated kind of function defined out of possible worlds, but which has coded into it, so to speak, the structure of a specific sentence. What a sentence *means*, on Lewis' account, is fine-grained; but what a person *believes* is coarse-grained, so believing set theory and believing set-theory-plus-Banach-Tarski are precisely the same thing.

Now formally speaking, it would be possible to simply take these fine-grained propositions and use them in a way that Lewis does not, as the objects of belief. But is is quite implausible to do so unless we think of beliefs as being represented in the head by sentences or something like sentences, for fine-grained propositions have the structure of specific sentences coded right into them. Consequently, Lewis and Stalnaker accept the idea that to believe set theory and to believe set-theory-plus-Banach-Tarski are the same things. Stalnaker has tried to explain away our strong feelings to the contrary as follows:

> There are only two mathematically true propositions, the necessarily true one and the necessarily false one, and we all know that the first is true and the second false. But the functions that determine which of the two propositions is expressed by a given mathematical statement are just the kind that are sufficiently complex to give rise to reasonable doubt about which proposition is expressed by a statement. *Hence it seems reasonable to take the objects of belief and doubt in mathematics to be propositions about the relations between statements and what they say* ([25], p. 88; italics mine).

But this will not do. Let 'the Banach-Tarski conditional' stand for the conditional whose antecedent is the conjunction of the axioms of set theory (including choice) and whose consequent is the Banach-Tarski theorem. Consider a person who doubts or disbelieves the Banach-Tarski result, *but who knows the semantic rules that relate sentences in the language of set theory to propositions.* According to Stalnaker, such a person doesn't really doubt or disbelieve the proposition expressed by the Banach-Tarski conditional, since that is a logical truth; what he does doubt or disbelieve is the proposition expressed by

(i)   the semantic rules for the language of set theory relate the Banach-Tarski conditional to the necessary truth.

But since the person knows what the semantic rules for the language of set theory are, the only way he can doubt or disbelieve the proposition expressed by (i) would be to doubt or disbelieve the proposition expressed by

(ii) the semantic rules _____ relate the Banach-Tarski conditional to the necessary truth,

where in the blank goes a statement of the semantic rules for the language of set theory. Unfortunately for Stalnaker, however, the proposition expressed by (ii) is itself a necessary truth, and hence on Stalnaker's coarse-grained possible worlds view there is no way that anyone could doubt or disbelieve it. The ascent from mathematical propositions to meta-linguistic propositions has gained nothing.

I take it, then, that it is clearly desirable to be able to divide propositions more finely than sets of possible worlds: and Lewis' analysis shows us how to do this, *if we can accept the idea that believing a proposition involves an attitude toward sentences.* To believe set theory is very roughly to believe* the conjunction of the axioms; to believe set-theory-plus-Banach-Tarski is very roughly to believe* the conjunction of those axioms plus the Banach-Tarski theorem. The sentences believed* have different fine-grained meanings, on Lewis' analysis; hence (1) assigns different fine-grained propositions to the two believers.

It might be thought however that this sentential approach induces *too* fine-grained a distinction among beliefs; it makes the belief that either Russell was hairless or snow is white differ from the belief that if Russell was not hairless then snow is white; how then can we confidently pass from the claim that someone has the first belief to the claim that he has the second? These are two possible lines of answer. The first, which I believe to be rather *ad hoc* and artificial, is to introduce a slight coarsening of the fine-grained propositions, by taking equivalence classes under a suitable equivalence relation. The second and more satisfactory is to grant that the beliefs are indeed distinct, but to explain why someone who has one belief will nearly always have the other. Such an explanation is easy enough to give: it involves the idea that belief* is dispositional. I will now elaborate on the dispositional nature of belief* (thus returning to subproblem (a)); in the course of doing so, it will become clear why someone who has one of the two beliefs about Russell will nearly always have the other.

The crudest approach to the problem of giving a materialistic account of belief* would be wholly non-dispositional: this approach would involve the assumption that a person could believe* a sentence only if the sentence were explicitly stored in the person's head. (Similarly for desire*. If we adhere to this non-dispositional approach we must suppose that there are at least two kinds of storage, storage-as-belief and storage-as-desire. The precise details of *how* sentences are stored-as-beliefs or stored-as-desires is of course not a matter that can be settled without detailed neuro-physiological investigation.) A defect of this approach is that people apparently believe infinitely many propositions; if so, then if we adopt (1) (and assume that the relation of *meaning that* is not one-many), it follows that people believe* infinitely many sentences. But there is no way that infinitely many sentences can be explicitly stored in a finite head, so the idea that a sentence must be explicitly stored to be believed* is false.

This argument suggests that some kind of dispositional approach to belief* is required. (This conclusion can in fact be argued for without the assumption that we have infinitely many beliefs.) The

simplest kind of dispositional account (suggested by Dennett)[9] is that an organism has stored within it certain explicitly represented beliefs, which Dennett calls *core beliefs;* and what we say a person *believes* are just *the obvious consequences of* his core beliefs. [Not: the obvious consequences of his *beliefs;* for then we could show recursively that even very unobvious consequences of beliefs had also to be beliefs (since unobvious inferences can be broken down into a large number of obvious ones).] If the core belief approach is correct, then it may be the notion of core belief rather than the notion of belief that would enter into any detailed psychological theory. But even if this is so, it is the notion of belief rather than the notion of core belief which is more useful to us in everyday life, for it is much easier to know what a person believes than what he core-believes. The reason is clear: when the proposition A is an obvious enough consequence of one's core beliefs, one is almost sure to add A to one's belief core whenever any question as to the truth of A arises; behaviorally, then, it will be hard to distinguish this case from the case where A was present in one's belief core all along. But there are many cases where it is perfectly clear that a belief is not part of one's belief core. For instance, suppose I tell you that no one dug a tunnel from here to China through the center of the earth in 1953. I'm sure that by telling you this I'm not telling you something you didn't already believe, but I'm equally sure that it was not part of your belief core — i.e., not one of your explicitly represented beliefs — before I told it to you.

This idea of core belief gives us a very natural proposal for solving subproblem (a). The idea is simply to say that one believes* a sentence if and only if that sentence is an obvious consequence of sentences that are explicitly stored (in that manner of storage appropriate to beliefs as opposed to say desires).[10] This kind of account would make clear why someone who believes that either Russell was hairless or snow is white would almost certainly also believe that if Russell was not hairless then snow is white: almost any stock of core beliefs from which the former was an obvious consequence would also be a stock of core beliefs from which the latter was an obvious consequence.[11] (This solves the problem from which we began.) The account also makes clear why there is a certain vagueness or indeterminacy in ascriptions of belief that are far removed from the core (e.g., of why, when a philosopher's beliefs show a deep inconsistency, there is no clear point to asking whether he believes or disbelieves a proposition about which he has expressed no opinion but which is both provable and refutable by equally unobvious reasoning from things that he has committed himself to). The indeterminacy comes in because of the use of the notion of obviousness in defining belief from core belief.[12] It is a striking advantage of the core-belief proposal that it explains these facts.

I think then that the core-belief approach to subproblem (a) is quite attractive. However, I do not want to insist on it: conceivably it is possible to develop a more subtle kind of dispositional approach to belief* — perhaps an approach which would require fewer sentences to be explicitly stored. (It seems quite unlikely, however, that one could do without stored sentences altogether.) I take no stand on whether an alternative to the core-belief approach would be preferable, for I think I have said enough to make it plausible that in some way or other subproblem (a) could be solved.

Before turning to subproblem (b) — the problem of giving a materialistically adequate account of the relation of *meaning that* (which we are temporarily assuming to relate sentences to sets of possible worlds) — I should mention the long-promised refinement that is needed in (1).

The need of the refinement arises from the fact that dogs, chimpanzees, and young children presumably have beliefs but have no language. One could of course simply insist that beliefs and desires are not to be attributed to these or any other language-less creatures. To do so however does not seem very plausible. After all, we do often explain the behavior of languageless creatures by postulating beliefs and desires; and while in some such cases the explanations are clearly anthropomorphic and the behavior can be explained in simpler ways, there are many cases involving psychologically complicated organisms where these are the only sorts of explanation available. It seems rather rash to conclude that all such explanations are false, and therefore we must modify (1). Fortunately only a minor modification is needed, if we accept the widely held view[13] that though a dog has no language, he does have some kind of system of internal representation, and that it is only *because* he has some system of internal representation that he can represent to himself, and believe, any proposition. Let us then modify (1) by abandoning the requirement that the entities which are believed* be literally *sentences*, let us require instead only that they be either sentences or *sentence-analogs* — where by a sentence analog I simply mean some psychological entity which represents propositions (or more neutrally, which has the kind of meaning or content which sentences have). (1) should be replaced, then, by

(1′)   X believes that p if and only if there is a sentence or sentence-analog S such that X believes* S and S means that p.

This shift has an independent virtue in connection with adult humans that do have a language: it allows for the possibility that they might have beliefs that go somewhat beyond the expressive capacity of their languages.

Many philosophers are hostile to

postulating systems of internal representation in languageless organisms; I will try
to remove some of that hostility later on
in the paper. But perhaps I can undercut
some of the hostility in advance by noting
that on my view, the system of internal
representation in which a chimpanzee
believes and desires would presumably
have a much simpler structure than
human languages have—its 'sentence-
analogs' would be much simpler syntactically than English sentences are, and by
calling them 'sentence-analogs' I do not
mean to be denying the existence of these
structural disanalogies. How simple could
an animal's 'system of internal representation' be and still count as a system of
representation? This seems to me an uninteresting question of terminology. If
you like, you could even allow that an
animal's 'system of internal representation' consisted of five sentences, each of
them syntactically unstructured. However, I don't think that there is much *point*
in saying that an animal believes or
desires things unless one attributes a reasonably complex system of beliefs and
desires to it; and (according to (1')) a
reasonably complex system of beliefs and
desires will require a reasonably complex
system of representation. So there is no
point in attributing a system of internal
representation at all unless one attributes
a reasonably complex one. But there is no
need to draw a precise line and say "something must be at least this complicated to
count as a system of internal representation"; where such a line would go is
merely a matter of how widely one wants
to extend the term 'belief'. My claim is independent of such terminological issues: it
is that *organisms which are sufficiently
complicated for the notions of belief and
desire to be clearly applicable have
systems of internal representation in
which the sentence-analogs have significant grammatical structure.*

Couldn't we avoid introducing
systems of internal representation, by an
alternative modification of (1)? The alternative revision would be to give up the requirement that an organism believe* a
sentence only if he understands it: we
could then say that dogs believe* sentences of human languages like English
and Serbo-Croatian. There are three
problems with this approach:

(A) The approach is not very useful as a step
toward solving Brentano's problem: on
this approach, believes* would become a
semantic relation—it would be a relation
between organisms and sentences of
English (or Serbo-Croatian) which holds
in virtue of the meanings of those
sentences. Consequently, the proposed
alternative to (1) would divide the
original belief relation between
organisms and propositions into *two*
semantic relations (since *means that* is
also semantic); and since semantic relations are just the sorts of relations that
Brentano thought were inexplicable, this
would appear to be a doubling of our
original problem.

(B) The second problem with the suggestion
is that the whole point of the notions of
belief and desire is to aid us in explaining
behavior. It seems rather bizarre to explain a chimpanzee's behavior via his
relation to sentences in a human
language that he doesn't understand;
facts about English sentences have
nothing whatever to do with why the
chimpanzee behaves as he does. So it is
important to leave English sentences out
of the account of belief and desire for
chimpanzees.

The third problem with the suggestion is
mentioned in Section III. Because of these
difficulties, I think that (1') is the only
reasonable modification of (1).

Let us turn, finally, to subproblem
(b), which because of the shift from (1) to
(1') is the problem of giving a materialistically acceptable account of what it is
for a sentence or a sentence-analog in a
system of internal representation to mean
that *p*. Recall that we are temporarily
construing *means that* as relating

sentences (and sentence-analogs) to sets of possible worlds (or to slightly more structured entities built up out of functions defined on possible worlds; but for simplicity let us ignore this more complicated account—it raises no new difficulties of principle for a materialist theory of belief). What set of possible worlds does a sentence (or sentence-analog) mean? It means the set of possible worlds at which the sentence is true. If then we can give a materialistically acceptable account of the relation between sentences and worlds of *being true at*, then we will have a materialistically acceptable account of (b).

Now, in another paper[14] I have argued that it *is* possible to give a materialistically adequate account of *truth* (i.e., of truth *at the actual world*). The idea of how this is done is simplest for the very simple languages that logicians usually discuss; there it involves giving a Tarski-type truth-definition. Such a truth-definition explains what it is for a sentence to be true (at the actual world) in terms of what it is for a name to denote an object (at the actual world), what it is for a predicate to have a certain extension (at the actual world), and so forth. In other words, such a truth-definition reduces the problem of what it is for a sentence to be true (at the actual world) to what it is for the one-word components of the sentence to stand (at the actual world) for certain entities or sets of entities. I argued that we have every reason to think that the relations of *standing for* (i.e., the relations of *denoting, having as an extension*, etc.) are explainable in a materialistically acceptable way, and so the truth definition gives us derivatively a materialistically acceptable account of truth (at the actual world). The above remarks hold for sentences of the simple languages to which Tarski's methods apply directly; but following Davidson[15] and many other philosophers, I believe that such methods are generalizable to natural languages, so

that for sentences in natural languages too we can say that truth can be explained in a materialistically acceptable way. And the same should be true for sentence-analogs, if we suppose that they are sufficiently like the sentences in natural languages.

I have claimed that we can give a materialistically adequate account of *truth*, i.e., truth *at the actual world*. But what we need, if we are to explain what it is to mean a Stalnaker-type proposition, is a materialistically adequate account of *truth at w* for an arbitrary possible world *w*. And this, it may seem, is much harder to come by: for if we relativize Tarskian semantics to an arbitrary possible world *w*, we find that it explains what it is for a sentence to be true at *w* in terms of *what it is for a name to refer to an entity at w* and *what it is for a predicate to have a set of entities as its extension at w*. That is, we need to invoke relations of words (in the actual world) standing for entities or sets of entities *in the possible world w*; and it is difficult to see how to explain such trans-world relations in a materialistically acceptable way.

This however is a very misleading way of looking at the matter: for in actual fact one can define truth at *w* purely in terms of relations between words (in the actual world) and entities *in the actual world*. For instance, for a sentence of form #P(b)# [*Editor's note*: In this anthology, "#" is used instead of the corner quote.] where *P* is a predicate and *b* a name, the definition will read

#P(b)# is true at *w* if and only if there is an object *x* that *b* denotes (in the actual world) and a property *Z* that *P* stands for (in the actual world), and *w* is a world in which *x* exists and has *Z*.

For example, 'Bertrand Russell is hairless' is true at any possible world *w* in which Bertrand Russell (i.e., the person denoted *in the actual world* by the name 'Bertrand Russell') exists and is hairless (i.e., has the property that the word 'hairless' stands for *in the actual world).* So truth at w is definable in terms of the relation of denotation for names together with the relation of standing for predicates, where it is now to be understood that a predicate stands for not a set (its extension) but for a *property* that exists in the actual world.[16]

So the problem of giving a materialistically adequate account of truth at w reduces to (i) the problem of giving a materialistically adequate account of actual-world-denotation for names, and (ii) the problem of giving a materialistically adequate account of actual-world-standing-for for predicates, where as I've said predicates are now to be construed as standing for properties rather than sets. But (i) is a problem that arose even in the account of truth in the actual world; I'm assuming (since I've argued it in the aforementioned article) that we have good reason to believe that that problem is solvable. With (ii) the situation is a bit different. What we need in any account of truth-in-the-actual-world is a materialistically adequate account of the relation between predicates and their actual world *extensions;* let us then assume that that problem is solvable. But (ii) requires something that is formally stronger; it requires a materialistically adequate account of the relation between predicates and *properties;* and since these properties determine but are not determined by the extensions of the predicates, what we need is formally stronger than what actual-world semantics would have to give us. A little reflection will show however that actual-world semantics is bound to give the formally stronger thing as well. For what could a materialistically adequate account of the relation 'is the extension of' be like? Such an account would have to tell us the kinds of facts about the way we use words in virtue of which the set of hairless things is the extension of the word 'hairless'. How could it do that? One possibility is that it would be a causal

theory of reference: it would state that some kind of causal connection between hairless individuals and our use of the word 'hairless' is responsible for our word having the set of hairless individuals as its extension. But surely we have not come into causal contact with *all* members of the extension of 'hairless' — after all, there are hairless things on remote planets, there are hairless things that exist only in the distant future, and so forth. How could causal contact with certain hairless individuals help in solving the problem of what makes our word 'hairless' have as its extension a set which includes such future hairless creatures (and which excludes the future hairy ones)? The only possible answer, I think, is that the extension of the term 'hairless' is determined by a property. What is *directly* associated with the predicate is not its *extension*, but a certain *property*. Perhaps the property of hairlessness is associated with the term 'hairless' by causal connection with a number of hairless individuals, as a causal theory of reference would have it; or perhaps there is some non-causal theory of reference which determines how the property of hairlessness is associated with the word. But however *that* association is made, the association of an extension with the word 'hairless' is a derivative one: the extension of 'hairless' is simply the set of objects (in the actual world) which have that property which in the actual world is associated with the word 'hairless'. If it were impossible to give a materialistically adequate account of how properties were associated with predicates, then it would be impossible to give a materialistically adequate account of how sets are associated with predicates, and so it would be impossible to give a materialistically adequate account of actual-world truth. So *the problem of giving a materialistically adequate account of truth-at-a-possible-world is no more difficult than the task of giving a materialistically adequate account of truth-in-the-*

actual-world; fundamentally, these apparently distinct problems are one and the same.

I now have all the pieces: let me put them in place. The task with which I have been occupied for most of Section I has been to explain one *possible* approach to giving a materialistically adequate account of belief; and I have been assuming for the time being that belief is to be construed as a relation between people and sets of possible worlds. The 'other-worldly' character of the assumed objects of belief might appear to rule out the possibility of a materialistic account of the belief relation, but, I have argued, that appearance is illusory. For we can say that a person believes a set *p* of possible worlds if and only if he believes* some sentence (or sentence-analog) *S*, and *p* is the set of possible worlds at which *S* is true. And (given the ontology of possible worlds) defining truth at a possible world requires no more resources than are required for defining genuine truth, i.e., truth at the actual world: both of these tasks require us to explain what makes the names in *S* denote whatever items in the actual world they do denote, and what makes the predicates in *S* stand for whatever properties in the actual world they do stand for,[17] and that is doubtless a difficult task; but I know of no reason to believe that the task is hopeless, and in fact (as I've argued in the aforementioned article) I think there is good reason to think it can be solved.

The account of believing that has just been elaborated has only been put forward as a *possible* account. It is in fact an account that I will want to revise in certain respects later on—e.g., by dropping all reference to propositions and possible worlds. But I will not revise the two central features of the account given so far: the idea that belief involves a relation to sentences or to something very much like sentences, and the idea that these sentences must be given a Tarski-like

semantics (including a theory of reference for the primitives). To a large extent, my adherence to these two ideas is based on an inability to conceive of what a solution to Brentano's problem that did *not* rely on these ideas would be like. I do not claim to have proved that there *could be* no alternative account of belief that solved Brentano's problem but did not have the two features mentioned above. However, I have never seen even a *clear sketch* of what such an alternative account would be like. The fact that the kind of account that I have sketched above would solve Brentano's problem, and that no alternative solutions to the problem are known, seems to me to provide a very strong reason for tentatively accepting the kind of account sketched.[18]

At this point the reader may feel that there is a well-known alternative account of belief that will either solve Brentano's problem, or show it to be a pseudo-problem. That alternative account (according to my hypothetical reader) is the account that Lewis and Stalnaker actually advocate: it is the functionalist alternative. In the next section I will examine the question of whether functionalism does indeed solve or dissolve Brentano's problem.

II. Functionalism

The Lewis-Stalnaker approach to belief involves the idea that believing is a functional state. Putting the view very roughly, a state of an organism is a state of believing that *p* if that state plays an appropriate role in the organism's psychology: that is, if it is causally connected to inputs and outputs and to other psychological states in the right sort of way. Now it certainly seems at first as if such a functional theory of belief allows for the possibility of beliefs independent of language or of inner representations: that is, why couldn't it be the case that an organism is in a state which is causally connected to inputs and outputs and to other states in the right sort of way for that state to satisfy the functional conditions for being a belief that p, even though that state does not involve a relation to any sentence or to any sentence-like item in any system of inner representation? Stalnaker has put the point as follows:

It is conceivable (whether or not it is true) that there are rational creatures who have beliefs and desires, but who do not use language, and who have no internal representations of their attitudes which have a linguistic form. I think this is true of many animals—even some rather stupid ones—but there might be clearer cases. Imagine that we discovered living creatures— perhaps on some other planet—who did not communicate, but whose behavior was predictable, for the most part, on the hypothesis that they engaged in highly sophisticated theoretical deliberation. Imagine further that we had this indirect evidence supporting our hypotheses: that the beliefs that our hypothesis attributed to these creatures could be causally explained, in many cases, in terms of their sensory inputs; and that the desires attributed to them by the hypothesis were correlated appropriately, for the most part, with the physical requirements for their survival. Finally, imagine that we test the hypothesis by manipulating the environments of these creatures, say by feeding them misleading 'evidence' and by satisfying or frustrating some of their alleged desires. If they continued to behave as predicted, I think we would be tempted to attribute to these creatures not just belief and desire analogues, but beliefs and desires themselves. We would not, however, have any reason to hypothesize that they thought in a mental language, or in any language at all ([25], p. 82).

Is Stalnaker right about this?

In order to evaluate Stalnaker's claims, we need to make the idea of a functional theory of belief much clearer than my crude description above makes it. According to the crude description above, a state of an organism is a state of

believing that p if the state is causally connected to inputs and outputs and to other psychological states in the right sort of way; but until we know what the other psychological states are that it must be causally connected to, and what is 'the right sort of way' for it to be connected to them, we are in no position to determine whether such a functional theory of belief requires a system of inner representation. (E.g., why couldn't one of the other states to which a state of belief that p must be causally connected be a state of having an inner representation of the proposition p?) This fact must be borne in mind in considering Stalnaker's story about the creatures on another planet. It is perfectly clear that in the situation Stalnaker describes, we could not be absolutely certain that the creatures thought in any internal system of representation. But it is also perfectly clear that we could not be absolutely certain that they had beliefs and desires. We couldn't be certain of this because (a) we have not observed all of their actual behavior, let alone all of their possible behavior, and (b) because even if we had, a claim about beliefs and desires is not simply a claim about behavior, it is a claim about how that behavior is produced. Of course, we do not need to have *detailed* knowledge of how that behavior is produced to know whether the organism has beliefs and desires—the whole point of functionalism is to provide a fairly abstract representation of an organism's inner states, so that *certain kinds* of information about the organism's inner states will be irrelevant to the question of whether it has beliefs and desires. But we do need *some* knowledge about how that behavior is produced in order to know that it has beliefs and desires: a functionalist's claim about an organism's inner states is a claim *about that organism's inner states*, and is not reducible to any claims about the organism's actual and possible behavior. (That fact is, I hope, common knowledge. It comes out very clearly in Lewis' precise explication of the functionalist claim, which I will give shortly.) Consequently, when we conclude of the creatures on the other planet that they have beliefs and desires, we do so because that is the best explanation we can find of their behavior. But now, if we can know that the creatures have beliefs and desires because belief-and-desire theory is the best available explanation of their behavior, why couldn't we also know that the creatures have a system of inner representation, by the same means? Whether the first inference has better inductive warrant than the second is not something that can be settled by a casual appeal to intuitions: it depends on whether it is possible to come up with an adequate functional account of belief and desire according to which belief and desire do not require internal representation. So the last sentence of the quotation from Stalnaker (or, if you like, the conjunction of the last two sentences) simply begs the question at issue. Perhaps its conclusion is correct, but we can show this only by a detailed examination of what a functional theory of belief would be like.

A full discussion of this topic would be two-fold. Part of such a discussion would involve the question of whether any adequate theory of belief would have to have assumptions about internal representation *explicitly built into it*. I am strongly inclined to think it would, and I think my remarks about core beliefs in Section I and the remarks about propositions in Section III provide *some* support for this claim; but the ultimate proof of the claims lies in the detailed development of psychological theory. In this section I will not deal with these matters, but will undertake a more modest task: I want to show that the functionalist approach to theories of believing and desiring does not provide an *alternative* to the idea that belief requires some system of representation.

In saying this I mean to be saying much more than that functionalism is compatible with there being some system of inner representation (involving sentences of natural language and/or sentence-analogs): that point is certainly not one that either Lewis or Stalnaker would deny. Both of them would certainly agree that if we opened up a person's head and found a blackboard inside on which various English sentences were written, and if we also found that the occurrence of those sentences on that blackboard entered in the right way into that person's behavior, then that would be strong reason to suppose that (for that person anyway) belief involved inner representation. This would of course not conflict with functionalism, for what we would be discovering is simply that the state which (in that person) is causally connected in the right sort of ways to inputs and outputs and to other states happens to be a state which involves inner representations. It is uncontroversial, then, that functionalism is compatible with the inner representation hypothesis. But I want to argue for a much stronger claim, one which I *suspect* Lewis and Stalnaker would deny (though I infer this more from the general tone of their discussions than from anything they explicitly say). What I suspect Lewis and Stalnaker hold is that without opening up people's heads, we can have little or no reason to *think* that believing anything involves a system of inner representation; the hypothesis that belief does involve a system of inner representation, then, is simply *unfounded neurophysiological speculation*. Now, in Section I I have given a *prima facie* argument that it was not just unfounded neurophysiological speculation: the inner representation hypothesis, I claimed, was *the only known possibility* for solving Brentano's problem, and this in itself provides good reason for tentatively accepting it. But in arguing that, I ignored the possibility of the functionalist approach.

What we must investigate now, then, is whether the functionalist approach alters the conclusion. My claim is that it does not, and *that* is what I mean when I say that functionalism provides no alternative to the view that belief *requires* some system of representation.

To put my claim in a sentence, then, it is that *functionalism does not provide a solution to Brentano's problem, nor does it in any way dissolve the problem.* That is the claim to be argued in this section.

The whole point of functionalism in psychology is to provide a fairly abstract representation of psychological properties, a representation that is not tied too closely to the details of the physical structure of particular organisms; in fact, a functional theory guarantees that if two organisms are, in a suitable sense, psychologically isomorphic, then they have precisely the same psychological properties, however different they may be in those aspects of physical structure that are not relevant to establishing the psychological isomorphism. A functionalist does not say that the physical structure of an organism is *irrelevant* to its psychological properties: nearly all functionalists are materialists, that is, they believe that all psychological properties require a *physical realization*.[19] This means for instance that for any organism X and any time t, X can have a 1-place psychological property F at t only if X has at t some physical property $R(F)$ which *realizes* F (in a sense soon to be made precise). But different physical properties can realize the same psychological properties in different organisms (or in the same organisms at different times); so organisms of very different structure can have the same psychological properties. It is because the functionalist allows the possibility of *different* realizations — not because he gives up the requirement of a realization altogether — that he achieves the goal of abstracting from the physical structure of particular organisms.[20]

It will be important in what follows to have a clear idea of what a realization of a psychological property is, and of what a psychological property itself is. The following account is David Lewis',[21] except for a few minor divergences (mentioned in footnotes) which make no difference to the argument at hand.

Suppose that H is a psychological theory that is intended to apply at any time t to all organisms which are of type K at t. (H might for instance be a theory intended to apply to all adult humans, or to all organisms capable of feeling pain, or to all rational beings.)[22] For simplicity, let us suppose that H is finitely axiomatized; then we can represent it as a single formula which I abbreviate as $A(x, t)$, where x is a variable ranging over organisms and t a variable ranging over times. [Then the theory is true of all the organisms in its intended range if and only if the following claim holds:

For any t and any x, if x is of type K at t then $A(x, t)$.

It is this last claim, rather than H, that is properly speaking true or false, so you might prefer to use the term 'theory' for the last claim rather than for H.] In giving crude formulations of psychological theories we often omit the variables (and initial quantifiers), but they must be understood as implicit: we say 'pain has such and such a causal role' when what we really mean is 'For any t and any x of type K at t, pain has such and such a causal role in x at t'. If we do not write the theory in this way, we cannot properly define the notion of a realization.[23]

Suppose that the specifically psychological[24] primitives in H are $T_1, \ldots, T_n$; then we can write H as $A(T_1, \ldots, T_n; x, t)$. For simplicity, I will assume that $T_1, \ldots, T_n$ are all predicates.[25] Let us say that an n-tuple $[P_1, \ldots, P_n]$ of properties *realizes H in organism X at time t* if and only if the formula $A(Y_1, \ldots, Y_n; x, t)$ is true of $[P_1, \ldots, P_n, X, t]$; and that such an n-tuple *uniquely realizes H in X at t* if it and no other n-tuple realizes H in X at t.

Now if H is a psychological theory with n primitive psychological predicates we can use it to define n *functional properties*. Suppose for instance that T_j is a predicate that stands for a 1-place property of organisms, the kind of property (like pain) of which it makes sense to say that the organism has it at one time but not at another. (Lewis calls properties of this sort 'states',[26] but I prefer to reserve this term for a different use.) If T_j is a predicate of this sort, then *the jth functional property associated with H is the property F defined as follows*:

(2) X has F at t if and only if there is some 1-place physical[27] property P such that
   (i) P is the jth component of a unique[28] realization of H in X at t
   (ii) X has P at t.

If F is the jth functional property associated with H, we can then say that a *realization of F in X at t* is simply the jth component of a unique realization of H in X at t. From this and (2) we derive

(2') X has F at t if and only if there is some 1-place physical property P such that
   (i) P realizes F in X at t, and
   (ii) X has P at t.

This machinery enables us to give a precise sense to the general remarks of five paragraphs back. What functionalism about pain claims is that *the property of pain[29] is a functional property associated with some theory H_p by* (2) (or by the analog of (2) with the word 'physical' replaced by 'non-functional' — see note 27). By taking functionalism in this way we can make precise sense of various vague notions appealed to in the general remarks (e.g., the notion of psychological isomorphism), and we can also verify the really important claim that if materialism is true, then for an organism to have the psychological property of pain it must have some physical property that realizes

that psychological property in the organism.

Now let us apply this machinery to the case of believing, where we assume as before that belief is a relation between an organism and a proposition. Belief, then, will be a functional relation associated with some theory H_b in which the term 'believes' occurs, say as the jth psychological term. We cannot of course apply the schema (2) to define such a functional property, since (2) made sense only in defining properties that correspond to *1-place* predicates, but it is clear enough how to generalize it to entities of another kind:

(3) X bears F to p at t if and only if there is some 2-place physical property R such that
   (i) R is the jth component of a unique realization of H in X at t
   (ii) X bears R to p at t.

No other generalization of (2) to the case of 2-place functional properties is possible.

Now the important thing to note about this is that it existentially quantifies over physical relations between people and propositions. If there is no physical relation of an appropriate sort between a person and a proposition, then according to (3) the person cannot stand in the functional relation F to the proposition. The functional relation F is not itself a physical relation; but if F is to relate an organism to a proposition at a time, there must be some physical relation $R(F)$ which realizes F and which relates the organism to the proposition. Thus even if we take belief to be a functional relation, we have to solve Brentano's problem: we have to show that there *are* physical (non-functional) relations between people and propositions. That is what I meant when I said earlier that *functionalism does not either solve or dissolve Brentano's problem. The only thing it says of relevance to that problem is something that probably no one ever* *doubted anyway:* that the physical relation that relates me now to the propositions I believe can differ from the one that relates dogs to the propositions they believe; and even from the one that relates other people to the propositions they believe, and from the one that related me twenty years ago to the propositions I believed then. In other words: *it is indeed legitimate to solve Brentano's problem in different ways for different organisms; but this does not remove the need for solving the problem within an organism.* I don't mean to downgrade the importance of the observation that we don't need to solve Brentano's problem in the same way in different organisms: that fact is crucial to the plausibility of the model of believing put forth in Section I, for no one could plausibly claim that the relation of believing* is physically the same across different species. All I am saying is that to admit the allowability and importance of such variation across organisms does not in any way diminish the force of the tentative argument for the model of believing put forth in Section I. It remains true that if no other model can be given of what a physical relation between people and propositions would be like, then we should tentatively accept the model there proposed.

The argument I have just given is I think an extremely obvious one: one would expect it to be obvious to anyone who thought about functionalism for a moment. Yet I have found in conversation that the conclusion of the argument is one that nearly all functionalists oppose: nearly all of them are convinced that functionalism somehow undermines the argument of Section I. One reason, I suspect, is a tendency to slip from functionalism to an extreme behaviorism according to which nothing inside an organism is relevant to determining its psychological properties. Another reason is perhaps a Leibnizian tendency to regard relations as less real than 1-place properties — not out of con-

scious doctrine but merely because of the fact that the word 'relation', unlike the word 'property', doubles as a word for a certain kind of set. But there is a third source of error that I now want to consider. It is equally crude, but I think that there are deep and subtle confusions that lead people to implicitly make it.

The third source of error is that even among people who explicitly advocate the view that belief is a relation between people and propositions, there seems to be a tendency to sometimes fall into the 'orthographic accident' view: the view that an adequate theory of belief could treat 'X believes that Russell was hairless', 'X believes that either Russell was hairless or snow is white', etc., as primitive 1-place predicates, and do without the 2-place predicate 'X believes that *p*' entirely. (The fact that the term 'believes that' occurs in both 1-place predicates would then be, from a theoretical view, of no significance, a mere orthographic accident; that fact that both contain 'Russell was hairless' would likewise be an orthographic accident.) It is not easy to take such a view seriously. But let us suppose it were true: what would follow? Well, the account would clearly obviate the need for a physical relation between people and propositions: since it didn't talk of a *psychological* relation between people and propositions, it is clear that no *physical* relation between people and propositions would be needed in a realization. But this of course does not refute the point I was making in this section, which is that if you *do* construe belief relationally, you need a physical realization of the belief relation.

In spite of the crudity of this mistake, I think that it is an easy one to make implicitly. In fact, in the opening paragraph of this section, when I tried to motivate the view that functionalism obviated the need of a system of representation, I found myself talking in a way that strongly suggested the orthographic accident view: I said "a state of an organism is a state of believing that p if that state plays the appropriate role in the organism's psychology." Now, for this to make any sense, the letter 'p' here must be understood as abbreviating a specific sentence—say 'Either Russell was hairless or snow is white.' Now, what is "the appropriate role" of the state of believing that either Russell was hairless or snow is white? I do not say that no sense can be made of such talk: if we give a functional account of the relation of believing which holds between organisms and propositions, such an account will certainly have *implications* about the state of believing the particular proposition that Russell was hairless or snow is white. I think however that talk of "the appropriate role" of the state of believing this particular proposition *strongly suggests* that we can give a direct functional definition of *this particular state*. And *that* strongly suggests that the kind of procedure used for 'pain' can be applied to 'believes that either Russell was hairless or snow is white': in other words, it suggests that *believing that either Russell was hairless or snow is white* can be regarded as a functional 1-place property defined by schema (2). That however is the orthographic accident view, for it presupposes that the theory H from which *believing that either Russell was hairless or snow is white* is to be functionally defined contains a primitive term that represents this property. The moral is that if you want to avoid the orthographic accident view, you should not regard 'X believes that p_0' for specific sentences p_0 as functionally definable in the way that 'X is in pain' is: you should regard them as defined non-functionally from a relational predicate 'X believes the p' which is functionally defined by (3). And that means that we must invoke physical relations between organisms and sets of possible worlds.

I believe that there is a deeper source of the tendency to slip into the orthographic accident view; it has to do with functional theories that invoke psychological *states*, where 'state' is not used in Lewis' sense (cf. note 26) but in the sense of 'type of inner occurrence'. There is nothing wrong with such functional theories, but they must be treated with care, as I will now explain. The reader may however wish to skip the explanation and move directly to Section III.

Let us first consider the case of pain. Linguistic usage suggests the following view:

(4) X feels pain at t if and only if there is an internal occurrence o such that
(i) X feels o at t, and
(ii) o is a pain.

Now suppose that we give a theory H_p' of the sortal property *being a pain* which was used in clause (ii) of (4). It is easy to see that the proper way to functionally define *being a pain* from such a theory is this:

(5) o is a pain if and only if there is some physical property P of inner occurrences such that
(i) P is the jth component of a unique realization of H_p' in X at t, and
(ii) o has the property P.

(Here t is the time of occurrence of o and X is the organism in which o occurred.) Putting this together with (4), we get

(6) X feels pain at t if and only if there is an internal occurrence o and a physical property P such that
(i) X feels o at t
(ii) o has the property P, and
(iii) P is the jth component of a unique realization of H_p' in X at t.

Now suppose we introduce the word 'state' for physical properties of inner occurrences. (That is, let us use it for *state-types*; if P is a state-type then the *state-tokens* are the inner occurrences that *have*

P.) If we also introduce the expression 'is in *P* at *t*' for 'feels at *t* some internal occurrence of type *P* (i.e., with the property *P*)', then we can rewrite (6) as

(7) *X* feels pain at *t* if and only if there is a physical state *P* such that
   (i) *X* is in *P* at *t*, and
   (ii) *P* is the *j*th component of a unique realization of H_p' in *X* at *t*.

The problem of finding a realization of pain-theory of this kind in *X* at *t*, then, is the problem of finding a *physical state* of pain in *X* at *t*; physical state in the sense of state-type, that is, in the sense of property of inner occurrences.

   Now the same thing done here for pain can be done for belief. The analog of (4) is

(4') *X* believes that *p* at *t* if and only if there is an inner occurrence *o* such that
   (i) *o* occurs in *X* at *t*, and
   (ii) *o* is a belief that *p*.

Functionally defining the relation *is a belief that*, analogously to (5) above, and combining the result with (4'), we get (in analogy to (6) above)

(6') *X* believes that *p* at *t* if and only if there is an internal occurrence *o* and a physical relation *R* between internal occurrences and propositions such that
   (i)   *o* occurs in *X* at *t*,
   (ii) *o* bears *R* to *p*, and
   (iii) *R* is the *j*th component of a unique realization of H_b' in *X* at *t*.

So far so good: the result makes clear that in using a psychological theory of belief of this sort, we need to find physical realizations of a relation between internal occurrences and propositions. Now suppose we want to introduce the term 'state' for a 1-place property of inner occurrences. There is no objection to doing so: for each sentence p_0, there is a 1-place property of bearing *R* to p_0, and we can call this a state (meaning of course a state-type). And we can go on to define what it is for

an organism to be in such a state: *X* is in the state Q_0 at *t* if and only if there occurs in *X* at *t* some inner occurrence of the type Q_0 (i.e., with the property Q_0). But now if we try to reformulate (6') in terms of state-types, we find that we get the following:

(7') *X* believes that p_0 at *t* if and only if there is a physical state Q_0 such that
   (i) *X* is in Q_0 at *t*, and
   (ii) *the relational component* of Q_0 is the *j*th component of a unique realization of H_b' in *X* at *t*.

(Q_0 is the property of bearing *R* to the specific sentence p_0; by the relational component of Q_0 I mean the relation *R*.) This is the *correct* way to introduce talk of state-types into a functional theory of belief.

   But, I suspect, many people do not bother to think the matter through. Seeing functionalism for pain formulated as (7), they immediately jump to the conclusion that belief-theory formulated in terms of states should read as

(7*) *X* believes that p_0 at *t* if and only if there is a physical state Q_0 such that
   (i) *X* is in Q_0 at *t*, and
   (ii) Q_0 is the *j*th component of a unique realization of H_b' in *X* at *t*.

Formulated in this way, H_b' has to be construed as a theory in which a term for being a state of believing p_0 (for the specific sentence p_0) appears as a primitive. And that of course is the orthographic accident view.

   The moral of all this is that the view that functionalism either solves or dissolves Brentano's problem results from confusion: the confusion of a relational theory of belief with an orthographic-accident theory of belief according to which belief is not a relation at all. I am sure that any functionalist would emphatically reject the idea that psychological theories of belief should have the orthographic-accident format; but if one thinks of states of believing as having functional roles not derivative on the functional role of the belief relation, then one is implicitly adhering to an orthographic accident account.

III. Dispensing with Propositions

At the beginning of Section II, I quoted an argument of Stalnaker's which suggested that a functional theory of belief would obviate the need for a system of internal representation. I remarked that in order to fully evaluate the argument, it was necessary to get clear on what a functional account of belief would be like. I have done that only in a very minimal sense: I have looked only at those features of a functional account of belief which follow from the nature of functionalism together with the (supposed) fact that belief involves a relation between people and propositions. But much more than this is involved in getting clear about what a functional account of belief would be like. For we have seen that on any functional account of belief, the relation of believing is a functional relation *associated with a certain theory H_b.* Part of what's involved in getting clear on what a functional account of belief would be like, then, is getting clear on what H_b would be like. I am strongly inclined to think that any adequate H_b would have to explicitly postulate a system of representation, and that this provides a reason to believe the internal representation hypothesis *independently of any considerations about Brentano's problem.* I will not however try to argue this claim here. Instead I will merely note a converse: that since (as I've argued) we appear to need a system of representation in order to solve Brentano's problem, we shouldn't have too much reluctance about explicitly incorporating such a system into our psychological theory H_b if doing so seems helpful.

One advantage of explicitly incorporating a system of representation into one's psychological theory is that it enables us to obtain most of the advantages of regarding belief and desire as relations between people and propositions, without the attendant liabilities. Suppose that for some reason or other we do not want to quantify over propositions; in that case, then apparently we will be unable to say things like

(8)   There are many things she believes about him, and none of them are at all complimentary

or

(9)   No one can perceive an object without coming to believe various things about it;

for apparently the 'things' quantified over in (8) and (9) are propositions. However I know of no reason why our purposes in uttering (8) and (9) wouldn't be equally well served by quantifying over objects of belief* rather than of belief: e.g. 'No one can perceive an object without coming to believe* various things about it'; here the 'things' quantified over are not propositions, but sentences in an internal system of representation. Of course, we could accept this reformulated version of (9) in our psychological theory only if we incorporated the inner representation hypothesis explicitly into the theory.

I think that by now the asterisks have become tiresome: so let us introduce the terminological convention that the word 'believes' is to be used in the way that I have heretofore used 'believes*'. On this way of talking, the objects of belief are sentences or sentence-analogs, and these sentences or sentence-analogs have content or meaning. Contrary to the suggestion in the first paragraph of Section I, this way of talking does not really remove Brentano's problem: that problem rearises as the problem of giving a materialistic account of *having content.* Unless such an account of content can be given, much of what we say about belief (e.g. that certain beliefs are *about Caesar*, that certain beliefs are *true*, and so forth) makes no sense at all. I have however suggested, at the end of Section I, that the problem of giving a materialistic account of content seems manageable: one way to manage it is to give a Tarski-like account of truth, supplemented by theory of reference.

My use of the word 'believes' to mean 'believes*' does not accord very well with the use of the term 'believes' in English: in English 'believes' is pretty much synonymous with 'believes that', and we can say even of organisms who know no English that they believe that snow is white. Let us then introduce a new technical term, 'believes that', which will serve the purposes that 'believe' and 'believe that' serve in English: let us say that a person 'believes that *p*' (where '*p*' abbreviates an English sentence S) if that person believes some sentence in his system of internal representation whose translation into English is S. In effect then 'believes that' is to be used for a relation between organisms and English sentences. It must be realized that the notion of translation employed in the definition of 'believes that' is a loose and sloppy one. For even those of us who are hostile to Quine's radical indeterminacy thesis are bound to recognize that translation *between languages of very different structure or expressive power* is highly indeterminate. (Part of the reason is that a sentence in language L_1 need not have exactly the same meaning as any sentence in language L_2, so that a translator of L_1 into L_2 has to settle for approximate sameness of meaning; and which approximation one picks depends on complicated pragmatic considerations.) Since the notion of *believing that* is to be applied to organisms whose system of internal representation is doubtless quite different from ours — e.g., chimpanzees, Martians, and (if Whorff is right) humans *whose spoken and written language* differs significantly from ours — then it would be

absurd not to recognize that the translation involved in the definition of 'believes that' is highly indeterminate. For this reason the notion of 'believing that' defined above is itself a highly indeterminate notion, and consequently it is a notion that we ought to avoid in our psychological theorizing.[30] Instead, we should use the notion of believing (i.e., believing*), together perhaps with various semantic notions applied to the sentences believed. (Another reason for avoiding use of 'believing that' (as defined above) in our psychological theories has already been mentioned in Section I — cf. (B).

I have introduced conventions about the use of 'believes' and 'believes that' according to which the first term relates organisms to sentences in their own system of representation and the second relates organisms to sentences in English. These terminological conventions are not intended to rule out the possibility that we need propositions in the analysis of belief and desire: it may be that we need propositions in our account of meaning for the sentences that are believed and desired. My own view however is

(a) that talk of propositions is best avoided (except as a dispensable manner of speaking) unless it can be shown to serve purposes that cannot be served otherwise; and it is doubtful that this condition is met

(b) that such talk commits us to semantic theses which (independently of ontological scruples) may well be false.

Let's take (a) first. That one should not posit entities needlessly is, I take it, uncontroversial: to do so would be to indulge in "unfounded ontological speculation." And that there is no particular need to introduce propositions — at least, no need to introduce propositions construed in terms of possible worlds — was implicit in my discussion at the end of Section I. There I argued that if one wanted to use the idea of possible worlds, and if one construed a proposition as a set of possible worlds, then the correlation of a particular proposition with a sentence posed no problem as long as we had an adequate truth-theoretic semantics for the language. Another way of putting this point is that talk of propositions adds nothing of semantic interest; everything that is semantically of interest is already there in the truth-theoretic semantics. (I'm speaking of course of a truth-theoretic semantics that assigns properties rather than sets to predicates.) In other words, instead of saying that a person is related to the set of possible worlds in which Russell was hairless (or to some fine-grained proposition constructed out of possible worlds), why not say instead that he is related to a sentence that consists of a name that stands for Russell copulated with a predicate that stands for hairlessness?[31]

One might try to respond to this question by holding (implausibly, I think) that names are non-rigid designators. But this response, while adequate to the question just asked, does not undercut the point I am trying to make (as has in effect been observed already, in note 16). For if 'Russell' is non-rigid, then to believe that Russell was hairless is to believe some sentence that contains a definite description, some sentence of the form 'G(the x such that Fx)' in which 'F' is an individuating description of Russell and 'G' stands for hairlessness. A truth-theoretic analysis of *this* sentence contains all the semantic information that is contained in a possible world analysis; so why bring in possible worlds? Again, they seem to be excess ontological baggage serving no semantic role.

Under (b) there are two points to be made. The first is that if one talks of propositions and also assumes that propositions must be explicable in terms of possible worlds, then one will be driven to postulate that proper names and theoretical terms like 'temperature' are non-rigid designators; and this postulate is

controversial at best. The second point is that whether or not one adheres to the possible worlds approach, talk of propositions commits one to a general relation of synonymy, and it is not at all obvious that there is any such general relation. I will develop these points, especially the second one, in Section VI. Their upshot is that the postulate of propositions involves not only unfounded ontological speculation but highly controversial semantic speculation as well. To me both the ontological and the semantic claims that underlie the postulate of propositions seem far more dubious than the postulate of a system of internal representation, especially since this last postulate appears to be a necessary one for the solution of Brentano's problem.

Let us say then that belief and desire are not attitudes toward propositions, but toward meaningful sentences in a system of internal representation. Presumably part of any adequate account of meaning for a system of internal representation is a truth-theoretic semantics; I will suggest in Section VI that there is another aspect of meaning as well. But first I would like to try to clarify the idea of a system of internal representation.

IV. Remarks on the Inner Representation Hypothesis

I have spoken of belief and desire as involving a system of *internal* representation; but I have allowed that in the case of organisms that have a genuine language, the system of internal representation might either be the language or include the language as a part.[32] This combination of claims may seem puzzling: if the only representation is in natural language, why call it internal representation? If there is internal representation, what sense does it make to say that the representation is in a natural language?

The answer to these questions lies in the distinction between types and tokens. I have talked of an organism as believing (i.e., believing*) sentence-types. But I said in Section I that (neglecting the complication about core beliefs) a person believes a sentence-type if and only if he employs that sentence-type in an appropriate way in reasoning, deliberating, etc.; and the only way to employ a sentence-type is to employ some of its tokens. Now, it is clear that in order to believe (or core believe) a sentence I can't be required to employ *spoken or written* tokens of it: no one writes down all of his beliefs (or all of his core beliefs). Consequently, if I believe sentences of my language, what I employ has to include *internal* tokens of those sentences. That explains why, even if all representation is in natural languages, we have to speak of internal representation: some of the tokens are certainly internal.

This brings us to the second question: does it make sense to speak of internal representation as representation *in natural language?* It makes sense if, and only if, it makes sense to speak of internal tokens as being of the same type as spoken or written tokens. One might argue that any claim of type-identity between internal tokens and spoken or written tokens is highly implausible: after all, it seems pretty absurd to suppose that there is much of a physical resemblance between internal tokens on the one hand and spoken or written tokens on the other. But this of course would be a very bad argument: after all, a spoken token can be said to be of the same type as a written token, and yet spoken and written tokens bear little physical resemblance to each other.

My own view is that the issue of whether we speak of internal tokens as type-identical to spoken or written tokens is partly a verbal issue, but that there are interesting empirical questions that underlie it, of which the most important is the extent to which (and the manner in which) linguistic development involves conceptual development. To put the point very vaguely: if (as seems to me quite like-

ly) learning a first language involves *extending* an initial representational system to include an isomorphic copy of the language being learned, then I think it is quite natural to view the isomorphism as establishing a criterion of type-identity between internal tokens and spoken or written tokens. However, the issues here are pretty complicated. (See Harman [10] for an interesting discussion which more or less supports the pro-type-identity position, and Fodor [7] (Ch. 2) for an interesting discussion in support of the other side.) My sympathies are much more with Harman than with Fodor on this matter, but I will try to remain neutral on the question in the rest of the paper.[33]

But there are other questions that need to be considered. First, I have talked of 'internal tokens'. What kinds of entities are these? Presumably they are inner occurrences of some kind, but *what* kind? Second, although I have begged off the question of what it is for an internal token to be of the same type as a spoken or written token, there is also the question of what it is for two internal tokens to be of the same type as each other; and since a psychological theory will clearly need to use the notion of type-identity between different tokens, this question cannot very well be ignored. Third, there is the question of syntactically characterizing internal tokens — what is it for an internal token to belong to a given syntactic category (e.g., what is it for it to be a sentence token)? Again, we will need to appeal to syntactic characterizations of inner tokens in developing the psychological theory, so this question is a fairly pressing one.

There are two possible strategies in dealing with such questions. The first strategy, which I think is the wrong one, is to try to answer the above questions prior to developing the psychological theory. Such a strategy is a bad one because it is hard to see how to carry it out without doing a great deal of neuro-physiological speculation: e.g., we would apparently have to specify two neuro-physiological properties P_1 and P_2 and a neurophysiological relation R, and say that an inner occurrence is an expression-token if and only if it has P_1, and is a sentence-token if in addition it has P_2, and that two inner occurrences with property P_1 are of the same type if one bears R to the other. The task of specifying P_1, P_2 and R is certainly not a task we are equipped for in our current state of knowledge, and I don't see how we could ever become equipped for it *prior* to the development of psychological theory.

The second strategy, which is the one I advocate, is to develop the syntax of the system of representations as part of the psychological theory: *we can then use the psychological theory to give a functionalist answer to the questions raised above.* That this is the right way to proceed seems completely obvious: it is simply an instance of the general rule that psychological theories ought to be construed functionally.

Let me be a bit more explicit about what is involved in this functionalist approach. If one were to write out in detail a theory H that postulates a system of inner representation, such predicates as 'x is an expression-token', 'x is a sentence-token', and 'x and y are expression tokens of the same type' would either appear as primitives or be explicitly definable (within set theory or higher order logic) from other such syntactic primitives. *Such syntactic primitives are to be included among the psychological primitives when we 'functionalize' H: that is, a realization of H is to be an n-tuple consisting of properties and relations corresponding to the syntactic predicates of the theory as well as to the more straightforwardly psychological predicates. If we* 'functionalize' the theory in this way then the answers to the questions raised above can be read right off of the theory H.[34] For

instance, suppose for simplicity that 'x and y are tokens of the same type' is a primitive of H. If we want to know what it is for two internal occurrences in an organism X at a time t to be tokens of the same type, the answer is simple: c and d are tokens of the same type if and only if there is a physical relation R which is the appropriate component of a unique realization of H in X at t, and c bears R to d.[35] [35a] (If 'x and y are tokens of the same type' is a defined term rather than a primitive, the answer is slightly more complicated; but again, it can be read right off of the theory.) The upshot is that there is no need in developing psychological theory to specify what R is; we can leave that to future neurophysiology. (Moreover, we can allow that there are different physical type-identity relations in different organisms.) The fact that we leave the question to future neurophysiology does not imply any unclarity in our theory: *in some sense, the theory implicitly specifies what it is for two inner tokens in a system of representation to be tokens of the same type.*

There is one final point to be made about theories that postulate a system of internal representation. I have said that the *syntax* of a system of internal representation should be explicitly stated in a psychological theory of belief and desire. Should the *semantics* of the system of internal representation *also* be stated as part of the psychological theory? That depends on what we want psychological theory for. If the task of psychology is to state

(i) the laws by which an organism's beliefs and desires evolve as he is subjected to sensory stimulations, and
(ii) the laws by which those beliefs and desires affect his bodily movements,

then I think that it is clear we do not need to use the semantics of the system of representation in stating the psychological laws: the sentences in the system of internal representation might as well be meaningless as far as the psychology is concerned.[36] This is not the only way to view a psychological theory—a broader conception of a belief-desire psychology will be suggested in the next section, and in it semantic notions would play a genuine role. But it is worth stressing the narrow kind of psychology at least momentarily. For we have seen that the syntax and type-identity conditions for a system of internal representation should be regarded as functionally characterized by a psychological theory in which they appear; and we can take that theory to be narrow psychology, that is, the kind of psychology that does not employ any semantic characterizations of the sentences in a system of representation. This is important, for it means that the syntax and conditions of type-identity for the system of representation could in principle be determined independently of any considerations about what the sentences in the system mean.

V. Truth

What would a theory of meaning for system of internal representation be like? In Sections I and III I have hinted at one aspect of my views on this question: a theory of meaning for a system of internal representation must consist in part of a truth-theoretic semantics of a more-or-less Tarskian kind. If we do not give a theory of truth for the system of internal representation, we cannot make sense of the idea that some of our beliefs are true and others are false; and I think we do want to be able to make sense of this idea (for reasons to be sketched shortly). Moreover, the only kind of theory of truth that I have ever heard of which is not obviously deficient is the Tarskian kind. The upshot, then, is that we need to give a Tarski-type semantic theory for the system of internal representation. In a recent article to which I am in most respects very sympathetic, Gilbert Harman has questioned this:

> . . . no reason has been given for a compositional theory of meaning for whatever system of representation we think in, be it Mentalese or English ([12], p. 286).

Presumably however if the notion of truth makes any sense, then truth and meaning must be related in the following way: the truth of the sentence 'Caesar crossed the Rubicon' should follow from the meaning of the sentence together with the fact that Caesar crossed the Rubicon. *In this sense* a theory of meaning must include a theory of truth-conditions. And as far as I can see, the theory of truth-conditions has to be a compositional theory of roughly the type that Tarski made famous.

Harman's critique of compositional semantics is based on an important insight. He points out in the article that there is a serious problem for those philosophers, like Davidson, who regard *knowledge of* truth-conditions as what is essential in semantics:

> Davidson would (presumably) say that the speaker understands [the sentence 'Snow is white'] by virtue of the fact that he knows it is true if and only if snow is white. The difficulty . . . is that [for the speaker to know any such thing he] needs some way to represent to himself snow's being white. If the relevant speaker uses the words 'snow is white' to represent in the relevant way that snow is white, . . . Davidson's [theory] would be circular. And, if speakers have available a form of Mentalese in which they can represent that snow is white, so that the [theory avoids] circularity, there is still the problem of meaning for Mentalese (p. 286).

But the moral to be drawn is that *knowledge* of truth-conditions is not what is important to the semantics of a system of internal representation. The theory must ascribe *truth-conditions*, not *knowledge of truth-conditions*, to the sentences of English or Mentalese; for if it doesn't ascribe truth-conditions to these sentences it will not have given sense to talk of our beliefs as being true or false.

I have assumed that we do want to make sense of the idea that some of our beliefs are true and others are false; I would also assume that we want to make sense of the idea that some of our beliefs are about Julius Caesar and that other of our beliefs are about quarks. It seems to me however that there is a serious question as to why we *should* want to make sense of these ideas. Is our desire to do so based on anything other than a naive metaphysics that has no place in a properly scientific account of the world?

That this question is not a silly one can be seen from a fact noted at the end of the previous section. If the task of psychology is to state

(i)   the laws by which an organism's beliefs and desires evolve as he is subjected to sensory stimulations, and

(ii) the laws by which those beliefs and desires affect his bodily movements,

then semantic characterizations of beliefs and desires are irrelevant to psychology: one can state the laws without saying anything at all about what the believed and desired sentences mean, or what their truth-conditions are or what their subject matter is. For instance, we might imagine a super-crude psychology that contained laws like the following:

there is some connective ' $\rightarrow$ ' in the system of internal representation such that for all sentences S_1 and S_2 in the system, whenever a person believes #$S_1 \rightarrow S_2$# and desires S_2 then he also desires S_1.

[*Editor's note:* In this anthology, " $\rightarrow$ " is used instead of the horseshoe and the arrow as the material conditional ("if . . . then").] The connective ' $\rightarrow$ ' that satisfied this law might mean 'only if', that is, it might obey the truth-table for the conditional; but the fact that it obeys this truth-table is not something we need to say in stating the psychological laws.[37] The psychology, since we are imagining it to

be super-crude, might also contain laws like this:

there is a privileged class of sentences in the system of representation, called the class of *observation sentences,* with the property that each sentence in the class has associated with it a particular type of sensory stimulation. Whenever a sensory stimulation of the appropriate type occurs, the organism believes the observation sentence.

Intuitively, we might expect that if a particular observation sentence is associated in this way with the class of retinal stimulations that are characteristically caused by nearby rabbits, then the observation sentence means something like 'there are rabbits nearby'; but even if this is true, the psychological theory need not say that it is true. Why then do we need to semantically characterize the sentences in the system of inner representation? Why not simply say that belief and desire are relations between people and meaningless sentences? Saying this would preclude us from speaking of beliefs as being true or as being about rabbits, but would anything of scientific value be lost?

Here is one answer to this question — not the whole story, I think, but the part of the story that is emphasized in the writings of such philosophers as Quine, Davidson, and Harman (and perhaps Lewis in [18]). Imagine that we find ourselves with a foreigner whose language we do not understand. A rabbit scurries by, in the foreigner's line of sight, and the foreigner raises his gun in its direction — by now we have rather overwhelming grounds for thinking that he believes that there is a rabbit nearby. But can we say so in the vocabulary of the narrow psychology considered heretofore? We can't say 'He believes the sentence . . .' (giving the name of the sentence): for we don't know his language. How about if we say instead 'He believes some sentence which is an observation sentence associated with sensory stimulations of type . . . (and which serves as evidence for syntactically related sentences according to laws . . ., and so forth)'. The difficulty is clear: only someone with a great deal of very detailed information about the psychology of our foreigner could fill in the blanks. A third possibility is much better:

> He believes some sentence of his language which plays approximately the role in his psychology that the sentence 'There's a rabbit nearby' plays in mine.

But this, it might be claimed, really involves a semantic notion! For isn't it really just a long-winded way of saying

> He believes some sentence of his language that *translates* into my language as 'There's a rabbit nearby'?

And isn't translation a semantic notion?

This answer does not satisfy me, for though it does definitely motivate the introduction of a notion of translation, it does not motivate the introduction of any non-translational semantic notions; that is, it motivates the introduction of a more-or-less[38] semantic notion about the relation of one language to another, but it does not motivate the introduction of any semantic notions like 'true' or 'refers' which relate language to the world. No reason has been offered, it seems to me, for regarding another person as having beliefs that are *true* or *about rabbits*. The Quinean reply, I would imagine, is that we need such notions as truth in connection with our own language (e.g., to state generalizations like 'Every sentence of the form 'p or not p' is true');[39] and that we can then use the notion of translation that we have motivated on other grounds to carry over the truth concept to foreign languages. I do not want to discuss this Quinean reply here; but it seems to me rather weak, and I would like to do better.

I think that the reason why we need to be able to apply semantic notions like truth and reference to the sentences that people believe and desire is that we hold

the theory that people's beliefs are, in many circumstances, reliable indicators about the world; and the only way to state this theory is to use the notion of truth (and probably the notion of reference as well). *Moreover, this theory is not a piece of gratuitous metaphysics that could easily be dispensed with:* it is central to our getting information about the world, for we are constantly using our opinions about other people's beliefs in forming opinions about the world. The fact that a child believes that he has done something I won't like (a fact that can often be inferred from his behavior) gives good reason to think he *has* done something I won't like; the fact that most physicists believe that there are gravitational waves (a fact that can be inferred from reading a few physics books) is good reason for me to believe that there *are* gravitational waves; and so forth. These inferences evidently proceed by means of certain *reliability principles*, principles that say under what conditions a person's beliefs about certain things are likely to be true. The principles we need are not easy to state: after all, the fact that a child believes in Santa Claus is not good reason for me to believe in Santa Claus, and the fact that most members of a certain religious cult believe that flying saucers will land on a certain farm in Arizona next month is not good enough reason for me to believe that flying saucers will land there. (I don't think that the failure of these inferences is due entirely to independent evidence as to the falsity of the conclusion.) We do evidently have a stock of reliability principles, though we can not explicitly formulate them; and one can imagine that they will someday be systematized into an explicit theory. In a suitably broad sense, we might even regard this 'reliability theory' as part of psychology.

What such a reliability theory would look like I do not know. My guess is that it would have to include not only the notion of truth but the notion of reference: for we want to be able to say in the theory that some people have very reliable beliefs *about physics* but very unreliable beliefs *about the state of the economy*, and so forth. We might imagine then that 'true', 'refers', etc. are primitives of the theory. If we do that—and if we imagine that the reliability theory is elaborated with such detail and precision that it is uniquely realized in each of the organisms to which the theory is intended to apply—then we could use this theory to give a functional account of truth and reference for systems of internal representation. Such a functional account would of course be desirable, for the reason that functional accounts are always desirable: it would allow for the possibility that the reference relation is realized by different physical relations in different organisms.[40]

VI. More on the Semantics of Internal Representation

Is there more to the semantics of a system of internal representation than is given by truth-theoretic semantics? I think that there is; and I think that this casts considerable doubt on the possible worlds analysis of propositions, even independently of ontological considerations. In fact, I think it casts some doubt (independent of ontological considerations) on whether *any* notion of proposition is possible. In explaining these matters, I will begin by discussing the semantics of spoken and written languages, since I want to discuss some points that Quine has made in the context of them; but what I say will carry over to systems of internal representation.

Many years ago Quine made the following observation:

A lexicographer may be concerned with synonymy between forms in one language and forms in another or . . . he may be concerned with synonymy between forms in the same language. It is an open question how satisfactorily the two cases can be sub-

sumed under a single general formulation of the synonymy concept . . . ([21] p. 56).

The point that Quine is making here is very relevant to the question of propositions: if one postulates propositions one is assuming a positive answer to Quine's 'open question'. For if sentences mean propositions, then apparently two sentences are synonymous if they mean the same proposition; and this would be a general concept of synonymy, it would apply both intra-linguistically and inter-linguistically.

Is Quine's 'open question' really open? Well, at least this much is true: intralinguistic synonymy seems a lot easier to define than interlinguistic synonymy. (Similarly, intraspeaker synonymy is easier to define than interspeaker synonymy, suggesting that there might be still further divergence in the synonymy concept.) That intralinguistic synonymy is easier to define than interlinguistic synonymy *at least for what Quine calls occasion sentences* is a point that Quine argues in Sections 9 and 11 of [22]: he points out that the difference in meaning between 'Everest' and 'Gaurisanker' (construed as one-word sentences) for a certain speaker is revealed by the fact that different sensory stimulations would prompt him to assent to one than to the other; and that the difference in meaning of these one-word sentences in a given linguistic community is revealed by the fact that these sentences are intra-subjectively non-synonymous for most members of that community. Now, it seems to me that this talk of 'prompting to assent' is much too behavioristic, and leads Quine into unnecessary worries, e.g., about "stimulations of second intention" (verbal stimulations like "Assent to one-word sentences that begin with 'E' or I'll beat your brains out")—cf. [22] pp. 48-49. Nevertheless, it seems to me that Quine's general point is correct: *we can explain intra-linguistic differences of meaning by evidential considerations.* I have developed this point elsewhere,[41] using a non-behavioristic (but, I admit, idealized) conception of evidence; and in addition to solving such humdrum difficulties with Quine's approach as the second-intention problem, it also obviates the need for restricting the account to occasion sentences. What is interesting about this approach I think is that it gives you differences of meaning where you would intuitively expect them, but where you do not get them on the possible worlds approach (without adopting implausible assumptions about non-rigid designation). For instance, the following pair of sentences come out equivalent in meaning on the possible worlds approach:

(10)   Everest is Gaurisanker

comes out equivalent to

(11)   Everest is Everest;

and

(12)   Temperature is mean molecular energy

comes out equivalent to[42]

(13)   Temperature is temperature.

But is should be pretty clear, even without looking up the details of my account, that these equivalences will not hold on any sufficiently sophisticated evidential criterion of intraspeaker synonymy, even for speakers who believe the sentences (10) and (12).

Such evidential considerations (coupled with truth-theoretic considerations if the latter are not redundant)[43] seem to me to provide a very natural account of intra-speaker synonymy. For inter-speaker synonymy however the situation is quite different, for here it is very hard to formulate any evidential criteria for two words differing in meaning. The source of the difficulty is clear: you and I may disagree about what counts as evidence for a certain sentence, not because that sentence means some-thing different to you than it means to me, but because of differences in the rest of our beliefs. One might try to find some rule of the form 'If there is an evidential difference of such and such a kind between your sentence and mine, then they differ in meaning'; this is the task that Quine refers to as "trying to strip away the effects of collateral information." Quine has cast considerable doubts on the possibility of carrying out this task ([22], Section 9), and I think that if you look at the question in terms of my formal model in [6] you will find that Quine's doubts are reinforced.

It seems to me that the criteria of inter-linguistic synonymy we actually employ are, *almost* exclusively, the criteria provided by truth-theoretic semantics.[44] This is not quite true; when there are two sentences S_1 and S_2 in one language that are equivalent from the point of view of truth-theoretic (or possible world) semantics, but which differ evidentially, and when there is a sentence S_3 in another language that is truth-theoretically equivalent to both S_1 and S_2 but is much more similar evidentially to S_1 than to S_2, then we regard it as definitely a mistake to translate S_3 as S_2 — the translation S_1 seems required. But except in such cases, little if any inter-subjective sameness of evidential role is required; if the Martians have singled out Everest, i.e., Gaurisanker, by their powerful telescopes and have named it 'Schrdlu', we would translate their name 'Schrdlu' by 'Everest' or by 'Gaurisanker' indifferently, however much we might want to say that 'Everest' and 'Gaurisanker' differ in meaning for us. One might object to this argument by saying that translation is a loose and pragmatic notion: the true situation (one might say) is that 'Schrdlu' differs in meaning *both* from 'Everest' *and* from 'Gaurisanker'; we translate the name indifferently by 'Everest' or by 'Gaurisanker' because these approximate 'Schrdlu' about equally well. I sympathize with this response, except for one thing: it assumes that there is *some* clear notion of inter-linguistic difference in meaning between words that refer to the same thing, and that is what I think needs to be established.

My view then is that truth-theoretic semantics — i.e., possible world semantics without the possible worlds — is almost enough, but that there are certain very fine-grained distinctions of meaning that it cannot explain. These fine-grained distinctions of meaning seem to be clearly drawable only intra-linguistically, and that fact appears to make the notion of proposition suspect.

It should be clear that these remarks about synonymy between sentences in public languages apply also to synonymy between sentences in systems of internal representation. It should also be clear that to define the evidential differences between sentences in the same system of internal representation, one does not need to employ any concepts that go outside psychology in the narrow sense. Consequently there seems to be no special problem in motivating the introduction of such evidential considerations into a semantic theory for the system of inner representation, in a way that there did seem to be a special problem of motivating the introduction of truth-theoretic concepts.

I want to conclude this paper by raising what I regard as an open question: what connections are there between a theory of meaning for a system of internal representation and a theory of meaning for a spoken or written language?[45] According to one influential approach[46] to the theory of meaning for spoken and written languages, the meaning of a sentence in such languages is to be explained in terms of beliefs (or desires, etc.) that are conventionally correlated with the sentence. Roughly, to know the meaning of 'Caesar was egotistical' is to know that this sentence is conventionally correlated with the belief that Caesar was egotistical;

and similarly for every other sentence in one's public language. (The conventional correlation must be spelled out recursively, of course.) This approach presupposes that one can explain what it is to believe that Caesar was egotistical *without relying at any point on the semantic features of the sentence 'Caesar was egotistical' in one's spoken or written language:* for if one relied on the semantic features of the spoken or written sentence in one's account of the belief, then to explain the meaning of the sentence in terms of the belief would involve a circularity. So a crucial question is whether that presupposition is correct.

Putting the presupposition in terms of internal representation, it is this: that one can explain what it is for a sentence in the internal system of representation to mean that Caesar was egotistical without relying in one's explanation on the fact that certain words and phrases in the public language stand for Caesar or that certain other words and phrases in the public language stand for the property of being egotistical. *If this presupposition is correct,* then the above approach to the theory of meaning is quite attractive: if worked out, it would reduce all questions about the semantics of the spoken or written language to the corresponding questions about the semantics of the system of internal representation; and those questions could then be answered without further reference to language. I am inclined to doubt however that the presupposition is true. My *guess* is that in a typical case, *part of* what makes a symbol in my system of internal representation a symbol that stands for Caesar is that this symbol acquired its role in my system of representation as a result of my acquisition of a name that stands for Caesar in the public language. If something of this sort is true, it would appear to defeat[47] the above approach to a theory of meaning for a public language. I believe however that the issues here are quite complicated, and deserve a great deal of further study.

An opposite approach to the theory of meaning would be to try to reduce the semantics of the system of internal representation to the semantics for public language. To do this would be to assume that although dogs, chimpanzees, etc. might have systems of internal representation which played an important role in the explanation of their behavior, these systems of representation would not be ones to which notions like meaning and truth applied: such semantic notions could be applicable only to the representational systems of organisms with a spoken or written language. To me, such a conclusion seems very implausible. It may nevertheless be that there is *something* to this approach, for it may be that *certain aspects* of meaning can be explained more directly for public language than for systems of internal representation. The suggestion is not that these aspects of meaning can be explained without reference to beliefs and desires, for two reasons. In the first place, in explaining the fact that the public word 'Caesar' referred to Caesar one could appeal freely to certain sorts of beliefs and desires, e.g., those beliefs and desires that a languageless organism could possess; for we have granted that such beliefs and desires can be accounted for in a language-independent way. In the second place, there is an important sense in which one could appeal to other beliefs and desires as well in our semantic theory for public language: we could appeal to beliefs and desires *construed as attitudes towards internal sentences* all we liked; the only restriction would be on which semantic features of those internal sentences we appealed to.

I do not want to draw any very definite conclusions from this last discussion. I merely want to say that it may well be necessary to develop the semantic theory for internal languages and the semantic theory for public languages together rather than developing one kind of semantics independently of the other and reducing the other kind to it. The reductionist strategy (particularly the strategy that tries to reduce public semantics to internal semantics) is worth pursuing, but alternative strategies are worth pursuing as well.[48]

Notes

1. See for instance Armstrong [1], Ch. 3, and Putnam [20].

2. Brentano's problem is discussed by Chisholm in [2], Ch. 11; references to Brentano can be found there.

3. See Stalnaker [25]. Lewis' remarks on functionalism are scattered throughout various writings; see [14], [15], [17], [18], and [19].

4. See Quine [22], Section 45.

5. *Believing** is thus different from *believing true*: a foreign speaker can believe an English sentence true while having no idea what it means, e.g., if he sees a headline in the *N.Y. Times*. To believe a sentence S true (i.e., to believe that S is true) is, if (1) is right, to believe* a sentence $S*$ which means *that S is true*. Believing true involves the concept of truth; believing* does not.

6. The Banach-Tarski theorem says roughly that a solid sphere can be decomposed into a finite number of disjoint 'pieces' in such a way that the 'pieces' can then be put back together again to form two solid spheres the same size as the original one. (For a more precise statement (and a proof) see [13], pp. 3-6.)

7. For pedants: I'm speaking of von Neumann set theory including the axiom of choice; it is finitely axiomatized.

8. [16], pp. 182ff.

9. [4], p. 410. Dennett seems to regard the introduction of the notion of core-believing as an *ad hoc* device to save stored-sentence approaches from the absurdity of requiring infinitely many sentences to be stored: but the following discussion will show I think that the notion can be given strong independent motivation.

10. To spell this out more fully, we'd need first to spell out the characteristic role of beliefs (as opposed to say desires) in reasoning, deliberating, and so on — call this characteristic

role Role B. Then the materialistic view of believing* that I am suggesting is roughly that in each believer there is some kind of physical storage of sentences such that the things stored in that way and their obvious consequences are the things that have Role B.

11. The 'almost' appears to be needed here because of the non-transitivity of 'is an obvious consequence of'. I doubt that there are any *clear cases* of believing that either Russell was hairless or snow is white but not believing that if Russell was not hairless then snow is white; but I regard this as more or less analogous to the fact that there are no clear cases of numbers *n* such that some individuals with less than *n* hairs are bald but no individual with *n* or greater hairs is bald. I would not want to assert that because there are no *clear* cases of such numbers, there are no such numbers, because that would lead to a Sorites paradox. Similarly, I would not want to assert that because there are no *clear* cases of believing *p* and not believing an obviously equivalent proposition *q*, there are no such cases; for that would lead by Sorites-like reasoning to the conclusion that one can't believe *p* and yet not believe the unobviously equivalent claim *r*.

12. The acceptance of indeterminacies of the kind mentioned here is a minor concession to an instrumentalistic view of ordinary belief-talk, but only a minor one; for even if it does not always make sense to ask whether a belief-ascription is true or false, we have seen no reason to deny that a core-belief ascription is always true or false; and that is close enough. (Another minor concession to an instrumentalistic view of our ordinary belief-talk will be made in Section III.)

13. See for instance Fodor [7] and Harman [11], Ch. 4, Section 2.

14. [5].

15. [3].

16. I have assumed in this paragraph that proper names are always rigid designators. Some people however deny this: they believe that when we use the name 'Bertrand Russell' we associate with this name a property *H* which we think picks out Russell uniquely; and that when we say 'Bertrand Russell is hairless', what we say is true at a world *w* if and only if there is exactly one thing in *w* with property *H* in *w*, and that thing is hairless in *w*. (The thing with *H* in *w* need not be the thing with *H* in the

actual world, i.e., it need not be Russell.) I find this doctrine that names can denote non-rigidly quite implausible; but the point I am making in the paper could be generalized so as to allow for names to be non-rigid designators for anyone who finds that desirable. To see this, reflect on how we would associate a property *H* with a name. The only way I can see to do that is to associate with that name some expression (in a natural language or in a system of internal representation) which stands for that property. What the advocate of non-rigid designation is saying, then, is that when we utter the sentence 'Bertrand Russell is hairless', that sentence merely serves to abbreviate the sentence (or sentence-analog) that we really mean, which is something of the form 'There is exactly one thing *x* such that *F(x)*, and *x* is hairless'. Truth-at-a-possible-world can then be defined for the sentences (or sentence-analogs) *that we really mean*, by the process described in the text; and we can say that derivatively, a sentence *S* containing the name 'Bertrand Russell' is true at *w* if and only if the associated sentence (or sentence-analog) *that we really mean when we utter S* is true at *w*.

17. I don't really mean to be assuming that the primitive symbols in the sentence-analogs are names or predicates; who knows what they are. All that the account I am suggesting assumes is that *whatever* problems of (actual world) reference such symbols raise are soluble in a materialistically acceptable manner.

18. I should add that the difficulty of constructing an alternative account of a relation between people and propositions is especially acute if one takes propositions to be fine-grained.

19. Lewis certainly believes this, and I suspect that Stalnaker does too.

20. This is true even of non-materialist functionalists; they too require realizations of psychological properties, they merely allow that the realizations be non-physical. (Only an instrumentalistic functionalist would deny the requirement of realizations entirely.)

21. [14], [15], and [17].

22. I do not impose Lewis' requirement that *H* be a *common sense* psychological theory. But if you want to add that (to my mind unnecessary) requirement, you may: the argument of this section of the paper will not be affected.

The restriction to common sense psychological theories *might* interfere with a proposal to be made later on: that we explicitly build the postulate of a system of internal representation into *H*. At first blush this would seem to conflict with letting *H* be a common sense theory, since common sense would not appear to be committed to systems of internal representation. However, Lewis is rather generous in what he regards common sense as committed to: he does not regard the fact that a theory postulates possible worlds other than our own as going against the requirement that it say only what is common sense. I believe that systems of internal representation are at least as close to being postulates of common sense as are possible worlds.

I have said that I think that the requirement that *H* be a common sense theory is unnecessary. I also think that it is harmful. For one thing, it is not at all clear that any of the common sense theories of belief are (or even come close to being) *uniquely* realized; the only way to get anything like *unique* realization may be to invoke non-common-sense suppositions. It may well be for instance that only a theory of belief that explicitly postulates a system of internal representation can come anywhere near to being uniquely realized. But I do not want to press this point here: the argument of this section goes through even if *H* itself does not postulate a system of internal representation or in any other way (apart from propositions!) strain the bounds of common sense.

23. Lewis' own account of what realizations are is strictly speaking inaccurate because he does not take the precaution I've recommended: as his account stands, something can serve as a realization of pain only if it realizes pain in *all* organisms at *all* times, thus depriving functionalism of its point (cf. Harman [11], Ch. 3, Section 4). But it is clear that what I have suggested (which is equivalent to what Harman suggests) is what Lewis really had in mind.

24. Here I oversimplify: we might imagine that $T_1, \ldots, T_n$, include non-psychological terms that are needed in the theory; and we might also imagine that some psychological terms needed in the theory are not included among $T_1, \ldots, T_n$, because their reference is fixed independently of *H*.

25. For reasons not relevant to the present paper, Lewis finds it convenient to imagine that the theory has been rewritten so that all the psychological terms are names. I have chosen not to do this, and the features of the next paragraph that do not look quite like anything explicitly in Lewis result from this fact. The conclusion I will derive however would have been forthcoming on his procedure as well.

26. "I take states to be attributes of a special kind: attributes of things at times" ([14], p. 165). When Lewis says that 'pain' refers to a state he does not of course mean that it refers to what might be called a *state-token*, that is, an individual inner occurrence (an occurrence of the type that the organism feels when it 'feels pain'). Nor does he mean what might be called a *state type*: a sortal property of such inner occurrences, a property that might be expressed by the predicate 'is a pain'. Rather, pain is taken to be an attribute *of organisms*, the attribute that is expressed by 'feels pain' (cf. [14], footnote 1). I think myself that the word 'state' is best reserved for what I've called state-tokens and state-types; for Lewis' use of the term helps foster a confusion between states in his sense and state-types in mine, and this can lead to a disastrous confusion to be noted later in this section. (Lewis himself does not fall into the confusion, as footnote 13 of [17] shows, but I think his terminology has led others to make it.)

27. Strictly speaking, it might be better to leave out the word 'physical' here: that way if materialism is only *contingently* true, then we can allow organisms in those possible worlds in which *H* is realized by irreducibly mental properties to have functional properties. This change in the definition of functional property would in no way affect the application of functional properties to organisms in those worlds where materialism is true; in particular, it would not affect the application of functional properties in the actual world, if as I am assuming materialism is indeed true. Since my own interest lies wholly in the actual world, my addition of the word 'physical' does no harm.

I chose to put in the word 'physical' partly to remind the reader of the materialist premise, and partly as a convenient way to introduce distinctions of *order*. For the method of defining properties used in (2) to make sense, the functional property being defined cannot be one of the properties in the range of property-quantifier. If we use the notion of 'physical property' narrowly, so that functional properties like those defined in (2) do not themselves count as physical, then this condition is met. On this narrow use of the term physical, the materialist thesis is that all non-functional properties are physical.

28. The uniqueness requirement is Lewis'. I think that it must be taken with a grain of salt, but I do not have the space here to explain my reservations or to develop the machinery needed to avoid it. (The word 'unique' in (2) cannot merely be dropped.)

29. According to Lewis, 'the property of being in pain' and 'pain' refer to different properties: 'the property of being in pain' refers to a functional property, and 'pain' refers (in the context of discussing a specific organism X at a specific time t) to the non-functional property which realizes the functional property in X at t. I have tried to remain neutral on the question of whether 'pain' refers to the functional property or refers (in a context-dependent way) to a realization of it.

30. This is not intended as an argument against using a notion of *believing that* which relates people to propositions, but only as an argument against using a notion which relates people to English sentences (or to utterances of English sentences). A theory involving propositions is exempt from the criticism, since if there are propositions at all then presumably there are propositions not expressible in English. (However, even if 'believes that' relates people to propositions, it is not clear that sentences attributing *particular* beliefs to organisms very unlike us could ever be literally true.)

31. Some people may feel that there is no ontological gain in quantifying over properties rather than over propositions. Such a person should read Putnam [20]. Putnam makes a good case (a) that quantification over properties is needed in science, and (b) that properties are quite distinct from meanings, in that two predicates like 'x has temperature 210° C' and 'x has mean molecular energy 10^{-20} joules' can turn out to stand for the same property even though they clearly differ in meaning.

32. I have allowed this by allowing for the possibility that the sentences which are believed be genuine sentences in a genuine language, rather than sentence-analogs.

33. Where neutrality of formulation is difficult to achieve without verbosity, I have frequently sacrificed the neutrality; but even in these cases it is not difficult to rephrase what I say so as to accord with the position that I am temporarily excluding.

34. This assumes that the syntactic theory is formulated in such a way that all syntactic predicates are predicates of tokens. To assume this is not to assume that the syntax can be given nominalistically, i.e., without quantifying over abstract entities like sets, or even like sequences which can be intuitively regarded as having more or less the role of expression-types. Once this is realized, the task of formulating the syntactic theory in the way required presents no difficulty.

Incidentally, I should remark that the syntactic theory can be formulated in such a way as to allow wide diversity in the grammars of the systems of representation of organisms to which the theory is intended to apply. (One way in which it might do this is to postulate a general system of syntactic categories. Different sub-sets of this general system could be instantiated in different organisms to which the theory applies, and in this way a wide syntactic diversity in systems of representation would be compatible with the general theory. See Lewis [16] for an illustration of the kind of general syntax I have in mind.)

35. Incidentally, R could perfectly well be a disjunctive relation, say of the form 'Either x and y are both occurrences in the left hemisphere of the brain and x bears R_1 to y, or x and y are both occurrences in the right hemisphere and x bears R_2 to y, or one is an occurrence in the left and the other in the right and the one in the left bears R_3 to the one in the right'. Disjunctive realizations are needed for other functional theories — e.g., it is perfectly possible that pain is realized in a given organism at a given time by a disjunctive property like 'is a stimulation of the C-fibers or a firing of the X-neurons' — and there is no reason to rule out the same flexibility in the theory of belief and desire. I make this point because I think that a main reason why many philosophers resist the inner representation hypothesis is that they tend to exaggerate its neurophysiological commitments.

35a. This only defines what it is for two tokens *in the same organism* to be of the same type; but the notion of type-identity between tokens in one organism and tokens in the other is not needed for psychological theory, and can be regarded as a meaningless notion.

36. I will elaborate on this point in the next section.

37. The proposed 'law' involving ' $\rightarrow$ ' is of course *exceptionally* crude: to get anything that looks at all plausible, one probably has to bring in something like *degrees* of belief and *degrees* of desirability. But the point I am making is unaffected: the degrees of belief and degrees of desirability can be regarded as attaching to sentences, and laws can be given relating the degrees of belief and desirability of a sentence of the form $\#S_1 \rightarrow S_2\#$ to the degrees of belief and desirability of the component sentences S_1 and S_2 and of other compound sentences containing S_1 and S_2. (E.g., if B is degree of belief, one law might be that

$B(S_1 \rightarrow S_2)$ is greater than or equal to max $[B(S_2), 1 - B(S_1)])$.

At no point do the meanings of the component sentences or of the logical connectives need to be mentioned.

38. I think that there is some question as to whether the notion of translation, used in the very loose and pragmatic way just explained, ought to count as a genuinely semantic notion; hence the 'more or less'.

39. Cf. Quine [23], p. 11.

40. Without a functional account, we can in a sense recognize this: we can let 'refers' stand for a certain physical relation in connection with organisms of one kind (say, organisms that speak some language of a certain general type), and also let 'refers' stand for a different physical relation in connection with organisms of another type; but without a functional account we do not have the means to explain what these two uses of 'refers' have in common. (Similarly for 'true'.)

41. [6].

42. Strictly, this equivalence holds only on the coarse-grained possible worlds approach. But we could imagine that a one-word phrase 'glub' had been introduced into the language by the stipulation that it was to (rigidly) denote the property of mean molecular energy; then 'Temperature is glub' would be equivalent to (13) even on the fine-grained possible worlds approach, but they would clearly be non-synonymous.

43. Whether they are redundant depends on whether one treats evidential considerations in a fine-grained or a coarse-grained manner; see [6], pp. 396-397.

44. Our criteria for inter-speaker but intra-linguistic synonymy are less clear: sometimes we treat this case like the inter-linguistic case, and sometimes we use the common language to extend considerations of intra-speaker synonymy across different speakers.

45. Here I am concerned primarily with the truth-theoretic aspects of meaning. Also, the question I am asking does not really presuppose what the formulation in the text suggests, that a person's system of internal representation is distinct from his public language. If we adopt the opposite presupposition, we can phrase the question as follows: in what ways if any does one need to bring in the fact that a system of internal representation is also used publicly, in giving a complete theory of truth-conditions for the system of internal representation; and in what ways does one need to bring in the fact that a public language is used for thinking, in giving a complete theory of meaning for it.

46. See Schiffer [24]. Lewis' approach in [19] is quite similar. Harman's suggestion in [9] that the "level 2 theory of meaning" presupposes the "level 1 theory of meaning" but not conversely seems to involve a similar idea.

47. It might not defeat it, if as suggested at the end of Section V we give a functional account of reference: for then we could grant that we need to specify the use of the word 'Caesar' in public language in order to specify a *realization* for the reference-relation as applied to the system of internal representation, but hold that we do not need to mention it *in the functional theory itself*. However, it does not seem to me at all *obvious* that we do not need to mention the public use of words in a satisfactory functional theory of truth-conditions for systems of internal representation; it seems to me that no one has developed any such theory in anywhere near enough detail for us to tell. It may well be for instance that a fairly detailed causal account of reference has to be explicitly built into reliability theory (or whatever other kind of broad psychological theory it is in which the notion of reference or of truth-conditions appears), and that such a detailed causal theory will have to explicitly mention acquisition of a public word that refers to something as one of

the mechanisms by which people can become causally related to an object in the way that is relevant to having beliefs about the object.

48. I have greatly benefited from discussion on these issues with David Lewis, Janet Levin, Brian Loar, and Stephen Schiffer. The latter two especially, by their relentless criticism of the way I expressed my ideas in conversation, have forced me to write a very much better paper than I would otherwise have written. I am also grateful to Ned Block, Tyler Burge, Michael Devitt, Keith Donellan, and David Hills for helpful comments on an earlier version.

References

[1] Armstrong, David, *A Materialist Theory of the Mind*. London: Routledge, Kegan, & Paul, 1968.

[2] Chisholm, Roderick, *Perceiving: A Philosophical Study*. Ithaca: Cornell U. Press, 1957.

[3] Davidson, Donald, 'Truth and Meaning', *Synthese* 17 (1967), pp. 304-323.

[4] Dennett, Daniel, 'Brain Writing and Mind Reading', in [8].

[5] Field, Hartry, 'Tarski's Theory of Truth', *Journal of Philosophy* 69 (1972), pp. 347-375.

[6] Field, Hartry, 'Logic, Meaning, and Conceptual Role', *Journal of Philosophy* 74 (1977), pp. 379-409.

[7] Fodor, Jerry, *The Language of Thought*, New York: Crowell, 1975.

[8] Gunderson, Keith, ed., *Language, Mind, and Knowledge*, (Minnesota Studies in the Philosophy of Science, Vol. 7). Minneapolis: U. of Minnesota Press, 1975.

[9] Harman, Gilbert, 'Three Levels of Meaning', *Journal of Philosophy* 65 (1968), pp. 590-602.

[10] Harman, Gilbert, 'Language Learning', *Nous* 4 (1970), pp. 33-43.

[11] Harman, Gilbert, *Thought*. Princeton: Princeton U. Press, 1973.

[12] Harman, Gilbert, 'Language, Thought, and Communication', in [8].

[13] Jech, Thomas, *The Axiom of Choice*. Amsterdam: North-Holland, 1973.

[14] Lewis, David, 'An Argument for the Identity Theory', in David Rosenthal (ed.), *Materialism and the Mind-Body Problem*. Englewood Cliffs: Prentice-Hall, 1971.

[15] Lewis, David, 'How to Define Theoretical Terms', *Journal of Philosophy* 67 (1970), pp. 427-446.

[16] Lewis, David, 'General Semantics', in Donald Davidson and Gilbert Harman (eds.), *Semantics of Natural Language*. Dordrecht: Reidel, 1972.

[17] Lewis, David, 'Psychophysical and Theoretical Identifications', *Australasian Journal of Philosophy* 50 (1972), pp. 249-258.

[18] Lewis, David, 'Radical Interpretation', *Synthese* 23 (1974), pp. 331-334.

[19] Lewis, David, 'Languages and Language', in [8].

[20] Putnam, Hilary, 'On Properties', in Putnam, *Philosophical Papers*, Vol. 1. Cambridge: Cambridge U. Press, 1975.

[21] Quine, Willard, 'The Problem of Meaning in Linguistics', in Quine, *From a Logical Point of View*. New York: Harper & Row, 1963.

[22] Quine, Willard, *Word and Object*. Cambridge: M.I.T. Press, 1960.

[23] Quine, Willard, *Philosophy of Logic*. Englewood Cliffs: Prentice-Hall, 1970.

[24] Schiffer, Stephen, *Meaning*. Oxford: Oxford U. Press, 1972.

[25] Stalnaker, Robert, 'Propositions', in Alfred Mackay and Daniel Merrill (eds.), *Issues in the Philosophy of Language*. New Haven: Yale Press, 1976.

[26] Krantz, Luce, Suppes and Tversky, *Foundations of Measurement*, Vol. 1. New York: Academic Press, 1971.

Postscript

David Lewis has informed me that there are two points on which he feels that I have slightly misrepresented his position. In addition, he has made an interesting suggestion that allows me to clarify and buttress my position on the central point of the paper.

(1) *Concerning Section I*, where I attribute to Lewis the view that the objects of belief are coarse-grained: Lewis informs me that, unlike Stalnaker, he has had no settled opinion as to whether the objects of belief are coarse-grained or fine-grained, and has tried to remain neutral on this issue in his publications.

There is little point in discussing here the considerations that led me to attribute Stalnaker's position to Lewis. (I admit that they were somewhat tenuous.) What is important, rather, is (i) that if Lewis were to resolve his neutrality by *accepting* Stalnaker's position, he would be stuck with the view that to believe set theory is to believe all of its consequences; thereby making it difficult or impossible to explain the behavior of mathematicians who try to prove results which later turn out to be refutable. And (ii) if Lewis were to resolve his neutrality by *rejecting* Stalnaker's position, then the argument for accepting an internal system of representation in order to solve Brentano's problem would be *reinforced:* since a fine-grained proposition has the structure of a specific sentence coded right into it, it is all the harder to see how one could believe such a proposition without believing* some sentence that means it.

(2) *Concerning Section II,* where I attribute to Lewis the view that the hypothesis of inner representation is unfounded: Lewis informs me that he thinks that the hypothesis of inner representation is plausible and fairly well founded; but no *so* well founded that he wants to presuppose it in doing philosophy. (He compares it to the axiom of choice: it's plausible, but it's better to do without it when one can.)

I sympathize with the idea of being cautious about such matters. To some extent, my position in the paper *is* cautious: for, as explained in Section IV, I interpret the hypothesis of inner representation functionalistically, and this reduces the degree to which I commit myself to neurophysiological assumptions. But the functionalist interpretation does not completely free us from neurophysiological commitment, so wouldn't it be better to do without the inner representation hypothesis altogether?

My reply is that caution is good, but that we have a choice as to which of two questions to leave open in doing philosophy: the question of a system of representation, and the question of the existence of propositions. We can't leave *both* questions open, because we need to invoke *either* propositions *or* internal representations in our account of belief, so as to make belief relational (and to avoid the anomalies discussed in the text which arise when we relate belief only to sentences in a language that the believer doesn't understand). Given this choice, I choose internal representations, for I believe the arguments for their existence are more compelling than arguments for the existence of propositions.

(3) *Concerning Brentano's problem:* Lewis has suggested comparing Brentano's problem to the following problem about numbers: "Many seemingly physical properties appear to relate physical things to non-physical entities called *numbers.* What kind of physical relation can a seven-gram stone bear to a non-physical abstract entity: the number seven?"

One solution to this problem is the nominalistic one: there are no numbers, and so there are no relations between physical entities and numbers. Let us put this solution aside (though it is more or less analogous to what I in fact believe about Brentano's problem, viz., that there are no propositions). Nominalism aside, there are two lines which one could take to the numerical analog of Brentano's problem. Let us see what light they shed on Brentano's problem itself.

The first line, which I don't like but which seems to be currently popular, is that various relations between physical objects and numbers — e.g., the mass relation — are used in axiomatizing physics, and this makes them "physical relations" in the only intelligible sense that can be given to that phrase. On this first line, then, the numerical analog of Brentano's problem is trivial. Could Brentano's problem likewise be trivialized? No: for no relation between people (or other physical objects) and *propositions* is used in the underlying physics, so there is no way to regard *such* a relation as *trivially* physical. (Relations between certain organisms and propositions may be used in *psychology*; but *no one* could think that the occurrence of a property or relation in *psychology* makes that property or relation physical: if *that* view were right there could be no mind-body problem.) The upshot is that even if the trivial "solution" to the numerical analog of Brentano's problem is adequate, which I very much doubt, still it would shed no light on Brentano's problem itself.

A much more interesting solution to the numerical analog of Brentano's problem is available. This second solution relies on results in the theory of measurement. The theory of measurement (see for instance [26]) explains why real numbers can be used to "measure" mass (better: to serve as a scale for mass). It does this in the following way. First, certain properties and relations among massive objects are cited—properties and relations that are specifiable without reference to numbers. Then a representation theorem is proved: such a theorem says that if any system of objects has the properties and relations cited, then there is a mapping of that system into the real numbers which "preserves structure." Consequently, assigning real numbers to the objects is a convenient way of discussing the intrinsic mass-relations that those objects have, but those intrinsic relations don't themselves require the existence of real numbers. The numerical analog of Brentano's problem is then solved: this

massive object bears to the number seven the relation of being mapped into that number by the unique structure-preserving mapping that accords with the convention laid down to determine the scale (i.e., the convention that determines the standard gram).

Can we solve Brentano's problem itself in an analogous way? To do so we would have to postulate a system of entities inside the believer which was related via a structure-preserving mapping to the system of propositions. The "structure" that such a mapping would have to preserve would be the kind of structure important to propositions: viz., logical structure. So the system of entities inside the believer would have to have logical structure, and this I think means that the system of entities inside the believer can be viewed as a system of sentences—an internal system of representation. In other words, I think it can be shown (at least if propositions are taken to be fine-grained, as I've argued they should be) that any system of entities that satisfies the condition of being related to the system of propositions via a structure-preserving map *is* a system of internal representation, according to the kind of functional definition of 'system of internal representation' suggested in Section IV. Consequently, the second line of solution to the numerical analog of Brentano's problem suggests precisely the kind of solution to Brentano's problem that was offered in Section I of the paper, before propositions were eliminated. (This may have been the point that Lewis had in mind in suggesting the comparison.)

Part Two

Imagery

Introduction: What Are Mental Images?

Georges Rey

Few issues in the philosophy of psychology are more entwined at one and the same time with abstract difficulties in philosophy and experimental details in psychology than the problem of so-called mental images. At first glance, the problem seems straightforward enough: most of us report having experiences that we are strongly inclined to describe as of "images." These range from outright hallucinations, to (for some people) "eidetic" images,[1] to dreams, to "afterimages," to "what we see with the mind's eye" when we "form an image of" (or *image*)[2] something, to what some people claim to see when they merely imagine something. Ignoring, for the moment, the very real and important differences among these cases, and looking only to the classification of a certain sort of *experience*, let us refer to experiences of this sort as "image-experiences."

Such experiences can be quite intense, a source of pleasure or pain, and some people claim that they can play a useful role in the solution of a great variety of problems, from puzzles about spatial arrangement to less pedestrian matters of conceptual relations, mathematical models, plans, strategies. It seems to help to "picture" things. And so it seems natural to suppose that there are at such times *pictures* that are being so pictured or, at any rate, some sorts of objects of these experiences, namely, the very *mental images* the experiences seem to be experiences of. But if there are such objects, what in the world might they be? Are they *physical* objects, or patterns of physical objects, like the images formed on an oscilloscope or a television screen? Or are they special, "private" objects, flitting about in the mysterious medium of the mind, necessarily observable only from "within"? (Here we are brought back to issues discussed in "Reductionism and Physicalism," volume 1, part two of this anthology.) And, if they do exist, do they really play a role in our reasoning? Or are they mere "epiphenomena," enlivening our experience, but playing, by themselves, no significant causal or computational role? (Here we continue to address the issues raised in part one of this volume, "Mental Representation," for the interesting question arises whether the representations over which our mental computations are defined include images, or whether they are, as the representations in all existing computer languages seem to be, entirely discursive or "propositional," that is, nonimagistic.)

Until recently, these questions were by and large confined to philosophical speculation. Chapter 6, by Daniel C. Dennett, represents some of the most developed results of that speculation, pursuing an argument for the unreality of mental images that grows out of the philosophical psychology of the last twenty-five years, the tradition (roughly) of Ludwig Wittgenstein and Gilbert Ryle. But, since the late 1960s, considerable experimental work in cognitive psychology — in particular, the elegant work of R. N. Shepard and his colleagues — has added a new dimension to the problem, presenting experimental data that can seem to preempt the previous philosophical speculation. This work is nicely summarized and supplemented by Stephen M. Kosslyn and James R. Pomerantz (chapter 8). The two remaining chapters, by Jerry A. Fodor (chapter 7) and Zenon W. Pylyshyn (chapter 9), taking what seem to be opposed views, represent welcome efforts to bring the philosophical and psychological discussions together.

But, as with many philosophical issues, these differences in perspective can lead one to wonder whether there is really just one straightforward problem being discussed. As things presently stand, a good part of the problem of mental images consists in saying specifically just what the problem really is, over the solution to which the different disputants can rightly be regarded to be disputing. What, for instance, distinguishes imagistic from nonimagistic representation? What sorts of evidence and argument are even relevant to establishing the reality of mental imagery; what sorts to establishing their utility? In the remainder of this introduction, an effort will be made to sort out the different problems with which the different writers below sometimes seem concerned, and to determine precisely at which points, if any, their different claims actually conflict.

We might gain some footing on the topic by discussing first not *mental* images, but what might be called *ordinary* images: reflections, photographs, television displays, retinal images, "realistic" paintings, maps, charts, diagrams. By virtue of what sorts of features of these diverse things are we inclined to classify them all, roughly, as "images"? What are the "rules of images in general," to which the writers here (for example, Dennett, chapter 6, and Fodor, chapter 7) are wont to advert?

Ordinary visual images presumably have something peculiarly to do with the visual system, and, in particular, with the properties to which that system is characteristically sensitive.[3] The central property here is that associated with light (and/or color). But, at least for human beings, other properties that are reliably indicated by light also seem to count importantly as visual properties. These are especially the *spatial* properties: length, width, depth, proportion, composition, and orientation of parts (what is part of what; what is right, left, above, below what). It seems to be a fairly unalterable fact about visual experience — in sharp contrast to experiences in most of the other modalities — that it almost always involves experiences *as if* of objects in at least *some* space. "Light patches," unlike odors or sounds, for instance, seem to be just that: like *patches*, having at least relative length and width. We seem decidedly unable to abstract away from these particular properties at least in the visual case. At any rate, all ordinary visual images seem to be forms or patterns that possess at least *some* spatial properties (see Dennett, chapter 6; Kosslyn and Pomerantz, chapter 8).

Something is an ordinary visual image usually by virtue of being an image *of* something. This "of" relation, however, can be quite diverse: an image can be *of* the thing(s) it resembles, or *of* the thing(s) that played a certain role in its production, or *of* the thing(s) that it is used to represent; and these things may be the same or different in different cases. For the purposes of the discussions below, however, we can restrict our attention to the "of" relation that is involved in *depiction:* the relation between an image and the spatiotemporal (token or type of) particular it purports to represent. Let us call the images that depict some object *X* the *X-depicting* images. Thus, Edward Steichen's photograph of Greta Garbo is a Garbo-depicting image.[4]

An *X*-depicting image is a particular kind of *representation* (see part one, "Mental Representation"). It seems to be a representation in which not only it, but also some of its visual properties, play representational roles: not only does the *X*-depicting image represent (an) *X*, but some of its visual properties represent some properties of (an) *X*. Moreover, these further representational roles are fulfilled through the exploitation of certain systematic correspondences between these properties of the *X*-depicting image and the properties of (an) *X* they represent. Thus the Garbo photograph depicts Garbo by virtue of certain visual properties of *it* (such as the arch of the eyebrow line) corresponding to and representing properties of Garbo herself (such as the arch of her actual brow); and a map of Topeka depicts Topeka by virtue of certain visual properties of *it* (such as the length of street lines) corresponding to and representing properties of Topeka (such as the lengths of actual streets). The correspondence is systematic in that it is lawlike, supporting a certain range of inferences and counterfactuals: under normal circumstances, and within certain limits, *were* Garbo's actual brow more arched, the imaged brow *would* be proportionally more arched; *were* the streets of Topeka longer, the lines representing them on the map *would* be proportionally longer. Indeed, on the basis of these correspondences, many properties of Garbo

and Topeka can be inferred from visual properties of the photo and the map: it is in just this way that the map serves to get us about. Let us call this use of a representation's properties to represent by virtue of such systematic correspondences *compositional exploitation:* an *X*-depicting image compositionally exploits some of its visual properties as representations of properties of (an) *X*.

This is a little rough. Qualifications need to be made for the conventionalities involved in our ordinary viewing of objects, typicalities involved in our typing of them, our tolerance of various sorts of distortion, our occasional granting of painterly license. But we need not lose ourselves in these intricacies here. It suffices for present purposes merely to notice that it is some such condition of compositional exploitation that would seem to be needed to distinguish imagistic from nonimagistic representation. Surely at least *one* visual property of a representation would have to be so exploited for it to count as *X-depicting,* and not merely as *X-denoting* or *X-describing.* No matter what Fodor may say about his (standard) inscriptions of 'tiger', none of them count as *depictions* of a *tiger.* They might serve as depictions of the word 'tiger' (be, that is, 'tiger'-depicting); or they might become *tiger*-depicting were a convention to evolve whereby, for instance, concrete nouns were to be colored the color of their referents. But, as things stand, words are generally not any sort of image of their referents; and that is because generally none of their visual properties systematically corresponds to and represents properties of those referents. We cannot infer any properties of tigers from visual properties of 'tiger's. Were tigers generally taller than they were long, or wider than they were short, had they three heads, seven tails, or forty-four legs, none of Fodor's inscriptions of 'tiger', but surely some of his images of tigers, would change. As it is, for all their distortion and poverty of detail, Fodor's stick figures do capture some distinctions between head and leg, for example, and do preserve the general continuities between the depicted parts.

If compositional exploitation is what distinguishes imagistic from nonimagistic representation, however, we are confronted with a number of problems in applying this criterion to the purported images of the mental sort. Chief among these is the fact that it is not at all obvious that mental images can literally be said to have any visual properties whatsoever, much less compositionally exploit them. They do not seem, themselves, to be produced by actual light, and so cannot be colored in anything like the way in which ordinary visual images—and for that matter most ordinary objects—are colored. And they do not seem to occupy ordinary space; or, at any rate, it is quite obscure how we are to go about relating these purported objects to other objects in ordinary space in anything like the way objects in ordinary space are related to one another. It is not even clear just what visual properties mental images even *seem* to have, in and of themselves: as Dennett points out, most mental images of tigers do not clearly have a determinate number of stripes; and it is not obvious that this is always due to the possible effects of blurriness, or to the rapidity with which the image passes before one's mind (see Fodor, chapter 7). The particular sort of indeterminacy seems, as an indeterminacy about images, rather unique.

It is essential to distinguish here, in a way that some of the discussions below do not (for example, Fodor, chapter 7; Pylyshyn, chapter 9), between the determinacy of certain properties as properties of the image *itself* and the determinacy of the *compositional exploitation* of those properties as representations of properties of the depicted object.[5] A tiger-depicting image may (and perhaps must) have a determinate number of stripes; but this does not imply that that number of stripes of the image represents anything whatsoever about tigers or any particular tiger. Which properties of an image must be exploited is an issue it seems reasonable to settle, as do both Dennett and Fodor, with utmost leniency: there need be but a single compositionally exploited property. But what properties an image must have, as an object by itself, is another matter, and remains puzzling. On the one hand, mental images seem to be presented to us in at least two dimensions—it seems impossible to abstract even to just one—and yet, on the other hand, they do not seem to be entirely determinate in those two dimensions.

By way of accommodation of some of these and other problems, there have been two main sorts of stances regarding the ontological status of mental images, dualist and straightforwardly physicalist. The first allows that there are special *mental* objects, distinct from any physical ones, that have special "phenomenal" properties and exist in a special "phenomenal" space. Mental images are just a species of these inner objects, satisfying in this way "phenomenal" analogs of the conditions on ordinary images.

This particular traditional stance has its traditional problems. Just what space is this mental space? Are there n (different?) spaces for each of the n people who have ever and will have ever existed? Are there laws for this space (or those spaces)? Are they Euclidean, Riemannian, or Lobachevskian? Or do they comprise some and yet uncharted space(s)? Can objects in these spaces causally interact with one another, and/or with objects in ordinary space? How must neurophysiology and the causal theory of perception be modified to account for them? How are we even to begin to answer these questions in our own, much less in our neighbor's case? These problems may not be insurmountable, a priori, as some philosophers may have sometimes supposed, but any defender of this view must be prepared to deal with them.

The straightforwardly physicalist stance simply bites the bullet and identifies mental images with configurations in our brains. They consequently enjoy precisely the same three full dimensions in ordinary space, and all the other determinate properties ordinarily accorded such configurations. We are simply, for the most part, woefully ignorant of most of these properties — in particular, perhaps, of exactly how many stripes the tiger-depicting image has — mostly owing to the peculiar, rather restricted access we have to them introspectively.

But there are traditional problems with this traditional stance as well. Mainly, they center around the difficulties presented to any such view by "Leibniz's Law": if two things are identical, then all the properties of the one are properties of the other and vice versa. If, in particular, mental images are identical to physical configurations, then all the properties of a mental image are properties of a physical configuration and vice versa. Plausibly, the oddness of attributing properties of the physical — say, electrical resistance, or contiguity with the hypothalamus — to the mental could be explained by our ignorance, and by whatever sympathy we may hae for one another form of dualism. But attributing properties of the mental to the physical is rather more problematic. Is the physical configuration really as brilliantly colored as the mental image? Are its parts contiguous in the ways the parts of the mental image seem to be? Does it really waver, flit by, grow larger and smaller as introspection suggests? Or its introspection just dead wrong about all this?

Moreover, just where in the brain might such spectacular configurations be displayed? To be sure, there are *retinal* images. But they could not be what any believer in imagery has in mind, since it is precisely for those image-experiences in which there is no retinal image that mental images are conjured up. Perhaps the images are elsewhere in the brain. If they are, there is, as yet, scant evidence of them (although interested readers may wish to pursue here the "holographic" suggestions recently advanced by Karl Pribram).[6]

Even if there are these images displayed somewhere in the brain, intact with all their introspectable properties, a deeper and darker question arises as to how they come to be "perceived." In this connection, the tempting analogy with images on an oscilloscope or on a television screen (Kosslyn and Pomerantz, chapter 8) can be misleading. These are images that are accessed by the *human eye looking* at the screen of the machine. But surely there is no further human eye located in the recesses of the brain! (And even if there were, surely this regress to eyes within eyes would have to end somewhere; at which point we would still be left with the question as to how the images available to the innermost eye are accessed.) There may be images somewhere in the brain, for God or for the poking neurosurgeon; but unless they are integrated into our cognition, they are not there for us.

For these and other reasons, all of the writers represented in this part tend (at least when they are explicit on the matter) to disavow what they call the "picture in the head" hypothesis. Even defenders of the reality of mental imagery, like Kosslyn and Pomerantz, claim that they are not interested in positing any sort of ordinary image either in the brain or "in the mind" (see chapter 8). It is not easy to discern just what alternative hypothesis they are proposing. There may be no single one. But it is worth setting out and distinguishing several that are plausible.

As I have just noted, what I have called the compositional exploitation of visual properties occurs ordinarily in relation to the human eye: it is by use of the eye that these properties, as they might appear, for example, on a television screen, are accessed and their compositional exploitation appreciated. This is not surprising, since this is how the visual properties are identified in the first place. Yet these very same properties could conceivably be accessed, and so exploited, in other ways. And the notion of an ordinary visual image could therefore be extended (as in many of the discussions below it seems implicitly to have been) to include these other ways.

The main alternative means of access most writers have in mind are the various means that might be employed in modern computational machinery. Thus a machine might be constructed that computed geographic distances by employing an internal gridlike display, calculating, for instance, the distance between towns as a function of the length of the shortest line on the grid connecting the dots that represent them (see chapter 8). Such a machine, at any rate, would certainly seem to be computing in a fashion quite distinct from one that simply computed the distance from numerical representations of the towns' locations. It would seem reasonable to regard at least part of this computer's system of representation (in this case, of locations and distances) as imagistic. Yet, of course, no actual *eye* might be employed, or even employable, in accessing the nonetheless compositionally exploited visual property (in this case, the length of the line). Let us call images accessed in this way *functional* images, as opposed to the *eye-accessible* images with which we have so far been concerned.

Several points bear emphasizing with regard to functional images. First of all, contrary to a great deal that has been written on the subject (see Kosslyn and Pomerantz, chapter 8; Pylyshyn, chapter 9),[7] the presence of a functional image in a machine does not by itself render that machine *analog*. Although a clear characterization of the distinction between digital and analog processes is still wanting, it seems easy to think of clear examples that cut across the distinction between the imagistic and nonimagistic. The above-mentioned distance-computer, for example, could well determine the length of the connecting line by counting the number of grid spaces the line traverses: presumably a discrete and therefore digital process. (Similarly, most newspaper photographs and Times Square light-bulb displays are entirely digitalized, eye-accessible images.) Conversely, an analog representation might be entirely nonimagistic: distances might be represented by continuous, and so presumably analog, variations in the voltage of an electric current; surely not a *visual* property (nor one of any other sensory modality either). A discussion of whether human mental processes are digital or analog is perhaps an interesting and important discussion for the philosophy of psychology; but it is not one that is central to a discussion of mental imagery.

It is also important to emphasize what we have already had occasion to notice, that not all images produced in or on a machine are therefore functional images. The image, to be functional for a machine, must have its visual properties accessed and exploited by the machine as part of the *machine*'s computations. Thus neither the wavelike image on the oscilloscope, nor the Garbo-like image on the television screen, is functional for the respective machines. They are entirely eye-accessible images, produced for the computational or other interests of their human *observers*. So far as the functioning of these machines is concerned, such images are mere "epiphenomena."

One last, almost definitional, but still sometimes surprising point: a functional image need not look or be arranged in a manner anything like an eye-accessible one. In particular, a functional *X*-depicting image need not be in the least eyeaccessibly X-depicting. Consider again the distance-computer: *we* need not be able to look inside and see a maplike display, or be able to compute the distance between the towns as a function of anything *we* can see. The grid spaces may not be physically contiguous, but interrupted by other bits of the machinery, even by other "irrelevant" grid spaces. Perhaps the relevant spaces are scattered far and wide about the machine! All that need obtain is that the machine, itself, access and compositionally exploit the spaces *as if* they were contiguous, that what we have identified as visual properties be accessed and exploited by the machine in its way, as we access and exploit them in ours. (Similarly, contrary to what Pylyshyn seems at one point to assume, the kinds of problems associated with a functional image may be quite different from those associated with an eye-accessible one: because of the very different means of access, there may be nothing about a functional image that corresponds to a photograph's being *blurred* or *torn* or, returning to Dennett's objection, having a determinate number of stripes.)

The proposal that there are functional images in the brain would seem to be an entirely live empirical hypothesis. It may be extremely difficult to sort out the evidence for and against such a hypothesis (and who said psychology was easy?), but it is by no means impossible. What is wanted is evidence—perhaps in terms of the times processes take, the relative difficulty of different tasks—that, in the processing of certain representations in the brain,[8] visual properties of those representations are accessed and compositionally exploited in something like the way, for example, the distance-computer accessed and exploited the length of the line on its grid. Much of the discussion by Kosslyn and Pomerantz and by Pylyshyn can be regarded as addressed to this issue. Especially in the light of Shepard's striking results, in which,

among other things, the response time for re-identification of rotated patterns is shown to be directly proportional to the angle of rotation of the pattern (see chapters 8 and 9), the hypothesis can be a very tempting one. Roughly, in the chapters below, Fodor, and Kosslyn and Pomerantz yield to this temptation, while Dennett and Pylyshyn try to find ways to resist it.

It is very important, however, to distinguish this hypothesis of functional imagery from a quite different, and much weaker, hypothesis that would also explain a great deal of both the experimental and the introspective data. This might be called the hypothesis of *quasi-perception:* the processes that underlie image-experiences are significantly like the processes that underlie actual perceptual experiences.[9] For example, whatever way in which data are presented to the nervous system for evaluation in the case of actual visual perception might be *mimicked* in the cases of image-experiences (see chapter 9). But then image-experiences would involve an actual image only if actual perceptual experiences did. And this latter hypothesis is by no means obviously true. It is true that there is, again, the retinal image; but it also seems to be true that that image is immediately *encoded* into electrical impulses along the optic nerve. That these impulses themselves form an image, or that an image is later reconstructed from them, are hypotheses, themselves, that have yet to be supported. They are certainly possibly false. In that case, image-experiences could be quasi-perceptual events, and there might be no mental images, functional or otherwise, at all! Kosslyn and Pomerantz actually claim at one point that it is only such a hypothesis of quasi-perception that they are seriously interested in defending. And it would seem to be the most reasonable hypothesis that most of Fodor's arguments could be taken to defend. Indeed, the results on "interference" and image-object comparisons (see chapter 7), as well as dreams, hallucinations, eideticism, and even the most vivid, introspected experiences, could much more economically be explained by appeal to quasi-perception than by functional imagery (see chapter 6).

But even if there are functional images, as at least the Shepard data do seem to suggest, still one might balk at *identifying* them with the seeming objects of image-experiences (to allow for the possible distinction of these latter purported objects, let us call them *phenomenal* images). There remain, after all, the problems with Leibniz's Law. Either the functional image has the visual properties claimed by introspection (for instance, contiguity of parts), in which case we are in the same position we were in with regard to the straightforward physicalist; or, more plausibly, its properties are merely such that it may be accessed by the brain *as if* it had those visual properties. However, something's having properties such that it may be accessed *as if* it had certain visual properties can be quite a different matter from its actually having those very visual properties themselves (consider the distance-computer with its "relevant" grid spaces scattered far and wide about the machine). In which case, we are in a worse position than we were with the straightforward physicalist, for now it would seem to be admitted from the start that the functional image might very well *not* have the properties of the phenomenal image, and so might very well not be identical to it. Perhaps there is a more sophisticated story on which the functional image does have the properties of the phenomenal, or on which the phenomenal does not in fact have the properties it seems to have. The burden rests on the defender of the identification to provide such a story. There is, of course, little doubt that, if functional images are being accessed when phenomenal images are being experienced, then the

properties of the phenomenal could likely be *explained* by properties of the functional. But *explanation* is one thing, *identification* quite another. Speakers of English there are who would feel such an identification would visit too great violence upon our ordinary ways of talk.

It can begin to seem as though every possible stance with regard to the ontology of at least phenomenal images raises greater problems than it settles. Is no position plausible? Well, there is the view, defended here both by Dennett and by Pylyshyn, that would dispense with such things as phenomenal images altogether. This view can sometimes seem outrageous — like "flying in the face of the data" — not to say barbarously behaviorist. But it need not be so, with sufficient attention to qualifying phrases.

We have, in general, abundant reason to know that people are frequently disposed to report on the (supposed) existence of things that we can also have abundant reason to know do not really exist. Thus people can report seeming to see apparitions over lagoons, ghosts in their attics, magnificent ranges of mountains over Arctic ice, demons, or just puddles of water on the hot road ahead. In some of these cases, there may be genuine objects (such as concentrations of mist or old clothes) that these people may be said, in some important sense, to be perceiving. But in others — for instance, in the case of closed-eyed hallucination of a demon — there may be *nothing* they are, in any sense, perceiving at all.[10] They just *think* there is something they are perceiving. But from the fact that someone *thinks* there is something she is perceiving, it does not follow that *there really is* something she is perceiving — any more than it follows from the fact that people hope for a Hereafter that there really is a Hereafter for which people hope. You can, after all, fool some of the people some of the time.

This is all a matter of what philosophers have called "logical form"; a matter in particular of which sentences to regard as genuinely existential (seriously asserting "there is" or "there really are"). And, at least since 1905,[11] those philosophers have been reminding us that a sentence in natural language does not always wear its logical form on its sleeve. We have to look past the "clothes," or surface form of words, to the *work* the sentence does, particularly to the inferential role it plays — which inferences need to be drawn, which can without loss be resisted — in our reasonable theories about the world. It is, for example, because our present reasonable theories by and large need to advert to material objects that we need to take seriously the existential claims concerning them. And it is because no reasonable theories advert to ghosts, demons, or the Hereafter that we need to resist inferences to them from statements of merely peoples' belief in them.

What, then, of the purported objects of image-experiences? By virtue of what reasonable theories about the world do we need to take them seriously? The theories needed to account for psychological *functioning*, as evidenced, for example, in Kosslyn and Pomerantz's chapter, can (and, I have argued, must) make do with *functional* images, if with any images at all. Perhaps the phenomenal image is identical with the functional one. But, perhaps in view of some of the problems already noticed, it is not. If it is not, then the only remaining evidence for the existence of phenomenal images is the image-experiences themselves, and the reports people are inclined to make of them. These, too, want explaining. Image-experiences and their reports *could*, however, be explained without positing images that are experienced or reported, just as hallucinations of demons, or hopes for a Hereafter, can be explained without recourse to demons or to a Hereafter. Indeed, just as in these latter cases, the experiences may simply in-

volve an *illusion*, that is, a false, but tempting belief.

There are a number of plausible sources of such an illusion. There is the surface grammatical form of our reports: we are tempted to infer 'There is a phenomenal image I'm experiencing' from 'I'm experiencing a phenomenal image', an inference that reflections on theory and form might lead us to resist. There is the related convenience and vivacity of objectual ways of speaking. There is, in many quarters, a lingering sympathy with one or another form of dualism. Perhaps most important, there is the strong possibility that image-experiences involve what I have called quasi-perceptions, which, for all their resemblance to genuine perceptual experiences, may not involve any image whatsoever. And then there is the interesting, apparently ineluctable, two-dimensional character to our visual experiences. It seems to us not only that there are some kinds of objects before us, but that there is even some sort of space in which they are contained. But this should no more persuade us that there really is such a space with such objects, than should a perspectival painting, with objects suggested at different places in its apparent depth, persuade us that there is any actual space, containing those objects, mysteriously inlaid in the canvas.[12]

On such a view, we would be left merely with the image-experiences and the reports people are inclined to make of them. However, these things, too, might be undermined, and might come in time to be regarded as involving something of an illusion. Perhaps upon more careful (and less philosophical) introspection, we will find that what we have regarded as image-experiences really are quite a motley lot, the differences among them, and between any of them and actual perceptual experiences, seeming far more striking and significant than their superficial similarities. We might even come no longer to make the reports many of us are presently inclined to make, and to revoke the description 'image-experience' from what may, for all that, remain precisely the same sorts of experiences they always were. And we might then come to wonder, as the reader of these and the following pages might, how it was that people ever came to worry about the reality and utility of mental images.[13]

Notes

1. "Eidetic" images are those images that seem to be involved in the phenomenon popularly called "photographic memory," in which a person seems to be able to "read off" features of a remembered visual scene quite as if she were actually perceiving the scene itself. For more discussion, see chapter 6, footnote 1.

2. Following the practice of many writers in this area, we ought to distinguish the activity of *imaging*, that is, deliberately forming an image, from *imagining*, which, in English, may often refer merely to *conceiving*, which may or may not involve imaging. This distinction should be borne in mind in reading many of the passages in this part, particularly, for example, Dennett's claim that one "cannot imagine the inside and outside of a barn at the same time."

3. Sensory images may, of course, arise in any of the sensory modalities. But problems about images seem to arise mainly in the visual case (see Dennett, chapter 6). For this reason, and reasons of space, the discussions here are confined to mental images of the visual sort.

4. Similarly, we might also speak of the X-like, the X-produced, and the more general X-representing. Notice that all these classifications may diverge: a Melvin Laird-produced image may be missile-like, man-depicting, and imperialism-representing. For further discussion of some of these distinctions—as well as of problems about images of nonexistent things, which do not bear upon the present discussion—see Nelson Goodman, *Languages of Art* (Indianapolis: Hackett, 1968), pp. 21-31.

5. I am indebted here to Josef Stern.

6. Karl Pribram, *Languages of the Brain* (Englewood Cliffs, N.J.: Prentice-Hall, 1971).

7. Goodman attempts to rest the distinction between the imagistic and nonimagistic almost entirely upon a distinction between analog and digital representations, peculiarly scorning any appeal to any sort of compositional exploitation at all. See *Languages of Art*, pp. 160, 226.

8. Notice that, as in the distance-computer, it is only *certain* representations that might be imagistic. All of the writers in this part seem to agree that an *entirely* imagistic, but still *representational*, system is impossible. This point is generally credited to Ludwig Wittgenstein—see *Philosophical Investigations* (New York: Macmillan, 1953), pp. 54-55 and scattered remarks in pp. 193-229—although, as Fodor points out, it can probably be traced back to Bishop Berkeley.

9. This hypothesis is quite like the "topic neutral descriptions" proposed by J. J. C. Smart, in his "Sensations and Brain Processes" (*Philosophical Review* 68 [1959]:141-156), to account for the meanings of reports of afterimages. I am not advancing it as any such account. Moreover, as Ned Block has pointed out to me, the hypothesis is quite independent of those reports: it may seem to people that image-experiences are quite like actual perceptual ones, but there may still be all the difference in the world between the processes responsible for them; and, conversely, the processes could be extremely similar, and yet the experiences seem very different.

10. Richard Rorty, in his defense of a view similar to that being presented here, encumbers his argument by failing to allow for this possibility. See "Mind-Body Identity, Privacy, and Categories," *Review of Metaphysics* 19, no. 1 (September 1965):24-54.

11. The tradition begins with Bertrand Russell's famous "On Denoting" (*Mind*, 1905) and continues through most of the work of the analysts, the positivists, Wittgenstein, W. V. Quine, and their followers. Discussions relevant to the present point may be found especially in Wittgenstein, *Philosophical Investigations*, pp. 100-103; and in Quine, "On What There Is," in *From a Logical Point of View* (Cambridge, Mass.: Harvard University Press, 1961), and *Word and Object* (Cambridge, Mass.: M.I.T. Press, 1960), chap. 7.

12. Perhaps an even more vivid analogy to the seeming "mental space" of mental images is afforded by the seeming "film space" of films. Indeed, one could imagine a stranger to our culture being taken in by our movies in ways

similar to the ways we sometimes seem to be taken in by our minds. The stranger might first try to enter the film directly (as Buster Keaton dreams he does in *Sherlock Jr.*); failing that, he then might posit a "different space" for the film (and perhaps *n* different spaces for all the *n* different films?); failing that, he might then propose identity theories between the "objects in the film space" and, for instance, complicated sets of particles on the silvered screen; and, finally, failing that as well, he might settle simply for the usual story about projectors, film, screens and darkened rooms, and the illusions created thereby—special objects and spaces be hanged.

13. Some of these latter remarks, in particular, were influenced by discussions with Rogers Albritton. I am grateful also to Ned Block, Amelie Rorty, and Josef Stern for criticisms of earlier drafts.

The Nature of Images and the Introspective Trap

Daniel C. Dennett

The view of awareness or consciousness developed in the last two chapters makes it quite clear that we are not aware (in any sense of the word) of mental *pictures*, and although few philosophers these days will express outright allegiance to the doctrine of mental imagery, these ghostly snapshots have not yet been completely exorcized from current thinking. Introspection is often held to tell us that consciousness is filled with a variety of peculiar objects and qualities that cannot be accounted for by a purely physical theory of mind, and this chapter is devoted to demolishing this view. The imagistic view of consciousness has been in the past a prolific source of confusions, such as the perennial problems of hallucinations, 'perceptual spaces' and colour qualities, to name a few. Once the distinction between the personal and sub-personal level is made clear and mental images are abandoned these problems vanish.

From *Content and Consciousness* (London: Routledge and Kegan Paul, 1969), pp. 132-141. Reprinted by permission of Routledge and Kegan Paul, Humanities Press, and the author. Chapter references are to *Content and Consciousness*. Notes have been renumbered for this edition.

Although the myth of mental imagery is beginning to lose its grip on thinkers in the field, it is still worth a direct examination and critique.[1] I shall restrict the examination to visual perception and mental imagery, since the results obtained there can be applied directly to the other sense modalities. We are less inclined to strike up the little band in the brain for auditory perception than we are to set up the movie screen, so if images can be eliminated, mental noises, smells, feels and tastes will go quietly.

The difficulty with mental images has always been that they are not very much like physical images — paintings and photographs, for example. The concept of a mental image must always be hedged in a variety of ways: mental images are in a different space, do not have dimensions, are subjective, are Intentional, or even, in the end, just quasi-images. Once mental images have been so qualified, in what respects are they *like* physical images at all? Paintings and photographs are our exemplary images, and if mental images are not like them, our use of the word 'image' is systematically misleading, regardless of how well entrenched it is in our ordinary way of speaking.

Let me propose an acid test for images. An image is a *representation* of something, but what sets it aside from other representations is that an image represents something else always in virtue of having at least one quality or characteristic of shape, form or colour in common with what it represents. Images can be in two or three dimensions, can be manufactured or natural, permanent or fleeting, but they must *resemble* what they represent and not merely represent it by playing a role — symbolic, conventional or functional — in some system. Thus an image of an orange need not be orange (e.g., it could be a black-and-white photograph), but something hard, square and black just cannot be an image of something soft, round and white. It might be intended as a *symbol* of something soft, round and white, and — given the temper of contemporary art — might even be labelled a *portrait* of something soft, round and white, but it would not be an image. Now I take the important question about mental images to be: are there elements in perception that represent in virtue of resembling what they represent and hence deserve to be called images?

First let us attack this question from the point of view of a sub-personal account of perception. Consider how images *work*. It is one thing just to be an image — e.g., a reflection in a pool in the wilderness — and another to function as an image, to be taken as an image, to be used as an image. For an image to work as an image there must be a person (or an analogue of a person) to see or observe it, to recognize or ascertain the qualities in virtue of which it is an image of something. Imagine a fool putting a television camera on his car and connecting it to a small receiver under the bonnet so the engine could 'see where it is going'. The madness in this is that although an image has been provided, no provision has been made for anyone or anything analogous to a perceiver to watch the im-

age. This makes it clear that if an image is to function as an element in *perception*, it will have to function as the raw material and not the end product, for if we suppose that the product of the perceptual process is an image, we shall have to design a perceiver-analogue to sit in front of the image and yet another to sit in front of the image which is the end product of perception in the perceiver-analogue and so forth *ad infinitum*. Just as the brain-writing view discussed in Chapter IV required brain-writing readers, so the image view requires image-watchers; both views merely postpone true analysis by positing unanalysed man-analogues as functional parts of men.

In fact the last image in the physical process of perception is the image of stimulation on the retina. The process of afferent analysis begins on the surface of the retina and continues up the optic nerve, so that the exact pattern of stimulation on the retina is 'lost' and replaced with information about characteristics of this pattern and eventually about characteristics of the environment.[2] The particular physiological facts about this neural analysis are not directly relevant to the philosophical problem of images. The nervous system *might* have transmitted the mosaic of stimulation on the retina deep into the brain and then reconstituted the image there, in the manner of television, but in that case the analysis that must occur as the first step in perception would simply be carried out at a deeper anatomical level. Once perceptual analysis has begun there will indeed be elements of the process that can be said to be representations, but only in virtue of being interrelated parts of an essentially arbitrary system (see Chapter IV). The difference between a neural representation of a square and that of a circle will no more be a difference in the shape of the neural things, than the difference between the *words* 'ox' and 'butterfly' is that one is heavier and uglier than the other. The upshot of this is that there is no room in the sub-personal explanation of the perceptual process, whatever its details, for images. Let us turn then to the personal level account of mental imagery to see if it is as compelling, after all, as we often think.

Shorter, in 'Imagination',[3] describes imagining as more like depicting — in words — than like painting a picture. We can, and usually do, imagine things without going into great detail. If I imagine a tall man with a wooden leg I need not also have imagined him as having hair of a certain colour, dressed in any particular clothes, having or not having a hat. If, on the other hand, I were to draw a picture of this man, I would have to go into details. I can make the picture fuzzy, or in silhouette, but unless something positive is drawn in where the hat should be, obscuring that area, the man in the picture must either have a hat on or not. As Shorter points out, my not going into details about hair colour in my imagining does not mean that his hair is coloured 'vague' in my imagining; his hair is simply not 'mentioned' in my imagining at all. This is quite unlike drawing a picture that is deliberately ambiguous, as one can readily see by first imagining a tall man with a wooden leg and then imagining a tall man with a wooden leg who maybe does and maybe does not have blond hair, and comparing the results.

If I write down a description of a person it would be absurd for anyone to say that my description cannot fail to mention whether or not the man is wearing a hat. My description can be as brief and undetailed as I like. Similarly it would be absurd to insist that one's imagining someone must go into the question of his wearing a hat. It is one thing to imagine a man wearing a hat, another to imagine him not wearing a hat, a third to imagine his head so obscured you can't tell, and a fourth to imagine him without going into the matter of headgear at all. Imagining is depictional or descriptional, not pictorial,

and is bound only by this one rule borrowed from the rules governing sight: it must be from a point of view — I cannot imagine the inside and outside of a barn at once.[4]

A moment's reflection should convince us that it is not just imagining, however, that is like description in this way; all 'mental imagery', including seeing and hallucinating, is descriptional. Consider the film version of *War and Peace* and Tolstoy's book; the film version goes into immense detail and in one way cannot possibly be *faithful* to Tolstoy's words, since the 'picture painted' by Tolstoy does not go into the detail the film cannot help but go into (such as the colours of the eyes of each filmed soldier). Yet Tolstoy's descriptions are remarkably vivid. The point of this is that the end product of perception, what we are aware of when we perceive something, is more like the written Tolstoy than the film. The writing analogy has its own pitfalls, as we saw in Chapter IV, but is still a good antidote to the picture analogy. When we perceive something in the environment we are not aware of every fleck of colour all at once, but rather of the highlights of the scene, an edited commentary on the things of interest.

As soon as images are abandoned even from the personal level account of perception in favour of a descriptional view of awareness, a number of perennial philosophical puzzles dissolve. Consider the Tiger and his Stripes. I can dream, imagine or see a striped tiger, but must the tiger I experience have a particular number of stripes? If seeing or imagining is having a mental image, then the image of the tiger *must* — obeying the rules of images in general — reveal a definite number of stripes showing, and one should be able to pin this down with such questions as 'more than ten?', 'less than twenty?'. If, however, seeing or imagining has a descriptional character, the questions need have no definite answer. Unlike a snapshot of a tiger, a description of a tiger need not go into the number of stripes at all; 'numerous stripes' may be all the description says. Of course in the case of actually seeing a tiger, it will often be possible to corner the tiger and count his stripes, but then one is counting real tiger stripes, not stripes on a mental image.[5]

Another familiar puzzle is Wittgenstein's duck-rabbit, the drawing that looks now like a duck, now like a rabbit. What can possibly be the difference between seeing it first one way and then the other? The image (on the paper or the retina) does not change, but there can be more than one description of that image. To be aware$_1$ of it first as a rabbit and then as a duck can be just a matter of the content of the signals crossing the awareness line, and this in turn could depend on some weighting effect occurring in the course of afferent analysis. One says at the personal level 'First I was aware of it *as* a rabbit, and then *as* a duck', but if the question is asked 'What is the difference between the two experiences?', one can only answer at this level by repeating one's original remark. To get to other more enlightening answers to the question one must resort to the sub-personal level, and here the answer will invoke no images beyond the unchanging image on the retina.

Of all the problems that have led philosophers to posit mental imagery, the most tenacious has been the problem of hallucinations, and yet it need hardly be mentioned that there is no problem of hallucinations *unless* one is thinking of awareness imagistically. On the sub-personal level, there can be little doubt that hallucinations are caused by abnormal neuronal discharges. Stimulation by electrode of micro-areas on the visual cortex produces specific and repeatable hallucinations.[6] Having a visual hallucination is then just being aware$_1$ of the content of a non-veridical visual 'report' caused by such a freak discharge. And where is this report, and what space does

it exist in? It is in the brain and exists in the space taken up by whatever event it is that has this non-veridical content, just as my description of hallucinations takes up a certain amount of space on paper. Since spatiality is irrelevant to descriptions, freak descriptions do not require ghostly spaces to exist in.[7]

The one familiar philosophical example that may seem at first to resist the descriptional view of perception and awareness in favour of the imagistic is the distinction, drawn by Descartes, between imagining and conceiving. We can imagine a pentagon or a hexagon, and imagining one of these is introspectively distinguishable from imagining the other, but we cannot imagine a chiliagon (a thousand-sided figure) in a way that is introspectively distinct from imagining a 999-sided figure. We can, however, *conceive* of a chiliagon (without trying to imagine one) and this experience is perfectly distinct from conceiving of a 999-sided figure. From this it might be tempting to argue that whereas conceiving might well be descriptional and not imagistic, imagining must be imagistic, for our inability to imagine a chiliagon is just like our inability to tell a *picture* of a chiliagon from the *picture* of a 999-sided figure. All this shows, however, is that imagining is like *seeing*, not that imagining is like making pictures. In fact, it shows that imagining is *not* like making pictures, for I certainly *can* make a picture of a chiliagon if I have a great deal of patience and very sharp pencils, and when it is done I can tell it from a picture of a 999-sided figure, but this deliberate, constructive activity is unparalleled by anything I can do when I 'frame mental images'. Although I can *put together* elements to make a mental 'image' the result is always bound by a limitation of seeing: I can only imagine what I could see in a glance; differences below the threshold of discrimination of casual observation cannot be represented in

imagination. The distinction between imagining and conceiving is real enough; it is
like the distinction between seeing and
listening to someone. Conceiving depends
on the ability to understand words, such
as the formula 'regular thousand-sided
figure', and what we can describe in
words far outstrips what we can see in one
gaze.

If seeing is rather like reading a novel
at breakneck speed, it is also the case that
the novel is written to order at breakneck
speed. This allows introspection to lay a
trap for us and lead us naturally to the
picture theory of seeing. Whenever we examine our own experience of seeing,
whenever we set out to discover what we
can say about what we are seeing, we find
all the details we think of looking for.
When we read a novel, questions can
come to mind that are not answered in the
book, but when we are looking at
something, as soon as questions come up
they are answered immediately by new information as a result of the inevitable shift
in the focus and fixation point of our eyes.
The reports of perception are written to
order; whatever detail interests us is immediately brought into focus and
reported on. When this occurs one is not
scanning some stable mental image or
sense-datum. One is scanning the outside
world — quite literally. One can no more
become interested in a part of one's visual
experience without bringing the relevant
information to the fore than one can run
away from one's shadow. For this reason
it is tempting to suppose that everything
one *can* know about via the eyes is *always*
'present to consciousness' in some stable
picture.

To sit and introspect one's visual experience for a while is not to examine normal sight. When one does this one is
tempted to say that it is all very true that
there is only a small, central part of the
visual field of which one is aware at any
moment, and that to describe the whole
scene our eyes, our fixation point, and

our 'focus of interest' must scan the sensory presentation, but that the parts we
are not scanning at any moment persist or
remain, as a sort of vague, coloured
background. Of this background we are
only 'semi-aware'. Here, however, introspection runs into trouble, for as soon
as one becomes interested in what is going
on outside the beam of the fixation point
one immediately becomes aware (aware$_1$)
of the contents of peripheral signals, and
this phenomenon is quite different from
the ordinary one. While it is true that one
can focus on a spot on the wall and yet
direct one's attention to the periphery of
one's visual field and come up with
reports like 'There is something blue and
book-sized on the table to my right; it is
vague and blurred and I am not sure it is a
book', it cannot be inferred from this that
when one is *not* doing this one is still
aware of the blue, booklike shape. We are
led to such conclusions by the natural
operation of our eyes, which is to make a
cursory scanning of the environment
whenever it changes and as soon as it
changes, and by the operation of short-
term memory, which holds the results of
this scanning for a short period of time. In
familiar surroundings we do not have to
see or pay attention to the objects in their
usual places. If anything had been moved
or removed we *would* have noticed, but
that does not mean we notice their
presence, or even that we had the experience (in any sense) of their presence.
We enter a room and we know what objects are in it, because if it is a familiar
room we do not notice that anything is
missing and thus it is filled with all the objects we have noticed or put there in the
past. If it is an unfamiliar room we
automatically scan it, picking out the objects that fill it and catch our attention. I
may spend an afternoon in a strange room
without ever being aware (in any sense) of
the colour of the walls, and while it is no
doubt true that had the walls been bright
red I would have been aware of this, it

does not follow that I must have been aware that they were beige, or aware that they were colourless or vaguely coloured — whatever that might mean.[8]

It is true, of course, that when we see we do not simply see *that* there is a table in front of us, but a table of a particular colour and shape in a particular position and so forth. All this need mean is that the information we receive is vivid and rich in detail. This is not true of the vision of many lower animals. The frog, for example, can see that there is a small moving object before him, but he cannot see that it is a fly or a bit of paper on a string. If the small object is not moving, *he cannot see it at all*, because motion signals are required for the production of the higher-level signals that will initiate a behavioural response. A frog left in a cage with freshly killed (unmoving) flies will starve to death, because it has no equipment for sending the signal: there is a fly (moving or still). Dangle a dead fly on a string and the frog will eat it.[9] The difference in degree of complexity and vividness between frog and human perception does not warrant the assumption that there is a difference in kind — however much we may feel that a picture is worth a thousand words.[10]

Notes

1. Optimists who doubt that mental images are still taken seriously in philosophy and even in science are invited to peruse two recent anthologies, R. J. Hirst, ed., *Perception and the External World*, New York, 1965, and J. R. Smythies, ed., *Brain and Mind, Modern Concepts of the Nature of Mind*, London, 1965. The wealth of cross-disciplinary confusions over mental images is displayed in both volumes, which both include papers by philosophers. psychologists and neurophysiologists. Neither editor seems to think that much of what he presents is a dead horse, which strengthens my occasionally flagging conviction that I am not beating one. On the other hand, there are scientists who have expressed clear and explicit rejections of imagistic confusions. See, e.g., G. W. Zopf, 'Sensory Homeostasis' in Wiener and Schadé, 1963, esp. p. 118, and D. M. MacKay, 'Internal Representation of the External World,' unpublished, read at the Avionics Panel Symposium on Natural and Artificial Logic Processors, Athens, July 15-19, 1963.

2. H. B. Barlow, 'Possible Principles Underlying the Transformations of Sensory Messages' in *Sensory Communication* (1961) offers a particularly insightful account of the 'editorial' function of afferent neural activity and the depletion of information that is the necessary concomitant of such analysis.

3. J. M. Shorter, 'Imagination', *Mind*, 61, 1952, pp. 528-42.

4. Counter-examples spring to mind, but are they really counter-examples? All the ones that have so far occurred to me turn out on reflection to be cases of imagining myself seeing — with the aid of large mirrors — the inside and outside of the barn, imagining a (partially) transparent barn, imagining looking in the window and so forth. These are all from a point of view in the sense I mean. A written description, however, is not bound by these limitations; from what point of view is the description: 'the barn is dark red with black rafters and a pine floor'?

5. In the unusual phenomenon of 'eidetic imagery', the subject *can* read off or count off the details of his 'memory image', and this may seem to provide the fatal counter-example to this view. (See G. Allport, 'Eidetic Imagery', *British Journal of Psychology*, 15, 1924, pp. 99-120.) Yet the fact that such 'eidetic memory images' actually appear to be projected or superimposed on the subject's normal visual field (so that if the subject shifts his gaze the position of the memory image in his visual field remains fixed, and 'moves with the eye') strongly suggests that in these cases the actual image of retinal stimulation is somehow retained at or very near the retina and superimposed on incoming stimulation. In these rare cases, then, the memory mechanism must operate *prior to* afferent analysis, at a time when there still is a physical image.

6. Penfield, 1958. Some of Penfield's interpretations of his results have been widely criticized, but the results themselves are remarkable. It would be expected that hallucinations would have to be the exception

rather than the rule in the brain for event-types to *acquire* content in the first place, and this is in fact supported by evidence. Amputees usually experience 'phantom limb' sensations that seem to come from the missing limb; an amputee may feel that he not only still has the leg, but that it is itching or hot or bent at the knee. These phenomena, which occur off and on for years following amputation, are nearly universal in amputees, with one interesting exception. In cases where the amputation occurred in infancy, before the child developed the use and coordination of the limb, phantom limb is rarely experienced, and in cases where amputation occurred just after birth, no phantom limb is ever experienced (see M. Simmel, 'Phantom Experiences following Amputation in Childhood', *Journ. of Neurology, Neurosurgery and Psychiatry* 25, 1962, pp. 69-78).

7. Other phenomena less well known to philosophers also favour a descriptional explanation. See, e.g., W. R. Brain's account of the reports of patients who have their sight surgically restored, in 'Some Reflections on Mind and Brain,' *Brain*, 86, 1963, p. 381; the controversial accounts of newly sighted adults' efforts to learn to see, in M. von Senden, *Raum- und Gestaltauffassung bei operierten Blindgeborenen vor und nach der Operation*, Leipzig, 1932, translated with appendices by P. Heath as *Space and Sight, the Perception of Space and Shape in the congenitally blind before and after operation*, London, 1960; I. Kohler's experiments with inverting spectacles (a good account of these and similar experiments is found in J. G. Taylor, *The Behavioral Basis of Perception*, New Haven, 1962); and the disorder called simultanagnosia, M. Kinsbourne and E. K. Warrington, 'A Disorder of Simultaneous Form Perception', *Brain*, 85, 1962, pp. 461-86 and A. R. Luria, *et al.*, 'Disorders of Ocular Movement in a Case of Simultanagnosia', *Brain*, 86, 1963, pp. 219-28.

8. Cf. Wittgenstein, 'But the existence of this feeling of strangeness does not give us a reason for saying that every object we know well and which does not seem strange to us gives us a feeling of familiarity', 1953, i. 596. See also i. 597, i. 605.

9. Muntz, *op. cit.* and Wooldridge, *op. cit.*, pp. 46-50.

10. Having found no room for images in the sub-personal account of perception, we can say that 'mental image' and its kin are poor candidates for referring expressions in science; having found further that nothing with the traits of genuine images is to be found at the personal level either allows us to conclude that 'mental image' is valueless as a referring expression under *any* circumstances.

References

Barlow, H. B. 1961. 'Possible Principles Underlying the Transformations of Sensory Messages.' In W. A. Rosenblith, ed., *Sensory Communication*. New York.

Penfield, W. 1958. *The Excitable Cortex in Conscious Man*. Liverpool.

Wittgenstein, L. 1953. *Philosophical Investigations*. Trans. G. E. M. Anscombe. Oxford: Blackwell.

Zopf, G. W. 1963. 'Sensory Homeostasis.' In N. Wiener and J. P. Schadé, eds., *Nerve, Brain and Memory Models. Progress in Brain Research*, vol. 2. Amsterdam: Elsevier.

7

Imagistic Representation

Jerry A. Fodor

If I have been unsympathetic about the empirical basis for the existence of stagelike changes in modes of internal representation, it is because I think it would be appalling if the data really did somehow require us to endorse that sort of view. I am, in fact, strongly inclined to doubt the very *intelligibility* of the suggestion that there is a stage at which cognitive processes are carried out in a medium which is fundamentally nondiscursive. I am not, of course, denying the empirical possibility that children may use images more than adults do, or that their concepts may be, in some interesting sense, more concrete than adult concepts. What I do deny, however, is that the difference could be qualitative in the kind of way that Bruner seems to require. That is, I don't think that there could be a stage at which images are the vehicle of thought in the strong sense that thinking is *identifiable* with imaging at that stage; not, at least, if images are representations that refer by resembling. All this needs considerable sorting out.

From The Language of Thought (New York: Crowell, 1975), pp. 177-195. Reprinted by permission of Harper & Row, Publishers, Inc., and the author. Notes and figures have been renumbered for this edition.

Imagine, *per impossible*, that adults think in English; i.e., that English sentences provide the medium in which adult cognitive processes are carried out. How, on this assumption, would children have to differ from adults if Bruner's ontogenetic doctrines are to hold? That is, if we take thinking in English as a clear case of thinking in symbols, what is to count as the corresponding clear case of thinking in icons? Well, one possibility is that the children use a representational system just like the one that the adults use except that the children have *pictures* where the adults have *words*. This suggestion surely *is* coherent; one can, for example, imagine devising a hieroglyphic orthography for English. English sentences would thus be sequences of pictures (rather than sequences of phones) but everything else stays the same. So we have assigned *a* sense to the proposal that children's thought is iconic and adults' thought is symbolic.

But, of course, it isn't the sense that Bruner has in mind. For icons, in Bruner's sense, aren't just *pictures*; they are pictures that resemble what they stand for. That is, it's not just that symbols *look* different from icons; it's also that they are differently related to what they symbolize. The reference of icons is mediated by resemblance. The reference of symbols is mediated by conventions. Or something.[1]

So English in hieroglyphs won't quite do. But we can fix things up. We can imagine a language just like English except that (a) words are replaced by pictures and (b) the only pictures allowed are such as resemble what the corresponding words refer to. Of course, the representational capacity of such a language would be very limited since we can only use it to refer to what we can picture. Still, it is a coherent suggestion that there could be such a language, and it is a coherent hypothesis that that is the language that children think in. The point of the exercise is that one way of understanding the idea that children think in icons is this: Children think in a language in which *pictures* (not just hieroglyphs) take the role that words play in natural languages.

I am pretty sure that this is not, however, the sort of account of children's mental processes that Bruner wants to commend either. For one thing, if the difference between children and us were just that we think in something like standard English while they think in (call it) Iconic English, then the difference between us and children might not come to much. For though Iconic English can refer to fewer things than standard English can, they can both express some of the same semantic relations among the things they do refer to. After all, some such relations are carried by grammatical features of standard English, and standard English and Iconic English have the same grammar. Since agency, predication, possession, and the rest are presumably expressible in Iconic English, it looks as though much of the cognitive incapacity that would be involved in using it would be a relative paucity of *vocabulary*. Bruner makes it pretty clear, however (1966, Chap. 2), that he takes the availability of grammatical structure in representations to be a proprietary feature of symbolic (i.e., noniconic) representational systems.

The preceding remarks are intended as something more than a commendation of syntax. The point is that we can make sense of Iconic English as a representational system precisely *because* the switch to Iconic English leaves the grammar of standard English unaltered. One way to put the point is this: In Iconic English, *words* resemble what they refer to, *but sentences don't resemble what makes them true*. Thus, suppose that, in Iconic English, the word 'John' is replaced by a picture of John and the word 'green' is replaced by a green patch. Then the sentence 'John is green' comes out as (say) a picture of John followed by a green picture. But *that* doesn't look like being green; it doesn't look much like anything. Iconic English provides a construal of the notion of a representational system in which (what corresponds to) *words* are icons, but it provides no construal of the notion of a representational system in which (what corresponds to) *sentences* are. Nor do I think that this can usefully be patched up; the notion that sentences could be icons *has* no construal. But if sentences couldn't be icons, thoughts couldn't be either.

The structure of the argument is this: If the role that images play in a representational system is analogous to the role that words play in a natural language, then having a thought *cannot* be simply a matter of entertaining an image, and this is true whether the image is motoric or iconic and quite independent of any particular empirical hypothesis about the nature of cognitive development. For thoughts are the kinds of things that can be true or false. They are thus the kinds of things that are expressed by *sentences*, not words. And, while (barring considerations to be reviewed below) it makes a sort of sense to imagine a representational system in which the counterparts of words resemble what they refer to, it makes no sense at all to imagine a representational system in which the counterparts of sentences do.

We have hypothesized a representational system — Iconic English — which differs from standard English in that all the words are pictures but where everything else stays the same. We have remarked that in *that* representational system there is a *noniconic* relation between sentences and what makes them true. Can we do better? What *would* it be like to have a representational system in which sentences are icons of their truth conditions?

For example, what would it be like to have a representational system in which the sentence 'John is fat' is replaced by a picture? Suppose that the picture that corresponds to 'John is fat' is a picture of John with a bulging tummy. But then, what picture are we going to assign to 'John is tall'? The same picture? If so, the representational system does not distinguish the thought that John is tall from the thought that John is fat. A different picture? But John will have to have some shape or other in whatever picture we choose, so what is to tell us that having the picture is having a thought about John's height rather than a thought about his shape? Similarly, a picture of John is a picture of John sitting or standing, or lying down, or it is indeterminate among the three. But then, what is to tell us whether having the picture is having the thought that John is tall, or having the thought that John is sitting, or having the thought that he is standing, or having the thought that he is lying down, or having the thought that one doesn't know whether John is sitting, standing, or lying down?[2]

There are lots of ways of making this sort of point. Suppose that John *is* fat and suppose that John's name is a picture of John. So thinking of John is having a picture which, presumably, shows John fat. And thinking that John is fat is *also* having a picture that shows John fat. But

then: What, on this account, is the difference between (just) thinking of John, on the one hand, and thinking that John is fat, on the other?[3]

Let's see where we have gotten to. The notion that thoughts are images — or that they were images when we were very young — is really viciously ambiguous. On the one hand, the proposal might be that we should identify having an image with thinking *of* something, and, on the other, it might be that we should identify having an image with thinking *that* something. These two proposals don't, by any means, come to the same thing. The former amounts to the suggestion that images might be the vehicle of *reference*, while the latter amounts to the suggestion that images might be the vehicle of *truth*.

So, e.g., if Iconic English were the language of thought, then *thinking* of John might consist of entertaining John's image; just as, in the standard use of ordinary English, *mentioning* John (referring to him) might consist just in uttering John's name. It is, in this sense, no more problematic that there should be a language in which reference is defined for images than that there should be a language in which reference is defined for words. I suppose it is just a matter of brute fact that all the natural languages that there are happen to be of the latter kind. But I see no way of construing the notion that there might be a language in which *truth* is defined for icons instead of symbols; in which, i.e., 'formulae' of the system are true of what they resemble. The trouble is *precisely* that icons are insufficiently abstract to be the vehicles of truth.

To a first approximation, the kind of thing that can get a truth value is an assignment of some property to some object. A representational system must therefore provide appropriate vehicles for expressing such assignments. Under what conditions, then, is a representation adequate to express the assignment of a property to an object? Well, one condition which surely must be satisfied is that the representation specify *which* property is being assigned and which object it is being assigned to. The trouble with trying to truth-value icons is that they provide no way of doing the former. Any picture of a thing will, of necessity, display that thing as having indefinitely many properties; hence pictures correspond (and fail to correspond) in indefinitely many ways to the things that they resemble. Which of these correspondences is the one which makes the picture true?

But if pictures correspond to the same world in too many different ways, they also correspond in the same way to too many different worlds. A picture of John with a bulging tummy corresponds to John's being fat. But it corresponds equally to John's being pregnant since, if that is the way that John *does* look when he is fat, it is also, I suppose, the way that he *would* look if he were pregnant. So, if the fact that John is fat is a reason to call a picture of John with a bulging tummy true, then the fact that John isn't pregnant is as good a reason to call a picture of John with a bulging tummy false. (A picture which corresponds to a man walking up a hill forward corresponds equally, and in the same way, to a man sliding down the hill backward; Wittgenstein, 1953, p. 139.) For every reason that we might have for calling a picture true, there will be a corresponding reason for calling it false. That is, there is no reason for calling it either. Pictures aren't the kind of things that can have truth-values.

Notice that symbols (as opposed to icons) are exempt from these worries; that's one of the respects in which symbols really *are* abstract. A picture of fat John is also a picture of tall John. But the sentence 'John is fat' abstracts from all of John's properties but one: It is true if he's fat and only if he is. Similarly, a picture of a fat man corresponds in the same way (i.e., by resemblance) to a world where

men are fat and a world where men are pregnant. But 'John is fat' abstracts from the fact that fat men *do* look the way that pregnant men *would* look; it is true in a world where John is fat and false in any other world.

Taken together, these sorts of considerations strongly suggest that there isn't much sense to be made of the notion that there might be an internal representational system in which icons are the vehicles of truth; i.e., in which entertaining an image is identical to thinking *that* such and such is the case. But we've seen that a certain kind of sense *can* be made of the suggestion that there is an internal representational system in which icons are the vehicles of reference; i.e., in which thinking *of* such and such is identical with entertaining an image. It should now be remarked that even this concession needs to be hedged about.

In Iconic English, John's name is a picture of John. So if the language of thought were Iconic English, then thinking of John might consist of entertaining an image of John, in just the sense that, in real English, referring to John might be identical with uttering 'John'. But what sense is that?

Clearly not every utterance of 'John' *does* constitute a reference to John. For example, I just sat back from my typewriter and said 'John'. But I referred to no one; a fortiori, I did not refer to John. One might put it as follows: In the case of natural languages, utterances of (potentially) referring expressions succeed in making references only when they are produced with the right intentions. I cannot, as it were refer by mistake; no utterance of 'John' counts as a reference to John unless it was at least produced with the intention of *making* a reference.

In natural languages, to put it succinctly, the vehicles of reference are utterances that are taken under (i.e., intended to satisfy) descriptions. In paradigm cases of referring to John, I utter 'John' intending, thereby, to produce a form of words, and moreover to produce a form of words standardly used to refer to John, and moreover to refer to John by producing a form of words standardly used to refer to John. But on other occasions when I make the sound 'John' none of these things are true, and in those cases (though not only in those cases) my utterances of 'John' don't count as references to John.

So sometimes uttering 'John' constitutes making a reference to John, but only when the speaker intends his behavior to satisfy certain descriptions; only when he intends his utterance in a certain way. I think the same kinds of remarks apply, *mutatis mutandis*, to the use of images as vehicles of reference in systems like Iconic English: If Iconic English were the language of thought, then there might be cases in which entertaining an image of a thing constituted thinking of it; but only when the image is taken to satisfy certain descriptions; only when it is entertained in the right way. Iconic English is, by hypothesis, a language where the referring expressions are images. But even in Iconic English resemblance wouldn't be a sufficient condition for reference since, even in Iconic English, what refers aren't images but images-under-descriptions. Iconic English doesn't succeed in being *very* nondiscursive after all.

Figure 7-1 is a picture of a pinwheel sort of thing. Close your eyes and form an image of it. If thinking is forming an image of a thing, and if images refer to whatever they resemble, then you must just have been thinking of a cube viewed from one of its corners. For the image you just entertained does, in fact, resemble a cube viewed from one of its corners, just as (and in just the same way that) Figure 7-2 resembles a cube viewed from one of its edges. But, surely, many readers will have formed the image and *not* have thought of the cube. Having the image

Figure 7-1. A pinwheel sort of thing. See text.

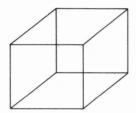

Figure 7-2. Schematic cube.

will have constituted thinking of a cube only for those readers who both formed the image and took it in a certain way: i.e., took the point in the center to be a corner of the cube, took the lines radiating from the point to be edges of the cube, etc.

The moral is: Yes, we can make a certain sort of sense of children having icons where we have symbols; viz., they have pictures where we have words (N.B.: words, not sentences).[4] But no, we cannot make much sense of the notion that the relation between thoughts and their objects is basically different for children and for us. To make sense of that, we would need to suppose that images refer by resembling while symbols refer by convention. (Or, as we remarked above, something.) And that they patently do not do. (Images usually don't *refer* at all. But when they do—as, e.g., in Iconic English—they do so in basically the same way that words and phrases do: viz., by satisfying, and by being taken to satisfy, certain descriptions.)

This is not, of course, to deny that pictures look like the things that they are pictures of. It is rather to deny that *looking like a thing* could be a sufficient condition for *referring* to that thing, even in a language like Iconic English, where pictures are the referring expressions. There is, in fact, a perfectly good way of using a picture to make a reference: viz., by embedding it in a description. So one might say 'I am looking for a man who looks like this . . .' and show a picture of a man. It's true that, in such a case, the form of words wouldn't usually succeed in communicating a reference unless the picture of the man looks like the man one is seeking. But, equally, the picture is no use without the description which tells you how it is intended to be taken. Compare the ways in which the picture would be used in 'I am looking for a man who (looks like/dresses like/is taller than) this . . . (picture of a short man wearing a toga)'. What carries the reference here is the picture *together with the 'symbols' that interpret it.*

I can, in short, see no way of construing the proposal that there might be a representational system in which resembling is a *sufficient* condition for referring; still less that there might be a representational system in which resembling and referring come to the same thing. To put it briefly, even if Bruner is right and the *vehicles* of reference are different for adults and children, the *mechanisms* of reference — whatever they are — must be pretty much the same for both.

I have been trying to undermine two notions about images that have played a long and dubious role in cognitive psychology: that thinking might *consist* of imaging, and that the means by which images refer to what they are images of might be fundamentally different from the means by which symbols refer to what they denote. But, of course, nothing I have said denies that images exist or that images may play an important role in many cognitive processes. Indeed, such empirical evidence as is available tends to support both claims. This is interesting from the point of view of the major preoccupations of this book. The fact that

the data come out the way they do throws light on the nature of the representational resources that people have available. And the fact that the data come out *at all* supports the view that the nature of such resources is a bona fide empirical question.

The relevant studies have recently been extensively reviewed (see, in particular, Paivio, 1971; Richardson, 1969). Suffice it here to sketch one or two of the findings which seem to argue forcibly for the psychological reality of images.

1. If there are images, and if, as introspection suggests, imaging is very like visual perception, one might plausibly expect that experimental tasks which elicit images should produce mode-specific interference with other cognitive processes in which vision is implicated. Tasks which require visual imagery, e.g., should induce decrements in the performance of simultaneous tasks which require visually guided responses. An elegant series of experiments by Brooks (1968) suggests that they do so. In one condition, Ss are asked to form a memory image of a figure like Figure 7-3. They are then asked to trace around the memory image following the arrows and indicating, for each corner, whether it occurs on a top edge of the figure. (The appropriate responses for Figure 7-3 are thus: 'no, yes, no, no, no, yes, yes, no, no, no'.) Depending on the experimental group to which the subject is assigned, responses are indicated either by pointing to written yeses and noes or by some form of nonvisually guided gesture (like tapping or saying 'yes' or 'no'). The relevant result is that performance is significantly better for subjects in the latter (nonvisually guided) groups. Visual images interfere with visually guided tasks.

Moreover, they interfere selectively. Brooks had another condition in which S's task was to produce sequences of yeses and noes depending on the form class of the words in a previously memorized

Figure 7-3. Stimulus diagram of the kind used by Brooks (1968).

sentence. A subject might be given a sentence like 'Now is the time for all good men to come to the aid of the party' and told to indicate 'yes' for each word that is a noun or verb and 'no' for each word that is neither. In this condition, the effect of response mode upon performance reversed the relation found in the visual image case: Performance was best for subjects who point or tap, worst for subjects who gave their responses verbally. Visually guided responses don't, apparently, much interfere with auditory images.

2. If there are images, and if, as introspection suggests, images are very much like pictures, then there ought to be demonstrable similarities between the processes of comparing an object with an image of that object and comparing two objects that look alike. There are, in fact, a number of experiments in the literature which suggest that this is so. (See, e.g., Cooper and Shepard, 1973.) The paradigmatic study is owing to Posner, Boies, Eichelman, and Taylor (1969).

To begin with, it is possible to show that there is a reliable difference in the speed with which subjects can make judgments of type identity in the case where the tokens are physically *similar*, on the one hand, and in the case where the tokens are physically *different*, on the other, Thus, e.g., Ss are presented with tachistascopic displays consisting of two letters and asked to respond 'yes' if the letters are the same and 'no' if they are different. In this situation, Ss are faster when the members of the positive pairs (i.e., the

pairs for which the correct response is 'yes') are of the *same case* (like *PP* or *pp*) than when they are of *difference case* (like *Pp* or *pP*).

Now suppose the paradigm is changed. Instead of presenting S with two letters in the visual mode, we present him first with an auditory case-and-letter designation, then with a *single visual* letter to match to the auditory description. So the subject might hear 'capital *P*' and then see *P* (to which his response would be 'yes') or *p* or *Q* or *q* (to all of which the right response would be 'no'). It turns out that Ss performance in this situation depends critically on the length of the interval between the auditory and the visual stimulus. Subjects for whom the visual stimulus comes on immediately after the auditory stimulus give response latencies comparable to those for visually presented letter pairs whose members *differ* in case. If, however, the interstimulus interval is increased to about 0.7 second, the response latencies *decrease* and approximate those for visually presented letter pairs whose members are *identical* in case. It is not mandatory, but it is extremely natural, to assume that what happens during the 0.7 second of interstimulus interval is that the subject constructs a letter image to fit the auditory description, and that it is that image which gets matched to the visual display. If this is true, and if, as we have supposed, matching images to things is fundamentally similar to matching things that look alike, we have some sort of explanation of the behavioral convergence between Ss who judge the relation between pairs of letters both of which they *see*, and Ss who judge the relation between pairs of letters one of which they only hear described.

The studies just reviewed are by no means the only possibilities for the empirical investigation of the psychological reality of mental images.[5] Consider just one further line of argument.

Discursive symbols, as Bruner remarked, are deployed in time. Or, rather, *some* discursive symbols are (viz., spoken sentences). Pictures (and written sentences), on the other hand, are deployed in space. There may be conventions for determining the order in which information is retrieved from a picture (as in certain kinds of didactic paintings which 'tell a story' and are meant to be scanned in a certain order) but, in general, there needn't be. In principle, all the information is available simultaneously and can be read off in whatever order the observer chooses.[6]

Suppose, then, that subjects *can* employ mental images to display the information pertinent to performing an experimental task, and suppose that mental images are relevantly similar to real pictures. One should then predict that Ss who can use images ought to enjoy considerable freedom in the order in which they can report the information that their images present, while Ss who use discursive forms of representation (e.g., sentences) ought to be relatively restricted in the order in which their information can be accessed. To take an extreme case, imagine an experiment in which the subject is shown a red triangle and then asked about what he has seen. Ss who stored an *image* ought to be about equally quick in answering 'Was it red?' and 'Was it triangular?' Ss who stored the sentence 'It was a red triangle' ought to be faster in answering the first question than in answering the second.[7]

As things stand this is, alas, largely a *gedanken* experiment; I mention it primarily as a further illustration of techniques that might be used to subject hypotheses about the nature of internal representations to experimental test. It is worth mentioning, however, that precisely this interpretation *has* been suggested by Paivio (1971) to account for differences in order-of-report effects exhibited by subjects in an experiment by

Haber (1966). Paivio remarks that "while the implications of the present analysis have not been independently tested using the appropriate perceptual tasks, evidence from several sources is consistent with the hypothesis" (p. 130).

The preceding should suggest that the existence and functioning of mental images can be handled as an experimental issue and that techniques more subtle than brute appeals to introspection can be employed in the experiments. This may strike the philosophical reader as surprising, since it has recently been fashionable to treat the nonexistence of images as demonstrable a priori. Before we round off this discussion, it is worth digressing to see what can be said for so implausible a view.

Dennett (1969) has put succinctly what appears to be the paramount philosophical worry about images.

> Consider the Tiger and his Stripes. I can dream, imagine or see a striped tiger, but must the tiger I experience have a particular number of stripes? If seeing or imaging is having a mental image, then the image of the tiger *must*—obeying the rules of images in general—reveal a definite number of stripes showing, and one should be able to pin this down with such questions as 'more than ten?', 'less than twenty?'. If, however, seeing or imagining has a descriptional character, the questions need have no definite answer. Unlike a snapshot of a tiger, a description of a tiger need not go into the number of stripes at all; 'numerous stripes' may be all the description says. Of course in the case of actually seeing a tiger, it will often be possible to corner the tiger and count his stripes, but then one is counting real tiger stripes, not stripes on a mental image. (pp. 136-137)

A number of philosophers appear to hold that this sort of argument provides something like a *demonstration* that there aren't mental images. If they are right it is an embarrassment since, as we have seen, there is some persuasive empirical evidence in the field, and it suggests that what goes on in imaging is very like picturing and very unlike describing. Moreover, the introspective plausibility of the image theory is enormous, so if the striped tigers do show what they are alleged to show we are without an explanation of either the introspections or the experimental data. Any theory is better than none; clearly, we should undermine the striped tiger argument if we can.

There are, I think, at least three ways that one might attempt to do so. I don't suppose that any of these counterarguments is conclusive, but I do think that, between them, they suggest that striped tigers don't clinch the case against images. Given the persuasiveness of the a posteriori arguments for imagery, that should be good enough.

To begin with, one might try simply denying what the striped tiger argument primarily assumes. That is, one might argue that there *is* some definite answer to 'How many stripes does the image-tiger have?' but that, because our images are labile, we usually can't hold on to them for long enough to count. It's to be said in favor of this view (a) that it seems introspectively plausible to many people who claim to have images (if you don't believe it, ask a few);[8] (b) it makes everyday mental images qualitatively like idetic images, from which even Dennett admits "the subject *can* read off or count off the details" (p. 137); (c) this view is anyhow less hard to swallow than the alternative suggestion: that what goes on when I think that I am picturing a thing is that I am, in fact, describing it to myself.[9]

This is, I think, the kind of suggestion that sophisticated philosophers take to be naive; perhaps because they are impressed by the following sort of argument. 'Having images is supposed to be part of the perceptual process. But now, if images themselves have to be perceived (scanned, etc.) to recover the information they contain, then surely we have taken the first step in a regress which will eventually require the postulation of images without number and endless perceivers to look at them'. This is, however, a bad argument. It assumes, quite without justification, that if recovering information from the external environment requires having an image, recovering information from an image must require having an image too. But why should we assume that? Moreover (and more to the present point), even if this were a *good* argument it would be no good here. For the most it could show is that images don't play a certain role in perception (i.e., that perceiving a thing couldn't always and everywhere require forming an image of that thing). It shows nothing about whether having and scanning an image might play a role in *other* mental processes (such as, e.g., comparing, remembering or imagining things).

The second point that one might want to make about striped tigers is this: It simply isn't true that a picture of a striped tiger must be determinate under such descriptions as 'has *n* stripes'.[10] Of course the *tiger* has to have precisely *n* stripes for some *n* or other (barring problems about the individuation of stripes), but there are all kinds of cases in which a picture of an *n*-striped tiger may not show any definite number of image stripes. Blurring is the main (but not the only) problem.[11]

What *is* true, what does follow from what Dennett calls "the rules of images in general" is that if what you've got is an image, then necessarily there will have to be *some* visual description under which it is determinate. For a picture in a newspaper, e.g., the pertinent description is one which specifies a 'gray-matrix'; an assignment of a value of black or white to each of the finitely many points that comprise the image. So far as I can see, this is the *only* kind of visual description under which newspaper pictures are *always* determinate. Whether a given such picture happens also to be determinate under some *other* visual description (as, e.g., has *n* stripes) will depend on such matters as what it's a picture of, the angle from which the picture was taken, how good the resolution is, etc.

If this is right, it means that the striped tiger argument is a good deal weaker than it started out to seem. What that argument shows *at most* is that there are *some* visual descriptions under which mental images *aren't* fully determinate. But what would need to be shown to prove that mental images fail to satisfy 'the rules of images in general', i.e., to prove that they aren't images, is that there are *no* visual descriptions under which they *are* fully determinate. Surely nothing that strong follows from the sort of observations Dennett makes.[12]

The third point to make against the striped tiger is that it is more dogmatic about the distinction between images and descriptions than there is any need to be. A paradigmatic image (say a photograph) is *nondiscursive* (the information it conveys is displayed rather than described) and *pictorial* (it resembles its subject). The present point, however, is that there is an indefinite range of cases in between photographs and paragraphs. These intermediate cases are, in effect, images under descriptions; they convey *some* information discursively and *some* information pictorially, and they resemble their subjects only in respect of those properties that happen to be pictured. In particular, they are determinate under the same visual descriptions as their subjects only for such properties.[13]

An example may help to make this clear. Dennett says: "Consider the film version of *War and Peace* and Tolstoy's book; the film version goes into immense detail and in one way cannot possibly be *faithful* to Tolstoy's words since the 'picture painted' by Tolstoy does not go into the details the film cannot help but go into (such as the colors of the eyes of each

filmed soldier" (1969, p. 136)). There are, however, other kinds of images than photographs. Consider, for example, *maps*. Maps are pictorial in respect of some of the information they convey; geographical relations are pictured when the map is oriented right. But they are, or may be, nonpictorial in respect of other information. Population densities or elevations above sea level may be given by coloring or shading, and then we need to use the legend to determine what the image means.

To put it briefly, since images under descriptions are images, they are typically pictorial vis-à-vis, some set of visual properties, and, of course, they will be determinate vis-à-vis any set of properties they picture. But since it is in part the description that determines what such an image is an image *of*, the properties for which the image has to be determinate can have arbitrarily little in common with the visual properties of whatever the image images. Images under descriptions share their nondiscursiveness with images *tout court*. What they share with descriptions is that they needn't look much like what they represent.

We can now say what all this has to do with the tiger's stripes. Suppose that what one visualizes in imaging a tiger might be anything from a full-scale tiger portrait (in the case of the ideticist) to a sort of transient stick figure (in the case of poor imagers like me). What makes my stick figure an image of a tiger is not that it looks much like one (my drawings of tigers don't look much like tigers either) but rather that it's *my* image, so I'm the one who gets to say what it's an image of. My images (and my drawings) connect with my intentions in a certain way; I *take* them as tiger-pictures for purposes of whatever task I happen to have in hand. Since my mental image *is* an image, there will be some visual descriptions under which it is determinate; hence there will be some questions whose answers I can 'read off' the display,[14] and the more pictorial the display is the more such questions there will be. But, in the case of any given image, there might be arbitrarily many visual properties which would not be pictured but, as it were, carried by the description under which the image is intended. The image will, ipso facto, not be determinate relative to these properties. We thus return, by a different route, to the conclusion mooted above: To show that mental images violate 'the rules of images in general', one would have to show not just that they are indeterminate under some visual description or other, but rather that they are determinate under no visual descriptions at all. There *may* be a way of showing this, but I doubt it and the striped tiger argument doesn't do it.

All this points toward some plausible speculations about how images may integrate with discursive modes of internal representation. If one recalls the Posner *et al.* experiment discussed above, one notices that there are two psychological processes postulated by the proposed explanation of the results. In the first phase, an image is constructed in accordance with a description. In the second phase, the image is matched against a stimulus for purposes of perceptual identification. The explanation thus implies (what common sense also suggests) that we have psychological faculties which can construct images which display the information that corresponding descriptions convey discursively; i.e., faculties which permit us to construct images *from* descriptions. The experiment demonstrates that having the information displayed *as* an image facilitates performance in certain kinds of tasks. (In effect, using the image rather than the description permits the subject to do the job of perceptual categorization in parallel rather than in series; he can check letter case and letter type *at the same time.*)

These remarks about the Posner experiment fit very well with the view that images under description are often the vehicles of internal representation. For insofar as mental images are constructed *from descriptions*, the descriptions can function to determine what the images are images of, and how their properties are to be interpreted. Here, then, is the general outline of the picture I have been trying to develop:

1. Some behaviors are facilitated when task-relevant information is non-discursively displayed (e.g., when it is displayed as an image).

2. One of our psychological faculties functions to construct images which accord with descriptions. That is, we have access to a computational system which takes a description as input and gives, as output, an image of something that satisfies the description. The exploitation of this system is presumably sensitive to our estimates of the demand characteristics of the task at hand.

3. The image that gets produced may be quite schematic since how the image is *taken* — what role it plays in cognitive processing — is determined not only by its figural properties but also by the character of the description it is paired with. We have seen that this point is important for evaluating the striped tiger argument. It may now be added that it goes some way toward meeting one of the empirical arguments that is frequently urged against taking mental images very seriously.

Psychologists who don't think that images could play any very important role in internal representation often insist upon the idiosyncratic character of the images that subjects report (see, e.g., Brown, 1958). Clearly the content of images does vary quite a lot from person to person, and it might well be that a given image can function to effect different representations in different computational tasks (what counts as the image of a duck for one purpose might count as the image of a rabbit for another). The present point is that if mental images are images under descriptions, then their idiosyncrasies might have very little effect on the role they play in cognitive processes. Suppose your image of a triangle is scaline and mine is isosceles. This needn't matter to how we use the images to reason about triangles so long as we agree on how the images are to be taken; e.g., so long as we agree that they are to represent *any* closed three-sided figure whose sides are straight lines.

This is, in fact, quite a traditional sort of point to make. The empiricists were on to it, though the significance of their views has frequently been overlooked. Thus, Hume acknowledged Berkeley's insight that images can't resemble the referents of abstract ideas, but held that there is a sense in which entertaining an abstract idea might be identical with having an image all the same. Hume says: "the image in the mind is only that of a particular object, tho' the application of it in our reasoning be the same as if it were universal" (1960 ed., p. 28). Viewed one way, this is tantamount to the abandonment of the image theory of thought, since the vehicles of internal representation are taken to be (not images *tout court* but) images under one or another interpretation; what we have been calling images under descriptions. What has been abandoned, in particular, is the doctrine that mental images refer to what they resemble and resemble what they refer to. But, viewed the other way, Hume's point is that the abandonment of the resemblance theory of reference is compatible with preserving the insight that (some) internal representations are, or may be, nondiscursive. The importance of distinguishing between these two claims — and the failure of lots of latter-day psychologists and philosophers to do

so — has, of course, been one of the main themes of our discussion.

What we have so far is not more than a sketch of a theory: The questions it leaves open are more interesting than the ones that it proposes answers to. For example, granted that there is such a thing as mental imagery, is there any reason to suppose that it plays more than a marginal role in internal representation? What kinds of tasks are facilitated by the availability of nondiscursive displays? What is it about nondiscursive displays that makes them useful in such tasks? How much freedom do we have in opting for nondiscursive representation in given cases? What are the mechanisms by which images are constructed from descriptions?[15] Above all, it would be interesting to know whether *all* mental images are generated from descriptions, or whether some psychological processes are, as it were, nondiscursive from beginning to end.[16] If, for example, I use images to recall the look or smell of a thing, do I invariably recruit information which was discursively represented at some stage in its history? Was what Proust had stored a *description* of how madeleines taste soaked in tea? Or are there psychological mechanisms by which nondiscursive engrams are established and deployed? Certainly the enormous amounts of information which get handled in some tasks where images are implicated makes it implausible that the information displayed went through a stage of digital encoding. The discussion has, in any event, returned to an area of straightforwardly empirical psychological research, and I propose to leave it there. Interested readers are referred to Pribram (1971), and Penfield and Roberts (1959).

Notes

1. Bruner stresses the *conventionality* of noniconic representational systems (like English), but, surely, it isn't their conven-

tionality which makes them noniconic; English would be a discursive (i.e., a symbolic; i.e., a noniconic) representational system even if it were innate (i.e., nonconventional). It is, in fact, a major problem in the philosophy of language to give a plausible account of the relation between symbols and what they symbolize. What Bruner's theory comes to is that icons refer by resembling and symbols refer in some other — as yet unspecified — way. The latter claim is certainly true.

2. This form of argument is owing to Wittgenstein (1953). It is, I think, entirely convincing.

3. The obvious way out of this won't do. Suppose thinking of fat John *doesn't* involve having a picture that shows John fat. Still, the picture one has will have to show John *somehow*; i.e., as having some properties or other. And then what will be the difference between just thinking of John and thinking that John has those properties?

4. I want to emphasize that I am not *endorsing* the view that the thinking of children is iconic in *any* sense. I am simply trying to make clear what a coherent version of that view might come to. As will be apparent by now, I find that proposal a good deal less transparent than some of the psychologists who have sponsored it seem to do.

5. The most impressive finding is perhaps that steroptic depth perception can be produced by imposing an idetic memory image upon a visual stimulus. (See the very remarkable findings reported by Stromeyer and Psotka, 1970. For a general discussion of ideticism, see Haber, 1966.) It seems hard to deny that imaging is like perceiving when it is possible to produce typical perceptual illusions whose objects are images rather than percepts. It's worth remarking, in this respect, that it has been known for some time that there are circumstances in which subjects can be induced to confuse (*nonidetic*) images with percepts (Perky, 1910; Segal and Gordon, 1968).

6. This point is related to one that Kant makes in the *Critique of Pure Reason*. Kant distinguishes between 'subjective' and 'objective' temporal sequences, where the latter, but not the former, are independent of the scanning strategies of perceiver. Thus, we may choose to examine the facade of a building from portal to pediment. But since all of the bits of the building are in fact contemporaneous, we could equally have chosen to go the other way around. Events which constitute an objective sequence, on the other hand, can be scanned in one order only. The same kind of point applies, *mutatis mutandis*, to the contrast between recovering information from pictures and from spoken sentences.

7. *S*s who stored, as it might be, the sentence 'It was a triangle and it was red' ought, of course, to show the reverse asymmetry. The point is that *some order of report effect or other* should be associated with any form of discursive representation, while imagists ought to be relatively free from such effects. If *S*s who claim that they are imaging turn out to be the ones who exhibit relatively weak order of report effects, that would be a reason for taking the hypothesis that they *are* using images seriously.

8. I *will not* get involved in the question whether introspection is infallible; but it seems to be perverse to hold that the deliverances of introspection are eo ipso always wrong. The subject's views about what he's doing appear to have as good a right to be considered as yours or mine or the experimenter's.

9. What's still harder to believe is that what goes on in typical cases of *perceiving* a thing is significantly like what goes on in typical cases of describing it. This is pertinent because the natural view of imaging is that to image a thing is to be in a psychological state qualitatively similar to the state that one would be in if one were perceiving the thing. If, therefore, imaging is like describing, perceiving must be too.

10. By stipulation, a picture is *determinate under a description* iff the statement that the picture satisfies the description has a determinate truth value.

11. Think of an out-of-focus photograph of a page of type. There is a definite answer to 'How many letters on the page?' Need there be a definite answer to 'How many image letters on the photograph?'

12. My discussion begs the question of what is to count as a 'visual' description. However, the striped tiger argument does too since, presumably, it is only for visual descriptions that it follows from 'the rules of images in

general' that images must be determinate.

13. It isn't even the case that images under descriptions are necessarily pictorial in respect of all the information in respect of which they are nondiscursive. Taking 'nondiscursive' and 'pictorial' as coextensive is one of the root sources of confusion in thinking about images. Thus, the line on the globe that shows where the equator is presumably conveys information nondiscursively. But it doesn't look like the equator. Such cases suggest how rough-and-ready the unanalyzed contrast between images and descriptions really is. For present purposes, I am using the materials at hand, but serious work in this area would require sharpening (and perhaps ultimately abandoning) the framework of distinctions that I have been assuming.

14. It is, presumably, because images do allow some information to be 'read off' that people bother with constructing images in memory tasks. A standard psychological anecdote concerns the man who can't tell you how many windows his house has unless he constructs an image of the house and then counts.

15. Some hints might be garnered from an examination of 'digital to analog' computer routines. It argues for the possibility of psychologically real devices which map descriptions onto images that machines can already be built to realize such functions. See Sutherland (1970).

16. I assume, for the kinds of reasons just discussed, that insofar as internal representations are images, they must be images-under-descriptions. What I regard as an open empirical question is the mechanisms by which descriptions and images are related. One way to relate them — the one sketched above — would be to generate the images *from* the descriptions. The present question is whether there are other ways and, if so, what they are.

It may be worth remarking, by the way, that there are similarities between what I have been saying about how images might be deployed in recognition tasks and the so-called 'analysis by synthesis' theories of perceptual categorization. The point of such theories is precisely that representations — in effect, templates — are generated from descriptions and then matched to the input that needs to be categorized. The description from which the template is generated then provides the perceptual analysis of the input. It is an attractive feature of such models that they provide for an infinite stock of templates, so long as the formation rules for the descriptions are iterative. (For discussion, see Halle and Stevens, 1964; Neisser, 1967.) I very much doubt that analysis by synthesis could yield anything like a general theory of perception, but it is quite plausible that such mechanisms are involved in perception *inter alia*.

References

Brooks, L. R. (1968). Spatial and verbal components of the act of recall. *Canadian Journal of Psychology*, 2, 349-368.

Brown, R. (1958). "Words and Things," The Free Press, New York.

Bruner, J. S. (1957). On perceptual readiness. *Psychological Review*, 64, 123-152.

Bruner, J. S., Goodnow, J. J. and Austin, G. A. (1956). "A Study of Thinking," Wiley, New York (Paperback Wiley Science Editions, 1962.)

Bruner, J. S., Olver, R. R. and Greenfield, P. M. (1966). "Studies in Cognitive Growth," Wiley, New York.

Cooper, L. A. and Shepard, R. N. (1973). Chronometric studies of the rotation of mental images. In "Visual Information Processing," (W. G. Chase, ed.), Academic Press, New York.

Dennett, D. C. (1969). "Content and Consciousness," Humanities Press, New York.

Haber, R. N. (1966). Nature of the effect of set on perception. *Psychological Review*, 73, 335-351.

Halle, M. and Stevens, K. N. (1964). Speech recognition: a model and a program for research. In "The Structure of Language: Readings in the Philosophy of Language" (J. A. Fodor and J. J. Katz, eds.), Prentice-Hall, Englewood Cliffs, New Jersey.

Hume, D. (1960). "A Treatise of Human Nature," Vol I. (Originally published 1739), Dent, London.

Kant, I. (1953). "Critique of Pure Reason," N. K. Smith (trans.). Macmillan, New York. (Originally published, 1781).

Neisser, U. (1967). "Cognitive Psychology," Appleton, New York.

Newell, A. and Simon, H. A. (1972). "Human Problem Solving," Prentice-Hall, Englewood Cliffs, New Jersey.

Paivio, A. (1971). "Imagery and Verbal Processes," Holt, New York.

Penfield, W. and Roberts, L. (1959). "Speech and Brain Mechanisms," Princeton Univ., Princeton, New Jersey.

Perky, C. W. (1910). An experimental study of imagination. *American Journal of Psychology*, 21, 422-452.

Posner, M. I., Boies, S. J., Eichelman, W. H. and Taylor, R. L. (1969). Retention of visual and name codes of single letters. *Journal of Experimental Psychology Monograph*, 79 (1, pt. 2).

Pribram, K. H. (1971). "Languages of the Brain," Prentice-Hall, Englewood Cliffs, New Jersey.

Richardson, A. (1969). "Mental Imagery," Springer, New York.

Segal, S. J. and Gordon, P. (1968). The Perky effect revisited: paradoxical thresholds or signal detection error? Paper presented at the 39th Annual Meeting of the Eastern Psychological Association.

Stromeyer, C. F. and Psotka, J. (1970). The detailed texture of eidetic images. *Nature*, 225, 346-349.

Sutherland, I. E. (1970). "Computer displays," *Scientific American*, 222, No. 6, 56-81.

Wittgenstein, L. (1953). "Philosophical Investigations," Blackwell, Oxford.

Imagery, Propositions, and the Form of Internal Representations

Stephen M. Kosslyn and James R. Pomerantz

Mental imagery has long played a central role in psychologists' and philosophers' accounts of cognitive processes and the representation of knowledge in the mind.[1] The construct of the image, however, has never been operationalized well enough to satisfy most psychologists, and so it is not surprising that imagery has disappeared periodically from the mainstream of Western psychology. Nevertheless, the concept has such magnetism that it has never stayed away for long, and it is currently enjoying remarkable popularity.

Given this state of affairs, it is appropriate that the notion of imagery be given a thorough logical examination. Pylyshyn's stimulating paper (1973) has given us an excellent starting point for this analysis. His paper deals with the general problem of the internal representation of knowledge and argues against considering imagery as a qualitatively distinct or theoretically adequate form of mental representation. We disagree with Pylyshyn, but the fact that many other

From *Cognitive Psychology* 9 (1977): 52-76. Reprinted, with revisions by the authors, by permission of Academic Press and the authors. Notes have been renumbered for this edition.

psychologists share his views (e.g., Anderson & Bower, 1973; Clark & Chase, 1972; Reid, 1974) makes it important to consider his (and closely related) arguments seriously.

Plan of the paper. This paper has four major sections. In the first section, we review the major thrusts of Pylyshyn's arguments against the construct of imagery and consider the basic arguments for what is called a "propositional system." In the second section, we submit these arguments to critical scrutiny. In the third section, we consider the usefulness of imagery and of propositions when they are used as constructs to account for several classes of empirical findings. In the fourth, concluding section, we summarize the major implications of our review and analysis.

I. Summary of the Basic Anti-Imagery Arguments

The Issue

The issue is whether imagery ought to be invoked as an explanatory construct in psychology. Debate over this issue has had two foci: First, one dispute concerns whether images are a *structurally* distinct form of internal representation, possessing a different *format* than other internal representations. The "format" is the structure of a code, as defined by the nature of the elements (e.g., discrete, continuous) and the nature of the relations between them. The content of an internal representation (i.e., what is represented) should not be confused with its format; any given content can be represented in terms of various formats (e.g., the same sentence can be represented in Morse code, in written print, spoken English or French, sequences of magnetic fluxes in a computer, etc.). The fact that certain contents (e.g., memory for pictures) are encoded into memory says nothing about the format of the internal representations.

The second focus of the present debate concerns whether or not images are a *functionally* distinct form of internal representation. The basic question is whether images function differently in cognition than do other sorts of internal representations. If not, and if images are represented in the same format as are other internal representations, then there are no grounds for maintaining the construct of imagery as an explanatory device in psychology. Let us now consider arguments of Pylyshyn and others for discarding imagery as an explanatory construct in psychology. We will postpone our critique of these arguments until the next section.

A. The Picture Metaphor

The visual image[2] has often been described as a "picture in the head," stored in memory much as a snapshot is stored in a photograph album. "Mental photographs," replicas of previous patterns of sensory activity at or near the receptor level, are stored in a raw undifferentiated form. Experiencing an image consists of retrieving and examining one of these mental photographs.

Interpretation and organization. The above notions, Pylyshyn maintains, are misleading in critical ways. The "picture metaphor," as it may be called, wrongly implies that images are reperceived much as pictures are perceived. The error lies in the fact that images, unlike pictures, are not in need of much fundamental perceptual processing such as contour sharpening or figure-ground segregation. Rather, images are preorganized into objects and properties of objects. We are never aware of having to interpret images as we sometimes have to interpret percepts, particularly complex or ambiguous percepts. In addition, when we forget part of an image, it is not a random part. It is not as if a corner were torn from a photographic picture in the head; if our image of a room were incomplete, for example, it would not be missing half a sofa or half a lampshade. Rather, images seem to be organized into meaningful parts, which in turn are remembered in terms of spatial relations among them (cf., Reed, 1974).

Imagery and seeing. The picture metaphor also introduces a host of inappropriate analogies between seeing and imaging. For example, a "mind's eye" is often said to "see" images internally. This notion seems to require a second processing system, or "mind's eye's brain," to interpret information from the mind's eye, which in turn would require another eye to interpret the images projected onto this internal brain, and so on in an infinite regression. The picture metaphor also leads us to speak of perceptual events like scanning and focusing in relation to image processing. These analogies are difficult to reconcile with the fact that no mind's eyeballs exist to do the scanning.

Capacity limitations. Pylyshyn argues that processing and storing of information in image form would be cumbersome, if not totally unworkable, because a huge storage capacity would be necessary to preserve all the information transmitted by the retina. The amount of stored information would soon exceed the capacity of the brain if people did indeed store the wealth of images they commonly claim to remember.

Accessibility. Even if all the unanalyzed images could be stored, it would be virtually impossible to search for one particular image among them, since uninterpreted images could not be organized into a format facilitating their retrieval. But people who experience imagery report no awareness of such searching: The desired image seems to come to mind directly and quickly. Thus it seems necessary to assume that some sort of "interpretation" is stored in memory along with each image. If this is granted, it would seem more economical to store only the interpretations and dispense with the images entirely.

B. Propositional Knowledge

Propositions are abstract structures that express precise relations between entities. They are not linguistic structures, since they may include concepts that lack verbal labels altogether, but they can often be approximated by simple sentences. A representation of a visual scene, for example, might consist of a set of propositions corresponding to the sentences: "The ball is red," "The ball is to the left of the pyramid," etc. Minsky and Papert's (1972) notion of "symbolic" representation is equivalent to propositional representation as here described. According to Pylyshyn, propositions are "abstract" in the same sense that linguistic "deep structure" is said to be abstract. Moreover, every proposition must be either true or false, and in addition, must be "well formed" (see Anderson & Bower, 1973).

The factual nature of knowledge. Pylyshyn argues that a propositional format is appropriate for representing knowledge, because what we know about the world is a set of facts or assertions that are necessarily either true or false. Mental pictures, on the other hand, do not have this property. Pictures do not assert anything, and hence are neither true nor false; they merely exist, with no truth value (although propositions about the picture and its correspondence to an object or scene do have truth value). Thus, images, if considered to be mental pictures, are inadequate for representing world knowledge.

C. Necessity of a Third Code

It has often been assumed that there are only two kinds of internal codes. *Verbal* codes must exist at some level simply because we can transmit and receive verbally encoded messages. Similarly, *perceptual* (e.g., visual) codes are necessary to account for our perceptual capacities. There is, however, good reason to postulate a third coding system, which is abstract (amodal), propositional, and not externalizable. According to Pylyshyn and others (e.g., Clark & Chase, 1972; Moscovitch, 1973), our ability to translate or exchange information between verbal and visual codes (as when we describe a picture) requires the existence of a third "interlingual" code, because the structual differences between visual and verbal representations preclude direct translation:

> But the need to postulate a more abstract representation — one which resembles neither pictures nor words and is not accessible to subjective experience — is unavoidable. As long as we recognize that people can go from mental pictures to mental words or vice versa, we are forced to conclude that there must be a representation (which is more abstract and not available to conscious experience) which encompasses both. There must, in other

words, be some common format or inter-lingua. (Pylyshyn, 1973, p. 5).

Ease of processing.   Since eventual translation into a third code is thus necessary, it would be more efficient simply to encode all information into the common format to begin with. This suggests that all knowledge is coded in an abstract propositional format, from which it can be translated into verbal or perceptual structures as needed.

Economy.   Use of a single amodal representational format would result in a considerable simplification of the mental machinery needed for retrieving informa-tion. The need for a perceptual inter-pretative device (a "mind's eye") in addi-tion to devices needed to retrieve nonpic-torial information would be eliminated if information were represented in a single format.

D. Introspective Evidence

Pylyshyn suggests that the common-ly reported *experience* of imagery should not be given much weight in theorizing. As compelling as imagery may be to some of us through our introspections, this does not justify the use of the concept in an ex-planatory way. The mere experience of imagery, as vivid and undeniable as it may be, does not imply that imagery plays any causal (as opposed to merely epiphenomenal) role in cognition. More-over, not everyone reports experiencing images, and those who do cannot always agree on the nature of their experience.

E. Definitional Problems for Imagery

Two further arguments can be levied against the construct of imagery as cur-rently used:

Fuzziness of concept.   The "image" is an ill-defined construct which is in need of further explication. Theorizing about im-agery has involved much arm waving,

and the actual operational definitions used in experiments have not followed explicitly, or always even implicitly, from theory. Furthermore, the operational definitions of imagery vary so widely from experiment to experiment as to obscure the common construct being ad-dressed.

Reduction to primitives.   Even given a consistent operational definition of imagery, the proper analysis of this con-struct is in terms of the most primitive, atomistic, and mechanistic elements possible. Imagery, however defined, is not a primitive construct and ought to be further reduced.

II. Critique of the Anti-Imagery Position

The arguments summarized above have two major thrusts: first, image representation is inadequate; second, propositional representation is not only more adequate but is actually required. The present section will assess the logical bases for both of these arguments while a later section will consider the usefulness of images and propositions in explaining actual experimental results.

There are two positions on which an imagery theorist could base a reply to the above arguments. The stronger stance holds that dual code theory, which assumes the existence of only perceptual and verbal codes, is sufficient to handle the representation problem without ap-pealing to abstract propositions at all. The weaker stance holds that imagery may work in conjunction with some form of propositional representation, making an essential contribution because images have emergent properties which proposi-tions lack. We shall concentrate on the stronger of these positions in our arguments below; however, the weaker stance will be addressed when ap-propriate.

A. The Picture Metaphor

Pylyshyn's attacks are based on a particular definition of imagery, namely, the picture-in-the-head hypothesis. We agree with Pylyshyn that this approach is untenable, but fail to see what is gained by attacking such a strawman. No serious student of imagery holds this view. The critical question is whether Pylyshyn's arguments bear with equal force on other conceptualizations of imagery.

Interpretation and organization. We do not believe it is fruitful to suppose that images are simply reembodiments of stored sensations. Although storage of primitive sensations is possible (e.g., in afterimages and, perhaps, in eidetic images), the products of higher perceptual activity can be stored as well. Perception is a process of information reduction whereby a welter of sensations is reduced into a simpler and more organized form. These organizational processes result in our perceptions being structured into units corresponding to objects and properties of objects. It is these larger units that will be stored and later be assembled into images that are experienced as quasi-pictorial, spatial entities resembling those evoked during perception itself (cf., Neisser, 1967). It is obviously wrong to consider the representation of an object during perception as photographic; by the same token, it is erroneous to equate image representations with mental photographs, since this would overlook the structure present within an image.

Imagery and seeing. No researcher in the field would seriously argue that images are like pictures; pictures are concrete objects that exist in the world, while images are ethereal entities that occur in the mind. A more serious claim is that the experience of an image resembles the experience of seeing the referent of the image. Similar internal representations are posited to underlie all forms of visual experience (whether perceptual or imaginal), and these representations may be activated by information from the sensory periphery (when one is viewing a scene or picture), or by information from long-term memory (when one is imaging; cf., Hebb, 1968). The internal representations then may be processed in ways appropriate to the processing of sensory data regardless of whether they are sensory or imaginal in origin (see Kosslyn, 1974, for an elaboration of this thesis). At some point in the data-processing stream, images and percepts have a common format, which differs from the format of representations of other (e.g., linguistic) sorts of information.

It could be argued that in equating imagery with perception we have gained little since perception itself is so poorly understood. We disagree with this argument on two counts. First, one does gain something in reducing the number of unknowns to be explained from two to one. Second, while perception is far from being totally understood, we do know some things about it, and this knowledge may be usefully applied in the study of imagery (cf. Hebb, 1968; Segal & Fusella, 1970).

Inappropriate metaphors? Many of the visual metaphors used in theorizing about imagery are not as ill-conceived as it might seem. For example, the fact that mobile eyeballs are not available for viewing images poses no insurmountable problems. In Sperling's (1960) famous experiments on scanning afterimages (or "icons"), eye movements were clearly irrelevant. Furthermore, Kaufman and Richards (1969) showed that where one's eyes are directed and where one thinks one is looking are not necessarily the same. What is required for scanning an image is a shift of attention from one part of the image to another. This no more requires physical motion than does the shift of a "pointer" within a data structure in a computer memory.

The mind's eye. Perception is not the inspection of some internal screen by a homunculus; it is the processing of sensory information. Such processing may take place in stages (see Sternberg, 1966), wherein the products of applying one operation are then processed anew by a further operation. We can think of the "mind's eye" as a processor that interprets perceptual representations (i.e., those underlying perceptual experience) in terms of "conceptual" categories. For example, the array depicting blocks in Guzman's (1968) computer program may be thought of as a "perceptual" representation, which then may be categorized (via template matching and the like) into conceptual categories (e.g., "block"); this classification stage is equivalent to a "mind's eye." When these interpretative processes are applied to remembered perceptual information instead of information that comes from the senses, an image rather than a percept will be experienced. Sophisticated computer programs (e.g., Guzman, 1968; Winston, 1970) have demonstrated that a homunculus is not required for an effective perceptual system. The routines used in these programs could, in principle, operate just as well on information being fed in from the computer's memory (imagery) as from a TV camera (perception). In fact, most of these programs dispense with external input and work only with memory representations.[3]

Capacity limitations. Pylyshyn claims that image representations would strain the limited capacity of the brain. This point remains moot because: (1) We do not know what the capacity limitation of the brain is, or even if it has one; and (2) we have no good measure of the amount of information contained in an image or a percept of a scene. Furthermore, the capacity-limit argument would be effective only against the picture theory, in which the image is thought to consist of relatively unprocessed sensations. If we treat images as being composed of relatively large, interpreted, perceptual "chunks," like the arms, legs, head, and trunk of a person, the number of informational units to be encoded may not be so large.

Accessibility. Pylyshyn's claim that an enormous amount of time would be necessary to retrieve a particular image assumes that images: (1) are uninterpreted, and thus cannot be "content addressed"; and (2) have no other information associated with them in memory which could be used to "look them up." It seems entirely possible that verbal labels or other codes associated with images could serve this purpose. If images are analogous to the displays generated on a cathode-ray tube by a computer program, for example, different data files (which store different images) could be named and later called up by name. In addition, it remains possible that all images are in fact randomly searched, just as Pylyshyn suggests, whenever a particular one is sought. We have no way of knowing what the speed of such a search might be and need not assume that the search would be apparent to consciousness (cf., Sternberg, 1966).

B. Propositional Knowledge

This section addresses the claim that a propositional format is necessary in order to account for our knowledge of structures and relations in the world. Contrary to Pylyshyn, we believe that mental imagery can represent such knowlege in its own right. There is no dispute, of course, that knowledge can be represented in terms of propositions. The invention of the "proposition" originally was motivated in part by a desire to capture the common "idea" underlying differently expressed but synonymous statements. Consequently, the construct of the proposition was formulated to be powerful and flexible enough to represent all knowledge. Nevertheless, propositions need not be the only way of modeling mental processes and structures. Sufficiency does not imply necessity.

Knowledge and information representation. A person does not have knowledge when he has a mental image any more than a camera has knowledge when it contains exposed film (see Wittgenstein, 1953). This point is hardly original. Nevertheless, images may contain information from which knowledge can be derived. If images are sensory patterns that have been partially processed and stored, the question of how knowledge can be derived from images is quite similar to the question of how knowledge is derived from ongoing sensory activity. Knowledge obviously is derived from perceptual representations, and there seems to be no reason why it should not also be gleaned in similar ways from mental images.

It also should be kept in mind that mere possession of representations in propositional format does not constitute knowledge either, any more than a page has knowledge because a sentence is written on it. It only makes sense to speak of knowledge in the context of some processes that make use of internal representations. If not a "mind's eye," some sort of "mind's frontal lobe" is necessary to interpret even abstract propositions (and yet we do not feel in danger of an "infinite regress" of propositions and "mind's frontal lobes"!). If knowledge is viewed in terms of active processes performed on data structures rather than in terms of the static structures themselves, then using propositions instead of images as the format for these structures does not necessarily gain us anything. In either case, processors must be postulated that operate on the data structures. The power of any representational format can be

assessed only by considering its compatibility with these processors.

Evaluating efficiency of formats. The different characteristics of representation systems can lead to differences in the nature, speed, and efficiency of the processing they support. Consider two formats for representing geographical information: a map, and a chart of intercity distances. These two systems may be completely isomorphic to each other in all important respects since they contain identical information and either one can be generated from the other. Nevertheless, they have obviously different properties. The map is an analog representation, which makes it suitable for rapid geometrical computations; the chart of intercity distances is digital, which makes it suitable for rapid arithmetic computations. If we want to know quickly whether three cities fall on a straight line, we consult a map; if we want to know the total distance of an air flight from New York to Los Angeles to Miami, we consult the chart. Clearly other forms of external representation besides these two are possible: lists of sentences expressing propositions such as "Miami is south of Atlanta," for example, or tree structures containing similar propositional information. It is likely that each of these formats would be optimal for some purposes but not for all. The "efficiency" of a representation, then, depends in part upon the purposes to which one puts that representation.

Given that different types of external representation formats have different characteristics, the same may apply to internal representations. There is good evidence (which we will summarize below) that information can be represented internally in at least two different formats, which differ in their suitability for different tasks. It is not necessary to assume that information must always be recorded into a common, propositional format. Even if images were generated or derived from propositional representations (as in our cathode-ray tube metaphor mentioned earlier), the information they contain might be more readily accessed from the emergent image rather than from the underlying structure.

Capacity considerations. In comparing the economy of representational systems using images and propositions, it is necessary to know how many propositions are necessary to represent a scene or an event. This question is difficult to answer because: (1) we lack the means to measure the amount of information in a scene or episode, and (2) we do not know which of an infinite number of sets of propositions best represents a scene or event. In any case, when one considers the models proposed to date (e.g., Baylor, 1971), one is impressed with the sheer number of propositions needed to represent even relatively simple objects. These numbers become even greater if one assumes, with Pylyshyn, that propositions are constructed to represent knowledge at several different levels of hierarchy at the same time. Thus, it might be much more wasteful to generate hordes of propositions at the time of encoding than to store a smaller number of perceptual units which could then be used at a later time for making deductions. If limited encoding or memory capacity is an important factor in internal representation, then it is advantageous to encode and store as little as possible and to deduce as much as possible when more detailed information is required. Although propositions could also be used for deduction, certain implicit relations can be derived much more easily from images (as discussed above in connection with discovering which cities fall along a straight line).

Since the storage capacity of the brain and its encoding systems is unknown, not much weight should be given to these considerations. However, it is clear that capacity arguments levied against imagery can be applied to propositions with equal force.

Predictive value. Making comparisons between the predictive value of models based on images and models based on propositions is difficult. Few image-based systems have been worked out with sufficient rigor to generate detailed predictions. However, virtually all of them have some assumptions in common, such as the sharing the mechanisms between imagery and like-modality perception. These assumptions have led to certain qualitative predictions, such as modality-specific interference between perception and imagery, which will be reviewed shortly.

The problem with propositional theories, on the other hand, is that they may be too powerful. They possess no inherent constraints, and the theorist must add restrictions onto his theory to make it conform with experimental observations. The propositional language is so powerful that one can use it to formulate almost any kind of theory that one desires, predicting with equal ease, it would seem, any experimental finding or its converse. The human representational system is limited while a propositional representational system in principle may not be limited; thus, one must find some way of introducing constraints into a propositionally based model to account for the constraints so apparent in human memory.

Requirements of propositional representation. Propositional format, by definition, requires explicit notation of a relation or operator distinct from the representations of the arguments (elements). Is propositional formatting, then, appropriate for both visual and verbal codes? Consider the sentence, "The ball is left of the cube," and a photograph of the same scene. In the sentence, the relation "is left of" is explicit, and the sentence seems easily converted into propositional format (which is abstract, but otherwise similar in structure to that of English sentence format). In the picture, however, the spatial relation is not given explicitly; it is defined implicitly by the positions of the objects. The relation simply cannot be expressed in this format without also depicting the ball and the cube. Clearly, a photograph is not propositional in its format. Is an iconic image? We think not. A long-term memory image? Although it may be possible to represent the information in such an image propositionally, if relations are not explicitly represented in images (which is an empirical question), it probably is best to consider imagery as a distinct format which is not equivalent to "propositional" format (which presumably characterizes memory for linguistic material).

C. Necessity of a Third Code

Pylyshyn argues that an interlingual code must be postulated since translation between verbal and perceptual codes cannot occur directly. Further, this third code should be amodal and propositional in nature. We find this argument unconvincing for the following reasons.

Transformational rules. To solve the translation problem, one must have a set of transformational rules that specify how one format is represented or mapped in terms of another. It would be a mistake, however, to equate these transformational rules with specific world knowledge as Pylyshyn appears to do. These rules would not represent information about the world, but only about the codes between which translation is required. These rules would take the form of processes or routines, which when applied to information coded in one format

would produce a corresponding representation in another format. No intermediate third form of representation need be involved.

Parsimony. Some form of perceptual code and some form of verbal code are required in order to account for our perceptual (input) and response (output) capacities. Clearly, if these two codes were shown to be sufficient, a dual code position (e.g., Paivio, 1971) would be more economical than a theory postulating an additional, third code. Moreover, those who have claimed that translation between verbal and perceptual codes requires a separate propositional representational system have never specified how this translation would be accomplished. It appears to us that this assumption simply pushes the problem back one step. How is translation to be accomplished between images and propositions? Between propositions and verbal codes? Translation problems exist for both dual-code theory and a three-code theory and may be more difficult for the latter if the *two* translational steps required (versus *one* for dual-code theory) are based on different operations. However translation between verbal and image codes may be achieved, it is not clear that an intermediate propositional representation would aid in this process.

D. Introspective Data

Three points should be made concerning introspective data:

A source of corroborative data. Introspections are not adequate in and of themselves to attest to the functional role of imagery in cognition. However, they are one source of evidence which, when taken together with behavioral performance data (e.g., the time necessary to make certain introspections—see Kosslyn, 1973, 1974, 1975, 1976), can assist in demonstrating that images have genuine functions in cognition.

Generality.   Although a theory that deals with publically observable behavior alone may be adequate for understanding a class of behaviors, one that can explain introspective evidence as well with no added complexity certainly is to be preferred.

Phenomenology.   The experience of imagery is undeniable, even if its functional role is an open question. This experience must arise as a consequence of some psychological processes; simply labeling it as "epiphenomenal" will not make it go away. The study of phenomenology is a legitimate enterprise in its own right, and any theory that serves to illuminate phenomenological issues achieves added value.

E. Problems of Definition

Fuzziness of concept.   The absence of a precise definition of "image" at present hardly constitutes grounds for deciding on the ultimate adequacy of imagery as a theoretical construct. Pylyshyn expresses concern that different theorists and experimenters operationalize imagery in different ways and that there is no single operation that can uniquely define the existence or functioning of the image. This is a common problem; "image" is not the only construct in cognitive psychology that lacks a unique operational definition. Most psychologists, however, have become comfortable with the use of converging operations to define entities that are not subject to direct observation. In fact, Garner, Hake, and Eriksen (1956) argue that unitary operational definitions should be avoided when dealing with inferred constructs, since such definitions confound the entity being measured with the instrument doing the measurement. Rather, a number of independent operations should be devised to "converge" on

the construct. In this approach, a good deal of research must be conducted before a satisfactory operational definition can be framed at all. Thus, it is legitimate for a scientific enterprise in its formative period to be engaged in research on a construct whose definition has not yet been precisely formulated. We believe that this accurately describes the current status of imagery research; we also believe that some imagery research has begun to converge successfully, as we shall show below.

Reduction to primitives: What is the proper level of analysis?   It seems likely that imagery can be described in terms of more basic processes, perhaps including propositional representations (as is evident in some of the more successful computer simulations of imagery tasks, e.g., Moran, 1973). But will this exercise increase our understanding of mental phenomena or merely cloud over important distinctions? As Putnam (1973) points out, we must take care to distinguish explanations from "parents of explanations." Consider Putnam's example of the appropriate explanation for why a certain square peg will not fit into a certain round hole. The proper level of analysis would not entail discussion of subatomic particles, but would make use of emergent properties like "rigidity" and "contour," properties that are not necessarily derivable from only a knowledge of the most molecular constitution of the objects involved. Similarly, one would not learn much about architecture simply by studying bricks, mortar, and other building materials. The proper focus on the imagery question, then, concerns finding the effective, functional internal representation, rather than the most "basic" irreducible one. The issue is *not* whether images may be derived from more primitive "propositional" or "symbolic" representations. Rather, it is whether a quasi-pictorial image – however derived—has emergent properties and so can serve as a distinct form of representation. If so, then images deserve a role as a useful theoretical construct. This assignment need not be made solely on a priori, logical grounds.

III. Consideration of Empirical Findings

A large body of literature is relevant to the topic under discussion. We will not try to review all the relevant experiments exhaustively, but will restrict the discussion to a few representative ones. Further detail and references can be obtained in other sources (e.g., Paivio, 1971).

Five classes of experiments will be described below. Following each description, we will briefly show how one possible imagery theory would deal with the typical findings of the experiments and then outline a possible propositional treatment of the same data. A short critical comparison of the two treatments will also be offered. These accounts are not intended as definitive statements of each position, but as representative examples of interpretations currently in vogue. This exercise should serve to make many of the points raised previously more concrete. Before proceeding, however, we must briefly describe the sorts of imagery and propositional theories on which our explanations will be based.

Assumptions of the Imagery Accounts

The imagery explanations will be based on a few central ideas:[4]

(1) An image is a spatial representation like that underlying the experience of seeing an object during visual perception. These images may be generated from underlying abstract representations (see Kosslyn, 1974), but the contents of these underlying representations are accessible only via generation of a surface (experienced) image.

(2) Only a finite processing capacity[5] is available for constructing and representing images. This limits the amount of detail that may be activitated at any one moment.

(3) Images, once formed, are wholes that may be compared to percepts in a template-like manner.

(4) The same structures that represent spatial information extracted during vision also support images.

(5) Many of the same operators (excluding peripheral functions) that are used in analyzing percepts are also applied to images.

Assumptions of the Propositional Accounts

Because propositional representation can be used to model practically any theory, we cannot state a definitive propositional explanation of any given result. We will base our accounts on a possible theory that uses propositional representation in a straightforward, parsimonious manner. Our treatments will be in the spirit of the computer simulations described by Anderson and Bower (1973), Rumelhart, Lindsay, and Norman (1972), Minsky and Papert (1972), Pylyshyn (1973), and others. These conceptions include no provision for a "surface" image, but attempt to model all processes in terms of underlying "abstract" propositional representations. The propositional explanations are based on the notions that:

(1) Material in memory is represented by networks of propositions.

(2) Only a limited number of propositions may be entered into active memory at one time. Time and effort are required to activate propositional structures.

(3) Networks may be accessed by a specified ordered search which scans node by node. Networks also may be compared to other networks node by node simultaneously.

(4) Networks can be constructed in a manner such that any desired spatial relations can be represented.

(5) Networks or portions of networks are similar to the extent that similar propositions (i.e., having the same relations and/or elements) are incorporated into them.

Selective Interference

Many studies have shown that imaging and perceiving in the same modality interfere with each other more than when two distinct modalities are involved. A classic result was obtained by Segal and Fusella (1970), who found that detection of a *visual* signal was more impaired by instructions to make irrelevant *visual* images at the same time than by concomitant *auditory* images, but vice versa for detection for an auditory signal. Brooks (1967, 1968), Byrne (1974), and others (summarized for the most part in Paivio, 1971) have reported corroborative findings. Of particular interest is Segal and Fusella's (1971) finding of modality-specific interference in six different sensory modalities (gustatory, tactile, kinesthetic, olfactory, visual, and auditory).

An imagery account. These results can be understood if the process of imaging in a specific modality utilizes some of the same mental machinery specialized for perceptual processing in that same modality, but not in other modalities. Visual imagery, for example, may occur within the same structures that are involved in processing stimulation from the retina. These two types of input might easily interfere with each other, or they might intermix, making it difficult to ascertain the original source of an input. Since the representational structures of the visual system are different than those involved in audition, visual imaging should impair simultaneous visual perception more than simultaneous auditory

perception. By the same token, auditory imagery involves some specialized auditory perceptual mechanisms (but not specialized visual perceptual ones), and hence will disrupt simultaneous auditory perception more than simultaneous visual perception.

A propositional account. Visual images are represented by propositions that incorporate various spatial relations (e.g., "left of," "above", etc.). These same relations appear in the descriptions generated by the perceptual apparatus. Since the propositions decribing images are similar in form to those describing percepts, they are difficult to distinguish from each other. In this case, a person might mistakenly interpret a percept to be an image, and thus fail to perceive the stimulus as such. If propositions representing material encoded in different modalities use different relations (as seems necessary), then it will be easier to distinguish these propositions from each other than if propositions encode material in the same modality (using similar relations and structure).

Critical comparison. The two explanations based on confusion and misclassification of source of origin seem indistinguishable. One possible difference between the two models suggests itself, however. If the propositional model is correct, one might be able to establish perception-like representations verbally, perhaps by describing a scene and asking a person to remember the content of the description. In this case, selective decreases in visual perceptual sensitivity ought to occur without imagery instructions. The imagery account, of course, makes no such prediction.

Mental Rotation

Recent experiments on analog properties of internal representations have produced results that must be dealt with by any theory of imaging. Shepard and Metzler (1971), Cooper and Shepard (1973a, b), and Cooper (1975) report experiments on the mental rotation of internal representations (of letters, digits, block-like forms, or Attneave figures). In a typical experiment, subjects must judge whether or not a test figure is the same as a standard or different from it (in which case it is usually a mirror-reversed version of the standard). The test figure has been rotated to one of several orientations before presentation. The major finding is that the further the figure has been rotated from the orientation of the standard, the longer are the subjects' decision-times. This result is consistent with the notion that subjects rotate a mental image of the stimulus to the standard orientation before deciding. In some experiments subjects were told the identity and orientation of an upcoming test figure in advance and asked to indicate when they were "ready" for it. These preparation times showed a similar pattern: The further the rotation, the more time was required. It may be important to note that these subjects were not explicitly told to use imagery in the tasks; when interviewed after the experimental session, however, most subjects reported performing the task by mentally rotating images of the stimuli.

An imagery account. The imagery explanation of this phenomenon is that subjects mentally rotate an image representation of the test figure into congruence with the standard. One question that this interpretation must answer is why rotation is necessary at all; that is, why is not the image of the test figure instantaneously transformed into the proper orientation for comparison with the standard? A possible answer rests on the claim that people try to minimize the effort necessary to perform any transformation. Generating a new image (of the object in a new orientation) may require more effort than transforming an already available image. There are many reasons why available images may be transformed gradually. The simplest explanation is that image transformations are constrained to behave in a fashion like analogous physical transformations. One often-cited use of imagery, after all, is as a model for anticipating the effects of physical manipulations. Thus, it is plausible that the imagery representational system would have evolved to mimic the sorts of gradual transformations that occur when one physically manipulates objects.

Other explanations involving specific mechanisms are possible. For example, one explanation posits that it may be optimal to transform available images a portion at a time to minimize the amount of effort expended any given moment. If images are transformed a part at a time, only relatively small transformations could be used or the image would seem to bend, warp, or fragment. Thus, "rotation" may consist of a series of stepwise transformations, each so small as to appear continuous. More time is required to rotate further distances because more intervening small transformations are performed.

A propositional account. An image of an object may be represented in terms of a network of propositions that describes how lines and arcs are interrelated. A letter "A," for example, might be described as two lines meeting at the top to form a vertex and bridged about halfway down by a short horizontal line. Rotation would proceed by replacing all relations with new ones, systematically altered in regard to spatial reference. When rotating 45° clockwise, for example "top" might be replaced by "northeastern orientation," and "right" by "southeastern orientation."

Critical comparison. The imagery account seems somewhat plausible and relatively straightforward. The propositional account seems less satisfactory: Aside from the problem of not knowing how to represent the letters in the first place, it is not clear why rotation is gradual in such a system. It should be especially easy to rotate an image 180° because all the relations could simply be reversed (e.g., right becomes left). To rotate an image 45° should be more difficult, because more complex substitutions must be implemented. Nevertheless, subjects take longer to rotate an imaged object 180° than 45°. It appears that people do not (or cannot) skip from one orientation of an image directly to another, but must proceed gradually. Such a prediction does not follow from basic concepts of propositional representation (for example, especially see Gips, 1974).

Image Size

Similar results have been obtained for the effects of image size. Hayes (1973) presented the subject with two letters in succession. He was instructed to retain an image of the initial letter, and then to decide whether or not the second "test" letter was the same letter of the alphabet as the first. "Same" decision times were faster when the test letter was the same size as the imaged letter than when a size disparity existed. This finding seems to demonstrate that images can represent different sizes of objects.

Kosslyn (1975) also examined the effects of imaged size. He argued that since it is hard to discriminate details of small stimuli in perception, we might expect similar effects in imagery. In fact, when subjects were asked to form images of animals at subjectively smaller sizes, the time they required to "see" internally represented details of the imaged animal (e.g., a cat's legs) increased. This result appeared not only when subjects were asked to adjust the relative size of images of isolated animals, but also when image size was manipulated indirectly. In the

latter case, the size of a target animal (e.g., a rabbit) was made relatively small by having subjects image it next to an elephant or relatively large by requesting that it be imaged next to an appropriately scaled fly. Furthermore, Kosslyn (1976) reports that smaller properties (e.g., a cat's claws) of animals require more time to affirm than larger ones (e.g., its head) when subjects use imagery; this was true despite the fact that smaller properties were more strongly associated with the animal in question than were the larger properties. In contrast, when subjects who were not requested to use imagery simply judged the appropriateness of presented properties for given animals, the smaller and more highly associated properties were responded to more quickly. Thus, the data clearly distinguish between cases where imagery was and was not encouraged (Cf., Smith, Rips & Shoben, 1974).

An imagery account. If images are like surface displays generated on a cathode-ray tube by computer, it should be easy to change their size scale.[6] An image representation might be placed "over" (e.g., displayed in the same matrix as) a representation evoked by a percept, and the two representations matched wholistically. If the image and perceptual representations were initially matched for size, this template-like comparison would be faster than if size adjustments had to be made. Thus, Hayes' finding makes sense within an imagery framework.

Kosslyn's results are explained if images can be "re-processed" by applying the same processes used in categorizing percepts and parts of percepts. These processes are assumed to require a minimal spatial extent upon which to operate efficiently (see Kosslyn, 1975). Thus, larger images should be more quickly categorized than smaller images. When subjects are not instructed to use imagery, some other form of internal representation is presumably accessed. For example, there may be lists of linguistic descriptions in which representations of the animal's properties are ordered in terms of associative strength. More highly associated properties would then be nearer the "top" of the list (i.e., the point of entry during search), and thus located more quickly.

A propositional account. Under imagery instructions, letters would be represented by networks of propositions that relate lines and arcs; these propositions also represent metric size and distance information. When subjects are asked to image letters at the same size as perceived letters, the internal representations are more similar (because the same metric information is listed propositionally, and more easily compared) than when sizes mismatch. This explanation accounts for Hayes' results.

Kosslyn's initial results for image size can be understood if an image of an animal corresponds to the activation of a list structure. This structure contains propositions representing characteristics of the animal and how they are related together. It could be assumed that the larger the size of an image, the more such representations are activated. As more representations are activated, the probability increases that a queried property's representation will be available. If so, a subject discovers it at once when probed; if not, he must consume time in activating it.

The results on the size of the probed part would be explained if it were assumed that larger properties are located higher (i.e., nearer the point of list entry) than smaller properties in the list describing an animal. Thus, subjects would discover larger properties more quickly because these properties are more likely to be activated and available at the time of the query. When images are not used, other lists — ordered in terms of associa-

tion strength — are accessed in the manner described above.

Critical comparison. The imagery account of Hayes' results seems much more plausible to us than the propositional account. The propositional representation of metric information seems less appropriate for the phenomena at hand, and the account of the size-congruence effect seems ad hoc. The propositional account of Kosslyn's results also seems less satisfactory than the imagery account: Why should people access less information about an object when asked to "image it small"? This seems ad hoc; a propositional model would not lead one to expect such effects. The requirement that people represent an object's properties in two differently ordered lists — one to be used in response to imagery instructions and one for use on other occasions — also seems strained.

Imagery and "Parallel Processing"

It is frequently claimed that imagery differs from other forms of internal representation in that much information is available simultaneously, instead of being accessible only by a sequential search (see Paivio, 1971). Perhaps the best examples of studies that support this notion are those of Smith and Nielson (1970) and Nielson and Smith (1973). Smith and Nielson asked subjects to decide whether a test face was identical to a standard presented just previously. Faces were constructed from a set of "features" (e.g., mouth, eyebrows) and varied with respect to 3, 4, or 5 features. In addition, test faces were presented either 1, 4, or 10 sec after the standard. The "same" reaction times (when the test face was identical to the standard) increased with the number of features incorporated, but only for the longer intervals (cf. Sekuler and Abrams, 1968). Nielson and Smith (1973) then tested the notion that an image of the initial face had been wholistically compared against the test face at short interstimulus intervals but not at longer ones. If so, they reasoned, then instructions to hold an image should eliminate the effect of number of features which had been observed at the longer intervals. This result was in fact obtained; when subjects intentionally maintained images of the originally presented face, the number of features no longer had any effect on "same" decisions even at intervals up to 10 sec.

An image account. This account is virtually the same as one offered for the Hayes results on imaged letter size. An image is constructed and subsequently used as a template. The number of features is irrelevant up to the point where image processing capacity is exceeded. Thus, images representing 3, 4, or 5 features may be held in memory with more or less equal ease and can subsequently be used like templates on the input.

Since most adults are accustomed to verbal encoding, a short time after presentation they describe the standard face to themselves and remember this verbal description, unless instructed otherwise. Such a description might resemble a list of features, which then must be compared sequentially to the features of the test face. Thus, after some seconds, inclusion of more features in a face should result in increased "same" reaction time.

A propositional account. The faces are represented as networks of propositions. The propositional structure initially formed to represent a face is extremely complex and elaborate. This propositional structure may be compared to like portions of similar structures exhaustively in parallel, corresponding parts being matched simultaneously. Parallel comparison rates remain constant when 3, 4, or 5 features are being compared.

After a given length of time it becomes difficult to maintain and compare such complex structures, and the propositions are reorganized into a simpler list. This list is then compared sequentially, proposition by proposition, to the corresponding propositions representing the perceived test face. Imagery instructions have the effect of causing subjects to retain the more detailed and complex representation.

Critical comparison. Both explanations seem to work, but each of them has some difficulty in explaining the transition from "image" to "list" representations with the passage of time. In the imagery account, one could hypothesize that images usually decay after a while; imagery instructions result in more-than-usual capacity being allocated to preserve them. The similar notion required by the propositional account is perhaps more arbitrary.

Scanning Visual Images

Although people seem to be able to keep many parts of an image in mind at once, they can also attend selectively to portions of images, Kosslyn (1973) tested the notion that images, once constructed, have spatial properties that allow them to be scanned. If so, he reasoned, it should take more time to scan further across the image. His subjects were asked to memorize a set of drawings, and later to visualize one drawing at a time. Subjects were asked to "focus" on one end of the object they had imaged (e.g., the rear portion of a speedboat). Following this, a possible property of the original picture was named; half of these properties had really been included on the picture and half had not. The measure of interest was the time necessary to decide whether the property had been present, as a function of how far one needed to scan to reach the appropriate location. And in fact, greater scanning distances resulted in longer retrieval times (it took more time to scan to the bow than to a porthole located midway across the boat). A second group of subjects, asked to keep the whole image in mind at once, showed no differences in time needed to retrieve properties located in different positions on the image. Thus, it appeared that images could actually be scanned.

Lea (1975) pointed out that in Kosslyn's experiment more properties fell between locations relatively far apart on an image than between locations closer together. Thus, distance and number of properties to be scanned over were confounded, and the distance effects could be an artifact of this confounding. Recent experiments (Kosslyn, Note 1) eliminated this confounding and still found strong effects of actual distance on time to scan across images. In one experiment, for example, time was linearly related to 21 different distances scanned between all possible pairs of 7 locations on an imaged map.

An imagery account. One interesting way of explaining the scanning of an image is to treat it as a kind of image transformation. Such an explanation posits that the entire image may not display uniform resolution or clarity. The center may be in "sharper focus" because more capacity is allocated for construction of details there. If so, then scanning may consist in moving the image such that different portions occupy the "center." (This sort of shifting account of scanning may sound counterintuitive, but the same thing happens on a TV or movie screen when the camera scans across an object — which is not seen as strange.) The reason the image is shifted gradually across the field, then, will be the same as that invoked in explaining mental rotation effects. One explanation would posit that parts are shifted step by step (to minimize capacity expended at any given moment), but only as far as can be done without fragmenting the image. Thus, an increasing number of small shifts (requiring more time) are performed as one scans further across an image.

A propositional account. Measures of distance between pairs of locations may be explicitly listed in memory. Time to respond is regulated by values associated with each entry, longer distances causing a longer lag in the output system prior to executing a response.

Critical comparison. The imagery account seems somewhat plausible, while the propositional account seems entirely ad hoc. A propositional framework based on discrete units and links is inherently ill-suited for representation of metric, analog information.

IV. Conclusions

We have found no reason to discard imagery as an explanatory construct in psychology, either on structural or functional grounds. There are no convincing arguments that images are not represented in a distinct format, nor can imagery phenomena be easily accounted for by appealing to propositional representations. In addition, there is some evidence that emergent properties of images do in fact play a functional role in cognition.

We have intentionally not committed ourselves to a "strong" or "weak" imagery position, as outlined earlier. These positions differ in whether images are thought to be derived from propositional representations or are thought to be a primitive, irreducible form of representation. This question may be basically unanswerable. In addition, the question of a strong or weak position is tangential to the one at hand. If images (surface representations) display distinct and unique properties, then imagery clearly deserves a special role as an explanatory construct. The current debate boils down to the question of whether or not images have emergent properties not directly derivable from properties of propositions. This issue will not be settled by taking an overly reductionistic tack, but rather should be addressed by concentrating on answerable empirical questions about the properties of surface images. We do not expect that further metatheoretical speculation about the underpinnings of imagery will lead to genuine progress in the field.

Notes

1. An earlier version of this paper was written in late 1974. Since then, Paivio (in press) has made some similar arguments, and Pylyshyn (in press, a, b) has further developed his ideas. We feel that Pylyshyn's recent elaborations of the anti-imagist position are also countered by the general sorts of arguments offered here, and thus we do not address these elaborations in detail at present. The authors wish to thank Robert Abelson, Howard Egeth, Steve Palmer, and Zenon Pylyshyn for helpful suggestions. We especially wish to thank Ulric Neisser, who did a superb job in editing our manuscript. This work was supported partly by Biomedical Sciences Grant 5 SO5 RR07041-09 awarded to The Johns Hopkins University by the Division of Research Resources, DHEW. In addition, the first author's work was supported by NIMH Grant R03 MH 27012.

2. Most of Pylyshyn's arguments are addressed to the topic of visual imagery. We will follow suit, although the reader should keep in mind that parallel arguments may be levied for and against imagery in other modalities as well.

3. The actual Guzman program itself does not work directly on a digitalized image, but operates on a list of points (vertices), lines (edges), and regions (surfaces). Guzman's program has reportedly been interfaced with the "Horn-Binford line finder" program, however, which constructs lists of the sort used by Guzman's program from a digitalized image. Thus, the description above is of the two programs working together, the Horn-Binford one acting as a preprocessor for Guzman's program.

4. S. M. Kosslyn and S. P. Shwartz have implemented a computer simulation that incorporates these assumptions.

5. "Processing capacity" is limited by the rate at which images may be constructed and the rate at which they fade. If too much detail must be filled in, initially constructed portions of the image may have decayed before the entire image is completed (and thus, the object or scene cannot be imaged all at once).

6. Although we may talk of a "large" image for convenience, it is understood that the image itself is not "large" or "small" or any size (it is not an object). Rather, the representations that compose the image register size in the same way that the corresponding representations evoked during perception register size. The same point applies to other aspects of images as well: color, movement, orientation, etc. (See Shepard & Chipman, 1970.)

References

Anderson, J. R., & Bower, G. H. *Human associative memory.* New York: V. H. Winston & Sons, 1973.

Baylor, G. W. *A Treatise on the mind's eye.* Unpublished Ph.D. thesis, Carnegie-Mellon University, 1971.

Bower, G. H. Mental imagery and associative learning. In L. Gregg (Ed.), *Cognition in learning and memory,* New York: Wiley, 1972.

Brooks, L. The suppression of visualization by reading. *Quarterly Journal of Experimental Psychology,* 1967, 19, 280-299.

Brooks, L. Spatial and verbal components of the act of recall. *Canadian Journal of Psychology,* 1968, 22, 349-368.

Byrne, B. Item concreteness vs spatial organization as predictors of visual imagery. *Memory and Cognition,* 1974, 2, 53-59.

Clark, H. H., & Chase, W. G. On the process of comparing sentences against pictures. *Cognitive Psychology,* 1972, 3, 472-517.

Cooper, L. A. Mental rotation of random two-dimensional shapes. *Cognitive Psychology,* 1975, 7, 20-43.

Cooper, L. A., & Shepard, R. N. Chronometric studies of the rotation of mental images. In W. G. Chase, (Ed.), *Visual information processing.* New York: Academic Press, 1973. (a)

Cooper, L. A., & Shepard, R. N. The time required to prepare for a rotated stimulus. *Memory and Cognition,* 1973, 1, 246-250. (b)

Garner, W. R., Hake, H. W., & Eriksen, C. W. Operationism and the concept of perception. *Psychological Review*, 1956, 63, 149-159.

Gibson, J. J. *The Senses Considered as Perceptual Systems*. Boston: Houghton Mifflin, 1966.

Gips, J. A syntax-directed program that performs a three-dimensional perceptual task. *Pattern Recognition*, 1974, 6, 189-199.

Guzman, A. *Computer recognition of three-dimensional objects in a visual scene*. MIT Artificial Intelligence Laboratory Project MAC-TR-59, 1968.

Hayes, J. R. On the function of visual imagery in elementary mathematics. In W. G. Chase, (Ed.), *Visual information processing*. New York: Academic Press, 1973.

Hebb, D. O. Concerning imagery. *Psycholgical Review*, 1968, 75, 466-477.

Kaufman, L., & Richards, W. Spontaneous fixation tendencies for visual forms. *Perceptions & Psychophysics*, 1969, 5, 85-88.

Kosslyn, S. M. Scanning visual images: some structural implications. *Perception & Psychophysics*, 1973, 14, 90-94.

Kosslyn, S. M. *Constructing visual images*. Unpublished Ph.D. dissertation, Stanford University, 1974.

Kosslyn, S. M. Information representation in visual images. *Cognitive Psychology*, 1975, 7, 341-370.

Kosslyn, S. M. Can imagery be distinguished from other forms of internal representation? Evidence from studies of information retrieval time. *Memory and Cognition*, 1976, 4, 291-297.

Lea, G. Chronometric analysis of the method of loci. *Journal of Experimental Psychology: Human Perception and Performance*, 1975, 104, 95-104.

Minsky, M., & Papert, S. *Research at the laboratory in vision, language, and other problems of intelligence*. MIT Artificial Intelligence Memo 252, 1972.

Moran, T. P. *The symbolic imagery hypothesis: A production system model*. Unpublished Ph.D. thesis, Carnegie-Mellon University, 1973.

Moscovitch, M. Language and the cerebral hemispheres: Reaction time studies and their implications for models of cerebral dominance. In P. Pliner, L. Kromes, & T. Alloway (Eds.). *Communication and affect: Language and thought*. New York: Academic Press, 1973.

Nielson, G. D., & Smith, E. E. Imaginal and verbal representations in short-term recognition of visual forms. *Journal of Experimental Psychology*, 1973, 101, 375-377.

Paivio, A. *Imagery and verbal processes*. New York: Holt, Rinehart & Winston, 1971.

Paivio, A. Images, propositions, and knowledge. J. M. Nicholas (Ed.), *Images, Perception and Knowledge, The Western Ontario Series in Philosophy of Science*. Dordrecht: Reidel, in press.

Putnam, H. Reductionism and the nature of psychology. *Cognition*, 1973, 2, 131-146.

Pylyshyn, Z. W. What the mind's eye tells the mind's brain: A critique of mental imagery. *Psychological Bulletin*, 1973, 80, 1-24.

Pylyshyn, Z. W. Imagery and artificial intelligence. In W. Savage (Ed.), *Minnesota studies in the philosophy of science*. In press. Vol. 9 (a)

Pylyshyn, Z. W. The symbolic nature of mental representations. S. Kaneff & J. F. O'Callaghan (Eds.), *Objectives and methodologies in artificial intelligence*. New York: Academic Press, in press. (b)

Reed, S. K. Structural descriptions and the limitations of visual images. *Memory and Cognition*, 1974, 2, 329-336.

Reid, L. S. Toward a grammar of the image. *Psychological Bulletin*, 1974, 81, 319-334.

Rumelhart, D. E., Lindsay, P. H., & Norman, D. A. A process model for long-term memory. In E. Tulving & W. Donaldson (Eds.), *Organization and memory*. New York: Academic Press, 1972.

Segal, S. J., & Fusella, V. Influence of imaged pictures and sounds on detection of visual and auditory signals. *Journal of Experimental Psychology*, 1970, 83, 458-464.

Segal, S. J., & Fusella, V. Effect of images in six sense modalities on detection of visual signal from noise. *Psychonomic Science*, 1971, 24, 55-56.

Sekuler, R. N., & Abrams, M. Visual sameness: A choice time analysis of pattern recognition processes. *Journal of Experimental Psychology*, 1968, 77, 232-238.

Shepard, R. N., & Chipman, S. Second-order

isomorphism of internal representations: shapes of states. *Cognitive Psychology*, 1970, 1, 1-17.

Shepard, R. N., & Metzler, J. Mental rotation of three-dimensional objects. *Science*, 1971, 171, 701-703.

Smith, E. E., & Nielson, G. D. Representation and retrieval processes in short-term memory: Recognition and recall of faces. *Journal of Experimental Psychology*, 1970, 85, 397-405.

Smith, E. E., Rips, L. J., & Shoben, E. J. Semantic memory and psychological semantics. In G. H. Bower (Ed.), *The psychology of learning and motivation*. New York: Academic Press, 1974. Vol. 8.

Sperling, G. The information available in brief visual presentations. *Psychological Monographs*, 1960, 74 (Whole No. 498).

Sternberg, S. High-speed scanning in human memory. *Science*, 1966, 153, 652-654.

Winston, P. H. *Learning structural descriptions from examples*. MIT Artificial Intelligence Laboratory Project AI-RT-231, 1970.

Wittgenstein, L. *Philosophical investigations*. New York: Macmillan, 1953.

Reference Note

1. Kosslyn, S. M. *Evidence for analogue representation*. Paper presented at the conference on Theoretical Issues in Natural Language Processing, Massachusetts Institute of Technology, Cambridge, MA, July 1975.

Imagery and Artificial Intelligence

Zenon W. Pylyshyn

1. Introduction

In this paper I shall attempt to summarize and extend some of the arguments I have advanced against the use of the notion of mental image as an explanatory construct in cognitive psychology (e.g., in Pylyshyn, 1973). In the first part (sections 2-4) I shall review some of my reasons for preferring to speak of cognitive representations — such as those involved in memory and thinking — as structured descriptions (albeit rather different from the usual linguistic descriptions) instead of images. I shall try to show that the facts of human perception, storage, and retrieval argue against the view that what is involved in such cognitive activity is some iconic and uninterpreted sensory pattern, as is implied when we speak of images. The point is not that there is no such object as an image, only that an adequate theory of the mental representation involved in imaging will depict it as having a distinctly nonpictorial character.

From C. W. Savage, ed., *Perception and Cognition. Issues in the Foundations of Psychology, Minnesota Studies in the Philosophy of Science*, vol. 9 (Minneapolis: University of Minnesota Press, 1978), pp. 19-55. Copyright © 1978 by the University of Minnesota. Reprinted by permission of the University of Minnesota Press.

Although the main arguments in the first part of the paper will be directed at the question of how knowledge is represented in long-term memory, most of the points apply equally to those transient structures constructed during imaging and thinking.

In the second part of this paper (sections 5-8) I shall examine the growing trend (at least in psychology) of referring to something called an analogical representation as a way of representing nonlinguistic information. I shall argue that much of the attraction of this notion stems from a failure to recognize some fundamental differences between the objects of perception (i.e., the physical environment) and the objects of cognition (i.e., mental representations). In this connection I shall examine some evidence frequently cited as supporting an analogical view of mental representation — in particular, experiments on such mental manipulations as "mental rotation" of figures.

2. What Is a Mental Representation Like?

It is schemata, not images of objects, which underlie our pure sensible concepts. No image could ever be adequate to the concept of a triangle in general. . . . Still less is an object of experience or its image ever adequate to the empirical concept; . . . The concept "dog" signifies a rule according to which my imagination can delineate the figure of a four-footed animal in a general manner, without limitation to any single determinate figure such as experience, or any possible image that I can represent *in concreto*, actually presents.

Emmanuel Kant,
Critique of pure reason, 1781

To begin, I shall give you an informal and somewhat discursive review of why I believe mental representations are appropriately thought of as a type of description. Consider what happens when a scene is perceived and becomes assimilated into our store of knowledge, and what happens when we later access this knowledge from memory in recalling the scene.

It is useful to distinguish two phases of the process that intervenes between the arrival of a proximal stimulus and its interpretation and assimilation as knowledge. There is some reason to believe there is an early phase in this process that has considerable autonomy—i.e., it does not depend upon higher cognitive processes except in a very general way, such as by adjusting peripheral receptors. Various phenomena that appear early in life and seem to be resistent to learning — such as figure-ground separation, certain illusions, gestalt laws of pragnanz, and perhaps some stereoscopic and temporal integration — may be identified with this phase. Roughly speaking, processes such as that which Julesz (1971) refers to as "cyclopean vision" or which Hochberg (1968) has characterized as the "mind's eye" in perception may occur immediately after this stage.

David Marr (1975) has investigated the computational requisites of this lowest level of vision and has proposed a model of this process up to figure-ground isolation. The process first computes a rich description of the optical intensity level differences present in the image; this description is called the "primal sketch."

Marr then posits certain "non-attentive" groupings and first-order discriminations acting on the primal sketch. Higher-level knowledge and purpose are brought to bear on only very few of the decisions taken during this processing.

I would argue that from a computational point of view it is appropriate to treat this early semi-autonomous phase of vision as a special purpose transducer, which takes physical magnitudes as inputs and produces symbol structures as outputs. Regardless of the precise details of this phase (it is not clear, for example, whether Julesz, Hochberg, and Marr are describing precisely the same level), there is reason to believe that: (a) there is a semi-autonomous, preattentive phase in visual perception, (b) this phase is initiated by energy arriving at the sense organs, (c) only the output of this phase, and not intermediate steps, are available for further perceptual analysis, and (d) such cognitive processes as "noticing" and the assimilation of sensory patterns into cognitive structures take place after this phase. These characteristics are ones that one would expect a "wired-in" transducer to possess.

Because of the nature of this transducer itself, it may be excluded from the process of imaging, since there are literally no adequate physical stimuli — no light patterns — to which it can apply. It is not so obvious, however, that the output of the transducer — say the aggregated primal sketch — cannot be stored in memory or even generated in the process of imaging. I shall argue, however, that it is extremely unlikely that any preconceptual, preassimilated, or knowledge-independent data are stored or otherwise used in thinking or imaging.

Consider what happens to the transducer output as it is assimilated into some cognitive structure and stored in memory for later retrieval. First of all, we are clearly highly selective in what (and how) we notice. We have to be, since not only the scene itself but the transducer output is literally unlimited in its potential for interpretation. So much is not controversial. But now let us look more closely at the *nature* of this selection or "noticing function." What follows is a sketch of some of the characteristics of the transformation that relates the output of a transducer and a memory representation of some event. Taken together, it seems to me, they provide a strong case against viewing cognitive (or memory) representations of perceptually acquired knowledge as consisting of unprocessed (unabstracted) records of transducer outputs. Note that this argument is being made not only against the view that memory consists of pictures, a view that may well be a straw man. It applies equally well if memory is thought to consist of collages of pictorial segments, sketches, dynamic motion pictures, holograms, encoded multidimensional intensity matrices, or any other form of record of a particular concrete event (the one-time output of the transducer). Properties of the transformation and of the memory representation that lead us to this view include the following.

(1) The transformation between transducer and memory does not simply produce a degradation of resolution (a blurring or a mapping of a coarser grid), since we clearly do not perceive (in any sense of that word) or remember something that is complete in all aspects but low in detail or in precision. As Bobrow (1975, p. 8) puts it, "Human visual memory does not seem to have (the) property of uniform extraction of detail, or of exhaustiveness."

(2) The transformation is not a continuous topological deformation of the pattern of stimulation. No continuous transformation results in such commonplace phenomena as, for example, failure to notice objects or relations in a scene, perceptual addition of features that were not there (e.g., "cognitive con-

tours"), or noticing the "what" but not the "where" or "when" of scene contents. Furthermore, the radical manner in which perception is influenced by such things as motivation, expectation (e.g., see the review by Bruner, 1957), prior knowledge, or even stage of cognitive development, attests not only to the general malleability of perception, but to the high degree of stimulus-independent knowledge-based *construction* that goes into the mental representation. Although this simple point is frequently forgotten, it has been made repeatedly and eloquently in the psychological literature by people like Hochberg (1968), Gombrich (1961), and Gregory (1974), and in the philosophical literature by people like Hanson (1953) and Goodman (1968).

(3) The representation of a scene contains many non-pictorial (and non-sensory) aspects — aspects that cannot realistically be said to be in the sense data at all. Examples of the latter are the perceived relation of causality (Michotte, 1963) or the relations of attack and defence on a chess board (Simon and Barenfeld, 1969). In fact I would argue that all relations are of this type: that there is no fundamental difference between the relations "is to the left of," "is under attack by," or "causes," inasmuch as none of them is any more "directly in the scene" than any other. These are all abstract conceptual relations far removed from the output vocabulary of the transducer.

(4) Although we often appear to go through a process of recalling an image of a scene and then of noticing or perceiving aspects of that image, this recall-reperceive sequence is extremely problematic. The fact that we can recall a scene, or part of a scene, by addressing aspects of the perceptually interpreted content of the scene argues that what we have stored is *already interpreted* and not in need of reperception as we supposed. Retrieval of images is clearly hierarchical

to an unlimited degree of detail and in the widest range of aspects. Thus, for example, I might image a certain sequence of events as I recall what happened at a conference session. Such images may be quite global and could involve a whole scene in a room over a period of time. But I might also image someone's facial expression, or the substance of his remarks, or my reactions to the papers, or the approximate location of a questioner in the audience, without first calling up the entire scene. Such perceptual attributes must therefore be available as interpreted integral units in my representation of the whole scene. Not only can such recollections be of fine detail, but they can also be of rather abstract qualities, such as the mood of the assembly. Furthermore, when there are parts missing from one's recollections, these are never arbitrary pieces of a visual scene. We do not, for example, recall a scene with some arbitrary segment missing, such as a torn photograph. What is missing is invariably some integral perceptual attribute or relation; for example, colors, patterns, events, or spatial relations (I might, for example, recall the people who were in the front row without recalling exactly where they were sitting or what they were wearing). When our recollections are vague, it is always in the sense that certain perceptual qualities or attributes are absent or vague, not that there are geometrically definable pieces of a picture missing. All of the above suggest that one's representation of a scene must contain already differentiated and interpreted perceptual aspects. In other words, the representation is far from being raw, and, so to speak, in need of "perceptual" interpretation. Because retrieval must be able to address perceptually interpreted content, the network of cross-classified relations must have interpreted objects (i.e., concepts) at its nodes.[1] This does not mean, of course, that what we retrieve cannot be further processed. The argument is simply that they are not subject to

perceptual interpretation the way pictures are interpreted; by "perceptual" I refer to the processes of transduction and of interpretation or assimilation into cognitive conceptual structures.

Because the representation is so obviously selective and conceptual in nature, referring to it as an image—a term that has pictorial or projective connotations—is very misleading. Although there are some who have no objections to speaking of "conceptual images," I prefer the term "description" or "structural description" because this carries certain desirable connotations. For example, it implies that the representation is something that (a) must be constructed out of a vocabulary of available concepts (Kant's "Categories of understanding"), (b) bears a referential relation to the object it represents rather than a relation of "resembling," and (c) has its semantics defined by an accessing function that is not assumed to be the entire visual apparatus (I shall have more to say about (b) and (c) in section 6 below). The structured description approach also gives one a psychologically appropriate way of talking about the complexity of a representation. Such complexity is not a property defined over a material layout (e.g., extent, dimensionality, number of topologically defineable segments, etc.) but rather a property defined over a symbol structure (e.g., number of symbols, relations, etc. or, better still, number of nodes at different levels of a tree structure—some details for the latter measure have been proposed and successfully tested in a limited context by Palmer, 1974). Complexity, in other words, is a measure over a description in symbolic or conceptual terms, not over a description in geometric or physical terms.

3. Some Illustrative Examples

To give an idea of what I believe can be gained by this approach to imagery, signalled as it were by the new terminology, I shall describe several phenomena — mostly ones observed in children (who incidentally have been shown to have particularly good "visual imagery" ability) — and then give an account of the phenomena in terms of the notion of "description."

Figure 9-1a schematically depicts some findings reported in Piaget and Inhelder (1956). When young children below the ages of four or five years are shown a colored fluid in an inclined transparent container and are later asked to draw (or to indicate by describing and pointing) what they saw, they typically indicate the fluid as being parallel to either the bottom or the side of the container. Two other related figural "errors" of reproduction or recognition that occur with young children are shown in Figures 9-1c and 9-1d. The first part of Figure 9-1c illustrates the well-known mirror image confusion common in children. Figure 9-1d (reported by Eve Clark, 1973) illustrates the following phenomenon. When young children are shown a small object being placed next to a container and are asked to imitate exactly the action they have just observed, they most frequently place the object *inside* the container. There are a number of other similar transformations that children systematically produce in imitating actions.

Such "errors" can be simply accounted for if we assume that children's internal vocabulary of descriptive concepts is limited or that the priorities they place on the use of such concepts differ from those of adults. For example, without a concept for the relation "is left of" or "is right of," no description of an asymmetrical figure is possible that distinguishes that figure from its mirror image (Figure 9-1c). Similarly, if a child lacks the concept of "geocentric level," his percept of the fluid in the inclined container may not be the same as an adult's. In such a case the nearest appropriate con-

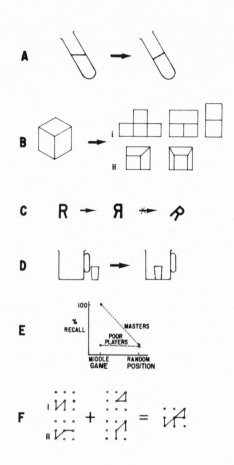

Figure 9-1. Examples of the conceptual nature of visual mental images. A: Typical recall error made by children who have not mastered the concept of "level" (Piaget & Inhelder, 1956). B: Common errors in children's drawings of a cube (adapted from Weinstein, 1974). C: Children are more likely to confuse a figure and its mirror image than a figure and a misoriented copy (e.g., Rock, 1973). D: When imitating the action of placing an object beside a container, a child is more likely to place the object inside the container (Clark, 1973). E: Chess masters superior "visual recall" of chess positions holds only when the positions are taken from real middle games (reported in Chase and Simon, 1973). F: When subjects are asked to synthesize a figure by mentally superimposing two given figures, their performance depends on the way the figure is decomposed (adapted from Palmer, 1974).

cepts (e.g., perpendicular, parallel) may be used, producing the observed errors. Of course such differences in the availability of figural concepts do not always produce a failure to make a distinction. In some cases they result in a failure to perceive similarities. Thus, as illustrated in the second part of Figure 9-1c, children tend to treat a figure in a different orientation as a different figure. For example (see Rock, 1973), young children make fewer orientation generalization errors, confusing figures in different orientations in a discrimination learning experiment, than their older counterparts. (The apparent indifference of young children to the orientation of pictures and print may simply be due to their failure to recognize the importance of orientation to recognition — see Rock, 1973.) In our terms, for the same form in different orientations to be perceived as similar it would have to be represented in terms of appropriate orientation-independent concepts (e.g., relations like centripetal-centrifugal).[2]

The case of imitation is very similar. For what is considered to be mere mechanical imitation must be mediated by a memory representation, which, we have been arguing, depends on the availability of descriptive concepts. Of course imitation also depends on other factors such as preferred response strategies. Eve Clark (1973) found that if she asked a child to imitate the experimenter's action of moving a small object and placing it beside a container, the child most frequently performed a similar movement but left the object *inside* the container (as depicted in Figure 9-1d). One might be inclined to say that the child saw an object being placed in some appropriate proximate relation to a container and constructed an internal representation that recorded this observation. In imitating, the child selects an action in his repertoire, according to some preferences such as discussed by Clark

(1973), which is compatible with this representation. For the child, then, the observed and produced actions fall in the same equivalence class — as captured by its internal representation — just as a figure and its mirror image are in the same class because the child's representation is conceptually less differentiated than that of the adult.

Figure 9-1b depicts a related situation in which children's drawings of a cube deviate from those made by adults. Notice that relative to the more familiar perspective drawing, the children's renderings are *more* faithful to a description of the cube (e.g., the angles are mostly 90°, faces are square and perpendicular to other faces, etc.). Weinstein (1974) found that older children produce hybrid drawings (such as the two on the second line) as they attempt to incorporate the perspective conventions that the Western adult community did not adopt uniformly until the Renaissance (and that, conceivably, are considered the veridical rendering because they represent the way cameras operate). The point is that "optical projection onto a single stationary point of view" is only one of a large number of ways of transforming a mental representation of a three-dimensional object into a two-dimensional drawing. Since the mental representation is necessarily not identical with any of the drawings, it does not independently determine one of them as the unique "correct" rendering. The process of selecting from among the set of drawings compatible with the mental representation of the object must depend on other, probably learned and culturally specific principles — often collectively called "drawing skill."

Because children do not have so refined a vocabulary of descriptive figure-concepts as adults do, their mental representations may tend to be less differentiated than those of adults. In addition, children have not mastered adult conventions and various physical principles, so their reproductions and imitations are a source of more dramatic illustrations of the abstract conceptual or descriptive nature of mental representation. The principle is not by any means, however, confined to children. Consider the following two published results from adult subjects.

Chase and Simon (1973) describe a series of ingenious experiments on the visual memory of chess players. Chess masters are known to have a vastly superior memory for board positions than mediocre chess players. The question arises whether chess ability rests in part on exceptionally good visual imagery ability. Chase and Simon conclude, in effect, that such ability is very important but that it does not consist simply of a general visual imagery talent. The superior performance of chess masters in reproducing a board position after only a few seconds' exposure is manifest *only* when it is a true board position taken from an actual chess game. The difference between masters and duffers disappears when a random arrangement of the same pieces is used as the stimulus (see Figure 9-1e). Thus what appears to be strictly visual memory is extremely sensitive to chess-specific patterns. Chase and Simon conclude that the exceptional visual memory of chess experts derives from their very large repertoire of familiar chess configurations. Such "configurations" are not defined simply by geometrical patterns, since they are independent of the shape, size, or color of chess pieces but are sensitive to nongeometrical relations such as attack, defence, control, etc., which may even be spatially nonlocal. In our terms chess masters may be said to have a rich internal vocabulary with which to construct a representation of the board. Their representation can thus be constructed rapidly and is also conceptually simple —i.e., it consists of a compact description constructed from a rich vocabulary ap-

propriate to the game of chess. Even though the memory is of an apparently visual pattern, the particular internal representation constructed depends on nonvisual factors. As a further corroborating example Eisenstadt and Kareev (1975) have shown that the pattern of errors in the recall of a particular Go board configuration depends on whether a subject perceives it as a position in the game of Go or in the game of Gomoku. In this case geometrically identical patterns are shown to be represented differently depending on highly cognitive factors.

Another study illustrating the large conceptual component involved in visual imagery was reported by Palmer (1974). He presented subjects with two patterns (each with the same number of line segments), which they were to superimpose to yield a third synthesized pattern. The difficulty subjects experienced (measured in terms of both latency and accuracy) in synthesizing a particular pattern depended on the way it had been presented as subpatterns to be superimposed. Thus the subpatterns designated as "good" configurations (e.g., Figure 9-1e(i)), which shared a larger number of major integrated substructures with the required figure (defined by Palmer in terms of a hierarchical description), were easier to synthesize.

Again, as in the other evidence cited above, Palmer found that in what appears to be fundamentally a visual imagery task it is the conceptual rather than some sort of graphic complexity that is the essential determiner of task difficulty. Apparently even when visual imagery seems clearly implicated, the underlying representation is best characterized as something more abstract and conceptual—i.e., what we have been calling a structured description. The point is not simply that there are tasks in which something beyond an iconic image is involved, but that even in cases in which visual images would appear to be the chief mode of representation, task complexity measures lead one to recognize that what serves as the mental representation is highly cognitive. Furthermore, the most perspicuous way of talking about such representations is in terms of such notions as a vocabulary of internal concepts, compactness of descriptions couched in this vocabulary, and other locutions much more appropriate to descriptions than to pictures. I should emphasize, however, that in using the term "description" I am not referring to linguistic objects in the conventional sense. Such internal descriptions (e.g., those discussed in the next section) cannot be directly externalized as sentences. The reasons for this are, first, that the symbols involved may not have corresponding lexical labels in any natural language and, second, that the descriptive structures are not discursive in the sense that they must be scanned in a fixed sequence (as in the case with sentences). The primary reason for persisting in calling them "descriptions" lies in the way these representations are related to what they represent, as discussed in (a)-(c) in section 2 above.

4. Symbol Structures for Imagery

Those who are familiar with work in artificial intelligence will recognize that most computational data structures (e.g., semantic networks) have properties that make them suitable candidates for internal descriptions. Although they are all articulated symbol structures, most have very different formal properties from those of natural language or even of predicate calculus. For example, they contain flexible access paths among symbols that can be tailored to specific goals, they may designate procedures that can be evoked at appropriate times, and they may contain propositional forms that are asserted only in appropriate contexts, when bindings for free variables are provided. Although the formal properties of such descriptive systems as a class are not

yet well understood (see Woods, 1975), it seems clear that they are at least a promising candidate as a formalism for internal representations, not only because of their descriptive power but also because of their structural flexibility. The latter quality is most important in the present context because we are presumably interested in finding a psychologically adequate form of representation as well as a logically adequate one. In particular we are interested in accounting for certain properties of natural intelligence. We would like to be able to give an account of why certain tasks are easier than others (e.g., why some take less time, or result in fewer errors), why certain types of systematic errors occur, how representations are transformed in memory and thought, etc. From this perspective there are good reasons for believing that different representational structures are used at different times and for different purposes. For example, representations that are temporarily constructed in the course of activity we call imaging have some properties not shared by those constructed during episodes we would describe as inner speech. Evidence for this need not rely solely on reports that these activities are accompanied by different subjective experiences. Various measures of access and manipulatory complexity (as assessed, for example, by reaction times) also supports this view. My contention is, however, that there is at present no good reason to reject the view that a common articulated descriptive system underlies all of these representations and that the apparent differences arise from such things as the particular vocabulary of symbols (i.e., designations of concepts and relations) that are used, accessibility paths that are set up among parts of the representation, and the particular operations that are evoked to process these symbol structures. For example, some characteristics of temporary symbol structures that have been developed to model aspects of imaging (as in the work of Baylor, 1972; Moran, 1973; Farley, 1974) include the following:

(1) Representations of physical objects and their attributes are *individuated* — i.e., individual objects are distinguished by distinct internal symbols, and attributes are often attached to them (i.e., attributes are accessible through these symbols). Thus individuals in such representations can be *counted*. For example, there would be no atomic symbol corresponding to "*n* windows." Rather *n* distinct symbols would be generated one for each imagined window. These might even have to be related to one another by relations such as "above," "to the right of," etc.

(2) Spatial and temporal relations in such imaginal data structures are often found to provide particularly good access paths. For example, given an object in such an imaginal structure, it is easier to retrieve an object that is in the relation "next to" or "above" to it than in the relation "larger than" or "same color as" to it (e.g., see Collins and Quillan, 1969).

(3) When a temporary data structure corresponding to an image is constructed, many "default values" are included so that ready access is provided to some details not obviously relevant to the task at hand.

(4) In such workspace data structures we would not have quantifiers or logical connectives (i.e., we would not have an "image symbol structure" for the proposition of "all red blocks"), although sometimes prototypical patterns might be made to serve some of these functions.

(5) Common symbol systems, particularly those designating spatial relations, might be shared by various modalities and by the motor functions as well as the perceptual and image functions. This may explain why coordination is possible and why phenomena such as stimulus-response compatability (Fitts

and Seeger, 1953) and intramodality interference (Brooks, 1968) are observed.

(6) We might even postulate that certain operations performed on objects in the "imaginal workspace" are computational primitives. Suggestion (2) above can be thought of in this way — i.e., given a reference to an element, retrieving the element that designates some spatially adjacent object may be computationally cheap. In fact this could be the theoretical interpretation of the claim that images are "spatially organized" — the reason is not that image data structures are distributed in space (whatever that could mean), but rather that spatial relations such as adjacency can be used as access paths. One must be careful, however, in positing computational primitives for the image workspace. As I shall argue it later, it is very tempting to posit as primitive operations, processes that conceal a major part of what one is trying to explain (as occurs if we take metaphors such as the "mind's eye" or "mental rotation" too literally).

But attempts to develop formal models of imagery are just beginning, and most of the story is yet to be told. Should it be possible to model all forms of cognition (in a manner that takes into account not only logical requisites but also psychological complexity evidence) in a single formalism, not only would we have achieved considerable theoretical parsimony, but we would also have made a significant contribution to bringing some integration to many classical philosophical puzzles of cognition.

I might remark that I have occasionally heard objections to such data structures on the grounds that the symbols are arbitrary atomic elements. As in mathematics, the symbol that designates some quality or some object is chosen for the theorist's convenience; hence in computer science the symbol is usually a string of letters forming a mnemonic word or phrase. What troubles some people is the fact that one must at some point bridge the gap between the symbol and the world outside. Thus, even admitting that much of the representation is symbolic, they would prefer to have some nonarbitrary symbolic content in the representation. For example, one proposal is that a fragment of a representation of a checkered tablecloth might be expressed as something like: "(TEXTURE TABLECLOTH ▦)," where the third term is a piece of template that can both designate checkeredness and be used to identify this texture in some transducer (the same might be done for TABLECLOTH but perhaps not for the more abstract concept TEXTURE). But although this hybrid expression may *look* different from a standard data structure, this is a property only of the way we have chosen to display it. It is no different from (TEXTURE TABLECLOTH Q137) provided the atom Q137 is used consistently (a) when a reference to a checkered pattern is intended; (b) when a checkered pattern is detected by the transducer hardware; (c) when a verbal reference to checkered patterns is received or generated, etc. (The last condition is contingent on the system having "learned" the relation between Q137 and a verbal label such as "checkered.") The nonarbitrariness of a symbol arises entirely from the system of symbols within which it occurs as well as the way in which input-output transducers are wired to translate between energy patterns and symbols.

5. Are Images Analogue?

Although enthusiasm for pictorial representations, which resemble what they represent, or for some kind of "sensory storage" may be waning (at least in the case of representations stored in long-term memory), many people do not subscribe to the view that articulated symbol systems are sufficient to account for many of the phenomena that have been studied by psychologists interested in imagery. These people feel we are forced into the position of admitting at least two radically different types of representations — one to encompass articulated, verbal, or factual information, and the other to capture continuous, analogical, sensory, or holistic types of phenomena implicated in imagery and perhaps other areas of cognition and thought. Within artificial intelligence the study of different types of representational systems is very much an active frontier, and it is impossible to rule out such a hypothesis — however vague the current notions of what constitutes an "analogical" representation. Whatever the outcome of this research, however, it nevertheless appears to me that the arguments and evidence that people have typically presented as favoring such nonarticulated representations have been far short of persuasive.

A wide variety of experimental phenomena has been cited in support of the claim that such nonarticulated imagery representations must be entertained. For example, there are experiments demonstrating differences in recall between concrete imaginable situations and abstract ones, and between performance under instructions to image vs. instructions to rehearse; experiments demonstrating confusion errors based on appearances as opposed to category membership; experiments showing intramodality interference during imaging; and more recently, experiments using reaction time measures, which show that relative difficulty of some tasks performed imaginally mirrors the relative difficulty of such tasks performed perceptually, i.e., while examining actual displays (see Kosslyn & Pomerantz, 1977). In addition there are a number of ingenious experiments (mostly by Roger Shepard and his students; e.g., Shepard, 1975; Cooper & Shepard, 1973; Metzler & Shepard, 1974) also using reaction time measures, which suggest that mental manipulation of images involves carrying out a sequence (or possibly a continuum) of transformations paralleling those that would be carried out in manipulating real objects. For example, the time taken to determine that two figures are identical except for their relative orientation has been found to be a linear function of the angle between them. This effect has been demonstrated in a variety of ways, including asking a subject to prepare mentally for the second of the two figures at some prescribed angle. The preparation time appears to be the same linear function of angular deviation (Cooper & Shepard, 1973). This is explained by saying that subjects rotate an image of the presented form at some constant rate.

Taken as a whole these studies have persuaded many psychologists that mental representations of objects, particularly in the visual modality, must be structurally isomorphic to the objects they represent. This is often phrased by saying that representations are *analogical* rather than descriptive or articulated and that they are transformed by holistic analogue processes. The argument is often made that although it *might* be possible to fabricate an account of how such results could arise from articulated descriptive representations, such accounts are always post hoc and unnatural. Accounts based on positing the manipulation of internal analogues are invariably more natural and are independently motivated by the observation that the same laws of perception and transformation can be applied to the internal representation as are known to apply to external stimuli. My response to this is threefold.

(1) If one takes the position I outlined earlier — viz., that perception involves the construction of an internal description — then it should not be surprising that cognitive operations (e.g., judgments) occurring during perception bear some strong relation to cognitive operations oc-

curring during imaging. On this account both involve the further processing of these internal descriptions.

Furthermore, it should not be surprising if operations upon internal representations show some systematic relationship to operations that would be carried out upon the corresponding objects in the world. We surely have some representation of physical operations as well as of objects. Our knowledge of what it means to manipulate objects derives at least in part from our experience in carrying out actions on real objects. Thus if someone asked me whether a piece of paper of a certain shape could be folded up to form a certain polyhedral form, I would not attempt to solve the problem by applying any arbitrary transformation to my representation of the paper. Instead I would go through a process of solving a series of subproblems, each of which involved answering the question, "What will happen to the shape if I make the following fold?" But this is far from being an argument for internal analogues, as many writers have claimed (e.g., Shepard, 1975). In any problem the solution method I use depends on both the demands of the task (e.g., in this case only physically possible transformations are legitimate) and on the way my knowledge about such transformations is structured. Presumably my knowledge of folding consists of such facts as what happens to the shape of an object when a single fold is made in it, just as my knowledge of addition consists of such atomic facts as $2 + 3 = 5$, which I use in the solution of more complex problems. But notice that all this implies only that I solve the problem in stages by applying operations to representations. There need literally be nothing in common between my mental representation of folding and actual folding, other than that one can be used in certain situations to compute the effect produced by the other — i.e., to compute what could result from actually completing a fold. In fact I shall argue in the next section that theoretical adequacy will force the mental operation to be unlike the physical operation in certain critical respects, giving the theory that "unnaturalness" that bothers many people.

If there were a high degree of correspondence between operations in the world and mental operations (including comparable complexities and constraints on what could be performed), one might perhaps be justified in speaking of the mental activities as in some sense "analogue." But the correspondence is highly partial: only certain aspects of some physical operations have correspondences. Although mental operations have few of the constraints that affect physical operations (i.e., it is easy to imagine physically impossible phenomena), they are also subject to many constraints for which there are no physical counterparts. There are countless simple operations that are impossible to imagine accurately. Sometimes we cannot keep track of all the relations. For example, imagine a familiar scene; now try to image it upside down, out of focus, viewed through a green filter, etc. Or sometimes we lack the tacit knowledge of the physical laws governing the phenomena. Examples of this are a child asked to imagine what will happen when a block is pushed over the edge of a table, or an adult asked to imagine the trajectory of a weight being dropped behind a screen. Ian Howard (1974) has discussed an interesting series of experiments in which he shows that adults' "perceptual schemata" are often not consonant with the laws of physics. In fact in a recent ingenious experiment, using trick 3-D photography and motion pictures, he showed that (a) about half the college students he tested could not articulate the principle that fluid levels in a container remain horizontal as the container is tilted, and (b) those who could not articulate this principle could not recognize gross anomalies (up to 30° from horizontal) in fluid levels, whereas those who did articulate the principles were very accurate in their detection of anomalies (Howard, 1978). The failure of "perceptual schemata" to be veridical has also been demonstrated for fluid levels by Thomas, Jamison, and Hummel (1973). The point is that even in perception, the detection of deviations from physical laws is far from automatic. Obviously in the case of imaging physical transformations, the ability to image the correct effect is highly dependent on what the subject knows and does not merely follow from the behavior of internal analogues. It is especially not a consequence of any intrinsic property of some analogue "medium," as I shall argue presently. I shall return to the differences between physical and mental operations in sections 7 and 8 when I discuss mental rotation experiments.

(2) Although there are similarities between cognitive operations in perception and in imaging, there are also some outstanding differences that may be more revealing of the underlying processes. For example, the order of scanning and the sorts of things that can be "noticed" in imaging are much more constrained than in perception. The reason for this is partly that a scene has a stable independent existence and can be reexamined at will to produce new interpretations. In contrast, the construction of an internal description from stored knowledge can hardly be divorced from its interpretation. While some reinterpretation is certainly possible, it surely is more like the derivation of new entailments from the stored knowledge than like the discovery of new aspects of an environment by the usual visual means. Discovering even moderately novel readings from a mental image such as those required to find simple embedded figures in a pattern, have been shown to be exceedingly difficult (Reed, 1974). Another important property of an image that distinguishes it from percep-

tion is that it is quite limited in its content. This limitation, however, does not appear to depend on any simple measure of geometrical complexity so much as on conceptual, or what I would call descriptive, complexity. The latter in turn varies depending on the availability of appropriate concepts for describing the display, as I have already argued.

(3) My third reaction to the arguments for analogical representation based on the parallels between imaging and perception is the following. I maintain that the reason why structured descriptions and the computational processes that go with them appear unnatural is precisely that they are an earnest attempt to make explicit the detailed structure of the entire cognitive system involved in imagery, down to the level of mechanically realizable processes. It seems that naturalness of theoretical accounts of imagery can be gained by sweeping a large part of the puzzle under one of two rugs: we can attribute some of the phenomena to unexplained properties of the "mind's eye" or some other interpreting process, or we can attribute some of them to intrinsic properties of the analogical representational *medium*. I shall suggest that both of these moves involve us in the game of *obscurum per obscurus*, an unreasonable price to pay for naturalness.

6. Properties of the Mind's Eye

I shall begin this sketch by giving the following caricature of a class of arguments for "analogical" or "direct" or "presentational" representations. Consider the parallel between the pairs "organism-environment" and "mental process-representation" (Figure 9-2a, b).

The system depicted in Figure 9-2a must surely have many properties in common with the system depicted in Figure 9-2b; otherwise thought would be irrelevant to action, and our chances of survival would be negligible. From this one is

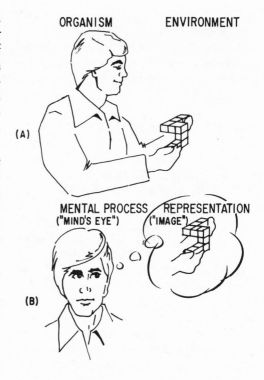

Figure 9-2. Because the object-organism relation depicted in A must share some functional properties with the "mental image"-"mind's eye" relation depicted in B, we can be seduced into attributing many object properties to the image and many perception properties to the mind's eye.

tempted to say that representations and the objects they represent must have much in common. Beginning with this innocent remark we are irresistibly and imperceptibly drawn towards the fatal error of attributing more and more of the properties of the environment, as described by the physical sciences, to the representation itself. If I were permitted to misappropriate other people's terms slightly, I might call this the tendency to commit the "stimulus error" after Titchner or to succumb to the "objective pull" after Quine. It is in the failure to emphasize the fundamental differences between the mental object, which we call the representation, and the physical object (i.e., the two right-hand elements in Figure 9-2) that we run ourselves into various traps. The physical object has a stable existence, its transformations are governed by natural laws, and it is open to as many readings or interpretations as are compatible with the cognitive powers of its perceiver. The representation, on the other hand, is already an interpretation or reading given to the object by an act of conceptualization, and any transformations of the representation are determined by cognitive operations that may or may not bear any relation to the laws of physics. These may seem like rather obvious differences, but I shall argue that the failure to keep them in focus has been behind some of the arguments for analogical representations.

The temptation to draw the external world inside the head leads to a classical dilemma of imaginal representation: if the representation is too similar to the world it represents, it is of no help in apprehending the world, since it merely moves the problem in one layer; but if it is too dissimilar, then how can it represent the world at all? This apparent dilemma turns on the use of the word "similar," which surely is appropriate only when two things are examined by the same process (e.g., when they are both viewed). This, however, is a gratuitous assumption that underlies and confuses much of the discussion of representation.

For example, one frequently hears that a "nonverbal" representation preserves the structure of the environment it represents. Such preservation of structure is taken by many to be a defining characteristic of analogical representations. Aaron Sloman (1971, pp. 216-217) makes the following comparison in contrasting analogical representations with a pedicate calculus formulation, or what he calls Fregean systems:

In an *analogical* system properties of and relations between parts of the representing configuration represent properties and relations of parts in a complex configuration, so that the structure of the representation gives information about the structure of what is represented. . . . By contrast, in a Fregean system there is basically only *one* type of 'expressive' relation between parts of a configuration, namely the relation between 'function-signs' and 'argument-signs'. . . . For example, the denoting phrase 'the brother of the wife of Tom' would be analyzed by Frege as containing two function-signs 'the brother of ( )' and 'the wife of ( )' and two argument-signs 'Tom' and 'the wife of Tom' as indicated in 'the brother of (the wife of (Tom))'. Clearly the structure of such a configuration need not correspond to the structure of what it represents or denotes.

Now this may sound like a reasonable claim until one tries to interpret the phrase "the structure of X." All the phrase can mean is that some function (which I have called the "semantic interpretation function") can give X an interpretation as a structure. There is literally nothing intrinsic in any object that can be called its "structure." Sloman's distinction is empty unless we are told which of an unlimited number of potential structures it refers to. For example, Sloman notes that in the above example the sign "Tom" is *part of* the sign "the wife of Tom," whereas in the situation represented, the thing designated by the sign "Tom" is certainly not part of the thing designated by the sign "the wife of Tom." Thus, he argues, the structure of the representation does not reflect the structure of what is represented. But the point is that so long as the function that interprets the phrase shows no inclination to attend to what you and I might call the relation "is a part of," or, if it does attend to such a relation, does not identify it with a similarly named (but in fact quite different) relation in the world, the problem does not arise. In this case "is a part of" is simply not a *signifying* relation. In fact it would be correct to say that from the point of view of the "semantic interpretation function" such a relation does not exist. Thus it is true that a potential relation in the representation does not signify a relation in the world. But neither does the relation "is heavier than" in a picture represent a relation in the scene depicted—e.g., the part of a picture corresponding to a cloud may weigh more than the part of the picture representing a building, but so long as the interpretation function does not attend to relative weights, this remains irrelevant. Or to take a less farfetched example, the relation among areas in a Mercator map projection is not signifying, although a compass direction is.[3]

Thus discussions about the nature of mental representations should really be discussions about representational *systems* consisting of the pair "representation" and "semantic interpretation function." Furthermore, my earlier claim that representations are descriptions should more properly be put as a claim that representations *function* as descriptions—i.e., they are related to the objects they represent in the way sentences are related to the objects they describe (i.e., via an interpretation or something like Wittgenstein's "laws of projection") rather than the way photographs are related to the objects they picture (i.e., via laws of optics and principles of projective geometry).

Occasionally writers have recognized the importance of the semantic interpretation function. In one recent case it has been used to resolve a long-standing philosophical puzzle relating to the indeterminateness of images. This is a problem that Dennett (1969) considers a serious difficulty with the imagery view. Recently, however, Fodor (1975, p. 191) has argued that such indeterminateness is not problematic for a pictorial view of images. Fodor's argument rests on a recognition that the content of a mental representation is always relative to some interpretation. This is precisely the point we have been discussing. Let us look briefly at Fodor's argument that what we call images can reasonably be understood as indeterminate.

What makes my stick figure an image of a tiger is not that it looks much like one (my drawings of tigers don't look much like tigers either) but rather that it's *my* image, so I'm the one who gets to say what it's an image of. My images (and my drawings) connect with my intentions in a certain way; I *take* them as tiger-pictures for purposes of whatever task I happen to have in hand. Since my mental image *is* an image, there will be some visual descriptions under which it is determinate; hence there will be some question whose answers I can 'read off' the display, and the more pictorial the display is the more such questions there will be. But, in the case of any given image, there might be arbitrarily many visual properties which would not be pictured but, as it were, carried by the description under which the image as intended.

This is an important and relevant observation. But notice what it has done to the notion of an image. The image has lost its essential quality. It has become an object that must be *read* via an intention and that can be read in many different ways. In other words, it contains forms or symbol tokens exactly as does a structured description.[4] What makes it pictorial, according to Fodor, is that there are many properties that can be "read off," presumable with low computational cost. But this is precisely what happens when we enrich a structured description by making it more elaborate and detailed. The advantages of thinking of this as the elaboration of a description, rather than of the image being more pictorial (apart from the vagueness of the notion of "degree of pictorialness"), are that (a) this interpretation gives recognition to the fact that the elaboration is done within the constraints of available concepts rather than by the addition of arbitrary pictorial fragments; (b) "reading off" becomes a well-defined symbol-matching operation rather than involving all of the perceptual apparatus driven by intentions; (c) no matter how much elaboration of detail is carried out, there will always be an arbitrarily large amount of indeterminateness in the resulting representation (it will always fail to be determinate with respect to some aspects which are not only determinate in the scene but which no picture would leave uncommitted), and furthermore, as noted in section 2 (1), the representation is not homogeneous in the amount of determinateness of various aspects; (d) this interpretation discourages the view, invariably associated with the term "image," that there exists an object that is interpreted the way a scene is interpreted (i.e., visually), that has a stable simultaneous existence so that it can be scanned perceptually for new readings, and that inherits certain intrinsic properties from the material medium in which it is embedded (e.g., rigidity under various transformations — see the discussion below).

Replacing "images" with "images under descriptions," as Fodor does, frees the term from many of the philosophical problems that plagued it in the past. The trouble with this move is precisely the problem of making clear the sense in which images under descriptions are to be distinguished from descriptions. Fodor (p. 190) puts it this way: "Images under description share their nondiscursiveness with images *tout court*. What they share with descriptions is that they needn't look much like what they represent." Thus discursiveness seems to be the crucial property. But, as we have seen, symbol structures are not discursive in the sense that sentences are — i.e., they need not be read in a prescribed order. The order of "scanning" is determined by the accessing algorithm and makes use of the relations that are the access paths of the structured description, just as a visual scan of an image would presumably be determined by

the intentions of the perceiver together with something like peripheral vision. This amounts to saying that we have yet to see a viable distinction among images, images under descriptions, and structured descriptions when any of these is embedded within a representational system — i.e., when paired with the appropriate semantic interpretation function. Given the advantages of the nonpictorial description option mentioned above, I see no reason to abandon this approach, which at least has some theoretical exemplars in current computational models.

It is important to keep in mind the central role the semantic interpretation function plays in the whole issue of representation. One of the reasons why imagistic representations appear so natural is that they can literally *resemble* the objects they depict, just as we might think of the contents of our recollections as resembling the recalled situation. But this can be paraphrased as saying that the relation between images (or pictures) and their designata is clear when the semantic interpretation function in both cases is nothing less than the whole of intelligent human perception. That this way of characterizing representations is plagued with difficulties has been amply discussed by Wittgenstein (1953), Goodman (1968), Dennett (1969), Fodor (1975), and others, so I shall pass up the opportunity to add my comments. However, there are also more subtle errors based on tacit assumptions regarding the nature of the interpretation function. For example, there are frequent claims that certain kinds of information are "directly available" in an analogue representation and need merely to be "read off," as opposed to being computed from a descriptive representation. But as we have seen above, such claims are not about the merits of one *form* of representation as opposed to another, but about which aspects of a situation are explicitly built into the representation in advance and which types of operations are primitive in the semantic interpretation function.

It has long been recognized in computer science that there is a trade-off between the complexity of data structures and the complexity of algorithms for processing them. For example, at one extreme one of the simplest forms of representation is a list of propositions in the predicate calculus. However, extracting answers from such a representation requires a combinatorially explosive theorem-proving system. At the other extreme are some exhaustively cross-referenced data networks from which most of the more frequent questions can be answered by pattern-matching and graph-processing techniques. The difference is that in one case the work is done when new information is entered, whereas in the other case it is done at the time information is retrieved. For the psychologist, choosing some intermediate ground between these is at least partly an empirical issue, since he wishes to model the accessing complexity exhibited by human cognition. The trap here is that representations appear "natural" in proportion to the intelligence attributed to the accessing function. The most natural representation (the picture in the head) requires a full-fledged homunculus for its interpretation. Few psychologists would opt for this alternative. Next in attractiveness comes the holistic analogue. What type of interpreting function this requires is not clear, but one that is sometimes hinted at would simply compute some similarity metric, such as implied by Quine's "quality space," or a function that recognizes something like Wittgenstein's "family resemblances." Such a function could thus indicate how similar some whole configuration was to, say, a prototypical one. Unfortunately we know nothing about how such similarity metrics can be "holistically" computed. Even if we dropped the "holistic" requirement, no one has been able to show general dimensional

characteristics of similarity. In fact what evidence there is, such as the failure to find dimensions of generalization or dimensions of similarity in multidimensional scaling of structured stimuli (Shepard, 1964), suggests that a dimensional approach to similarity is probably doomed to failure.

As we depart from these direct or analogue representations and build more complex articulated descriptions, we find we can get away with somewhat better understood symbol-processing algorithms. What we lose in naturalness of representation we gain in approaching realizeable systems. Since we are still far from an adequate overall model of imagery, it is not a closed issue as to whether we will eventually run into fundamental difficulties. But at least the problems are out in the open — in all their unnatural nakedness — where they can be examined, rather than hidden in metaphors, such as that imagery involves perception.

7. Properties of the Medium

In the first place, I declare to you, sir, that when one has only confused ideas of thought *and of* matter, *as one ordinarily has, it is not to be wondered at if one does not see the means of solving such questions.*

Leibniz,
New essays on the understanding, 1704

The second rug under which people have attempted to hide some of the puzzle of representation has been the representational medium itself. This approach is often taken in attempting to account for certain mental operations performed on representations. Before describing this approach I should like to describe a problem known as the "frame problem," which researchers in artificial intelligence have studied in the context of robot-planning, since it illuminates a relevant point.

Suppose we have a robot that has perceptual and motor capabilities and can be directed to move about, grasp objects, and generally follow a simple sequence of commands while observing what is going on around it. Such a robot has no difficulty with inconsistencies in its world model, since it merely observes what happens and updates its knowledge base. Sooner or later we would want to be able to give the robot more general goals that would require it to plan out an effective series of actions in advance. This, it turns out, is a qualitatively very different task from the one it has been performing. For now there is a problem of consistency. After each planned action the robot must, in effect, recompute its representation of the entire state of the world, since it must take into account all the possible effects of the action on every aspect of the environment. Such a recomputation may in fact involve referring to the laws of physics. The problem of reasoning about actions, in contrast with merely acting, gets us into a very difficult set of problems stemming from the interdependence of actions. A number of approaches to this so-called frame problem have been proposed (see Simon, 1972; McCarthy & Hayes, 1969; Raphael, 1971). All of them appear somehow to be unduly complex and unnatural. It is clear, however, that part of their unnaturalness rests on the fact that a great deal of knowledge must explicitly be brought to bear in reasoning about actions that we are not aware of using and that indeed we may not have to use when we operate directly on the world. In the latter case relevant interactions are given to us for free by the environment. In the case of reasoning, however, the relations are not free. We must in some way explicitly build in the knowledge regarding what effects do and do not follow from any action.[5]

It seems to me that the notion of an analogue representation medium is in part an attempt to get this information for free again. Consider the claim that data on the time-course of mental rotation (e.g., Shepard, 1975) argues that the process is analogue (since, as some people have been known to ask innocently, "How can you rotate a data structure through its intermediate positions?"). This carries the implication that once we start a rotation the medium will take care of maintaining the rigidity of the total pattern and carry along all the parts for us — just as the laws of physics take care of this for us in the real environment. But, as in the frame problem, we are overlooking the fact that the person must know what will and will not happen to the bottom part when the top part starts to rotate. In a descriptive structure this is precisely what makes "mental rotation" appear awkward and computationally unduly costly. But this is unavoidable unless we have an analogical modeling medium which intrinsically follows the laws of physics.[6] Unless we are willing to ascribe such laws to brain tissue (which, to some extent, is what Gestalt psychologists attempted to do), we are stuck with locating knowledge of such laws explicitly in some part of the total representation or in what I have called the semantic interpretation function (which does not, incidentally, preclude such knowledge from being a distributed computation attached to the data structure itself). If we admit this, however, we lose one of the main attractions of the "analogical medium" gambit. For now actions such as rotations must be accounted for by cognitive operations that are themselves not prima facie analogue, since they must in turn refer to knowledge about what happens to forms under certain transformations (we shall return to the notion of image rotation in the next section). Observations of children by Piaget as well as the experiments by Howard cited in section 5(1) show that when such "operational knowledge" is not available, imagining actions does not lead to veridical conclusions, the supposedly analogical nature of the representation notwithstanding.

The phenomenon of attributing to the intrinsic nature of a representation some of the crucial aspects that need to be taken into account (because these are so intuitively obvious to the theorist) is not confined to analogical representations. Woods (1975) has recently shown that we frequently commit the same oversight in the case of semantic networks. For this reason it is important to attempt to simulate a significant portion of cognition by machine (although even here the existence of such built-in functions as an arithmetic processor may create the illusion that we get magnitudes for free — i.e., we need not account for how they are mentally represented).

8. What Is Rotated in Mental Rotation?

The mental rotation example raises a number of other related problems worth exploring. Let us suppose that an empirically adequate computational model of some cognitive process — say, for comparison of rotated forms, as in the Shepard (1975) experiments — is developed. What then would be the status of a description of the comparison process which used phrases such as "the image is mentally rotated"? There are several ways of approaching this question. One is to say that no rotation in fact takes place, since all behavorial data are accounted for by a model which contains no rotating entities. The only thing conceivably left to explain is why the subject reports "rotating an image."[7] This question might then be approached as Dan Dennett does in his "Toward a cognitive theory of consciousness" (1978), which explores the source of introspective reports about cognitive processes.

A second approach is to say that "rotation" is the name we give to the result of a certain subprocess within the model that at a more microscopic level may or may not be carried out by a discrete symbolic computation. In other words, the "mental rotation" account is simply a description in a higher level language of a certain computation that takes place in

the cognitive system. Furthermore, it could be argued that this is not just any arbitrary higher-level description but one that is particularly appropriate because (a) it is consonant with subjects' reports of what they do and (b) it alone accounts for the empirical constraints on the transformations applied to the representation — i.e., of all the logically possible ways of solving the comparison problem by transforming the symbol structure that is the mental representation of the stimulus, only the one describable as "rotation" (or, in other contexts, as "enlargement" or some such equally plausible pictorial manipulation) offers a natural account of the empirical regularities. Thus "rotation" is more than a convenient global description of the computation involved; the term has additional explanatory power because it captures the significant generalization, as the linguist would say, which underlies the empirically observed, as opposed to the logically possible, transformations.

In fact one might even cast the computational model or simulation in a higher-level language that had ROTATE as one of its primitive operations. This would make the computational model, in a sense, isomorphic to the imagery account (although presumably more complete in its detail and not necessarily analogue in any strong sense).

Such a defence of the "image rotation" account, if correct, would reduce the distinction between the imagery approach and the artificial intelligence approach. It would not entirely eliminate the distinction, since the latter group, not satisfied with an *explanation* that rests on the statement that comparisons require a subject first to "rotate an image," demands a more complete explication of the entire process. It would, however, eliminate some of the arguments over what is meant by words like "rotation" used in a technical theoretical sense.

Unfortunately such a translation from the language of images and rotations leaves some residual difficulties. In particular there are reasons for resisting the use of global operations like ROTATE as computational primitives. Presumably any operation that is a computational primitive need not be decomposed (i.e., no new understanding of the underlying *psychological* process is gained by expressing the primitive operation in terms of still smaller steps, even though such an analysis may be required in order to get it to execute on some particular device or perhaps to relate it to neurophysiology). But if the operation is to be treated as a single computational step, then surely the amount of computational resources (time and memory capacity) the operation uses must be independent of the context in which it is used. In particular the amount of computational resources used by a primitive operation should be independent of the representation to which it is applied.

Thus it should take *t* seconds to "rotate" a representation by *D* degrees regardless of what it is a representation of. If this were not the case, then we should further want to know what made one stimulus faster and another slower to rotate, which would be tantamount to asking what process takes place within the primitive operation ROTATE.

This approach reflects a general phenomenon in cognitive psychology. In constructing theories we often have the option of either postulating a large number of independent processes or else postulating a smaller number of more primitive interacting processes. In the former case variety of computations is accomplished by a variety of elementary processes, whereas in the latter case the variety comes from the way a few primitive processes interact. Given the option, the latter approach is usually preferred as providing the more powerful explanation — i.e., as being able to capture more significant generalizations with fewer theoretical entities.

Although such discussion rapidly gets into some deeper issues concerning the appropriate level of description of psychological processes, which cannot be discussed in general terms in this paper, the particular example of rotation should be clear enough. If the empirical evidence were compatible with the existence of a primitive cognitive operation for rotating a percept or an imaginal representation (which proceeded at some fixed rate of so many degrees per second), then it would be useful to speak of image-rotation as a description of part of the cognitive process. If, on the other hand, we have to qualify this description by saying that the cognitive process appears to be like a rotation of 360° per second for this kind of figure but of 60° per second for that kind of figure, or that some parts of a figure behave as if they were rotated but others do not, or that only certain kinds of figures can be subjected to rotation or only certain kinds of properties are contained in the rotated figure, then we have lost the most important currency this term had.[8] It then no longer acts like a primitive cognitive operation, since we are forced to expose the underlying computations covered by the term in order to account for the qualifying conditions. In addition it no longer has the virtue of distinguishing between permissible and impermissible transformations on representations, since clearly more is going on than simple rotation. So the usefulness of the image rotation account turns on a set of empirical questions.

Although there is not a great deal of evidence bearing on the kinds of possibilities raised above, there is some reason to believe that the hypothetical examples cited may very well be the case. In the first place, the ability to "mentally rotate" a presented figure clearly depends on the nature and complexity of that figure. For example, people find it almost impossible to recognize faces from inverted photographs (Rock, 1973) by performing a "mental rotation." The difficulty here does not seem to be associated with such geometrical attributes of the figure as its extent or the number of its components or attributes, as one might expect if the percept were thought of as some sort of iconic display. Numerous experiments have shown that the ability to recall a display (Chase and Simon, 1973), to construct an image mentally from a description (Moran, 1973), or to synthesize a composite figure mentally from component subfigures (Palmer, 1974) depends on the conceptual or descriptive complexity of the figures. Although I know of no published studies showing that the ability to manipulate images (e.g., by rotation) depends on conceptual complexity, this would certainly be a reasonable expectation, given, for example, the instability of complex images and the variable difficulty in retrieving different kinds of information from apparently clear initial images that are subjected to different transformations (e.g., in such tasks as the Guilford Spatial Visualization test — see Baylor, 1972).

In the second place, there is reason to believe that apparent rates of mental rotation depend on conceptual complexity. Metzler and Shepard (1974) found that line drawings of simple three-dimensional figures were rotated at only 60° per second, whereas Cooper and Shepard (1974) obtained a rate of 360° per second with letters of the alphabet. Hochberg and Gellman (1977) also report evidence that the apparent rate of rotation does depend on figural complexity, and in particular on the presence of "landmark features" in the figures. In fact, where salient landmark features are absent (as with certain patterns of filled and empty dots), *no* evidence of rotation is found (Hochberg & Gellman, 1976). I have also obtained data (Pylyshyn, 1979) showing that apparent rates of rotation of line drawings are sensitive to such factors as practice and the

type of discriminations that are to be performed on the rotated figures, suggesting that what passes for rotation in such experiments is not simply a rigid angular transformation of a gross iconic image.

There are, of course, many other proposals that could be made to account for data such as those cited here. These include proposals for various hybrid models involving iterating over features of the figure using some kind of relaxation method. Such iterations could involve small local rotations, rotations of a skeletal frame followed by partial reconstruction of the figure, or even iterations over descriptions with no obvious analogue (in the sense of continuous spatial function) processes involved. In the absence of a model worked out in detail, as well as of additional experimental analyses of factors affecting rotation, it is not clear how such proposals would fare. In any event it would seem that a major part of the evidence cited in support of "mental rotation" will be accounted for by computational processes of various kinds and not by properties of some analogue medium.

In conclusion let me reiterate that I do not claim to have made an argument against analogical modes of representation, and still less am I satisfied that semantic networks, procedures, etc. are adequate to handle all forms of knowledge. I have simply tried to argue that many of the reasons people have for jumping on the "analogical" (whatever that may be) bandwagon are insufficient. Furthermore, we are so far from understanding the semantics of discrete data structures (as Woods has cogently argued) that any mass movement to abandon them, or even augment them with something radically different is at the very least premature.[9]

Notes

1. One might respond to Kant's objection that "concepts without percepts are blind" by

pointing out that (a) 'concepts' in our sense can refer to an equivalence class of transducer outputs — i.e., they may correspond to perceptual patterns; and (b) nodes need not be iconic or sense-resembling in order to represent percepts (see the last paragraph of section 4 for more on this point).

2. It is also worth pointing out another advantage of thinking of such figures as being represented by structured descriptions. This approach resolves an old psychological puzzle of why figures' shapes remain perceptually invariant, for both adults and children, when we view them lying down or with our heads at an angle: if the figures are described in relation to their background the description remains the same.

3. This is not to suggest that no useful distinction can be made between analogical and Fregean or between pictorial and discursive representations. The point here is that one cannot make the distinction by simply examining the representation itself. One must, in addition, know something about how it is being used or interpreted. In fact the notion of isomorphism between representations is not a useful one. A more useful notion of isomorphism is the one that appears in algebra — i.e., isomorphism between systems.

4. When it is sometimes claimed that a painting or sketch can be abstract, this surely means that it can be interpreted to bear an abstract relation to the object depicted. The picture itself is never abstract or vague. But this simply means that two-dimensional displays can sometimes, in certain respects, do the work of descriptions.

5. This is not to suggest that people solve the frame problem as it is described. In fact there is good reason to believe that our ability to plan, anticipate, etc. is rather limited precisely because we cannot bring all relevant facts to bear. The point is merely to argue that when we do anticipate successfully we bring to bear multifarious knowledge, including tacit knowledge of physical laws. In some cases we can design representational structures in such a way that certain consequences appear to follow without explicit appeal to stored principles. For example, by choosing a list representation for objects related by a total ordering and by examining the list serially we seem to obtain the transitivity property of such relations as a by-product. Finding such

representations is an important goal in building efficient computational models. From a psychological point of view, however, it should be noted that (at least in this example) a commitment to transitivity is made along with the decision to place particular objects on a particular list, and this decision (and hence the representation of transitivity) may then simply fall outside the domain of what is being modeled. But in general we shall want to model the implicity knowledge of such principles. The need to model intellectual structures explicitly arises because of the kind of independence of properties of thought and properties of the world that we see in cognitive development in children as well as in the nonveridical nature of perceptual schemata discussed in section 5 (2).

6. The more general problem, one that vexed Leibniz in the above quotation is that the most tempting way to represent property P is to attribute P to the representation. However, when P is a *physical* predicate and we are dealing with *mental* representations, we must guard against reifying the physical world in the mind. The seductiveness of applying physical predicates (e.g. those pertaining to physical magnitudes) to images appears to be almost irresistible. For example, in a recent response to my critique of imagery, Kosslyn and Pomerantz (1977, p. 13) begin by carefully noting that images themselves are neither large nor small but that they only "register size in the same way that the corresponding representations evoked during perception register size." Now this unexceptionable position does not itself say anything about the form of the representation. However, in each case in which they find that "imaginal" accounts are more "natural" than "propositional" accounts, this is the case precisely because a *literal* interpretation of terms like "large-small" or "near-far" is being applied to images projected onto a hypothetical screen. The Kosslyn and Pomerantz paper is one of most carefully argued expositions of the imagery position, one that emerged after considerable communication with the author of the present paper. The reader is invited to consult the Kosslyn and Pomerantz paper for a revealing sample of how precipitous the "analogical" slope can get and how arguments in psychology can slip past one another in recycling classical philosophical puzzles.

7. Whether or not at even a pretheoretical

level, the relevant phenomena are best described as "rotation" or something else, such as serial piece-by-piece analysis of where relevant portions of a figure would be were a rotation of the object actually carried out, is an empirical question. Although adequate fine-grain data bearing on this question are not available at present, such tentative evidence as introspective reports (e.g., gathered in our laboratory) and preliminary eye-movement evidence mentioned by Metzler and Shepard (1974) suggest that serial scanning and recomputation may in fact be a better description of the processes occurring in the comparison experiment than wholesale rotation. Recently detailed monitoring of eye-movements by Just and Carpenter (1976) has confirmed that there are several distinct phases to the rotation task, many of which clearly involve piecemeal search and comparison operations. In certain cases, however, such as closing one's eyes and imagining a rotating object, rotation may be the appropriate phenomenological description, so we shall stick with this for the time being.

8. There remains of course the serious methodological problem of empirically estimating the computational complexity of an operation. Presumably response latency arises from several sources that may interact in various ways. This, however, is a problem for everybody's theory, and we are here simply taking the current first-order view that variation in reaction time directly reflects changes in computational complexity of the primary operation. The next step would involve a theory of how such factors as attention and memory load interact with latency—i.e., a theory of computing under limited resources.

9. I wish to thank Jerry Fodor for his careful and critical reading of an earlier draft of this paper. Part of the work of writing this paper was done while I was a visiting faculty member at the Artificial Intelligence Laboratory of M.I.T. Discussions with various members of the laboratory were invaluable in clarifying many problems in my earlier thinking (which is not to say that no errors of confusions remain in the present version). Research reported herein was supported by the National Research Council of Canada, Operating Grant A4092.

References

Baylor, G. W. A treatise on the mind's eye: An empirical investigation of visual mental imagery. (Unpublished doctoral dissertation, Carnegie-Mellon University.) Ann Arbor, Mich. University Microfilms, no. 72-13, 699, 1972.

Bobrow, D. G. Dimensions of representation. In D. G. Bobrow & A. Collins (Eds.), *Representation and understanding: Studies in cognitive science.* New York: Academic Press, 1975.

Brooks, L. R. Spatial and verbal components in the act of recall. *Canadian Journal of Psychology*, 1968, 22, 349-368.

Bruner, J. S. On perceptual readiness. *Psychological Review*, 1957, 64, 123-152.

Chase, W. G. & Simon, H. A. Perception in Chess. *Cognitive Psychology*, 1973, 4, 55-81.

Clark, E. V. Non-linguistic strategies and the acquisition of word meanings. *Cognition*, 1973, 2, 161-182.

Collins, A. M., & Quillian, M. R. Retrieval time from semantic memory. *Journal of Verbal Learning and Verbal Behavior*, 1969, 8, 240-247.

Cooper, L. A., & Shepard, R. N. Chronometric studies of the rotation of mental images. In W. G. Chase (Ed.), *Visual information processing.* New York: Academic Press, 1973.

Dennett, D. C. *Content and consciousness.* New York: Humanities Press, 1969.

Dennett, D. C. Toward a cognitive theory of consciousness. In C. W. Savage (Ed.), *Perception and cognition. Issues in the foundations of psychology.* Minneapolis: University of Minnesota Press, 1978.

Eisenstadt, M., & Kareev, Y. Aspects of human problem solving: The use of internal representations. In D. A. Norman & D. E. Rumelhart (Eds.), *Explorations in cognition.* San Francisco: W. H. Freeman, 1975.

Farley, A. VIPS: A visual imagery and perception system. Unpublished doctoral dissertation, Computer Science Department, Carnegie-Mellon University, Pittsburgh, 1974.

Fitts, P. F., & Seeger, C. M. SR compatibility: Spatial characteristics of stimulus and response codes. *Journal of Experimental Psychology*, 1953, 46, 199-210.

Fodor, J. *The language of thought*. New York: Crowell, 1975.

Gibson, J. J. The information available in pictures. *Leonardo*, 1971, 4, 27-35.

Gombrich, E. H. *Art and illusion: A study in the psychology of pictorial representation*. Princeton: Princeton University Press, 1961.

Goodman, N. *Languages of art: an approach to a theory of symbols*. New York: Bobbs-Merrill, 1968.

Gregory, R. L. Choosing a paradigm for perception. In E. C. Carterette & M. P. Friedman (Eds.), *Handbook of perception* (Vol. 1). New York: Academic Press, 1974.

Hanson, V. R. *Patterns of discovery*. Cambridge: Cambridge University Press, 1953.

Hochberg, J. In the mind's eye. In R. N. Haber (Ed.), *Contemporary theory and research in visual perception*. New York: Holt, Rinehart and Winston, 1968.

Hochberg, J., & Gellman, L. Feature saliency, "mental rotation" times, and the integration of successive views. Mimeo, 1976.

Hochberg, J., & Gellman, L. The effect of landmark features on mental rotation times. *Memory and Cognition*, 1977, 5, 23-26.

Howard, I. P. Proposals for the study of anomalous perceptual schemata. *Perception*, 1974, 3, 497-513.

Howard, I. P. Recognition and knowledge of the water-level principle. *Perception*, 1978, 7, 151-160.

Julesz, B. *Foundations of Cyclopean Perception*. Chicago: The University of Chicago Press, 1971.

Just, M. A., & Carpenter, P. A. Eye fixations and cognitive processes. *Cognitive Psychology*, 1976, 8, 441-480.

Kosslyn, S. M. & Pomerantz, J. R. Imagery, propositions and the form of internal representation. *Cognitive Psychology*, in press.

Marr, D. Analysing natural images: A computational theory of texture vision. M.I.T. A.I. Laboratory memo 334, 1975.

McCarthy, J. & Hayes, P. Some philosophical problems from the standpoint of artificial intelligence. In B. Meltzer & D. Minchie (Eds.), *Machine Intelligence 4*. Edinburgh University Press, 1969.

Metzler, J. & Shepard, R. N. Transformational studies of the internal representation of three-dimensional objects. in R. L. Solso (Ed.), *Theories of cognitive psychology, The Loyola Symposium*. Hillsdale, N.J.: Lawrence Erlbaum, 1974.

Michotte, A. *Perception of Causality*, Lonon: Methuen, 1963.

Moran, T. The symbolic imagery hypothesis: A production system model. Unpublished doctoral dissertation, Carnegie-Mellon University, 1973.

Neisser, U. Changing conceptions of imagery. In P. W. Sheehan (Ed.), *The function of nature of imagery*. New York: Academic Press, 1972.

Palmer, S. E. Structural aspects of perceptual organization. Unpublished doctoral dissertation, University of California, San Diego, 1974.

Piaget, J. & Inhelder, B. *The child's conception of space*. New York: The Humanities Press, 1956.

Pylyshyn, Z. W. What the mind's eye tells the mind's brain: A critique of mental imagery. *Psychological Bulletin*, 1973, 80, 1-24.

Pylyshyn, Z. The rate of "mental rotation of images: A test of a holistic analogue hypothesis. *Memory and Cognition*, 1979, 7, 19-28.

Raphael, B. The frame problem in problem-solving systems. In N. V. Findler & B. Meltzer (Eds.), *Artificial intelligence and heuristic programming*. Edinburgh: Edinburgh University Press, 1971.

Reed, S. K. Structural descriptions and the limitations of visual images. *Memory and Cognition*, 1974, 2, 329-336.

Rock, I. *Orientation and Form*. New York: Academic Press, 1973.

Shepard, R. N. Attention and the metric structure of the stimulus space. *Journal of Mathematical Psychology*, 1964, 1, 54-87.

Shepard, R. N. Form, formation and transformation of internal representations. In R. Solso (Ed.), *Information processing and cognition: The Loyola Symposium*. Hillsdale, N.J.: Lawrence Erlbaum Assoc., 1975.

Shepard, R. N. & Metzler, J. Mental rotation of three-dimensional objects. *Science,* 1971, 171, 701-703.

Simon, H. A. On reasoning about actions. In H. A. Simon and L. Siklossy (Eds.), *Representation and meaning.* Englewood Cliffs, N.J.: Prentice-Hall, 1972.

Simon, H. A. & Barenfeld, M. Information-processing analysis of perceptual processes in problem solving. *Psychological Review,* 1969, 76, 473-483.

Sloman, A. Interactions between philosophy and artificial intelligence: The role of intuition and non-logical reasoning in intelligence. *Artificial Intelligence,* 1971, 2, 209-225.

Thomas, H., Jamison, W., & Hummell, D. D. Observation is insufficient for discovering that the surface of still water is invariantly horizontal. *Science,* 1973, 181, 173-174.

Weinstein, E. L. The influence of symbolic systems on perspective drawings: A developmental approach. Unpublished M.Sc. thesis, Department of Psychology, University of Toronto, Canada, 1974.

Wittgenstein, L. *Philosophical investigations.* Oxford: Blackwell, 1953.

Woods, W. What's in a link: Foundations for semantic networks. In D. Bobrow & A. Collins (Eds.), *Representation and understanding: Studies in cognitive science.* New York: Academic Press, 1975.

Part Three

The Subject Matter of Grammar

Introduction: Some Notes on What Linguistics Is About

Jerry A. Fodor

All the chapters in this part are about what it is for a lingusitic theory to be true. The question what it is for a linguistic theory to be true is an *interesting* question and should be sharply distinguished from the question what it is for a true theory to be linguistic. The question what it is for a true theory to be linguistic is a *boring* question. Very often, in these chapters, the authors appear to be discussing the second question when they are in fact discussing the first. This is quite a standard tactic in philosophical argument. Philosophers like to appear to be discussing boring questions (such as how the word "good" is used) when they are in fact discussing interesting questions (such as what it is for something to be good). Heaven knows *why* philosophers like to do this, but they do and the reader is hereby forewarned. The question at issue in these papers is *not*: who gets to call his research real linguistics (as opposed to mere psychology or mere mathematics)? The question at issue is: what is it for a linguistic theory to be true?

Truth is (of course) correspondence to the facts. So, if we want to know what it is for a linguistic theory to be true, we have to know (a) which facts a true linguistic theory corresponds to and (b)

what relations to these facts are constitutive of the correspondence. Most of the discussion in these chapters centers on (a) since, presumably, whatever correspondence is, it's the same wherever truth claims are at issue. It might be that linguistic theories, when they are true, correspond to the facts in a different way than, say, physical theories do when *they* are true. But, so far, no one has suggested that this is so, and there is reason to hope that no one is about to.

So the question is: what facts are such that the truth of a linguistic theory consists in its correspondence to *those* facts, whatever correspondence may itself consist in? There are, as it turns out, really only two schools of thought on this question, though it may be a little hard to see that this is so, partly because other issues keep getting in the way, and partly because some of the players keep changing sides. One school (roughly, the forces of darkness) holds that the question is susceptible of a priori settlement; in fact, that we can even now specify a priori some set of facts such that the truth of a linguistic theory consists in its correspondence to *them*. The other school (roughly, the forces of light) holds that the question what facts a true linguistic theory corresponds to is answerable only a posteriori; in fact, only after adequate linguistic theories have been developed. The borders between these two positions are slightly vague, as, indeed, the borders between light and darkness are forever wont to be. But, to a first approximation, the two accounts are exclusive and exhaustive. Moreover, how you choose between them will determine your views on most of the rest of the methodological issues in the field.

The idea that it is possible to enumerate a priori the kinds of facts a scientific theory is required to account for has a considerable provenance in the history of philosophical discussions of scientific methodology. So, in the positivist tradition, it used to be believed that the truth of a scientific theory consists in its correspondence to those facts that constitute its *data*. This idea amounted to more than a triviality since the notion of data was proprietary. For example, the data might consist of just those facts that can be reported in a *data language*, where a data language, in turn, is one whose predicates subsume only "directly observable" objects, or only middle-sized objects, or only qualia, or whatever. The motives for holding this sort of view were usually epistemological (a desire to confine inductive risk to some level of theory distinct from its data sentences) and they need not concern us in detail. Suffice it to remark upon two tenets of positivist philosophy of science that appear to have survived the positivist's epistemology: that the data base for a theory can be delimited antecedent to the construction of theory, and that the truth claims a theory makes are exhausted by what it says about its data base. (All theories that entail the same data sentences are therefore equivalent unless they are distinguishable in respect of simplicity.)

Linguistics since 1957 has been busy rewriting its history in the approved Kuh-

nian fashion, and I make no claims about what real "taxonomic" linguists really thought that they were doing. But there is a taxonomic straw man with whom we are all acquainted and he, at least, was a positivist in the sense just specified. That is, he thought (a) that there is a specifiable data base for linguistic theories; (b) that this data base can be specified antecedent to theory construction; (c) that the empirical content of linguistic theories consists of what they say about the data base; and (d) that the data base for linguistics consists of the corpora of utterances that informants produce (or, in some versions, would produce given specified forms of prompting). Forget the epistemology and alter (d) to read "the data base for linguistics consists of the intuitions (about grammaticality, ambiguity, and so on) that informants produce (or would produce . . .)" and you get the view that seems to be common to Stephen P. Stich in "Grammar, Psychology, and Indeterminacy" (chapter 10) and Jerry Katz in "The Real Status of Semantic Representations" (chapter 13). I need a name for this view. I shall call it the Wrong View.

Thus, the Wrong View and Positivist View are in pretty fair agreement that the question what linguistics is about is one that can be settled a priori. But it is essential to bear in mind that the arguments currently being advanced for the Wrong View are really quite different from the ones that used to be advanced for the Positivist View. If positivists thought themselves warranted in identifying the empirical content of a theory with the data sentences that it entails, that was often because they thought that meaningfulness is a matter of verifiability, or that theoretical entities are fictions, or that theoretical terms must be definable in an observation vocabulary, and so on. There may be those who hold the Wrong View for these sorts of reasons, but you will not find their writings in this volume. I think (if I may momentarily abandon the posture of perfect neutrality that I have thus far assumed) that the Wrong View is certainly wrong. But the standard antiverificationist arguments aren't what one has against it.

I want to discuss the arguments against the Wrong View at some length. First, however, let me set out, quite briefly, the alternative position (which I shall call the Right View). The Right View is the one enunciated in Noam Chomsky and Jerry Katz's "What the Linguist Is Talking About" (chapter 11) and assumed in Janet D. Fodor, Jerry A. Fodor, and Merrill F. Garrett's "The Psychological Unreality of Semantic Representations" (chapter 12).[1] What it amounts to is the following claims. (a) Linguistic theories are descriptions of grammars. (b) It is nomologically necessary that learning one's native language involves learning its grammar, so a theory of how grammars are learned is *de facto* a (partial [?]) theory of how languages are learned. (c) It is nomologically necessary that the grammar of a language is internally represented by speaker/hearers of that language; up to dialectical variants, the grammar of a language is what its speaker/hearers have in common by virtue of which they are speaker/hearers of the *same* language. (d) It is nomologically necessary that the internal representation of the grammar (or, equivalently for these purposes, the internally represented grammar) is causally implicated in communication exchanges between speakers and hearers insofar as these exchanges are mediated by their use of the language that they share; talking and understanding the language normally involve exploiting the internally represented grammar.[2]

Never mind, for the moment, whether the Right View is right. My present purpose is to emphasize a glaring difference between the Right View and its antagonist. According to the latter, as we have seen, there is a proprietary body of data (the speaker/hearer's linguistic intui-

tions according to the most popular version) such that, a priori, the facts that a true linguistic theory corresponds to are exhausted by those data, and such that any theories that predict the same such data are *ipso facto* "empirically equivalent."[3] Whereas, according to the Right View, *any* facts about the use of language, or about how it is learned, or about the neurology of speaker/hearers, or, for that matter, about the weather on Mars, could, in principle, be relevant to the choice between competing linguistic theories. This is because, according to the Right View, linguistics is embedded in psychology (it offers a partial theory of the capacities and behaviors of speaker/hearers) and is thus sensitive to whatever information about the psychology of speaker/hearers we are able to bring to bear. Moreover, *sensitive to* is, in this respect, a transitive relation: if we get our neurology (or our astronomy) to bear on some part of our psychology, then if that part of our psychology bears on our linguistics, then so too do our neurology and our astronomy.

It is thus a consequence of the Right View that there is no a priori distinction between linguistic data and psychological data (or, indeed, between linguistic data and data of *any* other kind). Such distinctions as we *are* able to draw are a posteriori; we find out more and more about which are the relevant data as we find out more and more about how grammars function in the mental processes of speaker/hearers. This seems to me to be precisely as it ought to be; it accords with our intuitions about how scientific practice should proceed. Suppose that, tomorrow, some very clever astro-linguist were to devise an argument that runs from observations of the Martian climate to some or other constraint on theories of human psychology and thence to the proper formulation of the English pseudocleft. *Surely* we would say, "Bravo and, well done," not "Ingenious but not pertinent."

200 Jerry A. Fodor

The alternative view is that the scientist gets to *stipulate* what data are to count as relevant to the (dis)confirmation of his theories, and my point is that that view simply isn't plausible given the way that real science is conducted. I take this to be a point of utmost methodological seriousness since it implies that either the Wrong View misdescribes linguistics or what linguists do is somehow an exception to the methodological principles that other sciences endorse. Here is one way that (barring the anachronisms) the argument between Ptolemy and Galileo might have gone:

Galileo. I have these telescopic observations, and they seem to show that Venus has phases. It's going to be awfully hard to square that with Venus and the Sun revolving around the Earth, so I think you guys have got trouble.

Ptolemy. Ingenious but not pertinent. The data of astronomy are [i.e., are exhausted by] observations of the positions of the stars and planets. Astronomy *is* [i.e., = *df*] the science that predicts such observations. It follows that any two theories that make the same such predictions are *ipso facto* (barring simplicity) equivalent theories. That one but not the other predicts phases for Venus *could not* be relevant to a choice between them. For: Nothing but astronomical data can be relevant to a choice between astronomical theories, and OBSERVATIONS OF THE PHASES OF VENUS DO NOT CONSTITUTE ASTRONOMICAL DATA. They constitute, to coin a phrase, *performance data.* There is a great deal that we do not know about telescopes.

The point is that the argument didn't go that way. If Ptolemy *had* tried stipulating a proprietary data base for astronomy, his problem would have been to make the stipulation stick; and, stipulations notwithstanding, anybody rational prefers a theory that predicts both the observed locations of the planets *and* the phases of Venus to a theory that predicts only the former.

Indeed, a stronger—and rather less familiar—point appears to be germane. It's not just that the observation of planetary positions has no *stipulated* position as the data par excellence of astronomy; it is also true that one requires a posteriori justification for the claim that such observations are relevant *at all*. This is not, of course, an idiosyncrasy of astronomy. Any science is under the obligation to explain why *what it takes to be* data relevant to the confirmation of its theories *are* data relevant to the confirmation of its theories. Typically one meets this condition by exhibiting a causal chain that runs from the entities that the theory posits, via the instruments of observation, to the psychological states of the observer. (So, the astronomer can argue, if there are such things as planets, and if they are at least roughly the sorts of things that his theories suppose them to be, then given the way that terrestrial astronomers are situated, and given the way that telescopes work, telescopic observations of the apparent positions of the planets *should* bear upon the confirmation of theories about how the planets are arranged in space.) Whereas, if there is reason to suppose that such a causal chain does *not* connect the observations to the postulated entities, the scientist has no warrant to appeal to those observations as data in support of his theories, however much tradition may sanction such appeals.

This all applies, *mutatis mutandis*, to linguistics, or so one would have thought. In particular, an adequate linguistics *should explain why it is that the intuitions of speaker/hearers constitute data relevant to the confirmation of grammars.* The Right View meets this condition. It says, "We can use intuitions to confirm grammars because grammars are internally represented and actually contribute to the etiology of the speaker/hearer's intuitive judgments." The Wrong View says only: "We do it because we have always done it," or "We do it by stipulation."

So far, I've been running the discussion on the assumption that linguistics works the way that science does, and of course that assumption might be false. I now want to look at some of the arguments that allege that linguistics is special in a way that exempts the linguist from adherence to the usual canons of scientific methodology; in particular, that because of the kind of discipline that linguistics is, linguists can (as Ptolemy could not) specify a priori what data are to bear on the confirmation of their theories.

The easiest of these arguments to understand (and to sympathize with) is one that I take to underlie much of Stich's chapter. Stich sees very clearly that the Right View is tenable only if sense can be made of the notion of internal representation. After all, the Right View construes learning a language as a process that eventuates in the internal representation of a grammar, and it construes the production/perception of speech as causally mediated by the grammar that the speaker/hearer learns. On both grounds, it is committed to a Realistic construal of the notion of internal representation; what isn't there has no effects or causes.

It is thus only because it allows itself free use of "the internally represented grammar (the internal representation of the grammar)" that the Right View can define truth-for-a-linguistic-theory in the way that it does: as correspondence between the grammar that the theory postulates and the grammar that the speaker/hearer learns. (See, in particular, Stich, chapter 10, note 14, where he doubts—correctly, I believe—that one can make sense of the notion of *learning* a grammar once the internal representation concept is abandoned). If, then, the no-

tion of internal representation is *not* coherent, the only thing left for a linguistic theory to be true of is the linguist's observations (*de facto*, the intuitions of the speaker/hearer as extrapolated by the formally simplest grammar). Take the notion of internal representation away from linguistic metatheory and you get positivism by subtraction.

Of course, this would constitute a serious argument for the Wrong View only if no sense could be made of the notion of internal representation, and that is a moot question as readers of this volume will doubtless already have gathered. (See, especially, part one, "Mental Representation.") Some philosophers think that there exists a distinguishable intellectual enterprise called "conceptual analysis." The idea is that, if a question should arise as to whether a notion can be made clear, you can answer the question by getting a philosopher to do some of this conceptual analyzing. When he is finished analyzing, the philosopher will tell you whether or not you are allowed to use the notion to do science with.

I do not think that this is how things work. Philosophers don't get to tell you what counts as a permissible scientific construct, any more than scientists get to tell you what counts as relevant scientific data. What determines which constructs are permissible (and which data are relevant) is: how the world turns out to be. We will find out whether we can make sense of "mental representation" *as we go along.* (The prospects look rather better now than they did a decade or two ago.)

I think that Stich thinks that claims about internal representations suffer from an inherent resistance to (dis)confirmation, and that this flaw irremediably infects theories that entail such claims. In particular, I take it to be Stich's view that (a) you can make sense of choosing among descriptively adequate grammars (*dags*)[4] only given a reputable notion of internal representation; but (b) no merely empirical result could license a choice among descriptively adequate grammars (so that no such result could require us to embrace the internal representation construct). I think that (a) is probably correct, but it is easy to imagine cases contrary to (b).

Indeed, such cases arise again and again in the actual practice of validating linguistic theories. For example, nobody is interested in grammars that *demonstrably could not be learned*, though there is no reason why some such grammars shouldn't be *dags* in Stich's sense. Or, consider the following unsubtle example. Suppose it turned out that, among the equally simple extrapolations of the adult's intuitions, there existed one (*G3*) that contained precisely three rules. And suppose it were also to turn out that, in learning English, a child goes through three distinguishable stages. In stage 1, he produces precisely the sorts of utterances (or intuitions) that he would produce if he knew only rule 1 of *G3*; in stage 2 he produces precisely the ones he would produce if he knew only rules 1 and 2 of *G3*; and in stage 3 he produces the typical adult corpus. It would surely be mad, under such circumstances, not to prefer *G3* to other *dags*, all other things being equal, for it could be claimed of *G3* — but, by assumption, not of any other *dag* — that it is learned *rule by rule*. This is to say that it would be mad, under these circumstances, not to do precisely what (according to Stich) requires you to embrace a notion of internal representation: namely, choose among descriptively adequate grammars. But it is conceptually possible that such circumstances might obtain; the world *could* turn out that way. So, it looks as though the world could turn out so as to license the use of the notion of internal representation, and could do so even if philosophers hadn't finished analyzing it at the time.

There are two arguments for the Wrong View that do not depend upon agnosticism about internal representations. These need to be looked at now. I'll move fairly quickly, since many of the relevant points have already been made.

It is sometimes suggested that the Wrong View can be defended by appeal to the competence/performance distinction. (This is a proposal that Katz appears to endorse in his discussion of "Competencism.") My own view is that there *is* a competence/performance distinction but that it has been much abused by some of its devotees. I often wish that it would go away. Still, at a minimum, something has to be said by way of showing that making the distinction in a defensible form doesn't commit one to the Wrong View of linguistic theories.

At heart, the competence/performance distinction is a distinction between *kinds of explanations.* "Competence theories" account for facts about the behaviors and capacities of a speaker/hearer by reference to properties of his internalized grammar, whereas "performance theories" account for facts about the behaviors and capacities of a speaker/hearer by reference to interactions between the internally represented grammar and other aspects of the speaker/hearer's psychology. So, to cite the classical example, we explain the speaker/hearer's ability to understand and produce novel linguistic forms by reference to the productivity of the grammar he has learned, but we explain the speaker/hearer's *in*ability to understand multiply center-embedded sentences by reference to the interactions between the mentally represented grammar and the (short-term) memory he employs in parsing the sentences that the grammar generates.

Notice that, so construed, the competence/performance distinction is clearly to be drawn a posteriori; we discover which aspects of the speaker/hearer's behavior/capacity are in the domain of theories of competence, and which are not, by discovering which explanations of the speaker/hearer's behavior/capacity are *true*. Notice also that the competence/performance distinction, so construed, is not a very *interesting* distinction. Its primary use is to explain (for example) why hiccoughs aren't part of English even though they *do* occur, from time to time, in the corpus of English utterances. The explanation goes; hiccoughs that occur during speech are produced by the interaction of the language mechanisms with the hiccough mechanisms. An adequate theory must, therefore, treat utterances that contain hiccoughs as interaction effects. It must not, in particular, attribute them to the functioning of the language mechanisms per se; were it to do so, the theory would not be *true*. It should be emphasized that, according to this analysis, it is the notion of truth, and not the performance/competence distinction, that is actually doing the work in constraining the linguist's theories. Similarly, in cases where we appeal to the competence/performance distinction to correct an informant's linguistic intuitions: What's wrong with the intuition that a multiply self-embedded sentence is ungrammatical is not that it somehow flouts the competence/performance distinction; it's simply that the intuition is false. The competence/performance distinction isn't, in short, a methodological constraint imposed upon linguistic theories over and above the demand for correspondence to the facts. On the contrary, we honor the performance/competence distinction when — and only when — we get the facts right.

A sensible discussion of the competence/performance distinction might well stop here. Beyond this point there are monsters. However.

You can, if you like, use the competence/performance distinction to introduce a notion of *Ideal Speaker/Hearer*. You do so as follows. Imagine what a real speaker/hearer would be like if his behavior did *not* exhibit certain effects that are consequences of interactions between the language mechanisms and other psychological states and processes. For example, if speaker/hearers had infinite short-term memories, then (assuming our current theories are true) they would be able to construe arbitrarily self-embedded sentences. And, perhaps, they would always be able to tell whether a string in their language was grammatical (though this is by no means obviously so). Well, then, an Ideal Speaker/Hearer is just like a real speaker/hearer except that, in explaining the behavior/capacities of the former, we do not need to refer to the effects of these interactions; we define the behaviors characteristic of Ideal Speaker/Hearers by abstracting from such effects. We can even add this: grammars per se are theories about Ideal Speakers/Hearers. This sounds wildly deep and ontological and sexy, but actually it is trivial and harmless. All it means is that grammars are not, per se, theories of the interaction effects. (Of course, there *is* a question of fact here, and it's not a small one: namely, which is the *correct* parsing of the speaker/hearer's psychology into "linguistic mechanisms" and "others." Only a characterization of the Ideal Speaker/Hearer that gets this parsing right will be of use for purposes of empirical theory construction.)

Finally, having gone this far, we can take the rest of the plunge and characterize a proprietary notion of "linguistic data." Linguistic data, in this proprietary sense, are those that, *de facto*, are explicable by reference to just the theoretical constructs appealed to in theories of the Ideal Speaker/Hearer. Since the grammar *is*, by assumption, a theory of the Ideal Speaker/Hearer, it will follow that linguistic data are data relevant to the confirmation of the grammar.

There are now two mistakes just aching to be made. One is to ignore the *"de facto"* and assume that you can somehow determine a priori *which* aspects of the behavior/capacities of the speaker/hearer are preserved under idealization (hence which data are linguistic in the proprietary sense). The other is to suppose that the linguistic data *exhaust* the facts that bear on the confirmation of a grammar. I take it that the first of these is *obviously* a mistake. The kinds of observations that linguists have thus far taken to bear on their theories about grammars are, almost certainly, a heterogeneous and fragmentary sample of the data that God would consider relevant. As our theories and techniques of observation get better, we will surely revise our views about which observations are germane; in what science is this not the case? The point is: because we know very little about the grammar and practically nothing about the way it interacts with other psychological faculties, *we do not know which capacities an Ideal Speaker/ Hearer has qua Ideal Speaker/Hearer.* Moreover, we aren't allowed to *stipulate* these capacities on pain of introducing a notion of Ideal Speaker/Hearer that is, *de facto,* useless for theory construction. (**Ptolemy:** The Sun *does* revolve around the Earth in an *Ideal* Solar System.) Again: What the capacities of the Ideal Speaker/Hearer are depends on which theory of real speaker/hearers is *true.*

But suppose we *did* know, a posteriori, what capacities an Ideal Speaker/Hearer has qua Ideal Speaker/ Hearer. Couldn't we then say that the simplest grammar that accounts for *those* capacities is *ipso facto* true? For example, suppose that it turned out, in light of the best theories we can devise, that the ability to formulate intuitions of grammaticality is the only such capacity. Couldn't we then say: the true grammar is the (simplest) one that predicts the grammaticality intuitions of the speaker/ hearer?

Patently not. For, suppose we had two equally simple grammars, *G* and *G',* which gave the same account of the grammaticality intuitions of speaker/hearers. And suppose we had a theory *M* of the organization of memory in human adults, such that *M* is independently highly confirmed. Finally, suppose that the conjunction of *M* and *G* predicted that multiply self-embedded sentences are not construable by human adults, whereas the conjunction of *M* and *G'* predicted the contrary. It would then be mad to deny that we had evidence for preferring *G* to *G',* even despite the fact that they make the same predictions about those behaviors/capacities that Ideal Speaker/ Hearers have qua Ideal Speaker/Hearers. Here, then, is another moral from the general philosophy of science: the data relevant to the confirmation of *T* include the data predicted by *the conjunction of T with any other theory that is independently well confirmed.*[5] In particular, they are *not* exhausted by the entailments of *T* taken alone. From the assumption that grammars are theories of the capacities of Ideal Speaker/Hearers, it does *not* follow that the confirmation base for a grammar is exhausted by the claims about the capacities of Ideal Speaker/Hearers that the grammar makes.

The short form of this discussion goes like this: there are no such things as "competence data" or "performance data" (just as there are no such things as "linguistic data" or "psychological data" or "astronomical data"). I mean that none of these classifications is *principled.* In principle, there are just the facts, on the one hand, and the totality of the available scientific theories, on the other. It is probably a historical accident that, so far, the best field of data for the confirmation of grammars has been the well-formedness intuitions of speaker/hearers. It is to be hoped (and, for once, optimism is rational) that new fields of data will become increasingly available as we learn more about how to use facts about the interactions between internally represented grammars and other psychological mechanisms to constrain both the theory of the grammar and the theory of the interactions.[6]

There is, however, one version of the Wrong View that does seem to me to be, in a certain sense, unassailable; it's the position that Katz calls Platonism. In effect, the Platonist is unmoved by any of the methodological morals that I have been drawing from general scientific practice because he doesn't think that linguistics is (empirical) science. What he thinks is that linguistics is a part of mathematics, and (I suppose) in mathematics you can stipulate whenever you are so inclined.

Hence, a possible position is this: "I am interested in the mathematical problem of formally specifying a grammar that predicts certain of the intuitions of speakers/hearers; more precisely, I am interested in this project insofar as such intuitions are not artifacts of memory limitations, mortality, lapses of attention and other 'performance factors.' I stipulate that any pair of equally simple theories that make the same such predictions are to count as equivalent for these purposes. There is therefore nothing that, for these purposes, could decide between two such theories." (Note that what counts as a "performance factor" in this view is itself determined by stipulation, and not, as previously, by reference to which etiology of the behavior of the speaker/hearer is true. Thus there is no particular reason why, in choosing a domain for his theory, the Platonist needs to attend to those of the speaker/hearer's capacities that are left when you eliminate contamination from memory limitations and the like. In principle, he might just as well attend to the construction of grammars that predict only intuitions about sentences with more than seven vowels, or sentences whose twelfth word is "grandmother," or sentences that happen to be uttered on Tuesdays. Once you start to stipulate, it's Liberty Hall.)

It is worth emphasizing that Platonism, so construed, isn't incompatible with the Right View. It doesn't deny that some grammars are learned (and thus internally represented) or that the grammar that is learned causally mediates the production/perception of speech. Indeed, a reasonable Platonist might well want to endorse these claims since he would presumably want *some* story about the etiology of the speaker/hearer's linguistic intuitions, and the internal representation story seems to be the only one in town. But while he denies none of this qua, as it were, mildly interested observer, he officially doesn't care one way or the other qua Platonist. Qua Platonist, he isn't interested in the empirical truth of linguistic theories any more than the geometer (qua geometer) is interested in the empirical truth of Euclidean theory (in whether physical space is Euclidean). Indeed, strictly speaking, the Platonist has no use for distinguishing among grammars in respect of *truth* at all, so long as they make the same predictions about the speaker/hearer's intuitions. Formal simplicity, for example, is not a truth criterion in Platonistic linguistics any more than it is in number theory.[7]

The only thing against Platonism, so construed, is that, deep down, nobody is remotely interested in it.[8] Mathematical linguists aren't, because what *they* care about is the formal properties of those grammars that are current or foreseeable candidates for theories of what the speaker/hearer learns when he learns his language (namely, for theories of internal representation). There isn't, after all, the remotest reason to believe that the class of generative sources that have in common *only* the ability to predict the intuitions of speaker/hearers has any mathematical interest whatever. (Indeed, there is some a posteriori reason to believe that it does not, since, so far at least, the intuitive data have failed to yield clear decisions among types of grammars of very different formal structure.)

A fortiori, practicing empirical linguists aren't Platonists, for the good and sufficient reason that Platonism is so much less interesting than the Right View. Suppose that we grant the Platonist proprietary use of the term "linguistics." So, by stipulation, linguistics is part of mathematics. But then, just down the road, there must be another science *just like linguistics* except that it *does* care about empirical truth because it cares about how the mind works. Suppose we call this other science "psycho-linguistics." Psycho-linguistics, so construed, is part of the theory of internal representation. If, as we now suppose, intuitions have construct validity for the theory of (internally represented) grammars, then we are guaranteed that the psycho-linguist's grammar will turn out to be one of the grammars that the Platonist is interested in. Like the Platonistic linguist, the psycho-linguist is interested in predicting the intuitions of speaker/hearers because he believes (*believes*, not *stipulates*) that intuitions are relevant to the confirmation of grammars. But, unlike the Platonistic linguist, the psycho-linguist thinks that other kinds of data can constrain the choice of grammars too. He is therefore professionally interested in how languages are learned, how utterances are understood, whether there are linguistic universals, whether transformations are innate, how cognition affects language, how language affects cognition, aphasic speech, schizophrenic speech, metaphorical speech, telegraphic speech, dolphin speech, chimp speech, speech production, speech acts, and, in short, all that stuff that got people interested in studying language in the first place. Go ahead, be a Platonist if you like. But the action is all at the other end of town.

I shall now once more relax the attitude of strict impartiality that I have hitherto assumed. The Right View is the right view *so far as we can now make out*. The italics are not, however, intended to be taken lightly. The Right View defines the goals of linguistics *ex post facto*, in light of the theories now in the field. It's certain that these theories aren't true in detail, and it's entirely possible that they are false root and branch. In that case, there will be a residual philosophical question whether we ought to say that linguistics was misconstrued by the Right View or that there is no such science as linguistics. I, for one, won't much care.

Notes

1. Katz thinks that Garrett and I once held the Wrong View (in the passage he cites from our "Some Reflections on Competence and Performance"), but he is wrong to think so. What we said was that "the internal evidence in favor of the structural descriptions modern grammars generate is so strong that it is difficult to imagine them succumbing to any purely experimental disconfirmation." N.B.: "hard to imagine," not "methodologically inconceivable." What we try to show in "The Psychological Unreality of Semantic Representations" (chapter 12) is that all of the internal evidence (all the evidence that linguists have thus far alleged) favoring lexical decomposition can be met equally well by using meaning postulates; and, moreover, that the latter approach can cope with the available experimental data.

I wouldn't fuss about these exegetical details except that I have changed my mind, at one time or another, about almost everything *but* the Right View, and I do claim credit for this little island of consistency. I suspect that what caused the confusion is that Katz takes such distinctions as "internal" versus "experimental" evidence to be principled, whereas it would never have occurred to Garrett or to me to view them as other than heuristic. This sort of point will loom large below.

2. A word about these nomological necessities. For all we now know, it is nomologically possible that there should be organisms (chimps? Martians? machines?) that could learn and use English without learning or

exploiting its grammar. So, for all we now know, these nomological necessities hold at most for *our* species (or for species with our sort of nervous system). Linguistics is certainly part of *human* psychology, according to the Right View; the rest is an empirical issue currently up for grabs.

This is not, of course, an *objection* to the Right View. Sciences often leave unspecified the domain of the nomological necessities they articulate. A biologist who says that respiration is necessary for (our kind of) life is not thereby denying the possibility of life forms *very* different from us. And some cosmologists think that even fundamental laws of nature may have restricted applicability: that they may not hold at very remote times or in very extreme states of matter.

A fortiori, it does not follow from these nomological necessities that "it would be logically absurd to claim that creatures with sufficiently different information processing mechanisms from ours also speak English" (Katz, chapter 13). The identification of the grammar of *L* as that system that is nomologically necessary for *us* to learn if we are to learn *L* is quite compatible with the assumption that that grammar plays *no* role in the use of *L* by other (nomologically possible but very different) kinds of creatures. Should it be proposed that the grammar of *L* is that system that is neutral between the ways in which *L* might be represented by any nomologically possible *L*-speakers, we would require arguments to show that there *is* a unique such system—or, indeed, that there are *any* such systems. I know of no such arguments.

3. "Empirically equivalent" theories cannot, in point of logic, compete in respect of truth. For (a) truth is correspondence to the facts; (b) the facts linguistic theories correspond to are, by assumption, the linguistic data; and (c) linguistic theories are empirically

equivalent iff they correspond to the same data in the same way. Hence, in particular, simplicity is not a truth criterion according to the Wrong View (though one may, of course, prefer the simplest of a set of empirically equivalent theories on grounds *other than* truth—for instance, on aesthetic grounds).

4. A *dag* is any adequately simple extrapolation of the adult corpus of intuitions that is compatible with the data in the corpus.

5. Assuming, of course, that the conjunction is consistent.

6. Just as the distinction between "linguistic" and "psychological" data is not principled, so, too, the distinction between collecting intuitions and running experiments (or between "on-line" and "off-line" mental processes) is heuristic from the point of view of specifying the data relevant to the confirmation of a linguistic theory. Of course, it *could* turn out a posteriori (that is, in light of a true theory of language processing) that only a specifiable class of observations (such as collecting intuitions, or collecting responses that it takes more than six minutes for the subject to produce, or, for that matter, weighing your grandmother) *in fact* bear on which grammar is true. But this would be a *discovery*, not part of a stipulative definition of "linguistic data." You don't get to stipulate what counts as construct validity for an experiment, any more than you get to stipulate which data are relevant to the truth of a theory.

7. See note 3 above.

8. I provisionally except certain "Montague grammarians," who do appear to have achieved the requisite detachment from the claims of mere fact. See, for example, Richmond Thomason's remarks in his introduction to R. Montague's *Formal Philosophy* (New Haven: Yale University Press, 1974) (which, however, are perhaps more enigmatic and less univocal than they may at first appear.)

Grammar, Psychology, and Indeterminacy

Stephen P. Stich

Significance is the trait with respect to which the subject matter of linguistics is studied by the grammarian.

Pending a satisfactory explanation of the notion of meaning, linguists in semantic fields are in the position of not knowing what they are talking about.

W. V. Quine

According to Quine, the linguist qua grammarian does not know what he is talking about. The goal of this essay is to tell him. My aim is to provide an account of what the grammarian is saying of an expression when he says it is grammatical, or a noun phrase, or ambiguous, or the subject of a certain sentence. More generally, I want to give an account of the nature of a generative grammatical theory of a language — of the data for such a theory, the relation between the theory and the data, and the relation between the theory and a speaker of the language.

I

Prominent among a linguist's pronouncements are attributions of grammaticality. What are we saying about a sentence when we say it is grammatical? One strategy for answering this question

From *Journal of Philosophy* 69, no. 22 (December 7, 1972): 799-818. Reprinted by permission of *Journal of Philosophy* and the author.

is to attend to the work of the grammarian. To be grammatical, a sentence must have those characteristics which the grammarian seeks in deciding whether a sentence is grammatical. So a reconstruction of the grammarian's work is a likely path to an explication of 'grammatical'. This is the strategy adopted by Quine,[1] and it will be of value to study his remarks in some detail. On Quine's account, *significance* rather than *grammaticality* "is the trait with respect to which the subject matter of linguistics is studied by the grammarian" (18). If the two are different, there is some inclination to take the grammarian at his name. So let us see what can be learned by taking Quine's proposal as an explication of *grammaticality*.

The problem for the grammarian may be posed as the segregating of a class *K* of sequences that we will call *grammatical*. On Quine's view, he attends to four nested classes of sequences, *H, I, J,* and *K*.

H is the class of observed sequences, excluding any which are ruled inappropriate in the sense of being non-linguistic or belonging to alien dialects. *I* is the class of all such observed sequences and all that ever will happen to be professionally observed, excluding again those which are ruled inappropriate. *J* is the class of all sequences ever occurring, now or in the past or future, within or without professional observation — excluding, again, only those which are ruled inappropriate. *K*, finally, is the infinite class of all those sequences, with the exclusion of the inappropriate ones as usual, which *could* be uttered without bizarreness reactions. *K* is the class which the grammarian wants to approximate in his formal reconstruction (53).

The linguist's data are *H*, and he checks his predictions against *I* minus *H* hoping that this will be a representative sample of *J*. It is when we come to *K* that philosophical eyebrows are raised; for what is the force of the 'could' which extends the class beyond *J*, commonly infinitely beyond? Quine's answer is that, besides *H* and future checks against *I*, the 'could' is the reflection of the scientist's appeal to simplicity. "Our basis for saying what 'could' be generally consists . . . in what *is* plus simplicity of the laws whereby we describe and extrapolate what is" (54).

Quine's proposal shares with other operational definitions the virtue of objectivity. Yet his solution is beset with problems. For Quine's procedure just does not pick out anything like the class we would pre-systematically hold to be grammatical — and this because his account fails to portray what the grammarian *actually does*. To see this, consider the case of a Quinean linguist ignorant of English setting out to segregate grammatical English sequences. He starts with *H*, the class of sequences he observes. But *H*, in addition to samples of what we would pre-systematically hold to be grammatical sequences, contains all manner of false starts, "lost thoughts," peculiar pauses ('aahhhh'!) and, unless he is uncommonly fortunate, a liberal sprinkling of blatantly incoherent speech. Yet Quine, if we take him literally, would have *H* included as a subset of *K*. What the resulting projection

might be is hard to imagine. But *K*, so constructed, would not be the class of grammatical sequences in English.

It might be thought that, appealing to simplicity, the linguist could toss out an occasional member of *H*, much as he excludes from *H* what he takes to be non-linguistic noise or intrusion from another tongue. But an hour spent attending carefully to unreflective speech will dispel this notion. There is simply too much to exclude.[2]

Quine succeeds in muddying the waters a bit by sprinkling the restriction that the sentences to be studied are those which could be uttered "without bizarreness reactions." It is not clear whether he takes such sentences to be excluded from *H* and *I* by virtue of their being observed *in situ* or whether he would have *H* and *I* further filtered. But it seems clear that, in either case, either this move is inadequate or it begs the question. If by 'bizarreness' Quine means *bizarreness*, then the exclusion will hardly accomplish his purpose. For many sorts of sequences that we would want to exclude from *K* (those with 'aahhh's' interspersed, for example, or those which change subject mid-sentence) are uttered all the time without bizarreness reactions. And many sentences we would want to include in *K* would surely evoke the strongest of bizarreness reactions. Indeed, though *K* will be infinite, only members of a finite subset could be uttered without evoking a bizarreness reaction. Sentences that take more than six months to utter are bizarre. If, however, the reaction Quine has in mind is the reaction (whatever it may be) characteristically displayed when an ungrammatical sequence is uttered, then, until he has provided some account of how this reaction is to be recognized, he has begged the question.[3]

II

Taking Quine's proposal as an explication of grammaticality has led to an impasse. In seeking our way around it we might do well to return to Quine's original insight and attend more closely to what the grammarian actually does. From the first, the generative grammarian has relied heavily on the fact that, with a modicum of instruction, speakers can be brought to make all manner of judgments about their language. In particular, they can be brought to make firm judgments on the oddness or acceptability of indefinitely many sequences. Provided with a few examples, speakers can go on to judge new sequences in point of grammaticality, and do so with considerable consistency for large numbers of cases. This suggests that we might try to remedy the difficulties with Quine's proposal by substituting *intuitive judgments* for observed utterances. On the revised account, H would be the class of those sequences which to date have been considered and judged to be grammatical. I would be the class of sequences ever reflected upon and judged clearly grammatical. And K is the infinite class projected along simplest lines from H and checked against I.

This modified account nicely circumvents the major shortcoming we found in Quine's proposal. Read literally, Quine's method did not pick out the class of sequences we would pre-systematically call grammatical. The class H on which his projection was based was already tainted with ungrammatical sequences. Our modified version avoids this difficulty by basing its projection on sequences intuitively taken to be grammatical. The projected class K can still miss the mark, failing to be compatible with I minus H. But this potential failure is the normal inductive one.[4]

We can now make a plausible first pass at depicting the grammarian's work. He proceeds by eliciting intuitive judgments about which sequences are in the informant's language and which are not. He then projects these clear cases along

simplest lines, checking his projected class against speakers' intuitions. Thus the task of the generative grammarian may be viewed as that of constructing a system of rules and a definition of 'generate' that define a terminal language containing phonetic representations for all the sequences judged by speakers to be clearly acceptable and containing no sequence judged to be clearly unacceptable. The sequences about which speakers have no firm or consistent intuitions can be relegated to the class of "don't cares" and decided by the simplest grammar that handles the clear cases.

Yet as it stands the account still will not do. One fault is its myopic concentration on intuitions. Speakers' judgments about acceptability are the most important data for the grammarian. But they are not his only data, nor are they immune from being corrected or ignored. The attentive grammarian will attend to many aspects of his subjects' behavior in addition to their response to questions about sentences' acceptability. And a proper explication of the grammarian's job must provide some account of the role these additional data play.

Perhaps the most important sort of evidence for the grammarian besides intuitions of acceptability is the actual unreflective speech of his subjects. An informant's protest that a given sequence is unacceptable may be ignored if he is caught in the act, regularly uttering unpremeditatedly what, on meditation, he alleges he doesn't say. In addition to actual speech, there is a host of further clues for the grammarian. Stress patterns, facts about how sentences are heard and data on short-term verbal recall are among them.[5] Others might be mentioned. To what use does the grammarian put this further evidence? Principally, I suggest, to shore up the evidence provided by speakers' intuitive judgments or to justify his neglect of them. A sentence whose acceptability to speakers is in some doubt will, with good conscience, be generated by a grammar if it ranks high in the other tests. And, on the other side, a sentence that has the blessings of speakers may be rejected—not generated by the grammar—if it fails to display the other characteristics of grammatical sequences.

We now have one justification the grammarian may use for rejecting speakers' intuitions. There is another. And consideration of it will lead to a fundamental revision of our account of grammaticality. Intuitive oddness may be explained by many factors. Some sentences seem odd because they are pragmatically odd, describing a situation that is bizarre. Others, perhaps, may be rejected as obscene or taboo. Most importantly, sentences may seem odd because they are simply too long and complicated. If the grammarian suspects that any of these factors explain speakers' rejection of a sentence, he may classify it as grammatical *even though it lacks all the characteristics in the cluster associated with grammaticality.*

Note that at this juncture two notions we have been conflating part company. Thus far I have been interchanging 'acceptability' and 'grammaticality' with studied equivocation. Intuitions of acceptability and the cluster of further characteristics usually accompanying sentences judged acceptable have been taken as (more or less) necessary and sufficient conditions for grammaticality. But the picture changes when a sentence may be classed as grammatical in spite of failing each relevant test. The motivation for separating acceptability and grammaticality is *broad theoretic simplicity.* It is simpler to generate an infinite class including the acceptable sentences than it is to draw a boundary around just those sentences which rank high in the several tests for acceptability. But in thus choosing the simpler task we must assume that some further theory or theories will account for those grammatical sentences which are

unacceptable. And we must also assume that the new theory combined with a grammatical theory will together be simpler than any theory attempting directly to generate all and only the acceptable sequences. In short, we are venturing that the best theory to account for *all* the data will include a grammar of infinite generative capacity. This is hardly a step to be taken lightly. For in allowing his grammar to generate an infinite number of sentences, the grammarian is countenancing as grammatical an infinite number of sentences that fail each test of acceptability. It might be thought that such prodigality could be avoided by simply cutting off the class of sentences generated by a grammar at an appropriately high point. But this is not the case. For there is no natural point to draw the line—no point at which the addition of another conjunct or another clause regularly changes a clearly acceptable sentence into a clearly unacceptable one. Nor would it do to pick an *arbitrary* high cut-off point. This would leave the grammarian as before with generated sentences that are unacceptable. And any account of *why* these sentences were unacceptable would likely also account for the sequences beyond the arbitrary cut-off point.

By now it is evident that grammaticality is best viewed as a *theoretical* notion. Like other theoretical notions, it is related to relevant data in several and complex ways. Simple grammatical sentences generally have several or all of the cluster of characteristics typical of acceptable sequences. More complex grammatical sentences may share none of these characteristics. They are grammatical in virtue of being generated by the grammar that most simply generates all the clearly acceptable sentences and holds the best promise of fitting into a simple total theory of acceptability.

There is, thus, a conjecture built into a proposed grammar—the conjecture that this generative system will fit comfortably into a total theory that accounts for all the data. In this respect a grammar is similar to the theory of ideal gases. The ideal-gas laws do a good job at predicting the behavior of light gases at high temperatures and low pressures. In less favorable cases, the laws predict poorly. They were accepted in the hope, later fulfilled, that further laws could be found to explain the difference between the behavior of real gases and the predicted behavior of ideal ones. The adoption of a given grammar or form of grammar might be viewed as setting up a "paradigm"[6] or framework for future investigation. The grammar serves to divide those phenomena still needing explanation (viz., unacceptable grammatical sequences) from those already adequately handled.

In our portrait of the grammarian's job, the emphasis has shifted from the concept of grammaticality to the notion of a correct grammar. A sequence is grammatical if and only if it is generated by a correct grammar for the language in question. And a grammar is correct only if it excels in the virtues lately adumbrated. But there are higher virtues to which a grammar may aspire, and more data to be reckoned with. So far we have taken into account data about speakers' intuitions of acceptability and data about a cluster of further characteristics common among acceptable sequences. But we have hardly exhausted the speaker's intuitions about matters linguistic. There is a host of other properties of sentences and their parts about which speakers have firm intuitions. With a bit of training speakers can judge pairs of sentences to be related as active and passive, or as affirmative and negative. They can pick out parts of speech, detect subjects and objects, and spot syntactic ambiguities. The list of these grammatical intuitions could easily be extended. A grammatical theory will not only try to specify which sequences are acceptable; it will also try to

specify the grammatical properties and relations of sentences as intuited by speakers. As in the case of intuitions of acceptability, the grammatical theory will be expected to agree with grammatical intuitions only for relatively short and simple sentences. The theory is an idealization, and, as before, we permit it to deviate from the intuited data in the expectation that further theory will account for the differences.

III

It might seem our job is finished. We set ourselves to giving an account of the grammarian's doings in building a grammar, and this we have done. But the reader conversant with competing accounts[7] will expect more. For, commonly, such accounts go on to talk of *linguistic theory, acquisition models, evaluation measures* and other notions related to the question of how a speaker acquires his grammar. Moreover the discussion of these notions is not a simple addition to the account of the grammarian's work in constructing a grammar. Rather it is an intrinsic part of that account. Yet why this is so is far from obvious. Constructing a theory of grammar acquisition is surely a fascinating project and one which would naturally catch a grammarian's eye. But, at first blush at least, it would seem to be a new project, largely distinct from the job of constructing grammars for individual languages. Why, then, do Chomsky and others view the study of acquisition as intrinsic to the construction of grammars for individual languages? This is the riddle that will occupy us in the present section. In the course of untangling it we will come upon some unexpected facts about grammar and its place among the sciences.

Let me begin with a puzzle. A grammar of English will generate structural descriptions for English sentences in the form of phrase markers or labeled bracketings. The labels on these brackets will be the familiar NP, VP etc. But now imagine a perverse variant of our grammar created by systematically interchanging the symbols NP and VP throughout the theory. If the change is thoroughgoing (made in all appropriate generative rules and definitions), then presumably the original theory and the variant will make exactly the same predictions about intuitions, etc. So the two would appear to be empirically indistinguishable. On what basis, then, are we to select one over the other?

To underscore the puzzle, consider a grammarian attending to the hitherto neglected tongue of some appropriately exploited and unlettered people. His grammar will likely end up generating labeled bracketings among whose labels are the familiar NP and VP. But what justification can there be for this grammar as contrasted with a variant interchanging NP and VP throughout, or yet another variant in which NP and VP are systematically replaced with a pair of symbols that occur nowhere in any grammar of English?[8]

There is a related puzzle that focuses not on the vocabulary of a grammar but on its rules. Consider any grammar or fragment of a grammar for English. With the grammar at hand it requires only modest ingenuity to produce a variant set of rules and definitions whose consequences (the entailed claims about grammaticality, grammatical relations and the rest) are identical with those of the original. Among the variants that might be produced some will differ only trivially, adding a superfluous rule perhaps, or capturing a generalization in two rules rather than one. But other variants exist which differ quite radically from the original.[9] A grammar is but an axiomatized theory, and it is a truism that a theory that can be axiomatized at all can be axiomatized in radically different ways. Yet each of these variants makes identical claims about the grammarian's data — not only the data on

hand, but *all* the data he might acquire. They may, of course, predict incorrectly on a given point; but if one variant predicts incorrectly they all will. How then is the grammarian to decide among them?

The point of these puzzles is that grammar is afflicted with an embarrassment of riches. It is a task demanding wit and perseverance to construct a grammar that correctly captures a broad range of speakers' intuitions. Yet when the job has been done there are indefinitely many variants each of which captures the known intuitions equally well and predicts unprobed intuitions equally well (or poorly). Somehow the grammarian does come up with a single theory. What principle can he use to guide his choice?

It is in attempting to answer this question that the study of acquisition looms large in Chomsky's writings. But exactly how a theory of grammar acquisition is supposed to motivate a choice among alternative grammars is far from clear. Part of the obscurity, I suspect, stems from the fact that Chomsky, perhaps without realizing it, pursues two rather different strategies in relating the study of acquisition to the problem of choosing among alternative grammars. One of these strategies, I will contend, is thoroughly misguided and rests on a mistaken picture of what grammar is. The other is quite compatible with the account of grammar developed above and suggests an illuminating solution to the puzzles of alternative grammars. Our first project will be to dissect out these alternatives for closer inspection.

Before we begin, some terminology will be helpful. Let us call a grammar *descriptively adequate* for a given language if it correctly captures the intuitions of the speakers of the language (and the rest of the grammarian's data) within the limits of accuracy allowed by idealization. The grammarian's embarrassment of riches arises from the fact that for each descriptively adequate grammar of a language there are indefinitely many alternatives all of which are also descriptively adequate.

Now the strategy I would disparage unfolds like this:[10] When a child learns a language, he learns a descriptively adequate grammar (*dag*). He somehow "internally represents" the rules of the grammar. So if we could discover which set of rules the child has "internalized" we would be able to choose a right one from among the *dags* of the child's language. The right one is simply that grammar which the child has in fact internally represented. The study of acquisition will be designed to give us a lead on which descriptively adequate grammar the child has learned.

Let us reflect on what the child must do to acquire his grammar. The learner is exposed to what Chomsky calls *primary linguistic data (pld)* which "include examples of linguistic performance that are taken to be well formed sentences, and may include also examples designated as non-sentences, and no doubt much other information of the sort that is required for language learning, whatever this may be" (*ibid.*, p. 25). When he has succeeded in learning his language the child will have internalized a *dag*. In two rather different ways this grammar will specify more information about the language than is to be gleaned from the *pld*. First, the *pld* contain a modest sample of the grammatical sentences of the language; the grammar acquired generates all the grammatical sentences. Second, the *pld* contain little or no information about the structural descriptions of sentences and the grammatical relations among them; the grammar assigns structural descriptions to each grammatical sentence and entails all the appropriate facts about grammatical relations. Thus a theory of grammar acquisition must explain how the child can acquire and internalize a grammar that is significantly more informative

about the sentences of the language than the *pld* he has been exposed to.

How might we build a theory that accounts for the child's accomplishment? What we seek is a model (or function) which, when given a complete account of the *pld* available to the child as input (or argument), will produce, as output (or value), the *dag* that the child acquires. Our problem is to design the model with sufficient structure so that it can correctly project from the limited *pld* to the full grammar of the language from which the data are drawn. What sort of information should the model contain?

Suppose it were discovered that certain features were shared by all known *dags*. If the grammars that shared the features were sufficiently numerous and diverse we might reasonably hypothesize that these features were universal among *dags* of natural language. We would, in effect, be hypothesizing that there is a restricted set of grammars that humans can in fact learn (in the normal way). Were such universal features to be found, our strategy suggests that we take account of them in our acquisition model. Since the output of the model must be a *dag*, we would want to build our model in such a way that the possible outputs (the range of the acquisition function) each had the features that were universal to all *dags*. We would thus take the specification of universal features to define the class of *humanly possible grammars (hpgs)*. The task of the acquisition model is to discover the correct grammar, the grammar of the language the child is actually exposed to, from among the humanly possible grammars.

There is great gain for the builder of an acquisition theory in discovering as rich a set of universal features as possible. For the stronger the restrictions on the *hpgs*, the smaller the class of such grammars will be. Thus the easier the task relegated to the other parts of the model.

What remains for the rest of the model is to compare the *pld* with the class of *hpgs* and exclude those possible grammars which are incompatible with the data.

Now it might happen that the universal features we discover so narrow down the class of *hpgs* that only one *hpg* is compatible with the *pld*.[11] If this is commonly the case, our acquisition theory need contain only a specification of *hpgs* and a device for excluding those *hpgs* which are incompatible with the *pld*. If, however, there are several *hpgs* compatible with all the data the child has accumulated by the time acquisition is essentially complete, we will have to seek some further principle of selection. The principle, the strategy suggests, is to be found in an evaluation measure or weighting of *hpgs*. Some of the *hpgs* that are compatible with all the *pld* will still fail to be descriptively adequate for the child's language. Some of these may simply project incorrectly beyond the sample of the language available to the child. They will then classify as grammatical sequences that are not grammatical. Others, while projecting correctly, may miss the mark on structural descriptions or grammatical relations, specifying that sentences are related in ways other than the ways speakers in fact intuit them to be related. So what we seek in our evaluation measure is some ranking of *hpgs* that has the following property: when we exclude from the *hpgs* those grammars which are incompatible with the *pld*, the highest ranked of the *remaining* grammars is a descriptively adequate grammar of the language the child acquires. The acquisition model would then proceed by first eliminating those *hpgs* which are not compatible with the *pld*, then selecting from among those which remain the one that is highest ranked. The grammar selected is unique among *dags*, for it is chosen by a model that explains how a child might go about acquiring the grammar he does acquire. It

is this "explanatorily adequate" grammar which the child actually internalizes and which the linguist seeks to uncover.

A more detailed account of the strategy we are sketching might now go on to worry about how the appropriate evaluation measure could be discovered or what we can say about linguistic universals in the light of present knowledge. But this will not be our course. For I think we have said enough to see that the strategy is wholly wrongheaded. To begin, let us consider the possibility, mentioned briefly a paragraph back, that the universals so constrict the class of *hpgs* that only one *hpg* will be compatible with the *pld*. A moment's reflection will reveal that this is not a real possibility at all. For recall the pair of puzzles that initially prodded our interest in acquisition models. Each puzzle pointed to the superabundance of descriptively adequate grammars for any natural language. For every *dag* there are alternatives which are also descriptively adequate. But the linguistic universals were taken to be properties of all *dags*.[12] Thus each *dag* for every natural language will be among the *hpgs*. So if any *dag* is compatible with the *pld*, all its alternatives will be as well. And we have made no progress at selecting a single *dag* as the right one.

What is more, the hunt for an evaluation measure is of no real value in narrowing down the class of *dags*. The job that was set for the evaluation measure was not a trivial one. Given any body of *pld*, the evaluation measure had to rank as highest among the *hpgs* which are compatible with the *pld* a *dag* of the language from which the data are drawn. Finding such a measure would likely be a task of considerable difficulty. But, and this is the crucial point, once such a measure *has* been found there will be indefinitely many alternative measures which select different *dags* for the same body of *pld*. If the sub-class of *hpgs* compatible with a given body of *pld* contains *one dag* of the language of which the data are a sample, it will contain many. Thus if we can design a measure which ranks any one of these *dags* highest in the sub-class, there will be another measure which ranks a different *dag* highest.[13] But whatever justification there is for holding the *dag* selected by one measure to be the grammar actually internalized is equally justification for holding that the other is. And we are back where we started, with too many *dags* each with equal claim to be the "right one."

The second strategy for solving the problem, the strategy I would endorse, sets out in quite a different direction from the first. It does not propose to select among *dags* by finding the one actually internalized. Indeed it is compatible with (but does not entail) the view that *no* grammar is, in any illuminating sense, internally represented in the speaker's mind or brain, and that there is no good sense to be made of the notion of "internal representation." The second strategy approaches the multiplicity of *dag* as a practical problem for the working linguist. At numerous junctures a linguist may find himself with data to account for and a variety of ways of doing so. Among the alternatives, more than one will handle all the data available and will coincide in their predictions about facts as yet unrecorded. How is the linguist to choose? What the linguist seeks, according to this strategy, is not the grammar actually in the head (whatever that may mean) but some motivated way to select among *dags*.

The motivation is to be found through the study of acquisition models, though the goals of an acquisition model must be reinterpreted. If we suspend interest in which grammar is "internally represented" we need no longer demand of an acquisiton model that, for a given body of *pld*, it produce as output a gram-

mar that a learner exposed to the data would internalize. Instead, we ask only that the acquisition model have as output *some* grammar that is true of the accomplished speaker (i.e., some grammar that correctly describes the sentences acceptable to him, his intuitions about grammatical relations, etc.). But let it not be thought that this is a trivial task. Such a model would be able to specify a grammar true of the speaker given only the (relatively scant) primary linguistic data to which the speaker was exposed. To do this would be a monumentally impressive feat realizable, for the foreseeable future, only in linguistic science fiction.

How can such a model be built? In attending to the more demanding model of the first strategy, our first move was to linguistic universals, the properties shared by all *dags*. The analogous role in the present strategy can be played by properties less difficult to discover. For suppose we have a single descriptively adequate grammar of a particular natural language. Might it not be reasonable to take as many properties of that grammar as possible as "quasi-universals"? "Quasi-universal" properties play just the role that universals did in the first strategy — they constrain the output of the acquisition model. The quasi-universals, then, define a class of "quasi-humanly possible grammars" which are the only possible outputs of the acquisition model. The terminology is adopted to stress the parallel with the first strategy. But there are important differences. For quasi-universals are in no sense universals — there is no claim that all *dags* must share them. Nor does the class of quasi-humanly possible grammars pretend to exhaust the class of grammars that humans can learn;[14] it simply coincides with the possible outputs of the acquisition model.

As was the case at the analogous point in the first strategy, there is profit in taking the quasi-universals to be as strong as we can. For the stronger the quasi-universals, the smaller the class of quasi-*hpgs* and thus the easier the task that remains for the rest of the model. Indeed, it would not be unreasonable as a first guess to take *all* the properties of the single *dag* as quasi-universals.[15] But this clearly will not do. For then the output class of the acquisition model would have but a single member. Rather, our principle in deciding whether to take features of our single *dag* as quasi-universal is this: take as quasi-universal as many features of the *dag* as possible, provided only that the resultant class of quasi-*hpgs* contains at least one quasi-*hpg* for each natural language. The remainder of the model will contain (at least) a component testing the compatibility of quasi-*hpgs* with the accumulated *pld*. Note that, on this second strategy, it is indeed possible that the quasi-universals so narrow down the class of quasi-*hpgs* that only one *hpg* will be compatible with any given body of *pld*. If this is the case, then a specification of the quasi-universals and a compatibility-testing device of the sort lately considered would complete an acquisition model. But if we cannot discover quasi-universals of this strength, we will again resort to an evaluation measure. As with the first strategy, what we seek is a ranking of quasi-*hpgs* which, when we exclude from the quasi-*hpgs* those grammars incompatible with a given body of *pld*, ranks highest among the remaining quasi-*hpgs* a grammar that is descriptively adequate for the language from which the *pld* was drawn. Since we are making no claim that the selected grammar is "actually internalized" we need not be concerned that there may be several such evaluation measures. Our project is the highly nontrivial project of producing a model that takes *pld* as input and yields an appropriate *dag* as output. *Any* evaluation measure that does the trick will be suitable.

The outline we have given of the construction of an acquisition model is, in crucial respect, misleading. For it suggests that the model builder is bound irrevocably by the first *dag* he constructs. He takes as quasi-universal as many properties of this grammar as he can get away with, weakening the quasi-universals only when he comes upon some language no *dag* of which would be included among the quasi-*hpgs* if the stronger quasi-universals are retained. Actually, of course, matters are much more flexible. There is room for substantial feedback in both directions as work proceeds on the model and on individual grammars. The overriding concern is to make both the individual grammars and the acquisition model as simple and as powerful as possible. If at a given juncture it is found that adhering to the working hypothesis about the acquisition model will substantially complicate construction of grammars for one or more languages, he will try to alter the model, even if this may require altering or abandoning the original grammar from which the earliest hypothesis about quasi-universals was drawn. And, on the other side, if in constructing a particular *dag* a certain choice of how to proceed would accord well with the working hypothesis about the acquisition model, then he will be inclined to make that choice even if the resulting grammar is somewhat less elegant than another which would result from an alternative choice. There is no circularity here, or at least, to crib a phrase, the circularity is virtuous. Through this process of mutual adjustment progress on the acquisition model and on particular grammars can take place simultaneously.

Notice, now, that the strategy we have been detailing will solve the puzzles with which we began. An acquisition model provides motivation for selecting one *dag* over another, though both do equally well at predicting intuitions and such. The grammar to be chosen is that which accords with the quasi-universals. And, if several do, the grammar chosen is the one the evaluation measure ranks highest. Thus the grammar chosen will be preferred to its descriptively adequate competitors because it is more closely parallel to successful grammars for other languages and integrates more successfully into a model of grammar acquisition.

The account we have given of the second strategy has the further virtue of according well with actual linguistic practice. It is simply not the case that, when speculating about "linguistic universals," Chomsky and his followers set out to survey a broad range of languages and collect those features common to all the grammars. Rather, speculation is based on the study of a single language, or at best a few closely related languages. A feature of a grammar will be tentatively taken as "universal" if it is sufficiently abstract (or nonidiosyncratic) to make it plausible that the feature could be readily incorporated into a grammar of every natural language. If "universals" are taken to be features common to all *dags*, this speculation about universals would be quite mad. But in the light of the second strategy the speculation appears as a thoroughly reasonable way to proceed.

An element of indeterminacy still lurks in our second strategy. And if I am right in identifying this strategy with the generative grammarian's practice, then the indeterminacy infuses his theory as well. In constructing an acquisition model, the first few plausible (approximations of) descriptively adequate grammars have a profound influence. For it is the abstract features of these grammars which are taken as quasi-universals. Yet the selection of these first *dags* over indefinitely many alternatives is completely unmotivated by any linguistic evidence. Which *dag* is first constructed is largely a matter of historical accident. But the accident casts its shadow over all future work. The acquisition model serves to direct future research into the channel forged by these first grammars, even

though there are indefinitely many other possible channels available. Nor does the flexibility we stressed three paragraphs back eliminate the indeterminacy. There we noted that, if an original choice of quasi-universals led to overwhelming difficulties in constructing a grammar for some previously neglected language, the universals might be patched and the early grammars that suggested them might be abandoned. But the new choice of quasi-universals has no more claim to uniqueness than the old. For they too will be abstracted from *dags* that were selected over competitors largely by virtue of historical accident.

To the appropriately conditioned reader this indeterminacy will appear familiar enough. It bears strong analogy with Quine's thesis of the indeterminacy of translation.[16] Quine's analytical hypotheses, like the first *dags*, are underdetermined by the data. The selection of one *dag* or one set of analytical hypotheses is largely a matter of cultural bias or historical accident. But once a *dag* or a set of analytical hypotheses has been formulated, it has profound effects on the remainder of the translation theory (for analytical hypotheses), or on the acquisition model and *dags* for other languages. Both analytical hypotheses and early *dags* are susceptible to later tampering; but neither a patched *dag* nor a patched analytical hypothesis has any more claim to uniqueness than the originals.

My departure from Quine comes on the score of the *implications* of the indeterminacy. Were Quine to grant that grammars and translation manuals share a sort of indeterminacy,[17] he would presumably conclude that for grammars, as for translations, modulo the indeterminacy, there is nothing to be right about. On this view there is no saying that one *dag* of a language is more correct than another, except relative to a given set of quasi-universals. Yet the selection of quasi-universals, like the selection of analytical hypotheses, is in part quite arbitrary. My dissent comes in the step that passes from recognition of arbitrariness in quasi-universals or analytical hypotheses to the claim that there is (modulo the indeterminacy) nothing to be right about. For I think that, *pace* Quine, the same indeterminacy could be shown lurking in the foundations of every empirical science. Grammar and translation are not to be distinguished, in this quarter, from psychology or biology or physics. If we are disinclined to say that in all science, modulo the indeterminacy, there is nothing to be right about, it is because the theories we are willing to allow as correct are those whose arbitrary features have the sanction of tradition. But all this is to stake out my dissent, not to defend it. The defense is a project I must postpone until another occasion.

IV

Our sketch of the grammarian's doings is all but complete. We have surveyed the data to which he attends and indicated the nature of the theory he builds upon his data. It remains to say something of the interest of the grammarian's theory and to set out the relation between his theory and the speakers whose intuitions and behavior are his data.

As I have depicted it, a grammar is a modest portion of a psychological theory about the speaker. It describes certain language-specific facts: facts about the acceptability of expressions to speakers and facts about an ability or capacity speakers have for judging and classifying expressions as having or lacking grammatical properties and relations.

The modesty of a grammar, on my account, stands in stark contrast to more flamboyant portraits. On Jerrold Katz's view, a grammar is a theory in physiological psychology whose components are strongly isomorphic to the fine structure of the brain. "The linguistic description and the procedures of sentence production and recognition," according to Katz, "must correspond to independent mechanisms in the brain. Componential distinctions between the syntactic, phonological, and semantic components must rest on relevant differences between three neural submechanisms of the mechanism which stores the linguistic description. The rules of each component must have their psychological reality in the input-output operations of the computing machinery of this mechanism."[18] Though Katz's claims about grammar are more expansive than those I have made, the evidence he uses to confirm a grammar is of a piece with the evidence indicated in my account. Thus it remains something of a mystery how the grammarian has learned as much as Katz would have him know about the structure of the brain, having left the skulls of his subjects intact.

Less imaginative than Katz's view, but still not so sparse as mine, is a story about grammar put forward by Chomsky.[19] On this account a grammar describes the speaker's "competence" — his knowledge of his language. The speaker is held to have a large and complex fund of knowledge of the rules of his grammar. The grammarian's theory mirrors or describes the knowledge that the speaker has "internalized" and "internally represented." Chomsky's view is intriguing, though an explicit unpacking of the metaphors of "internalization," "representation," and the rest can prove an exasperating task. My own view is that the notion of competence is explanatorily vacuous and that attributing knowledge of a grammar to a speaker is little more plausible than attributing knowledge of the laws of physics to a projectile whose behavior they predict. But the issues are complex, and I have aired my views at length elsewhere.[20] I will not rehash them here. What is important to our present project is the observation that, on the account of grammar and acquisition models we have constructed, no knowledge claim is *needed*. A grammar is a theory describing the facts of acceptability and intuition; a grammar-acquisition model is a theory specifying a grammar which comes to be true of a child, as a function of the linguistic environment in which he is placed. Grammar and the theory of grammar acquisition are bits of psychological theory.

If our account of the grammarian's activity is accurate, then it is perhaps misleading to describe him as constructing a theory of the language of his subjects. Rather he is building a description of the facts of acceptability and linguistic intuition. A theory of a language seriously worthy of the name would provide some insight into what it is to *understand* a sentence, how sentences can be used to communicate and to deal more effectively with the world, and into a host of related questions that we have yet to learn to ask in illuminating ways. But a grammar does none of this. Indeed, it is logically possible that there be a person whose linguistic intuitions matched up near enough with our own, but who could neither speak nor understand English. Such a person would serve almost as well as an English speaker as an informant for constructing a grammar of English, provided only that we shared a metalanguage in which we could question him about the sequences of sounds he did not understand. What is important about this bit of fiction is that it is *only* fiction. It is an empirical fact that comprehension and intuition run in tandem. And this fact provides the beginning of the answer to a question that will likely have begun to trouble the reader: Of what interest is a grammar? If a grammar is not, in any exciting sense, a theory of a language, why bother constructing it?

The answer is twofold. First, there is substantial correspondence between the grammatical sentences and the sentences we do in fact use for thought and communication; grammatically related sentences are understood in similar ways[21] (though in our present state of ignorance we have no serious understanding of what it is to "understand sentences in similar ways"); the ability to speak and understand a language is an empirically necessary condition for the possession of linguistic intuitions about the expressions of the language. So one reason for studying grammar is the hope that these overlaps and correlations can be exploited to yield deeper insight into the exciting phenomena of comprehension and communication. Once we have the sort of description of acceptability and linguistic intuition provided by a grammar we can begin to seek an explanation of these facts. We can ask what psychological mechanisms underlie the speaker's ability to judge and relate sentences as he does. The parallels between linguistic intuition and other language-related phenomena make it reasonable to hope that insight into the mechanisms underlying intuition will explain much else about language as well. But hope is not to be confused with accomplishment. If we fail to recognize how modest a theory a grammar is, we can expect only to obscure the extent of our ignorance about language, communication, and understanding.

A second reason for doing grammar is that it is something to do. In grammar, at least, we have a coherent set of data that we know how to study, intelligible questions to ask, and some clear indication as how we can go about answering them. Acceptability and grammatical intuitions are language-related phenomena about which we have the beginnings of an empirical theory. Few other approaches to the phenomena of natural language fare as well. Thus grammar is a natural focus of attention for the investigator concerned with language. It is an entering wedge to a theory of a language, and, for the present at least, there are few competitors.

Notes

1. *From a Logical Point of View*, 2d ed., revised (New York: Harper & Row, 1963), essay III.

2. Much the same point is made by Jerrold Katz and Jerry Fodor in "What's Wrong with the Philosophy of Language?," *Inquiry*, 5 (1962): 197-237.

3. Significance is likely a more inclusive notion than grammaticality, more liberal in the constructions it will allow and tolerating a richer sprinkling of 'aahhh's, 'I mean's, and 'you know's. Thus perhaps Quine's proposal does rather better when taken as advertised. But whatever its interest, significance as characterized by Quine is not the property studied by grammarians of a generative bent.

4. Note that Quine's "bizarreness reactions" could be taken as negative judgments when the subject is queried about a sequence's acceptability. If this is Quine's intention, his proposal and the present account converge.

5. Cf. George A. Miller and Stephen Isard, "Some Perceptual Consequences of Linguistic Rules," *Journal of Verbal Learning and Verbal Behavior*, 2 (1963): 217-228.

6. In a sense that may be intended by T. S. Kuhn, *The Structure of Scientific Revolutions* (Chicago: University Press, 1962).

7. For example, those in Noam Chomsky, "Current Issues in Linguistic Theory," in Fodor and Katz, eds., *The Structure of Language* (Englewood Cliffs, N.J.: Prentice-Hall, 1964); in Chomsky, *Aspects of the Theory of Syntax* (Cambridge, Mass.: MIT Press, 1965), ch. I; and Katz, *The Philosophy of Language* (New York: Harper & Row, 1966).

8. Much the same puzzle is hinted at by Quine in "Methodological Reflections on Current Linguistic Theory," *Synthese*, 21, 3/4 (October 1970): 386-398, pp. 390 ff.

9. Such variants often require considerable effort to construct. Nor is it always a trivial matter to prove the equivalence of a pair of grammars.

10. I think this strategy is often suggested by what Chomsky says (e.g., in *Aspects of the Theory of Syntax*, pp. 24-27 and elsewhere). But my concern here is to scotch the view, not to fix the blame. So I will not bother to document details of its parentage.

11. Chomsky suggests this possibility, *ibid.*, pp. 36-37.

12. It is essential that the linguistic universals be taken as the properties common to each descriptively adequate grammar of every natural language. An alternative notion that took the linguistic universals as the features common to each of the actually internalized grammars of every natural language would be useless in the present context, since our project is to discover which among the *dags* of a given language is internalized. And until we *know* which grammars are internalized we cannot discover which features are universal to such grammars.

13. As is the case with alternative *dags*, some alternative measure functions will be trivially cooked up variants of the original. (E.g., simply select an arbitrary *dag* of the language from which the *pld* is drawn and place it highest under the evaluation measure, leaving the rest of the measure unchanged.) Others will exist which differ from the original in more substantial ways.

14. Indeed, if we abandon the notion of internal representation, it is no longer clear that it makes sense to speak of a child "learning" a grammar. When the child succeeds in mastering his mother tongue, each *dag* of that tongue is true of him. But he surely has not learned *all* these *dags*. What, then, is the "cash value" of the claim that he has learned any one of them?

15. During the John Locke Lectures at Oxford in 1969, Chomsky suggested that were a Martian linguist to come to earth in the midst of an English-speaking community, his most reasonable first hypothesis would be that the ability to speak English is entirely innate. I suspect that Chomsky's remark and the present observation are directed at basically the same point.

16. Cf. "Speaking of Objects," *Proceedings and Addresses of the American Philosophical Association*, 31 (1957/8): 5-22; "Meaning and Translation," in Fodor and Katz, *The Structure of Language, op. cit.*; *Word and Object* (Cambridge, Mass.: MIT Press, 1960), ch. II; and "Ontological Relativity," *Journal of Philosophy* 65, 7 (April 4, 1968): 185-212, reprinted in *Ontological Relativity, and Other Essays* (New York: Columbia, 1969).

17. There is evidence that he would. Cf. "Methodlogical Reflections . . .," *op. cit.*

18. "Mentalism in Linguistics," *Language*,

40, 2 (April/June 1964): 124-137, p. 133.

19. In *Aspects of the Theory of Syntax*, *op. cit.*, and elsewhere.

20. "What Every Speaker Knows," *Philosophical Review*, 80, 4 (October 1971): 476-496, and "What Every Grammar Does," to appear in *Philosophia 3, 1*.

21. Cf. Chomsky *Syntactic Structures* (The Hague: Mouton, 1957), p. 86: "the sentences (i) *John played tennis* [and] (ii) *my friend likes music* are quite distinct on phonemic and morphemic levels. But on the level of phrase structure they are both represented as *NP-Verb-NP; correspondingly, it is evident that in some sense they are similarly understood.* (Last emphasis added.)

What the Linguist Is Talking About

Noam Chomsky and Jerrold J. Katz

At the beginning of his article "Grammar, Psychology, and Indeterminacy," Stephen Stich announces that his goal is to tell the linguist "what he is talking about" [see chapter 10. — Ed.] The implication is that linguists are confused about important issues in the theory of grammar which Stich will proceed to clarify for them. In fact, much of Stich's essay recapitulates familiar descriptions of the theory of grammar. Where he departs from these, his approach seems to us fundamentally mistaken, though it does touch on important issues. The most important of such issues is Quine's indeterminacy thesis. Stich claims that, on his description of the theory of transformational grammar, this theory itself attributes indeterminacy to natural languages as an inherent feature. Thus, if

From *Journal of Philosophy* 71, no. 12 (June 27, 1974): 347-367. Reprinted by permission of *Journal of Philosophy* and the authors. This work was supported by Grant 5P01 MH 13390-07 from the National Institute of Mental Health. Notes have been renumbered for this edition. [The second author wishes it to be said that since this article was written he has changed his mind about the nature of linguistics. He now thinks that the linguist *qua* linguist talks about abstract objects. See his *Language and Other Abstract Objects* (Totowa: Rowman and Littlefield, 1980). —Ed.]

Stich's interpretation of the present theory of grammar were right, indeterminacy would be implied by the theory, rather than merely a controversial philosophical doctrine urged on linguistics from the outside by Quine and his followers. Stich's argument is directed specifically against views that we have developed in various publications. We believe that his criticism is not well founded on this and other issues and that Stich's alternative descriptions of the theory of grammar are seriously in error.

Sections I and II of Stich's essay review the methodological backgrounds of current linguistic theory along conventional lines. A grammar is a theory of the language, an idealization similar to those in other branches of science such as the theory of gases. Grammars are constructed on the basis of various types of data that linguists have available to them: data on acceptability, ambiguity, relatedness of utterances and their parts, etc. The rules of a grammar assign a structural description to each of the infinitely many sentences of the language. The structural description of a sentence is in principle a complete account of its grammatical (i.e., semantic, syntactic, and phonological) properties. Grammars, moreover, form part of a more comprehensive theory of language use which takes into account such factors as the structure of memory and perceptual strategies in order to explain linguistic behavior and the judgments speakers make about sentences. In this way, the linguist seeks a full account of the entire range of linguistic data concerning a language.[1]

At this point Stich departs from familiar formulations, and undertakes a critical discussion of them. Before proceeding to investigate the problems and solutions he presents, let us review briefly what is actually proposed in the account to which he specifically refers (*ibid.*, 24-27).

In addition to accounting for linguistic data concerning particular languages, the linguist seeks to construct a general linguistic theory expressing the grammatical properties essential to all human languages. A grammar, regarded as a theory of an individual language, "is *descriptively adequate* to the extent that it correctly describes the intrinsic competence of the idealized speaker." In contrast, "*a linguistic theory is descriptively adequate* if it makes a descriptively adequate grammar [*dag*] available for each natural language," each system that is a possible language for this particular organism. A linguistic theory "meets the condition of *explanatory adequacy*" to the extent that it "succeeds in selecting a *dag* on the basis of primary linguistic data [*pld*]," namely, the kind of data that suffice for language acquisition. Such a theory would offer an explanation, not merely a description, of particular judgments that constitute part of the linguist's data, in that it offers a principled reason for the selection by the speaker-hearer of the grammar that entails these judgments. The theory is falsifiable in many ways: e.g., "by showing that it fails to provide a *dag* for *pld*" for some language. The linguistic theory may be

regarded as an abstract theory of language acquisition: it postulates certain "innate predispositions" that enable the child to develop competence on the basis of *pld*. The linguistic theory "constitutes an explanatory hypothesis about the form of language as such," and, at the same time, "an account of the specific innate abilities that make [the achievement of language acquisition] possible."

For convenience of exposition, we will refer to the approach summarized so far as the "standard account" of "what the linguist is talking about."

Stich argues that the standard account is badly confused about the relation between grammars, linguistic theory, and acquisition models. There is, according to Stich, a "riddle" here:

> Constructing a theory of grammar acquisition is surely a fascinating project and one which would naturally catch a grammarian's eye. But, at first blush at least, it would seem to be a new project, largely distinct from the job of constructing grammars for individual languages. Why, then, do Chomsky and others view the study of acquisition as intrinsic to the construction of grammars for individual languages? (805/6)

We find nothing puzzling in this. Linguists who concern themselves with acquisition models do so in the belief that grammar construction gains its primary intellectual significance from the role it plays in the study of language acquisition. Grammar construction is a worth-while enterprise in itself, but the study of language bears directly on philosophical and psychological issues, specifically, we have argued, on issues of rationalism and empiricism.[2] For this reason, we and others have been particularly concerned with developing a general theory that has something of the character of traditional "universal" or "philosophical" grammar. We have argued that the study of these more abstract questions leads to a rationalistic account of the acquisition of language. The speaker-hearer does not acquire competence by inductive generalization from regularities in a corpus of *pld*; rather, a rich framework of linguistic universals defines a set of what Stich calls "humanly possible grammars" (*hpgs*). Language learning is a process of determining which of these is the actual grammar of the language to which the child is exposed. The procedure, we suggest, is akin to theory construction. Learning of language is a matter of selecting among *hpgs*, filling in details in a fixed framework or schematism. Generative grammars of individual languages thus provide the empirical basis for construction of a theory that deals with the common structure of natural languages. This theory leads to specific hypotheses about the innate principles underlying language acquisition.[3]

Stich believes that the study of acquisition and the related concern with general linguistic theory (universal grammar) are motivated by the "puzzle" of how to choose among alternative *dags*. The puzzle he sees is that there are variant grammars "each of [which] makes identical claims about the grammarian's data — not only the data on hand, but *all* the data he might acquire . . . grammar is afflicted with an embarrassment of riches" (807).

We have already given the answer to Stich's "riddle": the study of acquisition and universal grammar does not arise as an ancillary problem in the course of constructing grammars, but is rather the focus of our interest — grammars interest us insofar as they contribute to these further investigations. Stich's "puzzle" is nothing more than his formulation of the defining characteristic of empirical science: nontrivial theories are underdetermined by data. If working linguists are unconcerned with the further problems that happen to intrigue us, they will simply exercise their acquired skills to formulate the best hypothesis they can with

regard to the grammar of the language under study. Like other working scientists, they will not worry about the problem of induction nor about rationally reconstructing criteria for choosing hypotheses. Rather, they will exercise a skill that might as well be on all fours with chicken sexing: linguists and other scientists use these skills without knowing the details about their nature. Stich gives no argument to show that linguists and other scientists are wrong to rely on such criteria and their skill in applying them.

We would argue, moreover, that the linguist who happens to be so lacking in curiosity as to be unconcerned with universal grammar is excluding significant data that bear on the choice of a grammar for the language. For us, data from language L' can contribute to the choice of a grammar for language L. Thus, suppose that two *dags* G_1 and G_2 are under consideration for L, but that only G_1 is an *hpg* in accordance with a general linguistic theory T which serves as a hypothesis concerning the human "language faculty" as such and which provides a basis for explaining how speaker-hearers of L' acquired a *dag* for L'. Any scientist would tentatively select G_1 over G_2 on this more extensive data base. Linguists unconcerned with linguistic theory would be forced to disregard this evidence, to the detriment of their work. For a linguist with broader interests, data from L' can be used to confirm or reject a hypothesis for L — on the reasonable assumption that speaker-hearers are not genetically predisposed to acquire L but not L', that the capacity to acquire language is a fixed human capacity, not differing for members of different races, political groupings, etc.

Stich presents several versions of his puzzle. He asks:

. . . what justification can there be for [a] grammar as contrasted with a variant interchanging NP and VP throughout, or yet another variant in which NP and VP are systematically replaced with a pair of symbols that occur nowhere in any grammar of English? (806)

And he asks how one decides among different sets of grammatical rules all of which make the same predictions about all the data a linguist might acquire. As far as interchange of symbols is concerned, this is merely a notational change unless linguistic theory presents — as we think it must and can — a set of substantive conditions on the choice of such symbols as NP and VP. As for the more general question that Stich raises, the linguist, like any scientist, will attempt to choose among variants that are empirically indistinguishable in principle by simplicity considerations and other methodological principles. Where such variants exists, choice of a best hypothesis in empirical science is not only underdetermined locally, that is, by particular samples from the data available in principle, but also globally: that is, even given "all data," there are variant hypotheses consistent with the data. But, assuming there could be nonequivalent hypotheses that are consistent with *all* relevant data (of any sort), there is no argument in Stich's essay to prevent us from saying what surely any other scientist would say: simplicity and other methodological criteria, applied by skilled scientists, may determine a unique best choice among these hypotheses.

According to the standard account, linguistic theory specifies the schematism for grammar, thus generating the class of *hpgs*, and furthermore provides an evaluation measure — an algorithm for selecting among *hpgs* that are compatible with given *pld*. Much of the linguistic work of recent years has been an effort to determine the character of the schematism and the evaluation measure. Plainly, all hypotheses about these matters are empirical; hence, if nontrivial, underdeter-

mined by evidence. Notice that the schematism and the evaluation measure are not to be confused with the criteria used by scientists (including linguists) in choosing among possible theories, whatever these criteria may be. The latter are general methodological criteria employed to select a preferred hypothesis; the former are hypotheses about the form of linguistic rules, conditions on rules, relations among subcomponents in grammars, linguistically significant generalizations, etc. That is, the latter constitute a hypothesis that falls within theoretical human psychology. This hypothesis concerning a schematism and an evaluation measure is itself to be judged on the basis of general methodological criteria that guide ordinary scientific practice.

Consider now Stich's approach to the "puzzle" and "riddle" that he has posed. He outlines two strategies: strategy I, which he "disparages," and strategy II, which he "endorses." Strategy I incorporates a determinacy thesis; strategy II, an indeterminacy thesis. Strategy I is "thoroughly misguided and rests on a mistaken picture of what a grammar is" (807). Strategy II, he contends, "suggests an illuminating solution to the puzzle of alternative grammars" (807). Stich's strategy I is alleged to be a summary of the standard account, recapitulated above. However, his strategy I misstates this account in a crucial respect, implying an absurdity which leads him to reject strategy I.

According to Stich's strategy I, linguists postulate "all known *dags*" for the languages for which they have data. They seek to determine "universal features" of "all known *dags*," incorporating such features in their "acquisition model." This model defines the class of *hpgs*. If the theory is not so restrictive that there is only one *hpg* compatible with *pld*, then the theory must also provide an "evaluation measure or weighting of *hpgs*," which selects the highest ranked among them as the grammar which, it is postulated, is "internally represented" by the speaker-hearer who has learned the language, who has acquired competence.[4] But, Stich remarks, this strategy is "wholly wrong-headed." The reason is that there is a

> . . . superabundance of *dags* for any natural language. For every *dag* there are alternatives which are also descriptively adequate. But the linguistic universals were taken to be properties of all *dags*. Thus each *dag* for every natural language will be among the *hpgs*. So if any *dag* is compatible with the *pld*, all its alternatives will be as well. And we have made no progress at selecting a single *dag* as the right one (810).

Furthermore, the same problem holds in the case of an evaluation measure:

> . . . once such a measure *has* been found there will be indefinitely many alternative measures which select different *dags* for the same body of *pld* . . . Thus if we can design a measure which ranks any one of these *dags* highest in the sub-class, there will be another measure which ranks a different *dag* highest (810).

Notice in the first place that Stich has misrepresented the account he is disparaging. The standard account defined a descriptively adequate theory as a theory that provides *some dag* for each set of *pld*. In Stich's version, we must first consider "all known *dags*" and then arrive at the theory inductively by considering features common to all of these. Naturally, this strategy will fail, given the superabundance of *dags*—that is, given the general underdetermination of theory by evidence. There will, to be sure, be mutually inconsistent grammars, all descriptively adequate so far as can be determined, but differing in their properties. We will get nowhere if we insist on first considering all known (imaginable, contrivable) grammars compatible with evidence, then proceeding to determine their common properties. But this was not the enterprise outlined. Rather, the account suggested that we construct a linguistic theory,

which defines *hpgs* and offers a measure to select among them, as a hypothesis about human language and the capacity to acquire language in the normal way on the basis of *pld*. We then test this theory for descriptive adequacy by determining whether it provides *a dag* (not *all dags*) for each human language. We test it for explanatory adequacy by determing whether it selects, on the basis of *pld*, a *dag* for each language. Replacing an existential by a universal quantifier, Stich converts a sensible and properly limited inquiry into one that is "utterly wrongheaded," but has never been suggested in the literature.

In formulating his strategy I, Stich argues that "It is essential that the linguistic universals be taken as the properties common to each descriptively adequate grammar of every natural language," as against "An alternative notion that took the linguistic universals as the features common to each of the actually internalized grammar of every natural language" (810). The latter notion, which is in fact that of the standard account, is "useless," Stich claims: "until we *know* which grammars are internalized we cannot discover which features are universal to such grammars" (810). But the objection is senseless. We cannot "know" which grammars are internalized in advance of constructing a linguistic theory. We can only *hypothesize* that certain grammars are internalized. The natural and appropriate strategy is to construct hypotheses with regard to particular grammars *and* with regard to linguistic theory, confronting the entire complex with data from various languages for confirmation. That is, we ask whether the grammars selected on the basis of *pld* by the postulated linguistic theory, with its definition of *hpg* and an evaluation measure, are, so far as can be determined, *dags*. We do not "know" that we are correct in these hypotheses. Nor will we ever be certain about this. All of this is commonplace, and it is perhaps surprising that it is necessary to reiterate it. Once it is recognized, however, it is plain that Stich has offered no objection at all to the account that has actually been proposed, though we agree with him in rejecting his strategy I, which misrepresents the standard account by a change of quantifiers. The latter seems to us quite adequate as far as it goes. The problems that arise are in principle no different from those which arise in any other empirical inquiry.

Of course, having constructed a linguistic theory meeting (to some extent) the conditions of descriptive and even explanatory adequacy, we will always be able to construct another theory, with a different characterization of *hpg* and a different evaluation measure, which will meet these conditions (to the same extent), selecting different *dags* that are just as compatible with evidence. Thus Stich is perfectly right in saying that "if we can design a measure which ranks any one of the *dags* highest in the subclass, there will be another measure which ranks a different *dag* highest" (810). This, he asserts, is the "crucial point." The point amounts to nothing more than the assertion that linguistics is an empirical science, not a branch of logic or mathematics. It thus has no force whatever with regard to the standard account, which of course also insists that linguistic theory, being a nontrivial empirical theory, is underdetermined by evidence.

Stich then expands the argument as follows:

> But whatever justification there is for holding the *dag* selected by one measure to be the grammar actually internalized is equally justification for holding that the other is. And we are back where we started, with too many *dags* each with equal claim to be the 'right one' (811).

The statement is uninteresting, no matter how we understand the notion "all evidence" that figures in the definition of *dag* and "justified linguistic theory." If by 'all the grammarian's data'[5] we mean "all available data," then the linguist faced with alternative theories that are equally justified by all the data would search for more data to choose among them. Furthermore, he would consider how general methodological criteria (not to be confused with the evaluation measure that forms part of empirical linguistic theory) apply to the choice between these theories. If by 'all the grammarian's data' we mean "all possible data" (granting some sense to this notion), then the linguists, by hypothesis, is restricted to methodological considerations. The linguist's "dilemma" would be exactly that of a physicist faced with the question: what would you do if you were presented with incompatible theories each "justified" in terms of all possible data?

Here we come to the real crux of the matter. Clearly, the physicist will reply that under such conditions the choice between these theories will be made on the basis of simplicity and other methodological criteria. What, then, would Stich say to this reply? He can only try to argue that the particular methodological criteria to which the physicist appeals are not the only criteria to which appeal could be made in choosing among these theories, and that — and here is the critical point — the criteria to which the physicist has appealed enjoy no special privilege among imaginable criteria. If philosophically informed and not caught napping, the physicist will surely point out that the criteria appealed to are justified by their success in other cases of scientific choice. For example, let the argument be about whether the physicist can motivate a choice of a specific curve to express the relation between the temperature and pressure of a gas on the basis of a set of observed values (supposing them to include every possible piece of data). Let us suppose further there are a number of curves $C_1, \ldots$ such that each passes through every observed point, and that the methodological criteria K to which our physicist appeals lead to selection of the curve with the least average curvature, say C_1. Then, if Stich suggests that there are other criteria K', K'', etc. that rank these curves differently, the physicist would, on our account, respond that K is preferable to the alternatives because in other cases in which K has been used to select a relationship between physical properties the subsequent evidence has confirmed the choice of K. Curves with the least average curvature, in general, turn out to state physical relationships more correctly than curves with any of the curvature properties that are evaluated more highly under K', K'', etc. Now, Stich has to reject such "empirical justification" by arguing that it depends on a second-level inductive extrapolation from similar cases in which K has been used and that such an extrapolation itself might be judged by varying criteria. But now Stich is in the position of asking that the physicist justify inductive criteria over counterinductive criteria, that the working physicist solve the Humean problem of induction in order to make practical decisions among competing theories. Unless Stich makes the solution of the philosophical problem of justifying an inductive policy a condition of scientific practice, he allows empirical justifications of methodological criteria of the kind that physicists and linguists use to choose hypotheses and theories. This concession, of course, means that in principle we may always be able to show, for any two *dags*, that they do not have "equal claim" to being the "right one," since only one of them may be in accord with the empirically justified evaluation measures. Thus Stich equivocates on the term 'justification'. If in asking for a justification of a simplicity criterion or other methodological criteria, he means 'justification' in the sense in which this term is used in connection with the

classical riddle of induction, then he is clearly asking too much of the scientist. On the other hand, if he is not asking too much, then the sense of 'justification' must allow empirical evidence in the form of higher-level inductions to count as justifying a simplicity criterion and other methodological criteria.

Suppose it were further argued that the totality of possible observations concerning dispositions to respond by verbal (or other) behavior is consistent with *dags* and linguistic theories that are incompatible with one another. This observation would not distinguish linguistics from physics, since it is also true of physical theory that it is underdetermined by all possible data regarding dispositions (again, granting that this is a coherent notion). Suppose it were further argued, as it has been by Quine,[6] that there is nevertheless a difference between physics and linguistics because "theory in physics is an ultimate parameter," and we must "go on reasoning and affirming as best we can within our ever underdetermined and evolving theory of nature, the best one that we can muster at any one time"; whereas in linguistics,[7] "there is no real question of right choice; there is no fact of the matter even to *within* the acknowledged underdetermination of a theory of nature" because there is no "right English answer which is unique up to equivalence transformations of English sentences" to the question: "What did the native say?" This effort to distinguish linguistics from physics amounts to nothing more than the unargued claim that meanings do not exist.[8] But if physicists were to argue, say, that vital forces or atoms do not exist, they could not merely appeal to the undeniable fact of underdetermination of theory by evidence. Rather, they would either show some incoherence in the postulation of vital forces or atoms or construct a better theory to account for the data without any such assumptions. In the case at issue, Quine does nothing of the sort. There is no sense in which theory is an "ultimate parameter" in physics, more so than in other domains of empirical inquiry (granting the vast differences in depth of theory and empirical confirmation). We see no force whatsoever to the claim that there is some fundamental problem here that distinguishes linguistics from physics, and until some alternative is proposed to the theories of semantic representation now being explored in various ways, we see no reason to accept the arbitrary and unargued assertion that these theories have nothing to be right or wrong about.

Moreover, there is something conceptually incoherent in Quine's position. Quine accepts atoms and other inferred entities in physics, but would refuse to accept meanings even if the best theory to explain linguistic phenomena were to posit them. But surely Quine would not reject in principle a reduction of linguistics together with meanings to physics, say, a reduction on which meanings are interpreted as equivalence classes of brain states. On this possibility, linguistics is part of physical theory and semantic theory is part of our theory of the brain. If physics is able to deal with questions of truth, then surely it can deal with such questions in connection with states of the brain. How, then, can there be no truth in translation when there is something to be right or wrong about in physics generally?

Let us now consider the strategy that Stich endorses, his strategy II. In accordance with this strategy, the linguist seeks to construct an "acquisition model [which gives] as output *some* grammar that is true of the accomplished speaker," some grammar that is selected as "true of the speaker" given *pld*. Note that this is exactly the standard account, with one exception: that account took the linguist's hypothesized *dag* to be a description of the postulated "internal representation" of linguistic competence, whereas Stich speaks of this *dag* as "true of the speaker."

Furthermore, Stich asserts that his strategy II does not "pretend to exhaust the class of grammars that humans can learn," whereas the standard account does propose that a theory meeting the condition of explanatory adequacy be taken as an empirical hypothesis concerning the intrinsic human ability to acquire language on the basis of *pld*. Thus we note two respects in which Stich's strategy II appears to differ from the account that is familiar in the linguistic literature.[9]

We have already noted that Stich offers no objection to the standard account. Let us now compare strategy II with the standard account. The latter proposes that linguistic theory is falsifiable by the demonstration that, on some *pld*, a speaker-hearer will acquire competence that is not as described by the grammar selected by the acquisition theory — or, in Stich's terms, that the grammar selected by the acquisition model will not be "true of the speaker." Since Stich does not impose on his acquisition model the condition that its outputs "exhaust the class of grammars that humans can learn," it would seem that he would not regard the result just described as a refutation of his model. On the other hand, since he does impose on his acquisition model the condition that, for each choice of *pld*, "the acquisition model have as output *some* grammar that is true of the accomplished speaker," it would seem that he should regard the result just described as a refutation of his theory. Suppose that we interpret him as saying that this result does refute the theory. In this case, his strategy II does not differ at all, in this respect, from the standard account. Suppose that he would not regard this result as refuting the theory. Then we will disregard his alternative and less exacting enterprise until he suggests some interesting empirical conditions that it must in fact meet.

Let us turn then to the issue that Stich seems to regard as more important, namely, the distinction between grammars "true of" speakers and grammars that correctly describe what is "internally represented" by speakers. Note that this issue has no relation to anything discussed so far. That much is plain when his misunderstanding of the standard account is corrected. Thus that account could have been formulated, throughout, referring to the *dags* as "true of speakers" rather than as descriptions of the internally represented linguistic competence. The question now at issue is, in essence, the question of realism. Are we willing to postulate that our *dags*, and our linguistic theory, describe properties of the speaker-hearer? Is the mature speaker-hearer to be regarded as a "system" with the properties spelled out in detail in the postulated *dag*, and is the child to be regarded as a "system" with the properties spelled out in detail in the postulated linguistic theory?

The standard account follows normal scientific practice in answering "yes" to both of these questions. Thus, imagine that a psychologist, investigating properties of visual perception, were led to postulate a theory involving analyzing mechanisms of various sorts, say, devices that analyzed stimuli into line, angle, motion, and so on. Would the psychologists propose that the theory is "true of" the organism or that it describes mechanisms possessed by the organism? If the former, the psychologists would be unconcerned if neurophysiological investigation were to demonstrate that visual perception actually proceeds in some entirely different way, with entirely different and unrelated mechanisms. The theory would still be "true of" the organism in Stich's sense of this notion. But any actual scientist regards a theory as subject to disconfirming or confirming evidence from other domains and would abandon the theory if it were shown that it is incompatible with such evidence, say, from neurophysiology. Comparably, a linguist who postulates a *dag* will not merely propose that

it is "true of" an organism in what appears to be Stich's sense of this notion. Thus suppose it were discovered, say, by neurophysiological investigation or by psycholinguistic study, that all the linguist's data (and more) can be better explained by assuming that the organism has a system of perceptual strategies not involving the principles of generative grammar in any manner. The linguist who postulates a *dag* as "true of" the organism will be unperturbed. Linguists who take the realist position, claiming that a *dag* actually describes the speech mechanisms at work, might well abandon their formerly held comprehensive performance theory, with its idealized components and its specific principles and properties.

Now it might be argued that the perceptual psychologist, in the analogue, need not take a "realist" position; rather, if it is shown by neurophysiological investigation that some other theory is "true of" the organism, accommodating the data and much else, providing better explanations and deeper understanding, etc., then the perceptual psychologist can shift to this new theory, regarding it as "true of" the organism but not describing properties of the organism. Similarly, generative grammarians, faced with the discovery that a theory of perceptual strategies is superior in explanatory power, may shift to this theory taking it to be "true of" the organism but not as attributing to the organism specific properties and devices. If this tack is taken, then the alternative to the normal realist approach of the scientist is revealed to be merely a terminological quibble. Thus the physicist, following this approach, would no longer say that atomic theory postulates that matter consists of atoms, electrons, and so on; rather, the physicist says nothing about the structure of matter, but merely maintains that atomic theory is "true of" the world.

Stich's strategy II, understood narrowly, seems to amount to nothing more than an expression of lack of interest in certain problems; the problem of determining the nature of universal linguistic structure, the capacities that make language learning possible, the relation of logic to language, and whatever further insight the study of language might provide for psychology, philosophy, or neurophysiology. If grammars are not taken as theories about the internally represented systems of rules correlating sound and meaning, there is no problem for a theory of language acquisition to address itself to, since there is no longer a linguistic competence to account for as the product of language acquisition. Moreover, the notion of "linguistic universal" also is abandoned, since linguistic universals are principles common to the competence of native speakers of every natural language.[10] Abandoning this notion, we also relinquish any interest in the common structure of natural languages (should it exist). Moreover, we abandon the project of discovering general principles that determine the logical form of sentences in natural language (for example, determining how they are used in valid reasoning) on the basis of properties of postulated underlying structures; the search for such principles is hopeless, it would appear, if there are no universal properties of these underlying structures. All this follows, of course, only if we interpret Stich rather narrowly. If, on the other hand, he is merely proposing a terminological revision of the sort discussed in connection with perceptual psychology, we conclude that he is raising no substantive issue.

What, then, does Stich offer by way of counterbalancing advantages? He cites two. First, strategy II avoids the "puzzle" he brought up in connection with strategy I: now there is no need to make a unique choice among *dags* since there is no claim in strategy II that the selected grammar is actually internalized. Thus, the fact that

there are competing evaluation measures for ranking *dags* is no problem. As Stich says:

> Our project is the highly nontrivial project of producing a model that takes *pld* as input and yields an appropriate *dag* as output. *Any* evaluation measure that does the trick will be suitable (813).

This, however, is hardly an advantage if, as argued above, the alleged puzzle amounts to nothing more than the observation that linguistics is an empirical science. The second of the advantages that Stich claims for strategy II is that it accords better with actual linguistic practice than strategy I. Chomsky and others, Stich asserts, do not really study a broad range of languages in attempting to construct theories about universal grammatical structure and language acquisition, but merely speculate on the basis of "a single language, or at best a few closely related languages" (814). Stich's assertion is both false and irrelevant. Transformational grammarians have investigated languages drawn from a wide range of unrelated language families. But this is beside the point, since even if Stich were right in saying that all but a few closely related languages have been neglected by transformational grammarians, this would imply only that they ought to get busy studying less closely related languages, not that there is some problem in relating grammar construction to the study of linguistic universals.

Stich confuses the matter further by introducing plainly irrelevant analogies. Thus he argues that "attributing knowledge of a grammar to a speaker is little more plausible than attributing knowledge of the laws of physics to a projectile whose behavior they predict" (816/7). Physicists postulate certain laws. Observing the behavior of a projectile, they attribute to it a structure that accounts for its behavior, given these laws. Thus, observing that the earth wobbles on its axis, physicists attribute to it the required bulge at the equator — and may go on to try to determine whether the earth is constructed as required by the theory. Following Stich's analogy, linguists postulate the "laws" of English grammar and attribute to the speaker a structure that accounts for its behavior, given these "laws." But what are the "laws," and what is the "structure"? Plainly, the "laws" are not like the laws of motion — they do not apply to rocks, or even to speakers of Japanese. In fact, under any intelligible formulation that has ever been offered, the "laws" apply only to an organism postulated to have an "internal representation" of the rules and principles of the grammar, along with other systems that interact with this internal representation to yield the judgments of grammaticality, acceptability, etc., that constitute the linguist's data, in accordance with the standard account. Since Stich does not address the problem why the "laws" do not apply to rocks or to speakers of Japanese, it is unnecessary for him to inquire into the structure of the organism that behaves in accordance with these "laws." Thus he is able to present such pointless and irrelevant analogies as the analogy to a projectile in motion that obeys the laws of physics.

Notice that a physicist might well conclude, observing a projectile, that it contains computing mechanisms that assess trajectory, change course, etc., employing an internal representation of the laws of physics. Thus, he might be led to this conclusion by observing how the projectile behaves under various modifications of the environment. If he were to obtain evidence suggesting that the projective has an internal computing structure, or even that it is not a servomechanism but seems to be aiming to reach a certain goal in some other fashion, or is acting in a still more complex way, he would not hesitate to postulate additional structure and to search for additional evidence of its existence and character. As a scientist, he would assume the reality of the structure he postulates in his theory of the projectile, and try to disconfirm or confirm this assumption. He would not be much interested if a philosopher were to tell him that he might rephrase his account of what he is doing, saying rather that he is attributing no structure or properties to the projectile but is "merely" proposing a theory that is "true of" the projectile.

There remains the question whether the structure that we attribute to the speaking person can properly be called "knowledge of a language," "knowledge of grammar," "possession of a cognitive state," or something else. Stich does not raise the issue here, but he has elsewhere. His conclusions in this regard seem to us unacceptable.[11] At best, it is an open question whether more than an uninteresting issue of terminology is involved.[12]

Stich observes that in his strategy II (the nonrealist version of the standard account) "an element of indeterminacy still lurks." This is quite true. Again, it is a defining characteristic of empirical science that theories are underdetermined by raw data. As already noted, Stich rejects Quine's conclusion that there is some special kind of indeterminacy that plagues the study of language beyond t'.at of physics. He then goes on to claim (815) "If we are disinclined to say that in all science, modulo the indeterminacy, there is nothing to be right about, it is because the theories we are willing to allow as correct are those whose arbitrary features have the sanction of tradition." Thus neither linguistics, nor biology, nor physics, has anything "to be right about," tradition aside. Stich promises elsewhere a defense of this position. It will be interesting to see whether his defense will amount to something more than (a) a *reductio ad absurdum* argument against the indeterminacy thesis as formulated, or (b) a terminological variant of familiar realist approaches. We remain skeptical. In any event, we see no reason for taking seriously Stich's proposal that physics and linguistics, as well as every other science, have nothing to be right about, tradition aside.

Moreover, Stich's claim that there is a "strong analogy" between his thesis about the selection of *dags* in strategy II and Quine's thesis about the indeterminacy of translation is, as far as we can see, both a misunderstanding of Quine's thesis and an unwarranted claim. Stich seems to think that the fact that a *dag* has no claim to uniqueness and that an analytical hypothesis on Quine's thesis has none either is enough to establish Stich's thesis as analogous to Quine's except for their implications (815). However, on Stich's strategy II, a *dag* "correctly captures the intuitions of the speakers of the language (and the rest of the grammarian's data) within the limits of accuracy allowed by idealization" (807). Hence, the *dag* correctly predicts phonological, syntactic, and semantic properties of sentences (though without hypothesizing anything about an internalization). Therefore, since Stich's strategy II allows for the selection of a *dag*, it ought to choose between alternative analytical hypotheses, since Quine's analytical hypotheses state predictions about semantic properties of sentences. For any analytical hypothesis, say, *X* is synonymous with *Y*, the *dag* will correctly predict whether it is true or not. The point is this: Quine's thesis is a thesis about the tenability of meanings and the clarity and scientific status of semantic properties. Stich's is not, at least as far as we can determine.

Stich apparently interprets his strategy II in such a way that it leaves linguistics without the least interest to other scientific disciplines. He observes that "the modesty of a grammar, on my account, stands in stark contrast to more flamboyant portraits" (816).[13] The "flamboyant portrait" turns out to be nothing more than the claim that the grammar in the form it would take in models of speech production and perception must structurally correspond to some features of brain mechanism. Stich wonders how a linguist could presume to know so much about "the structure of the brain, having left the skulls of his subjects intact" (816). His skepticism seems to derive from some variant of instrumentalism. Clearly, the linguist does not produce a priori pronouncements on the details of neural connections and pathways, but rather presents a modest inference from some very general features of effects to very general features of their causes, providing a sketch of what the causes would have to be like to be capable of producing the effect.[14]

But, given Stich's charge, it is perhaps worth while to sketch the rationale for such realistic inferences from effects. Such inferences are standard practice in science. Early physicists had no opportunity to look at the microstructure of matter, but, like present-day linguists, had to leave the "skulls of their subjects intact." Nonetheless, they were able to determine a great deal about the microstructure of matter from its behavior. For instance, they could infer that matter is discontinuous, composed of many tiny particles that are invisible, because on this account they were able to explain such phenomena as diffusion. But to explain observable effects like the change of the color of water when dye is put in it in terms of the migration of dye molecules into the spaces between the water molecules commits scientists to the reality of the unobserved causal conditions, since such explanations make sense only if we adopt the realistic assumption that the theoretical terms in which they are couched actually refer to things in nature. If one were to say that the term 'molecule' in the foregoing explanation is a mere *façon de parler*, that it denotes nothing real, the "explanation" would become nonsense.

These considerations are quite general, applying to linguistic explanations as much as to explanations in physics. We postulate certain properties of the brain, e.g., that it must contain some neural mechanism that stores the information in the grammar,[15] on the grounds that properties of linguistic behavior can be explained by assuming them to be causal consequences of brain mechanisms with access to such information. To explain the grammatical judgments of speakers on the basis of such a hypothesized causal chain while denying the existence of essential links in the chain makes no more sense than to explain diffusion while denying the existence of molecules.[16] Stich asserts:

> Though Katz's claims about grammar are more expansive than those I have made, the evidence he uses to confirm a grammar is of a piece with the evidence indicated in my account. Thus, it remains something of a mystery how the grammarian has learned as much as Katz would have him know (816).

In reply, we can point out that some people may well be interested in making hypothetical inferences about underlying causes on the basis of certain evidence, while others with different interests and outlook may choose to restrict their attention more narrowly to the evidence. We can certainly imagine that some early physicists might have been quite happy to accept diffusion and similar phenomena at face value, chiding their Democritean colleagues for "flamboyant portraits" of atoms.

Finally, Stich argues that it is "perhaps misleading" for the grammarian to claim that he is "constructing a theory of the language of his subjects. Rather he is building a description of the facts of acceptability and linguistic intuitions" (817).

Apparently this remains true even if the grammarian succeeds in the task that Stich correctly regards as "a monumentally impressive feat," namely, constructing an acquisition model in accordance with his strategy II. The reason why even this feat would produce only a description, not a theory, is that "A theory of a language seriously worthy of the name would provide some insight into what it is to *understand* a sentence, how sentences can be used to communicate and to deal more effectively with the world, . . . But a grammar does none of this" (817; see our note 13). Stich continues: "Indeed it is logically possible that there be a person whose linguistic intuitions matched up near enough with our own, but who could neither speak nor understand English" (817). Stich's point is that, since such a person would be equivalent to a native speaker for the purposes of grammar construction, grammar construction has no contribution to make to explain how speakers use and understand sentences. Since this is the only argument Stich offers to show that Chomsky's notion of grammatical competence is "explanatorily vacuous" and that grammars provide no "insight into what it is to *understand* a sentence,"[17] it is worth considering it in some detail.

To begin with, we agree — in fact, we insist — that grammars are not full theories of sentence use. Indeed, this is the essence of the competence-performance distinction. But to conclude that theories of competence are "explanatorily vacuous" or mere descriptions is plainly a *non sequitur*. With equal force, one might argue that physics is explanatorily vacuous and provides only descriptions, not theories, because it gives us no insight into human behavior; who, after all, could be interested in mere inanimate objects and their properties? Plainly the distinction between "theory" and "description" and the notion of "explanatory force" are not dependent on the extent to which one or another person may be intrigued by the subject matter under discussion.

Pursuing Stich's argument, since we adopt the competence-performance distinction, we agree with him that it is logically possible that some creature might have full linguistic competence but lack the devices that are postulated in the more comprehensive theory of language use. Since, on Stich's account, the *dag* that is "true of" this speaker describes all his intuitions about grammatical properties and relations, then it describes in particular all semantic properties and relations. For each sentence, it determines whether it is meaningful, analytic, how many senses it has, to what sentences it is synonymous (on some reading), etc.[18] We fail to see, then, how this *dag* can describe all the speaker's intuitions about such properties and relations while offering no insight into how sentences are used and understood—though the creature postulated in Stich's logically possible case would, by hypothesis, not be able to proceed to use and understand sentences as do persons with the same linguistic competence embedded in a performance system. The fact that there could, in principle, be a creature whose linguistic intuitions "match up near enough with our own but who could neither speak nor understand English" shows no more than what the standard account assumes: a more comprehensive theory of performance must be constructed, incorporating grammars, to account for the use and understanding of speech.

In effect, Stich is arguing that a certain type of aphasia is logically possible: a case in which a speaker can give judgments about sentences and thus "serve almost as well as an English speaker as an informant for constructing a grammar of English," while being unable to speak and understand the language. From this observation he concludes that it is misleading to describe a grammar as a

theory of the language of the linguist's subject. The conclusion, if anything, should be quite the opposite. The existence of this type of aphasia would be most congenial to the standard account, since it would indicate that it is possible for the competence system to function even when it is "disconnected" from one component of the performance system in which the standard account assumes it to be embedded. Whereas the standard account does not imply that such a case must exist, discovery of such a case would surely confirm its specific empirical assumptions about the speaker.

In summary, we see no reason to believe that Stich has offered any coherent challenge to the standard account of what the linguist is talking about.[19]

Notes

1. Cf. Chomsky, *Aspects of the Theory of Syntax* (Cambridge, Mass.: MIT Press, 1965), ch. I, and other sources.
2. Cf. *ibid.*, ch. I, and Katz, *The Philosophy of Language* (New York: Harper & Row, 1966), pp. 240-282.
3. Transformational analysis inherently reflects this concern with more abstract questions. For one thing, in revealing underlying levels of sentence structure, transformational analysis overcomes structuralist objections to many of the claims of traditional universal grammar, namely, apparent counterexamples to cross-language generalizations based on features of surface structure. A transformational-generative grammar reveals deeper levels and more abstract properties which appear to be more uniform across languages, thus permitting the formulation of nontrivial general hypotheses about language structure. Furthermore, it seems reasonable to expect that important aspects of the traditional distinction between "logical form" and "grammatical form" can be explicated on the basis of syntactic structure and its semantic interpretation; Katz, *Semantic Theory* (New York: Harper & Row, 1972).
4. He refers to the selected grammar as "this 'explanatorily adequate' grammar which

the child actually internalizes and which the linguist seeks to uncover." Notice that in the account he is attempting to reproduce, "explanatory adequacy" is a property of linguistic theory, not of grammars.

5. Stich defines a *dag* as a grammar that "correctly captures the intuitions of the speakers of the language (and the rest of the grammarian's data) within the limits of accuracy allowed by idealization" (807).

6. "Replies," in D. Davidson and J. Hintikka, eds., *Words and Objections: Essays on the Work of W. V. Quine* (Dordrecht: Reidel, 1969), pp. 303/4.

7. It is unclear to us whether Quine intends to restrict his remarks about indeterminacy in linguistics to "indeterminacy of translation," which he explicitly discusses, or to indeterminacy of all linguistic theory that goes beyond the Gedankenexperiment on "stimulus meaning" to which he arbitrarily restricts attention at certain points in his exposition. It is obvious and uninteresting that, given an arbitrary restriction on permissible evidence, there will be incompatible hypotheses compatible with this evidence. It is less obvious that there are incompatible hypotheses such that no imaginable evidence can bear on the choice between them. We will not pursue this matter, since, even if we were to grant the latter claim, it would in no way distinguish linguistics in principle from other empirical inquiries. Stich, incidentally, agrees with our conclusion that Quine's arguments do not distinguish linguistics from physics, a matter to which we return. For further discussion of Quine's efforts to distinguish linguistics from physics, see Chomsky, *Current Issues in Linguistic Theory* (The Hague: Mouton, 1964); and "Quine's Empirical Assumptions," in Davidson and Hintikka, *op. cit.*

8. As is shown in Katz, *Semantic Theory*, pp. 286-292.

9. Stich suggests another respect in which his strategy II differs from the standard account, namely, he is concerned only with "quasi-universals" which are properties of all the outputs of the acquisition model, but "are in no sense universals – there is no claim that all *dags* must share them" (812). Again, this observation reflects his misunderstanding of the standard account, which did not hold that universals are properties of all *dags* but rather of those *dags* that are in fact descriptions of linguistic competence. In fact, Stich's "quasi-universals" are exactly the universals of the standard account, if we add the realist assumptions just noted.

10. Stich continues to use the term 'acquisition model' in connection with strategy II, but this usage seems to us incomprehensible on his grounds.

11. See Graves, Katz, *et al.*, "Tacit Knowledge," *Journal of Philosophy*, 70, 11 (June 7, 1973): 318-330.

12. See Chomsky, "Knowledge of Language," *Times Literary Supplement*, 15 May 1969, excerpted from an essay to appear in K. Gunderson and G. Maxwell, eds., *Minnesota Studies in Philosophy of Science*, vol. 6. And also *Problems of Knowledge and Freedom* (New York: Pantheon, 1971), ch. I.

13. Note that in Stich's view the best that one can say for doing grammar is to hope that it may lead to "deep insights into exciting phenomena of comprehension and communication" and "that it is something to do." Vague hopes and busy hands.

14. Katz, "Mentalism in Linguistics," *Language*, 40, 2 (April/June 1964): 133.

15. This is the disputed question: cf. Stich, 816.

16. Katz, *Semantic Theory*, pp. 28/9.

17. Stich 816/17. We are, of course, bypassing the question of attributing knowledge of a grammar to a speaker, which does not really play an essential role in the present discussion. Cf. Stich, "What Every Speaker Knows," and Graves, Katz, *et al., op. cit.*

18. Cf. Katz, *Semantic Theory*, ch. 1.

19. We would like to thank William Morris for his helpful comments and criticism.

The Psychological Unreality of Semantic Representations

Janet D. Fodor, Jerry A. Fodor, and Merrill F. Garrett

It is one of the consolations of philosophy that the benefit of showing how to dispense with a concept does not hinge on dispensing with it.

W. V. Quine
on definition without elimination

I. Introduction

As everybody knows, the treatment of semantics within generative grammars has been controversial even by the standards prevalent in linguistics. Neither the properties of semantic representations nor the way they relate to syntactic structures is generally agreed upon, though these are surely among the basic issues that any adequate semantic theory must decide.

However, some consensus is to be found: much of the recent literature assumes at least implicitly that the grammar must contain a semantic level that satisfies the following three conditions.

A. Semantic representations are psychologically real in the sense that, given appropriate idealizations, understanding a sentence requires the recovery of its semantic representation.

B. A variety of properties and relations that are pretheoretically identified as

From *Linguistic Inquiry* 6, no. 4 (1975): 515-531. Reprinted by permission of *Linguistic Inquiry* and the authors.

semantic are formally definable over representations at the semantic level. These have traditionally included synonymy, anomaly, and ambiguity, but in recent years discussion has come to center on entailment (Katz 1972, Lakoff 1970). In particular, something like the following is supposed to be a constraint on the semantic level: if, according to the intuitions of speaker/hearers, sentence S_1 of language L entails sentence S_2 of L, then the argument from the semantic representation of S_1 to the semantic representation of S_2 must be formally valid.

C. Not every lexical item of the natural language corresponds to a syntactically simple expression at the semantic level. That is, there are definable lexical items of L, and these are to be represented by defining *phrases* of the language in which semantic representations are couched. A standard example is the English word *bachelor*, which is supposed to be defined at the semantic level by some such phrase as 'unmarried, adult, male human'. An intended consequence of this is that sentences that are related in the way that *John is a bachelor* is related to *John is an unmarried man* should have identical representations at the semantic level.

The major contention of this article is that there are persuasive empirical grounds for believing that no level meeting conditions B and C will also meet condition A. This is to say that the semantic level, as linguists have generally conceived of it, does not exist. Before considering the evidence for this claim, we need to review a number of points about the status of conditions A-C and their relations to other assumptions about the character of generative grammars.

I.I. Condition A

The sort of psychological reality claim that A expresses is presumably not specific to the semantic level. In fact, those who hold that the semantic level ought to satisfy A usually do so because they endorse the psychological reality of structural descriptions at all the levels that the grammar postulates. This condition is presumably the weakest that a grammar can satisfy if it is to contribute to a psychological model of the speaker/hearer at all. Thus, for example, claims for the psychological reality of grammatical operations entail claims for the psychological reality of structural descriptions, but not vice versa. (For further discussion, see Fodor, Bever, and Garrett 1974).

It is important to emphasize however, that the particular psychological status attributed to semantic representations by A does not follow from the mere claim that semantic representations are psychologically real. Condition A assigns semantic representations a role in the comprehension of sentences, but it is possible to imagine that they play no role in that process but are engaged instead by some other psychological states or computations. As far as we can see, however, memory for sentences would be the only other plausible candidate, and the available evidence seems to show decisively that what is recalled in remembering a sentence corresponds to none of its linguistically motivated representations. (See Bartlett 1932, Bransford, Barclay, and Franks 1972, Johnson-Laird and Stevenson 1970 and the discussion in Fodor, Bever, and Garrett 1974).

Moreover, the view that semantic representations are implicated in the sentence comprehension process is independently plausible since it provides for an extremely natural account of communication exchanges between speakers and hearers. On this account, the formal objects that are encoded and recovered in speech exchanges are semantic representations. It seems that any psychological model of such exchanges must recognize some formal object which captures the notion of the message standardly communicated by uttering a sentence. The view we are considering here — which, in fact, we endorse — requires that this object be among the structural descriptions that the grammar assigns to the sentence. If grammars do contain a level meeting conditions B and C, then representations at that level are the obvious candidates for the job of specifying messages. In other words, it would be distinctly strange (though not logically incoherent) to recognize a linguistic level meeting conditions B and C that does not meet condition A.

I.2. Conditions B and C

These conditions, unlike A, are intended to be proprietary to the semantic level. Moreover, they are intimately interrelated, since C provides one of the means for satisfying B. For example, if, at the semantic level, definable words are replaced by their definitions, then the synonymy relation can perhaps be reconstructed in terms of identity of semantic representation (Katz 1972). Condition C is also presumed to permit inferences turning on "content" words of the language to be captured in essentially the same way as inferences that turn on

240 Janet D. Fodor, Jerry A. Fodor, and Merrill F. Garrett

"logical" words like *and, or, if, some, all,* etc. Thus, the argument from *John is a bachelor* to *John is unmarried* is reconstructed at the semantic level as an argument from 'John is unmarried and adult and male and human' to 'John is unmarried',[1] which is itself an instance of the valid inference scheme *If a is F & G then a is F.*[2]

This brings us to the third point about A-C, namely that they are neutral in the controversy between generative and interpretive semantics since they are presupposed by both. Both theories appeal to eliminative definitions to capture the validity of inferences that turn on content words. Viewed from this perspective, the major dispute between these schools is over how, not whether, defining expressions are assigned to definable lexical items in the natural language.

This is not to claim that the issues between generative and interpretive theories are exhausted by their respective accounts of the lexicon, or even that either kind of theory is inherently committed to eliminative definitions. Chomsky's recent accounts of the "extended standard theory", for example, propose what is clearly an interpretive model of the relation between syntactic and semantic representations, but they in no way rely upon the decomposition of lexical items. The remarks that follow are intended to apply only to those theories that do employ eliminative definitions.

Generative and interpretive theories agree that a dictionary is one of the essential components of a semantic theory. In the sense they have in mind, a dictionary consists of a finite set of *entries*, where each entry is an object language lexical formative together with its defining expression. According to interpretive theories, the input to the semantic component consists of syntactic structures drawn from one or more levels of the grammar. The process of constructing semantic representations for object language sentences exploits the dictionary to replace the formatives in these syntactic structures by their defining expressions. The rules for applying the dictionary are sui generis and in particular do not satisfy constraints on syntactic transformations. In a generative semantic theory, by contrast, the rules that relate object language formatives to their definitions are construed as a special case of substitution transformations, and are thus required to meet the usual conditions on such transformations. Semantic representations thus constitute the domain of transformational operations, and object language formatives are introduced by transformations which, in effect, substitute them for their definitions. In short, generative and interpretive theories differ on where, in the course of derivations, rules of definition operate, and on the formal character of such rules. However, there seems to be a general consensus that grammars contain some rules of eliminative definition.

But despite the central role that has been accorded to definitions in so much recent semantic theorizing, alternative approaches to word meaning have, from time to time, been suggested (Carnap 1956; Bar-Hillel 1967), and linguists have occasionally taken these suggestions seriously as supplements to the classic definitional approach (Fillmore 1971; Lakoff 1970). In what follows we shall argue for abandoning the definitional approach entirely since, so far as we can tell, it is inherently unable to account for a variety of pertinent facts about the way in which people understand sentences.

2. Some Psychological Evidence

In this section, we will review two kinds of considerations that seem to us to militate against the psychological reality of eliminative definitions, and hence against the existence of a level of grammatical representation that simultaneously satisfies A and C. The first of these considerations is as yet only a matter of informal observation; the second turns on some experimental results.

2.1. Intuitive Evidence

Theories that assume that the application of eliminative definitions is a prerequisite to understanding sentences appear to be committed to certain intuitively implausible predictions about sentence complexity: in particular, that, all other things being equal, the relative complexity of a pair of sentences should be a function of the relative complexity of the definitions of the words that the sentences contain. Thus, to pursue our very simple example, the sentence *John is a bachelor* should be more complex than the sentence *John is unmarried*, given that the semantic representation of the former properly includes the semantic representation of the latter. And, by a similar argument, *Floyd broke the glass* should be more complex than *Floyd saw the glass* if, as has been proposed, causative verb constructions are analyzed, at the semantic level, into structures containing (at least) two clauses, one of which has an explicit verb of causing and the other an inchoative verb. Again, *Cats chase mice* ought to be more complex than *Cats catch mice* if, as Katz (1972) has suggested, the semantic analysis of *chase* involves its decomposition into some structure that includes explicit reference to an intention to catch.

Which predictions one makes about the relative complexity of particular pairs of sentences depends, of course, on which definitions one assumes for the language in question. But any definition that is postulated should result in asymmetries of the kind just mentioned: the semantic representation of a sentence containing the defined term will possibly require more operations to recover, and will certainly require more memory space to display, than that of a corresponding sentence containing only a part of the definition. Experimental results addressed

to this question are hard to come by, so, as things stand, one is forced to rely largely on intuition. However, it is demonstrable (Schwartz, Sparkman, and Deese 1970) that intuitions of relative *syntactic* complexity are reliably correlated with experimentally derived rankings, so they have a prima facie claim to construct validity in the present case too. And they do not appear to support the asymmetries of semantic complexity that definitional theories predict.

It might be supposed — it might even be the case — that if the predicted asymmetries are not actually observed, that is only because they are too small to be registered by linguistic intuition. However, it should be noticed that in the kinds of cases cited above, the difference between the members of a sentence pair runs to a whole underlying clause. It does not seem unreasonable to suppose that differences of this magnitude ought to have some influence upon intuitions of relative sentence complexity. There are also standard candidates for definitional relations where the difference between surface sentences of intuitively comparable complexity would amount to several clauses at the level of semantic representation. Thus, for example, the Russellian eliminative definition of *the* renders *The man I met is bald* as (Ex) (I met x and x is a man and x is bald and (y) (if y is a man then (either (I didn't meet y) or $(y = x)$))). [*Editor's note:* In this anthology, the ordinary "E" is used instead of the backward "E" as the existential quantifier.] (Roughly: 'I met a man and he is bald and I met no man other than him.') On the other hand, *A man I met is bald* is analyzed as (Ex) (I met x and x is a man and x is bald). If, then, we assume that these definitions are both displayed at the semantic level, we must predict a difference of three clauses in the semantic representation of *The man I met is bald* vs. *A man I met is bald*, a difference of six clauses in *A man hit a ball* vs. *The man hit the ball*, and so on.

Patently, intuition does not support any such differences in complexity.

One might, quite plausibly, seek to avoid this kind of embarrassment by suggesting that *the* and *a* should both be treated as primitive (that is, unanalyzed) expressions at the semantic level. The Russellian schema would then function not as an eliminative definition in the sense of B and C, but rather as a "meaning postulate" in approximately the sense of Carnap (1956). But if one is prepared to rule out eliminative definitions by such a move in one case, the question immediately arises why one should not do so in every case, thereby removing definitions from their present central role in the system that assigns semantic representations to sentences. Of course, this would have the consequence that grammatical theory would not recognize a semantic level of the kind characterized by B and C. It is, in fact, our view that the failure of correlation between definitional and psychological complexity is so considerable as to suggest that this is the right move to make. We shall return to this later in the article.[3]

2.2. Experimental Evidence

The second sort of consideration that militates against the psychological reality of eliminative definitions is really just a special case of the failure of correlation between definitional and intuitive complexity just noted. In this case, however, differences in complexity are predicted not on the basis of the *number* of elements in semantic representations but on the basis of *which* elements are present. In particular, we will be concerned with the contribution of negative elements to determining the intuitive complexity of sentences.

Prima facie, there are four different sources for the element 'negative' in a semantic representation, i.e. there are four kinds of lexical formative that may contribute a negative element to the

semantic representation of sentences that they occur in. To begin with, 'negative' may be inherited from an *explicitly negative free* morpheme; *not* is an obvious example. Second, 'negative' may be inherited from a bound morpheme such as *in-, un-, im-,* etc. We shall call words containing such morphemes *morphological negatives.* Third, 'negative' may be inherited from an *implicitly negative* morpheme, viz. one that is negative in sense and whose scope exhibits such typical reflexes of negation as *any, much, give a damn,* etc., but which has no obvious morphological decomposition in terms of explicit negation. *Doubt, deny, fail,* etc. are paradigm examples of this class, though the border between morphological and implicit negation is hard to draw: *neither* is a morphological negative if its morphological analysis is *not + either,* but an implicit negative if it is morphologically simple. For present purposes, however, the issue is not how to distinguish the first three classes from each other, but rather the existence of a fourth source of 'negative' in semantic representation that is clearly distinct from any of these others. We have in mind here words that have 'negative' as an element of their definitions, but which contain no negative morpheme and which do not constitute syntactic environments for negative polarity items and so are not implicitly negative by that criterion. As it happens, several of the classic candidates for definitional analysis belong to this fourth class. Thus *bachelor* is supposed to mean 'man who has not ever been married', *kill* has been claimed to mean 'cause to become not alive', and on at least one standard representation of the meaning of *the* there is a negated clause in the "uniqueness" condition.

Let us call items of the fourth type *pure definitional negatives* (PDNs). In doing so, we stress that if 'negative' appears in their linguistic representations at all, it does so only at a level where definitions replace lexical items. The interest of PDNs is that they constitute a test case for the existence of such a level; if it can be demonstrated that their linguistic representations do contain 'negative', that would argue for the psychological reality of definitions, and hence for the existence of a semantic level in the sense of conditions A-C. Conversely, if it can be shown that their linguistic representations do not contain 'negative', that would argue for the unreality of definitions, and hence for the nonexistence of a semantic level of the kind that A-C postulate. We will argue that the linguistic representation of PDNs does not, in fact, contain 'negative'. If this is right, then there are at least some morphemes which are definable in principle but which must be undefined at any level of grammatical representation with claims to psychological reality.

There exists a litmus that can be used for detecting the negativity of a linguistic item: namely, such items typically interact with quantifiers and with each other to produce a noticeable increase in the complexity of a sentence. This is true not only for explicit negatives (as in *It's not true that nobody came*) but also for implicit negatives (as in *It's false that they denied that he was ill*). We have recently conducted an experiment which seeks to use this phenomenon to determine whether there is a negative element in the linguistic representation of PDNs. The detailed results of this study will be reported in a later publication, but the general outline can be given here.

Subjects were requested to evaluate the validity of a number of arguments, each of which contained a quantifier or explicit negative element together with either (a second) explicit negative, or a morphological negative, or an implicit negative, or a PDN. The stimulus materials were so arranged that performance on each of the three latter kinds of arguments could be compared with performance on an argument of the first kind. That is, the result allowed us to evaluate explicit negative vs. morphological negative, explicit negative vs. implicit negative, and explicit negative vs. PDN. In each of these comparisons, the paired arguments differed only with respect to the negative formatives they contained. (So, for example, the comparison between explicit negative and PDN might be made with respect to such sentences as: *If practically all of the men in the room are (not married/bachelors), then few of the men in the room have wives.*) The dependent variable was reaction time to a correct evaluation of the validity of the argument.

The results may be summarized as follows.

1. Both morphological and implicit negatives tended to be easier than their explicit counterparts, though in neither case is this tendency statistically significant on our current data.

2. The difference between morphological negatives and explicit negatives is quite comparable to the difference between implicit negatives and explicit negatives. Nothing in the results distinguishes subjects' performance on morphological and implicit negatives.

3. Arguments containing PDNs, however, were significantly easier than the paired arguments containing explicit negatives. Moreover, and most important, the difference between PDNs and explicit negatives was significantly greater than the difference between explicit negatives and either implicit or morphological negatives. We take this result to suggest strongly that PDNs do not act as though they contain a negative element in their linguistic representation; and therefore, that PDNs are not semantically analyzed at any level of linguistic representation.[4]

3. Overview and Conclusions

We have now considered two lines of evidence suggesting that there is no semantic level meeting conditions A-C; in particular, that no level that meets B and C is psychologically real. Of course, we do not view this evidence as literally establishing that claim. But it seems to us sufficiently persuasive to warrant raising the question of what the grammar and the psycholinguistics might look like if we assume that there is, in fact, no such level.

So far as we can see, there are three broad options.

1. We could hold to B and C while abandoning A. That is, we could give up the claim for the psychological reality of structural descriptions, either in general or for the special case of semantic representations. Clearly there is nothing in principle to stop one from taking this line, since it amounts merely to weakening the empirical conditions by which grammars have usually been constrained. However, anyone who argues this way owes an account of what is at issue between competing claims about the structural descriptions of sentences, and how, even in principle, such claims can be resolved.

On the view that structural descriptions are psychologically real, the answers to such questions are clear in principle (even though hard to establish in practice). Hypotheses about structural descriptions are true when they correspond to the relevant facts, and the relevant facts concern the internal representations that speaker/hearers compute when they produce and understand the sentences of their language. But if it isn't internal representations that make structural descriptions true, what is it?

It is becoming fashionable to try to answer this question by viewing the grammar merely as a representation of a certain abstract object — the language — and characterizing truth for the grammar as correspondence between the statements that it makes and the properties of that object. The intended analogy is to the purely formal sciences like logic and mathematics, since it is claimed that what makes theories in such sciences true is a correspondence between the statements that they make and the properties of abstract objects such as numbers, propositions, and functions. In particular, a formal science like mathematics makes no claims for the psychological reality of the entities it describes.

The difficulty with this position, however, is that it seems to make the empirical methodology of linguistics virtually unintelligible. Linguists normally take the intuitions of speaker/hearers to be the data to which structural descriptions are required to correspond. But this practice would be quite unwarranted unless it were assumed that speaker/hearers do have access to internal representations of sentences and that these provide a reliable source of information about the character of the abstract object (the language) which, on any view, the grammar is ultimately intended to describe.

In short, the primary data of linguistics are psychological data. Purity of method would thus suggest either that we use no psychological information, including intuitions, to constrain the grammar, or that we use all the pertinent psychological information to constrain it. However, the former alternative is not a serious option, since it would, in effect, limit the empirical data for linguistics to regularities in the corpus, which, as everyone now knows, hopelessly underdetermine grammatical descriptions. On the other hand, the latter alternative makes both intuitive and experimental data germane, in principle, to the validation of existence claims for linguistic levels, and this brings us back to the view that structural descriptions are intended to be psychologically real.[5]

2. The second possibility is to claim that conditions A-C *would* define a linguistic level if there were any arguments whose validity turned on the meaning of terms in the nonlogical vocabulary,

but that there are in fact no such arguments. This would be to embrace an austere notion of validity such that the only deductively valid arguments are those that turn on the meanings of the logical words. The argument from *is a bachelor* to *is unmarried* is then not deductively valid; that bachelors are unmarried is just a contingent truth. This approach preserves B and C since it takes them to be vacuously satisfied, but it does so by sacrificing all the textbook examples of lexical decomposition.

Many linguists find this sort of position so counterintuitive as to be untenable. But it should be noted that, whatever the case may be with *bachelor* and *unmarried*, a number of other classic examples of putative truths of definition (e.g. *Cats are animals*) have recently come under attack on epistemic grounds of the familiar Quineian variety (cf. Putnam, forthcoming). The point of these arguments is that scientific advances might lead us to abandon such statements, and that this shows them to be empirical rather than necessary. And, presumably, if they are not necessary, then they cannot be true by definition.

We cannot engage in this debate here.[6] For present purposes, we will assume that provision does need to be made for arguments whose validity turns on the meaning of content words, and hence for some mechanisms which will do what B and C do in standard semantic theories. But we allow that it may turn out that there are very few such arguments, and hence little work for this mechanism to do.

3. The third option requires some preliminary exposition.

One way of understanding conditions A-C is to see them as incorporating a certain claim about the relation between understanding a sentence and determining what it entails. Thus, if A-C are true, then merely understanding *John is a bachelor* amounts to recognizing that it entails that John is an unmarried man. This is because understanding a sentence requires recovering its semantic representation, and, by hypothesis, the semantic representation of *John is a bachelor* is 'John is an unmarried man'. No further inferential principles are required to capture the entailment.

Contrast this case with the inference from *John is a bachelor* to the conclusion that John is a bachelor or John is a fool. According to A-C, one can understand the sentence without, as it were, recovering the fact that it has this entailment.[7] That is, having recovered the representation of *John is a bachelor* as 'P', one must then resort to the logic to determine that 'P' entails 'P or Q'. Thus A-C constitute a hypothesis about the dividing line between sentence comprehension and the inferential processes that are defined for sentences. This is because A-C make the claim that sentences containing definable expressions are ipso facto not in normal form for the application of rules of inference; normalizing them requires replacing the definable expressions by their definitions. Any theory which translates sentences into a normal form to which inference rules apply thereby draws a line between comprehension and inference; comprehension is identified with recovering the normal form and inference with operating on it.[8]

There is, however, no a priori reason for drawing the line between comprehension and inference at the point that A-C specify rather than at some other point. In principle, we could have a more abstract notion of normal form (e.g. one at which *not not P* and *P* are identically represented in the output of the comprehension system). Or we could have a less abstract notion of normal form (e.g. one in which the normal form for a sentence respects its surface vocabulary; viz. in which definitions do not replace definables). Of course, compensating adjustments of the inferential system would be required in either case. So, if *not not P* and *P* have identical semantic representations, then, to that extent, the inferential system need contain no rule of double negation. On the other hand, if *bachelor* and *unmarried man* have distinct semantic representations, then (if we consider *if bachelor then unmarried man* to be valid) some principle to the effect that *x* is a bachelor only if *x* is an unmarried man will have to appear among the rules of inference. Such principles are traditionally called meaning postulates.

To summarize: we have given arguments that there is no semantic level in the sense of conditions A-C; in particular, our proposal is that to each morpheme of the surface vocabulary of a natural language there corresponds a primitive expression in the vocabulary of the representational system. (It should be clear that this proposal does not require that the vocabulary of semantic representations is identical with that of any natural language; we do not suppose, for example, that the formatives of the semantic level are phonologically interpreted. All that we require is that formatives of the natural language should correspond to formatives in the representational system, whatever these latter may turn out to be.) If our arguments are sound, then it appears practically mandatory to assume that meaning postulates mediate whatever entailment relations between sentences turn upon their lexical content. That is, meaning postulates do what definitions have been supposed to do by theories which endorse A-C.[9]

There are, we believe, several further considerations which support the meaning postulate approach. We shall mention just two of them here.

First, notice that the distinction between processes that are involved in understanding a sentence and processes that are involved in drawing inferences from it corresponds to a distinction between mandatory, on-line psychological processes and optional, long-term psychological processes. For, by hypothesis, the output of the sentence comprehension system is that representation of the sentence which must be recovered by anyone who understands it. But the application of principles of inference is presumably largely context-determined. What inferences we draw from what we hear must be a question of what we take to be relevant to the task at hand. (Clearly, we cannot draw *all* the inferences since there are typically infinitely many.)

Now, the overwhelmingly puzzling problem about sentence comprehension is how people manage to do it so fast. For example, there is evidence that subjects can perform tasks which depend on recognizing meaning relations in sentences with latencies as low as 250 msec; that is, with latencies which approximate the length of a CV syllable or the lower bound on a two-choice reaction task (see Marslin-Wilson 1973). Given this consideration, it seems clear that, barring decisive evidence to the contrary, we should assume that the semantic representation of a sentence is as much like the surface form of the sentence as we can. For, in doing so, we reduce the load on processes that must be assumed to be performed on-line. In particular, then, given a choice between assigning a process to the comprehension system and assigning it to the inferential system, all other things being equal we should choose the latter option. That is precisely what hypothesizing meaning postulates in place of eliminative definitions permits us to do.

Second, it seems clear that even if we do have definitions in our grammar, meaning postulates are still indispensable. For, as has been widely recognized, there will almost certainly be residual inferences that turn on "content" words even after the process of definitional decomposition has gone through. So, for example, even if we have replaced *kill* by 'cause to die', we will still need some apparatus to mediate the inference from 'x cause y to die' to, say, 'y die'. Such a principle would have to be sensitive to the meaning of 'cause' (notice that 'x intend y to die' does not entail 'y die') and would thus have precisely the character of a meaning postulate.

There is at least one further argument which suggests the indispensability of meaning postulates even in semantic theories that acknowledge eliminative definitions. Some of the recent skepticism about analytic definitions (though by no means all of it) has concerned the possibility of giving logically sufficient conditions for something being F, even though the possibility of giving logically necessary conditions for being F is not called into question. In traditional terms, it is often easier to specify the genus than the differentia. For example, many who admit that, necessarily, every case of killing is a case of causing to die, nevertheless deny that every case of causing to die is a case of killing. Nor is it obvious that there is any property of an action (except, of course, being a killing) such that, necessarily, an act of causing to die which has that property constitutes a killing. The problem may be clearer if one considers the relation between *red* and *colored*. Presumably x *is red* entails x *is colored*. But, surely, there is no property F which is logically independent of the property of being colored and such that x *is F and x is colored* entails x *is red*. If this is correct, and if it is analytic that whatever is red is colored, then there is at least one analyticity which does not rest on a definition. For definitions are required to be symmetrical (i.e. they provide sufficient as well as necessary conditions for the application of a term). Meaning postulates, however, are not so constrained. They would thus appear to be the only available mechanism in the present case. (For an elaboration of this argument see J. D. Fodor, forthcoming.)

In fact, all the theories which embrace A-C that have so far been proposed do employ meaning postulates under one guise or other. (In Katz's work, for example, they appear as "redundancy rules".) Since any entailment that can be captured with meaning postulates and definitions can equally be represented with the former alone, it seems clear that the least hypothesis is that definitions are otiose.

We close this discussion by briefly considering three lines of argument which might be held to substantiate the claim that lexical items are decomposed at the semantic level even in face of the counterevidence that we have been assembling.

1. There are claimed to be "purely linguistic" considerations which militate in favor of assigning structure to lexical items.

For example, there have been arguments for lexical decomposition based on the search for a principled distinction between "possible" and "impossible" words. There have been arguments based on the claim that adverbs can have scope over internal semantic components of words. And there have been arguments based on similarities of distribution between words and their defining phrases. Many of these arguments are ingenious and deserve serious examination. It is our belief that there are alternative explanations of the data which do not assume semantic decomposition of lexical items and which are at least as plausible as the ones that do, but establishing this is well beyond the scope of the present article. We must make do with one brief comment on the argument from distributional symmetry and one remark on a matter of general principle.

The distributional arguments we have in mind are those which appeal to the existence of selectional symmetries between items that are similar in meaning to support the claim that such items must have identical representations somewhere in the grammar. Our point is that such arguments beg the question that is primarily at issue in this article. For, it simply cannot be taken as a self-evident methodological principle that selectional symmetry is necessarily the product of identity of underlying linguistic representation. On the contrary, there is an empirical claim at issue, and what we have been arguing implies that certain distributional symmetries — viz. those between words and their defining phrases — should not be so treated. Nor is it hard to think of alternatives. For example, McCawley (1971) has argued that sentences which violate selection restrictions are simply special cases of sentences with incompatible entailments. If this is so, then it seems that any theory which correctly determines the entailments of sentences could accommodate cases where lexical items and their defining phrases are subject to identical selection restrictions. In particular, a theory which determines entailments by appeal to meaning postulates should be able to do so.

The general point of principle is this. Suppose there were some widely accepted pattern of purely linguistic argumentation that entailed the existence of eliminative definitions. Then if, as we have maintained, eliminative definitions are not psychologically real, that would constitute a reductio ad absurdum of the pattern of linguistic argument, which would then have to be abandoned. This is simply to endorse Chomsky's insight that the metatheoretical principles that are used to evaluate alternative grammatical arguments and analyses must themselves be empirically justified. In particular, they must be chosen so that they select the correct grammar for each language, viz. the grammar whose constructs are psychologically real.

2. It is claimed that there are fundamental semantic properties and relations which the grammar is required to mark, and the only way to mark them is by assuming a classical semantic level over whose structures they can be formally defined.

The following discussion will suggest the sort of point that is at issue. It is sometimes argued that there is a principled difference between sentential synonymy and logical equivalence of sentences. The suggestion is that this difference can be reconstructed only on the assumption that sentences are synonymous if and only if they receive identical representations at the semantic level. Logically equivalent sentences are then the ones which are interconvertible by valid rules of inference. (A similar contrast is supposed to exist between analyticity on the one hand and (mere) logical necessity on the other.)

To begin with, however, it is worth remembering that the existence of a principled distinction between analytic and logical equivalence has been repeatedly challenged in the philosophical literature. Certainly it is hard to argue that intuitions are clear enough to justify making that distinction correspond to a distinction of levels in the grammar.

But, in any event, there is no reason to suppose that the desired distinction cannot be drawn within the logic: viz. without reference to a semantic level. For example, one can imagine that intuitions of analyticity might correspond to arguments which employ only a designated subset of the inferential rules (including, of course, the meaning postulates). It is true that, on this view, one might have to list, for each such pattern of inference, whether it preserves analyticity. This may not seem to have much explanatory value, but notice that we do essentially the same thing when we list the dictionary entries and say that analyticity is preserved by applying them.

A different theory of analyticity might have it that intuitions of analyticity are essentially intuitions about the length of arguments under some canonical formalization. Roughly, the longer the argument from P to Q, the less analytic the sentence *if P then Q*. If this is true, it would argue for the meaning postulate treatment against a radical division of analytic from logical truth. At the very least, the fact that judgments of analyticity appear to be graded suggests that this might be right.

3. There is a class of psychological effects whose explanation has been held to require the kind of semantic cross-classification of the lexicon which decomposition of lexical items provides.

The best candidates we know of for such effects are slips of the tongue (see Fromkin 1971, Shattuck 1975), the tip of the tongue phenomenon (see Brown and McNeil 1966), and semantic generalization (see Osgood 1953). Without going into details, the point of each of these examples is the intrusion into a subject's performance in the experimental task of lexical items semantically related to the intended target item. Such intrusions suggest that the speaker/hearer's access to the contents of the lexicon may be via some system of semantic features. (Thus, for example, the words one thinks of when one attempts to recover some word that is on the tip of one's tongue are often semantically related to the desired item. So, the subject trying to remember *sextant* might say *astrolabe* instead.)

We think these observations are interesting and pertinent but not decisive. Though the existence of semantic intrusion is certainly compatible with the semantic decomposition of lexical items, it quite clearly does not require that view. Any accessing system which makes semantically similar items "closer" than semantically dissimilar ones would yield the same effect even without embracing lexical decomposition. Among the candidate systems are "networks", multidimensional spaces where the dimensions are semantically interpreted, "semantic fields", and, surely, many others that ingenuity might devise. The point to bear in

mind is that the assumption that lexical items are semantically decomposed does not follow from the assumption that the lexicon is semantically cross-classified (though, admittedly, if decomposition did occur that would provide a convenient mechanism for cross-classification).

Moreover, it is really quite unclear to what extent these intrusions *are* semantic in nature, if *semantic* is construed in the disciplined sense that linguists have in mind, such that semantic representation is intimately concerned with the determination of entailment. Our impression is that at least some of the psychological phenomena turn on *associative* connections which do not meet this stringent condition. So, for example, *table* is a likely slip for *chair* and *stool* is not. Yet, from the point of view of pure semantics, the amount of overlap in meaning is greater in the latter case than in the former. The difficulty is, of course, that many semantically related words are also high associates, so factoring out the respective contributions of meaning and association to the observed phenomena is no small matter. In any event, it tells against the view that these phenomena are the consequences of lexical decomposition that they appear to hold for proper names as well as for words which have meanings in the linguist's proprietary sense. Slips of the tongue that involve proper names often blend (or otherwise confuse) them with the names of related people: the name that comes to mind when one is trying to think of Smith's name is often that of someone one thinks of as related to Smith, and the names one conflates with *Rubinstein* are likely to be the names of pianists. We do not propose a theory of any of these processes, but patently they would not justify the lexical decomposition of names.

In conclusion: almost all of the recent discussion about semantics in linguistics, and much of the recent discussion of semantics in psychology, has concerned the detailed arrangement of representations at the semantic level. It seems to us, however, that there is no very convincing evidence for the existence of such a level, and that there is more than a little reason to believe that no such level does exist. Perhaps the reason that semantic representations have proved to be so elusive is simply that, after all, there aren't any.[10]

Notes

1. We shall put semantic representations in single quotation marks. Presumably semantic representations are couched in the vocabulary of some universal metalanguage. Since, however, we have no idea of what that language looks like, we will allow English expressions to stand as surrogates for its formulae. However, nothing in the discussion to follow turns upon our doing so.

2. We are not, of course, imputing the details of this example to all — or, indeed, any — of the semantic theories that have been developed in the recent linguistic literature. Even in such simple cases, a variety of different assumptions is possible concerning the nature of the defining expressions and the rules of inference that apply to them. Current theories do, in fact, differ on just such matters.

3. Since this was written, Professor Edward Martin has called our attention to the work of Kintsch (1974). Kintsch performed a number of experiments that were designed to test the relative psychological complexity of sentences that differed in the definitional complexity of their constituent lexical items. Among the experimental procedures he employed was the "phoneme monitor" task (see Foss 1969), which has generally proved a reliable instrument for measuring differences in the difficulty of understanding sentences. Kintsch's results uniformly failed to exhibit the asymmetries of complexity that definition-based theories of semantic representation predict. On the basis of these findings, Kintsch argues that meaning postulates are a more plausible mechanism than definitions for reconstructing the contribution of items in the nonlogical vocabulary to the determination of entailment relations between sentences. His view is fundamentally similar to the one that

we will develop here, though there are significant differences of detail.

4. It might be suggested that since implicit negatives are not significantly different from explicit ones, the former are negative by the complexity tests; and that this would require that *some* words have definitions even if some others (PDNs) do not. However, this argument is inconclusive. The fact that words like *doubt* and *deny* exhibit the characteristic interactions with quantifiers and overt negative elements shows that they must somehow be classed with negative words by the grammar. One way to so classify them would be to decompose them into a negative element plus further content material (so that *doubt* becomes 'not believe', *deny* becomes 'state that not', etc.). An alternative treatment, however, is simply to acknowledge a class of negative primitives that includes both the explicit and the implicit negatives.

In short, the fact that implicit negatives behave like explicit negatives in the relevant respects is compatible with representing the latter as containing negative elements at some level, but it does not literally require that treatment. On the contrary, one might argue that given some words (PDNs) that could be defined but are not, one should opt for the nondefinitional treatment of implicit negatives as well. Otherwise, we might have to tolerate an uninterpreted degree of freedom in the linguistic theory. Clearly, we should prefer a theory that requires all definables to be defined or a theory requiring that none of them be, as compared to a theory that allows definitions just when it happens to feel like doing so. At the very least, a "mixed" theory would need some principled distinction between the words that are defined and the ones that are not. (For an attempted defence of a mixed theory, see Lakoff 1970.)

5. Of course, we do not take all linguistic intuitions to be veridical. Nor need all the experimental data which seem prima facie relevant to constraining grammars turn out to be so. In some cases, we may conclude that the observations are not captured directly by the grammar, but rather by the interaction of the speaker/hearer's internal representation of his language with other psychological entities, states, and processes. But such conclusions need positive justification; merely appealing to

a "performance/competence" distinction does not absolve the linguist from the obligation to account for the data. So, in the present case, if the sorts of evidence we have cited are judged compatible with the existence of a traditional semantic level, one needs an explanation which shows how they are compatible, and one needs some independent evidence for accepting that explanation.

6. The situation is complicated by the consideration that the Quineian argument is directed, in the first instance, not against lexical decomposition per se but rather against the *necessity* of such statements as *Cats are animals*. It is thus germane to the issues we have been discussing only insofar as theories which assume that lexical items are decomposed also assume the analyticity (hence, the necessity) of the statements that decomposition gives rise to. It is possible to imagine a kind of semantic theory which makes the first assumption but not the second. Indeed, many of the decompositionalist theories of the lexicon that psychologists have proposed appear to be of that kind; the claim is that they provide a warranted account of the internal representation of lexical items rather than a theory of modal statements.

7. To put this more precisely, the semantic level does not distinguish between the argument *If John is a bachelor then John is a bachelor* and the argument *If John is a bachelor then John is an unmarried man*. But it does distinguish between both of these and the argument *If John is a bachelor then John is a bachelor or John is a fool.*

8. It should be emphasized that the line which A-C draws between understanding and inference does not fall at the same place as the line between analytic inferences and the others. Thus, it requires an inference, albeit a minimal one, to get from the premise *John is a bachelor* to the conclusion *John is unmarried*, though *If John is a bachelor then John is unmarried* is presumably analytic.

9. It is sometimes alleged that theories which employ meaning postulates are just "notational variants" of theories that use definitions (see Katz and Nagel 1974). But, as we have seen, such theories disagree on at least the following: (a) the primitive vocabulary of the language in which semantic representations are couched; (b) the abstractness of the semantic

level; (c) the relation between comprehension and inference; and (d) a host of psychological consequences, two of which were examined above.

10. We wish explicitly to exempt from these remarks those sorts of representations which are supposed to capture the "logical form" of sentences (as contrasted with the internal structure of their lexical items). Our arguments are not germane to the claim that there exists a level of representation which formalizes such relations as those between quantifiers and the variables they bind, those between relational terms and their arguments, or those between operators and what they operate upon. Nor do our arguments commit us, one way or the other, on the relation of that level of representation (if it exists) to the levels of deep and surface syntactic structure. It seems to us that arguments similar in spirit to the ones that we have given can be brought against some of the standard proposals about what representations of logical form are like (cf. Martin 1975). However, we have not tried to give such arguments here.

References

Bar-Hillel, Y. (1967) "Dictionaries and Meaning Rules," *Foundations of Language* 3, 409-414.

Bartlett, F. C. (1961) (first published in 1932) *Remembering*, Cambridge University Press, London.

Bransford, J. D., J. Barclay, and J. J. Franks (1972) "Sentence Memory: Constructive vs. Interpretive Approach," *Cognitive Psychology* 3, 193-209.

Brown, R., D. McNeil (1966) "The Tip of the Tongue Phenomenon," *Journal of Verbal Learning and Verbal Behavior* 5, 325-327.

Carnap, R. (1956) "Meaning Postulates," in *Meaning and Necessity*, Phoenix Books, The University of Chicago Press, Chicago, Illinois.

Fillmore, C. (1971) "Entailment Rules in a Semantic Theory," in J. Rosenberg and C. Travis, eds., *Readings in the Philosophy of Language*, Prentice-Hall, Englewood Cliffs, New Jersey.

Fodor, J. D. (forthcoming) *Semantics*, Crowell Inc., New York.

Fodor, J. A., T. G. Bever, M. F. Garrett (1974) *The Psychology of Language*, McGraw-Hill, New York.

Foss, D. J. (1969) "Decision Processes During Sentence Comprehension," *Journal of Verbal Learning and Verbal Behavior* 8, 457-462.

Fromkin, V. A. (1971) "The Non-Anomalous Nature of Anomalous Utterances," *Language* 47, 27-52.

Johnson-Laird, P. N. and R. Stevenson (1970) "Memory for Syntax," *Nature* 227, 412-413.

Katz, J. J. (1972) *Semantic Theory*, Harper and Row, New York.

Katz, J. J. and R. Nagel (1974) "Meaning Postulates and Semantic Theory," *Foundations of Language* 2, 311-340.

Kintsch, W. (1974) *The Representation of Meaning in Memory*, John Wiley and Sons, New York.

Lakoff, G. (1970) *Linguistics and Natural Logic, Studies in Generative Semantics*, no. 1, Phonetics Laboratories, University of Michigan, Ann Arbor, Michigan.

Marslin-Wilson, W. (1973) *Speech Shadowing and Speech Perception*, unpublished Doctoral dissertation, Dept. of Psychology, MIT, Cambridge, Massachusetts.

Martin, E. (1975) "The Psychological Unreality of Quantificational Representations," mimeographed paper, MIT, Cambridge, Massachusetts.

McCawley, J. (1971) "Interpretative Semantics Meets Frankenstein," *Foundations of Language* 7, 2, 285-296.

Osgood, C. E. (1953) *Method and Theory in Experimental Psychology*, Oxford University Press, New York.

Putnam, H. (forthcoming) "The Meaning of Meaning," in *Minnesota Studies in the Philosophy of Science* (Gunderson, ed.).

Schwartz, D., J. P. Sparkman, and J. Deese (1970) "The Process of Understanding and Judgements of Comprehensibility," *Journal of Verbal Learning and Verbal Behavior* 9, 87-93.

Shattuck, S. R. (1975) *Speech Errors and Sentence Production*, unpublished Doctoral dissertation, Dept. of Psychology, MIT, Cambridge, Massachusetts.

The Real Status of Semantic Representations

Jerrold J. Katz

This article replies to Fodor, Fodor, and Garrett's "The Psychological Unreality of Semantic Representations".[1] Their claim that there is no level of semantic representation in grammars is based on a methodological position about how to understand the theories linguists construct about natural languages. According to this underlying position, a grammar is a mentalistic theory and

. . . every aspect of a mentalistic theory involves psychological reality. . . . The rules [of each component of the grammar] must have their psychological reality in the input-output operations of the computing machinery . . .
. . . since the psychologist and the mentalistic linguist are constructing theories of the same kind, i.e., theories with the same kind of relation to the neurophysiology of the human brain, it follows that the linguist's theory . . . be consistent with the neurophysiologist's theories concerning the type of existing brain mechanisms. . . . Further, by subjecting a linguistic theory to this requirement we make it more easily testable. For the requirement enables us to refute a linguistic theory if we can find

From *Linguistic Inquiry* 8, no. 3 (1977): 559-584. Reprinted by permission of *Linguistic Inquiry* and the author.

psychological theories or facts that are inconsistent with it. (Katz (1964, 133-134))

My reply to FFG is made on behalf of a different methodological position, one expressed in the following passage:

It should be emphasized that, in showing a predicted complexity order fails to obtain, one has not shown that the grammar is disconfirmed. A grammar is simply an axiomatic representation of an infinite set of structural descriptions, and the internal evidence in favor of the structural descriptions modern grammars generate is so strong that it is difficult to imagine their succumbing to any purely experimental disconfirmation. Rather, one would best interpret negative data as showing that an acceptable theory of the relation between competence and performance models will have to represent that relation as abstract, the degree of abstractness being proportional to the failure of formal features of derivations to correspond to performance variables. (Fodor and Garrett (1966, 152))

The first quotation is from my "Mentalism in Linguistics", and the second is from Fodor and Garrett's "Some Reflections on Competence and Performance". I will thus be arguing here against my former position, as FFG update it and apply it to semantics, and in favor of Fodor and Garrett's former position, as I will update it and apply it to this discipline.

FFG begin with the assumption that there is a consensus among linguists that the semantic level of grammars ought to satisfy, inter alia, the condition A (p. 515):

> (A) Semantic representations are psychologically real in the sense that, given appropriate idealizations, understanding a sentence requires the recovery of its semantic representation.

They also observe that A is not to be regarded as an isolated thesis about semantic representation (p. 516):

> The sort of psychological reality claim that A expresses is presumably not specific to the semantic level. In fact, those who hold that the semantic level ought to satisfy A usually do so because they endorse the psychological reality of structural descriptions at all the levels that the grammar postulates.

In fact, the stronger claim might be made that those who endorse A are, other things being equal, committed to endorsing the psychological reality of structural descriptions at other levels. It might reasonably be supposed that a "principle of universalizability" governs the introduction of constraints like A, namely that *what is required for one level of grammatical representation is required for all, insofar as a generalization can be made.*

There are two conspicuous omissions here that constitute serious deficiencies in FFG's overall argument. One is the failure to mention sentence production in their treatment of the conditions for the psychological reality of grammars. In the absence of a discussion of sentence production, one might concede (for the sake of argument) that semantic representations play a negligible role in sentence comprehension, but argue that they have a role in sentence production that justifies

their existence. FFG might have had symmetry considerations in mind in passing over sentence production, but the general differences between production and recognition tasks make such generalization from sentence recognition dubious. The other omission is the absence of a psychological reality requirement on the operations in a grammar that generate structural descriptions. This omission, which seems to be a matter of principle, raises the further question of just what the point of performance oriented constraints on grammars can be if the imposition of such constraints is arbitrarily restricted to structural descriptions. One might guess, however, that FFG make no mention of operations because, on the one hand, the evidence now seems to go against the derivational theory of complexity, and on the other, proposals for transformation-reduced grammars, though available, are not yet firmly entrenched. Thus, performance oriented constraints that cover operations run the risk of ruling out too much of standard syntactic theory. But if this risk is not taken, FFG leave us wondering why they make a distinction between what in the grammar requires credentials of psychological reality and what does not when there seems to be no relevant difference between them.

The function of A in FFG's argument is to support their inference from the existence of certain *psychological data* to the existence of *linguistic evidence* against a level of semantic representation. Without A, one might reasonably take such data to be irrelevant to semantic representation. One might hold that a grammar is a perfectly good scientific theory of a natural language just in case it is the simplest formal system that predicts and explains each grammatical (i.e. phonological, syntactic, and semantic) property and relation of every sentence in the language.[2] It is not at all obvious why one would also have to show that its rules are the ones that speakers unconsciously use in producing and comprehending utterances. FFG's methodological position, which I will call "performancism", tries to explain why grammars ought also be accounts of the speaker's mental mechanisms. Because this methodological position purports to supply the rationale needed to make psychological data relevant to questions of grammar, it is crucial at the outset to see what one is committed to in accepting it and what the alternatives are.

One of the alternatives is what I will call "competencism". This is the classical Chomskyian position: it makes a strict competence/performance distinction, separating "the speaker-hearer's knowledge of the language" from "the actual use of language in concrete situations", and it takes a grammar "to be the description of the ideal speaker-hearer's competence, not of the use of language" (Chomsky (1965, 4)). On this position, the semantic component of a grammar generates semantic representations and pairs them with meaningful sentences without reference to facts about the role of semantic representations in speech production and comprehension. As with phonological and syntactic representations, the correctness of the pairing is judged on the basis of evidence about whether the predictions about a sentence's semantic properties and relations that follow from the semantic representation(s) assigned to it are confirmed by speakers of the language. The important point emphasized by Fodor and Garrett is that failure to predict experimental results such as complexity orderings does not count against representations at any grammatical level: grammars are to be judged not by their success in predicting such results but by "the internal evidence in favor of the structural descriptions [they] generate". The notion of internal evidence, within the theory of competencism, is that something constitutes such evidence just in case it reflects the fact that

some sentence (or one of its constituents) has some *grammatical* property or relation. Competencism, then, does not impose A on semantic representations, although, as we shall see below, it does require them to be psychologically real in a different sense. In this respect, it differs from the other alternative to performancism, the position I will call "Platonism".

Performancism requires that, beyond accounting for semantic properties and relations, semantic representations serve as part of the description of what is recovered in the understanding of utterances. FFG say (p. 516) that A "assigns semantic representations a role in the comprehension of sentences", and that this role, together with their role in "other psychological states or computations", constitutes their sole claim to existence. The critical difference between competencism and performancism concerns this narrow sense of psychological reality. Competencism treats this sense of psychological reality as a condition on performance models only, while performancism requires semantic representations, and structural descriptions generally, to be psychologically real in this narrow sense. An optimal grammar, according to competencism, has only to be the simplest theory of the language that predicts each grammatical property and relation of every one of its sentences.

In their overview (p. 522-523), FFG state that they find such an account unsatisfactory. One major problem with their argument is that they take this account of the notion of an optimal grammar to be a unique feature of the Platonist position, the view that grammar is an abstract science like arithmetic. So taking it, they argue that one has to choose between their performancist position, which, as they are at pains to point out, is methodologically respectable, and Platonism, which as they claim, amounts to methodological mysticism. Therefore, the existence of competencism, as a

distinct position, is an embarrassment to
their general argument. Given competencism, even assuming the worst about
Platonism, there is an alternative to performancism. Thus, it is important to see
how competencism differs from performancism and Platonism.

Competencism envisions a theory of
language that bases grammars on the
idealization of the objects hypothesized
to account for the internal evidence.[3]
Idealization creates perfect objects whose
flawlessness is designed to introduce no
unnecessary complication in the statement of explanatory laws. In physics,
laws are stated for ideal objects like
molecules in random motion, perfect
vacuums, and frictionless planes. In
grammar, laws are stated for ideal objects
like the rules that comprise the knowledge
of the ideal speaker-hearer. In both
disciplines, positing ideal objects is controlled by strong evidential constraints.
Thus, even though a grammar is a theory
of the ideal speaker-hearer's perfect
knowledge of the language, it is based on
evidence reflecting intuitions of actual
speakers about their less-than-perfect
knowledge. Moreover, these intuitions,
being mental acts of inner apprehension,
occur in real time. But this fact no more
makes theories of the grammatical structure of a language into performance
models than the fact that ideal objects in
physics are rooted in real-time observations makes theories like the kinetic
theory of gases into engineering models.

All idealization abstracts away from
certain things, thus allowing the scientist
to construct theories without paying attention to certain data. Competencism
claims that idealizations in grammar proceed only from intuitions of grammatical
properties and relations. Data pertaining
to the nature of events in tasks involving
high speed operations, such as errors and
reaction times, do not enter into the
evidential constraints in grammar construction. Such events are different in

kind from mental acts of inner apprehension. They reflect aspects of the way
speakers exercise their knowledge rather
than features of the knowledge itself. Accordingly, the competencist can give a
priori grounds for considering the sorts of
data that FFG use to argue their case
against semantic representation to be just
the sorts of data that a linguist should ignore in grammar construction: insofar as
performance normally involves high
speed calculation of appropriate
responses to complex situations, it is
natural to expect that grammatical information will assume a strategically abbreviated and incomplete form. It could
hardly serve the purpose of expediting on-
line processing operations if it didn't.
Hence, error scores and reaction-time differences, which indicate such abbreviation and incompleteness, are just what,
under a theory of competencism, ought to
be abstracted away from in the construction of grammars, "the degree of abstractness", as Fodor and Garrett say, "being
proportional to the failure of formal
features of derivations to correspond to
performance variables".

Disregarding data about the exercise
of competence and refusing to require
representations in the theory of competence to be psychologically real in the
sense of on-line processing in speech production and comprehension does not
make competencism less methodologically respectable than performancism.
Idealization provides sufficiently strong
constraints on theory construction, even
though the theories are framed in terms of
ideal objects. The constraints follow the
methodological principle M.

(M)   As real conditions more closely ap-
      proximate to ideal ones, the predic-
      tions of the laws formulated over
      ideal objects must approximate to ac-
      tual observations more and more
      closely.

Of course, real conditions can never reach

ideal ones, but, then, confirmation always involves inductive extrapolation.

Theories that talk about ideal objects like molecules in random motion, perfect vacuums, and frictionless planes are no less physical theories because such objects do not exist in this imperfect physical world. Such theories belong to theoretical physics. Similarly, theories that talk about ideal objects like perfect grammatical knowledge, surface and deep syntactic structure, and analytic definitions are, according to competencism, no less psychological theories because such objects do not exist in the imperfect world of performance mechanisms and on-line operations. Such theories, as Chomsky has repeatedly stressed, belong to theoretical psychology.

Here, then, is the source of competencism's notion of psychological reality: the psychological reality of a construct consists in its having a place in the vocabulary of theoretical psychology. The competencist might thus introduce principle R as the counterpart of A.

(R) A grammar of a language must be psychologically real in the sense that it represents an idealization of the knowledge that speakers of the language have about its grammatical structure, that is, it represents an ideal of their knowledge in the sense of M.

This, however, is not the only possibility. The competencist might not wish to impose such a constraint, but only to claim that an optimal grammar in the above sense *is* (as a matter of fact) psychologically real in the sense of being an idealization of actual speaker-hearers' grammatical knowledge. It is, I think, not clear which of these possibilities Chomsky takes, and it doesn't matter here which is preferable, because both of them complete the formulation of a position between performancism and Platonism. The existence of such a position in and of itself shows that FFG's failure to provide the

support their overall argument needs to prove that the existence of psychological data of the kind they claim to have found is evidence against a level of semantic representation. Principle A cannot be justified as the only alternative to methodological mysticism.

FFG's attempt to justify A can also be challenged on the grounds that Platonism can hardly be so easily dismissed.[4] FFG charge that a Platonist position on the nature of grammars makes the methodology of linguistics "virtually unintelligible". They argue as follows (p. 523). On the one hand, "a formal science like mathematics makes no claim for the psychological reality of the entities it describes", and on the other, "the intuitions of speaker-hearers [are taken by linguists] to be the data to which structural descriptions are required to respond"; "this practice," they claim, "would be quite unwarranted unless speaker-hearers do have access to internal representations of sentences." From this, they draw the conclusion that *since* "the primary data of linguistics are psychological data", either "we use no psychological information, including intuitions, to constrain the grammar, or . . . we use all the pertinent psychological information to constrain it. However, the former alternative is not a serious option, since it would, in effect, limit the empirical data for linguistics to regularities in the corpus."

If this argument were a good argument, we could easily establish that the methodology of mathematics, too, is "virtually unintelligible". Mathematics also traffics in intuitions. From the humblest intuitions of ordinary plane geometry to the most sophisticated intuitions of topology, this basis of justification provides the facts to which descriptions of geometrical and arithmetical structures are required to respond. Further, such justification would be unwarranted unless mathematicians have access to internal representations of geometrical and arithmetical structures. But, since "a formal science like mathematics makes no claim for the psychological reality of the entities it describes", it can use no psychological information, including intuition, to constrain its descriptions. Consequently, mathematics bases its theories on information it has no right to employ, and since there is no other information for it to base its theories on, its methodology is unintelligible.

The fact that, by parity of argument, we can arrive at such a conclusion shows that something is wrong with the form of argument FFG use to dismiss Platonism. The fallacy is that from the fact that mathematics and linguistics do not make claims about psychological reality, it does not follow that a mathematician or linguist cannot legitimately employ psychological data. The problem is that the term "psychological data" conveys two distinct notions, one having to do with how we come by the data and the other having to do with what the data are about.[5] If we distinguish the *source* sense from the *import* sense, FFG's objection vanishes. The Platonist can claim that intuition provides the facts to which the theories of mathematicians and linguists are required to respond and that such a methodology is intelligible because the intuitions that provide the mathematician and linguist with data involve access to internal representations. Such intuitions may be conceptualized as acts in which information in internal representations is made consciously available. Thus, the source of the data in mathematics and linguistics *is* psychological. Their import, on the other hand, is not. They are not about something psychological. The internal representations in question do not represent the structure of psychological objects, states, or events, in the manner of introspections about what one knows, feels, or imagines. The internal representations involved in intuitions represent

abstract entities, numbers, spaces, etc., on the one hand, and sound patterns, senses, etc., on the other. Only the conflation of source and import makes Platonism seem committed to an unacceptable limitation on the data for theories in linguistics. (see Katz, (1980))

Thus, it is also fallacious for FFG to use the fact that the source of primary data in linguistics is psychological to argue that an intelligible methodology uses "all pertinent psychological information" to constrain grammars, where this expression includes performance variables. The conclusion requires the same illicit shift from data that are psychological in the sense of source to data that are psychological in import.

We may sum up the difference between Platonism and the other positions. Platonists in mathematics or linguistics do not deny that access to internal representations is the source of their data, but what makes them Platonists rather than adherents of competencism or performancism is their insistence that such representations depict the structure of abstract entities rather than the structure of idealized mental objects or processing mechanisms. Platonists think that both competencism and performancism have a mistaken view about the nature of linguistic data, though Platonists think the latter's view is wider of the mark. Against performancists like FFG, the Platonist would argue that data about on-line operations in sentence processing cannot constitute evidence to confirm or disconfirm theories of semantic structure. Information about such on-line operations, like introspective information, concerns features of human psychology. Information about errors and reaction times for performance tasks like sentence comprehension thus has the wrong import. It is not about the language. Such information is, therefore, no more relevant to grammar than information about errors and reaction times for tasks like rapid addition is relevant to mathematics. Against competencists like Chomsky, the Platonist would argue, similarly, that data about the speaker-hearer's *knowledge* of the language do not directly confirm or disconfirm specific grammars because such data, too, are about features of human psychology. They are, therefore, no more relevant to grammar than information about what human beings must be presumed to tacitly know to add is relevant to mathematics. We return to some of these matters below.

We now pass from the philosophical positions underlying the present controversy about semantic representation to the particular points at issue in it. FFG's principal claim is that the "analytic approach" now widely practiced by both interpretive and generative semanticists should be abandoned. This approach is a modernized version of the classical theory of definition. Its theoretical objective is to construct a semantic level in generative grammars at which sentences are assigned semantic representations that meet conditions B and C:

(B) Semantic properties and relations of sentences, in particular, their entailment relations, must be definable over semantic representations.

(C) Some syntactically simple lexical items are explicated in semantic representations as having the same semantic structure as syntactically complex phrases of the language.

FFG's claim (p. 517) is that the analytic approach is "inherently unable to account for a variety of pertinent facts about the way in which people understand sentences". They advocate a grammar without a semantic level, coupled with a theory of how people understand sentences in which implication relations are stated exclusively by Carnapian meaning postulates (see Carnap (1956)).

Let me make a few preliminary remarks. Although FFG deal with only a small number of examples, their conclu-

sion expresses a quite general approach to logical structure at the lexical level. Since, moreover, they present no argument to show that the examples they do not deal with can be expected to be like those they do (in the relevant respects), there is, supposing that what they say about their examples is true, the possibility that each approach is preferable for some but not all items.[6] But this possibility is surely the least interesting, because only on the analytic approach or on FFG's do we obtain a uniform treatment of logical structure at the lexical level. Thus, I will confine my discussion to FFG's examples and the criticisms they base on them, assuming, as they do, that these examples are representative.

The validity of these criticisms depends entirely on just what facts are pertinent to semantics. A general line of argument I wish to use in reply to FFG's criticisms of the analytic approach is that the facts they cite are not pertinent because they are "purely experimental", not "internal evidence". My point is that FFG's criticisms, whatever their other deficiencies, will be inconclusive because these facts are pertinent only if A can be established; but performancism has not been shown preferable to competencism and Platonism, and A is unacceptable to both these positions.[7] (On both of them, psychological reality in the sense of A is only a condition on models of the language user.[8])

The facts FFG bring up in their principal criticisms are intended to provide "intuitive evidence" and "experimental evidence" against the analytic approach. I will structure my replies as follows. I will present their claims in turn, following each with a specific criticism of it, and then I will develop some general criticisms against any such claim, which apply equally to the claim about intuitive evidence and to the claim about experimental evidence.

FFG claim that, although the analytic

approach predicts an asymmetry in the complexity of sentences like (1) and (2) — because of the greater decompositional richness of *chase* compared to *catch* — people do not intuitively detect this asymmetry.

(1)   Cats chase mice.

(2)   Cats catch mice.

Judgments based on intuition, they claim (p. 518), disconfirm the predicted complexity order, relative to a criterion like D.

(D)   All other things equal, the relative complexity of a pair of sentences should be a function of the relative complexity of the definitions of the words that the sentence contains.

FFG are unclear about what they are referring to under the term "intuition" in this connection. On the one hand, they might be taken to mean people's notions of the underlying grammatical structure of sentences, i.e. their sense of the structure that structural descriptions explicate formally. If this is what they mean, then their only statement about cases like (1) and (2) or *bachelor* and *unmarried*, namely, "[intuitions] do not appear to support the asymmetries of semantic complexity that definitional theories predict" (p. 519), is rather feeble support for their claim. Clearly, a great number of people have the intuition that the semantic structure of cases like *catch* and *unmarried* is contained in the semantic structure of cases like *chase* and *bachelor*. Otherwise, the cry would have gone up long before this. On the other hand, FFG might be using "intuition" to refer to people's sense of the difficulty of understanding sentences.[9] But, on this analysis, the judgments in question are not judgments about the language; the data that they provide are psychological in import as well as in source.[10] The judgment that a sentence like (1) is as easy to understand as a

sentence like (2) is different from a judgment about English that the sense of *try to catch* is a component of the sense of *chase*. Intuitions about relative difficulty in comprehension are like introspections about one's thoughts, feelings, and imaginings. In *these* cases, people are making claims about their psychological states. This is clear from the fact that judgments about the language are about something objective, while a judgment that a sentence like (1) is as easy to understand as a sentence like (2) is about our subjective experience of the comprehension process. If today I make one judgment about the relative ease of understanding two sentences and tomorrow or a year from now I make the opposite judgment, both can be correct. But, if today I make one judgment about a semantic or syntactic relation between two sentences and at another time I make the opposite judgment, only one can be correct. The compatibility of the judgments in the former case shows that they are about my different psychological states at the times I made the judgments. Therefore, on this analysis, the data that FFG cite to show that people fail to intuit the predicted comprehension asymmetries is irrelevant to the claims of the analytic approach, since the "intuitive evidence" does not bear on its claims about the language.

FFG claim that there is experimental evidence to show that words like *bachelor* and *kill* cannot be handled by the analytic approach. FFG call such words "purely definitional negatives", "PDN", because the analytic approach takes such words to contain negative elements that are unrealized morphologically. PDNs contrast, on the one hand, with cases of "explicitly negative free morphemes", such as *not*, and of "morphological negatives", such as *unhappy* or *impossible*, and on the other hand, with "implicit negatives", such as verbs like *doubt*, *deny*, and *fail*. The important distinguishing feature of implicit negatives is that their "scope exhibits such typical reflexes of negation as *any, much, give a damn,* etc." (pp. 520-521), that is, these negatives involve a special syntactic relation governing their cooccurrence with other constituents.[11]

Although FFG do not present any experimental data to support their claim that, contrary to what the analytic approach holds, PDNs do not contain a negative, they summarize their results. According to their summary, the findings consist of reaction times to correct evaluations of the validity of arguments like (3) and (4) involving PDNs and explicit negative constructions.

(3) If practically all of the men in the room are not married, then few of the men in the room have wives.

(4) If practically all of the men in the room are bachelors, then few of the men in the room have wives.

Comparing reaction times of subjects, it was found that reaction times were faster for sentences with PDNs in them like (4). FFG put their results as follows (p. 522):

> Arguments containing PDNs . . . were significantly easier than the paired arguments containing explicit negatives. Moreover, and most important, the differences between PDNs and explicit negatives was significantly greater than the differences between explicit negatives and either implicit or morphological negatives.

These results, they conclude, constitute evidence against the analytic approach.

This, however, is not the case. Their results are easily explained independently of their hypothesis that words like *bachelor* and *kill* are not analytically defined. We would expect FFG's results simply from the fact that it ought to take longer to perform more syntactic computations than fewer. Thus, (4) ought to be the easier of the two arguments to evaluate because subjects are required to look up three morphemes in the case of

(3), namely, *not, marry,* and ——*ed,* but only two morphemes in the case of (4), namely, *bachelor* and *Plural.* Similarly, we would also expect the morphological negatives and the implicit negatives to line up with the explicit negatives in this contrast, since they, too, require the subject in the experiment to perform more syntactic computation, namely, the extra computation tasks introduced by the special syntactic restrictions that implicit negatives impose on appropriate constituents in their scope. Of course, some examples of sentences with implicit negatives might not have such constituents in their scope, but this ought not to matter insofar as the existence of such special syntactic restrictions will require some extra computation to determine that no appropriate constituent is present. Anyway, the whole matter becomes ethereal, at this point, since we have no notion of the relevant computation time scales, nor even if such examples appeared in the stimulus material that FFG used in their experiment(s).

We now turn to the general criticisms. The first is that their argument based on this intuitive and experimental evidence to show the superiority of their meaning postulate approach over the analytic approach fails because the results, if sound, cut both ways. Both approaches assume that for items like *bachelor* or *chase* there is some fixed number of properties n that constitutes the minimal properties required to determine the class of implications that depend on the item. The meaning postulate approach will represent them by n meaning postulates of the form "$(x)(I_x$ materially implies $E_x)$", where "I" is a lexical item and "E" an expression standing for one of the properties. The analytic approach will represent them by a lexical reading for the item containing n semantic markers, each standing for one of the properties. The number of independent semantic specifications, meaning postulates in the one case and semantic markers in the other, cannot be less than n without the account of logical structure in question being incomplete. Such incompleteness can, of course, occur in accounts based on either approach. Incomplete accounts fail to give an adequate description of the lexical basis for the class of implications. Therefore, on both approaches, accounts of logical structure must provide appropriate semantic specifications for an item like *bachelor* if, and only if, there is an implication between bachelorhood and the absence of a wife. Consequently, assuming that we know that $P_1, \ldots, P_n$ are the appropriate properties for *bachelor*, the formalizations of this knowledge, on accounts under both approaches, contain the same number of semantic specifications. So FFG also have to predict that the reaction times of subjects to (4) are no faster than to (3), since, presumably, there is no reason why the computation of n meaning postulates should take less time than the computation of n semantic markers. Moreover, it does FFG no good to claim that on their account the computation underlying the evaluation of (4) need refer just to the one of the n meaning postulates that relates *bachelor* to *unmarried*, since, on the analytic approach, the computation underlying this evaluation need refer to no more than the one of the n semantic markers in the reading of *bachelor* that relates this word to *unmarried*. Hence, evidence of the kind FFG claim to have found would count equally against their approach.[12]

The second general criticism is that the main assumption that FFG need for claiming that the intuitive judgments and experimental data constitute evidence against the analytic approach is false. It is not the case that semantic representations are required to predict differences in the complexity of senses. The relation of relative complexity of sense is not a *semantic* relation (a relation falling under B). If this is so, then the analytic approach does not have to use semantic representations that can predict asymmetries in sense complexity, and the semantic representations the approach does use can no more be considered deficient for not predicting facts about differences in complexity than they can for not predicting facts about rhyme, intelligence, and elections. The intuitive judgments and experimental data about complexity, if they reveal facts at all, do not reveal *semantic* facts.

The explanation is based on a distinction that has been neglected in linguistics. This is the distinction between *what may be predicted from a formalism at a grammatical level* and *what may be calculated from a formalism at a grammatical level*. For example, the tree representations of the phrase structure of two sentences, say S_1 and S_2, may enable us to calculate that S_1 contains exactly 17,375,031 morphemes more than S_2 or that the ratio of phrases to clauses in S_1 is the same as the ratio of occurrences of *fudge* in S_1 to occurrences of *jelly-beans* in S_2. None of these facts is predicted by these representations. The representations predict such things as that S_1 and S_2 are both well-formed, that they have different subjects, and that S_1 is an interrogative while S_2 is an imperative. The point is that what a formalism for a grammatical level predicts is relative to the grammatical properties and relations defined at that level. The features of the formalism that can be said to predict something are just those that enter into the definitions of these properties and relations. There are, then, a great many relations in the formalism utilized for writing grammars that contribute nothing to their predictive power. What I am claiming is that relative complexity of senses is such an indolent relation.

Let us make this claim more specific.

Suppose that we have semantic representations for *chase* and *catch*, say R_1 and R_2, that are the simplest formalisms that explicate the contribution of the senses of these words to the meanings of the sentences they appear in. Suppose, further, that R_1 represents a more complex sense, that is, R_1 has more component semantic markers than R_2. Even so, the only semantic predictions to which R_1 and R_2 can give rise are ones about the speaker's judgments of synonymy, ambiguity, entailment, anomaly, and other semantic properties and relations. If the relation of relative complexity of sense is not in the set of semantic properties and relations, then nothing that can be calculated about the relative complexity of senses of sentences on the basis of R_1 and R_2 is relevant per se to confirming or disconfirming the hypotheses that R_1 and R_2 express about *chase* and *catch*. Thus, even though we may calculate complexity differences from such semantic representations and compare the calculations with data about the complexity of sentences like (1) and (2), if, as I am claiming, the relation of relative complexity of sense is not one for which semantic representations must account in an optimal grammar, then the results of the comparison are not evidence (pro or con) about the structure of semantic representation.

To establish my claim, or any similar one, there is only one way to argue. It has to be shown that the class of pretheoretically clear cases of the properties and relations for the level does not contain the questioned relation and no legitimate extension of this class does either. Since it is obvious that the class of pretheoretically clear cases of semantic properties and relations contains synonymy, ambiguity, meaningfulness, and entailment but not relative complexity, the issue is now whether there is a legitimate extension of these clear cases that includes relative complexity.

Before trying to show that there is not, we should observe that the discussion already reveals a gap in FFG's argument. Since they have, on their side, given no reason for thinking that relative complexity belongs to some legitimate extension, we have no reason, at this point, for supposing that it does or that it doesn't belong to the set of properties and relations for which semantic representations must account. Hence, no reason now exists for taking FFG's data to be evidence against the analytic approach.

To show that there is no legitimate extension of the pretheoretically clear cases of semantic properties and relations that includes "x is a more complex sense than y", we require a conception of when the addition of a new property or relation to a pretheoretically identified set further articulates the domain and when it leads the science to overstep its boundaries. Fodor (1968, 10) suggests what I think is the right conception, namely, that ". . . a science has to discover what it is about; it does so by discovering that the laws and concepts it produced in order to explain one set of phenomena can be fruitfully applied to phenomena of other sorts as well". On this conception, a science ultimately learns what it has to explain by determining what further phenomena fit the pattern in what it has thus far explained.

What about what a science does *not* have to explain? It is clear that we cannot *logically conclude* from the fact that a new phenomenon does not fit the pattern in what has so far been explained that the phenomenon is outside the domain of the science. But, although what phenomena a science is or is not about cannot be known with certainty, it can be known on the basis of strong enough inductive grounds to decide questions pertaining to the science. We can make the inductive inference that a new phenomenon that fails in principle to fit the explanatory pattern to which the various phenomena in the sample conform is outside the population of phenomena with which the science deals.[13] We are thus led to formulate the principle Z:

(Z) A property or relation K not belonging to the set of clear cases of semantic properties and relations is semantic if, and only if, the definitions of the members of this set enable us to define K.[14]

Assuming that meaningfulness is a semantic property and synonymy is a semantic relation, we can use Z to show that the new property of redundancy, exhibited by (5) but not (6), is also semantic:

(5) naked nude

(6) naked nudist

(7) satisfies the requirement in Z.

(7) A modifier-head construction E is redundant = df. the modifier is meaningful and E is synonymous with the head of the construction by itself.[15]

We can also use Z to argue that the relation of rhyme is nonsemantic: the condition for rhyme is a correspondence of terminal sounds, but the definitions of synonymy, ambiguity, entailment, anomaly, and so on do not refer to phonological representations at all, and consequently, these definitions do not enable us to define rhyme; hence, by Z, rhyme is a nonsemantic relation.

We now show that relative complexity, like rhyme, is nonsemantic. We assume that synonymy, ambiguity, and the other clear cases of semantic properties and relations cited above constitute a fair sample. To meet the requirement in Z, we must be able to use the definitions of these cases to formulate a condition that determines exactly the set of ordered pairs of senses for which the relation "x is a more complex sense than y" holds. It will be possible to formulate such a condition for the proper subset containing related pairs like the senses of bachelor

and male. In such cases, the condition for one sense being more complex than the other is that the former includes but is not included by the other, and the condition for one sense being as complex as the other is just identity. But the extension of "x is a more complex sense than y" contains indefinitely many pairs of senses outside this proper subset. In such cases, neither sense is identical to a component sense of the other, and the apparatus for determining sense inclusion and for identifying instances of the same sense does not enable us to formulate the condition required. To determine the extension of "x is a more complex sense than y" for these cases, it is necessary to go beyond this apparatus by introducing a counter device to compute the components in the formal representation of each sense and to order the senses in terms of complexity on the basis of the computation. The fact that such a device is necessary means that the definitions of the clear cases of synonymy and the other semantic properties and relations do not suffice to define the relation of relative complexity of sense. We can thus infer from Z that the inductive support for the semantic theory in which the definitions of synonymy, ambiguity, etc. have been given is also grounds for thinking that the relation of relative complexity of sense is nonsemantic.

It is instructive to observe that our treatment of relative complexity of sense is parallel to Chomsky's treatment of complexity of center-embedding in a sentence (1965, 10-15). Chomsky points out that the aspects of structural descriptions that define syntactic properties and relations do not suffice to determine differences in the amount of center-embedding that correlate with differences in degree of intelligibility. He argues that in order to make such a determination it would be necessary to go beyond standard syntactic apparatus by introducing a counter device to compute the number of center-embeddings in a sentence and to compare the result of the computation with the result of such a computation for another sentence (or with some constant representing the upper bound on immediate memory if we wish to predict the point of unintelligibility in an absolute sense). ". . . it is clear," Chomsky writes, "that we can characterize unacceptable sentences only in terms of some 'global' property of derivations and the structures they define—a property that is attributable, not to a particular rule, but rather to the way in which the rules interrelate in a derivation" (1965, 12). Chomsky resists the introduction of such novel apparatus into syntactic theory and chooses instead to take the characterization of unacceptable sentences to fall outside grammar. To handle such unintelligibility as a case of ungrammaticality would require a radical change in the grammar, but by distinguishing the competence property of grammaticality from the performance property of acceptability, it is possible to avoid such a change and provide a natural explanation of unintelligibility phenomena in terms of hypotheses about the procedures that a language user employs in syntactic recognition.

The close parallel between our reasons for refusing to grant relative complexity of sense the status of a grammatical relation at the semantic level and Chomsky's reasons for not granting relative complexity of center-embedding the status of a grammatical relation at the syntactic level provides further grounds for thinking that relative complexity is nonsemantic.

In our preliminary remarks, prior to examining FFG's claims to have contrary evidence to the analytic approach, we pointed out that, without A, no relation is established between their data and semantic representations, so that such data do not count as contrary evidence.[16] FFG consider the response to their argument that A be abandoned. Abandoning A,

they say, "amounts to weakening the empirical conditions by which grammars have usually been constrained" (p. 522). This is a strange reply, in light of the fact that the empirical conditions by which grammars have usually been constrained do not include A, and for very much the reasons Fodor and Garrett give in the initial quotation from their "Some Reflections on Competence and Performance". Moreover, experiments designed to elucidate the role of transformations in the processing of sentences have, over a number of years, produced results indicating that grammatical transformations are not psychologically real in the sense of A.[17] Nonetheless, most linguists and psycholinguists, including Fodor, Bever, and Garrett,[18] have interpreted these results as bearing only on the performance system. No one, to my knowledge, has argued that these results motivate a return to the taxonomic theory of grammar.[19]

It is, of course, true to say that the empirical conditions by which grammars have usually been constrained include R, so the strangeness of FFG's reply might be explained by a conflation of A with R.

FFG could advocate that A ought to be adopted as a further condition on grammars, even though A is not such a condition at present. They might argue that such a new condition should be especially welcome now that linguists are coming to appreciate that grammars are far too loosely constrained in the metatheory. Although further restrictions on the class of possible grammars would be a significant addition to the present metatheory, we do not want to accept a condition as such a restriction unless it is legitimately a *grammatical* constraint. Thus, there exists the logically prior question of whether A is a grammatical constraint or (as I have tried to show above) simply a constraint on performance models. This question must be appropriately settled in order to establish that A ought to be adopted as a new condition on grammars. Hence, the reply under consideration begs the question.

FFG also argue that anyone who abandons A ". . . owes us an account of what is at issue between competing claims about the structural descriptions of sentences, and how, even in principle, such claims can be resolved" (p. 523). This reply is based on the false presumption that A contributes significantly to the basis on which linguists decide what is at issue between competing claims about structural descriptions and about how to choose among them. After all, if A is merely a condition on performance theories, then rejecting A as a condition on competence theories would create no such obligation. The reply begs the question at issue.

What is at issue in competing claims about structural descriptions and the criterion for deciding which, if any, are right is, I think, clear independently of A and even of R. The issue between such competing claims is the nature of a particular natural language — whether, for example, it is transformational, contains a case system like some other language, has an underlying SVO syntactic structure, relates meanings using only syntactic information in the deep structure of a sentence, and so on. The criterion for choosing one claim over another is the holistic principle that we choose the claim whose incorporation into our present best system of grammatical rules brings the system closest to being an optimal grammar of the language, where a grammar is optimal for a language if, and only if, the grammar is the simplest (or among the simplest) formal system(s) that predicts and explains each grammatical property and relation of every sentence in the language. Equally simple predictively and explanatorily equivalent grammars are *notational variants* in linguistics because they make exactly the same claims about the nature of the language. This criterion

permits linguists to choose freely among grammars that are notational variants.

Taking this line of thought a step further, we can argue that linguists are better off without A as part of their criterion for choosing grammars.[20] If linguists were saddled with A, their account of a natural language, say English, would have to reflect the idiosyncratic features of the speech production and comprehension mechanisms of human English speakers. Then, if there were creatures, Martians or perhaps porpoises, with sufficiently different speech production and comprehension mechanisms, but with whom we could communicate in English as easily as with any human English speaker, we would have to make the absurd claim that they do not speak English. Even though an optimal grammar of their language based on the above-mentioned criterion might be the same (or a notational variant) of the optimal grammar for human English speakers, the radical differences in processing mechanisms would force linguists saddled with A to deny that these creatures speak English. To bring the absurdity out more starkly, note that it could turn out that human beings whom we presently suppose to speak English, say Australians, have processing mechanisms as different from ours as these creatures we have been imagining. Would we want to say then that Australians are not speakers of English?

FFG end their article with some considerations that they think support their meaning postulate approach over the analytic approach. I shall conclude this article with an examination of these considerations, showing that none offers such support. Their first consideration is that ". . . no a priori reason exists for drawing the line between comprehension and inference at the point that A-C specify rather than at some other point" (p. 525). As a claim about performance, this is true but hardly exciting. It is hard to imagine how one could decide a priori which aspects of the on-line processing of sentences in speech comprehension are a matter of recovering semantic representations and which a matter of inference. But, as a claim about competence, it is both interesting and false. Its interest stems from the fact that, if true, the claim provides grounds for preferring the apparatus of meaning postulates over the apparatus of semantic representations for grammars. The former apparatus treats implications like (8) and (9) uniformly, while the latter does not.

(8)   If John is a bachelor, then John is male.

(9)   If John is a bachelor, then John is a bachelor or a fool.

Therefore, if there is no distinction between meaning and inference, such that the implication (8) holds solely by virtue of meaning but (9) holds by virtue of meaning and the inference principle p materially implies $p \lor q$, meaning postulates provide a more appropriate formalism.

It is peculiar for FFG to put their claim in the form of so flat and categorical a denial: Wittgenstein and other contemporary philosophers have argued plausibly enough on behalf of such a distinction for the entire issue to be controversial; see for example Wittgenstein (1974, 247-249). FFG neither explain why they do not count such arguments as a priori reasons nor do they offer arguments of their own against the distinction. Thus, this first consideration provides no support for the meaning postulate approach.

On the other hand, if there is a distinction between implications that rest only on definitions of words and implications that also require certain principles to be truths of logic, their claim is false and semantic representations provide the more appropriate formalism. Elsewhere, I have presented an argument establishing just this (see Katz (1977a)). I will try to

convey the crux of the argument. The question is whether there are nondefinitional implications involving expressions in the so-called "extralogical" vocabulary of a natural language. The notion of a definitional implication is that of an implication that holds *solely* in virtue of the logical form or meaning of the sentences, where a semantic specification about the logical form or meaning of a sentence is warranted just in case it is required as the basis on which to explain one of its implications or one of its semantic properties or relations. The implication of (11) by (10) is nondefinitional.

(10)   Sue is smarter than Moe and Moe is smarter than Lem.

(11)   Sue is smarter than Lem.

Even if we take the meaning postulate (12) to be a semantic specification about the logical form or meaning of the comparative in these sentences, the implication (10) materially implies (11) is not definitional.

(12) $(x)(y)(z)(($smarter than$_{x,y}$ & smarter than$_{y,z}$) materially implies (smarter than$_{x,z}$))

On inspection, one can see that there is nothing in the premise (10) solely in virtue of which the implication holds: (10) is a conjunction whose first conjunct compares the intelligence of Sue and Moe and whose second, and only other, conjunct compares the intelligence of Moe and Lem. No part of the logical form of (10) compares the intelligence of Sue and Lem. The individual constants *Sue* and *Lem* do not appear as coarguments of a predicate in (10) unless we take part of the logical form of (10) to be (12) instantiated with *Sue* for x, *Moe* for y, and *Lem* for z. But, even then, the implication of (11) by (10) cannot be established to hold without applying modus ponens to detach the consequent "smarter than$_{Sue, Lem}$". Therefore, the implication holds partly in virtue of the principle modus ponens being a truth of logic, and so not *solely* in virtue of the logical form or meaning of the sentences (10) and (11).

Thus, this implication contrasts with definitional implications like that of *John is male* by *John is a bachelor*, and the existence of such contrasting cases shows that there is an a priori reason for drawing the line between meaning relations and logical connection at the point B and C specify. The argument, which I am trying to convey the gist of here, shows that systems of meaning postulates, because they provide an account of implications based exclusively on meaning relations, which is continuous with implications based on logical connections (such as the implication of (11) by (10)), fail minimum conditions of adequacy on an appropriate formalism for describing meaning in natural language, whereas systems of semantic representations, because they provide an account of implications based exclusively on meaning relations, which is discontinuous with implications based on logical connections, easily satisfy these conditions of adequacy.[21]

The fact that FFG, on principle, do not distinguish between meaning and implication creates a serious difficulty for their position. Logically speaking, each sentence has an infinite number of implications, and hence, in order to avoid the absurd consequence that, on their position, the comprehension of a sentence never ends, FFG have to draw some sort of line between comprehension and inference. Since they cannot consistently draw this line at the natural point between processing that concerns only components of the meaning of a sentence and processing that also concerns laws of logic, it is hard to see how they can avoid making ad hoc stipulations (e.g. specifying a numerical upper limit on the implications computed, say as a function of time, task complexity, etc.). Without such an ad hoc stipulation, they will be committed to the embarrassing claim that no sentence is ever fully understood, but, with such a stipulation, they will be committed to a claim whose only recommendation is that it saves them from a more embarrassing one.

FFG's next consideration in favor of the meaning postulate approach is that meaning postulates might help solve the puzzle about how people manage to understand utterances as fast as they do (p. 526). FFG hypothesize that what has to be recovered in speech comprehension reflects meaning postulates expressed in a primitive vocabulary where there is a predicate for each surface content word. On this hypothesis, they propose to account for the speed of human sentence recognition in terms of the relatively light computational load "on processes that must be assumed to be on-line" (p. 526).

This account provides no support for the meaning postulate approach because its explanation of the speed with which people understand speech does not really require the assumption that lexical information is stated in meaning postulates. Rather, the critical assumption of the explanation is that the information recovered in understanding sentences is very close in form to the content words in the surface structure of the sentences. To bring this point home, I want to embody this assumption in semantic representations. Imagine, contrary to what the analytic approach has always claimed about predicate structure on the basis of empirical evidence, that the dictionary is set up in accord with this critical assumption about the relation between the formalism for predicates in semantic representations and surface content words. Then, the representations accessed in speech comprehension will contain few semantic markers, each corresponding fairly directly to surface constituents, and accordingly, we obtain the same explanation, in terms of a light computational load, for the speed with which people can understand utterances. Furthermore, the meaning postulate approach, correspondingly, can abandon the critical assumption. We can imagine a system of meaning postulates built out of a vocabulary of predicates that are extremely different in form from surface content words. Such a system could no longer explain the speed of sentence comprehension in terms of the small number of computations required to recover the semantic information. Meaning postulates are not essential in the explanation of the speed of sentence comprehension.

Even assuming that meaning postulates are somehow essential, still, there is no basis for FFG to claim that their position on the existence of a level of semantic representation in grammars is supported by such an explanation of the facts about speed of comprehension. For a parallel explanation of these facts is available without elimination of the level of semantic representation and without changing it in any substantive way. What is required is nothing more than what Bever (1970) has already proposed as an explanation of the speed with which humans process the syntactic structure of utterances.[22] Bever imagines coupling a syntactic component generating standard structural descriptions with a performance model containing *perceptual strategies* for expediting the recognition of constituent structure. Similarly, we can hypothesize coupling a semantic component generating standard semantic representations with a performance model containing meaning postulates, perhaps of the kind FFG propose, to expedite the recovery of logical structure. With meaning postulates framed in accord with the critical assumption that function as "strategies" at the semantic stage of speech processing, we obtain an equally good explanation of the speed of comprehension.

FFG's last consideration to support their meaning postulate approach is that ". . . it seems clear that even if we do have

definitions in our grammar, meaning postulates are still indispensable" (p. 526). One argument they give for this claim is the following: "For, as has been widely recognized, there will almost certainly be residual inferences that turn on 'content' words even after the process of definitional decomposition has gone through" (p. 526). There is an ambiguity here. It is widely recognized that present attempts to describe the semantic structure of words like *cause, kill, chase,* etc. have left a residue of inferences unaccounted for. This, however, is irrelevant because the residue might exist only because such attempts are not so far fully successful (though ultimately they will be). The other possible interpretation of their claim is that, even if the attempts to describe the semantic structure of such words have gone as far as they can go, so that the descriptions are complete from the semantic point of view, there is a residue of unexplained inferences. Now, although it is not widely recognized, I would be prepared to grant that this could happen if the residual inferences remain unexplained because they rest on more than meaning. That is, like the inference from (10) to (11), an appeal to the laws of logic must be made to account for these inferences. Thus, the issue here is the same as the earlier issue of whether there is a distinction between implications that rest only on definitions of words and implications that also require certain principles to be truths of logic. If there is such a distinction, then the fact that a complete semantic description of the vocabulary of the language leaves some inferences unexplained is all the reason needed to count these inferences as logical rather than semantic, and hence the fact that they are left unexplained is irrelevant to semantic representation. Finally, it is not widely recognized and I certainly would not grant that a *complete* semantic description could leave inferences that are semantic, not logical, unexplained. Since a complete semantic description of a set of words is one that predicts and explains their contribution to the semantic properties and relations, including entailments, of every sentence in which they appear, this situation is impossible.

Another argument FFG offer for the indispensability of meaning postulates is that ". . . all theories which embrace A-C that have so far been proposed do employ meaning postulates under one guise or other" (p. 527). FFG go on to claim that "In Katz's work, for example, they appear as 'redundancy rules'" (p. 527). We will show that this latter claim is false and therefore that meaning postulates are dispensable in semantic description.

A closer look at meaning postulates and redundancy rules shows unequivocally that these are quite different principles. Carnap introduced meaning postulates to fill a gap in his account of the intensions of expressions in first order languages. Two expressions have the same intension, in Carnap's (1956) use of the term, just in case they are assigned the same extension in each state-description. Carnap realized that such intensions offer no treatment of meaning and synonymy, and consequently, he introduced meaning postulates so that he could redefine the notion of the intension of an expression in terms of the extensions of the expression assigned in those state-descriptions under which all the meaning postulates are true. Meaning postulates thus enable us to handle sentences like (8) in a fashion exactly parallel to logical truths like (9): they come out, in an appropriately formulated formalized language, to be L-truths. Meaning postulates allow the author of such a language to reflect hypotheses about the meaning relations between expressions as necessary connections between their extensions, relative to the formalized language.

Redundancy rules were introduced not to fill such a gap, but to make statements about relations between terms

in the vocabulary of semantic theory that enable us to abbreviate lexical readings in an empirically adequate dictionary. We write such abbreviatory rules in the manner of (13).

(13) $(M_1), (M_2), \ldots, (Artifact), \ldots, (M_n)$ should be rewritten as $(M_1), (M_2), \ldots, (Artifact), \ldots, (M_n),$ (Physical Object)

[*Editor's note*: In this chapter only, "should be rewritten as" is used instead of the rewrite arrow.] Redundancy rules express an invariance over lexical readings. The symbols in such rules are metasymbols referring to the semantic markers in the basic vocabulary of semantic representation. In (13), the invariance is that every lexical reading that contains the semantic marker "(Artifact)" also contains the semantic marker "(Physical Object)". (13) makes the latter marker predictable. The function of redundancy rules like (13) is to make it unnecessary for the semantic marker "(Physical Object)" to appear in any lexical reading having the semantic marker "(Artifact)". In capitalizing on invariances in this way, redundancy rules effect an enormous economy over the dictionary as a whole.

Since redundancy rules supply the predictable semantic markers in the process of semantic interpretation, they can be taken as part of the projection rule. They apply as soon as lexical readings from the dictionary (in compressed form) are assigned to occurrences of lexical items in phrase markers undergoing semantic interpretation. At this stage, they supply the lexically omitted semantic markers, whose presence will now be required to determine which of the selection restrictions involved in the semantic interpretation process are satisfied.[23] Formally, then, redundancy rules are instructions about how to expand readings in abbreviated form, in which the arrow is the rewriting instruction. The rule (13) thus says to rewrite readings having the form represented by the schema on the lefthand side of the arrow as readings having the form represented by the schema on the righthand side (Katz (1972, 44-47)).

It follows from these explanations that redundancy rules are not meaning postulates. Meaning postulates make claims about the extensions of expressions; they make claims about what are possible and impossible states of affairs. Redundancy rules make no such claims. The meaning postulate (14)

(14) $(x)(A_x$ materially implies $PO_x)$

makes the claim that the extension of the expression *artifact* is included in the extension of the expression *physical object*, whereas the redundancy rule (13) makes a claim, not about the sets of things to which *artifact* and *physical object* refer, but about semantic derivations in some grammar. Because the symbols in redundancy rules refer to semantic markers in readings, these rules express an obligatory operation in semantic interpretation, and hence they embody a claim about the nature of the derivation that takes us from the first to the second stage of the projection process.

One further significant difference between meaning postulates and redundancy rules is that the latter, being mere abbreviatory devices, can be wholly eliminated from the theory of a language without loss of descriptive power. The description of its semantic structure becomes a great deal less economical, but no less true. In contrast, meaning postulates cannot be eliminated from the theory of a language without loss in its descriptive power. Theories using meaning postulates rely on them, as we indicated above, to fill exactly the gap for which Carnap first proposed them.

FFG end by offering an explanation of why semantics is in such a controversial and unsettled state. Their explanation is that its practitioners have set themselves a mistaken goal, namely, the discovery of semantic representations. "Perhaps," they suggest (p. 530), "the reason that semantic representations have proved to be so elusive is simply that, after all, there aren't any." It seems incumbent on me, having reached the conclusion that FFG are wrong about the existence of semantic representations, to end this article with an alternative explanation of why semantics is not better off.

I think semantics is at present in the state it is in for essentially three reasons. First, the semantic structure of natural languages is extremely complex and the attempt to describe it formally (i.e. within generative grammar) began only very recently. Second, this attempt began in a climate of intense hostility and skepticism about the value of the notion of meaning. This climate existed both in linguistics, as the result of Bloomfield's work, and in philosophy, as the result of Quine's. The effort to clear the notion of meaning of the stigma of occultism is, at least in philosophy, still underway. Third, aspects of the extensionalist position underlying this skepticism about meaning exert a strong influence on the work even of those linguists and philosophers who are no longer inhibited from addressing themselves to questions of meaning. These linguists and philosophers, principally Carnap and his followers, continue to assume that the old familiar postulational apparatus of applied predicate calculi is perfectly adequate to handle anything new that might be discovered about the semantic structure of natural language. Even though such apparatus was devised especially for the limited vocabulary of the so-called logical words, it is presumed adequate for describing logical form over the entire range of nouns, adjectives, verbs, etc. in natural languages.[24] This assumption does not, of course, prevent these linguists and philosophers from attempting to describe the semantic basis of implications that turn on so-called extralogical words, but it strongly influences the character of the descriptions by favoring ones that take the same form as the customary descriptions of implications that turn on truth-functional connectives and other logical words. The effect of this influence is to be found in compromises with intensionalist goals, for example, in FFG's failure to distinguish semantic entailment from logical implication, and in the strange bedfellows it makes, for example, in FFG's appeal to arguments of extensionalists like Quine and Putnam against analyticity (p. 524).[25] In my opinion, this third factor is the most important: the greatest single obstacle at present to progress in semantics is the use of extensionalist apparatus to carry out the intensionalist program of describing meaning in natural language. Revealing semantic descriptions will stop being so elusive when linguists and philosophers start to recognize that the complex semantic structure of natural languages cannot be described by the simple apparatus devised for the limited vocabulary of logical words.[26], [27]

Notes

1. Fodor, Fodor, and Garrett (1975). Henceforth I will refer to these authors by the designation "FFG" and will cite this article by page number only.

2. I will discuss this somewhat more below, and in much greater detail in another paper; see Katz (1980). Here I should make clear that I use *predict* in the sense that a grammar G predicts that a sentence S has the property or relation R just in case linguistic theory defines R as a grammatical property or relation and the structural description of S in G together with the definition of R implies that S has R. Also, I should make clear that I use *explain* in a sense close to that used in other sciences. Roughly, to explain something is to provide an account of the underlying conditions that show how or why it happens. For example, it was always puzzling to me why *flammable* and *inflammable* are synonymous rather than antonymous (e.g. express the same

warning). The explanation, as I learned, is that their derivations are different: *flammable* is an adjective formed from the noun *flame*, while *inflammable* is an adjective formed from the verb *inflame*, so *in* is not a negative prefix.

3. This, of course, is not to deny that performance theories, too, involve idealization, but to make clear that the idealizations are carried out with respect to different sets of properties and relations in the two theories.

4. I try to develop a tenable version of the Platonist position in Katz (1980).

5. See the discussion of this distinction in Dretske (1974).

6. I am indebted to one of the referees for raising this possibility.

7. The only other motivation FFG offer for A is their claim that if grammars contain a level meeting B and C, then "it would be distinctly strange" if that level does not also meet A (p. 517). But this experience of strangeness is one that can only be had within the framework of performancism. Within competencism, there is nothing strange about a level meeting B and C but not A. Since on this position grammars are about competence, it is an independent question how much of the information in the representations of sentences at the semantic level plays a role in "the comprehension of sentences" and in "other psychological states and computations". This is a psycholinguistic, not a linguistic, question: it is the task of the independent discipline of psycholinguistics to find the answer on the basis of experimental manipulation of performance variables. Moreover, this has been the received view since the early days of psycholinguistics. Chomsky and Miller (1963) set the question of what aspects of the grammar's account of competence can be shown to have psychological reality, and they offered the first hypothesis about this, namely, that the grammar as a whole is represented in the performance model.

8. Fodor, Fodor, and Garrett say something like this in claiming of A that "This condition is presumably the weakest that a grammar can satisfy if it is to contribute to a psychological model of the speaker/hearer at all" (p. 516). The claim that A is the weakest such condition is, however, false. We might reasonably require only that some portion of semantic representations in the grammar be

psychologically real in their sense, and we might leave it to further research in linguistics and psycholinguistics to discover what portion it is. This research would be a matter of working out a criterion for saying that a particular psychological model is a theory of the use of a particular language, in terms of the information in the structural descriptions of sentences that is experimentally found to have psychological reality in the on-line sense.

9. I am not happy about this interpretation, but I feel forced to it by the fact that Fodor, Fodor, and Garrett's claims on the other interpretation simply take no notice of the obvious, and crushing, replies. In the case of their first claim that intuitions of relative complexity "do not appear to support the asymmetries of semantic complexity that definitional theories predict", as mentioned in the text, there is the plethora of intuitive evidence accumulated over the years in linguistic discussions of *bachelor, broke, chase,* and other overworked examples. In the case of their claim about the Russellian prediction that sentences with definite articles like *The man hit the ball* ought to be more complex than sentences with indefinite articles like *A man hit a ball,* namely, "Patently, intuition does not support any such differences in complexity" (p. 519), there is the reply that Russell's eliminative definition of *the* is a funny case to foist on intensionalists, since it offers not an analysis of the meaning of *the* but only sentences without *the* that will be true and false under the same conditions as sentences with *the.* Fodor, Fodor, and Garrett might have made their point more forcefully by comparing *There is one god* with *There are a billion people.*

10. I owe this insight to Virginia Valian.

11. It ought to be observed, too, that inclusion of the so-called implicit negatives is not as uncontroversial as Fodor, Fodor, and Garrett lead us to think. Jespersen says: "There seem to be words with inherent negative meaning though positive in form: compare pairs like *absent: present, fail: succeed.* But though we naturally look upon the former in each of these pairs as the negative (*fail = not succeed*), nothing hinders us from logically inverting the order (*succeed = not fail*). These words, therefore, cannot properly be classed with such formally negative words as *unhappy,*

etc." See Jespersen (1917, 42). Klima (1964, 315) cites the fact that *fail, doubt,* and other implicit negatives exhibit the typical reflexes of negation as evidence against Jespersen, but, although this is evidence of a syntactic relation between such verbs and occurrences of indefinites, *much less* constructions, etc., in their scope, it is not clear whether it counts against Jespersen's semantic claim.

12. I owe this point to a suggestion from Scott Soames.

13. We are dealing here with what Reichenbach calls "second and higher level" inductive inferences. See Reichenbach (1938, 363-373) and Reichenbach (1949, 311-333).

14. The skeptic about meaning often misses the fact that the principle Z or something like it is an integral part of the explication undertaken in the construction of a semantic theory. See Katz (1975).

15. I owe the idea for the definition to Fred M. Katz.

16. There is, for example, no prediction from the grammar as to which sentences in pairs like (3) and (4) ought to be easier for subjects to identify as a valid argument. The reaction time data are thus not inconsistent with the analytic approach, so much as irrelevant to it.

17. There is a large literature, but see, for instance, Fodor and Garrett (1967). The statement in the text requires qualification on the basis of the very recent evidence for a version of the derivational theory of complexity in Valian and Wales (1976).

18. See the paper cited in the previous footnote, and also Fodor, Bever, and Garrett (1974, 221-372).

19. These authors accept the conception of grammars as theories of competence rather than performance: although they argue that structural descriptions rather than grammatical operations, i.e. transformations, are psychologically real, they do not take the experimental evidence to show that there are no transformations in the grammar of English.

20. A fuller development of this argument is found elsewhere (see Katz (1980)), where it is applied to R also.

21. Katz (1977a) shows that the argument in Katz and Nagel (1974) is wrong in its claim that theories of grammar using meaning postulates are simply notational variants of

theories using semantic markers and readings. Fodor, Fodor, and Garrett's footnote 9 (p. 526) is correct in what it says under cases (a) and (b). What it says under cases (c) and (d), however, involves assumption A, which does not enter into the comparison that Nagel and I made.

22. One example of such strategies is the one Bever calls "strategy E'," which says that it is heuristically desirable to close a noun phrase after the first noun following the determiner unless that noun is followed by a relative pronoun (pp. 322-326). Such a strategy imposes the correct constituent structure on expressions like *the pencil fell . . .* , *the nice pencil broke . . .* , *the very nice pencil broke . . .* , and *the very nice pencil that fell broke . . . .* It will, of course, fail to impose the correct constituent structure on expressions like *the plastic pencil fell . . .* because the lexicon marks *plastic* as a noun as well as an adjective. Bever suggests that the strategy might be restated to incorporate a scale of the degree of "noun-likeness" of adjectives in the sense of Vendler (1963). But, as a heuristic, such strategies must make some mistakes if they are to achieve the advantage of fast recognition of constituent structure. Thus, they are required to be coupled with a *fail-proof procedure* that contains a criterion that determines the true constituent structure of noun phrases in the language. Thus, such strategies presuppose the grammar's account of the syntactic structure of constituents, and accordingly, we may say that meaning postulates understood as semantic strategies presuppose the grammar's account of the semantic structure of constituents, which, of course, may take the form of semantic markers and readings.

23. Another interpretation is also possible insofar as the selection restrictions can be defined over the set of redundancy rules as well as the readings assigned to constituents, but it makes such rules, if anything, even more different from meaning postulates.

24. See Katz (1977a), Katz (1977b).

25. The reply to Putnam's arguments that scientific advances can lead us to abandon analytic statements can be found in Katz (1977c).

26. See Katz (1977a), Katz (1977b).

27. I wish to thank Virginia Valian for her extensive help with matters of both form and content. I also want to thank Ned Block for comments on an earlier draft.

References

Bever, T. G. (1970) "The Cognitive Basis for Linguistic Structures," in J. R. Hayes, ed., *Cognition and Language Learning*, Wiley, New York.

Carnap, R. (1956) "Meaning Postulates," in *Meaning and Necessity*, enlarged edition, University of Chicago Press, Chicago.

Chomsky, N. (1965) *Aspects of the Theory of Syntax*, MIT Press, Cambridge, Massachusetts.

Dretske, F. I. (1974) "Postscript" to "Explanation in Linguistics," in D. Cohen, ed., *Explaining Linguistic Phenomena*, Hemisphere, Washington, D.C.

Fodor, J. A. (1968) *Psychological Explanation*, Random House, New York.

Fodor, J. A., T. G. Bever, and M. F. Garrett (1974) *The Psychology of Language*, McGraw-Hill, New York.

Fodor, J. A. and M. F. Garrett (1966) "Some Reflections on Competence and Performance," in J. Lyons and R. Wales, eds., *Psycholinguistic Papers*, Edinburgh University Press, Edinburgh.

Fodor, J. A. and M. F. Garrett (1967) "Some Syntactic Determinants of Sentential Complexity," *Perception and Psychophysics*, 289-296.

Fodor, J. D., J. A. Fodor, and M. F. Garrett (1975) "The Psychological Unreality of Semantic Representations," *Linguistic Inquiry* 6.4, 515-532.

Jespersen, O. (1917) *Negation in English and Other Languages*, Copenhagen.

Katz, J. J. (1964) "Mentalism in Linguistics," *Language* 40.2.

Katz, J. J. (1972) *Semantic Theory*, Harper and Row, New York.

Katz, J. J. (1975) "Exorcising Skepticism," *Philosophical Studies* 33, 83-89.

Katz, J. J. (1977a) "The Advantage of Semantic Theory over Predicate Calculus in the Representation of Logical Form in Natural Language," in R. B. Marcus, ed., *New Directions in Semantics* (*The Monist* Vol. 60).

Katz, J. J. (1977b) *Propositional Structure and Illocutionary Force*, T. Y. Crowell, New York.

Katz, J. J. (1977c) "A Proper Theory of Names," *Philosophical Studies* 31, 1-80.

Katz, J. J. (1980) *Language and Other Abstract Objects*, Roman and Littlefield, Totowa, 1980

Katz, J. J. and R. I. Nagel (1974) "Meaning Postulates and Semantic Theory," *Foundations of Language* 2, 311-340.

Klima, E. (1964) "Negation in English," in J. A. Fodor and J. J. Katz, eds., *The Structure of Language: Readings in the Philosophy of Language*, Prentice-Hall, Englewood Cliffs, New Jersey.

Miller, G. A. and N. Chomsky (1963) "Finitary Models of Language Users," in R. D. Luce, R. Bush, and E. Galanter, eds., *Handbook of Mathematical Psychology*, John Wiley, New York.

Reichenbach, H. (1938) *Experience and Prediction*, University of Chicago Press, Chicago.

Reichenbach, H. (1949) *The Theory of Probability*, University of California Press, Berkeley.

Valian, V. V. and R. Wales (1976) "What's What: Talkers Help Listeners Hear and Understand by Clarifying Sentential Relations," *Cognition* 4.2, 155-176.

Vendler, Z. (1963) *Adjectives and Nominalizations*, Mouton, The Hague.

Wittgenstein, L. (1974) *Philosophical Grammar*, University of California Press, Berkeley.

Part Four

Innate Ideas

Introduction: What Is Innateness?

Ned Block

No organism can learn without a mechanism that accomplishes this learning. Hence at least one learning mechanism must be innate (if only a mechanism for acquiring other learning mechanisms). Although this is not a deductively valid argument (since it remains logically possible that learning mechanisms are inserted at birth by one's fairy godmother), it is nonetheless empirically persuasive, since there is no plausible alternative to an innate learning mechanism. Even Skinnerian behaviorists must (and often do) allow that there is an innate learning mechanism—one that causes the strength of a response to increase when the response is reinforced.[1] Without postulating such a mechanism, behaviorists would have no way of accounting for the alteration of behavior by reinforcement. According to *cognitive* theorists, learning mechanisms embody learning principles, and a commitment to innate learning mechanisms is normally a commitment to innate learning principles. Much of the debate about nativism with respect to language has focused not on the existence of such innate principles or strategies, but rather on their nature. The nativist view defended here by Chomsky, Katz, and Fodor, Bever, and Garrett argue that these principles contain very detailed information about language (including, according to Chomsky, principles of universal grammar) and hence that the principles underlying the acquisition of language are likely to be special to the domain of language. Antinativists such as Hilary Putnam argue that the facts of language learning can be accommodated by the hypothesis that language is acquired by general learning principles (themselves innate) of the sort that enable us to learn science, games, and everything else.

This issue is broadly empirical in nature. Both sides are willing to use a rough and ready notion of innateness (though Putnam expresses some doubts in chapter 15, but not in chapter 19). Both sides talk about roughly the same range of facts (though there are disagreements about some of them): mistakes children do *not* make; the linguistic accomplishments of chimpanzees; the fact that children learn language in a few years on the basis of degenerate evidence at a time when their capacities to learn other subject matters is limited; the existence of language "universals." But each side claims the facts are better accommodated by its theory.

The reader may wonder why the issue just described counts as *philosophical*. After all, questions about what the data are and what theory best explains them are normally left to scientists. The answer is that this issue, like many others discussed under the heading of "philosophy of psychology" is not easily pigeonholed either as science or as philosophy. Discussing it requires skills and knowledge of both sorts. As a matter of sociological fact, many such issues in the hard sciences tend to be discussed mainly by scientists, simply because philosophers rarely have the requisite scientific competence. But there are reasons why philosophers ought to have as much interest in such issues as do scientists. First, it is a typically philosophical matter to decide whether the concept of innateness is clear enough to allow meaningful empirical debate. Putnam and Chomsky apparently think it is, but other philosophers (Nelson Goodman, for example) would disagree. Second, both the nativist and the antinativist positions are somewhat speculative at this stage. My point is not that it is the business of philosophers to speculate, but rather that as the "distance" between theory and evidence increases, deciding what theory best explains the data increasingly involves complex and subtle reasoning of the sort philosophers are trained in. Third, the issues involved in adjudicating between the nativist and antinativist positions connect with partly empirical, partly conceptual issues of *other sciences*. For example, Putnam and Chomsky appeal to the nature of a semantic theory and conceptual issues having to do with evolution. A multiscientific issue is no less *scientific*, but it does fall in the domain of those who study *many* sciences.

In the remainder of this introduction, I shall briefly discuss one issue that, surprising as it may seem, is left untouched by most of the philosophical literature on innateness: what innateness *is*. The reader would not go wrong if he understood the authors of the chapters in this part as taking the content of knowledge or capacities to be innate just in case the knowledge and capacities are represented in and determined by the genes, rather than learned or otherwise determined by the environment. This suggestion is of some use, but its utility is limited by the fact that each of its central notions is itself in need of clarification.

The most obviously problematic notion is representation of information in the genes. Information can be represented in books and in the mind, although some philosophers will balk at the idea of nonconscious mental representation that looms so large in part four, "Mental Representation." Representation of information in the genes is yet more problematic. Further, the idea of genetic representation itself involves the as yet unexplicated notion of *genetic determination*. If an explosion produced a clump of molecules that happened, by a cosmic coincidence, to be identical in molecular structure to a human gene, the clump would not represent any knowledge solely in virtue of this molecular structure. After all, any pebble on the beach is a "gene" for some logically possible creature. If genes represent information, they do so in virtue of their causal role in determining characteristics of the creatures who *have* the genes. So if we want to say what it is for genes to represent information, we shall have to say what genetic determination is. Saying what learning is would raise similar problems, since we would have to explicate the difference in mechanisms of environmental determination that distinguish learning from other types of environmental determination of information—for instance, Fodor's Latin pill (Fodor, 1976).

The most obvious way to characterize genetic determination is to state that a characteristic is genetically determined just in case it is caused by features or states of the genes. There is a problem with such senses of genetic determination, however: it can plausibly be argued that every human characteristic is *both* genetically *and* environmentally determined. An environment without genes would produce no human characteristics, and genes without an appropriate environment would produce no human characteristics, either. Further, each of my characteristics (at least each of my distinctively human characteristics) is such that some difference in my genes would have produced an individual without that characteristic. And the same differences could have been produced by differences in my womb (or later) environment. Appropriate chemical or surgical intervention in the womb can, in principle, cause any sort of change that a genetic difference can cause. For example, had my genes been different, I might have had no arms; the same result might have been produced by an environmental difference (such as a drug like Thalidomide). So in an important sense, all human characteristics are caused both by genes and by the environment. A sense of 'genetically determined' in which some characteristics are genetically determined and *not* environmentally determined remains to be explicated.

Of course, we commonly single out *one* of a number of causal contributions as "the cause," and it may be that the way to go about explicating genetic determination is to rely on this commonsense notion of "the cause." Along these lines, we would say that a characteristic is genetically determined just in case "the cause" is some feature or state of the genes. However, such notions of causation are notoriously pragmatic, so the result would be a pragmatic conception of innateness.

While much work needs to be done to give a satisfactory account of innateness, it would be a mistake to conclude that no sense can be made of par-

ticular questions of whether this or that is innate. For example, newborns less than one minute old turn their heads in the direction of a sound. It is hard to imagine how the capacity to coordinate movements with sounds could have been learned in the womb or in the one minute of life outside it, so it seems likely that this capacity is innate according to any reasonable analysis of innateness. More strikingly, Bower (1977) has shown that newborns are startled when they swipe at a virtual image (an image that looks just like a real object) and their hand goes through the image. Since the womb is dark, and the neonates have not yet had swiping experiences outside the womb, it would seem that some aspects of knowledge of objects must be innate (see Eibl-Eibesfeldt, 1979, for a survey of ethological evidence; see also, Block, 1979). In sum, if a capacity or item of knowledge is present at birth, and if there seems no way it could have been learned (or otherwise environmentally acquired), then it is reasonable to suppose it is genetically represented and determined; and since what it is to be innate is to be genetically represented and determined rather than environmentally determined, it is reasonable to suppose it is innate.

Notes

1. There is evidence that some conditioning mechanisms are innate in people (see Bower, 1977).

References

Block, N. 1979. "A Confusion about Innateness." *Behavioral and Brain Sciences* 2, no. 1 (March): 27-29.

Bower, T. G. 1977. *A Primer of Infant Development.* San Francisco: Freeman.

Eibl-Eibesfeldt, I. 1979. "Human Ethology — Concepts and Implications for the Sciences of Man." *Behavioral and Brain Sciences* 2, no. 1 (March): 1-26.

Fodor, J. A. 1976. *The Language of Thought.* New York: Crowell.

14

Innate Ideas

Jerrold J. Katz

Rationalists such as Plato, Descartes, Leibniz, and Kant argued that men are born with a stock of ideas which determine to a very large extent both the form and content of their mature knowledge, while empiricists like Hobbes, Locke, Berkeley, and Hume argued that at birth men are a virtual *tabula rasa* on which experience writes its lessons according to the principles of associative learning. The rationalists claimed that our concepts originate in principles that form the inborn constitution of the mind, and the empiricists claimed that all our ideas come originally from experience. The controversy is fundamentally a conflict between two opposed hypotheses to account for how conceptual knowledge is built up from experience by the operation of innate principles of mental functioning. The basis for the controversy is not, as it is often conceived in popular discussions, that empiricists fail to credit the mind with any innate principles, but rather that the principles which are accorded innate

From *The Philosophy of Language* (New York: Harper & Row, 1966), pp 240-268. Copyright © 1966 by Jerrold J. Katz. Reprinted by permission of Harper & Row, Publishers, Inc., and the author. Notes have been renumbered for this edition.

status by empiricists do not place any substantive restrictions on the ideas that can qualify as components of complex ideas or any formal restrictions on the structure of associations which bond component ideas together to form a complex idea. On the empiricist's hypothesis, the innate principles are purely combinatorial devices for putting together items from experience. So these principles provide only the machinery for instituting associative bonds. Experience plays the selective role in determining which ideas may be connected by association, and principles of association are, accordingly, unable to exclude any ideas as, in principle, beyond the range of possible intellectual acquisition.

Thus, the empiricist's account of how conceptual knowledge develops is essentially this. Experience provides examples of things of a certain kind which are somehow copied by the mind to form a simple idea of such things. Empiricists differ among themselves about the sort of things that are represented as simple ideas, but this has no bearing on the present discussion. Simple ideas are combined to form complex ideas, and these are combined to form still more complex ideas, without any limit on the level of complexity that may be reached. Such combinations are dictated by the regularities exhibited in experience. The network of associative bonds instituted to form a complex idea from simpler ones is itself a copy of the pattern of regularities which connect items in experience, where these regularities are represented as associative bonds. Since the associative machinery does not place restrictions either on the intrinsic characteristics of the items from experience to determine which of them can be represented as simple ideas or on the structure of the complex ideas resulting from the process of combining ideas, any logically possible concepts can, given the appropriate experience, be realized in the mind in the form of some simple or complex idea. Since any simple ideas whatever are possible, since any simple ideas can become the elements associated in the formation of a complex idea, and since any complex idea is just a network of associative bonds whose ultimate elements can be nothing other than simple ideas derived from experience, it follows that the empiricist's principles of mental operation are, as it were, neutral with respect to which ideas from the totality of all logically possible ones are chosen for use in making sense of our actual experience. In this regard, these principles defer to experience to provide a basis for choice among the totality. To explain how this choice is made, empiricists introduce the doctrine that the causally effective factor in learning is the frequency of presentations of spatially and temporally contiguous items together with perhaps other precipitating factors such as drive reduction.[1] The components of every complex idea are bonded together by links forged by the operation of enumerative techniques of inductive generalization from frequently repeated instances of contiguously occurring items in experience.

Contrary to this, rationalists claim that the principles of mental operation

with which man is innately equipped place quite severe restrictions on what a simple idea can be and on what ways simple ideas can combine with one another and with complex ideas in the production of complex ideas. To account for the attainment of conceptual knowledge, such restrictions are incorporated in the rationalist hypothesis in the form of a system of innately fixed conceptual forms which sharply limit the set of those ideas which the mind is capable of acquiring to a very small subset of the set of all logically possible ideas. These innate conceptual forms, or innate ideas, contribute directly to our stock of abstract concepts and indirectly organize the content of experience by serving as models for the construction of particular concepts, which, accordingly, have the structure of the abstract concepts on which they are modeled. For example, an abstract concept such as our concept of an object with spatially and temporally contiguous parts is not learned by copying experienced objects but is manifested as a functional component of our conceptual knowledge under precipitating sensory conditions. Similarly, experience does not present instances of a particular concept such as that of a stone or animal which the mind copies without the benefit of a template. Experience sets off a process in which such particular concepts are manufactured from the same innately fixed conceptual form which gives rise to the abstract concept that determines the category to which those particular concepts belong.

Hence, the rationalist is no more claiming that all our ideas arise from innate forms in a way that is wholly independent of a selective effect of experience than the empiricist is claiming that there are no innate principles of mental operation. "Necessary truths," wrote Leibniz, ". . . must have principles whose proof does not depend on examples, nor consequently upon the testimony of the senses, although without the senses it would never have occurred to us to think of them."[2] According to the rationalists, conceptual knowledge is a joint product of the mind and the senses, in which sense experience serves to realize the innately fixed form of mature conceptual knowledge. Leibniz phrased this point in terms of a particularly revealing analogy. He wrote, ". . . I have taken as illustration a block of veined marble, rather than a block of perfectly uniform marble or than empty tablets, that is to say, what is called by philosophers *tabula rasa*. For if the soul were like these empty tablets, truths would be in us as the figure of Hercules is in a block of marble, when the block of marble is indifferently capable of receiving this figure or any other. But if there were in the stone veins, which should mark out the figure of Hercules rather than other figures, the stone would be more determined towards this figure, and Hercules would somehow be, as it were, innate in it, although labor would be needed to uncover the veins and to clear them by polishing and thus removing what prevents them from being fully seen. It is thus that ideas and truths are innate in us, as natural inclinations, dispositions, habits or powers, and not as activities . . . ."[3] The rationalist thus denies the empiricist contention that all of our ideas come from sense experience, arguing instead that sense experience serves to activate such natural inclinations, dispositions, habits or powers, i.e., to transform the latent unperceived ideas with which men are innately equipped into clearly perceived, actual ideas. The senses, to return to Leibniz's analogy, play the role of the sculptor who by polishing and clearing away extraneous marble reveals the form of Hercules.

Rationalists claim that the set of possible ideas from which experience selects those that are actually acquired by us is a far narrower set than those which it is possible to imagine or formulate. Consequently, in denying the empiricist's con-

tention that all our ideas come from experience, the rationalist is putting forth a stronger hypothesis about the innate contribution to conceptual knowledge. The controversy is, then, whether some version of this stronger hypothesis or the empiricist's weaker one best explains how a conceptual system of the sort that mature humans possess is acquired on the experience they have accumulated.

We make no effort here to review the traditional arguments of empiricists and rationalists. Instead we shall consider the form that the issue over innate ideas takes in the case of language acquisition. The reason for thus narrowing the issue is that in so doing we deal with the crux of the issue in terms of a case about which enough is now known in the theory of language to afford a substantial basis for deciding between the empiricist and rationalist hypotheses.

The major fact to be explained by the contending hypotheses is that a child who undergoes the transition from nonverbal infant to fluent speaker of a natural language on the basis of an exposure to a sample of speech has acquired an internal representation of the rules that determine how sentences are constructed, used, and understood. These internally represented rules constitute his competence in his native language. Thus, at the final stage of the nonverbal infant's transformation into fluent speaker, the product of the process of language acquisition is an internal representation of a linguistic description. This internal representation is, then, the object whose acquisition has to be explained by the contending empiricist and rationalist hypotheses. Accordingly, we may conceive of the nonverbal infant as initially equipped with a language acquisition device of undetermined constitution, and we may think of the empiricist and rationalist hypotheses as hypotheses about its constitution. Since the input to (D) is a sample of utterances over a certain maturational period, and perhaps

other linguistically relevant sensory information as well, and its output is an internalization of the rules of the language from which the sample was drawn, the best hypothesis about (D) is that hypothesis which accounts in the most revealing way for how such an output is produced on the basis of such an input. Therefore, our approach to deciding whether the empiricist or rationalist hypothesis is best will be to study the properties of the input and output of (D) to determine the kind of mechanism that can convert an input with the properties that the input to (D) is found to have into an output with the properties that the output of (D) is found to have. Whichever hypothesis thus provides the most fruitful model of the internal structure of the language acquisition device will be accepted as the best hypothesis.

The empiricist hypothesis claims that the language acquisition device operates essentially by principles of inductive generalization which associate observable features of utterances with one another and with other relevant sensory information to obtain an internalization of the rules of a linguistic description. These principles have been given a precise statement in various, from our point of view, equivalent forms in the work of taxonomic linguistics in the Bloomfieldian tradition and learning theorists in the tradition of American behaviorist psychology.[4] Such statements are attempts to work out a simulation model of the device (D). On the other hand, the rationalist hypothesis, which attributes a far richer structure to the device (D), has never been expressed in a precise enough form for it to receive serious consideration as a competing explanation. The rationalist hypothesis claims that the language acquisition device contains a stock of innate ideas that jointly specify the necessary form of language (realized in any actual natural language) and thus the necessary form of a speaker's internal representation of the rules of his language. But no rationalist has given a precise formulation of these innate ideas, or an exact account of the process by which abstract and particular concepts are created from the interaction of innate conceptual forms and sensory stimulation. Thus, one might even say that there is no definite rationalist hypothesis, but just a general notion about the character of such a hypothesis. These difficulties with the formulation of the rationalist hypothesis have been one major factor which has discouraged cultivation of such an alternative to the empiricist conception of intellectual acquisitions. Another difficulty is the somewhat greater initial plausibility that the empiricist hypothesis has by virtue of its apparent greater simplicity. Consequently, we consider the empiricist hypothesis first, and ask whether there are fundamental inadequacies in it that force us to resort to the rationalist's apparently more complicated account of language acquisition and to take on the burden of trying to give their account a more precise formulation. This means that we shall examine the output and input to (D) to find out if an empiricist model of associative learning can provide an account of how the input is transformed into the output which squares with what is known about them.

For a predetermined output from an input-output device, there is a functional relationship between the input and the richness of the internal structure of the device. Namely, the weaker the input in structural organization, the richer the internal structure of the device must be in order to give the fixed output from the input, i.e., in order to make up for the poverty of the input. Let us take a rather mundane example. A very intelligent person can obtain the solutions to certain mathematical problems (the output) given just the barest formulation of the problems (the input) whereas a very unintelligent person might have to be virtually told the solutions before he gets them. Thus, we often infer the poverty of someone's intellect from how much has to be given him at the outset for him to arrive at the solution to a problem. Similarly, here we will try to show that the input to the language acquisition device would be too impoverished for it to be able to produce an internalization of the rules of a linguistic description were it to be constructed in accord with the empiricist hypothesis. That is, we shall try to establish that operations of inductive generalization and association cannot produce an internalization of a linguistic description from the kind of speech and other data that is available to the child.

One fundamental assumption of any associative theory of learning is that what is learned can be broken down into elements which have been each associated with observable and distinguishable constituents of the input in the following sense. The elements of the input which can have something associated with them must be distinguishable in terms of the discriminative and analytic capacities of the perceptual mechanism that codes the input into discrete parts and analyzes those parts as units within one or another category. Thus, limitations on the perceptual mechanism based on the discriminative and analytic distinctions it can make are also limitations on the richness of the information which the input provides for the associative machinery. Similarly, insufficiencies in the input itself are also limitations on the richness of the information with which the associative machinery can work. Therefore, if the associationist theory is to successfully explain the case of language learning, the physical speech sounds, or utterances, from which the child acquires his knowledge of the rules of the linguistic

description must contain, or be analyzable into, observable and distinguishable elements such that for each constituent of the meaning of an utterance whose meaning has been acquired there is an observable and distinguishable component of its phonetic shape with which that semantic constituent can be associated. Since learning the meanings of the sentences of a language is conceived of as a process of associating semantic elements of some kind with observable features of the phonetic shape of the sentences to which the child is exposed, these observable features must provide a rich enough basis of distinct elements for each semantic component of the meaning of such sentences to have a distinct phonetic element(s) with which it can be correlated by association. If, therefore, we can show that this fundamental assumption is false — that there are, in the case of certain essential semantic elements, literally no observable features of the phonetic shape of sentences with which these semantical elements can be associated — then we will have established that the input to (D) is structurally too impoverished for the rules of a linguistic description to be derived from it by principles of inductive generalization and association. That is what we shall now attempt to establish.

To show this, we first define two notions, that of the *observable grammatical features of a sentence* and that of the *unobservable grammatical features of a sentence*. To define the first of these notions, we refer back to our earlier discussion of final derived phrase markers. It will be recalled that these phrase markers are the objects on which the phonological rules, the rules that determine the pronunciation of sentences, operate. These rules map phonetic interpretations onto final derived phrase markers. Since it is only the speech sounds represented by such phonetic interpretations which the child encounters in acquiring his fluency in the language — since, that is, this is the only data about the language that he can observe, it is natural to define the notion of observable grammatical features in terms of properties of final derived phrase markers, along with properties of their phonological interpretations where these are relevant. *Thus, we define the observable grammatical features of the sentence S to be any features of S which can be predicted directly from its final derived phrase marker or any feature that can be predicted directly from its phonological representation, and nothing else.* Anything that requires information from other sources, such as the rules of the linguistic description or other phrase markers of the sentence, in order to be predicted is *ipso facto* not an observable grammatical feature. . .

Note that this definition of a sentence's observable grammatical features, although it seems natural in the sense that it permits us to count anything that we would intuitively regard as an observable grammatical feature as such, is nonetheless, overly generous to the empiricist. That is, it is overly liberal in the sense that it counts much more information about the grammar of a sentence as observable than a nonverbal child could be expected to be able to inductively extract from the sounds he actually encounters. For one thing, it is quite obvious that the child is in no sense given a classification of the constituents of a sentence into their syntactic categories. Furthermore, the essentially inductive techniques of data cataloguing devised by taxonomic linguists in order to provide a mechanical discovery procedure for final derived phrase markers on the basis of their phonological representation have always proved a dismal failure, not because there was little skill employed in their development, but because, without the general definitions of the grammatical properties they were to identify in particular cases, they lacked the conceptual apparatus to do their job.[5] For another

thing, and perhaps more significantly, it has been found in recent work in acoustic phonetics that the physical sounds of speech do not themselves provide a complete basis for identifying the significant phonological units of sentences. These two points are by themselves a strong argument against the empiricist hypothesis about language acquisition, but we shall not develop them here. If on the basis of this overly liberal definition of an observable grammatical feature we can show that the observable features of sentences are insufficient to enable a child to acquire the rules of his language by operations of inductive generalization and association, then we have an adequate refutation of the empiricist conception of language learning.

Final derived markers do not, and could not, adequately specify all the information about the syntactic structure of sentences. This means that the syntactic structure of a sentence is not given by a single phrase marker which segments it into continuous constituents and labels these segments but must be given by other phrase markers also. These other phrase markers are connected with the final derived phrase marker by a system of transformational rules which convert underlying phrase markers into derived phrase markers, and these into still further derived phrase markers, until the final one is reached. The underlying phrase markers may be thought of, in contrast to the final derived phrase markers, as reconstructing the unobservable, theoretically inferred, features of sentences.

Now, in terms of the underlying phrase markers, we can define the notion unobservable grammatical feature of a sentence. *An unobservable grammatical feature of S is any syntactic feature of S which can be predicted directly from its underlying phrase marker but cannot be predicted from its final derived phrase marker.* In general, if we compare final derived phrase markers with their corresponding underlying phrase markers, we find that the unobservable grammatical features of sentences form quite an impressive collection. The occurrence of a 'you' subject in normal English imperative sentences is one example of an unobservable grammatical feature. . . . Such features cannot be detected in the perceptible or physically definable properties of the data in the sample of the language which a language learner encounters, but, nevertheless, they must, as we have already shown, be theoretically posited by the linguist as part of the structure of sentences in order that his linguistic description successfully explain observable grammatical features. Thus, the unobservable features of a sentence as well as its observable features must be considered as information that a speaker utilizes to produce it on the appropriate occasion and to understand it when it is produced by other speakers.

That unobservable grammatical features of sentences bear semantic content which makes an essential contribution to the meaning of sentences, i.e., that the meaning of sentences having such features is not complete without the semantic contribution made by them, is obvious from the examples we have already given. Thus, it follows that any hypothesis to explain how the rules of a language are acquired must explain how the semantic content contributed by unobservable grammatical features becomes part of the full meaning of sentences. Otherwise, the hypothesis fails to explain how a speaker knows what sentences with unobservable grammatical features mean. Now, the empiricist hypothesis claims that the meanings of sentences are learned by a conditioning process in which inductive generalization and association provide the steps of language acquisition. Since such steps must proceed exclusively from observable features of the utterances to which the

child is exposed, the empiricist hypothesis is claiming that the meaning of sentences can be learned solely on the basis of operations of associating semantic elements with observable grammatical features of sentences. But this is simply false. First, the observable grammatical features account for only a small fraction of the semantic content of sentences; and, second, on the empiricist hypothesis, there is no means of associating the semantic content of unobservable grammatical features with the sentences whose meaning contains that semantic content. We conclude, then, that the empiricist hypothesis is, in principle, incapable of accounting for the acquisition of a natural language, whereby acquisition is meant mastery of rules that provide the full meaning of any sentence in the language.

To put the matter another way, since the observable structure of sentences is often quite severely impoverished from the point of view of semantic interpretation and since principles of inductive generalization and association add nothing structural or substantive to these structures on which they operate, it follows that such principles cannot account for the full range of semantic as well as syntactic, properties on which the interpretation of sentences, essential to communication with them, depends.

* * *

In discussing the nature of lawlike statements, Goodman[6] exhibited a paradox in a current version of confirmation theory which shows that on this theory any prediction about unknown cases is confirmed by any evidence whatever about the known cases. Goodman argued as follows: "Suppose that all emeralds examined before a certain time t are green. At time t, then, our observations support the hypothesis that all emeralds are green; and this is in accord with our definition of confirmation. Our evidence statements assert that emerald *a* is green, that emerald *b* is green, and so on; and each confirms the general hypothesis that all emeralds are green. So far, so good. Now let me introduce another predicate less familiar than 'green.' It is the predicate 'grue' and it applies to all things examined before *t* just in case they are green but to other things just in case they are blue. Then at times *t* we have, for each evidence statement asserting that a given emerald is green, a parallel evidence statement asserting that that emerald is grue. And the statements that emerald *a* is grue, that emerald *b* is grue, and so on, will each confirm the general hypothesis that all emeralds are grue. Thus, according to our definition, the prediction that all emeralds subsequently examined will be green and the prediction that all will be grue are alike confirmed by the evidence statements describing the same observations. But if an emerald subsequently examined is grue, it is blue and hence not green. Thus although we are well aware which of the two incompatible predictions is genuinely confirmed, they are equally well confirmed according to our present definition. Moreover, it is clear that if we simply choose an appropriate predicate, then on the basis of these same observations we shall have equal confirmation, by our definition, for any prediction whatever about other emeralds—or indeed about anything else."[7] We will adapt this argument so that, instead of dealing with a definition of confirmation intended as a reconstruction of the techniques for confirming laws in science, it deals with the empiricist's hypothesis about language acquisition. Goodman's argument then becomes a refutation of a psychological hypothesis rather than an epistemological theory. The adaptation is possible because the empiricist's psychological hypothesis about how languages are acquired employs the same principles of inductive generalization as those on which the conception of confirmation, which

Goodman criticizes by this argument, rest.

According to the empiricist, (D) operates by inductive principles which associate contiguously occurring elements in the sensory input when their contiguous occurrence is repeated frequently enough. Thus, if *a* is always accompanied contiguously by *b*, we form the association *ab*, expecting *b* when *a* occurs again. Now, suppose that a child learning a language has encountered a sufficiently large number of instances, say *N*, in which two linguistic events *a* and *b* have occurred together, where *a* is a word in its phonetic form and *b* is a meaning. For example, *a* might be the word /*suwp*/ and *b* the meaning of the English word 'soup.' In analogy to Goodman's construction of the predicate 'grue,' we can construct other 'Goodman-type' meanings, representing other logically possible concepts, among which will be the case *c*. *c* is the concept which is the meaning of 'soup' during the period when the *N* instances of *a* and *b* were observed to occur together and the meanings of 'salad' at any time after that period. Now, by parity of argument, the empiricist must infer not only that the child associates *b* with *a*, thus giving /*suwp*/ the meaning of 'soup' but also that the child associates *c* with *a*, thus giving it a different meaning. Moreover, he must also predict that the child associates *d*, *e*, *f*, etc., with *a*, where these are also 'Goodman-like' meanings and are each, like *c*, incompatible with *b* and one another. For parallel to the *N* contiguous occurrences of *b* with *a*, there are *N* contiguous occurrences of *c* with *a*, of *d* with *a*, of *e* with *a*, and so on. This implies that the empiricist must predict that, for any occurrence of /*suwp*/ which takes place after the period when the *N* cases were observed, it is understood not only to mean what the English word 'soup' means but also what the word 'salad' means, what the word 'stones' means, what the word 'monkeys' means, and so forth.

Thus, with respect to the set of specifiable concepts, it will be taken to mean anything at all. Since this sort of adaptation of Goodman's argument can be made for grammatical features as well as for any meanings of any word in the language, what is shown is that the empiricist hypothesis completely underdetermines the output of (D), which means that the empiricist hypothesis completely fails to account for language acquisition.

* * *

Finally, we may briefly mention another criticism of the empiricist hypothesis. The previously discussed difficulties of this hypothesis stem from the fact that associationist principles fail to place constraints on what can qualify as a simple idea. The difficulty we will now consider arises because such principles do not place any contraints on the nature of the bonds that link ideas together to form complex ideas. That is, there is just one notion of connection between ideas, that of a pure association between them. The fact that there is only one way in which ideas can be connected to one another means that different conceptual relations must be expressed in terms of differences in the strength of the associative bonds connecting component ideas (together with differences in the component ideas and differences with respect to which components are connected with which other components in each particular case). However, such different conceptual relations as sameness of meaning, meaning inclusion, difference in meaning, incompatibility of meaning, and so on are wholly unexpressable in these terms. Given that two ideas are associated, each with a certain strength of association, we cannot decide whether one has the same meaning as the other, whether the meaning of one is included in that of the other, whether they are different in meaning, whether they are incompatible in meaning, etc. Strongly associated expressions like 'ham' and 'eggs' or 'one' and 'two' are

not for that reason strongly related in meaning, and weakly associated expressions like 'eye-doctor' and 'oculist' or 'natatorium' and 'indoor swimming pool' can be equivalent in meaning. Similarly, no invariant feature of association separates synonyms from antonyms or pairs of sentences exhibiting a logical entailment from pairs exhibiting a causal relation. The fact that such conceptual relations are unrepresentable in terms of associative connections means that the empiricist hypothesis provides no way to explain how the speaker's acquisition of language equips him to determine such relations. What is required is a wide variety of different kinds of connections, not one type of connection with possible variations in the degree of its strength.

Of course, classical empiricists such as Hume were aware of this difficulty and thus posited relations between ideas, such as resemblance, contrariety, etc., which they made no effort to reduce to networks of associative connections. But such posits must be regarded as concessions to the rationalist's position, as Leibniz pointed out,[8] since they have to be construed as positing the existence of innate ideas.

* * *

Notes

1. E.g., the law of effect or pattern of presentations, as in C. B. Ferster and B. F. Skinner, *Schedules of Reinforcement*, Appleton-Century-Crofts, 1957.
2. G. W. Leibniz, *New Essays Concerning Human Understanding*, A. C. Langley (trans. and ed.), Open Court Publishing Company, La Salle, Ill., 1949.
3. *Ibid.*
4. Cf. N. Chomsky, "Current Issues in Linguistic Theory" and "A Transformational Approach to Syntax," in Fodor and Katz (eds.), *The Structure of Language: Readings in the Philosophy of Language*; also Postal, *Constituent Structure*, provides a discussion of tax-

onomic linguistics; for behaviorist learning theory, a convenient survey is provided by W. K. Estes et al., *Modern Learning Theory*, Appleton-Century-Crofts, 1954.

5. Cf. Chomsky, *Syntactic Structures*, footnotes 3 and 7 of chapter 6.

6. N. Goodman, *Fact, Fiction, and Forecast*, Harvard University Press, 1955.

7. *Ibid.*

8. Leibniz, *New Essays Concerning Human Understanding.*

The "Innateness Hypothesis" and Explanatory Models in Linguistics

Hilary Putnam

I. The Innateness Hypothesis

The "innateness hypothesis" (henceforth, the I.H.) is a daring — or apparently daring; it may be meaningless, in which case it is not daring — hypothesis proposed by Noam Chomsky. I owe a debt of gratitude to Chomsky for having repeatedly exposed me to the I.H.; I have relied heavily in what follows on oral communications from him; and I beg his pardon in advance if I misstate the I.H. in any detail, or misrepresent any of the arguments for it. In addition to relying upon oral communcations from Chomsky, I have also relied upon Chomsky's paper "Explanatory Models in Linguistics," in which the I.H. plays a considerable role.

To begin, then, the I.H. is the hypothesis that the human brain is "programmed" at birth in some quite *specific* and *structured* aspects of human natural language. The details of this programming are spelled out in some detail in "Explanatory models in Linguistics." We should assume that the speaker has "built

From *Synthese* 17, no. 1 (1967): 12-22. Reprinted by permission of D. Reidel Publishing Company and the author.

in"[1] a function which assigns weight to the grammars G_1, G_2, G_3, . . . in a certain class S of transformational grammars. S is not the class of all *possible* transformational grammars; rather all the members of S have some quite strong similarities. These similarities appear as "linguistic universals" — i.e., as characteristics of *all* human natural languages. If intelligent non-terrestrial life — say, Martians — exists, and if the "Martians" speak a language whose grammar does not belong to the subclass S of the class of all transformational grammars, then, I have heard Chomsky maintain, humans (except possibly for a few geniuses or linguistic experts) would be unable to learn Martian; a human child brought up by Martians would fail to acquire language; and Martians would, conversely, experience similar difficulties with human tongues. (Possible difficulties in *pronunciation* are not at issue here, and may be assumed *not* to exist for the purposes of this argument.) As examples of the similarities that all grammars of the subclass S are thought to possess (above the level of phonetics), we may mention the *active-passive* distinction, the existence of a *nonphrase-structure* portion of the grammar, the presence of such major categories as *concrete noun, verb taking an abstract subject,* etc. The project of delimiting the class *S* may also be described as the project of defining a *normal form for grammars.* Conversely, according to Chomsky, any nontrivial normal form for grammars, such that correct and perspicuous grammars of all human languages can and should be written in the normal form, "constitutes, in effect, a hypothesis concerning the innate intellectual equipment of the child."[2]

Given such a highly *restricted* class *S* of grammars (highly restricted in the sense that grammars not in the class are perfectly conceivable, not more "complicated" in any absolute sense than grammars in the class, and may well be employed by nonhuman speakers, if such there be), the performance of the human child in learning his native language may be understood as follows, according to Chomsky. He may be thought of as operating on the following "inputs"[3]: a list of utterances, containing both grammatical and ungrammatical sentences; a list of corrections, which enable him to classify the input utterances *as* grammatical or ungrammatical; and some information concerning which utterances count as *repetitions* of earlier utterances. Simplifying slightly, we may say that, on this model, the child is supplied with a list of grammatical sentence *types* and a list of ungrammatical sentence *types.* He then "selects" the grammar in *S* compatible with this information to which his weighting function assigns the highest weight. On this scheme, the general *form* of grammar is not learned from experience, but is "innate," and the "plausibility ordering" of grammars compatible with given data of the kinds mentioned is likewise "innate."

So much for a statement of the I.H. If I have left the I.H. vague at many points, I believe that this is no accident—for the I.H. seems to me to be *essentially* and *irreparably* vague—but this much of a statement may serve to indicate *what*

belief it is that I stigmatize as irreparably vague.

A couple of remarks may suffice to give some idea of the role that I.H. is supposed to play in linguistics. Linguistics relies heavily, according to Chomsky, upon "intuitions" of grammaticality. But *what* is an intuition of "grammaticality" an intuition *of?* According to Chomsky, the sort of theory-construction programmatically outlined above is what is needed to give this question the only answer it can have or deserves to have. Presumable, then, to "intuit" (or assert, or conjecture, etc.) that a sentence is grammatical is to "intuit" (or assert, or conjecture, etc.) that the sentence is generated by the highest-valued G_i in the class *S* which is such that it generates all the grammatical sentence types with which we have been supplied by the "input" and none of the ungrammatical sentence types listed in the "input."[4]

Chomsky also says that the G_i which receives the highest value must do *more* than agree with "intuitions" of grammaticality; it must account for certain ambiguities, for example.[5] At the same time, unfortunately, he lists no semantical information in the input, and he conjectures[6] that a child needs semantical information only to "provide motivation for language learning," and not to arrive at the *formal* grammar of its language. Apparently, then, the fact that a grammar which agrees with a sufficient amount of "input" must be in the class *S* to be "selected" by the child is what rules out grammars that generate all and only the grammatical sentences of a given natural language, but fail to correctly "predict"[7] ambiguities (cf. E. M. in L., p. 533).

In addition to making clear what it *is* to be grammatical, Chomsky believes that the I.H. confronts the linguist with the following tasks: To *define* the normal form for grammars described above, and to *define* the weighting function. In *Syntactic Structures* Chomsky, indeed, gives this as an objective for linguistic theory: to give an *effective* procedure for choosing between rival grammars.

Lastly, the I.H. is supposed to justify the claim that what the linguist provides is "a hypothesis about the innate intellectual equipment that a child brings to bear in language learning."[8] Of course, even if language is *wholly* learned, it is still true that linguistics "characterizes the linguistic abilities of the mature speaker,"[9] and that a grammar "could properly be called an explanatory model of the linguistic intuition of the native speaker."[10] However, one could with equal truth say that a driver's manual "characterizes the car-driving abilities of the mature driver" and that a calculus text provides "an explanatory model of the calculus-intuitions of the mathematician." Clearly, it is the idea that *these* abilities and *these* intuitions are close to the human *essence*, so to speak, that gives linguistics its "sex appeal," for Chomsky at least.

II. The Supposed Evidence for the I.H.

A number of empirical facts and alleged empirical facts have been advanced to support the I.H. Since limitations of space make it impossible to describe all of them here, a few examples will have to suffice.

(a) The *ease* of the child's original language learning. "A young child is able to gain perfect mastery of a language with incomparably greater ease [*than an adult*—H.P.] and without any explicit instruction. Mere exposure to the language, and for a remarkably short period, seems to be all that the normal child requires to develop the competence of the native speaker."[11]

(b) The fact that reinforcement, "in any interesting sense," seems to be unnecessary for language learning. Some children have apparently even learned to speak without *talking*,[12] and then displayed this ability at a relatively late age to startled adults who had given them up for mutes.

(c) The ability to "develop the competence of the native speaker" has been said not to depend on the intelligence level. Even quite low I.Q.'s "internalize" the grammar of their native language.

(d) The "linguistic universals" mentioned in the previous section are allegedly accounted for by the I.H.

(e) Lastly, of course, there is the "argument" that runs *"what else* could account for language learning?" The task is so incredibly complex (analogous to learning, at least implicitly, a complicated physical theory, it is said), that it would be miraculous if even one tenth of the human race accomplished it without "innate" assistance. (This is like Marx's "proof" of the Labour Theory of Value in *Capital*, Vol. III, which runs, in essence, *"What else* could account for the fact that commodities have different value *except* the fact that the labor-content is different?")

III. Criticism of the Alleged Evidence

A. The Irrelevance of Linguistic Universals

1. Not surprising on any theory. Let us consider just how surprising the "linguistic universals" cited above really are. Let us assume for the purpose a community of Martians whose "innate intellectual equipment" may be supposed to be as different from the human as is compatible with their being able to speak a language at all. What could we expect to find in their language?

If the Martians' brains are not vastly richer than ours in complexity, then they, like us, will find it possible to employ a practically infinite set of expressions only if those expressions possess a "grammar"—i.e., if they are built up by recursive rules from a limited stock of basic forms. Those basic forms need not be built up out of a *short* list of phonemes — the Martians might have vastly greater memory capacity than we do — but if Martians, like humans, find rote learning difficult, it will not be surprising if they too have *short* lists of phonemes in their languages.

Are the foregoing reflections argument *for* or *against* the I.H.? I find it difficult to tell. If belief in "innate intellectual equipment" is *just* that, then how *could* the I.H. be false? How could something with *no* innate intellectual equipment *learn* anything? *To be sure,* human "innate intellectual equipment" is relevant to language learning; if this means that such parameters as memory span and memory capacity play a crucial role. But what rank Behaviorist is supposed to have ever denied *this*? On the other hand, that a particular mighty arbitrary set *S* of grammars is "built in" to the brain of *both* Martians and Humans is *not* a hypothesis we would have to invoke to account for *these* basic similarities.

But for what similarities above the level of phonetics, where constitutional factors play a large role for obvious reasons, *would* the I.H. have to be invoked *save* in the trivial sense that memory capacity, intelligence, needs, interests, etc., are all relevant to language learning, and all depend, in part, on the biological makeup of the organism? If Martians are such strange creatures that they have no interest in physical objects, for example, their language will contain no concrete nouns; but would not this be *more*, not *less* surprising, on any *reasonable* view, than their having an interest in physical objects? (Would it be surprising if Martian contained devices for forming truth-functions and for quantification?)

Two more detailed points are relevant here. Chomsky has pointed out that no natural language has a phrase structure grammar. But this too is not surprising. The sentence "John and Jim came home quickly" is not generated by a phrase-structure rule, in Chomsky's formalization of English grammar. But the sentence "John came home quickly and Jim came home quickly" *is* generated by a phrase-structure rule in the grammar of mathematical logic, and Chomsky's famous "and-transformation" is just an abbreviation rule. Again, the sentence "That was the lady I saw you with last night" is not generated by a phrase-structure rule in English, or at least not in Chomsky's description of English. But the sentence "That is the x such that x is a lady and I saw you with x last night" is generated by a phrase-structure rule in the grammar of mathematical logic. And again the idiomatic English sentence *can* be obtained from its phrase-structure counterpart by a simple rule of abbreviation. Is it really surprising, does it really point to anything more interesting than *general intelligence,* that these operations which break the bounds of phrase-structure grammar appear in every natural language?[13]

Again, it may appear startling at first blush that such categories as noun, verb, adverb, etc. have "universal" application. But, as Curry has pointed out, it is too easy to multiply "facts" here. If a language contains nouns — that is, a phrase-structure category which contains the proper names — it contains noun phrases, that is, phrases which occupy the environments of nouns. If it contains noun phrases it contains verb phrases — phrases which when combined with a noun phrase by a suitable construction yield sentences. If it contains verb phrases, it contains adverb phrases — phrases that, when combined with a verb phrase yield a verb phrase. Similarly, adjective phrases, etc., can be defined in terms of the *two* basic categories "noun" and "sentence." Thus the existence of nouns is all that has to be explained. And this reduces to explaining two facts: (1) The fact that all natural languages have a large phrase structure portion in their grammar, in the sense just illustrated, in spite of the effect of what

Chomsky calls "transformations." (2) The fact that all natural languages contain proper names. But (1) is not surprising in view of the fact that phrase-structure rules are extremely simple algorithms. Perhaps Chomsky would reply that "simplicity" is subjective here, but this is just not so. The fact is that all the natural measures of complexity of an algorithm — size of the machine table, length of computations, time, and space required for the computation — lead to the same result here, quite independently of the detailed structure of the computing machine employed. Is it surprising that algorithms which are "simplest" for virtually any computing system we can conceive of are also simplest for naturally evolved "computing systems"? And (2) — the fact that all natural languages contain proper names — is not surprising in view of the utility of such names, and the difficulty of always finding a definite description that will suffice instead.

Once again, "innate" factors are relevant *to be sure* — if choosing *simple* algorithms as the basis of the grammar is "innate," and if the need for identifying persons rests on something innate — but what Behaviorist would or should be surprised? Human brains are computing systems and subject to some of the constraints that affect all computing systems; human beings have a natural interest in one another. If *that* is "innateness," well and good!

2. Linguistic universals could be accounted for, even if surprising, without invoking the I.H. Suppose that language-using human beings envolved *independently* in two or more places. Then, if Chomsky were *right*, there should be two or more *types* of human beings descended from the two or more original populations, and normal children of each type should fail to learn the languages spoken by the other types. Since we do not observe this, since there is only *one* class S built into *all* human

brains, we have to conclude (if the I.H. is true) that language-using is an evolutionary "leap" that occurred only *once*. But in that case, it is overwhelmingly likely that all human languages are descended from a single original language, and that the existence today of what are called "unrelated" languages is accounted for by the great lapse of time and by countless historical changes. This is, indeed, likely even if the I.H. is false, since the human race itself is now generally believed to have resulted from a single evolutionary "leap," and since the human population was extremely small and concentrated for millennia, and only gradually spread from Asia to other continents. Thus, even if language using was learned or invented rather than "built in," or even if only some general dispositions in the direction of language using are "built in,"[14] it is likely that some one group of humans first developed language as we know it, and then spread this through conquest or imitation to the rest of the human population. Indeed, we do know that this is just how *alphabetic* writing spread. In any case, I repeat, this hypothesis — a single origin for human language — is certainly *required* by the I.H., but much weaker than the I.H.

But just this *consequence* of the I.H. is, in fact, enough to account for "linguistic universals"! For, if all human languages are descended from a common parent, then just such highly useful features of the common parent as the presence of some kind of quantifiers, proper names, nouns, and verbs, etc., would be expected to survive. Random variation may, indeed, alter many things; but that it should fail to strip language of proper names, or common nouns, or quantifiers, is not *so* surprising as to require the I.H.

B. The "Ease" of Language Learning Is Not Clear

Let us consider somewhat closely the "ease" with which children do learn their native language. A typical "mature" college student seriously studying a foreign language spends three hours a week in lectures. In fourteen weeks of term he is thus exposed to forty-two hours of the language. In four years he may pick up over 300 hours of the language, very little of which is actual listening to native informants. By contrast, direct method teachers estimate that 300 hours of direct-method teaching will enable one to converse fluently in a foreign language. Certainly 600 hours — say, 300 hours of direct-method teaching and 300 hours of reading — will enable any adult to speak and read a foreign language with ease, and to use an incomparably larger vocabulary than a young child.

It will be objected that the adult does not acquire a perfect accent. So what? The adult has been speaking one way all of his life, and has a huge set of habits to unlearn. What can equally well be accounted for by learning theory should not be cited as evidence for the I.H.

Now the child by the time it is four or five years old has been exposed to *vastly* more than 600 hours of direct-method instruction. Moreover, even if "reinforcement" is not neceessary, most children are consciously and repeatedly reinforced by adults in a host of ways — e.g., the constant repetition of simple one-word sentences ("cup," "doggie") in the presence of babies. Indeed, any foreign adult living with the child for those years would have an incomparably better grasp of the language than the child does. The child indeed has a better accent. Also, the child's grammatical mistakes, which are numerous, arise not from carrying over previous language habits, but from not having fully acquired the first set. But it seems to me that this "evidence" for the I.H. stands the facts on their head.

C. Reinforcement Another Issue

As Chomsky is aware, the evidence is today slim that *any* learning requires reinforcement "in any interesting sense." Capablanca, for example, learned to play chess by simply watching adults play. This is comparable to Macaulay's achievement in learning language without speaking. Nongeniuses normally do require practice both to speak correctly and to play chess. Yet probably anyone *could* learn to speak *or* to play chess without practice if muffled, in the first case, or not allowed to play, in the second case, with sufficiently prolonged observation.

D. Independence of Intelligence Level an Artifact

Every child learns to speak the native language. What does this mean? If it means that children do not make serious grammatical blunders, even by the standards of descriptive as opposed to prescriptive grammar, this is just not true for the young child. By nine or ten years of age this has ceased to happen, perhaps (I speak as a parent), but nine or ten years is enough time to become pretty darn good at *anything*. What is more serious is what "grammar" *means* here. It does not include mastery of vocabulary, in which even many adults are deficient, nor ability to understand *complex* constructions, in which many adults are *also* deficient. It means purely and simple the ability to learn what every *normal* adult learns. Every normal adult learns what every normal adult learns. What this "argument" reduces to is "Wow! How complicated a skill every normal adult learns. What else could it be but *innate.*" Like the preceding argument, it reduces to the "What Else" argument.

But what of the "What Else?" argument? Just how impressed should we be by the failure of current learning theories to account for complex learning processes such as those involved in the learning of language? If Innateness were a *general* solution, perhaps we should be impressed. But the I.H. *cannot* by its very nature, be generalized to handle all complex learning processes. Consider the following puzzle (called "jump"):

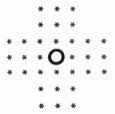

To begin with, all the holes but the center one are filled. The object of the game is to remove all the pegs but one by "jumping" (as in checkers) and to end with the one remaining peg in the center. A clever person can get the solution in perhaps eight or ten hours of experimentation. A not so clever person can get a "near-solution" — two pegs left — in the same time. No program exists, to my knowledge, that would enable a computer to solve even the "near solution" problem without running out of both time and space, even though the machine can spend the equivalent of many human lifetimes in experimentation. When we come to the discovery of even the simplest mathematical theorem the situation is even more striking. The theorems of mathematics, the solutions to puzzles, etc., cannot on *any* theory be *individually* "innate"; what must be "innate" are heuristics, i.e., learning strategies. In the absence of any knowledge of what *general multipurpose learning strategies* might even look like, the assertion that such strategies (which absolutely must exist and be employed by all humans) cannot account for this or that learning process, that the answer or an answer schema must be "innate," is utterly unfounded.

I will be told, of course, that *everyone* learns his native language (as well as everyone does), and that not everyone solves puzzles or proves theorems. But everyone does learn pattern recognition, automobile driving, etc., and everyone in fact can solve many problems that no computer can solve. In conversation Chomsky has repeatedly used precisely such skills as these to support the idea that humans have an "innate

conceptual space." Well and good, if true. *But that is no help. Let a complete seventeenth-century Oxford University education be innate if you like;* still the solution to "jump" was not innate; the Prime Number Theorem was not innate; and so on. *Invoking "Innateness" only postpones the problem of learning; it does not solve it.* Until we understand the strategies which make general learning possible — and vague talk of "classes of hypotheses" and "weighting functions" is utterly useless here — no discussion of the *limits* of learning can even begin.

Notes

1. What "built in" means is highly unclear in this context. The weighting function by itself determines only the relative ease with which various grammars can be learned by a human being. If a grammar G_1 can be learned more easily than a grammar G_2, then doubtless this is "innate" in the sense of being a fact about human learning *potential*, as opposed to a fact about what has been learned. But this sort of fact is what learning theory tries to account for; *not* the explanation being sought. It should be noticed that Chomsky has never offered even a schematic account of the sort of device that is supposed to be present in the brain, and that is supposed to do the job of selecting the highest weighted grammar compatible with the data. But only a description, or at least a theory, of such a device could properly be called an innateness *hypothesis* at all.

2. Noam Chomsky, "Explanatory Models in Linguistics" (hereafter cited as E. M. in L.), p. 550.

3. E. M. in L., pp. 530-531.

4. I doubt that the child really is told which sentences it hears or utters are *ungrammatical*. At most it is told which are *deviant* — but it may not be told which are deviant for *syntactical* and which for *semantical* reasons.

5. Many of these — e.g., the alleged "ambiguity" in "the shooting of the elephants was heard" — *require coaching to detect.* The claim that grammar "explains the ability to recognize ambiguities" thus lacks the impressiveness that Chomsky believes it to have. I am grateful to

Paul Ziff and Stephen Leeds for calling this point to my attention.

6. E. M. in L., p. 531, n. 5.

7. A grammar "predicts" an ambiguity, in Chomsky's formalism, whenever it assigns two or more structural descriptions to the same sentence.

8. E. M. in L., p. 530.

9. E. M. in L., p. 530.

10. E. M. in L., p. 533.

11. E. M. in L., p. 529.

12. Macaulay's *first* words, it is said, were: "Thank you, Madam, the agony has somewhat abated" (to a lady who had spilled hot tea on him).

13. Another example of a tranformation is the "active-passive" transformation (cf. *Syntactic Structures*). But (a) the presence of this, if it *is* a part of the grammar, is not surprising — why should not there be a systematic way of expressing the *converse* of a relation? — and (b) the argument for the existence of such a "transformation" at all is ex-

tremely slim. It is contended that a grammar which "defines" active and passive forms separately (this can be done by even a phrase-structure grammar) fails to represent something that every speaker knows, *viz.* that active and passive forms are *related*. But why must every *relation* be mirrored by *syntax*? Every "speaker" of the canonical languages of mathematical logic is aware that each sentence (x) $(Fx \longrightarrow Gx)$ is related to a sentence (x) $(Gx \longrightarrow Fx)$; yet the definition of "well formed formula" fails to mirror "what every speaker knows" in this respect, and is not inadequate on that account. [*Editor's note:* In this anthology, " $\longrightarrow$ " is used instead of the horseshoe and the arrow as the material conditional ("if . . . then").]

14. It is very difficult to account for such phenomena as the spontaneous babbling of infants without *this* much "innateness." But this is not to say that a class S and a function f are "built in," as required by the I.H.

Reply to Putnam

Noam Chomsky

It seems to me that Hilary Putnam's arguments are inconclusive, primarily, because of certain erroneous assumptions about the nature of the acquired grammars. Specifically, he enormously underestimates, and in part misdescribes, the richness of structure, the particular and detailed properties of grammatical form and organization that must be accounted for by a "language acquisition model," that are acquired by the normal speaker-hearer and that appear to be uniform among speakers and also across languages.

To begin with, Putnam assumes that at the level of sound structure, the only property that can be proposed in universal grammar is that a language has "a short list of phonemes." This uniformity among languages, he argues, requires no elaborate explanatory hypothesis. It can be explained simply in terms of "such parameters as memory span and memory capacity," and no "rank Behaviorists" would have denied that these are innate

From "Linguistics and Philosophy," in Sidney Hook, ed., *Language and Philosophy* (New York: New York University Press, 1969), pp. 60-94. Copyright © 1969 by New York University. Reprinted by permission of New York University Press and the author.

properties. In fact, however, very strong empirical hypotheses have been proposed regarding the choice of universal distinctive features, the form of phonological rules, the ordering and organization of these rules, the relation of syntactic structure to phonetic representation, none of which can conceivably be accounted for on grounds of memory limitations. Putnam bases his account largely on my "Explanatory Models in Linguistics," which examines in some detail the principle of cyclic application of phonological rules, a principle that, if correct, raises some rather serious problems. We must ask how the child acquires knowledge of this principle, a feat that is particularly remarkable since, as already noted, much of the evidence that leads the linguist to posit this principle is drawn from the study of percepts and is thus not even available to the child. Similar questions arise with respect to many other aspects of universal phonology. In any event, if the proposals that have been elaborated regarding sound structure are correct or near correct, then the similarities among languages at this level, and the richness of the knowledge acquired by the child, are indeed remarkable facts, and demand an explanation.

Above the level of sound structure, Putnam assumes that the only significant properties of language are that they have proper names, that the grammar contains a phrase-structure component, and that there are rules "abbreviating" sentences generated by the phrase-structure component. He argues that the specific character of the phrase-structure component is determined by the existence of proper names; that the existence of a phrase-structure component is explained by the fact that "all the natural measures of complexity of an algorithm . . . lead to the . . . result" that phrase-structure systems provide the "algorithms which are 'simplest' for virtually any computing system," hence also "for naturally evolved 'computing systems' "; that there is nothing surprising in the fact that languages contain rules of abbreviations. Hence, he concludes, the only innate conditions that must be postulated are those that apply to all reasonable "computing systems," and no Behaviorist should feel any surprise at this.

Each of the three conclusions, however, is vitiated by a false assumption. First, it is obvious that there are many different phrase-structure grammars consistent with the assumption that one of the categories is that of proper names. In fact, there is much dispute at the moment about the general properties of the underlying base system for natural languages; the dispute is not in the least resolved by the existence of proper names as a primitive category in many languages.[1]

As to the second point, it is simply untrue that all measures of complexity and speed of computation lead to phrase-structure rules as the "simplest possible algorithm." The only existing results that have even an indirect relevance to this matter are those dealing with context-free phrase-structure grammars and their automata-theoretic interpretation. Context-free grammars are a reasonable model for the rules generating deep structures, when we exclude the lexical items and the distributional conditions they meet. But even apart from this fundamental discrepancy, the only existing results relate context-free grammars to a class of automata called "nondeterministic pushdown storage automata," and these have no particularly striking properties insofar as speed or complexity of computation are concerned, and are certainly not "natural" from this point of view. In terms of time and space conditions on computation, the somewhat similar but not formally related concept of real-time deterministic automaton would seem to be far more natural. In short, there are no results demonstrating that phrase-structure grammars are optimal in any computational sense (nor, certainly, are there any results dealing with the much more complex notion of base structure with a context-free phrase-structure grammar and a lexicon, with much richer properties, as components).

But there is no point in pursuing this matter, since what is at stake, in any event, is not the "simplicity" of phrase-structure grammars but rather of transformational grammars that contain a phrase-structure component, the latter playing a role in the generation of deep structures. And there is absolutely no mathematical concept of "ease of computation" or "simplicity of algorithm" that even suggests that such systems have some advantage over the various kinds of automata that have been investigated from this point of view. In fact, these systems have never really been considered in a strictly mathematical context, though there are interesting initial attempts to study some of their formal properties.[2] The source of the confusion is a misconception on Putnam's part as to the nature of grammatical transformations. These are not, as he supposes, rules that "abbreviate" sentences generated by phrase-structure rules. Rather, they are operations that form surface structures from underlying deep structures, which are generated, in part, by phrase-structure rules. Although there has been considerable evolution of theory since the notions of transformational generative grammar were first proposed, one assumption that has remained constant is that the phrase-structure rules generate only abstract structures, which are then mapped onto surface structures by grammatical transformation—the latter being structure-dependent operations of a peculiar sort that have never been studied outside of linguistics, in particular, not in any branch of mathematics with which I am familiar. To show that transformational grammars are the "simplest possible" one would have to demonstrate that an optimal computing system would take a string of symbols as input and determine its surface structure, the underlying deep structure, and the sequence of transformational operations that relate these two labeled bracketings. Nothing known about ease or simplicity of computation gives any reason to suppose that this is true; in fact, the question has never been raised. One can think of certain kinds of organization of memory that might be well adapted to transformational grammars, but this is a different matter entirely.[3] I would, naturally, assume that there is some more general basis in human mental structure for the fact (if it is a fact) that languages have transformational grammars; one of the primary scientific reasons for studying language is that this study may provide some insight into general properties of mind. Given those specific properties, we may then be able to show that transformational grammars are "natural." This would constitute real progress, since it would now enable us to raise the problem of innate conditions on acquisition of knowledge and belief in a more general framework. But it must be emphasized that, contrary to what Putnam asserts, there is no basis for assuming that

"reasonable computing systems" will naturally be organized in the specific manner suggested by transformational grammar.

I believe that this disposes of Putnam's main argument, namely, that there is "nothing surprising," even to a Behaviorist, in the linguistic universals that are now being proposed and investigated. Let me then turn to his second argument, that even if there were surprising linguistic universals, they could be accounted for on a simpler hypothesis than that of an innate universal grammar, namely, the hypothesis of common origin of languages. This proposal misrepresents the problem at issue. As noted earlier, the empirical problem we face is to devise a hypothesis about initial structure rich enough to account for the fact that a specific grammar is acquired, under given conditions of access to data. To this problem, the matter of common origin of language is quite irrelevant. The grammar has to be discovered by the child on the basis of the data available to him, through the use of the innate capacities with which he is endowed. To be concrete, consider again the two examples discussed above: the association of nominal phrases to base structures and the cyclic application of phonological rules. The child masters these principles (if we are correct in our conclusions about grammar) on the basis of certain linguistic data; he knows nothing about the origin of language and could not make use of such information if he had it. Questions of common origin are relevant to the empirical problems we are discussing only in that the existing languages might not be a "fair sample" of the "possible languages," in which case we might be led mistakenly to propose too narrow a schema for universal grammar. This possibility must be kept in mind, of course, but it seems to me a rather remote consideration, given the problem that is actually at hand, namely, the problem of finding a schema rich enough to account for the development of the grammars that seem empirically justified. The discovery of such a schema may provide an explanation for the empirically determined universal properties of language. The existence of these properties, however, does not explain how a specific grammar is acquired by the child.

Putnam's discussion of the ease of language-learning seems to me beside the point. The question whether there is a critical period for language-learning is interesting,[4] but it has little relevance to the problem under discussion. Suppose that Putnam were correct in believing that "certainly . . . 600 hours [of direct method instruction] will enable any adult to speak and read a foreign language with ease." We would then face the problem of explaining how, on the basis of this restricted data, the learner has succeeded in acquiring the specific and detailed knowledge that enables him to use the language with ease, and to produce and understand a range of structures of which the data presented to him constitute a minute sample.

Finally, consider the alternative approach that Putnam suggests to the problem of language-acquisition. He argues that instead of postulating an innate schematism one should attempt to account for this achievement in terms of "general multi-purpose learning strategies." It is these that must be innate, not general conditions on the form of the knowledge that is acquired. Evidently, this is an empirical issue. It would be sheer dogmatism to assert of either of these proposals (or of some particular combination of them) that it *must* be correct. Putnam is convinced, on what grounds he does not say, that the innate basis for the acquisition of language must be identical with that for acquiring any other form of knowledge, that there is nothing "special" about the acquisition of language. A nondogmatic approach to this problem can be pursued, through the

investigation of specific areas of human competence, such as language, followed by the attempt to devise a hypothesis that will account for the development of such competence. If we discover that the same "learning strategies" are involved in a variety of cases, and that these suffice to account for the acquired competence, then we will have good reason to believe that Putnam's empirical hypothesis is correct. If, on the other hand, we discover that different innate systems (whether involving schemata or heuristics) have to be postulated, then we will have good reason to believe that an adequate theory of mind will incorporate separate "faculties," each with unique or partially unique properties. I cannot see how one can resolutely insist on one or the other conclusion in the light of the evidence now available to us. But one thing is quite clear: Putnam has no justification for his final conclusion that "invoking 'Innateness' only postpones the problem of learning; it does not solve it."[5] Invoking an innate representation of universal grammar does solve the problem of learning (at least partially), in this case, if in fact it is true that this is the basis (or part of the basis) for language-acquisition, as it well may be. If, on the other hand, there exist general learning strategies that account for the acquisition of grammatical knowledge, then postulation of an innate representation of universal grammar will not "postpone" the problem of learning, but will rather offer an incorrect solution to this problem. The issue is an empirical one of truth of falsity, not a methodological one of stages of investigation. At the moment, the only concrete proposal that is at all plausible, in my opinion, is the one sketched above. When some "general learning strategy" is suggested, we can look into the relative adequacy of these alternatives, on empirical grounds.

Notes

1. Not, incidentally, in all. Although this is hardly important here, it seems that many languages do not have proper names as a primitive category, but rather form proper names by recursive processes of an elaborate sort. See, for example, G. H. Matthews, *Hidatsa Syntax*, Mouton, The Hague, 1965, pp. 191f.

2. See, for example, S. Peters and R. Ritchie, "On the Generative Capacity of Transformational Grammars," *Information and Control*, forthcoming, and J. P. Kimball, "Predicates Definable over Transformational Derivations by Intersection with Regular Languages," *Information and Control*, 2 (1967), pp. 177-95.

3. For some speculations on this matter, see G. A. Miller and N. Chomsky, "Finitary Models of Language Users," part II, in R. D. Luce, R. Bush, and E. Galanter (eds.), *Handbook of Mathematical Psychology*, Vol. 2, Wiley, 1963.

4. See E. H. Lenneberg, *Biological Foundations of Language*, Wiley, 1967, for evidence bearing on this issue.

5. Or for his assumption that the "weighting functions" proposed in universal grammar constitute the "sort of fact . . . [that] . . . learning theory tries to account for; *not* the explanation being sought." No one would say that the genetic basis for the development of arms rather than wings in a human embryo is "the kind of fact that learning theory tries to account for," rather than the basis for explanation of other facts about human behavior. The question whether the weighting function is

learned, or whether it is the basis for learning, is an empirical one. There is not the slightest reason to assume, a priori, that it is to be accounted for by learning rather than genetic endowment, or some combination of the two.

There are other minor points in Putnam's discussion that call for some comment. For example, he asserts that since certain ambiguities "require coaching to detect," it follows that "the claim that grammar 'explains the ability to recognize ambiguities' . . . lacks the impressiveness that Chomsky believes it to have." But he misconstrues the claim, which relates to competence, not performance. What the grammar explains is why "the shooting of the hunters" (the example he cites) can be understood with hunters as subject or object but that in "the growth of corn" we can understand "corn" only as subject (the explanation, in this case, turns on the relation of nominalizations to deep structures, noted earlier). The matter of coaching is beside the point. What is at issue is the inherent sound-meaning correlation that is involved in performance, but only as one of many factors. Putnam also misstates the argument for assuming the active-passive relation to be transformational. It is not merely that the speaker knows them to be related. Obviously that would be absurd; the speaker also knows that "John will leave tomorrow" and "John will leave three days after the day before yesterday" are related, but this does not imply that there is a transformational relation between the two. Syntactic arguments are given in many places in the literature. See, for example, my *Syntactic Structures*, Mouton, 1957; *Aspects of the Theory of Syntax*.

On Cognitive Capacity

Noam Chomsky

Why study language? There are many possible answers, and by focusing on some I do not, of course, mean to disparage others or question their legitimacy. One may, for example, simply be fascinated by the elements of language in themselves and want to discover their order and arrangement, their origin in history or in the individual, or the ways in which they are used in thought, in science or in art, or in normal social interchange. One reason for studying language — and for me personally the most compelling reason — is that it is tempting to regard language, in the traditional phrase, as "a mirror of mind." I do not mean by this simply that the concepts expressed and distinctions developed in normal language use give us insight into the patterns of thought and the world of "common sense" constructed by the human mind. More intriguing, to me at least, is the possibility that by studying language we may discover abstract principles that govern its structure and use, principles that are

universal by biological necessity and not mere historical accident, that derive from mental characteristics of the species. A human language is a system of remarkable complexity. To come to know a human language would be an extraordinary intellectual achievement for a creature not specifically designed to accomplish this task. A normal child acquires this knowledge on relatively slight exposure and without specific training. He can then quite effortlessly make use of an intricate structure of specific rules and guiding principles to convey his thoughts and feelings to others, arousing in them novel ideas and subtle perceptions and judgments. For the conscious mind, not specially designed for the purpose, it remains a distant goal to reconstruct and comprehend what the child has done intuitively and with minimal effort. Thus language is a mirror of mind in a deep and significant sense. It is a product of human intelligence, created anew in each individual by operations that lie far beyond the reach of will or consciousness.

By studying the properties of natural languages, their structure, organization, and use, we may hope to gain some understanding of the specific characteristics of human intelligence. We may hope to learn something about human nature; something significant, if it is true that human cognitive capacity is the truly distinctive and most remarkable characteristic of the species. Furthermore, it is not unreasonable to suppose that the study of this particular human achievement, the ability to speak and understand a human language, may serve as a suggestive model for inquiry into other domains of human competence and action that are not quite so amenable to direct investigation.

The questions that I want to consider are classical ones. In major respects we have not progressed beyond classical antiquity in formulating clear problems in this domain, or in answering questions that immediately arise. From Plato to the present time, serious philosophers have been baffled and intrigued by the question that Bertrand Russell, in one of his later works, formulated in this way: "How comes it that human beings, whose contacts with the world are brief and personal and limited, are nevertheless able to know as much as they do know?" (Russell, 1948, p. 5). How can we gain such rich systems of knowledge, given our fragmentary and impoverished experience? A dogmatic skeptic might respond that we do not have such knowledge. His qualms are irrelevant to the present point. The same question arises, as a question of science, if we ask how comes it that human beings with such limited and personal experience achieve such convergence in rich and highly structured systems of belief, systems which then guide their actions and interchange and their interpretation of experience.

In the classical tradition, several answers were suggested. One might argue, along Aristotelian lines, that the world is structured in a certain way and that the human mind is able to perceive this structure, ascending from particulars to species to genus to further generalization and thus attaining knowledge of universals from perception of particulars. A "basis of pre-existent knowledge" is a prerequisite to learning. We must possess an innate capacity to attain developed states of knowledge, but these are "neither innate in a determinate form, nor developed from other higher states of knowledge, but from sense-perception." Given rich metaphysical assumptions, it is possible to imagine that a mind "so constituted as to be capable of this process" of "induction" might attain a rich system of knowledge.[1]

A more fruitful approach shifts the main burden of explanation from the structure of the world to the structure of the mind. What we can know is determined by "the modes of conception in the understanding";[2] what we do know, then, or what we come to believe, depends on the specific experiences that evoke in us some part of the cognitive system that is latent in the mind. In the modern period, primarily under the influence of Cartesian thought, the question of what we can know became again a central topic of inquiry. To Leibniz and Cudworth, Plato's doctrine that we do not attain new knowledge but recover what was already known seemed plausible, when this doctrine was "purged of the error of preexistence."[3] Cudworth argued at length that the mind has an "innate cognoscitive power" that provides the principles and conceptions that constitute our knowledge, when provoked by sense to do so. *"But sensible things themselves* (as, for example, light and colors) *are not known and understood either by the passion or the fancy of sense, nor by anything merely foreign and adventitious, but by intelligible ideas exerted from the mind itself, that is, by something native and domestic to it . . ."*[4] Thus knowledge "consisteth in the awakening and exciting of the inward active powers of the mind," which "exercise[s] its own inward activity upon" the objects presented by sense, thus coming "to know or understand, . . . actively to comprehend a thing by some abstract, free and universal ratio's, reasonings. . . ." The eye perceives, but the mind can compare, analyze, see cause-and-effect relations, symmetries, and so on, giving a comprehensive idea of the whole, with its parts, relations, and proportions. The "book of nature," then, is "legible only to an intellectual eye," he suggests, just as a man who reads a book in a language that he knows can learn something from the "inky scrawls." "The primary objects of science and intellection," namely, "the intelligible essences of things," "exist no where but in the mind itself, being its own ideas. . . . And by and through these inward ideas of the mind itself, which are its primary objects, does it know and understand all external individual things, which are the secondary objects of knowledge only."

Among the "innate ideas" or "common notions" discussed in the rich and varied work of seventeenth-century rationalists are, for example, geometrical concepts and the like, but also *relational ideas or categories which enter into every presentation of objects and make possible the unity and interconnectedness of rational experience,"*[5] including such "relative notions" as "Cause, Effect, Whole and Part, Like and Unlike, Proportion and Analogy, Equality and Inequality, Symmetry and Asymmetry," all *"relative ideas . . . [that are] . . . no material impresses from without upon the soul, but her own active conception proceeding from herself whilst she takes notice of external objects."*[6] Tracing the development of such ideas, we arrive at Kant's rather similar concept of the "conformity of objects to our mode of cognition." The mind provides the means for an analysis of data as experience, and provides as well a general schematism that delimits the cognitive structures developed on the basis of experience.

Returning to Russell's query, we can know so much because in a sense we already knew it, though the data of sense were necessary to evoke and elicit this knowledge. Or to put it less paradoxically, our systems of belief are those that the mind, as a biological structure, is designed to construct. We interpret experience as we do because of our special mental design. We attain knowledge when the "inward ideas of the mind itself" and the structures it creates conform to the nature of things.

Certain elements of the rationalist theories must be discarded, but the general outlines seem plausible enough. Work of the past years has shown that much of the detailed structure of the visual system is "wired in," though triggering experience is required to set the system in operation. There is evidence that the same may be true of the auditory structures that analyze at least some phonetic distinctive features. (Cf. Eimas et al., 1971.) As techniques of investigation have improved, Bower argues, "so has the apparent sophistication of the infant perceptual system." He reviews evidence suggesting that "the infant perceptual system seems capable of handling all of the traditional problems of the perception of three-dimensional space"—perception of solidity, distance, size-distance invariants, and size constancy. Thus, "contrary to the Berkeleian tradition the world of the infant would seem to be inherently tridimensional" (Bower, 1972). There is evidence that before infants are capable of grasping, they can distinguish graspable from ungraspable objects, using purely visual information (Bruner and Koslowski, 1972).

Gregory observes that "the speed with which babies come to associate the properties of objects and go on to learn how to predict hidden properties and future events would be impossible unless some of the structure of the world were inherited—somehow innately built into the nervous system."[7] He suggests further that there may be a "grammar of vision," rather like the grammar of human language, and possibly related to the latter in the evolution of the species. Employing this "grammar of vision"—largely innate—higher animals are able to "read from retinal images even hidden features of objects, and predict their immediate future states," thus "to classify objects according to an internal grammar, to read reality from their eyes." The neural basis for this system is gradually coming to be understood since the pioneering work of Hubel and Wiesel (1962). More generally, there is every reason to suppose that "learning behavior occurs via modification of an already functional structural organization"; "survival would be improbable if learning in nature required the lengthy repetition characteristic of most conditioning procedures," and it is well known that animals acquire complex systems of behavior in other ways (John, 1972).

Despite the plausibility of many of the leading ideas of the rationalist tradition, and its affinity in crucial respects with the point of view of the natural sciences, it has often been dismissed or disregarded in the study of behavior and cognition. It is a curious fact about the intellectual history of the past few centuries that physical and mental development have been approached in quite different ways. No one would take seriously a proposal that the human organism learns through experience to have arms rather than wings, or that the basic structure of particular organs results from accidental experience. Rather, it is taken for granted that the physical structure of the organism is genetically determined, though of course variation along such dimensions as size, rate of development, and so forth will depend in part on external factors. From embryo to mature organism, a certain pattern of development is predetermined, with certain stages, such as the onset of puberty or the termination of growth, delayed by many years. Variety within these fixed patterns may be of great importance for human life, but the basic questions of scientific interest have to do with the fundamental, genetically determined scheme of growth and development that is a characteristic of the species and that gives rise to structures of marvelous intricacy.

The species characteristics themselves have evolved over long stretches of time, and evidently the environment provides conditions for differential reproduction, hence evolution of the species. But this is an entirely different question, and here too, questions can be raised about the physical laws that govern this evolution. Surely too little is known to justify any far-reaching claims.

The development of personality, behavior patterns, and cognitive structures in higher organisms has often been approached in a very different way. It is generally assumed that in these domains, social environment is the dominant factor. The structures of mind that develop over time are taken to be arbitrary and accidental; there is no "human nature" apart from what develops as a specific historical product. According to this view, typical of empiricist speculation, certain general principles of learning that are common in their essentials to all (or some large class of) organisms suffice to account for the cognitive structures attained by humans, structures which incorporate the principles by which human behavior is planned, organized, and controlled. I dismiss without further comment the exotic though influential view that "internal states" should not be considered in the study of behavior.[8]

But human cognitive systems, when seriously investigated, prove to be no less marvelous and intricate than the physical structures that develop in the life of the organism. Why, then, should we not study the acquisition of a cognitive structure such as language more or less as we study some complex bodily organ?

At first glance, the proposal may seem absurd, if only because of the great variety of human languages. But a closer consideration dispels these doubts. Even knowing very little of substance about linguistic universals, we can be quite sure that the possible variety of languages is sharply limited. Gross observations suffice to establish some qualitative conclusions. Thus, it is clear that the language each person acquires is a rich and complex construction hopelessly underdetermined by the fragmentary evidence available. This is why scientific inquiry into the nature of language is so difficult and so limited in its results. The conscious mind is endowed with no advance knowledge (or, recalling Aristotle, with only insufficiently developed advance knowledge). Thus, it is frustrated by the limitations of available evidence and faced by far too many possible explanatory theories, mutually inconsistent but adequate to the data. Or—as unhappy a state—it can devise no reasonable theory. Nevertheless, individuals in a speech community have developed essentially the same language. This fact can be explained only on the assumption that these individuals employ highly restrictive principles that guide the construction of grammar. Furthermore, humans are, obviously, not designed to learn one human language rather than another; the system of principles must be a species property. Powerful constraints must be operative restricting the variety of languages. It is natural that in our daily life we should concern ourselves only with differences among people, ignoring uniformities of structure. But different intellectual demands arise when we seek to understand what kind of organism a human really is.

The idea of regarding the growth of language as analogous to the development of a bodily organ is thus quite natural and plausible. It is fair to ask why the empiricist belief to the contrary has had such appeal to the modern temper. Why has it been so casually assumed that there exists a "learning theory" that can account for the acquisition of cognitive structures through experience? Is there some body of evidence, established through scientific inquiry, or observation, or introspection, that leads us to regard mental and physical development in such different ways? Surely the answer is that there is not. Science offers no reason to "accept the common maxim that there is nothing in the intellect which was not first in the senses," or to question the denial of this maxim in rationalist philosophy.[9] Investigation of human intellectual achievements, even of the most commonplace sort, gives no support for this thesis.

Empiricist speculation and the "science of behavior" that has developed within its terms have proved rather barren, perhaps because of the peculiar assumptions that have guided and limited such inquiry. The grip of empiricist doctrine in the modern period, outside of the natural sciences, is to be explained on sociological or historical grounds.[10] The position itself has little to recommend it on grounds of empirical evidence or inherent plausibility or explanatory power. I do not think that this doctrine would attract a scientist who is able to discard traditional myth and to approach the problems afresh. Rather, it serves as an impediment, an insurmountable barrier to fruitful inquiry, much as the religious dogmas of an earlier period stood in the way of the natural sciences.

It is sometimes argued that modern empiricism overcomes the limitations of the earlier tradition, but I think that this belief is seriously in error. Hume, for example, presented a substantive theory of "the secret springs and principles, by which the human mind is actuated in its operations." In his investigation of the foundations of knowledge, he suggested specific principles that constitute "a species of natural instincts." Modern empiricists who disparage Hume have simply replaced his theory by vacuous systems that preserve empiricist (or more narrowly, behaviorist) terminology while depriving traditional ideas of their substance. I have discussed this matter elsewhere (cf. chapter 4), and will not pursue it here.

In recent years, many of these issues, long dormant, have been revived, in part in connection with the study of language. There has been much discussion of the so-called "innateness hypothesis," which holds that one of the faculties of the mind, common to the species, is a faculty of language that serves the two basic functions of rationalist theory: it provides a sensory system for the preliminary analysis of linguistic data, and a schematism that determines, quite narrowly, a certain class of grammars. Each grammar is a theory of a particular language, specifying formal and semantic properties of an infinite array of sentences. These sentences, each with its particular structure, constitute the language generated by the grammar. The languages so generated are those that can be "learned" in the normal way. The language faculty, given appropriate stimulation, will construct a grammar; the person knows the language generated by the constructed grammar. This knowledge can then be used to understand what is heard and to produce discourse as an expression of thought within the constraints of the internalized principles, in a manner appropriate to situations as these are conceived by other mental faculties, free of stimulus control.[11] Questions related to the language faculty and its exercise are the ones that, for me at least, give a more general intellectual interest to the technical study of language.

I would now like to consider the so-called "innateness hypothesis," to identify some elements in it that are or should be controversial, and to sketch some of the problems that arise as we try to resolve the controversy. Then, we may try to see what can be said about the nature and exercise of the linguistic competence that has been acquired, along with some related matters.

A preliminary observation is that the term "innateness hypothesis" is generally used by critics rather than advocates of the position to which it refers. I have never used the term, because it can only mislead. Every "theory of learning" that is even worth considering incorporates an innateness hypothesis. Thus, Hume's theory proposes specific innate structures of mind and seeks to account for all of human knowledge on the basis of these structures, even postulating unconscious and innate knowledge. (Cf. chapter 4.) The question is not whether learning presupposes innate structure—of course it does; that has never been in doubt—but rather what these innate structures are in particular domains.

What is a theory of learning? Is there such a theory as *the* theory of learning, waiting to be discovered? Let us try to sharpen and perhaps take some steps towards answering these questions.

Consider first how a neutral scientist—that imaginary ideal—might proceed to investigate the question. The natural first step would be to select an organism, O, and a reasonably well delimited cognitive domain, D, and to attempt to construct a theory that we might call "the learning theory for the organism O in the domain D." This theory—call it LT(O,D)—can be regarded as a system of principles, a mechanism, a function, which has a certain "input" and a certain "output" (its domain and range, respectively). The "input" to the system LT(O,D) will be an analysis of data in D by O; the "output" (which is, of course, internally represented, not overt and exhibited) will be a cognitive structure of some sort. This cognitive structure is one element of the cognitive state attained by O.

For example, take O to be humans and D language. Then LT(H,L) — the learning theory for humans in the domain language — will be the system of principles by which humans arrive at knowledge of language, given linguistic experience, that is, given a preliminary analysis that they develop for the data of language. Or, take O to be rats and D to be maze running. Then LT(R,M) is the system of principles used by rats in learning how to run mazes. The input to LT(R,M) is whatever preliminary analysis of data is used by rats to accomplish this feat, and the output is the relevant cognitive structure, however it should properly be characterized as a component of the state achieved by the rat who knows how to run a maze. There is no reason to doubt that the cognitive structure attained and the cognitive state of which it is a constituent will be rather complex.

To facilitate the discussion, let us make two simplifying assumptions. Assume first that individuals of the species O under investigation are essentially identical with respect to their ability to learn over the domain D — for example, that humans do not differ in language-learning capacity. Second, assume that learning can be conceptualized as an instantaneous process in the following sense: assume that LT(O,D) is presented with a cumulative record of all the data available to O up to a particular moment, and that LT(O,D), operating on that data, produces the cognitive structure attained at that moment. Neither of these assumptions is true: there are individual differences, and learning takes place over time, sometimes extended time. I will return later to the qustion of just "how false" these assumptions are. I think that they give a useful first approximation, helpful for the formulation of certain issues and possibly much more.

To pursue the study of a given LT(O,D) in a rational way, we will proceed through the following stages of inquiry:

1. Set the cognitive domain D.

2. Determine how O characterizes data in D "pretheoretically," thus constructing what we may call "the experience of O in D" (recall the idealization to "instantaneous learning").

3. Determine the nature of the cognitive structure attained; that is, determine, as well as possible, what is learned by O in the domain D.

4. Determine LT(O,D), the system that relates experience to what is learned.

Step 4 relies on the results attained in steps 2 and 3.

To avoid misunderstanding, perhaps I should stress that the ordering of steps is a kind of rational reconstruction of rational inquiry. In practice, there is no strict sequence. Work at level 4, for example, may convince us that our original delimitation of D was faulty, that we have failed to abstract a coherent cognitive domain. Or, it may lead us to conclude that we have misconstrued the character of what is learned, at step 3. It remains true, nevertheless, that we can hope to gain some insight at the level of step 4 only to the extent that we have achieved some understanding at levels 2 and 3 and have selected, wisely or luckily, at level 1. It is senseless to try to relate two systems — in this case, experience and what is learned — without some fairly good idea of what they are.

Parenthetically, we might observe that step 3 is missing in many formulations of psychological theory, much to their detriment. In fact, even the concept "what is learned" is missing in familiar "learning theories." Where it is missing, the basic questions of "learning theory" cannot even be formulated.

How does the study of behavior fit into this framework? Surely a prerequisite to the study of behavior is a grasp of the nature of the organism that is behaving — in the sense of "prerequisite" just explained. An organism has attained a certain state through maturation and experience. It is faced with certain objective conditions. It then does something. In principle, we might want to inquire into the mechanism M that determines what the organism does (perhaps probabilistically) given its past experience and its present stimulus conditions. I say "in principle," because I doubt that there is very much that we will be able to say about this question.

No doubt what the organism does depends in part on its experience, but it seems to me entirely hopeless to investigate directly the relation between experience and action. Rather, if we are interested in the problem of "causation of behavior" as a problem of science, we should at least analyze the relation of experience to behavior into two parts: first, LT, which relates past experience to cognitive state,[12] and second, a mechanism, M_{CS}, which relates present stimulus conditions to behavior, given the cognitive state CS.

To put it schematically, in place of the hopeless task of investigating M as in (I), we may more reasonably undertake research into the nature of LT as in (II) and M_{CS} as in (III).

(I) M: f(experience, stimulus conditions) = behavior

(II) LT: f(experience) = cognitive state CS

(III) M_{CS}: f(stimulus conditions) = behavior (given CS)

I think that we can make considerable progress towards understanding LT as in (II); that is, towards understanding particular LT(O,D)'s, for various

choices of D given O, and the interaction among them. It is this problem that I want to consider here. I doubt that we can learn very much, as scientists at least, about the second of these two parts, M_{CS}.[13] But it seems to me most unlikely that there will be any scientific progress at all if we do not at least analyze the problem of "causation of behavior" into the two components LT and M_{CS} and their elements. An attempt along the lines of (I) to study directly the relation of behavior to past and current experience is doomed to triviality and scientific insignificance.

Returning to the problem of learning, suppose that we have determined a number of LT(O,D)'s, for various choices of organism O and cognitive domain D. We can now turn to the question: What is "learning theory"? Or better: Is there such a theory as learning theory? The question might be put in various ways, for example, the following two:

(1) Is it the case that however we select O and D, we find the same LT(O,D)?

(2) Are there significant features common to all LT(O,D)'s?

Before considering these questions, let us return to the first of our simplifying assumptions, namely, with regard to variability within the species O. I would like to suggest that the interesting questions of "learning theory," those that might lead to a theory that is illuminating and that will ultimately relate to the body of natural science more generally, will be those for which our first assumption is essentially correct. That is, the interesting questions, those that offer some hope of leading to insight into the nature of organisms, will be those that arise in the investigation of learning in domains where there is a nontrivial structure uniform for members of O (with certain parameters relating to rapidity of learning, scope of learning, rate of forgetting, and other such marginal phenomena for which variability is to be expected). These are the questions that deal with significant characteristics of the species, or perhaps, of organisms generally. Again, I see no reason why cognitive structures should not be investigated rather in the way that physical organs are studied. The natural scientist will be primarily concerned with the basic, genetically determined structure of these organs and their interaction, a structure common to the species in the most interesting case, abstracting away from size, variation in rate of development, and so on.

If we can accept this judgment, then LT(O,D) can be characterized for O taken not as an individual but as a species — hence for individuals apart from gross abnormalities. And we may proceed to qualify question (1), asking whether LT(O,D) is identical with LT(O′,D′) apart from such matters as rapidity, facility, scope, and retention, which may vary across species and, to a lesser extent, among individuals of a given species.

Consider now question (1), so qualified. Surely the answer must still be a firm No. Even the crudest considerations suffice to show that there is no hope of reaching a positive answer to this question. Take O to be humans (H) and O′ rats (R); D to be language (L) and D′ maze running (M). If even some vague approximation to question (1) had a positive answer, we would expect humans to be as much superior to rats in maze-learning ability as they are in language-learning ability. But this is so grossly false that the question cannot be seriously entertained. Humans are roughly comparable to rats in the domain M but incomparable in the domain L. In fact, it seems that "white rats can even best college students in this sort of learning" — namely, maze-learning (Munn, 1971, p. 118). The distinction between the pair (LT(H,L), LT(R,L)) on the one hand and the pair (LT(H,M), LT(RM)) on the other cannot be attributed to sensory processing systems and the like, as we can see by "transpos-

ing" language into some modality accessible to rats. (Cf. chapter 4, note 14.) As far as is now known — and I say this despite suggestions to the contrary — the same is true if we consider other organisms (say, chimpanzees) in place of rats. Putting this interesting but peripheral question to the side, it is surely obvious at once that no version of question (1) is worth pursuing.

Let us turn to the more plausible speculation formulated in question (2). No answer is possible, for the present. The question is hopelessly premature. We lack an interesting conception of LT(O,D) for various choices of O and D. There are, I believe, some substantive steps possible towards LT(H,L), but nothing comparable in other domains of human learning. What is known about other animals, to my knowledge, suggests no interesting answer to (2). Animals learn to care for their young, build nests, orient themselves in space, find their place in a dominance structure, identify the species, and so on, but we should not expect to find significant properties which are common to the various LT(O,D)'s that enter into these achievements. Skepticism about question (2) is very much in order, on the basis of the very little that is known. I should think that for the biologist, the comparative physiologist, or the physiological psychologist, such skepticism would appear quite unremarkable.

Thus, for the present, there seems to be no reason to suppose that learning theory exists. At least, I see no interesting formulation of the thesis that there is such a theory that has initial plausibility or significant empirical support.

Within the odd variant of empiricism known as "behaviorism," the term "learning theory" has commonly been used, not as the designation of a theory (if it exists) that accounts for the attainment of cognitive structures on the basis of experience (namely, (II) above), but rather as a theory that deals with the relation of experience to behavior (namely, (I) above). Since there is no reason to suppose that learning theory exists, there is certainly no reason to expect that such a "theory of behavior" exists.

We might consider contentions more plausible than those implicit in questions (1) and (2). Suppose that we fix the organism O, and let D range over various cognitive domains. Then we might ask whether there is some interesting set of domains $D_1, \ldots, D_n$ such that:

(3) $LT(O,D_i) = LT(O,D_j)$; or $LT(O,D_i)$ is similar in interesting ways to $LT(O,D_j)$.

There might be some way of delimiting domains that would yield a positive answer to (3). If so, we could say that within this delimitation, the organism learns in similar or identical ways across cognitive domains. It would be interesting, for example, to discover whether there is some cognitive domain D other than language for which LT(H,L) is identical to or similar to LT(H,D). To date, no persuasive suggestion has been made, but conceivably there is such a domain. There is no particular reason to expect that there is such a domain, and one can only be surprised at the dogmatic view, commonly expressed, that language learning proceeds by application of general learning capacities. The most that we can say is that the possibility is not excluded, though there is no evidence for it and little plausibility to the contention. Even at the level of sensory processing there appear to be adaptations directly related to language, as already noted.[14] The proposal that language learning is simply an instance of "generalized learning capacities" makes about as much sense, in the present state of our knowledge, as a claim that the specific neural structures that provide our organization of visual space must be a special case of the class of systems involved also in language use. This is true,

so far as we know, only at a level so general as to give no insight into the character or functioning of the various systems.

For any organism O, we can try to discover those cognitive domains D for which the organism O has an interesting LT(O,D) — that is, an LT(O,D) that does not merely have the structure of trial-and-error learning, generalization along physically given dimensions, induction (in any well-defined sense of this notion), and so on. We might define the "cognitive capacity" of O as the system of domains D for which there is an interesting learning theory LT(O,D) in this sense.[15] For D within the cognitive capacity of O, it is reasonable to suppose that a schematism exists delimiting the class of cognitive structures that can be attained. Hence it will be possible, for such D, for a rich, complex, highly articulated cognitive structure to be attained with considerable uniformity among individuals (apart from matters of rate, scope, persistence, etc.) on the basis of scattered and restricted evidence.

Investigating the cognitive capacity of humans, we might consider, say, the ability to recognize and identify faces on exposure to a few presentations, to determine the personality structure of another person on brief contact (thus, to be able to guess, pretty well, how that person will react under a variety of conditions), to recognize a melody under transposition and other modifications, to handle those branches of mathematics that build on numerical or spatial intuition, to create art forms resting on certain principles of structure and organization, and so on. Humans appear to have characteristic and remarkable abilities in these domains, in that they construct a complex and intricate intellectual system, rapidly and uniformly, on the basis of degenerate evidence. And structures created by particularly talented individuals within these constraints are intelligible and appealing, exciting and thought-provoking even to those not endowed with unusual creative abilities. Inquiry, then, might lead to non-trivial LT(H,D)'s, for D so chosen. Such inquiry might involve experimentation or even historical investigation — for example, investigation of developments in forms of artistic composition or in mathematics that seemed "natural" and proved fruitful at particular historical moments, contributing to a "mainstream" of intellectual evolution rather than diverting energy to an unproductive side channel.[16]

Suppose that for a particular organism O, we manage to learn something about its cognitive capacity, developing a system of LT(O,D)'s for various choices of D with the rough properties sketched above. We would then have arrived at a theory of the mind of O, in one sense of this term. We may think of "the mind of O," to adapt a formulation of Anthony Kenny's,[17] as the innate capacity of O to construct cognitive structures, that is, to learn.

I depart here from Kenny's formulation in two respects, which perhaps deserve mention. He defines "mind" as a second-order capacity to acquire "intellectual abilities," such as knowledge of English — the latter "itself a capacity or ability: an ability whose exercise is the speaking, understanding, reading of English." Moreover, "to have a mind is to have the capacity to acquire the ability to operate with symbols in such a way that it is one's own activity that makes them symbols and confers meaning on them," so that automata operating with formal elements that are symbols for us but not for them do not have minds. For the sake of this discussion, I have generalized here beyond first-order capacities involving operations with symbols, and am thus considering second-order capacities broader than "mind" in Kenny's quite natural sense. So far there is no issue beyond terminology. Secondly, I want to consider mind (in the narrower or broader sense) as an innate capacity to form cognitive structures, not first-order capacities to act. The cognitive structures attained enter into our first-order capacities to act, but should not be identified with them. Thus it does not seem to me quite accurate to take "knowledge of English" to be a capacity or ability, though it enters into the capacity or ability exercised in language use. In principle, one might have the cognitive structure that we call "knowledge of English," fully developed, with no capacity to use this structure;[18] and certain capacities to carry out "intellectual activities" may involve no cognitive structures but merely a network of dispositions and habits, something quite different.[19] Knowledge, understanding, or belief is at a level more abstract than capacity.

There has been a tendency in modern analytic philosophy to employ the notion "disposition" or "capacity" where the more abstract concept of "cognitive structure" is, I believe, more appropriate. (Cf. chapter 4; also Chomsky, 1975a.) I think we see here an unfortunate residue of empiricism. The notions "capacity" and "family of dispositions" are more closely related to behavior and "language use"; they do not lead us to inquire into the nature of the "ghost in the machine" through the study of cognitive structures and their organization, as normal scientific practice and intellectual curiosity would demand. The proper way to exorcise the ghost in the machine is to determine the structure of the mind and its products.[20] There is nothing essentially mysterious about the concept of an abstract cognitive structure, created by an innate faculty of mind, represented in some still-unknown way in the brain, and entering into the system of capacities and dispositions to act and interpret. On the contrary, a formulation along these lines, embodying the conceptual competence-performance distinction (cf. Chomsky,

1965, chap. 1) seems a prerequisite for a serious investigation of behavior. Human action can be understood only on the assumption that first-order capacities and families of dispositions to behave involve the use of cognitive structures that express systems of (unconscious) knowledge, belief, expectation, evaluation, judgment, and the like. At least, so it seems to me.

Returning to the main theme, suppose that we now select a problem in a domain D that falls outside of O's cognitive capacity. O will then be at a loss as to how to proceed. O will have no cognitive structure available for dealing with this problem and no LT(O,D) available to enable it to develop such a structure. O will therefore have to proceed by trial and error, association, simple induction, and generalization along certain available dimensions (some questions arise here, which I put aside). Taking O to be humans, we will not expect the person to be able to find or construct a rich and insightful way to deal with the problem, to develop a relevant cognitive structure in the intuitive, unconscious manner characteristic of language learning and other domains in which humans excel.

Humans might be able to construct a conscious scientific theory dealing with problems in the domain in question, but that is a different matter — or better, a partially different matter, since even here there are crucial constraints. An intellectually significant science, an intelligible explanatory theory, can be developed by humans in case something close to the true theory in a certain domain happens to fall within human "science-forming" capacities. The LT(H,D)'s involved in scientific inquiry, whatever they may be, must be special and restrictive, or it would be impossible for scientists to converge in their judgment on particular explanatory theories that go far beyond the evidence at hand, as they customarily do in those few fields where there really is significant progress, while at the same time rejecting much evidence as irrelevant or beside the point, for the moment at least. The same LT(H,D)'s that provide for the vast and impressive scope of scientific understanding must also sharply constrain the class of humanly accessible sciences. There is, surely, no evolutionary pressure that leads humans to have minds capable of discovering significant explanatory theories in specific fields of inquiry. Thinking of humans as biological organisms in the natural world, it is only a lucky accident if their cognitive capacity happens to be well matched to scientific truth in some area. It should come as no surprise, then, that there are so few sciences, and that so much of human inquiry fails to attain any intellectual depth. Investigation of human cognitive capacity might give us some insight into the class of humanly accessible sciences, possibly a small subset of those potential sciences that deal with matters concerning which we hope (vainly) to attain some insight and understanding.

As a case in point, consider our near-total failure to discover a scientific theory that provides an analysis of M_{CS} as defined in (III) — that is, our very limited progress in developing a scientific theory of any depth to account for the normal use of language (or other aspects of behavior). Even the relevant concepts seem lacking; certainly, no intellectually satisfying principles have been proposed that have explanatory force, though the questions are very old. It is not excluded that human science-forming capacities simply do not extend to this domain, or any domain involving the exercise of will, so that for humans, these questions will always be shrouded in mystery.

Note, incidentally, how misleading it would be to speak simply of "limitations" in human science-forming capacity. Limits no doubt exist, but they derive from the same source as our ability to construct rich cognitive systems on the basis of limited evidence in the first place.

Were it not for the factors that limit scientific knowledge, we could have no such knowledge in any domain.[21]

Suppose that in investigating organisms, we decide, perversely, to restrict ourselves to tasks and problems that lie outside their cognitive capacity. We might then expect to discover simple "laws of learning" of some generality. Suppose further that we define a "good experiment" as one that provides smooth learning curves, regular increments and extinction, and so on. Then there will be "good experiments" only in domains that lie outside of O's cognitive capacity. For example, there will be no "good experiments" in the study of human language learning, though there may be if we concentrate attention on memorization of nonsense syllables, verbal association, and other tasks for which humans have no special abilities.

Suppose now that some branch of inquiry develops, limited in principle to "good experiments" in something like this sense. This discipline may, indeed, develop laws of learning that do not vary too greatly across cognitive domains for a particular organism and that have some cross-species validity. It will, of necessity, avoid those domains in which an organism is specially designed to acquire rich cognitive structures that enter into its life in an intimate fashion. The discipline will be of virtually no intellectual interest, it seems to me, since it is restricting itself in principle to those questions that are guaranteed to tell us little about the nature of organisms. For we can learn something significant about this nature only by inquiry into the organism's cognitive capacity, inquiry that will permit no "good experiments" in the strange sense just specified, though it may lead to the discovery (through experiment and observation) of intricate and no doubt highly specific LT(O,D)'s. The results and achievements of this perversely limited, rather suicidal discipline are largely an ar-

tifact. It will be condemned in principle to investigation of peripheral matters such as rate and scope of acquisition of information, the relation between arrangement of reinforcers and response strength, control of behavior, and the like. The discipline in question may continue indefinitely to amass information about these matters, but one may question the point or purpose of these efforts.

A more elaborate study of cognitive capacity raises still further questions. Thus, some intellectual achievements, such as language learning, fall strictly within biologically determined cognitive capacity. For these tasks, we have "special design," so that cognitive structures of great complexity and interest develop fairly rapidly and with little if any conscious effort. There are other tasks, no more "complex" along any absolute scale (assuming that it is possible even to make sense of this notion), which will be utterly baffling because they fall beyond cognitive capacity. Consider problems that lie at the borderline of cognitive capacity. These will provide opportunity for intriguing intellectual play. Chess, for example, is not so remote from cognitive capacity as to be merely a source of insoluble puzzles, but is at the same time sufficiently beyond our natural abilities so that it is challenging and intriguing. Here, we would expect to find that the slight differences between individuals are magnified to striking divergence of aptitude.

The study of challenging intellectual tasks might give some insight into human intelligence, at the borders of cognitive capacity, just as the study of the ability to run a four-minute mile may give useful information about human physiology. But it would be pointless to study the latter feat at a very early stage of our understanding of human locomotion—say, if we knew only that humans walk rather than fly. Correspondingly, in the present state of our understanding of mental abilities, it seems to me that, for example, the study of chess-playing programs may teach something about the theory of chess, but is unlikely to contribute much to the study of human intelligence. It is good procedure to study major factors before turning to tenth-order effects, to study the basic character of an intricate system before exploring its borders, though of course one can never know in advance just what line of inquiry will provide sudden illumination.[22]

In the case of human cognition, it is the study of the basic cognitive structures within cognitive capacity, their development and use, that should receive priority, I believe, if we are to attain a real understanding of the mind and its workings.

The preceding discussion is not very precise. I hope that it is at least suggestive as to how a rational study of learning might proceed. Let me now turn to the particular questions in the "theory of learning" that concern language.

Let us take O to be humans (H) and D to be language (L). What is LT(H,L)? Of the two simplifying assumptions mentioned earlier, the first — invariability across the species — is, so far as we know, fair enough. It seems to provide a close approximation to the facts. Let us therefore accept it with no further discussion, while keeping a cautious and skeptical eye on the second assumption, that learning is "instantaneous." I will return to the latter in chapter 3.

LT(H,L) is the system of mechanisms and principles put to work in acquisition of knowledge of language — acquisition of the specific cognitive structure that we are calling "grammar" — given data which are a fair and adequate sample of this language.[23] The grammar is a system of rules and principles that determine the formal and semantic properties of sentences. The grammar is put to use, interacting with other mechanisms of mind, in speaking and understanding language. There are empirical assumptions and con-

ceptual distinctions embedded in this account, and they might be wrong or misguided, but I think it is not unreasonable, given present understanding, to proceed with them.

To relate these remarks to earlier discussion, note that I am insisting that the relation of experience to action be subdivided into two systems: LT(H,L), which relates experience to cognitive state attained, and M_{CS}, which relates current conditions to action, given cognitive state attained ((II)-(III) above). One of the cognitive structures entering into the cognitive state CS attained and put to use by M_{CS} is grammar. Again, I see few present prospects for the scientific study of M_{CS}, though the study of LT(H,L), it seems to me, can be profitably pursued.

Let us define "universal grammar" (UG) as the system of principles, conditions, and rules that are elements or properties of all human languages not merely by accident but by necessity — of course, I mean biological, not logical, necessity. Thus UG can be taken as expressing "the essence of human language." UG will be invariant among humans. UG will specify what language learning must achieve, if it takes place successfully. Thus UG will be a significant component of LT(H,L). What is learned, the cognitive structure attained, must have the properties of UG, though it will have other properties as well, accidental properties. Each human language will conform to UG; languages will differ in other, accidental properties. If we were to construct a language violating UG, we would find that it could not be learned by LT(H,L). That is, it would not be learnable under normal conditions of access and exposure to data. Possibly it could be learned by application of other faculties of mind; LT(H,L) does not exhaust the capacities of the human mind. This invented language might be learned as a puzzle, or its grammar might be discovered by scientific inquiry over the course of generations, with the intervention of individual genius, with explicit articulation of principles and careful experimentation. This would be possible if the language happened to fall within the bounds of the "science-forming" component of human cognitive capacity. But discovery of the grammar of this language would not be comparable to language learning, just as inquiry in physics is qualitatively different from language learning.

UG will specify properties of sound, meaning, and structural organization. We may expect that in all of these domains, UG will impose conditions that narrowly restrict the variety of languages. For familiar reasons, we cannot conclude from the highly restrictive character of UG that there is a translation procedure of any generality or significance, even in principle (cf. Chomsky, 1965). And quite obviously, nothing is implied about the possibility of translating actual texts, since a speaker or writer naturally presupposes a vast background of unspecified assumptions, beliefs, attitudes, and conventions. The point is perhaps worth noting, since there has been much confusion about the matter. For some discussion, see Keyser (1975).

We can gain some insight into UG, hence LT(H,L), whenever we find properties of language that can reasonably be supposed not to have been learned. To make the discussion more concrete, consider a familiar example, perhaps the simplest one that is not entirely trivial. Think of the process of forming questions in English. Imagine again our neutral scientist, observing a child learning English. Suppose that he discovers that the child has learned to form such questions as those of (A), corresponding to the associated declaratives:

(A)   the man is tall — is the man tall? the book is on the table — is the book on the table? etc.

Observing these facts, the scientist might arrive at the following tentative hypothesis as to what the child is doing,

assuming now that sentences are analyzed into words:

Hypothesis 1: The child processes the declarative sentence from its first word (i.e., from "left to right"), continuing until he reaches the first occurrence of the word "is" (or others like it: "may," "will," etc.); he then preposes this occurrence of "is," producing the corresponding question (with some concomitant modifications of form that need not concern us).

This hypothesis works quite well. It is also extremely simple. The scientist has every right to be satisfied, and will be able to find a great deal of evidence to support his tentative hypothesis. Of course, the hypothesis is false, as we learn from such examples as (B) and (C):

(B)   the man who is tall is in the room — is the man who is tall in the room?
(C)   the man who is tall is in the room — is the man who tall is in the room?

Our scientist would discover, surely, that on first presentation with an example such as "the man who is tall is in the room," the child unerringly forms the question (B), not (C) (if he can handle the example at all). Children make many mistakes in language learning, but never mistakes such as exemplified in (C). If the scientist is reasonable, this discovery will surprise him greatly, for it shows that his simple hypothesis 1 is false, and that he must construct a far more complex hypothesis to deal with the facts. The correct hypothesis is the following, ignoring complications that are irrelevant here:

Hypothesis 2: The child analyzes the declarative sentence into abstract phrases; he then locates the first occurrence of "is" (etc.) that follows the first noun phrase; he then preposes this occurrence of "is," forming the corresponding question.

Hypothesis 1 holds that the child is employing a "structure-independent rule" — that is, a rule that involves only analysis into words and the property "earliest" ("left-most") defined on word sequences. Hypothesis 2 holds that the child is employing a "structure-dependent rule," a rule that involves analysis into words and phrases, and the property "earliest" defined on sequences of words analyzed into abstract phrases. The phrases are "abstract" in the sense that neither their boundaries nor their categories (noun phrase, verb phrase, etc.) need be physically marked. Sentences do not appear with brackets, intonation boundaries regularly marking phrases, subscripts identifying the type of phrase, or anything of the sort.

By any reasonable standards, hypothesis 2 is far more complex and "unlikely" than hypothesis 1. The scientist would have to be driven by evidence, such as (B), (C), to postulate hypothesis 2 in place of the simpler and more elementary hypothesis 1. Correspondingly, the scientist must ask why it is that the child unerringly makes use of the structure-dependent rule postulated in hypothesis 2, rather than the simpler structure-independent rule of hypothesis 1. There seems to be no explanation in terms of "communicative efficiency" or similar considerations. It is certainly absurd to argue that children are trained to use the structure-dependent rule, in this case. In fact, the problem never arises in language learning. A person may go through a considerable part of his life without ever facing relevant evidence, but he will have no hesitation in using the structure-dependent rule, even if all of his experience is consistent with hypothesis 1. The only reasonable conclusion is that UG contains the principle that all such rules must be structure-dependent. That is, the child's mind (specifically, its component LT(H,L)) contains the instruction: Construct a structure-dependent rule, ignoring all structure-independent rules. The principle of structure-dependence is not learned, but forms part of the conditions for language learning.

To corroborate this conclusion about UG (hence LT(H,L)), the scientist will ask whether other rules of English are invariably structure-dependent. So far as we know, the answer is positive. If a rule is found that is not structure-dependent, the scientist will be faced with a problem. He will have to inquire further into UG, to discover what additional principles differentiate the two categories of rules, so that the child can know without instruction that one is structure-dependent and the other not. Having gotten this far, the scientist will conclude that other languages must have the same property, on the assumption that humans are not specifically designed to learn one rather than another language, say English rather than Japanese. On this reasonable assumption, the principle of structure-dependence (perhaps, if necessary, qualified as indicated above) must hold universally, if it holds for English. Investigating the consequences of his reasoning, the scientist would discover (so far as we know) that the conclusion is correct.

More complex examples can be produced, but this simple one illustrates the general point. Proceeding in this way, the scientist can develop some rich and interesting hypotheses about UG, hence LT(H,L). Thus, learning theory for humans in the domain of language incorporates the principle of structure-dependence along with other more intricate (and, I should add, more controversial) principles like it. I will return to some of these in the third chapter.

Keeping this single example of a principle of UG in mind, let us return now to the "innateness hypothesis." Recall that there is no issue as to the necessity for such a hypothesis, only as to its character.

Assuming still the legitimacy of the simplifying assumption about instantaneous learning, the "innateness hypothesis" will consist of several elements: principles for the preliminary, pretheoretic analysis of data as experience, which serves as input to LT(H,L); properties of UG, which determine the character of what is learned; other principles of a sort not discussed in the foregoing sketch.

We might, quite reasonably, formulate the *theory of language* so as to reflect this way of looking at LT(H,L). A theory is a system of principles expressed in terms of certain concepts. The principles are alleged to be true of the subject matter of the theory. A particular presentation of a theory takes some of the concepts as primitive and some of the principles as axioms. The choice of primitives and axioms must meet the condition that all concepts are defined in terms of the primitives and that all principles derive from the axioms. We might choose to formulate linguistic theory by taking its primitive concepts to be those that enter into the preliminary analysis of data as experience, with the axioms including those principles expressing relations between the primitive concepts that enter into this preliminary analysis (thus, the primitive notions are "epistemologically primitive"; they meet an external empirical condition apart from sufficiency for definition). The defined terms belong to UG, and the principles of UG will be theorems of this theory. Linguistic theory, so construed, is a theory of UG incorporated into LT(H,L) in the manner described.

The "innateness hypothesis," then, can be formulated as follows: Linguistic theory, the theory of UG, construed in the manner just outlined, is an innate property of the human mind. In principle, we should be able to account for it in terms of human biology.

To the extent that our simplifying assumption about instantaneous learning must be revised, along lines to which I will return, we must accordingly complicate the "innateness hypothesis."

A fuller version of the "innateness hypothesis" for humans will specify the various domains belonging to cognitive capacity, the faculty of mind LT(H,D) for each such domain D, the relations between these faculties, their modes of maturation, and the interactions among them through time. Alongside of the language faculty and interacting with it in the most intimate way is the faculty of mind that constructs what we might call "common-sense understanding," a system of beliefs, expectations, and knowledge concerning the nature and behavior of objects, their place in a system of "natural kinds," the organization of these categories, and the properties that determine the categorization of objects and the analysis of events. A general "innateness hypothesis" will also include principles that bear on the place and role of people in a social world, the nature and conditions of work, the structure of human action, will and choice, and so on. These systems may be unconscious for the most part and even beyond the reach of conscious introspection. One might also want to isolate for special study the faculties involved in problem solving, construction of scientific knowledge, artistic creation and expression, play, or whatever prove to be the appropriate categories for the study of cognitive capacity, and derivatively, human action.

Notes

1. Aristotle, *Posterior Analytics* 2. 19 (ed. McKeon, 1941), pp. 184-6.

2. Cudworth (1838), p. 75. Except for those otherwise identified, quotations that follow in this paragraph are from the same source: respectively, pp. 65, 51, 49, 87, 122-3.

3. Leibniz, *Discourse on Metaphysics* (trans. Montgomery, 1902), p. 45. For a similar view, see Cudworth (1838), p. 64. For quotations and further discussion, see Chomsky (1966), Section 4.

4. Cudworth, *True Intellectual System of the Universe*, cited by Lovejoy (1908).

5. Lovejoy (1908).

6. Henry More, "Antidote Against Atheism," cited by Lovejoy (1908).

7. Gregory (1970). Gregory suggests further that the grammar of language "has its roots in the brain's rules for ordering retinal patterns in terms of objects," that is, "in a take-over operation, in which man cashed in on" the development of the visual system in higher animals. This seems questionable. The structure, use, and acquisition of language seem to involve special properties that are, so far as is known, not found elsewhere. Language is based on properties of the dominant hemisphere that may also be quite specialized. There seems to be no obvious relationship to the structure of the visual cortex in relevant respects, though so little is known that one can only speculate. It is not clear why one should expect to find an evolutionary explanation of the sort that Gregory suggests. For more on these matters, see the chapters by R. W. Sperry, A. M. Liberman, H.-L. Teuber, and B. Milner in Schmitt and Worden (1974).

8. This view, popularized in recent years by B. F. Skinner, is foreign to science or any rational inquiry. The reasons for its popularity must be explained on extrascientific grounds. For further discussion, see my "Psychology and Ideology," reprinted in Chomsky (1973b); also Chomsky (1973c); and the discussion of liberalism and empiricism in Bracken (1972, 1973a).

9. Antoine Arnauld (1964), p. 36. On the importance of considering "language as a biological phenomenon [comparable] to other biological phenomena" and some implications for epistemology and the philosophy of language and mind, see Moravcsik (1975b).

10. See, for example, the references of note 8.

11. Appropriateness is not to be confused with control, nor can the properties of language use noted here (what I have elsewhere called "the creative aspect of language use") be identified with the recursive property of grammars. Failure to keep these very different concepts separate has led to much confusion. For discussion of the creative aspect of language use in rationalist theory, see Chomsky (1966) and (1972a).

12. By LT I mean here the system of LT(O,D)'s, O fixed, D an arbitrary domain. In the terminology suggested, each LT(O,D) constructs a cognitive structure. Operating in concert and interaction, the LT(O,D)'s for given O form a cognitive state.

13. Hence I will not even raise the further question whether there is anything to say about M_2(CS, stimulus conditions), namely, a possible general mechanism ranging over cognitive states that might be called a "general theory of behavior."

14. See Eimas et al. (1971) and the references of note 7 above.

15. Thus we take cognitive capacity to be the set of such domains with whatever further structure this complex may have.

16. Consider the argument of Bourbaki that "as a matter of empirical fact, the bulk of mathematically significant notions can be analyzed profitably in terms of a *few* basic structures such as groups or topological spaces. They regard this fact as a discovery about our thinking . . ." (Kreisel, 1974).

17. Anthony Kenny, "The Origin of the Soul," in Kenny et al. (1973).

18. Imagine some hypothetical form of aphasia in which knowledge is unimpaired but all systems involving performance, i.e., putting knowledge to use, are destroyed. For discussion of this matter, see Stich (1972) and Chomsky and Katz (1974).

19. Thus my use of the term "cognitive capacity" (p. 21) might be misleading, though I have not found a term less likely to mislead.

20. I have discussed elsewhere why I think that modern criticisms of "Descartes's myth" by Ryle and others simply miss the point. Cf. Chomsky (1966), p. 12; (1972a), p. 13; (1975a).

21. On this matter, see Chomsky (1972a), pp. 90ff.; (1971), pp. 20ff.

22. To avoid misunderstanding, I am not making the absurd suggestion that science should study what is familiar and commonplace rather than search for perhaps exotic data that shed light on deeper principles. In the study of language no less than physics, this would be a self-defeating program. Gross coverage of familar phenomena can be achieved by very different theories; it is generally necessary to seek unusual data to distinguish them. To cite an example, idioms in natural

language are (by definition) abnormal, but the capacity of various linguistic theories to deal with their character and peculiarities has often proved quite relevant for distinguishing empirically among these theories.

23. Note that the notions "fair" and "adequate" are yet to be made precise, as biological properties of humans, though it is no great problem to place some reasonable bounds.

The Specificity of Language Skills

Jerry A. Fodor, Thomas G. Bever, and Merrill F. Garrett

It is sometimes said, in a rough-and-ready way, that while the American tradition in psychology is largely empiricist, the view of language learning characteristic of psycholinguists working in the tradition of generative grammar is nativistic. This way of talking is harmless unless it leads one to suppose that empiricist theories of learning are somehow able to do without assumptions about the character of the innate information that organisms bring to learning tasks. It is important to understand that no theorist whose views of learning are coherent can avoid such assumptions [for a discussion of this issue, see Harman (1969) and Chomsky (1969)]. We shall presently see that there *is* a real disagreement between the American tradition in learning theory and the views most psycholinguists now hold about the nature of language acquisition; our present point is that the disagreement is not properly captured by saying that one position is nativistic and the other is not.

For the empiricist, the learning of

From *The Psychology of Language* (New York: McGraw-Hill, 1974), pp. 436-441, 449-462. Copyright © 1974 by McGraw-Hill, Inc. Used with permission of McGraw-Hill Book Company and the authors.

languages is primarily a matter of discrimination learning: the ability to distinguish between utterances of sentences and nonsentential sounds is treated as a learned perceptual discrimination, and the ability to produce linguistically regular utterances is treated as a learned response discrimination. To understand why any such theory must be committed to fairly strong assumptions about the innate contribution of the organism to its performance in learning tasks, we must consider the discrimination-learning paradigm in some detail.

Whenever an organism learns a discrimination as the result of training, certain very general conditions must be satisfied. In the first place, there must be a *training period* during which the organism experiences correlations between reinforcement and certain other events. In typical discrimination-learning experiments, these "other events" are stimulus-response pairs. Second, it is a logically necessary condition for the occurrence of discrimination learning that the responses of the organism toward some potential future stimuli must be modified as a result of training. Finally, it is a logically necessary condition for the occurrence of discrimination learning that there be potential stimuli toward which training does *not* modify the organism's behavior. (A response that transfers to everything is not a discriminated response.)

Let us call the set of events with which reinforcement is coincident during the training period the *positive training set*. We will say that other events experienced by the organism during the training period constitute the *negative training set*. Finally, we will call the events toward which the organism's future behavior is modified by training the *positive transfer set* and the events toward which the organism's future behavior is *not* modified the *negative transfer set*.

We may now think of what happens in discrimination-learning experiments as a "game" the psychologist plays with the experimental organism. This game is played in the following way: the experimenter specifies the training sets by manipulating the reward contingencies. The experimental animal is then required to choose a corresponding transfer set. The animal wins (i.e., continues to be reinforced) if the positive transfer set it chooses is related to the positive training set in the right way (i.e., if it shares with the members of the positive training set those properties upon which reward is, in fact, contingent). On the other hand, the animal loses (i.e., ceases to be reinforced) if it chooses a positive transfer set whose members do *not* exhibit those properties upon which reward is contingent.

In short, what happens in the discrimination experiment is that the animal "bets" on which positive transfer set a given positive training set belongs to. There is, however, a more illuminating way of looking at it: having experienced a set of reinforced events, the animal is required to decide which properties the members of that set share with one another, but not with unreinforced events.

Notice that these two ways of characterizing the animal's problem are actually equivalent. This is because each hypothesis that the animal can devise about what property distinguishes unreinforced from reinforced training trials automatically determines a pair of positive and negative transfer sets. Thus, if the animal bets that P is that property, it thereby chooses events exhibiting P as belonging to the positive transfer set.

Now, given any finite set of reinforced events, there are obviously indefinitely many properties its members have in common with one another but not with the unreinforced events the animal has experienced. That is, there are indefinitely many hypotheses that will be true of all reinforced events and no unreinforced events, whatever the objective schedule of reinforcement happens to have been. Here then is the puzzle that a substantive theory of learning must solve. There are indefinitely many distinct bets that the animal can, in principle, make about what property defines the positive training set. Each such bet determines a different pattern of transfer: i.e., each bet determines a projection of the positive training set onto a different positive transfer set. Hence for any given training set there are infinitely many corresponding transfer sets among which the animal must choose. Question: What determines the choice?

In the case of animals in Skinner boxes, the empiricist may plausibily argue that the organism doesn't do anything like choosing among an infinity of possible transfer sets when it learns. It may be, says the empiricist, that there are an infinity of *predicates* that the events in the positive training set satisfy and that are not satisfied by the events in the negative training set. But it is a fallacy to think of the animal as somehow sorting through these predicates in order to find the one which names the property upon which reinforcement is contingent. For of that infinity of possible descriptions of the positive training set, there is only one (or only a few) that the animal could be conceived of as entertaining. Thus descriptions of the reinforcement set that refer, for example, to the abstract numerical properties of its members, to their geographical properties, or to their astrological properties simply do not occur to the animal. What does occur to it (or, to put it less tendentiously, what the animal does respond to) is things like color, sound, odor, rudimentary configurational properties, motion, and whatever other sensory properties it has sensory mechanisms for detecting. Only if the reinforced property of the members of the positive training set is one of these, or perhaps a simple Boolean function of them, does the animal learn. In short, there is no problem of "choosing a transfer set" because the choice is determined by the organism's *peripheral physiology*.

It is important to notice, however, that this way out of the problem (which, so far as we know, has been accepted by every psychologist who has discussed the problem at all) is itself nativistic. The suggestion, after all, is simply that the organism comes prewired to choose its transfer sets in a certain way (by reference to the sensory properties of its members) and not in other ways (not by reference to their number-theoretic or astrological properties). It is obvious, moreover, that the nativist move is the right move to make here. Unless one makes it, one creates an insuperable difficulty about how the organism ever makes the right induction from the observed contingencies of reinforcement.

Indeed, the most profound students of learning, be they empiricists or nativists, have generally acknowledged that there can be no explanation of generalization of training which does not eventually refer to the innate organization of the organism. Pavlov assumes as a matter of course that the pattern of

generalization typical of a species must reflect the "spread of neural excitation," the character of which is in turn determined by the local organization of the organism's nervous system. Similarly, the philosopher Quine argues that the possibility of learning presupposes, on the part of the organism, an innate quality space and an innate distance measure. The argument in both cases is essentially the same: there cannot be coherent transfer of training unless there are some general principles that determine which transfer set is selected by a given training set; and, on pain of infinite regress, we cannot assure that these principles themselves are all learned.

We can summarize the preceding discussion as follows: *Any* theory of discrimination learning must consist of two components. The first answers the question, What hypotheses does the organism have available for defining possible relations between training sets and transfer sets? The second answers the question, What considerations determine which of two such hypotheses the organism chooses in a specific learning situation? Answers to the latter question are generally given by theories constructed in terms of reinforcement variables. Such theories can profitably be construed as partial specifications of confirmation metrics, according to which the probability that the organism will accept a hypothesis is taken to be some complicated function of the frequency with which acting upon that hypothesis has yielded "confirming" data (i.e., rewards). Practically all traditional learning theory has this character, except that "probability of acceptance of a hypothesis" is usually called "response strength," "habit strength," etc.

The first kind of question is widely ignored in the learning theoretic tradition. However, as we have seen, any theory of learning must make some assumptions about the range of hypotheses available to the organism in the learning situation, and, in the long run, the assumptions one makes must be determined by what one supposes the innate cognitive structure of the organism to be. It is in this sense that no one can avoid being nativistic about learning, and it is in this sense that the controversy between classic and contemporary views of language acquisition is *not* a controversy over nativism.

But while it is a conceptual point that any organism which learns must have inherent principles for projecting its past experience to new cases, it is a question of brute fact whether such principles are species-specific, task-specific, or both. For example, it is a factual question whether the learning principles that underlie human-language acquisition are similar to those which underlie the acquisition of birdsong or, for that matter, the acquisition of nonlinguistic skills in humans. *It is, in short, the questions of species-specificity and task-specificity, rather than the question of innateness, that underlie the current disputes between empiricists and psycholinguists.* It is to these questions that we now turn.

The Species-Specificity of Language

A good one-sentence summary of the traditional American view of the psychology of language might be: "Verbal behavior differs in complexity but not in kind from learned behavior in animals." The consequences of this view were pursued with relentless consistency by American learning theorists. For example, Mowrer (1960) argued that given the essential homogeneity of verbal and nonverbal learning, the fact that humans and no other animals have achieved speech can be attributed only to the relatively advanced development of motor control of the vocal system in man. "It can hardly be doubted that the greatest single 'mutation' which separates man from other anthropoids consists precisely

of this: new and more abundant neural connections between the speech center in the brain and the speech organs!" (p. 111).

Indeed, the literature of this period abounds in attempts to train animals to talk, thereby demonstrating the essential homogeneity of human-language learning with infrahuman learning of motor skills. It seems to have been assumed that success in teaching language to an infrahuman organism is a critical experiment in demonstrating the interspecific character of the learning mechanisms involved in language acquisition.

These early attempts to teach animals to talk were, however, uniformly unsuccessful (cf. Kellogg and Kellogg, 1933; and the review by Brown, 1970). Nevertheless, theorists were surprisingly willing to draw morals for human-language learning from the putative facts about animals.

It is apparent that birds learn to talk when and only when the human teacher becomes a *love object* for them, . . . In terms of psychoanalytic theory, the bird, as a result of developing "positive cathexis" (love) for its human trainer or "foster parent," identifies with or tries to *be like* that person. . . . So far as can be determined at present, essentially the same account holds, at least up to a point, for acquisition of speech by human infants. . . . Human infants, like birds, are vocally versatile creatures and in the course of random activities in this area will eventually make sounds somewhat similar to those which have already acquired pleasant connotations [Mowrer, 1960, pp. 79-80].

Whatever one may think about the advisability of applying psychoanalytic theory to mynah birds, it *is* clear that the early failures to teach speech to animals are equivocal. For organisms that can produce speech-like sounds (parrots, mynah birds, etc.) are not remarkably plausible candidates for learning complex symbolic systems. Conversely, organisms whose general intelligence seems even remotely comparable to that of man (chimpanzees and possibly dolphins) have articulatory systems that are not well adapted to the production of speech sounds.

Two recent studies (both still in progress) have attempted to circumvent these difficulties by teaching a nonverbal language to chimpanzees. We shall briefly review these studies, concentrating on what they show about the chimpanzee's ability to master syntactic structures comparable to those found in human languages. [*Editor's note*: The review has been omitted, but it is summarized below.]

* * *

Summary

What has the work with Washoe and Sarah shown us? This question divides four ways: What has it shown us about chimpanzees? What has it shown us about whether chimpanzees can learn languages? What has it shown us about the species-specificity of the mechanisms involved in human-language learning? What has it shown us about human languages?

—What have the chimpanzee studies shown us about chimpanzees? Primarily, that chimpanzees are intelligent animals, and that they parse the world more or less the way that we do. In a variety of circumstances, Sarah and Washoe make discriminations and identifications in ways that make sense to us. Perhaps it is some comfort to have our ontology seconded by one of the higher primates. At any event, it is clear that the methodological decision to allow the chimpanzee to use nonverbal responses in signaling its classifications has been more than justified by the results.

—What have the chimpanzee studies shown us about the chimpanzees' ability to learn human language? Neither Washoe nor Sarah appears to have mastered a productive syntactic system;

in neither case do the animals' responses give clear evidence of constituent structure, to say nothing of transformational structure. In Washoe's case, it is at best extremely doubtful that any of the human grammatical relations are syntactically coded in her language. In Sarah's case, constituent order clearly performs such a coding, but perhaps only because discrimination training was explicitly employed to distinguish the reward conditions associated with distinct constituent orders. Since Sarah mastered none of the mechanisms that her language provides for generating novel constitutent sequences, this factor demonstrates only that chimpanzees can be conditioned to discriminate ordinal relations and apparently has no other significance.

We do not, of course, claim that no one will ever succeed in training an animal to use a language with a productive syntax. But it is remarkably clear from the studies of Washoe and Sarah that learning such systems is not a natural and spontaneous accomplishment for chimpanzees; apparently, that is, years of exposure to a language environment is not sufficient. The best one can say is that the present experiments provide no evidence that chimpanzees can learn a formal system in any important way similar to a natural language.

—What have the chimpanzee studies shown about the species-specificity of language-learning capacities in humans? It seems to us that the answer must be that these studies would not have been relevant to that question even if they had been fully successful.

Linguistic information is innate in humans if and only if it is represented in the gene code. Whether other animals can be taught to talk is irrelevant to answering this question. If they cannot be taught to talk, it need not be because they lack the relevant genetic endowment but only that they lack, for example, the relevant motivation. Conversely, if they can be taught to talk, they may still lack whatever innate species-specific language-handling capacities humans are endowed with; e.g., they may learn to talk in a different way from the way that humans do.

This last point is rather more than a quibble, since there are very many clear cases in which an organism with one kind of innate endowment can be trained to mimic the behavior of an organism with a quite different kind of innate endowment. The fact that a dog can be trained to walk on its hind legs does not prejudice the claim that bipedal gait is genetically coded in humans. The fact that we can learn to whistle like a lark does not prejudice the species-specificity of birdsong. It is hard to see, then, why a successful attempt to teach a chimpanzee to talk should have any bearing on the innateness of language in people.

—What have the chimpanzee studies shown us about language? Literally, nothing.

Given that the chimpanzee studies provide no decisive evidence against the claim that the human ability to talk a language is based on a species-specific genetic endowment, what positive arguments can be adduced in favor of the view that language skills are species-specific? The claim at issue is that when humans learn their language, they exploit a genetic endowment that other types of organisms do not have. It is to the character of this endowment, rather than to their "general intelligence," that the human capacity for language is attributed.

As Lorenz (1965) has remarked, the standard ethological method for establishing that behavior is species-specific, in the sense of being the consequence of specific phylogenetically adapted mechanisms, is the employment of the deprivation experiment. In such experiments one withholds "from the young organism information concerning certain well-defined givens of its natural environ-ment" (p. 83). Behavior patterns which the organism exhibits in spite of this sort of deprivation are considered to be genetically coded.

This method cannot be applied in the study of language learning: the crucial experiment, in which the character of the child's exposure to linguistic inputs is systematically manipulated, cannot be run. Moreover, the nativist need not claim that the human infant deprived of linguistic inputs would nevertheless exhibit verbal behavior. There are a variety of ethological precedents for the claim that the appearance of innately specified behavior is sometimes triggered only when the environment provides appropriate "releasing" stimuli. Very often the character of the stimuli that can serve to release innate behavior may itself be innately specified, either diffusely or in considerable detail (cf. Tinbergen, 1969, for examples). Thus the nativist and the empiricist can agree that experience is essential for the development of language behavior even though they disagree over the kind of role experience is alleged to play. For the empiricist, whatever information the organism uses to structure its behavior is abstracted from regularities in its environment. For the nativist, environmental information serves largely to elicit behavior whose principles of organization are genetically coded.

It is clear, at any event, that claims for species-specificity of language-learning mechanisms in humans cannot rest upon the relatively direct evidence that deprivation experiments provide. There are, however, five kinds of indirect evidence that can be brought to bear. We turn now to a review of this evidence.

1. There are a number of types of evidence which suggest a degree of dissociation between cognitive and linguistic development. For example, we have already seen that chimpanzees exhibit no clear ability to learn language.

The mental age of a mature chimpanzee is usually said to be comparable to that of a 3-year-old child, and 3-year-old children are verbal organisms. Similarly, there is evidence that the child's acquisition of language skills proceeds in roughly the same fashion in normal and pathological populations. This suggests that the character of language development is not particularly sensitive to general cognitive impairment and hence that language development is not simply an expression of general intellectual development.

Investigators have remarked upon the relatively unlabile character of certain features of language development in brain-damaged children and in children with congenital neurological disorders: the types of linguistic structures available to a child of a given *mental* age appear to be similar for pathological and normal groups. There are at least two relevant studies. The first is by Lenneberg, Nichols, and Rosenberger (1964), who examined 84 Mongoloid and feeble-minded children. A number of interesting findings emerged. For example, Lenneberg et al. found that the same sort of correlation between motor and linguistic development typical of normals also holds for Mongoloids. Thus even though handedness emerges much later for Mongoloids than for normals, it is correlated with the earliest predominance of words and phrases over random babbling in both groups. Moreover, analysis of errors produced by Mongoloids and young normals on sentence-repetition tests again suggests that the ontogenetic sequencing for the Mongoloids is similar to that of normals of comparable mental age.

When very young children (24 to about 30 months) are compared with the mongoloids in terms of their respective performance on the sentence repetition test, we are impressed with the similarity. Unfortunately, there is no reliable method available at present to quantify this impression, but the in-

accuracies, mistakes, and occasional forays into parroting-strategies appear to be strikingly alike. Thus the intellectual limitation does not produce bizarre language behavior; it merely results in arrest at primitive, but "normal," stages of development [Lenneberg, 1967, pp. 319-320].

In an analogous study, Lackner (1968) investigated the linguistic capacities of five grossly retarded children of mental ages 2-3 (2 years, 3 months): 2-11; 3-0; 4-9; and 8-10. These retarded children were compared with a group of normal children of corresponding mental age. Lackner found that the grammatical structures that had been mastered by brain-damaged children of a given mental age were, in general, also available in normal children of corresponding mental age. However, the grammatical structures that had been mastered by brain-damaged children of more advanced mental age were not, in general, comprehensible to the younger normals. From this Lackner infers that the *order* of development of syntactic forms is essentially the same for the two groups, i.e., that the primary difference between the groups is in the *rate* of development and the point at which development stops. As Lackner remarks,

These results are noteworthy in that an ordering is maintained between the complexity of the grammars and the mental ages of the retarded children and the chronological ages of the normal children. This result should not be interpreted as meaning that the language behavior of a retarded child of a given mental age is equivalent to that of a normal child of a particular chronological age. Rather, these findings suggest that the language behaviors of normal and retarded children are not qualitatively different, that both groups follow similar developmental trends, but that the most severely retarded children become arrested in their development and remain at a lower level of normal language acquisition [p. 309].

There is another sort of indirect

evidence which bears on the question of the genetic determination of the process of human-language acquisition by suggesting that there is a restriction on the period of a child's life during which "normal" language learning can take place. There may be a "sensitive period" during which first language learning *must* occur if it is to occur at all. If so, then the capacity for language acquisition exhibits a cutoff for which general cognitive development offers no obvious analog.

Lenneberg (1967) provides strong evidence for such a claim through an analysis of the symptoms and recovery rates for victims of traumatic aphasias. Lenneberg notes that the likelihood of a full recovery from aphasia is strikingly different for pre- and postpubescent populations. Children who suffer an aphasia as the result of cerebral damage incurred roughly before age 11 show almost 100 percent recovery, and the younger the child, the more certain this becomes. For older aphasics, however, the rate of full recovery is much lower — 60 percent at best.

The symptomatology in these cases is also revealing. For the very young children the course of recovery is often a recapitulation of the normal ontogenetic sequence, i.e., the child appears to be able to "start from scratch" and follow the normal course of language acquisition for a second time. This is never true of adult recovery, however. Lenneberg remarks:

When aphasic symptoms subside in the adult patient, he does not traverse the infant's stages of language learning. There is no babbling, single-word stage followed by a two-word-phrase stage. There is no semantic overgeneralization nor a gradual emergence of the more complex grammatical constructions. . . . Recovery from aphasia . . . means arrest of interference with established habits. This is very different from the emergence and assembly of speech and language phenomena

throughout the synthesizing process of language acquisition [pp. 143-144].

We have had occasion to refer to the observation that the order of stages in the language development of retarded children parallels the order of developmental stages in normal children. It may now be added that the termination of language development in retardates also honors the "critical period" for language acquisition in normals. Both Lackner (1968) and Lenneberg (1967) note that retardate language development proceeds until about the onset of puberty, at which point progress is arrested and no further elaboration of basic grammatical skills takes place; the retarded child can learn a great deal after this period, but *not* about the syntax of his language. His general problem-solving abilities continue to enable him to learn, but the mechanism which mediates the establishment of basic linguistic skills apparently ceases to function. [There is much more to the discussion of both the developmental sequence and symptomatology of language skills in aphasics and retardates than we are able to present here. Further information can be found in Lenneberg (1967), Thorpe (1961), and Penfield and Roberts (1959).]

Finally, under the general head of the relative independence of language learning from the development of intelligence, we may briefly consider the anecdotal evidence that the learning of a *second* language is easier for monolingual children than for monolingual adults. If this is true, it cannot be simply a matter of greater or lesser "retroactive inhibition," since both groups — children and adults — have fully functional linguistic skills. If language acquisition is to be accounted for simply in terms of general intelligence, it is difficult to understand why a mature organism should be *less* adept at learning languages than an immature one.

In fact, the linguistic facility of the 5-year-old as compared with that of the

15-year-old would appear to be a severe embarrassment for any traditional learning theoretic account of language acquisition. Clearly, inasmuch as the capacity for language acquisition appears to operate independently of general problem-solving skills, or survives their gross impairment, it ought not to be considered a special case of the application of those skills. The alternative hypothesis would appear to be that at least some important features of language acquisition are determined by fixed, autonomous, species-specific biases that the human infant brings to the language-learning situation but which are unavailable to the adult humans just as they are unavailable to intelligent infrahuman organisms.

2. The second line of empirical evidence consonant with this hypothesis stems from the existence of linguistic universals: i.e., of profound formal and substantive similarities between all natural languages, including those that are, presumably, historically unrelated.

As we saw in Chapter 3, natural languages resemble one another in rather surprising ways. For example, they share properties with one another that they do not share with artificial "languages" like the ones we use for talking to computers and the ones we use for formalizing logical inferences. There is, of course, no way of *proving* that such resemblances between natural languages are not the product of convergence brought about by similar environmental, cultural, or cognitive pressures operating on historically unrelated and initially heterogeneous codes. In fact, we saw in Chapter 6 that there are some universal linguistic properties for which precisely this sort of explanation appears plausible. But in most cases it is difficult to see why time should preserve, or the environment select, the quite arbitrary kinds of features that seem to be characteristic of natural

languages. At the very least, we have no a priori grounds for rejecting the suggestion that there are linguistic universals because there are genetic universals: e.g., that human languages are similar to one another for very much the same sorts of reasons that bee "languages" are similar to one another, the common behavioral properties being in either case dictated by a common genetic endowment.

3. There is surprisingly little evidence that reinforcement, or indeed any sustained form of explicit teaching, plays an important facilitating role in language learning. Indeed there exists some experimental evidence which suggests that explicit instruction in the child's first language fails to be facilitating. If reinforcement theory is the alternative to the view that language learning is the expression of species-specific genetic mechanisms, this evidence supports the latter rather than the former theory.

Luria and Yudovich (1959), for example, found short-term acceleration due to a program of first-language training but apparently failed to produce lasting differences between trained twins and their siblings. Thus *ten* months after the initation of training, the differences between the trained and untrained twins were less striking than the differences after *three* months of training; that is, the control twin was catching up with the experimental one, despite the special attention afforded the latter. Luria and Yudovich remark: "Special speech training, which made speech the object of conscious perception, accelerated the conscious application of speech and helped the child to acquire an extended grammatical structure of speech; nevertheless, it is clear that the special training played only a subsidiary role, leaving the leading place to the formative influence of direct speech communication" (pp. 75-76).

It may be remarked that this pattern

of short-term acceleration without significant long-term effect is often also observed in cases where attempts were made to
employ training to speed the child's
mastery of performances which, like
walking and climbing, are patently
genotypically determined.

Gesell and Thompson (1929) introduced the
now famous co-twin method of study [for
the investigation of maturational vs. environmental variables] . . . , observing the
progress of identical twins T and C. When
the twins were on the verge of climbing activities, twin T was given ten minutes of
training every day for 6 weeks, while the
control twin C received no training and was
prevented from climbing stairs. At the end
of the six weeks, twin C was given a brief 2
week training period. Performances of the
twins were then compared. On the initial
tests, twin T was more skillful, but twin C
also managed to climb the stairs unaided.
Two weeks later twin C was just as profi-
cient as her sister [Zubek and Solberg,
1954].

A study by Cazden (1965) is directly
relevant. Her results suggest that explicit
correction of the child's speech in the form
of "expansions" of his "telegraphic" utterances tends actually to inhibit grammatical development. Children in
Cazden's experimental group received
daily sessions in which the experimenter
provided the fully grammatical adult
sentence corresponding to each abbreviated sentence the child uttered.
(Thus, for example, if the child were to utter a sequence like "train run," the experimenter would provide an utterance
like "the train runs" or "the train is running.") Children in a second group received analogous daily periods of topic-
oriented free conversation with the experimenter, but received no expansions.
Cazden found that at the end of the experiment, the children who had received
expansions had made significantly *less*
progress in grammatical development, as
measured by a variety of test procedures,

than the children who had received no expansions.

This study suggests that the richness
of the child's verbal environment and the
extent of his opportunities to engage in
conversation with adults have more im-
pact upon his grammatical development
than does the occurrence of explicit training. A more recent study of Cazden's
strengthens this suggestion. Cazden examined a corpus consisting of dialogues
between three mothers and their children.
She compared the correlation between the
child's mastery of three syntactic variables
(the use of prepositions and prepositional
phrases, the ability to respond appropriately to *wh*-questions, and the use
of noun and verb inflection) with the extent to which the mother provided expansions of each of these forms and with the
frequency of each of these forms in the
mother's speech. The result of this comparison appears to be that frequency
variables correlate better with developmental variables than does the
mother's tendency to provide expansions.
For example, the child whose mother produced the smallest proportion of expansions of the child's uninflected utterances
was the one who was most advanced in
the use of inflections. Cazden (1967)
remarks that "it is hard to reconcile this
finding with our original hypothesis that
expansion should provide the most usable
information for the acquisition of all
types of functors" (p. 64). It is also hard to
reconcile this with any account of
language which makes *training* an important factor in the child's linguistic
development. As is often the case with the
maturation of endogenously determined
behaviors, language development apparently makes only quite diffuse
demands upon the character of the environment in which the learning occurs:
the structure of the mature behavior
reflects the mental structure of the
organism rather than the detailed
organization of its environment.

It is, in short, difficult to find evidence that the normal development of syntax requires any sort of training or reward on the part of the adult community. Perhaps that is why the adult community does not normally selectively reinforce syntactic well-formedness, learning theorists to the contrary notwithstanding. As Ervin-Tripp (1971) remarks in commenting on Staats (1971):

> Reinforcement appears to play a strong role in Staats' theory of acquisition. I can't imagine what kind of interaction he has been watching, but it is rarely the case that we spend much effort correcting the formal structure of children's speech. . . . Adults listening to children speak are usually listening to the message, just as they are when they listen to adults. Our evidence is that they comment on the form only in the case of socially marked deviations such as obscenities, lower class nonstandard forms, and in the case of black families, forms believed to be "country speech." Such formal correction occurred much more when the children were five or older than at the age of interest here [p. 196].

Learning theories which have not supposed that reinforcement is the primary mechanism of language acquisition have tended to coopt that role for imitation (sometimes construed as a "self-reinforcing" activity). However, the available evidence does not support the claim that imitation plays an essential role in acquiring a first language any more than it supports the claim that reinforcement does.

To begin with, it seems clear that imitation cannot be an essential mechanism in first-language learning since it appears that many normal children do not spontaneously imitate linguistic forms. (Cf. Leopold, 1939, and Bloom, in press.) Again, if the child's tendency to imitate adult forms is to play any important role in his learning of the adult language, this tendency must at least be "progressive" in

the sense that the child must frequently imitate forms which he has not previously mastered. But it is unclear whether or not children's imitations satisfy even this prerequisite to relevance in language learning. Though it is known that children can be trained to imitate forms that are grammatically more mature than their freely produced speech (see Frazer, Bellugi, and Brown, 1963), it is quite doubtful that they regularly do so spontaneously. For example, Ervin (1964) compared the grammatical maturity of spontaneously produced imitations by five children with the grammatical maturity of their free speech. In four of the five cases, the level of maturity was identical (i.e., the child's imitations were not progressive). In the fifth case, the imitations were *more primitive* than the free speech. In light of this kind of finding, McNeill concludes a recent discussion of the data on language imitation with the remark that "the contribution of parental speech to language acquisition is not to supply specimens for children to imitate" (1970, p. 107).

It may be added that however the empirical findings about the progressiveness of imitation turn out, appeals to imitation are incapable on purely conceptual grounds of accounting for the important features of the child's performance in learning his language.

There are two points to notice in this regard. The first is that theories of language learning which are based on imitation are, by that very fact, incapable of accounting for the child's mastery of productive systems. What the speech community offers the child as models for him to imitate are, at best, *examples* of sentences. (Probably what it offers are often examples of nonsentences, i.e., of sentence fragments.) At any event, the speech community does *not* offer the child examples of the structural facts that underlie sentences. If, then, the child's behavior is ever to go beyond rote repeti-

tion to the production of novel sentences, he must somehow learn from the examples he hears not just the conditions under which an imitation of this or that sentence is acceptable but also the general conditions an utterance must satisfy if it is to be in his language. In short, for the child to learn to talk, he must determine the relation between the sentences he hears and the possible sentences of his language. Even if it were true that the child imitates correctly *every* sentence he hears, reference to that fact would shed no light whatever on the question of how this relation is learned.

Imitation, then, obviously cannot account for the learning of productive systems. A less obvious, but equally important, conceptual point is that the imitation model fails even to provide a convincing answer to the question of how the child learns to repeat utterances. The relevant consideration is that the relation between an utterance and its repetition is often extremely abstract: in this respect there is a difference between repetition and mimicry. One way to put it is that the conditions for accurate repetition cannot be given in terms of *acoustic* correspondences between the child's utterances and those of the adult model since what is necessary and sufficient for one utterance to be a repetition of another is that they have the same *phonetic* representation. The question that the imitation theory begs is thus: How does the child learn the formidable system of abstractions required to master the correspondences between acoustic and phonetic descriptions?

It is clear, in point of fact, that the child *does* master this system. Spectograms of children imitating the utterances of their parents exhibit radical acoustic disparities between the signal produced by the adult and the signal produced by the child. If the child is to learn to imitate, he must learn to tolerate this disparity; *how* he learns this is, however,

a question about which the imitation model has nothing whatever to say.

None of this discussion, of course, denies that the tendency to imitate may play an important, or even essential, role in facilitating language acquisition in some children: e.g., in fixing attention and in providing occasion for rehearsals. The present point is that even if imitation *were* to prove an essential condition for language learning, an explanation of how the child learns a language could not consist primarily of an appeal to the tendency to imitate. [For speculations about the roles that imitation and rehearsal may have in facilitating language learning, see Weir (1962).]

One final remark should be made about the inadequacies of selective reinforcement and imitation theories of language learning. The most striking feature of a child's productions is clearly their spontaneity. By this we mean not only that the child, like the adult, is master of a productive system of rules rather than a fixed inventory of responses but also that the utterances of the child (even when he "imitates") diverge regularly and reliably from anything he hears in his speech community. Thus, for example, Ervin (1964) notes:

Omissions bulked large in our cases of imitation. These tended to be concentrated on the unstressed segments of sentences, on articles, prepositions, auxiliaries, pronouns, and suffixes. For instance: "I'll make a cup for her to drink" produced "cup drink"; "Mr. Miller will try," "Miller try"; "Put the strap under her chin," "Strap chin." Thus the imitations had three characteristics: they selected the most recent and most emphasized words, and they preserved word order [p. 169].

When one considers the child's free, as opposed to imitated, utterances, the disparity between his linguistic preferences and those of the adult are still more striking. Bellugi (1967), for example, has noted a preference for uncontracted forms in the dialect of the children she studies (thus her children said "do not" and "have not" whereas their parents regularly said "don't" and "won't"); and Slobin (in press) states that the phrase-order preferences of Russian children differs systematically from those of adult Russian speakers: children employ the "'base-structure" order *subject phrase verb phrase object phrase*, whereas for the adult order is essentially free. Analogously, Bellugi has demonstrated a systematic and orderly development of the negative in children's speech, where almost all the early forms that children typically use are ungrammatical, and presumably never occur in the adult dialect. Forms like "no daddy hat" are regular in the child's earliest negative productions and surely have no models in the adult language. Examples of this sort are legion; everyone knows that children speak a special dialect — the dialect we attempt to mimic when we talk "baby talk."

It is extremely difficult to see how a shaping model, or an imitation model, could account for this spontaneity in the child's productions. In the latter case, the best we can hope to do is to explain rote repetition. In the former case, *random* variability in verbal behavior is assumed; but this is not to the point, since the child's dialect is apparently quite regular even though it diverges from that of the adult speech community. In short, there appears to be structure in the child's productions which is in no obvious sense a copy of the structure on display in his verbal environment. A natural way to answer the question, "Where does this structure come from?" is by appealing to endogenous organismic variables.

4. There exists very little *direct* experimental evidence on the hypothesis that some features of the child's linguistic competence are determined by his innate species-specific genetic endowment. However, some recent work has been done on the perceptual constancies involved in phone recognition, and these results do point in the direction of a nativistic account.

It will be recalled from the discussion in Chapter 6 that it is characteristic of adult speech perception to impose discrete categories on continuously varying physical magnitudes. A classic case is the voiced-voiceless distinction among stop consonants. Apparently, one of the important acoustic cues for this distinction is the relation of temporal onset between f_1 and f_2. In the optimal voiced consonant, onset of f_1 and f_2 is roughly simultaneous; and in the optimal unvoiced consonant, f_2 precedes f_1 by about 60 milliseconds. The important point for the present discussion is that the degree to which two stimuli are likely to be perceived as differing in voicing is not proportional to the magnitude of the physical difference between their formant onset relations. Rather, any signal with an onset relation roughly between 0 and 25 milliseconds will tend to be perceived as voiced, and any signal with an onset relation of longer than 25 milliseconds will tend to be perceived as unvoiced.

In a recent experiment, Eimas, Siqueland, Jusczyk, and Vigorito (1971) undertook to show that infants' perception of such signals is categorical in very much the same way as is adults'. The experimental procedure consisted of playing recordings of signals with varying formant onset relations to infants of between 1 and 4 months. The signals were what adults hear as either [b] followed by vowel or [p] followed by vowel. Subjects were habituated to each such signal and tested for generalization of habituation to each of the others. The extent of generalization was determined by monitoring changes in the infant's sucking response.

Eimas et al. found less generalization of habituation when two stimuli were drawn from categories that were phonetically distinct for adults than otherwise. This was true even where differences in the absolute magnitudes of the onset relations were equated across stimuli. This discontinuity of discriminability at the same region that marks the adult phoneme boundary should be taken as evidence that speech sounds are categorized by the preverbal infant and that his categories are similar to those of the adult.

A demonstration with the same point was provided by Fodor and Garrett (in press) using differential reinforcement of head-turning responses in 3- to 4-month-old infants. It will be recalled that there are striking cases of variation in the acoustic properties of a given consonant when it appears in different vowel environments (see Chapter 6, page 291). Fodor and Garrett found that their infant subjects responded selectively to a given phone across several different vowel environments (e.g., that they identified /p/ in the environment /a/ with /p/ in the environment /i/). This indicates that infants' perceptual capacities allow them to respond to syllables in terms of the internal phonetic structure that permits a segmental analysis of adult speech. This study and that of Eimas et al. thus provide evidence that quite complex kinds of information about the linguistic analysis of speech are available at any age when infants could *not* have had experience with the distributional evidence required to infer those analyses. It seems inescapable that most of this information is endogenously determined.

5. What probably has had most effect in convincing psychologists of the specificity of language-learning mechanisms is simply complexity of the information that is internalized as a result of the operation of these mechanisms. There is, of course, no way to quantify this concept. But it does seem clear that

the child must internalize an extremely elaborate generative system in an extremely short time if his language acquisition is to proceed normally. To the extent that parts of this system are assumed to be innately given, the remarkable facility with which children learn to talk is rendered corresponding intelligible.

We have reviewed some of the evidence for and against the claim that the mechanisms of language acquisition are species-specific. It seems to us that the most persuasive of these arguments is the one which seeks to explain language universals as the expression of the genetic endowment of speaker-hearers. If grammars do have the universal form that transformational theory says they do, that fact will have to be explained; and it is hard to believe that an exhaustive explanation could be couched largely in terms of environmental variables.

What can be said with certainty is that language acquisition is not explicable by reference to the intraspecific learning mechanisms to which empiricists have usually appealed: selective reinforcement and imitation. It is conceivable that some account of first-language learning in terms of other intraspecific mechanisms will eventually be forthcoming. If so, it will have to be quite different from anything that has yet been proposed.

References

Bellugi, U. 1967. The acquisition of negation. Unpublished doctoral dissertation, Harvard University.

Bloom, L. 1973. One word at a time: The use of single word utterances before syntax. The Hague: Mouton.

Brown, R. W. 1970. *Psycholinguistics*. New York: The Free Press.

Cazden, C. B. 1965. Environmental assistance to the child's acquisition of grammar. Doctoral dissertation, Harvard University.

Cazden, C. B. 1967. The role of parent speech in the acquisition of grammar. *Project Literacy Report No. 8.*

Chomsky, N. 1969. Linguistics and philosophy. In *Language and philosophy*, ed. S. Hook. New York: New York University Press.

Eimas, P., Siqueland, E., Jusczyk, P., and Vigorito, J. 1971. Speech perception in infants. *Science* 171:303-306.

Ervin, S. 1964. Imitation and structural change in children's language. In *New directions in the study of language*, ed. E. Lenneberg. Cambridge, Massachusetts: M.I.T. Press.

Ervin-Tripp, S. 1971. An overview of theories of grammatical development. In *The ontogenesis of grammar*, ed. D. I. Slobin. New York: Academic Press.

Fraser, C., Bellugi, U., and Brown, R. W. 1963. Control of grammar in imitation, comprehension, and production. *Journal of Verbal Learning and Verbal Behavior* 2:121-125.

Gesell, A., and Thompson, H. 1929. Learning and growth in identical twins: an experimental study by the method of co-twin control. *Genet Psychological Monograph* 8:1-123.

Harman, G. 1969. Linguistic competence and empiricism. In *Language and Philosophy*, ed. S. Hook. New York: New York University Press.

Kellogg, W. N., and Kellogg, L. A. 1933. *The ape and the child*. New York: McGraw-Hill.

Lackner, J. A. 1968. A developmental study of language behavior in retarded children. *Neuropsychologia* 6:301-320.

Lenneberg, E. H. 1967. *Biological foundations of language*. New York: Wiley.

Lenneberg, E. H., Nichols, I. A., and Rosenberger, E. F. 1964. Primitive stages of language development in mongolism. *Disorders of Communication*, Vol. 42: *Research Publications*. Baltimore, Maryland: A.R.N.M.D. Williams and Wilkins.

Leopold, W. F. 1939-1949. *Speech development of a bilingual child*. 4 vols. Evanston, Illinois: Northwestern University Press.

Lorenz, K. 1965. *Evolution and modification of behavior*. Chicago, Illinois: University of Chicago Press.

Luria, A. R., and Yudovich, F. I. 1959. *Speech and the development of mental processes in the child*. Ed. Joan Simon. London: Staples.

McNeill, D. 1970. *The acquisition of language*. New York: Harper and Row.

Mowrer, O. H. 1960. *Learning theory and the symbolic processes*. New York: Wiley.

Penfield, W., and Roberts, L. 1959. *Speech and brain mechanisms*. Princeton, New Jersey: Princeton University Press.

Quine, W. V. O. 1960. *Word and object*. Cambridge, Massachusetts: M.I.T. Press.

Skinner, B. F. 1938. *The behavior of organisms*. New York: Appleton-Century-Crofts.

Skinner, B. F. 1957. *Verbal behavior*. New York: Appleton-Century-Crofts.

Slobin, D. I. In press. Early grammatical development in several languages with special attention to Soviet research. In *The structure and psychology of language*, ed. T. Bever and W. Weksel. The Hague: Mouton.

Staats, A. W. 1971. Linguistic-mentalistic theory versus an explanatory S-R learning theory of language development. In *The ontogenesis of grammar*, ed. D. I. Slobin. New York: Academic Press.

Thorpe, W. H. 1961. Sensitive periods in the learning of animals and men: A study of imprinting with special reference to the induction of cyclic behavior. In *Current problems in animal behavior*, eds. W. H. Thorpe and O. L. Zangwill. London: Cambridge University Press.

Tinbergen, N. 1969. *The study of instinct*. London: Oxford University Press.

Weir, R. 1962. *Language in the crib*. The Hague: Mouton.

Zubeck, J. P. and Solberg, P. A. 1954. *Human development*. New York: McGraw-Hill.

What Is Innate and Why

Hilary Putnam

I shall begin with Chomsky's arguments. The argument concerns "the process of formation of simple yes-or-no questions in English." Chomsky considers "such declarative-question pairs" as:

(1) The man is here. — Is the man here?

   The man will leave. — Will the man leave?

And he considers two hypotheses "put forth to account for this infinite class of pairs" (of course, H_1 has never been "put forth" by anyone, nor would any sane person put it forth):

H_1: process the declarative from beginning to end (left to right), word by word, until

This chapter, the reply by Noam Chomsky (chapter 20), and the rejoinder by Hilary Putnam (chapter 21) are extracts from a larger debate. The papers originated at a conference in Paris, attended by Chomsky, J. A. Fodor, Seymour Papert, Jean Piaget, and others. Putnam was unable to attend, but wrote his comments after listening to tape recordings of the meetings. The views of Chomsky he criticizes here are essentially the same as those expressed in Chomsky's "On Cognitive Capacity," reprinted as chapter 17, this volume. The entire debate appears in Massimo Piattelli-Palmarini, ed., *Language and Learning: The Debate between Jean Piaget and Noam Chomsky* (Cambridge, Mass.: Harvard University Press, 1980). Reprinted by permission of Editions du Seuil, Harvard University Press, Routledge and Kegan Paul, and the author.

reaching the first occurrence of the words *is, will,* etc.; transpose this occurrence to the beginning (left), forming the associated interrogative.

H_2: same as H_1, but select the first occurrence of *is, will,* etc., following the first noun phrase of the declarative.

Chomsky then writes:

Let us refer to H_1 as a "structure-independent rule" and H_2 as a "structure-dependent rule." Thus, H_1 requires analysis of the declarative into just a sequence of words, whereas H_2 requires an analysis into successive words and also abstract phrases such as "noun phrase." The phrases are "abstract" in that their boundaries and labeling are not in general physically marked in any way; rather, they are mental constructions.

A scientist observing English speakers, given such data as (1), would naturally select hypothesis H_1 over the far more complex hypothesis H_2, which postulates abstract mental processing of a nontrivial sort beyond H_1. Similarly, given such data as (1) it is reasonable to assume that an "unstructured" child would assume that H_1 is valid. In fact, as we know, it is not, and H_2 is (more nearly) correct. Thus consider the data of (2):

(2) The man who is here is tall. — Is the man who is here tall?

The man who is tall will leave. — Will the man who is tall leave?

These data are predicted by H_2 and refute H_1, which would predict rather the interrogatives (3):

(3) Is the man who here is tall?
    Is the man who tall will leave?

Now the question that arises is this: how does a child know that H_2 is correct (nearly), while H_1 is false? It is surely not the case that he first hits on H_1 (as a neutral scientist would) and then is forced to reject it on the basis of data such as (2).

Chomsky's conclusion from all this is the following:

Such observations suggest that it is a property of S_0 — that is, of LT(H,L) — that rules (or rules of some specific category, identifiable on quite general grounds by some genetically determined mechanism) are structure-dependent. The child need not consider H_1; it is ruled out by properties of his initial mental state, S_0.

I wish to discuss this example by considering two different questions: (1) can we account for the child's selection of "structure-dependent" hypotheses and concepts in the course of language learning on the basis of general intelligence, without postulating that the preference for H_2 over H_1 is built in, or that a template of a typical human language is built in, as Chomsky wishes us to do; and (2) can we account specifically for the preference of H_2 over H_1 without assuming that such a specific preference is built in? Before discussing these questions, however, I want to consider the vexed question, "What is a grammar?"

The Nature of Grammars

A grammar is some sort of system which — ideally — generates the "grammatical sentences" of a language and none of the ungrammatical ones. And a grammatical sentence is one generated by *the* grammar of the language (or by any adequate one, if one believes as Zellig Harris

does that there is no such thing as *the* grammar of a language).[1] This is obviously a circular definition. But how does one break the circularity?

Chomsky suggested long ago (in "Explanatory Models in Linguistics")[2] that a child *hears* people classing sentences as "grammatical" or "ungrammatical" — not, of course, in those words, but by hearing them correct each other or the child — and that he projects a grammar as a simplest extrapolation from such data satisfying some innate constraints.

The trouble with this view is that the factual premise is clearly false. People don't object to all and only *ungrammatical* sentences. If they object at all, it is to *deviant* sentences — but they do not, when they correct each other, clearly say (in a way that a child can understand) whether the deviance was syntactic, semantic, discourse-theoretic, or whatever.

Chomsky asserts that the child is, in effect, supplied with "a list of grammatical sentences" and "a list of ungrammatical sentences" and has to extrapolate from these two lists. But this is surely false. If anything, he is supplied rather with a list of acceptable sentences and a list of sentences that are deviant-for-some-reason-or-other; a grammar of his language will generate (idealizing somewhat) all of the acceptable sentences in the first list, but unfortunately, it will not be the case that it generates none of the deviant sentences in the other list. On the contrary, the grammatical sentences will be a superset of the (finite list of) acceptable sentences, which is *not disjoint from* the (finite list of) deviant sentences.

Moreover, the second list does not have to exist at all. Chomsky has cited evidence that children can learn their first language without being corrected; and I am sure he also believes that they don't need to hear anyone else corrected either. Chomsky might reply to this by scrapping the hypothetical second list (the list of "ungrammatical," or at least, "unacceptable" sentences). He might say that the grammar of an arbitrary language is the simplest projection of any suitable finite set of acceptable sentences satisfying some set of innate constraints. This throws the whole burden of defining what a grammar is on the innate constraints. I want to suggest a different approach: one that says, in quite traditional fashion, that the grammar of a language is a property of the *language*, not a property of the brain of *Homo sapiens*.

Propositional Calculus

Let us start with a simple and well-understood example: the artificial language called "propositional calculus" with its standard interpretation. The grammar of propositional calculus can be stated in many different but equivalent ways. Here is a typical one:

(I)   A propositional variable standing alone is a well-formed formula.

(II) If A and B are well-formed formulas, so are $-A$, $(A \& B)$, $(A \lor B)$ and $(A \rightarrow B)$.[3]

(III) Nothing is a well-formed formula unless its being so follows from (I) and (II).

[*Editor's note:* In this anthology, "$\rightarrow$" is used instead of the horseshoe and the arrow as the material conditional ("if . . . then").]

The fact that a perfectly grammatical sentence may be deviant for semantic reasons, which is a feature of natural languages, is possessed also by this simple language, since "$p \& - p$" (for example) is perfectly grammatical but would not be "uttered" for obvious semantic reasons.

Now consider the "semantics" of propositional calculus as represented by the following inductive definition of *truth* in terms of *primitive truth* (truth for propositional variables, which is left undefined). The fact that primitive truth is left undefined means that this can be thought

of as an *interpretation-schema*, which becomes an interpretation when joined to any definition of primitive truth.
Definition:

(i) $-A$ is true if and only if A is not true.

(ii) $(A \& B)$ is true if and only if A and B are both true.

(iii) $(A \lor B)$ is true if and only if at least one of A, B is true.

(iv) $(A \rightarrow B)$ is true unless A is true and B is not true.

Notice that the inductive definition of *truth* in propositional calculus parallels (in a sense which could be made precise, but which I will not attempt to make precise here) the inductive definition of *grammatical* in propositional calculus. Now, there are other ways of defining grammatical in propositional calculus with the property that corresponding to them there exist parallel inductive definitions of truth in propositional calculus. But if we limit ourselves to those that are computationally feasible (that is, the corresponding decision program is short, when written in any standard format, and the typical computation is also short), not a great many are known, and they are all extremely similar. In this sense, propositional calculus as an interpreted system possesses an *intrinsic* grammar and semantics.

Let me elaborate on this a little. If Martians exist, very likely they have hit upon propositional calculus, and it may be that when they use propositional calculus their logicians' brains employ different heuristics than our logicians' brains employ. But that does not mean that propositional calculus has a different grammar when used by a Martian and when used by a Terrestrian. The grammar is (any one of) the simplest inductive definition(s) of the set of strings in the alphabet of propositional calculus for which truth is defined—that is, the simplest inductive definition(s) with the property that there exist parallel inductive definitions of truth. Given the semantics of propositional calculus (and no information about the brains of speakers), the class of reasonable grammars is fixed by that semantics, *not* by the structure of the brains that do the processing.

It may seem that I have begged too many questions by introducing the predicate "true"; but it is not essential to my argument. Suppose we do not define "true," but rather "follows from." Any reasonably simple definition of the relation "x follows from y" in propositional calculus will have the property that it presupposes a syntactic analysis of the standard kind. In other words, checking that something is an axiom or a proof, etc., will involve checking that strings and components of strings have the forms (p & q), −p, (p V q), (p —+ q). The grammar (I), (II), (III) not only generates the set of strings over which the relation "follows from" is defined, but it generates it in a way that corresponds to properties of strings referred to in the definition of "follows from."

Coming to natural language: suppose we think of a natural language as a very complicated formalized language whose formalization is unknown. (This seems to be how Chomsky thinks of it.) Suppose we think of the speaker as a computer that, among other things, computes whether certain strings are "true," given certain inputs, or if you don't like "true," as a computer that computes whether certain sequences of strings are "proofs," or computes the "degree of confirmation" of certain strings, and so forth. The fact is that any one of these semantic, or deductive logical, or inductive logical notions will have an *inductive definition* whose clauses parallel or at least presuppose a syntactic analysis of the language.

To come right out with it: I am suggesting (1) that the declarative grammar of a language is the inductive definition of a set of strings which is the set over which

semantic, deductive-logical, inductive-logical (and so on) predicates are defined;[4] (2) that it must be in such a form that the inductive definitions of these predicates can easily "parallel" it; (3) that the corresponding decision program must be as computationally feasible as is consistent with (1) and (2). If a language is thought of in this way—as a system of strings with a semantics, with a deductive logic, with an inductive logic, and so on—then it is easy to see how the grammar can be a property of the *language* and not of the speakers' *brains*.

The Nature of Language Learning

Let us consider the linguistic abilities of Washoe (the chimpanzee brought up to use a certain amount of deaf-mute sign language by Alan and Beatrice Gardner). No doubt Chomsky will point out that Washoe lacks many of the syntactic abilities that humans have, and on these grounds he would claim that it is wrong to apply the term "language" to what she has learned. But the application of this term is not what is important. What is important is the following:

1. There is a certain class of words, which I will call *nouns-for-Washoe*, which Washoe associates with (classes of) *things*. For example, Washoe associates the word "grape" (in sign language) with more-or-less stereotypical grapes, "banana" with more-or-less stereotypical bananas, and so forth.

2. There is a *frame*, ⸻ gives ⸻ (to) ⸻, which Washoe has acquired (for example, "Alan gives apple to Trixie").

3. She can project *new* uses of this frame. If you teach her a new word, say "date," she will figure out herself the use she is expected to make of "⸻ gives *date* (to) ⸻."

4. She can use the word "and" to combine sentences. She can figure out the expected use of *p and q* from the uses of p and q separately.[5]

Actually Washoe's abilities go far beyond these four capacities; but let us just consider these for now. The only plausible account of what has occurred is that Washoe has "internalized" a rule to the effect that if X is a *noun-for-Washoe*, and A, B, and C are people's names — counting Washoe (of course) as a person — then "A gives X to B" is a sentence, and a rule to the effect that if p, q are sentences so is *p and q*. And these are *structure-dependent rules* which Washoe has learned *without benefit of an innate template for language.*

Nor is this really surprising. Let us introduce a semantic predicate to describe the above tiny fragment of Washoe's "language" (where the "shudder-quotes" are inserted to avoid the accusation of question-begging), say, the predicate "corresponds to the condition that." Here are the "semantic rules" for the fragment in question:

(I) If X is a *noun-for-Washoe* and B, C are people-names, and X corresponds to things of kind K and b, c are the people corresponding to B, C, then "B gives X (to) C" corresponds to the condition that b gives something of kind K to c.

(II) If p, q are *sentences-for-Washoe*, *p and q* corresponds to the condition that the condition corresponding to p and the condition corresponding to q both obtain.

Now, I submit that Washoe is not really interested in learning that certain *uninterpreted* strings of gestures have a certain *uninterpreted* property called "grammaticality." She is interested for practical reasons — reward, approval, and so forth — in learning (I) and (II). But learning (I) and (II) automatically involves learning the grammatical facts that:

(i) If B, C are people's names and X is a *noun-for-Washoe*, "B gives X (to) C" is a sentence-for-Washoe.

(ii) If p, q are sentences-for-Washoe, so is *p and q*.

For the set of sentences "generated" by the "grammar" (i), (ii) is precisely the set over which the semantic predicate — "corresponds to the condition that _____" — is defined by the inductive definition (I), (II); and the clauses (I), (II) presuppose precisely the syntactic analysis given by (i), (ii). Given that Washoe is trying to learn the *semantics* of Washoe-ese, and the syntax is only a *means* to this end, there are only two possibilities: either her intelligence will be too low to internalize "structure-dependent" rules like (I), (II), and she will fail; or her intelligence will be high enough, and as a corollary we will be able to ascribe to Washoe "implicit knowledge" of the syntactic rules (i), (ii) — not because she "knows" (I), (II) *and in addition* "knows" (i), (ii), but because having the "know-how" that constitutes implicit knowledge of (I), (II) *includes* implicit knowledge of (i), (ii).

But the same thing is true of the child. The child is not trying to learn a bunch of *syntactic* rules as a kind of crazy end-in-itself. He is learning, and he wants to learn, *semantic* rules, and these *cannot* be stated without the use of structure-dependent notions. There aren't even plausible candidates for structure-independent semantic rules. So *of course* (given that his intelligence is high enough to learn language), *of course* the child "internalizes" structure-dependent rules. And given that he must be building up an "inner representation" of abstract structural notions such as *sentence*, *noun*, *verb phrase*, and so on in learning to understand the language, the mere fact that H_2

uses such notions and H_1 does not, does *not* make H_2 so much less plausible than H_1.

Chomsky has, so to speak, "pulled a fast one" on us. He presents us with a picture of the child as being like an insanely scientistic linguist. Both are looking at language as a stream of uninterpreted noises; both are interested in an occult property of "grammaticality." From this (crazy) point of view, it is not surprising that H_1 seems infinitely "simpler" than H_2. So — Chomsky springs his carefully prepared trap — "Why doesn't the child try the simpler-but-false hypothesis H_1 *before* the correct hypothesis H_2?"

But this isn't what children (or sane linguists) are like at all. The child is in the process of trying to *understand* English. He has already tumbled (if Washoe can, so can he!) to the fact that he needs to internalize structure-dependent notions to do this. So the mere fact that H_2 *uses* such notions doesn't at all make it implausible or excessively complex. The point is that *the learning of grammar is dependent on the learning of semantics*. And there aren't even any candidates for structure-independent semantic rules (if there are, they get knocked out pretty early, even by a chimpanzee's brain).

H_1 Considered More Closely

So far I have argued that H_2 is not nearly as weird from the point of view of the intelligent brain unaided by an innate template of language as Chomsky wants to make it seem. But I haven't argued against H_1. So still the question remains, why doesn't the child try H_1?

Let us try applying to this problem the conception of grammar we just sketched (grammar as, so to speak, semantics minus the semantic predicates). H_1 will only be "tried" by the child if the child "tries" some *semantic* hypotheses that correspond to H_1. The child wants to *understand* questions, not just to "flag" them as questions. But it is plausible to assume (and Chomsky himself would assume) that understanding questions involves recovering the underlying declarative. This means that the question-transformation must have an *inverse* the child can perform. H_1 is indeed simple, but *its inverse is horribly complicated*. Moreover, *its inverse uses the full resources of the grammar*; all the notions, such as "noun phrase," that H_1 does not employ have to be employed in recovering the declarative from the output of our application of H_1. So it is no mystery that the child (or its brain) never "tries" such an unworkable semantic theory, and hence never "tries" H_1.

Incidentally, H_1 itself employs "abstract" notions, since it contains the phrase-structure concept "declarative," and applying it, if it were a rule of English, would therefore involve working with notions such as "noun phrase," since these have to be used to recognize declaratives. And some languages do have question-transformations that are as "structure-independent" as H_1 is; for example, in Hebrew one can form a question from a declarative by just prefixing *na im*. But this prefixing operation *does* have a simple inverse, namely, deleting *na im*.

I would like now to discuss Chomsky's more abstract remarks at the beginning of his paper. Let me begin with what he says about intelligence.

Chomsky on General Intelligence

So far I have assumed that there is such a thing as general intelligence; that is, that whatever else our innate cognitive repertoire may include, it *must* include *multipurpose* learning strategies, heuristics, and so forth. But Chomsky appears to deny this assumption explicitly. I quote:

More generally, for any species O and cognitive domain D that have been tentatively identified and delimited, we may, correspondingly, investigate LT(O,D), the "learning theory" for the organism O in the domain D, a property of the genetically determined initial state. Suppose, for example, that we are investigating the ability of humans to recognize and identify human faces. Assuming "face-recognition" to constitute a legitimate cognitive domain F, we may try to specify LT(H,F), the genetically determined principles that give rise to a steady state (apparently some time after language is neurally fixed, and perhaps represented in homologous regions of the right hemisphere, as some recent work suggests). Similarly, other cognitive domains can be studied in humans and other organisms. We would hardly expect to find interesting properties common to LT (O,D) for arbitrary O,D; that is, we would hardly expect to discover that there exists something that might be called "general learning theory." As far as I know, the prospects for such a theory are no brighter than for a "growth theory," intermediate in level between cellular biology and the study of particular organs, and concerned with the principles that govern the growth of arbitrary organs for arbitrary organisms.

The key notion in this argument is the notion of a "domain." How wide is a domain? Is all of mathematics one domain? If so, what about empirical science? Or are physics, chemistry, and so on, all *different* domains?

If Chomsky admits that a domain can be as wide as empirical science (that there can be a "learning theory for empirical science"), then he has granted that something exists that may fittingly be called "general intelligence." (Chomsky might retort that only exceptionally intelligent individuals can discover new truths in empirical science, whereas everyone learns his native language. But this is an extraordinarily elitist argument: the abilities of exceptionally intelligent men must be *continuous* with those of ordinary men, after all, and the relevant mechanisms must be present at some level of functioning in all human brains.) Even

if only physics, or just all of solid-state physics, or just all of the solid-state physics of crystals is one domain, the same point holds: heuristics and strategies capable of enabling us to learn new facts in these areas must be extraordinarily multipurpose (and we have presently no idea what they are). Once it is granted that such multipurpose learning strategies exist, the claim that they *cannot* account for language learning becomes highly dubious, as I argued long ago.[6] (Consider Washoe!)

On the other hand, if domains become so small that each domain can use only learning strategies that are highly specific in purpose (such as "recognizing faces," "learning a grammar"), then it becomes really a miracle that evolution endowed us with all these skills, most of which (for example, higher mathematics, nuclear physics) were not used at all until *after* the evolution of the race was complete (some 100,000-odd years ago). And the analogy with organ growth does not then hold at all: the reason there does not have to be a multipurpose learning mechanism is that there are only limited numbers of organs, whereas there are virtually unlimited numbers of "domains."

The Prospects of General Learning Theory

Chomsky feels that the "prospects" of "general learning theory" are bad. I tend to agree. I see no reason to think that the detailed functioning of the human mind will ever be transparent to the human mind.[7] But the existence of general intelligence is one question; the prospect for a revealing *description* of it is another.

Incidentally, if the innateness hypothesis is right, I am also not optimistic about the prospects for a revealing description of the innate template of language. The examples Chomsky has given us of how to go about inferring the structure of the template (such as the argument about H_1 and H_2) are such bad arguments that they cast serious doubt on the feasibility of the whole program, at least at this point in history (especially if there exist *both* general intelligence *and* an innate template).

On the other hand, we may well be able to discover interesting facts and laws about general intelligence without being able to describe it completely, or to model it by, say, a computer program. There may be progress in studying general intelligence without its being the case that we ever succeed in writing down a "general learning theory" in the sense of a mathematical model of multipurpose learning.

Chomsky on Evolution

Chomsky dismisses Piaget's question regarding how such a thing as an innate template for language might have evolved. But he should not dismiss it. One answer he might have given is this: primitive language first appeared as an *invention*, introduced by some extraordinary member of the species and learned by the others as Washoe learns her fragment of language. Given such a beginning of the instrument, genetic changes to enable us to use the instrument better (including the enlargement of the so-called speech center in the left lobe of normal humans) could have occurred, and would be explained, if they did occur, by natural selection. Presumably Chomsky did not give this answer because (1) he wants to deny that there exists such a thing as general intelligence, and to deny that even the simplest grammar could be internalized by general intelligence alone; and (2) he wants to deny that Washoe's performance is continuous with language learning, and to deny that it has any interest for the study of language learning. But this is surely perverse. If the first language user *already* had a complete innate template, then this could only have been a miraculous break in the evolutionary sequence, as Piaget in effect points out.

Chomsky remarks that we don't know the details of the development of the motor organs either, and this is surely true. We do postulate that they develop bit by bit. This poses difficulties, however, since there are no creatures with two thirds of a wing! But there have been impressive successes in this direction (for example, working out the evolution of the eye). We have found creatures with gliding membranes which are, in a sense, "two thirds of a wing." And we have found eyes with only rods (no cones) and eyes with only cones (no rods). Since the first draft of this paper was written, there have been exciting new suggestions in evolutionary theory.[8]

It is one thing to say that we cannot scientifically explain how certain structures were produced (and the theory of natural selection does not even claim that those structures were *probable*), and quite another to say that we now have scientific reason to postulate a large number of "mental organs" as specific as the various domains and subdomains of human knowledge. Such a mental organization would not be scientifically explicable at all; it would mean that God simply decided to produce these structures at a certain point in time because they were the ones we would need a half a million (or whatever) years later. (Although I don't doubt that God is ultimately responsible for what we are, it is bad scientific methodology to invoke Him as a *deus ex machina*. And, in any case, this is such a *messy* miracle to attribute to Him! Why should He pack our heads with a billion different "mental organs," rather than just making us smart?) On the other hand, if our language capacity did develop bit by bit, even with "jumps," a description of the first bit will almost certainly sound like a description of Washoe. But then we will have conceded that *some* internalization of linguistic rules (at least in prototype form) can be accounted for without innateness.

A Better Argument

But this suggests that there *is* an argument for *some* "innateness" that Chomsky might have used. Consider the phenomenon called "echo-location" in the bat. The bat emits supersonic "noises," which are reflected from the prey (or whatever — for example, a single insect), and the bat can "steer" by these sound-reflections as well as if it had sight (that is, it can avoid fine wires, catch the mosquito that is trying to avoid it, and so forth). Now, examination of the bat's brain shows that there has been a tremendous enlargement of the centers connected with hearing (they fill about seven-eighths of the bat's brain), as compared to other mammals (including, presumably, those in its evolutionary past). Clearly, a lot of the bat's echo-locating ability is *now* "innate."

Suppose Chomsky were to grant that Washoe has proto-speech, and thereby grant that general intelligence can account for *some* language learning. He could then *use evolution as an argument for (some) "innateness."* In other words, we could argue that, given the enormous value of the language ability (as central to human life as echo-location is to bat life), it is *likely* that genetic changes have occurred to make the instrument better — for example, the development of the "speech center" in the left lobe. (But caution is needed: if the left lobe is damaged early, speech *can* develop in the right lobe.) This argument is the only one I know of that makes it plausible that there is *some* innate structuring of human language that is not simply a corollary to the innate (that is, genetically predetermined) structuring of human cognition in general. But the argument is not very strong: it could be *general intelligence* that has been genetically refined bit by bit and not a hypothetical language template. Indeed, even species-specific and functionally

useless aspects of all human languages could be the product of unknown but genetically predetermined aspects of the overall functioning of the human brain and not clues to the character of a language template; so the mere existence of such aspects is no evidence at all for the template hypothesis.

Notes

1. Z. S. Harris, *Methods in Structural Linguistics* (Chicago: University of Chicago Press, 1951).

2. N. Chomsky, "Explanatory Models in Linguistics," in *Logic, Methodology and Philosophy of Science*, ed. E. Nagel, P. Suppes, and A. Tarsk (Stanford, Calif.: Stanford University Press, 1962).

3. Each formula can be associated with a corresponding statement expressed in ordinary language, namely, "not-A," "A and B," "A or B," "if A, then B."

4. By "declarative grammar" I mean that part of the grammar that generates the declarative sentences of the language. The usual assumption — made also by Chomsky — is that interrogatives, imperatives, and so on are somehow derived from declaratives.

5. What I have given here is a very oversimplified account of Washoe's actual abilities. The interested reader should consult the following works: B. Gardner and R. A. Gardner, "Two-Way Communication with an Infant Chimpanzee," in *Behavior of Non-Human Primates*, ed. A. Schrier and F. Stollnitz (New York and London: Academic Press, 1971), vol. 4, pp. 117-184; B. Gardner and R. A. Gardner, "Teaching Sign Language to the Chimpanzee Washoe" (16-mm sound film), State College of Pennsylvania, Psychological Cinema Register, 1974; B. Gardner and R. A. Gardner, "Comparing the Early Utterances of Child and Chimpanzee," in *Minnesota Symposia on Child Psychology*, ed. A. Pick (Minneapolis, Minn.: University of Minnesota Press, 1974); B. Gardner and R. A. Gardner, "Evidence for Sentence Constituents in the Early Utterances of Child and Chimpanzee," *Journal of Experimental Psychology: General* 104:244-267, 1975. The last of these references bears directly on Washoe's ability to learn "structure-dependent" rules.

6. See chapter 5 of my *Mind, Language, and Reality* (Cambridge: Cambridge University Press, 1975).

7. I discuss this in my 1976 John Locke Lectures, *Meaning and the Moral Sciences* (London: Routledge and Kegan Paul, 1978).

8. For an account of some of these suggestions, I recommend Stephen Gould's *Ontogeny and Phylogeny* (Cambridge, Mass.: Harvard University Press, 1977).

Discussion of Putnam's Comments

Noam Chomsky

Putnam's discussion of what he calls "the innateness hypothesis" extends an earlier critical analysis of his to which he refers.[1] The earlier criticism, I believe, is based on a series of specific errors and a mistaken conception of the problem at hand. I have discussed all of this in detail elsewhere[2] and will not recapitulate here. Putnam's current "Comments" (see chapter 19) contain some new arguments, all of them, I believe, erroneous. I will not review them all, but will concentrate on those that are directed specifically to my paper. [*Editor's note:* The paper to which Chomsky refers is similar in content to chapter 17, this volume.]

According to Putnam, I advocate the "innateness hypothesis" as he formulates it, and I (and Fodor) attribute to "associationists"—the adversary—the mistake of "denying innate structure (*laws* of learning) altogether." The second of these claims is utterly false. I have repeatedly, consistently, and clearly insisted that all rational approaches to the problems of

From Massimo Piattelli-Palmarini, ed., *Language and Learning: The Debate between Jean Piaget and Noam Chomsky* (Cambridge, Mass.: Harvard University Press, 1980). Reprinted by permission of Editions du Seuil, Harvard University Press, Routledge and Kegan Paul, and the author.

learning, including "associationism" and many others that I discuss, attribute innate structure to the organism.[3] I am sure that the same is true of Fodor.[4] The question is not whether innate structure is a prerequisite for learning, but rather what it is. Furthermore, the literature is clear and explicit about this point.

For just this reason I have never used the phrase "the innateness hypothesis" in putting forth my views, nor am I committed to any particular version of whatever Putnam has in mind in using this phrase (which, to my knowledge, is his and his alone) as a point of doctrine. As a general principle, I am committed only to the "open-mindedness hypothesis" with regard to the genetically determined initial state for language learning (call it S_0^L), and I am committed to particular explanatory hypotheses about S_0^L to the extent that they seem credible and empirically supported. In my paper, I outlined one possible research strategy for determining the nature of S_0^L and sketched a number of properties that it seems reasonable to attribute to S_0^L, pursuing this strategy. Putnam investigates one of these examples, namely, the "structure-dependent" property of syntactic rules, arguing that the point is not well established. He contends that this particular property derives from "general intelligence." If indeed Putnam could characterize "general intelligence" or "multipurpose learning strategies" in some manner, and indicate, however vaguely, how the structure-dependent property of syntactic rules follows from the assumption that innate structure is as characterized, I would be happy to consider the hypothesis that this property should be attributed to "general intelligence" rather than to S_0^L, as I presently suppose to be the case. Nothing will follow, obviously, about the other properties that I argue can plausibly be attributed to S_0^L. Furthermore, if it can be shown that all properties of S_0^L can be attributed to "general intelligence," once this mysterious notion is somehow clarified, I will cheerfully agree that there are no special properties of the language faculty. But Putnam offers not even the vaguest and most imprecise hints as to the nature of the "general intelligence" or "multipurpose learning strategies" that he believes to exist. Therefore, his claim that some particular property of S_0^L can be explained in terms of these notions cannot be assessed.[5] It has the form of an empirical hypothesis, but not the content of one. Furthermore, his specific arguments with regard to the single example he discusses are all based on errors of fact or reasoning. Therefore, I see no reason to qualify the tentative suggestions in my paper with regard to structure dependence.

Putnam considers my two hypotheses H_1 and H_2, advanced to explain the formation of yes-or-no questions in English. He observes that the structure-independent rule H_1 would not be put forth by any "sane person," which is quite true, but merely constitutes part of the problem to be solved. The question is: Why? The answer that I suggest is that the general principles of transformational grammar belong to S_0^L, as part of a schematism that characterizes "possible human languages." It can easily be shown that H_2 can be directly formulated as a transformational rule in accordance with these principles, whereas H_1 cannot. In other words, the property "main verb" or "first occurrence of *is* (etc.) following the first noun phrase" is easily expressed in this particular theory, whereas the property "first occurrence of *is* (etc.)" cannot be expressed without a vast enrichment of theory (technically, it requires quantifiers in structural descriptions of transformations, whereas the former property does not). It follows, then, that a language learner equipped with the principles of transformational grammar as part of S_0^L will formulate H_2 rather than H_1 on the basis of data consistent with both. These principles are not, of course, invented ad hoc for this example; there is independent evidence to support them. Therefore, we have a plausible explanation for the fact that children automatically make the correct "induction" to a hypothesis which on general grounds would be regarded as more complex. Similarly, "sane persons," who also have an intuitive, pretheoretical grasp of the nature of language, will not put forth H_1, despite its great simplicity as compared with H_2. On the other hand, a Martian scientist, not equipped with the principles of transformational grammar as a schematism for human language, would have no hesitation in putting forth H_1. He would not be "insane," but merely "nonhuman"; that is, he lacks S_0^L.

Putnam offers several arguments to the contrary, which I will consider in turn. The first has to do with the data available for language learning. I have argued that we can, under an appropriate idealization, think of the language learner as being supplied with a sample of well-formed sentences and (perhaps) a sample of ill-formed sentences—namely, corrections of the learner's mistakes. No doubt much more information is available, and may be necessary for language learning, although little is known about this matter.

Nothing that Putnam says in this connection has the slightest bearing on my (rather innocuous) proposal, as it has actually been formulated. Thus his "false premise" that people object to all and only ungrammatical sentences is one that I have never proposed, and his discussion of deviance is compatible with my views on this subject, as expressed since the mid-1950s. Therefore, I will not comment further on these remarks, which have no relevance to the issue at hand or, as far as I can see, to my expressed views on language learning.

Putnam objects to my conclusion that "the whole burden of defining what a grammar is [falls] on the innate constraints," arguing rather that the grammar of a language is a property of the "language." I find it difficult to make much sense of this part of his discussion, which seems to me quite confused. Before considering his "different approach," consider what he rejects. Is he proposing that only part of the burden of defining what a grammar is falls on the innate constraints? If so, which part? Which part of the burden falls elsewhere, why, and in what manner? No answer is suggested; therefore it is not clear that, and if so how, he is objecting to my conclusion. Note that he could hardly be claiming that none of the burden falls on the innate constraints, that is, that there are no innate constraints on what is a possible grammar, hence a possible human language. Thus even if language is constrained only by Putnam's "general intelligence," it follows that the burden of defining what a language is falls on the innate constraints, and hence the burden of "defining what a grammar is" falls on the innate constraints, if grammar is, as he claims, a property of "language." Thus to begin with, it is quite unclear to what view Putnam believes he is objecting.

In fact, Putnam's counterproposal suggests that he has something different in mind, and that his objection is just misstated. His counterproposal is that "the grammar of a language is a property of the *language*, not a property of the brain of *Homo sapiens*." But this formulation refers to the grammar of a particular language, say English, not to the innate constraints on possible languages and grammars. Apparently, Putnam is confusing the grammars of particular languages (the topic of his counterproposal) with "universal grammar," his notion of "what a grammar is" (the topic of his objection). Let us turn now to his counterproposal, as he formulates it.

The two counterposed views, then, are these: (1) my view, that grammars are represented in the brains of mature speakers, that languages are determined by these grammars, and that speakers of language can communicate to the extent that the languages characterized by the grammars in their brains are alike; (2) Putnam's view, that grammars are not represented in the brains of speakers but are properties of "languages."

It is difficult to compare these views, because Putnam's seems to me barely intelligible and, insofar as it is clear, inconsistent with other positions that he maintains. Let us put aside the fact that such notions as "the English language" are not linguistically definable, but are rather sociopolitical in nature. Consider now Putnam's "different approach." Note first that Putnam agrees, of course, that language is neurally represented (namely, in "the speech center in the left lobe," or the right lobe under early injury; see his "better argument"). It follows, then, that my language is a property of my brain. But Putnam claims that the grammar is a property of this language. Therefore, it is also a property of my brain, contrary to what Putnam asserts. If, as Putnam claims, grammars *are not* properties of brains but *are* properties of languages, then it follows that neither languages nor grammars are "properties of the brain of *Homo sapiens*," which is to say that my knowledge of English (and ability to use English) is not a property of my brain and is not represented in my brain, in the "speech center" or anywhere else. But this is surely not Putnam's view. One might take a different tack and argue that grammar is just an artifact of some sort, but that is not Putnam's approach; he is, it seems, a "realist" as far as grammar is concerned.

One can, perhaps, choose to think of propositional calculus (Putnam's example) as a "mathematical object" with whatever kind of existence we attribute to such "objects," but that has nothing to do with the empirical problem of determining the properties of natural systems such as some human language, as represented (I assume) in the brains of individuals in their mature state, or the problem of determining the properties of S_0^L, whatever these may be. Putnam gives no explanation of his alternative and allegedly "traditional" approach. I doubt that a coherent account is possible as a real alternative to the approach he wants to reject, which takes grammar to be a property of a brain and the "definition" of grammar to belong, in effect, to the theory of S_0^L. I see no need to comment further on Putnam's remarks about propositional calculus, except to note that even these are not free from error.[6]

Putnam proposes that the "declarative grammar of a language is the inductive definition of a set of strings which is the set over which semantic, deductive-logical, inductive-logical (and so on) predicates are defined" and that it must facilitate these definitions, be computationally feasible, etc. Let us grant all of this, for the sake of discussion, putting aside an ample literature that is concerned with the alleged "parallel" between semantic and syntactic properties of natural language.[7] From Putnam's suggestion, nothing follows about grammars being a property of "language" rather than "the speakers' brains," contrary to what Put-

nam asserts, without argument. The suggestion is entirely compatible with the view that grammars are represented in the brain, and represented in such a way that semantic (etc.) predicates have definitions whose clauses "parallel . . . syntactic analysis" (though I think there are adequate grounds to suspect that the latter conclusion is incorrect — an empirical question, which I cannot consider here).

Putnam next turns to Washoe, arguing that she has developed structure-dependent rules. His discussion, however, is vitiated by an equivocation with respect to the notion "structure-dependent." Note that both of my hypotheses, H_1 and H_2, present rules that apply to a sentence, deforming its internal structure in some way (to be precise, the rules apply to the abstract structures underlying sentences, but we may put this refinement aside). Both the structure-independent rule H_1 and the structure-dependent rule H_2 make use of the concepts "sentence," "word," "first," and others; they differ in that H_2 requires in addition an analysis of the sentences into abstract phrases. A rule that does not modify the internal structure of a sentence is neither structure-dependent nor structure-independent. For example, a phrase structure rule, part of a phrase structure grammar in the technical sense of the term, is neither structure-dependent nor structure-independent.

The rule for conjunction that Putnam discusses in his Washoe comments takes two sentences p and q and combines them to form $p \mathbin{\&} q$; in the framework of my discussion, it is phrase structure rule rather than a transformational rule. It is neither structure-dependent nor structure-independent in my sense of these terms, since it does not require an internal analysis of the sentences to which it applies as a sequence of words *or* as a system of phrases. The rule does nothing to the internal structure of the sentences, and thus lies outside the bounds of the present discussion altogether.

Notice that in discussing question formation, I counterposed a structure-dependent and a structure-independent hypothesis, H_2 and H_1, respectively, and raised the question of why one is selected over the other on evidence compatible with both. In discussing conjunction, Putnam does not put forth competing hypotheses. The reason is that neither the notion "structure-dependent" nor the notion "structure-independent" applies in this case. There is no "structure-independent" counterpart to his rule, because it is neither structure-dependent nor structure-independent. Thus even if we were to grant that Washoe has learned her rule, and can form $p \& q$ (in principle) for arbitrary sentences p, q, nothing at all follows with regard to structure dependence or the choice between H_1 and H_2. The other Washoe examples also fall outside the domain of our discussion. They having nothing to do with structure dependence or structure independence; they illustrate substitution of items in a fixed frame. There is, to my knowledge, no evidence that chimpanzees use structure-dependent (or structure-independent) rules, in the sense of my discussion. Clearly, Putnam's account involves no rules of either sort. Therefore, we can put aside the discussion of Washoe, which has no more relevance to the problem under consideration than the discussion of propositional calculus. Both concern a kind of syntax to which the concepts under discussion do not even apply (in the case of propositional calculus, context-free phrase structure grammar; in the case of Washoe, an extremely limited finite-state grammar, perhaps even without any cycles). The same is true of Putnam's Hebrew example, which involves a nontransformational phrase structure rule like the rule introducing an abstract question marker in many treatments of English grammar.

Putnam later argues that my H_1 is itself structure-dependent, again equivocating on the term. I did not patent the terms and Putnam is free to use them as he likes, but in my usage, the rule is plainly not structure-dependent.

It is not clear why Putnam introduced propositional calculus and Washoe into the discussion of structure dependence. Perhaps his argument is that since the child (like Washoe, allegedly) can learn the rule for conjunction, and since this rule is "structure-dependent" (in Putnam's sense, though not mine), then the child will, by some kind of induction, choose the structure-dependent H_2 over the structure-independent H_1. I hesitate to suggest that this is Putnam's implicit argument (there is no explicit argument), since it would be inconsistent with his assertion that both H_1 and H_2 are structure-dependent (in his sense); if this is so, then either could have been posited by "induction," so the original problem remains. Or perhaps Putnam means to suggest that the concept of "structure dependence" in his sense is a notion of "general intelligence" (since Washoe allegedly has it). But that is of no help to his argument, since Washoe also undoubtedly has the notion "before" in time and probably "first," so that these too, by the argument, form part of general intelligence. We are still faced with the problem of why the child selects H_2 over H_1, which "general intelligence" makes available (since it involves only the notions "before" or "first," applying to word sequences). Similarly, if both hypotheses are (as Putnam alleges) "structure-dependent" (in his sense), then we are still left with the original problem: Why is H_2 selected?

Whether or not Putnam has something like this in mind, in case anyone else might be misled into supposing that there is an argument here based on some kind of "induction," let me add a few remarks. Imagine some new concept of "structure dependence" (call it SD*) under which the rule of conjunction and H_2 are structure-dependent (have the property SD*) but not H_1. Suppose further that the child learns the rule of conjunction and others like it which have the property SD*. Can we then account for his choice of H_2, which has the property SD*, over H_1, which does not? Only if we suppose that the predicate SD* is "available" as a projectable predicate for induction. But that is to beg the very question at issue. That is, we can now ask why the child carries out an induction with the predicate SD* instead of another, equally good predicate SI*, which holds of the rule of conjunction and H_1, but not H_2 (for example, consider the property of being a rule that does not deform a sentence in accordance with its internal phrase structure). In short, this pseudo-argument requires that the predicate SD* but not SI* be available for "induction" (learning). The question then arises: why SD* but not SI*? But that is just a variant of our original problem—we have just another variant of the familiar Goodman paradox, except that in this case we cannot even tell which is "grue," SD* or SI*, since neither seems a reasonable choice as a "projectable" predicate.

Putnam next turns to H_1 and H_2 directly, presenting his first real argument that the child "of course" uses structure-dependent rules. He argues that this follows from the fact that the child wants to learn "semantic rules" which cannot be stated without structure-dependent notions. Let us assume, for the sake of argument, that the semantic rules are structure-dependent. Does this explain why the child selects H_2 over H_1? Obviously not. Suppose that in fact English used the structure-independent rule H_1 to form yes-or-no questions. This would pose no problem at all for the formulation of the appropriate semantic rule. The rule for yes-or-no questions merely requires that these be distinguished from declaratives; they can be distinguished by H_1, by H_2, by painting them green, by standing on one's head while saying them,

or in any other way, as far as the semantic rule is concerned. The rule asks: Is the corresponding declarative true or false? (Actually, the matter is more complex, but in no way that bears on this discussion.) We will turn in a moment to the matter of finding the "corresponding declarative." But Putnam offers no argument at all to support his claim that H_2 facilitates statement of the relevant semantic rule in a way that H_1 does not. Furthermore, there is no such argument, as the semantics makes clear. I should add that it is very common in discussions of language learning to appeal to "semantics" or "pragmatics" when problems arise. It is often not appreciated just what is at stake. Putnam's argument, which is completely without force, is a clear example of this unfortunate tendency.

Putnam argues that the child must use abstract phrase structure to understand the language, and that therefore H_2 is natural. He fails to add that the child also uses the notions "word" and "first" (presupposed by both H_1 and H_2) to understand the language; thus H_1 is no less "natural," in this regard. We then face again our original question: Why does the child use H_2, which employs analysis into phrases in addition to the notions presupposed in H_1? Putnam's argument is neutral with respect to this question, and therefore goes the way of the preceding ones.

Putnam next claims that (A) *"the learning of grammar is dependent on the learning of semantics."* He offers (A) as an apparent paraphrase of his earlier assertion that the grammar must provide for the definition of semantic predicates, but it is certainly no paraphrase of this assertion. Elsewhere, Putnam has been quite clear about the distinction and has indeed advanced a very different and more plausible thesis.[8] Indeed, it is not easy to reconcile (A) with Putnam's earlier observation that the inductive definitions of semantic notions "parallel or at least presuppose a syntactic analysis of the language." If the definitions of the semantic notions presuppose a syntactic analysis (that is, a formal grammar that assigns phrase structure, determines well-formedness, and so on), then how can the learning of this grammar be "dependent on" a (prior?) learning of semantics?[9] But putting this question aside, suppose that (A) is true, in some sense that remains to be explained. Does anything follow concerning H_1 and H_2? Not as far as Putnam has argued or shown. The semantics of yes-or-no questions prefers neither H_1 nor H_2.

Putnam next argues that H_2 is preferable to H_1 because its "inverse" is simple, whereas the inverse of H_1 is "horribly complicated." He does not explain why he believes that this is so. As far as I can see, it is not; the inverses are very similar. In each case, the inverse operation requires that we find the position from which *is* (etc.) has been moved—a position immediately before the predicate. Given H_1, we seek the first such position (and if someone wanted to argue that the inverse of H_1 is in fact simpler, he might note that our search is facilitated by the presence of the word *who* [etc.] in this case). Given H_2, we will seek the "main" position, using the full phrase structure analysis. One can think of various algorithms, none of which, as far as I can see, differentiates between H_1 and H_2. Since Putnam offers no argument, I have to leave it at that.

Note, incidentally, that even if the inverse algorithm must be "structure-dependent," that has no bearing on the choice between H_1 and H_2, that is, on the question of whether it is the first occurrence of *is* (etc.) or the "main" occurrence that is proposed. We cannot argue that because (by assumption) the inverse is structure-dependent, then so is the rule. In fact, even if one were to put forth this illegitimate argument, it would not bear on the essential point. We could then rephrase our original query, asking why it is that the occurrence of *is* after the main noun phrase is moved, rather than the first occurrence after a noun phrase (that is, the leftmost occurrence in "The man who is here is tall").

To allay any lingering confusion about this matter, consider the three relevant question forms:

(I) Is — the man here?

(II) Is — the man who is here tall?

(III) Is — the man who here is tall?

Both Putnam and I are assuming that the language learner is presented with many examples such as (I), and formulates either H_1 or H_2 to account for them. The facts of (II) and (III) show that H_2 was correct. To apply the inverse algorithm in (I), (II), and (III), the child must be able to detect where *is* is missing in the form to the right of — in these expressions. The question has never been studied, but it seems likely that at the stage of language acquisition when children can freely form sentences such as (II) (using H_2), they would have no difficulty in determining where *is* is missing in any of the forms to the right of — in (I), (II), and (III). Indeed, I would not be surprised to learn that they can solve the problem more easily for (III) than for (II). But ability to solve this problem is all that is required for the inverse algorithm to operate. Therefore, Putnam's unargued assertion that the inverse operation for H_1 is "horribly complicated" as compared with the inverse for H_2 seems far from the mark. If in fact it is easier to solve the problem for (III) than for (II), we would have an additional puzzle for the Martian observer, who might have taken this as further support for the obvious hypothesis that H_1 is to be preferred.

These comments exhaust Putnam's arguments concerning structure dependence. As far as I can see, none of them have any force. My conclusions, therefore, remain as stated.

Next, Putnam turns to the question of "general intelligence," beginning with the following assertion:

(IV) "So far I have assumed that there is such a thing as general intelligence," including *"multipurpose* learning strategies, heuristics, and so forth."

Actually, (IV) is a rather misleading assertion. All that Putnam has so far assumed is that S_0^L, whatever it may be, contains only the general mechanisms for learning. Recall that he gives no hint as to what these are. To invoke an unspecified "general intelligence" or unspecified "multipurpose learning strategies" is no more illuminating than his reference, at one point, to divine intervention. We have no way of knowing what, if anything, Putnam has assumed. The point is worth stressing, since it illustrates a common fallacy in discussions of this sort. The use of words such as "general intelligence" does not constitute an empirical assumption unless these notions are somehow clarified. As matters now stand, very little is asserted by (IV).

Putnam claims that his "multipurpose learning strategies" enable us to learn and create physics. He seems to feel that I should also grant something of the sort, since I insist, naturally, that these achievements are possible. But I am not committed to an empty claim. If Putnam tells us what these "multipurpose learning strategies" are, even in the most vague and informal way, I will be glad to join him in inquiring as to their efficacy in accounting for our learning of physics, etc. In the absence of any proposal, I have nothing to say about the problem. Nor does Putnam, it is crucial to emphasize.

There are, in fact, striking and obvious differences between language learning and the learning (or discovery) of physics. In the first case, a rich and complex system of rules and principles is at-tained in a uniform way, rapidly, effortlessly, on the basis of limited and rather degenerate evidence. In the second case, we are forced to proceed on the basis of consciously articulated principles subjected to careful verification with the intervention of individual insight and often genius. It is clear enough that the cognitive domains in question are quite different. Humans are designed to learn language, which is nothing other than what their minds construct when placed in appropriate conditions; they are not designed in anything like the same way to learn physics. Gross observations suffice to suggest that very different principles of "learning" are involved.

As for the proper delimitation of cognitive domains and their nature, I have nothing to add here to earlier discussion, at the Royaumont conference and elsewhere.[10] Where a rich and intricate system of belief and knowledge is rapidly attained in a uniform way on the basis of limited and degenerate evidence, it makes sense to suppose that some "mental organ" with special design is involved, and to try to determine the nature and properties of this "organ" and the cognitive domain related to it, as well as its relations to other systems that form part of the general structure of mind. Progress in delimiting these domains and determining their nature may come through studies analogous to those I have discussed in the case of language, or perhaps in other ways. Putnam asserts that the number of domains is "virtually unlimited" and that the strategies we use "must be extraordinarily multipurpose," although he adds that "we have presently no idea what they are." I know no more about these strategies than Putnam does, or about the delimitation of domains, or about their number or specific character. As far as I can see, we differ here only in that I am disinclined to put forth what appear superficially to be empirical hypotheses where, as we both admit, we have "no idea" as to what the facts may be. I would urge that Putnam too should adopt the "open-mindedness hypothesis" and refrain from putting forth assertions such as (IV) and others that appear in that section of his "Comments."

Putnam argues that if there are such cognitive domains as "learning a grammar," "recognizing faces," and others that are "so small" and have such "highly specific-purpose" learning strategies, then "it becomes really a miracle that evolution endowed us with all these skills," since most of them (for example, mathematics) weren't used until after the evolution of the race was complete. I see no miracle here. Consider the human ability to handle fairly deep properties of the number system. I suppose that this ability is genetically determined for humans, though it is hard to imagine that it contributed to differential reproduction. But we need not suppose that this is a miracle, if true. These skills may well have arisen as a concomitant of structural properties of the brain that developed for other reasons. Suppose that there was selection for bigger brains, more cortical surface, hemispheric specialization for analytic processing, or many other structural properties that can be imagined. The brain that evolved might well have all sorts of special properties that are not individually selected; there would be no miracle in this, but only the normal workings of evolution. We have no idea, at present, how physical laws apply when 10^{10} neurons are placed in an object the size of a basketball, under the special conditions that arose during human evolution. It might be that they apply in such a way to afford the brains that evolved (under selection for size, particular kinds of complexity, etc.) the ability to deal with properties of the number system, continuity, abstract geometrical space, certain parts of natural science, and so on. There are innumerable problems here, but I see no need to appeal to miracles. Nor

do the problems that arise seem qualitatively different from familiar problems in accounting for the evolution of physical structures in organisms.

Putnam's further remarks about evolution seem to me mystifying. He feels that I have "dismissed" Piaget's concerns about evolution, but that is quite false. Rather, I remarked that the structures I have been led to postulate for S_0^L, though "biologically unexplained," are not, as Piaget asserts, "biologically inexplicable." Furthermore, I see no specific problem that arises in this connection beyond those that are familiar (if often mysterious) in the case of physical organs. Putnam's further discussion seems to indicate that he agrees. Therefore, I assume that he has somehow misunderstood what I said about this matter.

In my earlier discussion of Putnam's criticisms of the "innateness hypothesis" (see note 2), I noted that his views about evolution seemed to me very curious. Thus in the paper to which he refers,[11] Putnam asserts that *invoking 'innateness' only postpones the problem of learning; it does not solve it.*" This is a very odd principle, one that would never be put forth in connection with the development of physical organs. If, in fact, the general properties of binocular vision or the fact that we grow arms instead of wings is genetically determined, then it would be senseless to say that "invoking 'innateness' only postpones the problem of the learning of binocular vision or the learning of arms rather than wings." There is no such problem to be "solved." True, a problem remains, but it is not the problem of learning; it is the problem of explaining the origin and development of structures that are innate. I see no reason to take a different approach when we study higher mental faculties. If, indeed, certain properties of language are genetically determined, then "invoking 'innateness'" does not "postpone the problem of learning" with regard to these properties, but rather is the proper move, since there is no "problem of learning" in these respects. Putnam seems to believe otherwise, but I have no idea why.

I will not comment on Putnam's "better argument," except to observe that it does not bear even in a remote way on the questions that I discussed and that seem to me to be the interesting ones, namely, what is the nature of S_0^L, how does it relate to other faculties of mind or to "general intelligence" (whatever it may be), and so on.

Putnam summarizes the view that he has been putting forward as follows: "Everything Chomsky ascribes to an innate template of language, a 'mental organ' specifically designed to enable us to *talk*, can, for all we know, be explained by general intelligence." And he suggests that this conclusion agrees "in broad outline" with Piaget's views. At the level of vagueness at which he discusses the problem, I would not disagree, once his specific arguments are dismissed as fallacious. Thus I agree that "for all we know" some notion of "general intelligence" about which we have "no idea" might explain everything I have ascribed to S_0^L. Similarly, there would be little point in debating the claim that "for all we know" some mysterious force, as to the character of which we have "no idea," might explain everything that physicists try to explain in terms of their complex constructions. Thus, contrary to what Putnam believes, I would not deny his contention. We differ only in that I dismiss it, whereas in contrast he seems to think the contention is important — why, I do not know.

Notes

1. See H. Putnam, *Mind, Language, and Reality* (Cambridge: Cambridge University Press, 1975), chapter 5.

2. See chapters 3 and 6 of my *Language and Mind*, extended edition (New York: Harcourt-Brace-Jovanovich, 1972). [Some of

this material is reprinted in chapter 16, this volume. — *Ed.*]

3. For a quite typical example, see chapter 1, section 8, of my *Aspects of the Theory of Syntax* (Cambridge, Mass.: MIT Press, 1965).

4. See J. A. Fodor, T. G. Bever, and M. F. Garrett, *The Psychology of Language* (New York: McGraw-Hill, 1974), pp. 436 ff.

5. We might even argue that his proposal, though nearly vacuous, can indeed be assessed, and rejected. The sole content of his proposal, as it stands, is that the properties of S_0^L are simply "general learning mechanisms," which apply freely in all cognitive domains. But there is evidence that S_0^L contains mechanisms and structures for which it is difficult to find even a vague analogue outside of language, for example, the specific principles of transformational grammar postulated to explain the structure dependence of rules (and much else). Consequently, the belief that the properties of S_0^L are in fact "general learning mechanisms" is quite implausible with regard to its minimal empirical content.

6. For example, when he asserts that "p & —p" is "deviant for semantic reasons," and "would not be 'uttered' for obvious semantic reasons." It is not deviant at all, and might well be "uttered" as a line in any proof by *reductio ad absurdum*.

7. See, for example, Otto Jespersen, *The Philosophy of Grammar* (London: Allen & Unwin, 1924); and for some recent discussion, my "Questions of Form and Interpretation," *Linguistic Analysis*, vol. 1, no. 1, 1975.

8. See Putnam's *Mind, Languages, and Reality*, volume 2, chapter 4.

9. Perhaps Putnam means that the learning of grammar is "dependent on" the learning of semantics in the sense that semantics provides the goal or motive for the learning of syntax. But if this is what he has in mind, the argument again fails, since as already noted, there is no problem in stating the semantics with the structure-independent rule.

10. See chapter 1 of my *Reflections on Language* (New York: Pantheon, 1975).

11. Putnam, *Mind, Language, and Reality*, chapter 5.

Comment on Chomsky's Reply

Hilary Putnam

1

The reply by Chomsky asserts that the notion of general intelligence is hopelessly vague (as opposed to such notions as "the genetically determined initial state reponsible for language learning," "universal grammar," and "the language faculty"). In fact, it is not vague at all. By "general intelligence" I mean the heuristics the brain uses for learning the answers to questions for which the answer (or an answer schema) is not genetically built in in the way in which Chomsky thinks a schema for the grammar of a human language is built in. Such heuristics certainly exist — subjective probability metrics over well-formed formulas in a suitable language are one mathematical model; the "trial and error" procedures for extrapolating functions from finite amounts of data studied by a number of workers in artificial intelligence are another. That such models are not realistic does not mean that the ability

From Massimo Piattelli-Palmarini, ed., *Language and Learning: The Debate between Jean Piaget and Noam Chomsky* (Cambridge, Mass.: Harvard University Press, 1980). Reprinted by permission of Editions du Seuil, Harvard University Press, Routledge and Kegan Paul, and the author.

they model is vague; we know what preference is, although our mathematical model of preference is certainly idealized and oversimplified. The notion of a faculty for *learning* is not a metaphysical notion. (Nor is it, as Fodor charges, the notion of a mysterious faculty for discovering whatever truths there are to be discovered — indeed, theorems on what inductive machines *cannot* learn from a considerable part of the literature.)

2

Much of Chomsky's reply to me rests on the mistaken assumption that anyone who denies that grammars describe *properties of the brain* is committed to denying that they are represented in the brain. This is a non sequitur. I deny that the grammar of propositional calculus is a description of properties of my brain; but I do not deny that, if I learn propositional calculus, some representation of that grammar (probably not the one I should use in writing a logic book) will be formed by my brain. The geography of the White Mountains is represented in my brain; but the geography of the White Mountains is not a description *of* my brain.

3

Chomsky also suggests that I may be confusing the grammar of a specific language (English, or propositional calculus) with "universal grammar"—the theory of the genetically determined normal form for all grammars learnable by human beings. This begs the point at issue, which is whether there *is* such a thing as "universal grammar" at all.

Of course, our constitution limits and determines what languages we can learn and what sports we can learn. Chomsky does not believe in a science called "universal sport" because he doubtless thinks that many different constraints, coming from many different aspects of our makeup and operating in different ways, determine what sports we can learn. Hence there is no reason to think that a normal form for what sports we can learn is necessary or possible. He believes that the constraints that determine what languages we can learn are, to quote a term he used in the *Russell Lectures*,[1] "language-specific"—which is why he thinks such a science as "universal grammar" is possible. After twenty years of vigorously espousing this point of view in print and in conversation, it is a little unfair of Chomsky to say that he is only advocating the "Open-mindedness hypothesis" with respect to our genetic makeup. Who could be against open-mindedness?

4

Chomsky admits that not all our abilities need be task-specific and specifically selected for by natural selection (unlike Fodor, who compares us to the beavers). In connection with mathematics, he speaks of "analytic processing" ("analytic processing" is apparently all right, although "general intelligence" is taboo), and says that our abilities in this area "may well have arise as a concomitant of structural properties of the brain that developed for other reasons." I agree emphatically. That is just what I think. But if this is true of mathematical ability, it could be true of linguistic ability as well.

5

Finally, I must say something about two of the technical points Chomsky raises.[2]

a. I regret if what I wrote left the mistaken impression that chimpanzees cannot learn that sentences have internal structure (beyond substitution in fixed frames); they certainly can. In particular, the structure-dependent semantic rule that a sentence of the form "the N Vs" is true just in case the object corresponding to "the N" has the property corresponding to "Vs" is clearly acquired by chimpanzees; and the alternative explanation Chomsky puts forward, that they learn "substitution in fixed frames," is refuted by a great deal of data.

b. The inverse of H_1 requires trying all possible positions for the moved "is," "does," etc.—at least I know of no other algorithm, and Chomsky suggests none. The inverse of H_2 requires only *locating the main break*; and, at least for phrase structure grammars, there are elegant algorithms for doing this without such a search, algorithms that were discovered by the Polish logicians many years ago.

Notes

1. N. Chomsky, *Problems of Knowledge and Freedom: The Russell Lectures* (New York: Random House, 1972).

2. I would like to discuss all of his points, but I have been asked by the editor to keep this discussion short.

Index

Wales, R., 273n17
Warrington, E. K., 134n7
Watson, J. B., 13
Weir, R., 335
Whorf, Benjamin L., 38, 58
Wiesel, T. N., 308
William of Ockham, 3, 13, 30-32
Winston, Patrick H., 155
Wittgenstein, Ludwig, 21-22, 31, 35, 38, 45, 118, 126nn8,11, 131, 134n8, 138, 147n2, 156, 184,

185, 186
Wollheim, Richard, 2
Woods, William, 177, 188, 190
Woolridge, D., 134n9

Yudovich, F. I., 332

Ziff, Paul, 298-299n5
Zopf, G. W., 133n1
Zubek, J. P., 333